IRISH FAMILY LEGISLATION HANDBOOK

Muriel Walls
Partner,
McCann Fitzgerald

David Bergin
Partner,
O'Connor & Bergin

Family Law

1999

Published by
Jordan Publishing Limited
21 St Thomas Street
Bristol BS1 6JS

British Library Cataloguing-in-Publication Data
A catalogue record for this book is available from the British Library.

ISBN 0 85308 500 5

Typeset by Mendip Communications Ltd, Frome, Somerset
Printed by MPG Books Ltd, Bodmin, Cornwall

PREFACE

The aim of this handbook is to make available in a convenient and up-to-date form the full text of the most important statutes and statutory instruments needed by family and child law professionals in Ireland. Publication of such a volume is long overdue. In its 1996 report on Family Courts (LRC 52–1996), the Law Reform Commission stated:

> 'The last twenty years have seen a growing recognition by society of the wide variety of problems associated with the breakdown of family relationships. Substantive family law has undergone a transformation during this period, with the introduction of a wide range of remedies and rights designed to protect vulnerable or dependent family members in the wake of breakdown, and to secure fair distribution of family assets.'

Intended in part as a companion volume to *The Law of Divorce in Ireland* (Walls and Bergin (Jordans, 1997)), the handbook also includes all relevant legislation relating to child care, adoption and child abduction. Inevitably in a book of this nature there will be legislation which it has been necessary to omit in order to keep the book to a reasonable size. The editors and publishers would welcome suggestions and comments from users of the book as to additional materials they would like to see included in the next edition.

Jordans
September 1999

BIOGRAPHIES

MURIEL WALLS

Muriel Walls obtained her Bachelor of Civil Law Degree in University College, Dublin in 1975 and qualified as a solicitor in 1977. She specialises in Family Law, and is a Fellow of the International Academy of Matrimonial Lawyers. She is a Member of the Law Society's Family Law Committee, and a Consultant to the Law Society on Family Law. She is a Member and former Chairperson of the Family Lawyers Association and an Associate of the Solicitors Family Law Association of England and Wales.

DAVID BERGIN

David Bergin obtained his Bachelor of Civil Law Degree in University College, Dublin in 1974 and qualified as a solicitor in 1976. He specialises in Family Law, and is a Fellow of the International Academy of Matrimonial Lawyers. He is Chairman of the Dublin Solicitors Bar Association Family Law Committee and is joint Vice Chairman of the Law Society's Family Law and Civil Legal Aid Committee. He is a Consultant to the Law Society on Family Law and a former Committee Member of the Family Lawyers Association.

They are the co-authors of *The Law of Divorce in Ireland* (Jordans, 1997).

CONTENTS

PART ONE: THE CONSTITUTION OF IRELAND

The Constitution of Ireland
Fundamental Rights

...

The Family

Article 41

1. 1° The State recognises the Family as the natural primary and fundamental unit group of Society, and as a moral institution possessing inalienable and imprescriptible rights, antecedent and superior to all positive law.

   2° The State, therefore, guarantees to protect the Family in its constitution and authority, as the necessary basis of social order and as indispensable to the welfare of the Nation and the State.

2. 1° In particular, the State recognises that by her life within the home, woman gives to the State a support without which the common good cannot be achieved.

   2° The State shall, therefore, endeavour to ensure that mothers shall not be obliged by economic necessity to engage in labour to the neglect of their duties in the home.

3. 1° The State pledges itself to guard with special care the institution of Marriage, on which the Family is founded, and to protect it against attack.

   2° A Court designated by law may grant a dissolution of marriage where, but only where, it is satisfied that—

       i. at the date of the institution of the proceedings, the spouses have lived apart from one another for a period of, or periods amounting to, at least four years during the previous five years,

       ii. there is no reasonable prospect of reconciliation between the spouses,

       iii. such provision as the Court considers proper having regard to the circumstances exists or will be made for the spouses, any children of either or both of them and any other person prescribed by law, and

       iv. any further conditions prescribed by law are complied with.

   3° No person whose marriage has been dissolved under the civil law of any other State but is a subsisting valid marriage under the law for the time being in force within the jurisdiction of the Government and Parliament established by this Constitution shall be capable of contracting a valid marriage within that jurisdiction during the lifetime of the other party to the marriage so dissolved.

Education

Article 42

1. The State acknowledges that the primary and natural educator of the child is the Family and guarantees to respect the inalienable right and duty of parents to provide, according to their means, for the religious and moral, intelectual, physical and social education of their children.

2. Parents shall be free to provide this education in their homes or in private schools or in schools recognised or established by the State.

3. 1° The State shall not oblige parents in violation of their conscience and lawful preference to send their children to schools established by the State, or to any particular type of school designated by the State.

    2° The State shall, however, as guardian of the common good, require in view of actual conditions that the children receive a certain minimum education, moral, intellectual and social.

4. The State shall provide for free primary education and shall endeavour to supplement and give reasonable aid to private and corporate educational initiative, and, when the public good requires it, provide other educational facilities or institutions with due regard, however, for the rights of parents, especially in the matter of religious and moral formation.

5. In exceptional cases, where the parents for physical or moral reasons fail in their duty towards their children, the State as guardian of the common good, by appropriate means shall endeavour to supply the place of the parents, but always with due regard for the natural and imprescriptible rights of the child.

PART TWO: STATUTES

Adoption Act, 1952

(1952 No 25)

ARRANGEMENT OF SECTIONS

PART I

PRELIMINARY AND GENERAL

PART II

ADOPTION ORDERS

PART III

EFFECTS OF ADOPTION ORDERS

An Act to provide for the adoption of children   [13 December 1952]

PART I

PRELIMINARY AND GENERAL

1 Short title

This Act may be cited as the Adoption Act, 1952.

2 Commencement

This Act shall come into operation on such day as the Minister may by order appoint.

3 Definitions

In this Act—

'adopted person' means a person in respect of whom an adoption order has been made;

'adoption order' means an order under section 9;

'the Board' means the body established by section 8;

'child' means (save where the context otherwise requires) any person under the age of 18 years;

'guardian', in relation to a child, means a person appointed, according to law, to be guardian of his person by deed or will or by order of a court of competent jurisdiction;

'interim order' means an order under section 17;

'the Minister' means the Minister for Health;

'orphan' means a child whose parents are dead;

'parent' does not include the natural father of an illegitimate child;

'prescribed' means prescribed by rules made under section 5;

'registered adoption society' means a body of persons entered in the Adoption Societies Register;

'relative' means grandparent, brother, sister, uncle or aunt, whether of the whole blood, of the half-blood or by affinity, relationship to an illegitimate child being traced through the mother only.

Amendments—Adoption Act, 1964, s 4; SI 1982/327; Adoption Act, 1988, s 6(1).

---

4   Making of arrangements for adoption

In this Act references to the making of arrangements for the adoption of a child shall be construed as including references to—

  (a) the making of any agreement or arrangement for, or facilitating, the adoption or maintenance of the child by any person, and

  (b) the initiation of or taking part in any negotiations of which the purpose or effect is the making of any such agreement or arrangement, and

  (c) the causing of another to initiate or take part in any such negotiations.

5   Rules

The Board, with the consent of the Minister, may make rules for the regulation of its procedure or for any matter referred to in this Act as prescribed.

6   Offences by bodies corporate

Where an offence under this Act is committed by a body corporate and is proved to have been facilitated by any neglect on the part of any person, being a director, manager, secretary or other officer of the body corporate, that person shall also be guilty of the offence and may be proceeded against and punished accordingly.

7   Expenses

The expenses incurred by a Minister of State or the Board in the administration of this Act shall, to such extent as may be sanctioned by the Minister for Finance, be paid out of moneys provided by the Oireachtas.

PART II

ADOPTION ORDERS

8   An Bord Uchtála

(1) There shall be a body to be known as An Bord Uchtála (in this Act referred to as the Board) to fulfil the functions assigned to it by this Act.

(2) The Board shall consist of a Chairman and eight ordinary members.

(3) The Chairman and the ordinary members shall be appointed by the Government.

(4) A person shall not be appointed Chairman unless he is or has been a Judge of the Supreme Court, the High Court or the Circuit Court or a Justice of the District Court or is a barrister or solicitor of at least ten years' standing.

(4A) The Government may appoint one of the ordinary members to be Deputy Chairman and the Deputy Chairman may act as chairman in the absence of the Chairman.

(4B) A person shall not be appointed Deputy Chairman unless he is qualified to be appointed Chairman.

(5) The Board may act notwithstanding the existence of one or more vacancies in its membership.

(6) The provisions of the First Schedule shall apply to the Board.

Amendments—Adoption Act, 1974, s 7; Adoption Act, 1991, s 11(1).

9   Power to make adoption order

(1) The Board may, on the application of a person desiring to adopt a child, make an order for the adoption of the child by that person.

(2) Where the applicants are a married couple the order shall be for the adoption of the child by them jointly.

10   Children who may be adopted

An adoption order shall not be made unless the child—

   (a) resides in the State, and
   (b) is, at the date of the application, not more than seven years of age, and
   (c) is illegitimate or an orphan.

Amendments—Adoption Act, 1974, s 13, Sch.

11   Persons who may apply for adoption order

(1) An adoption order shall not be made unless—

   (a) the applicants are a married couple who are living together, or
   (b) the applicant is the mother or natural father or a relative of the child, or
   (c) the applicant is a widow.

(2) Save in the case of a married couple living together, an order shall not be made for the adoption of a child by more than one person.

(3) An adoption order shall not be made unless—

(a) the applicant and, if the applicants are a married couple, each of them has attained the age of thirty years, or

(b) the applicant has attained the age of twenty-one years and is the mother, natural father or a relative of the child, or

(c) the applicants are a married couple and the wife is the mother of the child and she or her husband has attained the age of twenty-one years, or

(d) the applicants are a married couple and one of them is the natural father or a relative of the child and each of them has attained the age of twenty-one years.

(4) An adoption order shall not be made unless the applicants are ordinarily resident in the State and have been so resident during the year ending on the date of the order.

(5) An adoption order shall not be made unless the applicant or, if the applicants are a married couple, the husband is an Irish citizen or has been ordinarily resident in the State during the five years preceding the date of the application.

Amendments—Adoption Act, 1964, s 5(2).

12 (*repealed*)

Amendments—Adoption Act, 1974, s 13, Sch.

13 Suitability of adopters

(1) The Board shall not make an adoption order unless satisfied that the applicant is of good moral character, has sufficient means to support the child and is a suitable person to have parental rights and duties in respect of the child.

(2) Where the applicants are a married couple, the Board shall satisfy itself as to the moral character and suitability of each of them.

14 Consents to adoption

(1) An adoption order shall not be made without the consent of every person being the child's mother or guardian or having charge of or control over the child, unless the Board dispenses with any such consent in accordance with this section.

(2) The Board may dispense with the consent of any person if the Board is satisfied that that person is incapable by reason of mental infirmity of giving consent or cannot be found.

(3) The consent of a ward of court shall not be dispensed with except with the sanction of the Court.

(4) A person may give consent to the making of an adoption order without knowing the identity of the applicant for the order.

(5) A consent shall be given in writing in the prescribed form.

(6) A consent may be withdrawn at any time before the making of an adoption order.

15   Validity of consent

(1) A consent shall not be valid unless it is given after the child has attained the age of six weeks and not earlier than three months before the application for adoption.

(2) The Board shall satisfy itself that every person whose consent is necessary and has not been dispensed with has given consent and understands the nature and effect of the consent and of the adoption order.

Amendments—Adoption Act, 1974, s 8.

16   Hearing of applications

(1) The following persons and no other persons shall be entitled to be heard on an application for an adoption order—

   (a) the applicants,
   (b) the mother of the child,
   (c) the guardian of the child,
   (d) a person having charge of or control over the child,
   (e) a relative of the child,
   (f) a representative of a registered adoption society which is or has been at any time concerned with the child,
   (g) a priest or minister of a religion (or, in the case of any such religion which has no ministry, an authorised representative of the religion) where the child or a parent (whether alive or dead) is claimed to be or to have been of that religion,
   (h) an officer of the Board,
   (i) any other person whom the Board, in its discretion, decides to hear.

(2) A person who is entitled to be heard may be represented by counsel or solicitor.

(3) The Board may hear the application wholly or partly in private.

(4) Where the Board has notice of proceedings pending in any court of justice in regard to the custody of a child in respect of whom an application is before the Board, the Board shall make no order in the matter until the proceedings have been disposed of.

Amendments—Adoption Act, 1974, s 13, Sch.

17   Interim orders

(1) On an application for an adoption order the Board, in circumstances in which it would be lawful to make the adoption order, may, if it thinks fit, adjourn the application and make an order (in this Act referred to as an interim order) giving the custody of the child to the applicant for a probationary period not exceeding two years.

(2) The Board may attach to the interim order conditions in regard to the maintenance, education and supervision of the welfare of the child.

(3) The Board may revoke the interim order and shall revoke it at the request of the person to whom custody of the child has been given or of the mother or guardian of the child.

(4) A person who contravenes, whether by act or omission, a condition of an interim order shall be guilty of an offence and shall be liable on summary conviction to a fine not

exceeding one hundred pounds or to imprisonment for a term not exceeding twelve months or to both.

18   Re-adoption

Where the adopters (or sole adopter) of a child have died, a further adoption order may be made in accordance with this Act in respect of the child and, for this purpose, the child shall be taken to be the lawful child of the deceased adopters or adopter.

19   (*repealed*)

Amendments—Adoption Act, 1964, s 11(1).

20   Case stated for High Court

(1) The Board may (and, if so requested by an applicant for an adoption order, the mother or guardian of the child or any person having charge of or control over the child, shall, unless it considers the request frivolous) refer any question of law arising on an application for an adoption order to the High Court for determination.

(2) Subject to rules of court, a case stated under this section may be heard *in camera*.

21   Correction of adoption order

The Board may amend an adoption order by correcting any error in the particulars contained therein.

22   Adopted children register

(1) An tArd-Chláraitheoir shall maintain an Adopted Children Register.

(2) An entry shall be made in the register with respect to each adopted child. The entry shall be in the form set out in the *Second Schedule*, or in such other form as may be approved from time to time by the Minister, with the consent of the Minister for Health and shall contain the particulars required by such form.

(3) If the date of the child's birth is unknown, the Board shall determine the probable date of birth and that date shall be entered as the child's date of birth and if the Board subsequently ascertains the actual date of the child's birth, the determination shall be cancelled and the adoption order relating to the child correspondingly amended and if the date of the child's birth is not the date determined as aforesaid, the entry shall be amended.

(4) The country of birth of the child shall be entered in the register if the Board, being satisfied thereof, so directs.

(5) An tArd-Chláraitheoir shall keep an index to make traceable the connexion between each entry and the corresponding entry in the register of births. That index shall not be open to public inspection, and no information from it shall be given to any person except by order of a Court or of the Board.

(6) If an adoption order is amended the entry relating to it shall be amended accordingly.

(7) If an adoption order is set aside the entry shall be cancelled.

PART TWO

(8) The Board shall send to an tArd-Chláraitheoir the particulars necessary to enable him to comply with this section.

(9) An tArd-Chláraitheoir shall keep at his office an index to the register, and persons shall be entitled to search that index and to have a certified copy of an entry in the register or of items contained in the entry on the same terms and conditions in all respects as to fees and otherwise as are applicable under the Births and Deaths Registration Acts, 1863 to 1952, or any other enactment in respect of the register of births, and such fees shall be collected and disposed of in the same manner as fees payable under the said recited Acts.

(10) Regulations under section 6 of the Vital Statistics and Births, Deaths and Marriages Registration Act, 1952 (No 8 of 1952), (which relates to the issue of abridged certificates) may provide for the issue, as respects any entry in the Adopted Children Register, of a certificate of such items contained in the entry as may be specified in the regulations.

(11) A certified copy of an entry in the Adopted Children Register, if purporting to be issued under the seal of Oifig an Ard-Chláraitheora, shall, without further proof, be received as evidence of the facts stated therein and any requirement of law for the production of a certificate of birth shall be satisfied by the production of such certified copy.

Amendments—Adoption Act, 1964, s 7; Adoption Act, 1974, s 10.

23 Contribution by public assistance authority towards expenses of adoption

A public assistance authority or a health authority may, at their discretion, contribute towards the expenses incurred by any person in connexion with an application for an adoption order in respect of a child towards whose support they are entitled to contribute.

Amendments—SI 1954/161.

PART III

EFFECTS OF ADOPTION ORDERS

24 Parental rights and duties

Upon an adoption order being made—

(a) the child shall be considered with regard to the rights and duties of parents and children in relation to each other as the child of the adopter or adopters born to him, her or them in lawful wedlock,

(b) the mother or guardian shall lose all parental rights and be freed from all parental duties with respect to the child.

25 (repealed)

Amendments—Irish Nationality and Citizen Act, 1956, s 11(2).

26 Property rights

(1) Where, at any time after the making of an adoption order, an adopter or the adopted person or any other person dies intestate in respect of any real or personal property (other than property subject to an entailed interest under a disposition made before the date of the adoption order), that property shall devolve in all respects as if the adopted person were the child of the adopter born in lawful wedlock and were not the child of any other person.

(2) In any disposition of real or personal property made, whether by instrument *inter vivos* or by will (including codicil), after the date of an adoption order—

    (a) any reference (whether express or implied) to the child or children of the adopter shall, unless the contrary intention appears, be construed as, or as including, a reference to the adopted person,

    (b) any reference (whether express or implied) to the child or children of the adopted person's natural parents or either of them shall, unless the contrary intention appears, be construed as not being, or as not including, a reference to the adopted person, and

    (c) any reference (whether express or implied) to a person related to the adopted person in any degree shall, unless the contrary intention appears, be construed as a reference to the person who would be related to him in that degree if he were the child of the adopter born in lawful wedlock and were not the child of any other person.

(3) For the purpose of the devolution of any property in accordance with this section and for the purpose of the construction of any disposition to which subsection (2) applies, an adopted person shall be deemed to be related to any other person being the child or adopted child of the adopter or, where the adopters are a married couple, of either of them—

    (a) where the adopters are a married couple and the other person is the child or adopted child of both spouses—as brother or sister of the whole blood,

    (b) in any other case—as brother or sister of the half-blood.

(4) Notwithstanding any rule of law, a disposition made by will or codicil executed before the date of an adoption order shall not be treated for the purposes of this section as made after that date by reason only that the will or codicil is confirmed by a codicil executed after that date.

(5) Where an adoption order is made in respect of a person who had been previously adopted, such previous adoption shall be disregarded for the purposes of this section in relation to the devolution of any property on the death of a person dying intestate after the date of the subsequent adoption order and in relation to any disposition of property after that date.

27 Succession duty, legacy duty, customs duty and stamp duty on land

For the purposes of—

    (a) succession duty and legacy duty,

    (b) the stamp duties chargeable on conveyances or transfers of land, and

(c) exemption from customs duty under paragraph (b) of section 18 of the Finance Act, 1936 (No 31 of 1936) (which relates to the importation of articles of inheritance)

an adopted person shall be considered as the child of the adopter or adopters born to him, her or them in lawful wedlock and not to be the child of any other person.

28 Fatal Accidents and Workmen's Compensation Acts

For the purposes of—

(a) (*repealed*), and
(b) the Workmen's Compensation Acts, 1934 and 1948,

an adopted person shall be considered as the child of the adopter or adopters born to him, her or them in lawful wedlock and not to be the child of any other person.

Amendments—Fatal Injuries Act, 1956, s 9, Sch.

---

29 Subsequent marriage of natural parents

(1) Subject to subsection (2), the validity of an adoption order in respect of an illegitimate child and the provisions of this Act in regard to the effects of the order shall not be affected by the subsequent marriage of his natural parents and the Legitimacy Act, 1931 (No 13 of 1931), shall not apply to the child unless the order is set aside.

(2) (a) Subsection (1) shall not apply where the child has been adopted by one of his natural parents and their subsequent marriage would, apart from that subsection, legitimate the child.
(b) In that case, the Legitimacy Act, 1931, shall apply and the adoption order shall cease to be in force.
(c) Upon the re-registration of the birth of the child under that Act an tArd-Chláraitheoir shall cancel the entry in the Adopted Children Register and notify the Board accordingly.

30 Assurance on life of adopted child under ten years of age

(1) For the purposes of the enactments for the time being in force relating to friendly societies and industrial assurance companies, which enable such societies and companies to insure money to be paid for funeral expenses and restrict the persons to whom money may be paid on the death of a child under ten years of age, an adopted child shall be considered as the child of the adopter or adopters born to him, her or them in lawful wedlock and not to be the child of any other person.

(2) Where, before the making of an adoption order, any such insurance has been effected by a person who, in pursuance of this Act, has given consent to the making of the order, the rights and liabilities under the policy shall by virtue of the adoption order stand transferred to the adopter (or, where a married couple are the adopters, to the husband) who shall, for the purpose of the said enactments, be treated as the person who took out the policy.

31 Affiliation orders, etc

(1) When an adoption order is made in respect of an illegitimate child, then, unless the mother is an adopter, any affiliation order in force with respect to the child and any

agreement whereby the natural father of the child has undertaken to make payments specifically for the benefit of the child shall cease to have effect, but without prejudice to the recovery of any arrears which are due under the order or agreement at the date of the adoption order.

(2) (*repealed*).

Amendments—Child Care Act, 1991, s 79, Sch.

32 Restriction of Part I of Children Act, 1908

Part I of the Children Act, 1908, as amended by the Children Act, 1934 (No 15 of 1934) (which relates to the nursing and maintenance of children for reward), shall, in relation to a child who is the subject of an adoption order or an interim order, not apply to an adopter or to a person in whose favour the interim order was made.

33 Termination of parental authority of public assistance authority

Upon an adoption order being made a resolution in force in respect of the child under section 45 of the Public Assistance Act, 1939 (No 27 of 1939), shall terminate.

PART IV

REGISTRATION OF ADOPTION SOCIETIES

34 Restriction on making arrangements for adoption

(1) It shall not be lawful for any body of persons to make or to attempt to make any arrangements for the adoption of a child or, for that purpose, to retain a child in its custody or to arrange to have a child retained by any other person or body.

(2) If any person takes any part in the management or control of a body of persons which exists wholly or in part for the purpose of making arrangements for adoption, that person shall be guilty of an offence and shall be liable on summary conviction to a fine not exceeding one hundred pounds or to imprisonment for a term not exceeding twelve months or to both such fine and such imprisonment.

(3) In any proceedings under subsection (2) of this section, proof of things done or of words written, spoken or published (whether or not in the presence of any party to the proceedings) by any person taking part in the management or control of a body of persons, or in making arrangements for adoption on behalf of the body, shall be admissible as evidence of the purpose for which that body exists.

(4) It shall not be lawful for any person to give a child, or to cause a child to be given, to any other person for the purpose of having that child adopted by that other person, or by any other person, unless either the first mentioned person is a parent of the child, or the person who intends to adopt the child is a relative, or the spouse of a relative, of the child.

(5) Any person who contravenes subsection (4) of this section shall be guilty of an offence and shall be liable on summary conviction to a fine not exceeding one hundred pounds or to imprisonment for a term not exceeding twelve months or to both such fine and such imprisonment.

(6) This section does not apply to registered adoption societies or to health boards.

Amendments—SI 1954/16; Adoption Act, 1974, s 6.

35   The Adoption Societies Register

(1) The Board shall keep an Adoption Societies Register (in this Part referred to as the register).

(2) The register shall be open to public inspection during ordinary office hours.

(3) Entries in the register shall be in the prescribed form and contain the prescribed particulars.

36   Registration of adoption societies

(1) Subject to the provisions of this section, the Board shall enter in the register any body of persons which applies to be registered and furnishes to the Board such information as the Board may think necessary to enable it to determine if the body is entitled to be registered.

(2) The Board shall not register any body of persons unless the Board is satisfied—

  (a) that the body is one which exists only for the purpose of promoting charitable, benevolent or philanthropic objects, whether or not any such object is charitable within the meaning of any rule of law, and

  (b) that the body is competent to discharge the obligations imposed upon registered adoption societies under this Act.

(3) The Board may refuse to register any body of persons if it appears to the Board that any person who takes part in the management or control of the body or who is engaged on its behalf in connection with the making of arrangements for adoption is not a fit and proper person to act.

37   Cancellation of registration

The Board may cancel the registration of a registered adoption society on any ground which would require or entitle the Board to refuse an application for the registration of the society or if it appears to the Board that the requirements of this Act are not being adequately complied with by the society or if an offence under this Act is committed by the society or by any person acting on its behalf.

38   Furnishing of information and inspection of books

(1) A registered adoption society and every officer of the society or other person taking part in its management or control shall—

  (a) furnish the Board with such information as the Board may from time to time by notice in writing require in regard to its constitution, membership, employees, organisation and activities,

  (b) at all reasonable times permit a member or authorised officer of the Board to inspect and make copies of all books and documents relating to adoption in the possession or control of the society.

(2) A person who contravenes, whether by act or omission, a provision of this section shall be guilty of an offence and shall be liable on summary conviction to a fine not exceeding one hundred pounds.

39   Explanation to mother or guardian as to effect of adoption

(1) Where the mother or guardian of a child proposes to place the child at the disposal of a registered adoption society for adoption under this Act the society shall, before accepting the child—

- (a) furnish that person with a statement in writing in the prescribed form explaining clearly—
  - (i) the effect of an adoption order upon the rights of a mother or guardian, and
  - (ii) the provisions of this Act relating to consent to the making of an adoption order, and
- (b) ensure that the person understands the statement and that he signs a document to that effect.

(2) In the case of a failure to comply with any of the requirements of subsection (1), the society, every person who takes part in its management or control and every person concerned in the acceptance of the child on behalf of the society shall be guilty of an offence and shall be liable on summary conviction to a fine not exceeding one hundred pounds.

PART V

MISCELLANEOUS

40   Restriction on sending children abroad

(1) No person shall remove out of the State a child under seven years of age who is an Irish citizen or cause or permit such removal.

(2) Subsection (1) shall not apply to the removal of an illegitimate child under one year of age by or with the approval of the mother or, if the mother is dead, of a relative for the purpose of residing with the mother or a relative outside the State.

(3) Subsection (1) shall not apply to the removal of a child (not being an illegitimate child under one year of age) by or with the approval of a parent, guardian or relative of the child.

(4) A person who contravenes this section shall be guilty of an offence and shall be liable on summary conviction to imprisonment for a term not exceeding twelve months or to a fine not exceeding one hundred pounds or to both.

41   Prohibition upon certain advertisements

(1) No person shall publish or cause to be published any advertisement indicating—

- (a) that a parent or guardian of a child desires to have the child adopted, or
- (b) that a person desires to adopt such a child, or
- (c) that a person (not being a registered adoption society or a health authority, board of assistance or board of public assistance) is willing to make arrangements for the adoption of such a child.

(2) A person who contravenes this section shall be guilty of an offence and shall be liable on summary conviction to a fine not exceeding one hundred pounds.

Amendments—SI 1954/161; Adoption Act, 1974, s 13, Sch.

PART TWO

42 Prohibition of certain payments

(1) An adopter, parent or guardian of a child shall not receive or agree to receive any payment or other reward in consideration of the adoption of the child under this Act.

(2) No person shall make or give or agree to make or give any payment or reward the receipt of which is prohibited by subsection (1).

(3) (a) A person who makes arrangements for the adoption of a child shall not receive, make or give any payment or other reward in consideration of the making of the arrangements or agree to do so.

    (b) This subsection does not apply to—
        (i) payments made for the maintenance of the child,
        (ii) solicitors' remuneration for professional services.

(4) A person who contravenes a provision of this section shall be guilty of an offence and shall be liable on summary conviction to imprisonment for a term not exceeding twelve months or to a fine not exceeding one hundred pounds or to both.

43 False statements

If any person knowingly makes any false statement or furnishes any false information to the Board or a member or authorised officer of the Board or aids or abets another person to do so, he shall be guilty of an offence and, without prejudice to any other penalty to which he may be liable, shall, on summary conviction, be liable to imprisonment for a term not exceeding twelve months or to a fine not exceeding one hundred pounds or to both.

FIRST SCHEDULE

AN BORD UCHTÁLA

1 Member

In this Schedule, unless the context otherwise requires, 'member' means the Chairman or an ordinary member.

2 Term of office

(1) Each member, unless appointed to fill a casual vacancy, shall be appointed for a period of five years.

(2) A member appointed to fill a casual vacancy shall be appointed for the remainder of the term for which his predecessor, if he had continued to be a member, would have held office.

(3) An outgoing member may be reappointed.

3 Removal and resignation

(1) The Government may remove a member from office for stated misbehaviour or incapacity or failure to attend meetings of the Board.

(2) A member may resign his office.

4 Substitutes

(1) Where a member is temporarily unable to act, the Government may appoint a person to act in his place.

(2) A person shall not be appointed to act in place of the Chairman unless he is qualified for appointment as Chairman.

(3) References in this Act to a member include references to a person so acting.

5 Remuneration

There may be paid to the Chairman such remuneration as the Minister, with the consent of the Minister for Finance, determines.

5A Remuneration of Deputy Chairman

There may be paid to the Deputy Chairman, in respect of any period when he acts as chairman, such remuneration as the Minister, with the consent of the Minister for Finance, determines.

6 Registrar and officers and servants

(1) The Minister shall appoint a person to be registrar of the Board and may with the consent of the Minister for Finance appoint such other officers and servants of the Board as he thinks necessary.

(2) The registrar, officers and servants of the Board shall hold office on such terms and receive such remuneration as the Minister for Finance determines.

7 Seal

(1) The Board shall have an official seal which shall be judicially noticed.

(2) The seal shall, when applied to a document, be attested by the signature of the Chairman or the registrar or of a person authorised by the Board to attest it.

(3) Every document purporting to be an instrument made by the Board, to be sealed with the seal and to be attested in accordance with this paragraph shall, unless the contrary is shown, be received in evidence and be deemed to be such instrument without further proof.

8 Procedure

(1) The quorum for a meeting of the Board shall be the Chairman and two ordinary members.

(2) Every question at a meeting shall be decided in accordance with the opinion of the majority of those present.

(3) In the case of an equal division of opinion, the question shall be decided in accordance with the opinion of the Chairman.

(4) The decision of the Board shall be pronounced by the Chairman or other member authorised by the Chairman and no other opinion, whether assenting or dissenting, shall be pronounced nor shall the existence of such an opinion be disclosed.

(5) Subject to this Act, the Board may regulate its own procedure.

PART TWO

9   Power to summon witnesses, etc

(1) The Board may for the purposes of any proceedings before it under this Act do all or any of the following things—

(a) summon witnesses to attend before it,

(b) examine on oath (which a member or the registrar of the Board is hereby authorised to administer) the witnesses attending before it,

(c) require any such witness to produce to the Board any document in his power or control.

(2) A witness before the Board shall be entitled to the same immunities and privileges as if he were a witness before the High Court.

(3) If any person—

(a) on being duly summoned as a witness before the Board makes default in attending, or

(b) being in attendance as a witness refuses to take an oath legally required by the Board to be taken, or to produce any document in his power or control legally required by the Board to be produced by him, or to answer any question to which the Board may legally require an answer,

he shall be guilty of an offence and shall be liable on summary conviction to a fine not exceeding twenty-five pounds.

(4) Where a witness (other than an applicant for an adoption order) attends before the Board in pursuance of a summons issued on the initiative of the Board, the Board may, if it thinks fit, pay to him a sum in respect of expenses incurred by him in connection with his attendance in accordance with a scale prescribed by the Minister, with the sanction of the Minister for Finance.

10   Evidence

The Board may take evidence orally or on affidavit.

11   Enquiries

(1) The Board may make such enquiries as it thinks necessary for the fulfilment of its functions.

(2) A member or officer of the Board may visit the homes of the child, the guardian of the child, the applicants for an adoption order and the person to whom custody of the child has been given under an interim order.

(3) The Board may authorise an officer of a Department of State or of a local authority to make enquiries and visits on behalf of the Board.

12   Service of documents

A summons, notice or other document required or authorised by or under this Act to be issued by the Board to any person may be served by registered post.

13   Annual report

(1) The Board shall, after the expiration of each year, publish a report giving the following information in relation to that year—

(a) the number of applications for adoption and the decisions of the Board thereon,

(b) the names of the registered societies concerned in the applications,

(c) the number of applications for registration of societies and the decisions of the Board thereon,

(d) the name and address of each society which is registered or the registration of which is cancelled during the year.

(2) The Board shall present a copy of the report to the Minister who shall cause it to be laid before each House of the Oireachtas.

14　Notices to be published in *Iris Oifigiúil*

(1) The Board shall cause to be published in *Iris Oifigiúil* a notice in the prescribed form of every registration and cancellation of registration in the Adoption Societies Register.

(2) A notice in regard to an adoption order shall not refer to the child's natural parents, former surname, place of birth or otherwise to his origin.

Amendments—Adoption Act, 1974, s 12; SI 1987/81; Adoption Act, 1988, s 8.

SECOND SCHEDULE　　　　　　　　　　Section 22

FORM OF ENTRY IN ADOPTED CHILDREN REGISTER

No of entry	Date and country of birth	Christian name or first name	Sex	Name, address and occupation of adopter or adopters	Date of adoption order	Date of entry and signature of an tArd-Chláraitheoir

PART TWO

Adoption Act, 1964

(1964 No 2)

ARRANGEMENT OF SECTIONS

An Act to amend and extend the Adoption Act, 1952 [5 February 1964]

1 Definitions

In this Act—

'adoption order' means an order under section 9 of the Principal Act;
'the Board' means An Bord Uchtála;
'the Principal Act' means the Adoption Act, 1952;
'registered adoption society' means a body of persons entered in the Adoption Societies Register kept by the Board under Part IV of the Principal Act.

2 Adoption of legitimated child

(1) (a) Notwithstanding anything contained in section 10 of the Principal Act, an adoption order may be made in the case of a child—
    (i) who has been legitimated or whose legitimation has been recognised in pursuance of the provisions of the Legitimacy Act, 1931, and
    (ii) whose birth has not been re-registered in pursuance of the provisions of the Schedule to that Act or in pursuance of the law of a country other than the State,
provided that the father of the child gives his consent to the making of an adoption order or such consent is dispensed with in accordance with section 14 of the Principal Act.
(b) The provisions of subsections (2) to (6) of section 14 of the Principal Act shall apply in relation to a consent referred to in the foregoing paragraph as they apply in relation to the consents referred to in subsection (1) of that section.

(2) In section 16, 17, 20, 24 and 39 of the Principal Act, any reference to the mother of a child shall, for the purposes of the foregoing provisions of this section, be construed as including a reference to the father of the child.

(3) Where—

(a) a child was illegitimate when the consent by the mother to the making of an adoption order was given or, in a case in which the Board has dispensed with that consent on the ground that the mother could not be found, when the child was born, and

(b) no evidence has been adduced to the Board, either by way of objection to the application for adoption or otherwise, that the child was subsequently legitimated,

the Board may assume, for the purposes of the Principal Act and this Act, that the child is illegitimate at the time the application is heard, and if the Board makes an adoption order and the child has in fact been legitimated, the order shall have the same validity as if the child had not been legitimated and the reference in section 24 of the Principal Act to the mother shall be construed as including a reference to the father.

(4) If, before the passing of this Act, an adoption order was made in respect of a legitimated child (being a child of whose legitimation the Board was not aware), the order shall have, and be deemed always to have had, the same validity as if the child had not been legitimated and the reference in section 24 of the Principal Act to the mother shall be construed as including a reference to the father.

3   Extension in certain circumstances of time for applying for adoption order

(1) Notwithstanding anything contained in section 10 of the Principal Act, where the Board is satisfied that in the particular circumstances of the case it is desirable to do so, it may make an adoption order in respect of a child who was more than seven years of age at the date of the application for the order.

(2) Before deciding if it will make an adoption order in relation to a child to whom this section applies, the Board shall give due consideration, having regard to his age and understanding, to the wishes of the child.

Amendments—Adoption Act, 1974, s 11(a)(b).

4   (Amends s 3 of the Principal Act)

5   Amendment of section 11 of Principal Act

(1) Notwithstanding anything contained in subsection (3) of section 11 of the Principal Act, an adoption order may be made on the application of a married couple who have been married to each other for not less than three years and each of whom has attained the age of twenty-five years.

(2) (Amends s 11 of the Principal Act)

6   (*repealed*)

Amendments—Adoption Act, 1974, s 13, Sch.

7   (Amends s 22 of the Principal Act)

8   Interim orders

Where, on an application for an adoption order in respect of a child, the Board is not satisfied as respects the matters referred to in section 13 of the Principal Act, it may make an order under section 17 of the Principal Act giving the custody of the child to the applicant for a probationary period if it is of opinion that, before the expiration of such period, it is likely to be satisfied as respects the matters referred to in the said section 17.

9   Adjournment of applications for adoption orders

For the removal of doubt, it is hereby declared that, where an application is made to the Board for an adoption order, the Board has, and always has had, power to adjourn from time to time the making of a decision whether to make or refuse to make the order.

10   (*repealed*)

Amendments—Child Care Act, 1991, s 79, Sch.

---

11   Repeal

(1) Section 19 of the Principal Act is hereby repealed.

(2) Subsection (1) of this section shall come into operation on the 1st day of January, 1966.

12   Short title, construction and collective citation

(1) This Act may be cited as the Adoption Act, 1964.

(2) The Principal Act and this Act shall be construed together as one.

(3) The Principal Act and this Act may be cited together as the Adoption Acts, 1952 and 1964.

PART TWO

Adoption Act, 1974

(1974 No 24)

ARRANGEMENT OF SECTIONS

SCHEDULE

An Act to amend and extend the Adoption Acts, 1952 and 1964   [29 July 1974]

1   Interpretation

In this Act—

    'adoption order' means an order under section 9 of the Principal Act;
    'the Board' means An Bord Uchtála;
    'the Principal Act' means the Adoption Act, 1952.

2   Welfare of child

In any matter, application or proceedings before the Board or any court relating to the arrangements for or the making of an adoption order, the Board or the court, in deciding that question, shall regard the welfare of the child as the first and paramount consideration.

3   Power to make adoption order in the absence of consent

(1) In the case where a person has applied for an adoption order relating to a child and any person whose consent to the making of an adoption order relating to the child is necessary and who has agreed to the placing of the child for adoption either—

    (a)   fails, neglects or refuses to give his consent, or
    (b)   withdraws a consent already given,

the applicant for the adoption order may apply to the High Court for an order under this section.

(2) The High Court, if it is satisfied that it is in the best interests of the child so to do, may make an order under this section—

(a) giving custody of the child to the applicant for such period as the Court may determine, and

(b) authorising the Board to dispense with the consent of the other person referred to in subsection (1) of this section to the making of an adoption order in favour of the applicant during the period aforesaid.

(3) The consent of a ward of court shall not be dispensed with by virtue of a High Court order under this section except with the sanction of the Court.

4   Religion

An adoption order shall not be made in any case where the applicants, the child and his parents, or, if the child is illegitimate, his mother, are not all of the same religion, unless every person whose consent to the making of the order is required by section 14 of the Principal Act or by section 2 of the Adoption Act, 1964, knows the religion (if any) of each of the applicants when he gives his consent.

5   Application by widower for adoption order

(1) Notwithstanding anything contained in section 11 of the Principal Act (as amended by section 5 of the Act of 1964), in any case where—

(a) a child is in the care of a married couple who have made an application for an adoption order in relation to that child, and

(b) the wife dies before the making of the adoption order;

the Board may make an adoption order relating to that child on the application of the widower: Provided that—

(i) the widower has, at the date of his application another child in his custody, and

(ii) every person, whose consent to the making of the adoption order is required by section 14 of the Principal Act or by section 2 of the Act of 1964, knows, when he gives his consent, that the applicant is a widower.

(2) In any case where an application for an adoption order is made under this section, any consent given to the making of an adoption order in respect of the child in favour of the married couple shall be disregarded.

6   (Amends s 34 of the Principal Act)

7   (Amends s 8 of the Principal Act)

8   (Amends s 15 of the Principal Act)

9   Restriction on making of adoption order

(1) Subject to subsection (2) of this section, an adoption order shall not be made in respect of a child unless the child has been in the care of the applicants for such period (if any) as may be prescribed.

(2) The Board may, having regard to the particular circumstances of the case, make an adoption order in respect of a child notwithstanding that the child has not been in the care of the applicants for the period prescribed pursuant to subsection (1) of this section.

10   (Amends s 22 of the Principal Act)

11   (Amends s 3 of the Adoption Act, 1964)

12   (Amends Sch 1 to the Principal Act)

13 Repeals

The enactments mentioned in the Schedule to this Act are hereby repealed to the extent specified in the third column of that Schedule.

14 Short title, construction and collective citation

(1) This Act may be cited as the Adoption Act, 1974.

(2) The Adoption Acts, 1952 and 1964, and this Act shall be construed together as one.

(3) The Adoption Acts, 1952 and 1964, and this Act may be cited together as the Adoption Acts, 1952 to 1974.

SCHEDULE   Section 13

REPEALS

Number and year (1)	Short Title (2)	Extent of Repeal (3)
No 25 of 1952.	Adoption Act, 1952.	In paragraph (b) of section 10, the words 'not less than six months and'. Section 12. In section 16(1)(g), the words 'recognised by the Constitution'. In section 41(1)(a), the words 'under seven years of age'.
No 2 of 1964.	Adoption Act, 1964.	Section 6.

PART TWO

Adoption Act, 1976

(1976 No 29)

ARRANGEMENT OF SECTIONS

An Act to amend and extend the Adoption Acts, 1952 to 1974   [13 July 1976]

1 Definitions

In this Act—

     'adoption order' means an order under section 9 of the Principal Act;
     'the Board' means An Bord Uchtála;
     'the Principal Act' means the Adoption Act, 1952.

2 Validity of certain adoption orders and consents to adoption orders

(1) Where, in relation to an adoption order made before the passing of this Act, the consent to the making of the order of every person whose consent was necessary and was not dispensed with was given in a form for that purpose contained at any time in rules under section 5 of the Principal Act—

    (a) the Board shall be deemed to have complied with section 15(2) of the principal Act,

    (b) a consent so given shall not be invalid, insufficient or otherwise defective by reason only of either or both of the following circumstances—

       (i) that the person who gave the consent was not aware that the consent could have been withdrawn at any time before the making of the order,

       (ii) that such person was not aware of the date on which the Board proposed to make the order, and

    (c) the order shall not be invalid by reason only of either or both of the following circumstances—

       (i) that a person who gave a consent to the order was not aware of his rights under section 16 of the Principal Act,

       (ii) that the Board had not information as to whether the person was aware of those rights.

(2) Where, in relation to an adoption order made after the passing of this Act, a consent to the making of the order was given before such passing in a form for that purpose contained at any time in rules under section 5 of the Principal Act—

(a) the Board shall be deemed to have complied with section 15(2) of the Principal Act in relation to the consent,

(b) the provisions of subsection (1)(b) of this section shall apply in relation to the consent, and

(c) the order shall not be invalid by reason only of either or both of the following circumstances—

   (i) that the person who gave the consent was not aware of his rights under section 16 of the Principal Act,

   (ii) that the Board had not information as to whether the person was aware of those rights:

Provided however that nothing in this subsection shall be construed as limiting the right of the Board to make or cause to be made any enquiries it considers necessary.

3 Information for persons consenting to adoption orders

(1) A person whose consent to the making of an adoption order is necessary—

(a) shall be informed before he gives the consent or as soon as may be after such giving—

   (i) that the consent may be withdrawn at any time before the making of the order, and

   (ii) that he is entitled to be heard on the application for the order, and

(b) shall, if he gives the consent, be asked, at the time of such giving or thereafter, to indicate in writing if he wishes—

   (i) to be informed of the date on which the Board will, if he wishes to be heard, hear him or his counsel or solicitor on the application for the order, or

   (ii) otherwise to be consulted again in relation to the application for the order.

(2) In case a person has indicated in pursuance of subsection (1) of this section that he does not wish to be informed of the date on which the Board will hear him or his counsel or solicitor on the application for the adoption order to which his consent related or otherwise to be consulted again in relation to the application, it shall not be necessary so to inform or consult him, but in any other case (including the case where he has not given an indication in pursuance of the said subsection (1)), he shall be so informed and consulted and, if he cannot be found, the Board shall deal with the application as if he had not given his consent.

(3) This section does not apply in relation to a consent to which section 2 of this Act applies.

4 Enquiries on behalf of Board

(1) For the purposes of compliance with section 15(2) of the Principal Act and section 3 of this Act, the Board may request and authorise any person either in or outside the State whom it considers suitable for the purpose to make enquiries on its behalf and the Board shall be entitled, if it so thinks fit and accepts the report of the person in relation to the enquiries, to regard such acceptance as compliance by it with the said section 15(2) of the Principal Act, and as sufficiently demonstrating compliance with section 3 of this Act, as respects the subject matter of the enquiries.

(2) The powers conferred on the Board by subsection (1) of this section may be exercised by it as an alternative or in addition to hearing a person whose consent to the making of an adoption order is being considered by the Board or having enquiries made of that person in pursuance of paragraph 11(3) of the First Schedule to the Principle Act.

5   Adoption orders not to be declared invalid if declarations not in best interests of children concerned

(1) An adoption order shall not be declared invalid by a court if the court, after hearing any persons who, in the opinion of the court, ought to be heard, is satisfied—

    (a) that it would not be in the best interests of the child concerned to make such a declaration, and

    (b) that it would be proper, having regard to those interests and to the rights under the Constitution of all persons concerned, not to make such a declaration.

(2) An adoption order shall be deemed for all purposes to be and at all times since its making to have been a valid adoption order unless it is declared invalid by a court.

6   Orders by court as to custody of children in certain cases

(1) If, in any proceedings, an adoption order is declared invalid by a court and the child concerned is in the custody of the person or persons in whose favour the adoption order was made or any other person or persons not being the person or persons who sought the declaration of invalidity, the court shall not then make an order as to the custody of the child unless such an order is sought and the court is satisfied that, by reason of the fact that any person having custody of the child has been joined in the proceedings and by reason of all the other circumstances of the case, it would be in the interests of justice that the question of the custody of the child should be determined then rather than in separate proceedings; but if the court decides, in accordance with this subsection, to determine the question of the custody of the child it shall do so subject to the provisions of section 3 of the Guardianship of Infants Act, 1964.

(2) Notwithstanding anything in subsection (1) of this section, the person or persons in whose favour an adoption order is made (or any other person or persons having custody of the child who is the subject of the order) shall not be joined or otherwise heard in any proceedings in a court in which the validity of the order is an issue without the consent of the court, and the court, in deciding whether to give such consent, may take into account submissions made to it by the Board or any other interested person relating to the identification at that time of the person or persons concerned or to any other relevant matter.

7   Construction of references to child in other Acts

Where, in any Act of the Oireachtas passed after the passing of this Act, there is a reference to a child of a person or persons, then, unless the contrary intention appears—

    (a) the reference shall be construed as including a reference to a child adopted by the person or persons, as the case may be, under the Adoption Acts, 1952 to 1976, and

    (b) a child so adopted shall be deemed, for the purposes of the Act, to be the child of the person or persons aforesaid born to him or them in lawful wedlock and not to be the child of any other person.

8   Privacy of records

A court shall not make an order under section 22(5) of the Principal Act or an order for the discovery, inspection, production or copying of any book, document or record of the Board (or of any extracts therefrom), or otherwise in relation to the giving or obtaining of information therefrom, unless it is satisfied that it is in the best interests of any child concerned to do so.

9   Short title, construction and collective citation

(1) This Act may be cited as the Adoption Act, 1976.

(2) The Adoption Acts, 1952 to 1974, and this Act shall be construed together as one.

(3) The Adoption Acts, 1952 to 1974, and this Act may be cited together as the Adoption Acts, 1952 to 1976.

Adoption Act, 1988

(1988 No 30)

ARRANGEMENT OF SECTIONS

ACTS REFERRED TO

Adoption Act, 1952   1952, No 25
Adoption Act, 1964   1964, No 2
Adoption Acts, 1952 to 1976

An Act to provide, in exceptional cases, where the parents for physical or moral reasons have failed in their duty towards their children, for the supplying, by the adoption of the children, of the place of the parents and for that purpose and other purposes to amend and extend the Adoption Acts, 1952 to 1976   [26 July 1988]

1 Definitions

(1) In this Act—

'the Act of 1964' means the Adoption Act, 1964,
'the Acts' means the Adoption Acts, 1952 to 1976,
'the Board' means An Bord Uchtála,
'adoption order' means an order under section 9 of the Principal Act,
'the Court' means the High Court,
'parents' includes a surviving parent and, in the case of a child in respect of whom an adoption order is in force, means the adopters or the adopter or the surviving adopter under the order,
'the Principal Act' means the Adoption Act, 1952.

(2) References in this Act to persons in whose favour the Board has made a declaration under section 2(1) or to persons applying for an adoption order are, in the case of such a declaration in favour of one person or such an application by one person, references to that person.

(3) (a) A reference in this Act to a section is to a section of this Act unless it is indicated that reference to some other enactment is intended.

(b) A reference in this Act to a subsection or paragraph is a reference to the subsection or paragraph of the provision in which the reference occurs unless it is indicated that reference to some other provision is intended.

2   Adoption orders in respect of children the subject of orders under section 3(1)

(1) Where—

(a) an application is made by any persons (referred to subsequently in this subsection as 'the applicants') to the Board for an adoption order,

(b) but for this Act, the board would have not power to make the order, and

(c) the Board (having heard the health board in whose functional area the applicants ordinarily reside, any persons specified in paragraphs (a) to (h) of section 16(1) (as adapted by this Act) of the Principal Act who wish to be heard and any other person whom the Board, in its discretion, decides to hear) is satisfied that, if an order under section 3(1) in relation to the child to whom the application for the adoption order relates were made in favour of the applicants, it would be proper, having regard to the Acts and this Act, to make the adoption order,

the Board shall adjourn the application and declare that, if the order is made under section 3(1), it will, subject to subsection (2), make the adoption order.

(2) Where—

(a) an order in made under section 3(1), and

(b) an appeal against the order is not brought or the order is confirmed on appeal by the Supreme Court,

the Board, if so requested by the persons in whose favour the order was made, shall, notwithstanding anything in section 10 of the Principal Act, unless it is satisfied that the relevant circumstances have so changed since the date of the making of the declaration under subsection (1) in relation to the matter that it would not be proper, having regard to the Acts and this Act, to do so, make an adoption order in relation to the child to whom the order under section 3(1) relates in favour of the persons aforesaid.

(3) Section 14 of the Principal Act, the proviso to paragraph (a) of section 2(1) of the Act of 1964 and paragraph (b) of the said section 2(1) do not apply to an adoption order made by the Board by virtue of this section.

(4) Section 17 of the Principal Act does not apply in relation to an application for the making of an adoption order by virtue of this section.

(5) Where an adoption order is made by virtue of this section in respect of a child in respect of whom a previous adoption order has been made, the child shall be taken, for the purposes of the first-mentioned order, to be the lawful child of the adopters under the said previous order.

3   Orders by High Court authorising adoption of children whose parents have failed in their duty towards them

(1) Where persons in whose favour the Board has made a declaration under section 2(1) (referred to subsequently in this subsection as 'the applicants') request the health board in whose functional area they ordinarily reside to apply to the Court for an order under this section—

(a) if the health board considers it proper to do so and an application therefor in accordance with paragraph (b) of this subsection has not been made by the applicants, the health board may apply to the Court for the order, and

(b) if, within the period of 3 months from the day on which the request was given to the health board, the health board either—

    (i) by notice in writing given to the applicants, declines to accede to the request, or

    (ii) does not give the applicants a notice under subparagraph (i) of this paragraph in relation to the request but does not make an application for the order under paragraph (a),

    the applicants may apply to the Court for the order,

and, if an application under paragraph (a) or (b) of this subsection is made and it is shown to the satisfaction of the Court—

(I) that—

    (A) for a continuous period of not less than 12 months immediately preceding the time of the making of the application, the parents of the child to whom the declaration under section 2(1) relates, for physical or moral reasons, have failed in their duty towards the child,

    (B) it is likely that such failure will continue without interruption until the child attains the age of 18 years,

    (C) such failure constitutes an abandonment on the part of the parents of all parental rights, whether under the Constitution or otherwise, the respect to the child, and

    (D) by reason of such failure, the State, as guardian of the common good, should supply the place of the parents,

(II) that the child—

    (A) at the time of the making of the application, is in the custody of and has a home with the applicants, and

    (B) for a continuous period of not less than 12 months immediately preceding that time, has been in the custody of and has had a home with the applicants,

    and

(III) that the adoption of the child by the applicants is an appropriate means by which to supply the place of the parents,

the Court may, if it so thinks fit and is satisfied, having had due regard for the rights, whether under the Constitution or otherwise, of the persons concerned (including the natural and imprescriptible rights of the child), that it would be in the best interests of the child to do so, make an order authorising the Board to make an adoption order in relation to the child in favour of the applicants.

(2) Before making an order under subsection (1), the Court shall, in so far as is practicable, give due consideration, having regard to his age and understanding, to the wishes of the child concerned.

(3) The Court may, of its own motion or on application to it in that behalf, make an order adding such other persons as it thinks fit as parties to proceedings under subsection (1), and may, in the case of a person added as a party to any such proceedings under this section, make such order as it considers just in respect of—

(a) the payment of any costs in relation to the proceedings that are incurred by the person and are not paid by another party to the proceedings if legal aid in respect of them under any scheme operated by or on behalf of the State for the provision of legal aid has been refused, or

(b) the payment by the person of any costs in relation to the proceedings that are incurred by any other party to the proceedings.

(4) The health board concerned shall be joined as a party to proceedings under subsection (1)(b).

(5) Proceedings under this section shall be heard otherwise than in public.

(6) The functions conferred on a health board by section 2(1) and subsection (1) of this section shall be functions of the chief executive officer and any deputy chief executive officer of the board.

(7) A request to a health board under subsection (1) may be given to the board by handing it, or sending it by prepaid post, to an officer of the board at premises of the board and the request shall be deemed, for the purposes of paragraph (b) of that subsection, to be given to the board on the day on which it is so handed or posted.

4   Evidence to Court

(1) Subject to the provisions of this section, the Court shall not make an order under section 3(1) without having heard the parents of the child concerned and any other persons who, in the opinion of the Court, ought to be heard by it.

(2) Where the parents concerned (or either of them), having been requested to give evidence to the Court at the hearing of an application for an order under section 3(1), fail or refuse to do so, the Court may, if it so thinks fit, notwithstanding the absence of the evidence of the parents or, as the case may be, of either of them, make the order.

(3) Where the parents concerned (or either of them) fail to respond to such a request as aforesaid, the failure may be taken by the Court, for the purposes of subsection (2), to be a failure by the parents or, as the case may be, by either of them to give evidence to the Court at the hearing concerned.

(4) Notwithstanding subsection (1), where the Court is satisfied—

(a) that the identity of the parents concerned (or of either of them) is not known to the persons applying for an order under section 3(1) and is not known to the Board and that all appropriate measures have been taken to ascertain that identity, or

(b) that the whereabouts of the parents concerned (or of either of them) at the time of the making of the application for such order, and their whereabouts during the period of 12 months immediately preceding such time, are not known to the parties making the application and are not known to the Board and that all appropriate measures have been taken to ascertain those whereabouts,

the Court may, if it so thinks fit, notwithstanding the absence of the evidence of the parents concerned or, as the case may be, of either of them, make the order.

(5) Notwithstanding subsection (1), where the Court is satisfied that the parents concerned (or either of them) are incapable by reason of mental infirmity of giving reliable evidence to the Court, the Court may dispense with their evidence or that of either of them, as the case may be, on the hearing of an application for an order under section 3(1) and may, if it so thinks fit, notwithstanding the absence of such evidence, make the order.

5   Court costs

(1) The health board concerned shall—

   (a) pay to the parents of the child concerned, in respect of any costs—

      (i)   that are incurred by them in relation to an application under section 3(1) or an appeal to the Supreme Court against the making of, or the refusal to make, an order under the said section 3(1),

      (ii) that are not paid by another party to the proceedings, and

      (iii) in relation to which legal aid under any scheme for the provision of legal aid operated by or on behalf of the State has been refused,

      either, as may be specified by the Court, the whole or a part so specified of those costs, as taxed by a Taxing Master of the High Court, or such amount as, in the opinion of the health board and those parents, would be equal to the amount, as may be specified as aforesaid, of those costs or of a part so specified of them if they were taxed as aforesaid, and

   (b) if any costs of another party to the proceedings in relation to the application or, as the case may be, the appeal are ordered by the Court or the Supreme Court to be paid by those parents and legal aid in respect of them under any scheme for the provision of legal aid operated by or on behalf of the State has been refused, pay to that other party either, as may be specified by the Court, the whole or a part so specified of those costs, as taxed by a Taxing Master of the High Court, or such amount as, in the opinion of the health board and that other party, would be equal to the amount, as may be specified as aforesaid, of those costs or of a part so specified of them if they were taxed as aforesaid.

(2) Where, on an application under paragraph (b) of section 3(1)—

   (a) (i)   the Court makes an order under section 3(1) and either an appeal is not brought against the order or the order is affirmed by the Supreme Court on appeal, or

      (ii) the Court refuses to make an order under section 3(1) but, following an appeal to the Supreme Court against the refusal, the order is made, and

   (b) legal aid for the persons bringing the application under any scheme operated by or on behalf of the State for the provision of legal aid has been refused,

the health board concerned shall pay to the persons bringing the application, in respect of any costs incurred by those persons in relation to the application or, as the case may be, the application and the appeal that are not paid by another party to the proceedings either, as may be specified by the Court, the whole or a part so specified of those costs, as taxed by a Taxing Master of the High Court, or such amount as, in the opinion of the health board and those persons, would be equal to the amount, as may be specified as aforesaid, of those costs or of a part so specified of them if they were taxed as aforesaid.

6   Amendment of section 3 of Principal Act

(1) (Amends s 3 of the Principal Act)

(2) Notwithstanding subsection (1), the Acts shall apply and have effect in relation to any person whatsoever who is under the age of 21 years and as respects whom an application for an adoption order was made and was not determined before the commencement of this Act as if subsection (1) had not been enacted.

PART TWO

7   Adaptation of sections 16, 20 and 24 of Principal Act

(1) References in sections 16, 20 and 24 of the Principal Act to the mother of a child shall, for the purposes of section 2 in so far as it applies to a child of married parents (other than a child in respect of whom an adoption order is in force), be construed as including references to the father of the child.

(2) References in the said sections 16, 20 and 24 to the mother of a child shall, for the purposes of section 2 in so far as it applies to a child in respect of whom an adoption order is in force, be construed as references to the adopters or the adopter or the surviving adopter under the order.

8   (Amends First Schedule to the Principal Act)

9   Short title, collective citation and construction

(1) This Act may be cited as the Adoption Act, 1988.

(2) The Acts and this Act may be cited together as the Adoption Acts, 1952 to 1988.

(3) The Acts and this Act shall be construed together as one.

Adoption Act, 1991

(1991 No 14)

ARRANGEMENT OF SECTIONS

ACTS REFERRED TO

Adoption Act, 1952   1952, No 25
Adoption Act, 1964   1964, No 2
Adoption Act, 1974   1974, No 24
Adoption Acts, 1952 to 1988
Health Act, 1970   1970, No 1

An Act to provide for the recognition of certain adoptions effected outside the State, to amend and extend the Adoption Acts, 1952 to 1988, and to make further provision in connection with the matters aforesaid   [30 May 1991]

1 Definitions

In this Act—

'adoption order' means an order under section 9 of the Principal Act;
'the Board' means An Bord Uchtála;
'health board' means a health board established under the Health Act, 1970;
'the Court' means the High Court;
'foreign adoption' means an adoption of a child who at the date on which the adoption was effected under the age of 21 years or, if the adoption was effected after the commencement of this Act, 18 years, which was effected outside the State by a person or persons under and in accordance with the law of the place where it was effected and in relation to which the following conditions are satisfied:

(a) the consent to the adoption of every person whose consent to the adoption was, under the law of the place where the adoption was effected, required to be obtained or dispensed with was obtained or dispensed with under that law,

(b) the adoption has essentially the same legal effect as respects the termination and creation of parental rights and duties with respect to the child in the place where it was effected as an adoption effected by an adoption order,

(c) the law of the place where the adoption was effected required an enquiry to be carried out, as far as was practicable, into the adopters, the child and the parents or guardian,

(d) the law of the place where the adoption was effected required the court or other authority or person by whom the adoption was effected, before doing so, to give due consideration to the interests and welfare of the child,

(e) the adopters have not received, made or given or caused to be made or given any payment or other reward (other than any payment reasonably and properly made in connection with the making of the arrangements for the adoption) in consideration of the adoption or agreed to do so,

and 'adopter' and 'adopted child' shall be construed accordingly,

'the Minister' means the Minister for Health,

'place' means a country or any of the following jurisdictions, that is to say, England and Wales, Scotland, Northern Ireland, the Isle of Man and the Channel Islands or, in relation to a country that has in matters of adoption two or more systems of law applying in different territorial units, any of the territorial units,

'the Principal Act' means the Adoption Act, 1952,

'the Register' means the Register of Foreign Adoptions established under *section 6* of this Act.

2 Foreign adoptions effected in place of domicile of adopters

(1) A foreign adoption (whether effected before or after the commencement of this Act) effected in, or recognised under the law of, a place in which either or both of the adopters were domiciled on the date on which the adoption was effected shall be deemed, unless such deeming would be contrary to public policy, to have been effected by a valid adoption order made on that date.

(2) This section and *sections 3, 4* and *5* of this Act are in substitution for any rule of law providing for the recognition of adoptions effected outside the State.

3 Foreign adoptions effected in place of habitual residence of adopters

A foreign adoption (whether effected before or after the commencement of this Act) effected in, or recognised under the law of, a place in which either or both of the adopters were habitually resident on the date on which the adoption was effected shall be deemed, unless such deeming would be contrary to public policy, to have been effected by a valid adoption order made—

(a) on that date, or

(b) on such commencement,

whichever is the later.

4   Foreign adoptions effected in place where adopters ordinarily resident

A foreign adoption (whether effected before or after the commencement of this Act) effected in, or recognised under the law of, a place in which either or both of the adopters were ordinarily resident for a period of not less than one year ending on the date on which the adoption was affected shall be deemed, unless such deeming would be contrary to public policy, to have been effected by a valid adoption order made—

(a) on the date, or

(b) on such commencement,

whichever is the later.

5   Foreign adoptions where adopters ordinarily resident in State

(1) A foreign adoption (whether effected before or after the commencement of this Act), other than an adoption specified in *section 2, 3* or *4* of this Act, shall be deemed, unless such deeming would be contrary to public policy, to have been effected by a valid adoption order made—

(a) on the date on which the adoption was effected, or

(b) on such commencement,

whichever is the later, if, but only if—

(i)   the adopters are persons coming within the classes of persons in whose favour an adoption order may, by virtue of *section 10* of this Act, be made,

(ii) the adopters were ordinarily resident in the State on the date on which the adoption was effected, and

(iii) (I)   in case the adoption was effected before the 1st day of April, 1991, the Board declares in writing that it is satisfied that the adopters are persons in whose favour an adoption order may, by virtue of the said *section 10*, be made, or

(II) in case the adoption was effected on or after the 1st day of April, 1991, the Board declares in writing before the date on which the adoption was effected—

(A) that it is satisfied that the adopters are persons coming within the classes of persons in whose favour an adoption order may, by virtue of the said *section 10*, be made, and

(B) that (having had regard to a report by the health board in whose functional area the adopters were ordinarily resident at the time of the assessment, or by a registered adoption society, of an assessment as respects the matters referred to in section 13 of the Principal Act in relation to the adopters carried out by the board or the society, as the case may be) it is satisfied in relation to the adopters as respects the matters referred to in the said section 13.

(2) Notwithstanding anything in *subsection (1)*, where a foreign adoption was effected on or after the 1st day of April, 1991, and before the 1st day of July, 1991, and the Minister for Justice had received a request in writing from the adopters before the said 1st day of April, 1991, for an assurance in writing addressed to them as to the admission to the State of a child the subject of a foreign adoption effected in their favour, the adoption shall be deemed, unless such deeming would be contrary to public policy, to have been effected by a valid adoption order made—

(a) on the date on which the adoption was effected, or

(b) on the commencement of this Act,

whichever is the later, if but only if—

  (i) the Minister for Justice gave such an assurance as aforesaid,
  (ii) the adopters are persons coming within the classes of persons in whose favour an adoption order may, by virtue of *section 10* of this Act, be made,
  (iii) the adopters were ordinarily resident in the State on the date on which the adoption was effected, and
  (iv) the Board declares in writing that it is satisfied that the adopters are persons coming within the classes of persons in whose favour an adoption order may, by virtue of the said *section 10*, be made.

(3) (a) The adopters or the adopted child in relation to a foreign adoption or any other person having an interest in the matter may apply to the Board for the making of a declaration under *paragraph (iii)(I)* of *subsection (1)* or *subsection (2)(iv)* of this section in relation to the adopters, and the Board shall, if it is satisfied that it is appropriate to do so having regard to the provisions of those subsections, make the declaration.

   (b) A person or persons to whom the said *subsection (1)* applies and who has or have applied, or proposes or propose to apply, for the effecting in his or their favour of a foreign adoption may, before the adoption is effected, apply to the Board for the making of a declaration under *paragraph (iii)(II)* of the said *subsection (1)* in relation to the person or persons, and the Board shall, if it is satisfied that it is appropriate to do so having regard to the provisions of that subsection, make the declaration.

   (c) A person making an application to the Board under this subsection shall furnish the Board with such information as it may reasonably require and the information shall be in such form (if any) as may be specified.

   (d) A document purporting to be a copy, and to be certified by an officer of the Board to be a true copy, of such a declaration as aforesaid shall—
       (i) be evidence of the facts stated therein, and
       (ii) be issued by the Board to any person on application by him to the Board in that behalf.

(4) For the purposes of this section, a person in whose favour a foreign adoption was effected at any time before the commencement of this Act and who was not a widow or the mother or father or a relative of the adopted child shall be deemed to be a person in whose favour an adoption order might, by virtue of *section 10* of this Act, have been made on the date on which the foreign adoption was effected.

(5) A declaration under *subsection (1)(iii)(II)* of this section shall be expressed to and shall apply only in relation to an adoption effected during the period of 12 months from the date of the making of the declaration or such longer period as, on application to it in that behalf by the persons concerned during the period of 12 months aforesaid, the Board, being satisfied that it is reasonable and proper to do so, endorses on the declaration.

6   Register of Foreign Adoptions

(1) The Board shall establish and maintain a register (to be known as the Register of Foreign Adoptions).

(2) (a) If, an application to the Board in that behalf, in relation to an adoption effected outside the State, being an application made by the person who was the subject of the adoption or a person by whom a person was adopted

pursuant to the adoption or any other person having an interest in the matter, the Board is satisfied that—

(i) the adoption is a foreign adoption to which *section 2, 3* or *4* of this Act applies, or

(ii) the adoption is a foreign adoption to which *section 5* of this Act applies, then, unless (in a case to which *clause (II)* of *section 5(1)(iii)* of this Act applies) the Board is satisfied that the relevant circumstances have so changed since the date of the declaration under that clause that it would not be proper, having regard to section 13 of the Principal Act and *section 10* of this Act, an entry shall be made in the Register with respect to the adoption.

(b) If the Court so directs under *section 7* of this Act, an entry shall be made in the Register concerning a specified foreign adoption.

(3) An entry in the Register shall be in such form and contain such particulars as may be prescribed by rules made under section 5 of the Principal Act.

(4) A person making an application to the Board under this section shall furnish the Board with such information as the Board may reasonably require and the information shall be in such form (if any) as may be specified by the Board.

(5) An error in an entry in the Register may be corrected and, if the Court so directs, a specified correction shall be made in the Register.

(6) If the Board is satisfied that an adoption in relation to which there is an entry in the Register has been set aside, annulled or otherwise rendered void under and in accordance with the law of the place where it was effected or if the Court so directs under *section 7* of this Act in relation to an entry in the Register, the entry shall be cancelled.

(7) A document purporting to be a copy, and to be certified by an officer of the Board to be a true copy, of an entry in the Register—

(a) shall be evidence of the fact that the adoption to which it relates is a foreign adoption and is deemed by this Act to have been effected by a valid adoption order made on the date specified in the copy, and

(b) shall be issued by the Board, to any person on application by him to it in that behalf and on payment by him to it of such fee as may be specified by the Board with the consent of the Minister,

and any requirement of the law for the production of a certificate of birth shall be satisfied by the production of such a document.

(8) Section 20 of the Principal Act shall apply to an application under *subsection (2)* of this section as it applies to an application for an adoption order with the modification that the Board shall refer any question in relation to public policy arising on such an application to the High Court for determination and with any other necessary modification.

7 Directions of High Court in relation to entries in Register of Foreign Adoptions

(1) If, on application to the Court in that behalf by a person who may make an application to the Board under *section 6(2)* of this Act, the Court is satisfied that an entry should be made in the Register with respect to an adoption or that an entry in the Register with respect to an adoption should be cancelled or that a correction should be made in an entry in the Register, the Court may by order, as appropriate—

(a) direct the Board to procure the making of a specified entry in the Register,

(b) direct the Board to procure the cancellation of the entry concerned in the Register, or

(c) direct the Board to make a specified correction in the Register.

(2) If the Court refuses to give a direction under *paragraph (a)* of *subsection (1)* of this section or gives a direction under *paragraph (b)* of the subsection, the adoption concerned shall be deemed not to have been effected by a valid adoption order.

(3) (a) The Court may direct that notice of an application under the said *subsection (1)* shall be given by the person making the application to such other persons (including the Attorney General and the Board) as it may determine and may, of its own motion or on application to it in that behalf by the person concerned or a party to the proceedings in relation to the application under the said *subsection (1)*, add any person as a party to those proceedings.

(b) The Attorney General, of his own motion or if so requested by the Court, may, without being added as party to proceedings in relation to an application under the said *subsection (1)*, make submissions to the Court in relation to the application.

(4) Proceedings under this section shall, if the Court so determines, be heard otherwise than in public.

8 Assessments by health boards and registered adoption societies

(1) Whenever a health board is so requested, for the purposes of *section 5(1)(iii)(II)* of this Act, by a person or persons who is or are ordinarily resident in its functional area, it shall, as soon as practicable—

(a) carry out an assessment of the person or persons as respects the matters referred to in section 13 of the Principal Act and shall prepare a report in writing of the assessment and shall transmit the report to the Board, or

(b) arrange for the carrying out of such an assessment and the preparation of such a report in relation thereto by a registered adoption society and shall transmit the report to the Board.

(2) Where—

(a) at the request of a person or persons, for the purposes of the said *section 5(1)(iii)(II)*, or

(b) pursuant to an arrangement under *subsection (1)* of this section,

a registered adoption society carries out an assessment of a person or persons as respects the matters referred to in the said section 13, it shall prepare a report in writing of the assessment and shall transmit it, in a case to which *paragraph (a)* of this subsection relates, to the Board and, in a case to which *paragraph (b)* of this subsection relates, to the health board concerned.

(3) Upon the making of a declaration under the said *section 5(1)(iii)(II)*, a copy of the report concerned under *subsection (1)* or *(2)* of this section shall be made available by the Board to the person or persons who are the subject of the declaration and to any person in the place where the adoption concerned is proposed to be effected having an interest in the matter.

(4) The functions of a health board under *subsection (1)* of this section shall be functions of the chief executive officer of the board or a person acting as deputy chief executive officer of the board in accordance with section 13 of the Health Act, 1970.

9   Proof of adoptions effected outside State

(1) (a)   A document, duly authenticated, which purports to be a copy of the document by which an adoption outside the State was effected shall without further proof be deemed to be a true copy of the document unless the contrary is shown and shall be admissible as evidence of the adoption.

(b)   Documents, duly authenticated, which purport to be copies of the documents by which an adoption outside the State was effected shall without further proof be deemed to be true copies of the documents unless the contrary is shown and shall be admissible as evidence of the adoption.

(2) A document purporting to be a copy of a document or of one of the documents by which an adoption outside the State is effected shall, for the purposes of this section, be regarded as being duly authenticated if it purports—

(a)   to bear the seal of the court or other authority or the person or persons by which or by whom it was issued or executed, or

(b)   to be certified—

(i)   by a person in his capacity as a judge or officer of that court or in his capacity as that authority or as a member or officer of that authority, or

(ii)   by the person or persons by whom it was issued or executed.

(3) (a)   The Minister may by regulations make provision in relation to the proof of adoptions effected outside the State and the regulations may make different provision as respects different places and different classes of adoptions.

(b)   Provisions of regulations under this subsection may be in addition to or in substitution for the provisions of *subsections (1)* and *(2)* of this section and may amend those provisions.

(4) Where an adoption is effected in a place outside the State, it shall be presumed, until the contrary is shown, that it was effected under and in accordance with the law of that place.

10   Eligibility to be granted an adoption order

(1) Subject to *subsection (2)* of this section, an adoption order shall not be made unless—

(a)   the applicants are a married couple who are living together, or

(b)   the applicant is the mother or father or a relative of the child, or

(c)   the applicant is a widow or a widower.

(2) Notwithstanding *subsection (1)* of this section, where the Board is satisfied that, in the particular circumstances of the case, it is desirable, an adoption order may be made in favour of an applicant who is not a person specified in *paragraph (b)* or *(c)* of *subsection (1)* of this section.

(3) Subject to *subsection (1)(a)* of this section, an adoption order shall not be made for the adoption of a child by more than one person.

(4) An adoption order shall not be made for the adoption of a child by an applicant who is married without the consent of the spouse of the applicant (which shall be given in such manner as may be determined by the Board) unless—

(a)   the couple are living apart under—

(i)   a decree of divorce *a mensa et thoro*, or

(ii)   a decree of judicial separation, or

      (iii) a deed of separation,
- (b) the spouse has deserted the applicant or conduct on the part of the spouse results in the applicant, with just cause, leaving and living separately and apart from him.

(5) An adoption order shall not be made unless—

- (a) the applicant and, if the applicants are a married couple, each of them has attained the age of 21 years, or
- (b) the applicants are a married couple and one of them is the mother or father or a relative of the child and either of them has attained the age of 21 years.

(6) An adoption order shall not be made unless the applicant or the applicants is or are ordinarily resident in the State and has or have been so resident during the year ending on the date of the order.

(7) Section 11 of the Principal Act, section 5 of the Adoption Act, 1964, and section 5 of the Adoption Act, 1974, are hereby repealed.

11   Amendment of section 8 of the Principal Act

(1) (Amends s 8 of the Principal Act)

(2) Notwithstanding paragraph 2(1) of the First Schedule to the Principal Act, the two persons first appointed, by virtue of the amendment of section 8 of the Principal Act effected by this section, to be members of the Board shall be appointed for such period ending on the 29th day of January, 1993, as the Government may determine.

12   Short title, collective citation and construction

(1) This Act may be cited as the Adoption Act, 1991.

(2) The Adoption Acts, 1952 to 1988, and this Act may be cited together as the Adoption Acts, 1952 to 1991.

(3) The Adoption Acts, 1952 and 1988, and this Act shall be construed together as one.

Age of Majority Act, 1985

(1985 No 2)

ARRANGEMENT OF SECTIONS

ACTS REFERRED TO

Social Welfare Acts, 1981 to 1984
Statute of Limitations 1957   1957, No 6
Succession Act, 1965   1965, No 27

An Act to amend the law relating to the age of majority and to the time when a person attains a particular age and to make other provisions connected with the foregoing

[12 February 1985]

1 Interpretation

(1) In this Act—

'full age' shall be construed in accordance with *section* 2;
'statutory provision' means any provision of a statute (within the meaning of section 3 of the Interpretation Act, 1937) or of a statutory instrument (within the meaning aforesaid) made under a power or authority conferred by such statute.

(2) A reference in this Act to a section or to the Schedule is a reference to a section of, or the Schedule to, this Act, unless it is indicated that a reference to some other statutory provision is intended.

(3) A reference in this Act to a subsection or paragraph is a reference to the subsection or paragraph of the provision in which the reference occurs, unless it is indicated that some other provision is intended.

(4) A reference to any other statutory provision shall, except where the context otherwise requires, be construed as a reference to that statutory provision as amended by or under any other statutory provision, including this Act.

2 Reduction of age of majority

(1) Where a person has not attained the age of twenty-one years prior to the commencement of this Act, he shall, subject to section 4, attain full age—

(a) on such commencement if he has attained the age of eighteen years or is or has been married, or
(b) after such commencement when he attains the age of eighteen years or, in case he marries before attaining that age, upon his marriage.

(2) Subsection (1) applies for the purposes of any rule of law and, in the absence of a definition or of any indication of a contrary intention, for the construction of 'age of majority', 'full age', 'infancy', 'infant', 'minor', 'minority' and of other cognate words and expressions in—

(a) any statutory provision passed or made before, on or after the commencement of this Act, and
(b) any deed, will, court order or other instrument (not being a statutory provision) made on or after such commencement.

(3) Where there is, in any statutory provision passed or made before the commencement of this Act, a reference to the age of twenty-one years, such provision shall, subject to subsection (4), be construed and have effect as if the reference therein were a reference to full age.

(4) (a) This section does not affect the construction of any reference to the age of twenty-one years, or of any word or expression to which subsection (2) relates, in any statutory provision to which this subsection applies.

(b) This subsection applies to—
  (i) the Marriages (Ireland) Act, 1844,
  (ii) the Marriage Law (Ireland) Amendment Act, 1863,
  (iii) the Matrimonial Causes and Marriage Law (Ireland) Amendment Act, 1870,
  (iv) the Marriages Act, 1972,
  (v) the Adoption Acts, 1952 to 1976,
  (vi) the Social Welfare Acts, 1981 to 1984,
  (vii) the Income Tax Acts and any other statutory provision dealing with the imposition, repeal, remission, alteration or regulation of any tax or other duty under the care and management of the Revenue Commissioners,
  (viii) any provision of the Illegitimate Children (Affiliation Orders) Act, 1930, the Guardianship of Infants Acts, 1964, or the Family Law (Maintenance of Spouses and Children) Act, 1976, that provides for payments to be made for maintenance or support of children up to the age of twenty-one years.
  (ix) any statutory provision that provides for the payment of a pension or other allowance for children up to the age of twenty-one years, and
  (x) any statutory provision relating to prisons, to Saint Patrick's Institution or to any other place for the custody of persons.

3   Description of person not of full age

A person who is not of full age may be described as a minor instead of as an infant and, accordingly, in this Act 'minor' means such a person.

4   Time at which person attains a particular age

(1) Subject to subsection (3), the time at which a person attains a particular age expressed in years shall, for the purposes of any rule of law or of any statutory provision, deed, will or other instrument, be the commencement of the relevant anniversary of the date of his birth.

(2) Subsection (1) applies only where the relevant anniversary falls on a date after that on which this Act comes into operation, and, in relation to any statutory provision, deed, will or other instrument, has effect subject to any provision therein.

(3) (a) The date on which a person attains the age of eighteen years shall, for the purposes of any statutory provision to which this subsection applies, be calculated in the same manner as it is calculated for the purpose of determining whether a person has the right to vote at an election for members of Dáil Éireann.
  (b) This subsection applies to—
    (i) the Electoral Acts, 1923 to 1983,
    (ii) the Presidential Elections Acts, 1937 to 1973,
    (iii) the Seanad Electoral (University Members) Acts, 1937 to 1973,
    (iv) the Referendum Acts, 1942 to 1984,
    (v) the Local Elections Acts, 1963 to 1974, and
    (vi) the European Assembly Elections Acts, 1977 and 1984.

5   (Amends ss 76 and 107 of the Defence Act, 1954)

6   (Amends s 11 of the Guardianship of Infants Act, 1964)

7   Transitional provisions and savings

(1) The transitional provisions and savings contained in the Schedule shall have effect in relation to Section 2.

(2) Notwithstanding any rule of law, a will or codicil executed before the commencement of this Act shall not be treated for the purposes of section 2 or the Schedule as having been made on or after such commencement by reason only of the fact that the will or codicil is confirmed by a codicil executed after such commencement.

(3) Where before the commencement of this Act a justice of the District Court, by virtue of section 2 of the Courts of Justice (District Court) Act, 1949, or a county registrar, by virtue of section 56 of the Courts (Supplemental Provisions) Act, 1961, is continued in office to a date which occurs on or after the day immediately prior to the commencement of this Act, the warrant by which he is so continued shall, for the purpose of extending the period to which that warrant relates, be construed and have effect so as to continue him in office up to but excluding the next anniversary date of his birth after such commencement.

8   Repeals

The following are hereby repealed:

   (a)   the Infant Settlements Act, 1855,
   (b)   the Infant Marriage Act, 1860,
   (c)   in section 6 of the Employers and Workmen Act, 1875, the paragraph numbered
          (1) and the last sentence, and
   (d)   section 13 (2) (d) of the Married Women's Status Act, 1957.

9   Short title and commencement

(1) This Act may be cited as the Age of Majority Act, 1985.

(2) This Act shall come into operation on the 1st day of March, 1985.

SCHEDULE   Section 7

TRANSITIONAL PROVISIONS AND SAVINGS

1 Funds in Court

Any order or directions in force immediately before the commencement of this Act by virtue of any rules of court or other statutory provision relating to the control of money recovered by, or on behalf of or otherwise payable to, an infant in any proceedings shall have effect as if any reference therein to an infant's attaining the age of twenty-one years were a reference to his attaining full age and any provision in such order or directions referring, whether expressly or by implication, to the period before which, or the time at which, a person attains the age of majority shall be construed accordingly.

2 Wardship and Custody Orders

(1) Any order in force immediately before the commencement of this Act—

- (a) making a person a ward of court, or
- (b) otherwise providing for the custody of, or access to, any person,

that is expressed to continue in force until the person who is the subject of the order attains the age of twenty-one years, or any age between the age of eighteen and twenty-one years, shall have effect as if the reference to his attaining that age were a reference to his attaining full age.

(2) This paragraph is without prejudice to any provision in any such order that provides or allows for the maintenance or education of a person after he has attained full age.

3 Power of Trustees to Apply Income for Maintenance of Minor

(1) Section 2 shall not affect section 42 or 43 of the Conveyancing Act, 1881, in their application to any estate or interest under an instrument made before the commencement of this Act.

(2) In any case in which (whether by virtue of this paragraph or paragraph 7) trustees have power, under subsection (4) of the said section 42 or subsection (1) of the said section 43, to pay income to the parent or guardian of any person who has attained full age, or to apply it for or towards the maintenance, education or benefit of any such person, they shall also have power to pay it to that person himself.

4 Powers of Personal Representatives During Minority of Beneficiary

In the case of a beneficiary whose interest arises under a will or codicil made before the commencement of this Act or on the death before that date of an intestate, section 2 shall not affect the meaning of 'infant' in sections 57 and 58 of the Succession Act, 1965.

5 Accumulation Periods

The change, by virtue of section 2, in the construction of section 1 of the Accumulations Act, 1892, shall not invalidate any direction for accumulation in a settlement or other disposition made by a deed, will or other instrument that was made before the commencement of this Act.

6 Limitation of Actions

The change by virtue of section 2 in the construction of section 48(1) of the Statute of Limitations, 1957, shall not affect the time for bringing proceedings in respect of a right of action that accrued before the commencement of this Act.

7 Statutory Provisions Incorporated in Deeds and Wills

Section 2 shall not affect the construction of any statutory provision which is incorporated in and has effect as part of any deed, will or other instrument the construction of which is not affected by that section.

PART TWO

Child Abduction and Enforcement of Custody Orders Act, 1991

(1991 No 6)

ARRANGEMENT OF SECTIONS

PART I

PRELIMINARY AND GENERAL

PART II

THE HAGUE CONVENTION

PART III

THE LUXEMBOURG CONVENTION

PART IV

SUPPLEMENTARY

PART V

MISCELLANEOUS

FIRST SCHEDULE

SECOND SCHEDULE

ACTS REFERRED TO

Judicial Separation and Family Law Reform Act, 1989   1989, No 6

An Act to give the force of law to the Convention on the Civil Aspects of International Child Abduction signed at The Hague on the 25th day of October, 1980, and the European Convention on Recognition and Enforcement of Decisions Concerning Custody of Children and on Restoration of Custody of Children signed at Luxembourg on the 20th day of May, 1980, and to provide for matters consequent upon and otherwise related to the matters aforesaid

[27 March 1991]

PART ONE

PART I

PRELIMINARY AND GENERAL

1   Short title, construction and commencement

(1) This Act may be cited as the Child Abduction and Enforcement of Custody Orders Act, 1991.

(2) The Courts (Supplemental Provisions) Acts, 1961 to 1988, and this Act, insofar as it affects the jurisdiction or procedure of any court in the State, shall be construed together as one.

(3) This Act shall come into operation on such day or days as the Minister shall fix by order or orders either generally or with reference to any particular purpose or provision and different days may be so fixed for different purposes and different provisions.

2   Interpretation

In this Act—

'Central Authority in the State' shall be construed in accordance with *section 8* or *22* (as may be appropriate) of this Act;

'child' where used in the context of the Children Act, 1908, includes a young person within the meaning of that Act;

'the Court' means the High Court;

'the Hague Convention' means the Convention on the Civil Aspects of International Child Abduction, signed at The Hague on the 25th day of October, 1980;

'health board' means a health board established under the Health Act, 1970;

'the Luxembourg Convention' means the European Convention on Recognition and Enforcement of Decisions concerning Custody of Children and on Restoration of Custody of Children, signed at Luxembourg on the 20th day of May, 1980;

'the Minister' means the Minister for Justice, Equality and Law Reform;

'prescribed' means prescribed by regulations made by the Minister under this Act;

'probation and welfare officer' means a person appointed by the Minister for Justice to be a probation and welfare officer or to be a welfare officer or probation officer.

Amendments—Family Law Act, 1995, s 55(a)(b); Children Act, 1997, s 18.

PART II

THE HAGUE CONVENTION

3   'Contracting State'

In this Part 'Contracting State' means a state in respect of which the Hague Convention is in force in accordance with the provisions of that Convention and shall be construed so that this Act shall have effect in relation to—

(a)   the states which have acceded to that Convention, or any states which may accede to that Convention, and in respect of which the State has made a declaration pursuant to Article 38 of that Convention, and

(b)   the places as respects which that Convention has effect by virtue of Articles 39 and 40 of that Convention.

4   Contracting States and declarations, reservations, withdrawals and denunciations under Hague Convention

(1) The Minister for Foreign Affairs may by order declare—

(a)   that any state specified in the order is a Contracting State, or

(b)   that—

(i)   a declaration (the text of which shall be set out in the order) has been made pursuant to Article 38, 39 or 40 of the Hague Convention, or

(ii)   a reservation, or a withdrawal thereof (the text of which shall be set out in the order) has been made pursuant to Article 24, 26 or (in the case of a withdrawal) 42 of that Convention, or

(iii) a denunciation (the text of which shall be set out in the order) has been made pursuant to Article 44 of that Convention,

to the Ministry of Foreign Affairs of the Kingdom of the Netherlands.

(2) An order that is in force under *subsection (1)* of this section shall, as the case may be, be evidence—

(a)   that any state specified in the order is a Contracting State;

(b)   that a declaration, a reservation, a withdrawal of a reservation or a denunciation set out in the order was made and of its contents.

(3) The Minister for Foreign Affairs may by order amend or revoke an order under this section (including an order under this subsection).

5   Evidence of decisions and determinations of authorities of Contracting States and other matters relating to Hague Convention

(1) For the purposes of Article 14 of the Hague Convention a document, duly authenticated, which purports to be a copy of a decision or determination of a judicial or administrative authority of a Contracting State other than the State shall without further proof be deemed to be a true copy of the decision or determination, unless the contrary is shown.

(2) For the purposes of Articles 14 and 30 of the Hague Convention the original or a copy of any such document as is mentioned in Article 8 of that Convention shall be admissible—

(a)   insofar as it consists of a statement of fact, as evidence of that fact, and

(b) insofar as it consists of a statement of opinion, as evidence of that opinion.

(3) A document which—

(a) purports to be a translation of a decision or determination of a judicial or administrative authority of a Contracting State other than the State or of a document mentioned in Article 8 of the Hague Convention, and

(b) is certified as correct by a person competent to do so,

shall be admissible as evidence of the translation.

(4) A document purporting to be a copy of a decision, determination or declaration of a judicial or administrative authority of a Contracting State shall, for the purposes of this Part, be regarded as being duly authenticated if it purports—

(a) to bear the seal of that authority, or

(b) to be certified by a person in his capacity as a judge or officer of that authority to be a true copy of a decision, determination or declaration of that authority.

6   Hague Convention to have the force of law

(1) Subject to the provisions of this Part, the Hague Convention shall have the force of law in the State and judicial notice shall be taken of it.

(2) The text of the Hague Convention in the English language is set out for convenience of reference in the *First Schedule* to this Act.

7   Jurisdiction of the Court for purposes of *Part II*

(1) For the purposes of this Part and the Hague Convention the Court shall have jurisdiction to hear and determine applications under that Convention.

(2) For the purposes of such applications the expression 'the judicial or administrative authority' where it occurs in the Hague Convention shall be construed as referring to the Court unless the context otherwise requires.

8   Central Authority for purposes of Hague Convention

(1) The Minister may by order appoint a Central Authority (referred to in this Part as the Central Authority in the State) to discharge the functions under the Hague Convention of a Central Authority.

(2) Notwithstanding *subsection (1)* of this section, unless and until the Minister appoints a Central Authority under this section, the said functions shall be discharged by the Minister and references in this Part to the Central Authority in the State shall be construed, accordingly, as references to the Minister.

(3) The Minister may by order amend or revoke an order under this section (including an order under this subsection).

9   Application for return of child removed to the State

(1) Any application, in such form as may be prescribed, made under the Hague Convention in respect of a child removed to the State may be addressed to the Central Authority in the State.

(2) Where the Central Authority in the State receives any such application and is satisfied that the application is an application to which the Hague Convention applies, it

shall take action or cause action to be taken under that Convention to secure the return of the child.

10 Application for return of child removed from the State

(1) Any application, in such form as may be prescribed, made under the Hague Convention in respect of a child removed from the State to another Contracting State may be addressed to the Central Authority in the State.

(2) Where the Central Authority in the State receives any such application and is satisfied that the application is an application to which the Hague Convention applies, it shall, on behalf of the applicant, take any action required to be taken by a Central Authority under that Convention.

(3) Nothing in *subsection (1)* of this section shall prevent the Central Authority in the State from dealing with any application made under the Hague Convention by or on behalf of a person in respect of a child removed from a Contracting State (not being the State) to another Contracting State (not being the State).

11 Operation of this Part not to affect jurisdiction of the Court

Nothing in this Part shall prevent a person from applying in the first instance to the Court, whether or not under the Hague Convention, in respect of the breach of rights of custody of, or breach of rights of access to, a child removed to the State.

12 Interim powers of the Court for the purposes of *Part II*

(1) Where an application has been made or is about to be made to the Court under the Hague Convention, the Court may of its own motion or on an application under this section, at any time before the application is determined, give such interim directions as it thinks fit for the purpose of securing the welfare of the child concerned, or preventing prejudice to interested persons or changes in the circumstances relevant to the determination of the application.

(2) An application for interim directions under this section may, where the case is one of urgency, be made *ex parte.*

13 Notice and stay of certain proceedings for purposes of *Part II*

(1) Any person who has an interest in proceedings in the Court or in proceedings about to be commenced in the Court under this Part in respect of a child removed to the State shall, where he knows that an application relating to the custody of the child is pending in or before any court in the State, give notice to that court of the proceedings, or pending proceedings (as the case may be), under the Hague Convention and that court, having notified the parties to the proceedings before it of that notice, shall stay in accordance with Article 16 of that Convention all further proceedings in the matter and shall notify the Court of the stay.

(2) For the purpose of this section an application relating to custody of a child shall be construed as including a reference to an application for—

    (a) an order making, varying or discharging an order regarding the custody of, or the right of access to, a child under the Guardianship of Infants Act, 1964;

    (b) an order made pursuant to Part II or IV of the Children Act, 1908, in relation to the care of a child;

(c) the recognition or enforcement of a decision relating to custody under *Part III* of this Act.

14 Reports for purposes of *Part II*

Where the Central Authority in the State is requested to provide information relating to a child under Article 7.(d) of the Hague Convention it may—

(a) request a probation and welfare officer to make a report to it in writing with respect to any matter relating to the child which appears to it to be relevant;

(b) request a health board to arrange for a suitably qualified person to make such a report to it, or

(c) request any court to which a written report relating to the child has been made to send it a copy of the report,

and any such request shall be duly complied with.

15 Declaration by the Court of wrongful removal of child

(1) The Court may, on an application made for the purposes of Article 15 of the Hague Convention by any person appearing to the Court to have an interest in the matter, make a declaration that the removal of any child from, or his retention outside, the State was wrongful within the meaning of Article 3 of that Convention.

(2) The Central Authority in the State shall take action or cause action to be taken to assist the person referred to in *subsection (1)* of this section in making an application under this section if a request for such assistance, in such form as may be prescribed, is made by him or on his behalf by the Central Authority of another Contracting State.

16 Provision of certain documents by courts in the State for purposes of Hague Convention

As respects a decision relating to custody made by a court in the State (including a declaration made by the Court under *section 15* of this Act) the registrar or clerk of the court shall, at the request of a person who wishes to make an application under the Hague Convention in a Contracting State other than the State or at the request on his behalf of the Central Authority in the State and subject to any conditions that may be specified by rules of court, given to the person or the Central Authority, as the case may be, the following documents—

(a) a copy of the decision duly authenticated;

(b) where the decision was given in default of appearance, the original or a copy, certified by the registrar or clerk of the court to be a true copy, of a document establishing that notice of the institution of proceedings was served on the person in default.

PART III

THE LUXEMBOURG CONVENTION

17 Interpretation of *Part III*

In this Part—

'Contracting State' means a state in respect of which the Luxembourg Convention is in force in accordance with the provisions of that Convention and shall be construed so that this Part shall have effect in relation to the places as respects which that Convention has effect by virtue of Articles 24 and 25 of that Convention;

'decision relating to custody' has the meaning given to it in Article 1 of the Luxembourg Convention;

'enforcement order' means an order of the Court for the recognition or enforcement of a decision relating to custody to which either Article 7 or 12 of the Luxembourg Convention applies.

18 Contracting States and declarations, reservations, withdrawals, notifications and denunciations under Luxembourg Convention

(1) The Minister for Foreign Affairs may by order declare—

  (a) that any state specified in the order is a Contracting State, or

  (b) that—

    (i) a reservation, or a withdrawal thereof (the text of which shall be set out in the order) has been made pursuant to Article 6.3, 17, 18 or (in the case of a withdrawal) 27 of the Luxembourg Convention, or

    (ii) a declaration (the text of which shall be set out in the order) has been made pursuant to Article 24 or 25 of that Convention, or

    (iii) a notification (the text of which shall be set out in the order) has been received pursuant to Article 2 of that Convention, or

    (iv) a notification of a decision or of an alteration or revocation of a decision (the text of which shall be set out in the order) has been made pursuant to Article 20 of that Convention, or

    (v) a denunciation (the text of which shall be set out in the order) has been made pursuant to Article 29 of that Convention,

  to or by, as the case may be, the Secretary General of the Council of Europe.

(2) An order that is in force under *subsection (1)* of this section shall, as the case may be, be evidence—

  (a) that any state specified in the order is a Contracting State;

  (b) that a reservation, a withdrawal of a reservation, a declaration, a notification or a denunciation set out in the order was made or received and of its contents.

(3) The Minister for Foreign Affairs may by order amend or revoke an order under this section (including an order under this subsection).

19 Evidence of decisions and declarations of authorities of Contracting States and other matters relating to Luxembourg Convention

(1) For the purposes of the Luxembourg Convention—

  (a) a document, duly authenticated, which purports to be a copy of a decision or declaration relating to custody of a judicial or administrative authority of a Contracting State other than the State shall without further proof be deemed to be a true copy of the decision or declaration, unless the contrary is shown, and

  (b) the original or a copy of any other document as is mentioned in Article 13 of the Luxembourg Convention shall be admissible—

    (i) insofar as it consists of a statement of fact, as evidence of that fact, and

    (ii) insofar as it consists of a statement of opinion, as evidence of that opinion.

(2) A document which—

    (a) purports to be a translation of a decision or declaration of a judicial or administrative authority of a Contracting State other than the State or any other document mentioned in Article 13 of the Luxembourg Convention, and

    (b) is certified as correct by a person competent to do so,

shall be admissible as evidence of the translation.

(3) A document purporting to be a copy of a decision or declaration relating to custody made by a judicial or administrative authority of a Contracting State shall, for the purposes of this Part, be regarded as being duly authenticated if it purports—

    (a) to bear the seal of that authority, or

    (b) to be certified by a person in his capacity as a judge or officer of that authority to be a true copy of a decision or declaration of that authority.

20   Application of this Part

This Part applies to any decision relating to custody (by whatever name called) that is a decision relating to custody for the purposes of the Luxembourg Convention.

21   Luxembourg Convention to have the force of law

(1) Subject to the provisions of this Part (including the restrictions on recognition and enforcement of a decision relating to custody contained in *section 28* of this Act), the Luxembourg Convention shall have the force of law in the State and judicial notice shall be taken of it.

(2) The text of the Luxembourg Convention in the English language is set out for convenience of reference in the *Second Schedule* to this Act.

22   Central Authority for purposes of Luxembourg Convention

(1) The Minister may by order appoint a Central Authority (referred to in this Part as the Central Authority in the State) to discharge the functions under the Luxembourg Convention of a Central Authority.

(2) Notwithstanding *subsection (1)* of this section, unless and until the Minister appoints a Central Authority under this section, the said functions shall be discharged by the Minister and references in this Part to the Central Authority in the State shall be construed, accordingly, as references to the Minister.

(3) The Minister may by order amend or revoke an order under this section (including an order under this subsection).

23   Jurisdiction of the Court for purposes of *Part III*

For the purposes of this Part and the Luxembourg Convention the Court shall have jurisdiction to hear and determine applications under that Convention for the recognition or enforcement of a decision relating to custody.

24   Applications for recognition and enforcement of custody decisions in the State

(1) Any application, in such form as may be prescribed, made by or on behalf of a person on whom any rights are conferred by a decision relating to custody made by an authority

in a Contracting State other than the State for the recognition or enforcement of the decision in the State may be addressed to the Central Authority in the State.

(2) Where the Central Authority in the State receives any such application and is satisfied that the application is an application to which the Luxembourg Convention applies, it shall take action or cause action to be taken under that Convention to secure the recognition or enforcement of the decision.

25   Applications in the first instance to the Court

Nothing in this Part shall prevent a person from applying in the first instance to the Court under the Luxembourg Convention for the recognition or enforcement of a decision relating to custody made by an authority in a Contracting State, other than the State.

26   Interim powers of the Court for the purposes of *Part III*

(1) Where an application has been made or is about to be made to the Court under the Luxembourg Convention for the recognition or enforcement of a decision relating to custody, the Court may of its own motion or on an application under this section, at any time before the application is determined, give such interim directions as it thinks fit for the purpose of securing the welfare of the child concerned, or preventing prejudice to interested persons or changes in the circumstances relevant to the determination of the application.

(2) An application for interim directions under this section may, where the case is one of urgency, be made *ex parte.*

27   Notice and stay of certain proceedings for purposes of *Part III*

(1) Any person who has an interest in proceedings in the Court under this Part for the recognition or enforcement of a decision relating to custody made by an authority in a Contracting State other than the State shall, where he knows that an application relating to custody of the child is pending in or before any court in the State and such proceedings were commenced before the proceedings in the Contracting State which resulted in the decision in respect of which recognition or enforcement is sought were instituted, give notice to the Court of those proceedings and the Court may stay all further proceedings in the application for recognition or enforcement until the other proceedings have been determined.

(2) Any person who has an interest in proceedings in the Court under this Part for the recognition or enforcement of a decision relating to custody made by an authority in a Contracting State other than the State shall, where he knows that an application relating to custody of the child is pending in or before any court in the State and such proceedings in the Contracting State which resulted in the decision in respect of which recognition or enforcement is sought were instituted, give notice to that court of the proceedings under the Luxembourg Convention and that court having notified the parties to the proceedings before it of that notice shall stay all further proceedings in the matter until the Court determines the application for recognition or enforcement. The court concerned shall notify the Court of the stay.

(3) For the purpose of this section an application relating to custody of a child shall be construed as including a reference to an application for—

(a) an order making, varying or discharging an order regarding the custody of, or the right of access to, a child under the Guardianship of Infants Act, 1964;

(b) an order made pursuant to Part II or IV of the Children Act, 1908, in relation to the care of a child.

28 Refusal of application for recognition or enforcement of custody decision in the State

(1) The Court shall refuse an application made under this Part for recognition or enforcement in the State of a decision relating to custody where—

(a) in relation to a decision to which Article 8 of the Luxembourg Convention applies, the Court is of opinion on any of the grounds specified in Article 10.1.(a), (b), (c), or (d) of that Convention that the decision should not be recognised or enforced in the State;

(b) in relation to a decision to which Article 9 or 10 of that Convention applies, the Court is of opinion on any of the grounds specified in the said Articles that the decision should not be recognised or enforced in the State;

(c) the Court is of opinion that the decision is not enforceable in the Contracting State where it was made and is not a decision to which Article 12 of the Convention applies.

(2) Where an application is made to the Court under this Part for recognition or enforcement in the State of a decision relating to custody and an application to the Court in respect of the child is pending under *Part II* of this Act the Court shall stay all further proceedings under this Part until the other proceedings have been determined.

(3) The references in Article 9.1.(c) of the Luxembourg Convention to the removal of the child are to his improper removal within the meaning of that Convention.

(4) For the purposes of this section a decision relating to custody includes a decision varying that decision.

29 Enforcement of custody decisions

A decision relating to custody in respect of which an enforcement order has been made shall be of the same force and effect and, as respects the enforcement of the decision, the Court shall have the same powers, and proceedings may be taken, as if the decision was a decision of the Court.

30 Reports for purposes of *Part III*

Where the Central Authority in the State is requested to make enquiries about a child under Article 15.1.(b) of the Luxembourg Convention the Central Authority may—

(a) request a probation and welfare officer to make a report to it in writing with respect to any matter relating to the child which appears to it to be relevant;

(b) request a health board to arrange for a suitably qualified person to make such a report to it;

(c) request any court to which a written report relating to the child has been made to send it a copy of the report,

and any such request shall be duly complied with.

31 Variation and revocation of custody decisions

(1) Where a decision relating to custody is varied or revoked by an authority in the Contracting State in which it was made, any person appearing to the Court to have an

interest in the matter may make an application to the Court for an order for variation or revocation of the order of recognition or enforcement of that decision.

(2) Where an application is made under *subsection (1)* of this section for revocation of an order the Court shall, if it is satisfied that the decision (in respect of which the order of recognition or enforcement was made) has been revoked by an authority in the Contracting State in which it was made, discharge the order and the decision shall cease to be enforceable in the State.

(3) Where an application is made under *subsection (1)* of this section for variation of an order, the Court may, if it is satisfied that the decision has been varied by an authority in the Contracting State in which it was made and, subject to the grounds of refusal specified in *section 28(1)* of this Act, make an order varying the order and a decision so varied shall be of the same force and effect, and as respects the enforcement of the decision so varied, the Court shall have the same powers and proceedings may be taken, as if the decision so varied was a decision of the Court.

(4) The Central Authority in the State shall assist the person referred to in *subsection (1)* of this section if a request for such assistance, in such form as may be prescribed, is made by him or on his behalf by the Central Authority of the Contracting State in question.

32   Applications for recognition and enforcement of custody decisions in another Contracting State

(1) A person on whom any rights are conferred by a decision relating to custody made by a court in the State or by an authority within the meaning of the Luxembourg Convention in another Contracting State may make an application, in such form as may be prescribed, to the Central Authority in the State under Article 4 of the Luxembourg Convention with a view to securing its recognition or enforcement in another Contracting State.

(2) Where the Central Authority in the State receives any such application and is satisfied that the application is an application to which Article 4 of the Luxembourg Convention applies it shall, on behalf of the applicant, take any action required to be taken by a Central Authority under that Convention.

33   Provision of certain documents by courts in the State for purposes of Luxembourg Convention

As respects a decision relating to custody made by a court in the State (including a declaration made by a court under *section 34* of this Act), the registrar or clerk of the court shall, at the request of a person who wishes to make an application under the Luxembourg Convention in a Contracting State other than the State or at the request on his behalf of the Central Authority in the State and subject to any conditions that may be specified by rules of court, give to the person or the Central Authority, as the case may be, all or any of the documents referred to in Article 13.1.(b), (c) and (d) of that Convention, that is to say—

(a) a copy of the decision duly authenticated;
(b) a certificate signed by the registrar or clerk of the court stating—
    (i)   the nature of the proceedings,
    (ii) the date on which the time for the lodging of an appeal against the decision will expire or, if it has expired, the date on which it expired,
    (iii) whether notice of appeal against, or, in any case where the defendant does not appear, a notice to set aside, the decision has been entered, and

    (iv) such particulars (if any) as may be specified by rules of court, and

  (c) in case the decision was given in default of appearance, the original or a copy, certified by the registrar or clerk of the court to be a true copy, of a document establishing that notice of the institution of proceedings was served on the person in default.

34 Declaration by a court of unlawful removal of child

(1) Where a court in the State makes a decision relating to the custody of a child who has been removed from the State that court may also, on an application made by any person for the purposes of Article 12 of the Luxembourg Convention, make a declaration that the removal of the child from the State was unlawful if it is satisfied that the applicant has an interest in the matter and that the child has been taken from or sent or kept out of the State without the consent of any of the persons having the right to determine the child's place of residence under the law of the State.

(2) The Central Authority in the State shall take action or cause action to be taken to assist the person referred to in *subsection (1)* of this section in making an application under this section if a request for such assistance, in such form as may be prescribed, is made by him or on his behalf by the Central Authority of another Contracting State.

PART IV

SUPPLEMENTARY

35 Termination of existing custody orders

Where the Court makes—

  (a) an order for the return of a child under *Part II* of this Act, or

  (b) an order recognising or enforcing a decision relating to the custody of a child (other than a decision relating only to rights of access) under *Part III* of this Act,

the Court may, on notice to any interested parties, discharge any order regarding the custody of, or the right of access to, the child.

36 Power of the Court to order disclosure of child's whereabouts

(1) Where—

  (a) in proceedings for the return of a child under *Part II* of this Act, or

  (b) on an application for the recognition or enforcement of a decision in respect of a child under *Part III* of this Act,

there is not available to the Court adequate information as to the whereabouts of the child, the Court may order any person who, it has reason to believe, may have relevant information to disclose it to the Court.

(2) Any person who is the subject of an order under *subsection (1)* of this section may, notwithstanding production of the child, be ordered to disclose any information that is relevant to proceedings under *Part II* or *III* of this Act.

(3) Where—

  (a) in proceedings in a Contracting State other than the State for the return of a child under the Hague Convention, or

(b) in proceedings for the recognition or enforcement of a decision in a Contracting State other than the State in respect of a child under the Luxembourg Convention,

or where such proceedings are about to be commenced, there is not available to the authorities in the Contracting State adequate information as to the whereabouts of the child, the Court may, on application made to it by any person, if it is satisfied that the applicant has an interest in the matter and that the child has been taken from or sent or kept out of the State without the consent of any of the persons having the right to determine the child's place of residence under the law of the State, order any person who, it has reason to believe, may have relevant information to disclose it to the Court.

(4) Any person who is the subject of an order under *subsection (3)* of this section may, notwithstanding production of the child in the Contracting State, be ordered to disclose any information that is relevant to proceedings in that state.

(5) A person shall not be excused from complying with any order under this section by reason that to do so may incriminate him or his spouse of an offence; but a statement or admission made in compliance with any such order shall not be admissible in evidence against either of them in proceedings for an offence other than perjury.

37 Power of Garda Síochána to detain a child and matters consequential upon such detention

(1) A member of the Garda Síochána shall have power to detain a child who he reasonably suspects is about to be or is being removed from the State in breach of any of the following orders of a Court in the State—

(a) an order regarding the custody of, or right of access to, the child (whether or not such an order contains an order prohibiting the removal of the child from the jurisdiction without leave of the court) or any order relating to the child made by the court in the exercise of its jurisdiction relating to wardship of a child;
(b) an order made pursuant to Part II or IV of the Children Act, 1908, in relation to the care of the child;
(c) an order made under *section 12* of this Act or an order made for return of the child under *Part II* of this Act;
(d) an order made under *section 26* of this Act or an order made for recognition or enforcement of a decision relating to custody under *Part III* of this Act,

or while proceedings for one of those orders are pending or an application for one of those orders is about to be made.

(2) Where a child is detained under this section a member of the Garda Síochána shall as soon as possible—

(a) return the child to the custody of a person (not being a health board) in favour of whom a Court has made an order referred to in *subsection (1)* of this section unless the member has reasonable grounds for believing that such person will act in breach of such order, or
(b) where the child has been in the care of a health board, return the child to that board, or
(c) in a case other than one to which *paragraph (a)* or *(b)* of this subsection applies, or where the member is of the belief referred to in the said *paragraph (a)*, deliver the child into the care of the health board for the area in which the child is for the time being.

(3) Where a member of the Garda Síochána delivers into the care of a health board a child in accordance with *subsection (2)(c)* of this section, he shall as soon as possible inform or cause to be informed—

(a)   a parent of the child, or

(b)   a person acting *in loco parentis*, or

(c)   the Central Authority referred to in *section 8* (in a case to which *subsection (1)(c)* of this section applies) or *section 22* (in a case to which *subsection (1)(d)* of this section applies) of this Act,

of such delivery.

(4) Where any child is delivered into the care of a health board in accordance with *subsection (2)(c)* of this section the health board shall arrange suitable care and accommodation for the child, which may include placing the child in foster care or residential care, pending the determination of an application under *subsection (5)* of this section by the health board.

(5) Where a child is delivered into the care of a health board under *subsection (2)(c)* of this section the health board shall apply at the next sitting of the District Court or, in the event that the next sitting is not due to be held within three days of the date on which the child is delivered into the care of the health board, at a specially arranged sitting of the District Court held within the said three days, for directions as to the child's release from such care or otherwise in relation to the child's care and the District Court may make such order as it thinks proper in the circumstances regarding custody of and, where appropriate, access to, the child, taking into account any order referred to in *subsection (1)* of this section relating to the child and without prejudice to proceedings that may be pending or any application that is about to be made for one of those orders in relation to the child.

(6) Any order containing a direction under *subsection (5)* of this section shall be of the same force and effect as if it were an order made by the District Court under section 11 of the Guardianship of Infants Act, 1964.

(7) The jurisdiction of the District Court in respect of proceedings under *subsection (5)* of this section may be exercised by the justice of the District Court for the time being assigned to the district court district where the child resides or was at a material time residing and where a justice for the district in which the proceedings are brought is not immediately available, an order may be made by any justice of the District Court.

PART V

MISCELLANEOUS

38   Rules of court

(1) Proceedings under *Part II* or *III* of this Act shall be commenced in a summary manner.

(2) Rules of Court may make provision for the expeditious hearing of an application under *Part II* or *III* of this Act.

39   (Amends s 45 of the Judicial Separation and Family Law Reform Act, 1989)

40   Costs

(1) The costs of any proceedings under any provision of this Act shall be in the discretion of the court concerned.

(2) Without prejudice to the generality of *subsection (1)* of this section, a court in making an order for costs in any proceedings under this Act—

    (a)   may direct the person who removed or retained a child, or who prevented the exercise of rights of access in relation to a child, to pay any necessary expenses incurred by or on behalf of the applicant in the proceedings, including travel expenses, any costs incurred or payments made for locating the child, the costs of legal representation of the applicant and those of returning the child;

    (b)   shall otherwise have regard to the provisions of Article 26 of the Hague Convention (where proceedings under *Part II* of this Act are concerned) or Article 5.3 of the Luxembourg Convention (where proceedings under *Part III* of this Act are concerned).

41   Regulations

(1) The Minister may make regulations for the purpose of giving effect to this Act.

(2) Without prejudice to the generality of *subsection (1)* of this section, regulations under this section may prescribe forms to be used in connection with any of the provisions of this Act.

42   Laying of orders and regulations before Houses of Oireachtas

Every order or regulation made by the Minister under this Act (other than an order made under *section 1(3)* of this Act) shall be laid before each House of the Oireachtas as soon as may be after it is made and, if a resolution annulling the order or regulation is passed by either such House within the next subsequent 21 days on which that House has sat after the order or regulation is laid before it, the order or regulation shall be annulled accordingly, but without prejudice to the validity of anything previously done thereunder.

43   Expenses

The expenses incurred in the administration of this Act by the Minister or a Central Authority appointed under *section 8* or *22* of this Act shall, to such extent as may be sanctioned by the Minister for Finance, be paid out of moneys provided by the Oireachtas.

FIRST SCHEDULE

TEXT OF THE CONVENTION ON THE CIVIL ASPECTS OF INTERNATIONAL
CHILD ABDUCTION

The States signatory to the present Convention

Firmly convinced that the interests of children are of paramount importance in matters relating to their custody,

Desiring to protect children internationally from the harmful effects of their wrongful removal or retention and to establish procedures to ensure their prompt return to the State of their habitual residence, as well as to secure protection for rights of access,

Have resolved to conclude a Convention to this effect, and have agreed upon the following provisions—

CHAPTER I

SCOPE OF THE CONVENTION

Article 1

The objects of the present Convention are:

- (a) to secure the prompt return of children wrongfully removed to or retained in any Contracting State, and
- (b) to ensure that rights of custody and of access under the law of one Contracting State are effectively respected in the other Contracting States.

Article 2

Contracting States shall take all appropriate measures to secure within their territories the implementation of the objects of the Convention. For this purpose they shall use the most expeditious procedures available.

Article 3

The removal or the retention of a child is to be considered wrongful where:

- (a) it is in breach of rights of custody attributed to a person, an institution or any other body, either jointly or alone, under the law of the State in which the child was habitually resident immediately before the removal or retention, and
- (b) at the time of removal or retention those rights were actually exercised, either jointly or alone, or would have been so exercised but for the removal or retention.

The rights of custody mentioned in sub-paragraph (a) above, may arise in particular by operation of law or by reason of a judicial or administrative decision, or by reason of an agreement having legal effect under the law of that State.

Article 4

The Convention shall apply to any child who was habitually resident in a Contracting State immediately before any breach of custody or access rights. The Convention shall cease to apply when the child attains the age of 16 years.

Article 5

For the purposes of this Convention:

- (a) 'rights of custody' shall include rights relating to the care of the person of the child and, in particular, the right to determine the child's place of residence;
- (b) 'rights of access' shall include the right to take a child for a limited period of time to a place other than the child's habitual residence.

CHAPTER II

CENTRAL AUTHORITIES

Article 6

A Contracting State shall designate a Central Authority to discharge the duties which are imposed by the Convention upon such authorities.

Federal States, States with more than one system of law or States having autonomous territorial organisations shall be free to appoint more than one Central Authority and to specify the territorial extent of their powers. Where a State has appointed more than one Central Authority, it shall designate the Central Authority to which applications may be addressed for transmission to the appropriate Central Authority within that State.

Article 7

Central Authorities shall co-operate with each other and promote co-operation amongst the competent authorities in their respective State to secure the prompt return of children and to achieve the other objects of this Convention.

In particular, either directly or through any intermediary, they shall take all appropriate measures—

(a) to discover the whereabouts of a child who has been wrongfully removed or retained;

(b) to prevent further harm to the child or prejudice to interested parties by taking or causing to be taken provisional measures;

(c) to secure the voluntary return of the child or to bring about an amicable resolution of the issues;

(d) to exchange, where desirable, information relating to the social background of the child;

(e) to provide information of a general character as to the law of their State in connection with the application of the Convention;

(f) to initiate or facilitate the institution of judicial or administrative proceedings with a view to obtaining the return of the child and, in a proper case, to make arrangements for organising or securing the effective exercise of rights of access;

(g) where the circumstances so require, to provide or facilitate the provision of legal aid and advice, including the participation of legal counsel and advisers;

(h) to provide such administrative arrangements as may be necessary and appropriate to secure the safe return of the child;

(i) to keep each other informed with respect to the operation of this Convention and, as far as possible, to eliminate any obstacles to its application.

CHAPTER III

RETURN OF CHILDREN

Article 8

Any person, institution or other body claiming that a child has been removed or retained in breach of custody rights may apply either to the Central Authority of the child's habitual residence or to the Central Authority of any other Contracting State for assistance in securing the return of the child.

The application shall contain—

(a) information concerning the identity of the applicant, of the child and of the person alleged to have removed or retained the child;

(b) where available, the date of birth of the child;

(c) the grounds on which the applicant's claim for return of the child is based;

(d) all available information relating to the whereabouts of the child and the identity of the person with whom the child is presumed to be.

The application may be accompanied or supplemented by—

(e) an authenticated copy of any relevant decision or agreement;

(f) a certificate or an affidavit emanating from a Central Authority, or other competent authority of the State of the child's habitual residence, or from a qualified person, concerning the relevant law of that State;

(g) any other relevant document.

Article 9

If the Central Authority which receives an application referred to in Article 8 has reason to believe that the child is in another Contracting State, it shall directly and without delay transmit the application to the Central Authority of that Contracting State and inform the requesting Central Authority, or the applicant, as the case may be.

Article 10

The Central Authority of the State where the child is shall take or cause to be taken all appropriate measures in order to obtain the voluntary return of the child.

Article 11

The judicial or administrative authorities of Contracting States shall act expeditiously in proceedings for the return of children.

If the judicial or administrative authority concerned has not reached a decision within six weeks from the date of commencement of the proceedings, the applicant or the Central Authority of the requested State, on its own initiative or if asked by the Central Authority of the requesting State, shall have the right to request a statement of the reasons for the delay. If a reply is received by the Central Authority of the requested State, that Authority shall transmit the reply to the Central Authority of the requesting State, or to the applicant, as the case may be.

Article 12

Where a child has been wrongfully removed or retained in terms of Article 3 and, at the date of the commencement of the proceedings before the judicial or administrative authority of the Contracting State where the child is, a period of less than one year has elapsed from the date of the wrongful removal or retention, the authority concerned shall order the return of the child forthwith.

The judicial or administrative authority, even where the proceedings have been commenced after the expiration of the period of one year referred to in the preceding paragraph, shall also order the return of the child, unless it is demonstrated that the child is now settled in its new environment.

Where the judicial or administrative authority in the requested State has reason to believe that the child has been taken to another State, it may stay the proceedings or dismiss the application for the return of the child.

Article 13

Notwithstanding the provisions of the preceding Article, the judicial or administrative authority of the requested State is not bound to order the return of the child if the person, institution or other body which opposes its return establishes that—

(a) the person, institution or other body having the care of the person of the child was not actually exercising the custody rights at the time of removal or retention, or had consented to or subsequently acquiesced in the removal or retention, or

(b) there is a grave risk that his or her return would expose the child to physical or psychological harm or otherwise place the child in an intolerable situation.

The judicial or administrative authority may also refuse to order the return of the child if it finds that the child objects to being returned and has attained an age and degree of maturity at which it is appropriate to take account of its views.

In considering the circumstances referred to in this Article, the judicial and administrative authorities shall take into account the information relating to the social background of the child provided by the Central Authority or other competent authority of the child's habitual residence.

Article 14

In ascertaining whether there has been a wrongful removal or retention within the meaning of Article 3, the judicial or administrative authorities of the requested State may take notice directly of the law of, and of judicial or administrative decisions, formally recognised or not in the State of the habitual residence of the child, without recourse to the specific procedures for the proof of that law or for the recognition of foreign decisions which would otherwise be applicable.

Article 15

The judicial or administrative authorities of a Contracting State may, prior to the making of an order for the return of the child, request that the applicant obtain from the authorities of the State of the habitual residence of the child a decision or other determination that the removal or retention was wrongful within the meaning of Article 3 of the Convention, where such a decision or determination may be obtained in that State. The Central Authorities of the Contracting States shall so far as practicable assist applicants to obtain such a decision or determination.

Article 16

After receiving notice of a wrongful removal or retention of a child in the sense of Article 3, the judicial or administrative authorities of a Contracting State to which the child has been removed or in which it has been retained shall not decide on the merits of rights of custody until it has been determined that the child is not to be returned under this

Convention or unless an application under this Convention is not lodged within a reasonable time following receipt of the notice.

Article 17

The sole fact that a decision relating to custody has been given in or is entitled to recognition in the requested State shall not be a ground for refusing to return a child under this Convention, but the judicial or administrative authorities of the requested State may take account of the reasons for that decision in applying this Convention.

Article 18

The provisions of this Chapter do not limit the power of a judicial or administrative authority to order the return of the child at any time.

Article 19

A decision under this Convention concerning the return of the child shall not be taken to be a determination on the merits of any custody issue.

Article 20

The return of the child under the provisions of Article 12 may be refused if this would not be permitted by the fundamental principles of the requested State relating to the protection of human rights and fundamental freedoms.

CHAPTER IV

RIGHT OF ACCESS

Article 21

An application to make arrangements for organising or securing the effective exercise of rights of access may be presented to the Central Authorities of the Contracting States in the same way as an application for the return of a child.

The Central Authorities are bound by the obligations of co-operation which are set forth in Article 7 to promote the peaceful enjoyment of access rights and the fulfilment of any conditions to which the exercise of those rights may be subject. The Central Authorities shall take steps to remove, as far as possible, all obstacles to the exercise of such rights.

The Central Authorities, either directly or through intermediaries, may initiate or assist in the institution of proceedings with a view to organising or protecting these rights and securing respect for the conditions to which the exercise of these rights may be subject.

CHAPTER V

GENERAL PROVISIONS

Article 22

No security, bond or deposit, however described, shall be required to guarantee the payment of costs and expenses in the judicial or administrative proceedings falling within the scope of this Convention.

Article 23

No legalisation or similar formality may be required in the context of this Convention.

Article 24

Any application, communication or other document sent to the Central Authority of the requested State shall be in the original language, and shall be accompanied by a translation into the official language or one of the official languages of the requested State or, where that is not feasible, a translation into French or English.

However, a Contracting State may, by making a reservation in accordance with Article 42, object to the use of either French or English, but not both, in any application, communication or other document sent to its Central Authority.

Article 25

Nationals of the Contracting States and persons who are habitually resident within those States shall be entitled in matters concerned with the application of this Convention to legal aid and advice in any other Contracting State on the same conditions as if they themselves were nationals of and habitually resident in that State.

Article 26

Each Central Authority shall bear its own costs in applying this Convention.

Central Authorities and other public services of Contracting States shall not impose any charges in relation to applications submitted under this Convention. In particular, they may not require any payment from the applicant towards the costs and expenses of the proceedings or, where applicable, those arising from the participation of legal counsel or advisers. However, they may require the payment of the expenses incurred or to be incurred in implementing the return of the child.

However, a Contracting State may, by making a reservation in accordance with Article 42, declare that it shall not be bound to assume any costs referred to in the preceding paragraph resulting from the participation of legal counsel or advisers or from court proceedings, except in so far as those costs may be covered by its system of legal aid and advice.

Upon ordering the return of a child or issuing an order concerning rights of access under this Convention, the judicial or administrative authorities may, where appropriate, direct the person who removed or retained the child, or who prevented the exercise of rights of access, to pay necessary expenses incurred by or on behalf of the applicant, including travel expenses, any costs incurred or payments made for locating the child, the costs of legal representation of the applicant, and those of returning the child.

Article 27

When it is manifest that the requirements of this Convention are not fulfilled or that the application is otherwise not well founded, a Central Authority is not bound to accept the application. In that case, the Central Authority shall forthwith inform the applicant or the Central Authority through which the application was submitted, as the case may be, of its reasons.

Article 28

A Central Authority may require that the application be accompanied by a written authorisation empowering it to act on behalf of the applicant, or to designate a representative so to act.

Article 29

This Convention shall not preclude any person, institution or body who claims that there has been a breach of custody or access rights within the meaning of Article 3 or 21 from applying directly to the judicial or administrative authorities of a Contracting State, whether or not under the provisions of this Convention.

Article 30

Any application submitted to the Central Authorities or directly to the judicial or administrative authorities of a Contracting State in accordance with the terms of this Convention, together with documents and any other information appended thereto or provided by a Central Authority, shall be admissible in the courts or administrative authorities of the Contracting States.

Article 31

In relation to a State which in matters of custody of children has two or more systems of law applicable in different territorial units—

(a) any reference to habitual residence in that State shall be construed as referring to habitual residence in a territorial unit of that State;
(b) any reference to the law of the State of habitual residence shall be construed as referring to the law of the territorial unit in that State where the child habitually resides.

Article 32

In relation to a State which in matters of custody of children has two or more systems of law applicable to different categories of persons, any reference to the law of that State shall be construed as referring to the legal system specified by the law of that State.

Article 33

A State within which different territorial units have their own rules of law in respect of custody of children shall not be bound to apply this Convention where a State with a unified system of law would not be bound to do so.

Article 34

This Convention shall take priority in matters within its scope over the *Convention of 5 October 1961 concerning the powers of authorities and the law applicable in respect of the protection of minors,* as between Parties to both Conventions. Otherwise the present Convention shall not restrict the application of an international instrument in force between the State of origin and the State addressed or other law of the State addressed for the purposes of obtaining the return of a child who has been wrongfully removed or retained or of organising access rights.

Article 35

This Convention shall apply as between Contracting States only to wrongful removals or retentions occurring after its entry into force in those States.

Where a declaration has been made under Article 39 or 40 the reference in the preceding paragraph to a Contracting State shall be taken to refer to the territorial unit or units in relation to which this Convention applies.

Article 36

Nothing in this Convention shall prevent two or more Contracting States, in order to limit the restrictions to which the return of the child may be subject, from agreeing among themselves to derogate from any provisions of this Convention which may imply such a restriction.

CHAPTER VI

FINAL CLAUSES

Article 37

The Convention shall be open for signature by the States which were Members of the Hague Conference on Private International Law at the time of its Fourteenth Session.

It shall be ratified, accepted or approved and the instruments of ratification, acceptance or approval shall be deposited with the Ministry of Foreign Affairs of the Kingdom of the Netherlands.

Article 38

Any other State may accede to the Convention.

The instruments of accession shall be deposited with the Ministry of Foreign Affairs of the Kingdom of the Netherlands.

The Convention shall enter into force for a State acceding to it on the first day of the third calendar month after the deposit of its instrument of accession.

The accession will have effect only as regards the relations between the acceding State and such Contracting States as will have declared their acceptance of the accession. Such a declaration will also have to be made by any Member State ratifying, accepting or approving the Convention after an accession. Such declaration shall be deposited at the Ministry of Foreign Affairs of the Kingdom of the Netherlands; this Ministry shall forward, through diplomatic channels, a certified copy to each of the Contracting States.

The Convention will enter into force as between the acceding State and the State that has declared its acceptance of the accession on the first day of the third calendar month after the deposit of the declaration of acceptance.

Article 39

Any State may, at the time of signature, ratification, acceptance, approval or accession, declare that the Convention shall extend to all the territories for the international relations of which it is responsible, or to one or more of them. Such a declaration shall take effect at the time the Convention enters into force for that State.

Such declaration, as well as any subsequent extension, shall be notified to the Ministry of Foreign Affairs of the Kingdom of the Netherlands.

Article 40

If a Contracting State has two or more territorial units in which different systems of law are applicable in relation to matters dealt with in this Convention, it may at the time of signature, ratification, acceptance, approval or accession declare that this Convention shall extend to all its territorial units or only to one or more of them and may modify this declaration by submitting another declaration at any time. Any such declaration shall be notified to the Ministry of Foreign Affairs of the Kingdom of the Netherlands and shall state expressly the territorial units to which the Convention applies.

Article 41

Where a Contracting State has a system of government under which executive, judicial and legislative powers are distributed between central and other authorities within that State, its signature or ratification, acceptance or approval of, or accession to this Convention, or its making of any declaration in terms of Article 40 shall carry no implication as to the internal distribution of powers within that State.

Article 42

Any State may, not later than the time of ratification, acceptance, approval or accession, or at the time of making a declaration in terms of Article 39 or 40, make one or both of the reservations provided for in Article 24 and Article 26, third paragraph. No other reservation shall be permitted.

Any State may at any time withdraw a reservation it has made. The withdrawal shall be notified to the Ministry of Foreign Affairs of the Kingdom of the Netherlands.

The reservation shall cease to have effect on the first day of the third calendar month after the notification referred to in the preceding paragraph.

Article 43

The Convention shall enter into force on the first day of the third calendar month after the deposit of the third instrument of ratification, acceptance, approval or accession referred to in Articles 37 and 38.

Thereafter the Convention shall enter into force—

(1) for each State ratifying, accepting, approving or acceding to it subsequently, on the first day of the third calendar month after the deposit of its instrument of ratification, acceptance, approval or accession;

(2) for any territory or territorial unit to which the Convention has been extended in conformity with Article 39 or 40, on the first day of the third calendar month after the notification referred to in that Article.

Article 44

The Convention shall remain in force for five years from the date of its entry into force in accordance with the first paragraph of Article 43 even for States which subsequently have ratified, accepted, approved it or acceded to it.

If there has been no denunciation, it shall be renewed tacitly every five years.

Any denunciation shall be notified to the Ministry of Foreign Affairs of the Kingdom of the Netherlands at least six months before the expiry of the five year period. It may be limited to certain of the territories or territorial units to which the Convention applies.

The denunciation shall have effect only as regards the State which has notified it. The Convention shall remain in force for the other Contracting States.

Article 45

The Ministry of Foreign Affairs of the Kingdom of the Netherlands shall notify the States Members of the Conference, and the States which have acceded in accordance with Article 38, of the following—

(1) the signatures and ratifications, acceptances and approvals referred to in Article 37;

(2) the accessions referred to in Article 38;

(3) the date on which the Convention enters into force in accordance with Article 43;

(4) the extensions referred to in Article 39;

(5) the declarations referred to in Articles 38 and 40;

(6) the reservations referred to in Article 24 and Article 26, third paragraph, and the withdrawals referred to in Article 42;

(7) the denunciations referred to in Article 44.

In Witness Whereof the undersigned, being duly authorised thereto, have signed this Convention.

Done at The Hague, on the 25th day of October, 1980, in the English and French languages, both texts being equally authentic, in a single copy which shall be deposited in the archives of the Government of the Kingdom of the Netherlands, and of which a certified copy shall be sent, through diplomatic channels, to each of the States Members of the Hague Conference on Private International Law at the date of its Fourteenth Session and to each other State having participated in the preparation of this Convention at this Session.

(Here follow signatures on behalf of certain States.)

SECOND SCHEDULE   *Section 21*

EUROPEAN CONVENTION ON RECOGNITION AND ENFORCEMENT OF DECISIONS CONCERNING CUSTODY OF CHILDREN AND ON RESTORATION OF CUSTODY OF CHILDREN

The member States of the Council of Europe, signatory hereto,

Recognising that in the member States of the Council of Europe the welfare of the child is of overriding importance in reaching decisions concerning his custody;

Considering that the making of arrangements to ensure that decisions concerning the custody of a child can be more widely recognised and enforced will provide greater protection of the welfare of children;

Considering it desirable, with this end in view, to emphasise that the right of access of parents is a normal corollary to the right of custody;

Noting the increasing number of cases where children have been improperly removed across an international frontier and the difficulties of securing adequate solutions to the problems caused by such cases;

Desirous of making suitable provision to enable the custody of children which has been arbitrarily interrupted to be restored;

Convinced of the desirability of making arrangements for this purpose answering to different needs and different circumstances;

Desiring to establish legal co-operation between their authorities,

Have agreed as follows:

Article 1

For the purposes of this Convention:

(a) *child* means a person of any nationality, so long as he is under 16 years of age and has not the right to decide on his own place of residence under the law of his habitual residence, the law of his nationality or the internal law of the State addressed;

(b) *authority* means a judicial or administrative authority;

(c) *decision relating to custody* means a decision of an authority in so far as it relates to the care of the person of the child, including the right to decide on the place of his residence, or to the right of access to him;

(d) *improper removal* means the removal of a child across an international frontier in breach of a decision relating to his custody which has been given in a Contracting State and which is enforceable in such a State; improper removal also includes:

   (i) the failure to return a child across an international frontier at the end of a period of the exercise of the right of access to this child or at the end of any other temporary stay in a territory other than that where the custody is exercised;

(ii) a removal which is subsequently declared unlawful within the meaning of Article 12.

PART I

Central authorities

Article 2

1. Each Contracting State shall appoint a central authority to carry out the functions provided for by this Convention.

2. Federal States and States with more than one legal system shall be free to appoint more than one central authority and shall determine the extent of their competence.

3. The Secretary General of the Council of Europe shall be notified of any appointment under this Article.

Article 3

1. The central authorities of the Contracting States shall co-operate with each other and promote co-operation between the competent authorities in their respective countries. They shall act with all necessary despatch.

2. With a view to facilitating the operation of this Convention, the central authorities of the Contracting States:

(a) shall secure the transmission of requests for information coming from competent authorities and relating to legal or factual matters concerning pending proceedings;

(b) shall provide each other on request with information about their law relating to the custody of children and any changes in that law;

(c) shall keep each other informed of any difficulties likely to arise in applying the Convention and, as far as possible, eliminate obstacles to its application.

Article 4

1. Any person who has obtained in a Contracting State a decision relating to the custody of a child and who wishes to have that decision recognised or enforced in another Contracting State may submit an application for this purpose to the central authority in any Contracting State.

2. The application shall be accompanied by the documents mentioned in Article 13.

3. The central authority receiving the application, if it is not the central authority in the State addressed, shall send the documents directly and without delay to that central authority.

4. The central authority receiving the application may refuse to intervene where it is manifestly clear that the conditions laid down by this Convention are not satisfied.

5. The central authority receiving the application shall keep the applicant informed without delay of the progress of his application.

Article 5

1. The central authority in the State addressed shall take or cause to be taken without delay all steps which it considers to be appropriate, if necessary by instituting proceedings before its competent authorities, in order:

    (a) to discover the whereabouts of the child;

    (b) to avoid, in particular by any necessary provisional measures, prejudice to the interests of the child or of the applicant;

    (c) to secure the recognition or enforcement of the decision;

    (d) to secure the delivery of the child to the applicant where enforcement is granted;

    (e) to inform the requesting authority of the measures taken and their results.

2. Where the central authority in the State addressed has reason to believe that the child is in the territory of another Contracting State it shall send the documents directly and without delay to the central authority of that State.

3. With the exception of the cost of repatriation, each Contracting State undertakes not to claim any payment from an applicant in respect of any measures taken under paragraph 1 of this Article by the central authority of that State on the applicant's behalf, including the costs of proceedings and, where applicable the costs incurred by the assistance of a lawyer.

4. If recognition or enforcement is refused, and if the central authority of the State addressed considers that it should comply with a request by the applicant to bring in that State proceedings concerning the substance of the case, that authority shall use its best endeavours to secure the representation of the applicant in the proceedings under conditions no less favourable than those available to a person who is resident in and a national of that State and for this purpose it may, in particular, institute proceedings before its competent authorities.

Article 6

1. Subject to any special agreements made between the central authorities concerned and to the provisions of paragraph 3 of this Article:

    (a) communications to the central authority of the State addressed shall be made in the official language or in one of the official languages of that State or be accompanied by a translation into that language;

    (b) the central authority of the State addressed shall nevertheless accept communications made in English or in French or accompanied by a translation into one of these languages.

2. Communications coming from the central authority of the State addressed, including the results of enquiries carried out, may be made in the official language or one of the official languages of that State or in English or French.

3. A Contracting State may exclude wholly or partly the provisions of paragraph 1.(b) of this Article. When a Contracting State has made this reservation any other Contracting State may also apply the reservation in respect of that State.

PART TWO

PART II

Recognition and enforcement of decisions and restoration of custody of children

Article 7

A decision relating to custody given in a Contracting State shall be recognised and, where it is enforceable in the State of origin, made enforceable in every other Contracting State.

Article 8

1. In the case of an improper removal, the central authority of the State addressed shall cause steps to be taken forthwith to restore the custody of the child where:

   (a) at the time of the institution of the proceedings in the State where the decision was given or at the time of the improper removal, if earlier, the child and his parents had as their sole nationality the nationality of that State and the child had his habitual residence in the territory of that State, and

   (b) a request for the restoration was made to a central authority within a period of six months from the date of the improper removal.

2. If, in accordance with the law of the State addressed, the requirements of paragraph 1 of this Article cannot be complied with without recourse to a judicial authority, none of the grounds of refusal specified in this Convention shall apply to the judicial proceedings.

3. Where there is an agreement officially confirmed by a competent authority between the person having the custody of the child and another person to allow the other person a right of access, and the child, having been taken abroad, has not been restored at the end of the agreed period to the person having the custody, custody of the child shall be restored in accordance with paragraphs 1 (b) and 2 of this Article. The same shall apply in the case of a decision of the competent authority granting such a right to a person who has not the custody of the child.

Article 9

1. In cases of improper removal, other than those dealt with in Article 8, in which an application has been made to a central authority within a period of six months from the date of the removal, recognition and enforcement may be refused only if:

   (a) in the case of a decision given in the absence of the defendant or his legal representative, the defendant was not duly served with the document which instituted the proceedings or an equivalent document in sufficient time to enable him to arrange his defence; but such a failure to effect service cannot constitute a ground for refusing recognition or enforcement where service was not effected because the defendant had concealed his whereabouts from the person who instituted the proceedings in the State of origin;

   (b) in the case of a decision given in the absence of the defendant or his legal representative, the competence of the authority giving the decision was not founded:

   (i) on the habitual residence of the defendant, or

   (ii) on the last common habitual residence of the child's parents, at least one parent being still habitually resident there, or

    (iii) on the habitual residence of the child;

   (c) the decision is incompatible with a decision relating to custody which became enforceable in the State addressed before the removal of the child, unless the child has had his habitual residence in the territory of the requesting State for one year before his removal.

2. Where no application has been made to a central authority, the provisions of paragraph 1 of this Article shall apply equally, if recognition and enforcement are requested within six months from the date of the improper removal.

3. In no circumstances may the foreign decision be reviewed as to its substance.

Article 10

1. In cases other than those covered by Articles 8 and 9, recognition and enforcement may be refused not only on the grounds provided for in Article 9 but also on any of the following grounds:

   (a) if it is found that the effects of the decision are manifestly incompatible with the fundamental principles of the law relating to the family and children in the State addressed;

   (b) if it is found that by reason of a change in the circumstances including the passage of time not including a mere change in the residence of the child after an improper removal, the effects of the original decision are manifestly no longer in accordance with the welfare of the child;

   (c) if at the time when the proceedings were instituted in the State or origin:

     (i) the child was a national of the State addressed or was habitually resident there and no such connection existed with the State of origin:

     (ii) the child was a national both of the State of origin and of the State addressed and was habitually resident in the State addressed:

   (d) if the decision is incompatible with a decision given in the State addressed or enforceable in that State, after being given in a third State, pursuant to proceedings begun before the submission of the request for recognition or enforcement, and if the refusal is in accordance with the welfare of the child.

2. In the same cases, proceedings for recognition or enforcement may be adjourned on any of the following grounds:

   (a) if an ordinary form of review of the original decision has been commenced;

   (b) if proceedings relating to the custody of the child, commenced before the proceedings in the State of origin were instituted, are pending in the State addressed;

   (c) if another decision concerning the custody of the child is the subject of proceedings for enforcement or of any other proceedings concerning the recognition of the decision.

Article 11

1. Decisions on rights of access and provisions of decisions relating to custody which deal with the right of access shall be recognised and enforced subject to the same conditions as other decisions relating to custody.

2. However, the competent authority of the State addressed may fix the conditions for the implementation and exercise of the right of access taking into account, in particular, undertakings given by the parties on this matter.

3. Where no decision on the right of access has been taken or where recognition or enforcement of the decision relating to custody is refused, the central authority of the State addressed may apply to its competent authorities for a decision on the right of access, if the person claiming a right of access so requests.

Article 12

Where, at the time of the removal of a child across an international frontier, there is no enforceable decision given in a Contracting State relating to his custody, the provisions of this Convention shall apply to any subsequent decision, relating to the custody of that child and declaring the removal to be unlawful, given in a Contracting State at the request of any interested person.

PART III

PROCEDURE

Article 13

1. A request for recognition or enforcement in another Contracting State of a decision relating to custody shall be accompanied by:

   (a) a document authorising the central authority of the State addressed to act on behalf of the applicant or to designate another representative for that purpose;
   (b) a copy of the decision which satisfies the necessary conditions of authenticity;
   (c) in the case of a decision given in the absence of the defendant or his legal representative, a document which establishes that the defendant was duly served with the document which instituted the proceedings or an equivalent document;
   (d) if applicable, any document which establishes that, in accordance with the law of the State of origin, the decision is enforceable;
   (e) if possible, a statement indicating the whereabouts or likely whereabouts of the child in the State addressed;
   (f) proposals as to how the custody of the child should be restored.

2. The documents mentioned above shall, where necessary, be accompanied by a translation according to the provisions laid down in Article 6.

Article 14

Each Contracting State shall apply a simple and expeditious procedure for recognition and enforcement of decisions relating to the custody of a child. To that end it shall ensure that a request for enforcement may be lodged by simple application.

Article 15

1. Before reaching a decision under paragraph 1(b) of Article 10, the authority concerned in the State addressed:

   (a) shall ascertain the child's views unless this is impracticable having regard in particular to his age and understanding, and
   (b) may request that any appropriate enquiries be carried out.

2. The cost of enquiries in any Contracting State shall be met by the authorities of the State where they are carried out.

Requests for enquiries and the results of enquiries may be sent to the authority concerned through the central authorities.

Article 16

For the purposes of this Convention, no legislation or any like formality may be required.

PART IV

RESERVATIONS

Article 17

1. A Contracting State may make a reservation that, in cases covered by Articles 8 and 9 or either of these Articles, recognition and enforcement of decisions relating to custody may be refused on such of the grounds provided under Article 10 as may be specified in the reservation.

2. Recognition and enforcement of decisions given in a Contracting State which has made the reservation provided for in paragraph 1 of this Article may be refused in any other Contracting State on any of the additional grounds referred to in that reservation.

Article 18

A Contracting State may make a reservation that it shall not be bound by the provisions of Article 12. The provisions of this Convention shall not apply to decisions referred to in Article 12 which have been given in a Contracting State which has made such a reservation.

PART V

OTHER INSTRUMENTS

Article 19

This Convention shall not exclude the possibility of relying on any other international instrument in force between the State of origin and the State addressed or on any other law of the State addressed not derived from an international agreement for the purpose of obtaining recognition or enforcement of a decision.

Article 20

1. This Convention shall not affect any obligations which a Contracting State may have towards a non-contracting State under an international instrument dealing with matters governed by this Convention.

2. When two or more Contracting States have enacted uniform laws in relation to custody of children or created a special system of recognition or enforcement of decisions in this field, or if they should do so in the future, they shall be free to apply, between themselves, those laws or that system in place of this Convention or any part of it. In order to avail themselves of this provision the States shall notify their decision to

the Secretary General of the Council of Europe. Any alteration or revocation of this decision must also be notified.

PART VI

FINAL CLAUSES

Article 21

This Convention shall be open for signature by the member States of the Council of Europe. It is subject to ratification, acceptance or approval. Instruments of ratification, acceptance or approval shall be deposited with the Secretary General of the Council of Europe.

Article 22

1. This Convention shall enter into force on the first day of the month following the expiration of a period of three months after the date on which three member States of the Council of Europe have expressed their consent to be bound by the Convention in accordance with the provisions of Article 21.

2. In respect of any member State which subsequently expresses its consent to be bound by it, the Convention shall enter into force on the first day of the month following the expiration of a period of three months after the date of the deposit of the instrument of ratification, acceptance or approval.

Article 23

1. After the entry into force of this Convention, the Committee of Ministers of the Council of Europe may invite any State not a member of the Council to accede to this Convention, by a decision taken by the majority provided for by Article 20(d) of the Statute and by the unanimous vote of the representatives of the Contracting States entitled to sit on the Committee.

2. In respect of any acceding State, the Convention shall enter into force on the first day of the month following the expiration of a period of three months after the date of deposit of the instrument of accession with the Secretary General of the Council of Europe.

Article 24

1. Any State may at the time of signature or when depositing its instrument of ratification, acceptance, approval or accession, specify the territory or territories to which this Convention shall apply.

2. Any State may at any later date, by a declaration addressed to the Secretary General of the Council of Europe, extend the application of this Convention to any other territory specified in the declaration. In respect of such territory, the Convention shall enter into force on the first day of the month following the expiration of a period of three months after the date of receipt by the Secretary General of such declaration.

3. Any declaration made under the two preceding paragraphs may, in respect of any territory specified in such declaration, be withdrawn by a notification addressed to the

Secretary General. The withdrawal shall become effective on the first day of the month following the expiration of a period of six months after the date of receipt of such notification by the Secretary General.

Article 25

1. A State which has two or more territorial units in which different systems of law apply in matters of custody of children and of recognition and enforcement of decisions relating to custody may, at the time of signature or when depositing its instrument of ratification, acceptance, approval or accession, declare that this Convention shall apply to all its territorial units or to one or more of them.

2. Such a state may at any later date, by a declaration addressed to the Secretary General of the Council of Europe, extend the application of this Convention to any other territorial unit specified in the declaration. In respect of such territorial unit the Convention shall enter into force on the first day of the month following the expiration of a period of three months after the date of receipt by the Secretary General of such declaration.

3. Any declaration made under the two preceding paragraphs may, in respect of any territorial unit specified in such declaration, be withdrawn by notification addressed to the Secretary General. The withdrawal shall become effective on the first day of the month following the expiration of a period of six months after the date of receipt of such notification by the Secretary General.

Article 26

1. In relation to a State which has in matters of custody two or more systems of law of territorial application:

   (a) reference to the law of a person's habitual residence or to the law of a person's nationality shall be construed as referring to the system of law determined by the rules in force in that State or, if there are no such rules, the system of law with which the person concerned is most closely connected;
   (b) reference to the State of origin or to the State addressed shall be construed as referring, as the case may be, to the territorial unit where the decision was given or to the territorial unit where recognition or enforcement of the decision or restoration of custody is requested.

2. *Paragraph 1(a)* of this Article also applies *mutatis mutandis* to States which have in matters of custody two or more systems of law of personal application.

Article 27

1. Any State may, at the time of signature or when depositing its instrument of ratification, acceptance, approval or accession, declare that it avails itself of one or more of the reservations provided for in paragraph 3 of Article 6, Article 17 and Article 18 of this Convention. No other reservation may be made.

2. Any Contracting State which has made a reservation under the preceding paragraph may wholly or partly withdraw it by means of a notification addressed to the Secretary General of the Council of Europe. The withdrawal shall take effect on the date of receipt of such notification by the Secretary General.

Article 28

At the end of the third year following the date of the entry into force of this Convention and, on his own initiative, at any time after this date, the Secretary General of the Council of Europe shall invite the representatives of the central authorities appointed by the Contracting States to meet in order to study and to facilitate the functioning of the Convention. Any member State of the Council of Europe not being a party to the Convention may be represented by an observer. A report shall be prepared on the work of each of these meetings and forwarded to the Committee of Ministers of the Council of Europe for information.

Article 29

1. Any Party may at any time denounce this Convention by means of a notification addressed to the Secretary General of the Council of Europe.

2. Such denunciation shall become effective on the first day of the month following the expiration of a period of six months after the date of receipt of the notification by the Secretary General.

Article 30

The Secretary General of the Council of Europe shall notify the member States of the Council and any State which has acceded to this Convention, of:

   (a) any signature;
   (b) the deposit of any instrument of ratification, acceptance, approval or accession;
   (c) any date of entry into force of this Convention in accordance with Articles 22, 23, 24 and 25;
   (d) any other act, notification or communication relating to this Convention.

In witness whereof the undersigned, being duly authorised thereto, have signed this Convention.

Done at Luxembourg, the 20th day of May 1980, in English and French, both texts being equally authentic, in a single copy which shall be deposited in the archives of the Council of Europe. The Secretary General of the Council of Europe shall transmit certified copies to each member State of the Council of Europe and to any State invited to accede to this Convention.

(Here follow signatures on behalf of certain States.)

Child Care Act, 1991

(1991 No 17)

ARRANGEMENT OF SECTIONS

PART II

PROMOTION OF WELFARE OF CHILDREN

PART III

PROTECTION OF CHILDREN IN EMERGENCIES

PART IV

CARE PROCEEDINGS

PART V

JURISDICTION AND PROCEDURE

PART VI

CHILDREN IN THE CARE OF HEALTH BOARDS

PART VII

SUPERVISION OF PRE-SCHOOL SERVICES

PART VIII

CHILDREN'S RESIDENTIAL CENTRES

PART IX

ADMINISTRATION

PART X

MISCELLANEOUS AND SUPPLEMENTARY

SCHEDULE

ENACTMENTS REPEALED

ACTS REFERRED TO

Defence Act, 1954	1954, No 11
Guardianship of Infants Act, 1964	1964, No 7
Health Act, 1953	1953, No 26
Health Act, 1970	1970, No 1
Health Acts, 1947 to 1986	
Health (Amendment) Act, 1987	1987, No 3
Interpretation Act, 1937	1937, No 38
Judicial Separation and Family Reform Act, 1989	1989, No 6
Local Government (Superannuation) Act, 1980	1980, No 8
Mental Treatment Acts, 1945 to 1966	
Misuse of Drugs Acts, 1977 and 1984	
Prevention of Cruelty to Children Act, 1904	4 Edw 7, c 15
Petty Sessions (Ireland) Act, 1851	14 & 15 Vict, c 93
Public Offices Fees Act, 1879	42 & 43 Vict, c 58
School Attendance Act, 1926	1926, No 17

An Act to provide for the care and protection of children and for related matters. [10 July 1991]

PART I

PRELIMINARY

1　Short title and commencement

(1) This Act may be cited as the Child Care Act, 1991.

(2) This Act shall come into operation on such days or days as, by order or orders made by the Minister under this section, may be fixed either generally or with reference to any particular purpose or provision, and different days may be so fixed for different purposes and different provisions.

2　Interpretation

(1) In this Act, except where the context otherwise requires—

'area', in relation to a health board, means functional area,
'child' means a person under the age of 18 years other than a person who is or has been married,
'functions' includes powers and duties,
'health board' means a health board established under the Health Act, 1970,
'the Minister' means the Minister for Health,
'parents' includes a surviving parent and, in the case of a child who has been adopted under the Adoption Acts, 1952 to 1988, or, where the child has been adopted outside the State, whose adoption is recognised by virtue of the law for the time being in force in the State, means the adopter or adopters or the surviving adopter,
'prescribed' means prescribed by regulation made by the Minister.

(2) In this Act—

(a) a reference to a Part, section or Schedule is to a Part, section or Schedule of this Act unless it is indicated that a reference to some other enactment is intended,

(b) a reference to a subsection, paragraph or subparagraph is to the subsection, paragraph or subparagraph of the provision in which the reference occurs, unless it is indicated that reference to some other provision is intended,

(c) a reference to any other enactment shall, unless the context otherwise requires, be construed as a reference to that enactment as amended or extended by or under any other enactment, including this Act.

PART II

PROMOTION OF WELFARE OF CHILDREN

3 Functions of health boards

(1) It shall be a function of every health board to promote the welfare of children in its area who are not receiving adequate care and protection.

(2) In the performance of this function, a health board shall—

   (a) take such steps as it considers requisite to identify children who are not receiving adequate care and protection and co-ordinate information from all relevant sources relating to children in its area,

   (b) having regard to the rights and duties of parents, whether under the Constitution or otherwise—

      (i) regard the welfare of the child as the first and paramount consideration, and

      (ii) in so far as is practicable, give due consideration having regard to his age and understanding, to the wishes of the child, and

   (c) have regard to the principle that it is generally in the best interests of a child to be brought up in his own family.

(3) A health board shall, in addition to any other function assigned to it under this Act or any other enactment, provide child care and family support services, and may provide and maintain premises and make such other provision as it considers necessary or desirable for such purposes, subject to any general directions given by the Minister under *section 69.*

(4) The provisions of the Health Acts, 1947 to 1986, and the Health (Amendment) Act, 1987, shall apply in relation to the functions of health boards and their officers under this Act and the powers of the Minister under those Acts shall have effect accordingly as if those acts and this Act were one Act.

4 Voluntary care

(1) Where it appears to a health board that a child who resides or is found in its area requires care or protection that he is unlikely to receive unless he is taken into its care, it shall be the duty of the health board to take him into its care under this section.

(2) Without prejudice to the provisions of *Parts III, IV* and *VI*, nothing in this section shall authorise a health board to take a child into its care against the wishes of a parent having custody of him or of any person acting *in loco parentis* or to maintain him in its care under this section if that parent or any such person wishes to resume care of him.

(3) Where a health board has taken a child into its care under this section, it shall be the duty of the board—

   (a) subject to the provisions of this section, to maintain the child in its care so long as his welfare appears to the board to require it and while he remains a child, and

   (b) to have regard to the wishes of a parent having custody of him or of any person acting *in loco parentis* in the provision of such care.

(4) Without prejudice to the provisions of *Parts III, IV* and *VI*, where a health board takes a child into its care because it appears that he is lost or that a parent having custody of him is missing or that he has been deserted or abandoned, the board shall endeavour to reunite him with that parent where this appears to the board to be in his best interests.

5 Accommodation for homeless children

Where it appears to a health board that a child in its area is homeless, the board shall enquire into the child's circumstances, and if the board is satisfied that there is no accommodation available to him which he can reasonably occupy, then, unless the child is received into the care of the board under the provisions of this Act, the board shall take such steps as are reasonable to make available suitable accommodation for him.

6 Provision of adoption service

(1) Each health board shall provide or ensure the provision in its area of a service for the adoption of children in accordance with the Adoption Acts, 1952 to 1988.

(2) For the purposes of this section, a health board may enter into arrangements with any adoption society for the time being registered in the Adoption Societies Register maintained by An Bord Uchtála under Part IV of the Adoption Act, 1952.

(3) A health board may take a child into its care with a view to his adoption and may maintain him in such care in accordance with the provisions of this Act until he is placed for adoption.

(4) Without prejudice to *Parts III, IV* and *VI*, nothing in this section shall authorise a health board to take a child into its care against the wishes of a parent having custody of him or of any person acting *in loco parentis* or to maintain him in its care under this section if that parent or any such person wishes to resume care of him.

(5) The provisions of *section 10* shall apply with any necessary modifications in relation to any arrangement made under *subsection (2)*.

7 Child care advisory committees

(1) A health board shall establish a child care advisory committee to advise the health board on the performance of its functions under this Act and the health board shall consider and have regard to any advice so tendered to it.

(2) A child care advisory committee shall be composed of persons with a special interest or expertise in matters affecting the welfare of children, including representatives of voluntary bodies providing child care and family support services.

(3) A person shall not receive any remuneration for acting as a member of a child care advisory committee, but a health board may make payments to any such member in respect of travelling and subsistence expenses incurred by him in relation to the business of the committee.

(4) Payments under this section shall be in accordance with a scale determined by the Minister, with the consent of the Minister for Finance.

(5) The Minister shall give general directions in relation to child care advisory committees which may include directions on any matter relating to the membership, constitution or business of committees (including a provision empowering a committee to co-opt one or more members) and each health board and child care advisory committee shall comply with any such directions.

(6) A health board may, with the consent of the Minister, and shall, if so directed by the Minister, establish more than one child care advisory committee for its area and where more than one committee is established the provisions of *subsection (1)* shall apply with the necessary modifications.

(7) Each child care advisory committee shall—

(a) have access to non-personal information in relation to child care and family support services in its area,

(b) consult with voluntary bodies providing child care and family support services in its area,

(c) report on child care and family support services in its area, either on its own initiative or when so requested by the health board,

(d) review the needs of children in its area who are not receiving adequate care and protection,

and where more than one child care advisory committee is established in a health board area, the provisions of this subsection shall apply with the necessary modifications.

8 Review of services

(1) A health board shall, within 12 months of the commencement of this Part and annually thereafter, have a report prepared on the adequacy of the child care and family support services available in its area.

(2) Without prejudice to the generality of *subsection (1)*, a health board in preparing a report under this section shall have regard to the needs of children who are not receiving adequate care and protection and, in particular—

(a) children whose parents are dead or missing,

(b) children whose parents have deserted or abandoned them,

(c) children who are in the care of the board,

(d) children who are homeless,

(e) children who are at risk of being neglected or ill-treated, and

(f) children whose parents are unable to care for them due to ill-health or for any other reason.

(3) A health board shall give notice of the preparation of a report under *subsection (1)* to—

(a) any child care advisory committee in its area,

(b) such bodies as the board sees fit whose purposes include the provision of child care and family support services,

and shall have regard to any views or information furnished by such committee or bodies in the preparation of the report.

(4) A health board shall submit a copy of any report prepared under this section to the Minister and may make copies of any such report available to such bodies as are mentioned in *subsection (3)(b)*.

9 Provision of services by voluntary bodies and other persons

(1) A health board may, subject to any general directions given by the Minister and on such terms or conditions as it sees fit, make arrangements with voluntary bodies or other persons for the provision by those bodies or other persons on behalf of the health board

of child care and family support services which the board is empowered to provide under this Act.

(2) Nothing in this section shall empower a health board to delegate to a voluntary body or any other person the duty conferred on it under *section 4* to receive certain children into care or the power to apply for an order under *Part III, IV or VI.*

10 Assistance for voluntary bodies and other persons

A health board may, subject to any general directions given by the Minister and on such terms or conditions as it thinks fit, assist a voluntary body or any other person who provides or proposes to provide a child care or family support service similar or ancillary to a service which the health board may provide under this Act—

(a) by a periodic contribution to funds of the body or person,
(b) by a grant,
(c) by a contribution in kind (whether by way of materials or labour or any other service).

11 Research

(1) The Minister may conduct or assist other persons in conducting research into any matter connected with the care and protection of children or the provision of child care and family support services.

(2) A health board may conduct or assist other persons in conducting research into any matter connected with the functions assigned to the board under this Act.

PART III

PROTECTION OF CHILDREN IN EMERGENCIES

12 Power of Garda Síochána to take a child to safety

(1) Where a member of the Garda Síochána has reasonable grounds for believing that—

(a) there is an immediate and serious risk to the health or welfare of a child, and
(b) it would not be sufficient for the protection of the child from such immediate and serious risk to await the making of an application for an emergency care order by a health board under *section 13,*

the member, accompanied by such other persons as may be necessary, may, without warrant, enter (if need be by force) any house or other place (including any building or part of a building, tent, caravan or other temporary or moveable structure, vehicle, vessel, aircraft or hovercraft) and remove the child to safety.

(2) The provisions of *subsection (1)* are without prejudice to any other powers exercisable by a member of the Garda Síochána.

(3) Where a child is removed by a member of the Garda Síochána in accordance with *subsection (1),* the child shall as soon as possible be delivered up to the custody of the health board for the area in which the child is for the time being.

(4) Where a child is delivered up to the custody of a health board in accordance with *subsection (3),* the health board shall, unless it returns the child to the parent having custody of him or a person acting *in loco parentis,* make application for an emergency care order at the next sitting to the District Court held in the same district court district

or, in the event that the next such sitting is not due to be held within three days of the date on which the child is delivered up to the custody of the health board, at a sitting of the District Court, which has been specially arranged under *section 13(4)*, held within the said three days, and it shall be lawful for the health board to retain custody of the child pending the hearing of that application.

13 Emergency care order

(1) If a justice of the District Court is of opinion on the application of a health board that there is reasonable cause to believe that—

(a) there is an immediate and serious risk to the health or welfare of a child which necessitates his being placed in the care of a health board, or

(b) there is likely to be such a risk if the child is removed from the place where he is for the time being,

the justice may make an order to be known and in this Act referred to as an 'emergency care order'.

(2) An emergency care order shall place the child under the care of the health board for the area in which the child is for the time being for a period of eight days or such shorter period as may be specified in the order.

(3) Where a justice makes an emergency care order, he may for the purpose of executing that order issue a warrant authorising a member of the Garda Síochána, accompanied by such other members of the Garda Síochána or such other persons as may be necessary, to enter (if need be by force) any house or other place specified in the warrant (including any building or part of a building, tent, caravan or other temporary or moveable structure, vehicle, vessel, aircraft or hovercraft) where the child is or where there are reasonable grounds for believing that he is and to deliver the child into the custody of the health board.

(4) The following provisions shall have effect in relation to the making of emergency care orders—

(a) any such order shall, subject to *paragraph (b)*, be made by the justice for the district in which the child resides or is for the time being,

(b) where a justice for the district in which the child resides or is for the time being is not immediately available, an order may be made by any justice of the District Court,

(c) an application for any such order may, if the justice is satisfied that the urgency of the matter so requires, be made *ex parte,*

(d) an application for any such order may, if the justice is satisfied that the urgency of the matter so requires, be heard and an order made thereon elsewhere than at a public sitting of the District Court.

(5) An appeal from an emergency care order shall not stay the operation of the order.

(6) It shall not be necessary in any application or order under this section to name the child if such name is unknown.

(7) (a) Where a justice makes an emergency care order, he may, of his own motion or on the application of any person, give such directions (if any) as he thinks proper with respect to—

(i) whether the address or location of the place at which the child is being kept is to be withheld from the parents of the child, or either of them, a person acting *in loco parentis* or any other person,

    (ii) the access, if any, which is to be permitted between the child and any named person and the conditions under which the access is to take place,

    (iii) the medical or psychiatric examination, treatment or assessment of the child.

  (b) A direction under this subsection may be given at any time during the currency of the order and may be varied or discharged on the application of any person.

14 Notification to be given by health board

(1) Where a child is delivered up to, or placed in the custody of, a health board under this Part, the board shall as soon as possible inform or cause to be informed a parent having custody of him or a person acting *in loco parentis* of that delivery or placement unless that parent or person is missing and cannot be found.

(2) For the purposes of this section, a person shall be deemed to have been informed of the placing of a child in the custody of a health board under *section 13* if he is given or shown a copy of the emergency care order made under that section or if that person was present at the sitting of the court at which such order was made.

15 Provision of accommodation for purposes of *Part III*

A health board shall provide or make arrangements with the registered proprietors of children's residential centres or with other suitable persons for the provision of suitable accommodation for the purposes of this Part.

PART IV

CARE PROCEEDINGS

16 Duty of health board to institute proceedings

Where it appears to a health board with respect to a child who resides or is found in its area that he requires care or protection which he is unlikely to receive unless a court makes a care order or a supervision order in respect of him, it shall be the duty of the health board to make application for a care order or a supervision order, as it thinks fit.

17 Interim care order

(1) Where a justice of the District Court is satisfied on the application of a health board that—

  (a) an application for a care order in respect of the child has been or is about to be made (whether or not an emergency care order is in force), and

  (b) there is reasonable cause to believe that any of the circumstances mentioned at *paragraph (a), (b)* or *(c)* of *section 18(1)* exists or has existed with respect to the child and that it is necessary for the protection of the child's health or welfare that he be placed or maintained in the care of the health board pending the determination of the application for the care order,

the justice may make an order to be known and in this Act referred to as an 'interim care order'.

(2) An interim care order shall require that the child named in the order be placed or maintained in the care of the health board—

  (a) for a period not exceeding eight days, or

(b) where the health board and the parent having custody of the child or person acting *in loco parentis* consent, for a period exceeding eight days,

and an extension or extensions of any such period may be granted (with the consent, where an extension is to exceed eight days, of the persons specified in *paragraph (b)*) on the application of any of the parties if the justice is satisfied that grounds for the making of an interim care order continue to exist with respect to the child.

(3) An application for an interim care order or for an extension of such an order shall be made on notice to a parent having custody of the child or to a person acting *in loco parentis* except where, having regard to the interests of justice or the welfare of the child, the justice otherwise directs.

(4) Where an interim care order is made, the justice may order that any directions given under *subsection (7)* of *section 13* may remain in force subject to such variations, if any, as he may see fit to make or the justice may give directions in relation to any of the matters mentioned in the said subsection and the provisions of that section shall apply with any necessary modifications.

18 Care order

(1) Where, on the application of a health board with respect to a child who resides or is found in its area, the court is satisfied that—

(a) the child has been or is being assaulted, ill-treated, neglected or sexually abused, or
(b) the child's health, development or welfare has been or is being avoidably impaired or neglected, or
(c) the child's health, development or welfare is likely to be avoidably impaired or neglected,

and that the child requires care or protection which he is unlikely to receive unless the court makes an order under this section, the court may make an order (in this Act referred to as a 'care order') in respect of the child.

(2) A care order shall commit the child to the care of the health board for so long as he remains a child or for such shorter period as the court may determine and, in such case, the court may, of its own motion or on the application of any person, extend the operation of the order if the court is satisfied that grounds for the making of a care order continue to exist with respect to the child.

(3) Where a care order is in force, the health board shall—

(a) have the like control over the child as if it were his parent, and
(b) do what is reasonable (subject to the provisions of this Act) in all the circumstances of the case for the purpose of safeguarding or promoting the child's health, development or welfare,

and shall have, in particular, the authority to—

(i) decide the type of care to be provided for the child under *section 36*,
(ii) give consent to any necessary medical or psychiatric examination, treatment or assessment with respect to the child, and
(iii) give consent to the issue of a passport to the child, or to the provision of passport facilities for him, to enable him to travel abroad for a limited period.

(4) Any consent given by a health board in accordance with this section shall be sufficient authority for the carrying out of a medical or psychiatric examination or

assessment, the provision of medical or psychiatric treatment, the issue of a passport or the provision of passport facilities, as the case may be.

(5) Where, on an application for a care order, the court is satisfied that—

   (a) it is not necessary or appropriate that a care order be made, and

   (b) it is desirable that the child be visited periodically in his home by or on behalf of the health board,

the court may make a supervision order under *section 19.*

(6) Between the making of an application for a care order and its determination, the court, of its own motion or on the application of any person, may give such directions as it sees fit as to the care and custody of, or may make a supervision order in respect of, the child who is the subject of the application pending such determination, and any such direction or supervision order shall cease to have effect on the determination of the application.

(7) Where a court makes a care order, it may in addition make an order requiring the parents of the child or either of them to contribute to the health board such weekly or other periodic sum towards the cost of maintaining the child as the court, having regard to the means of the parents or either of them, thinks fit.

(8) An order under *subsection (7)* may be varied or discharged on application to the court by the parent required to contribute or by the health board.

19 Supervision order

(1) Where, on the application of a health board, with respect to a child who resides in its area, the court is satisfied that there are reasonable grounds for believing that—

   (a) the child has been or is being assaulted, ill-treated, neglected or sexually abused, or

   (b) the child's health, development or welfare has been or is being avoidably impaired or neglected, or

   (c) the child's health, development or welfare is likely to be avoidably impaired or neglected,

and it is desirable that the child be visited periodically by or on behalf of the health board, the court may make an order (in this Act referred to as a 'supervision order') in respect of the child.

(2) A supervision order shall authorise the health board to have the child visited on such periodic occasions as the board may consider necessary in order to satisfy itself as to the welfare of the child and to give to his parents or to a person acting *in loco parentis* any necessary advice as to the care of the child.

(3) Any parent or person acting *in loco parentis* who is dissatisfied with the manner in which a health board is exercising its authority to have a child visited in accordance with this section may apply to the court and the court may give such directions as it sees fit as to the manner in which the child is to be visited and the health board shall comply with any such direction.

(4) Where a court makes a supervision order in respect of a child, it may, on the application of the health board, either at the time of the making of the order or at any time during the currency of the order, give such directions as it sees fit as to the care of the child, which may require the parents of the child or a person acting *in loco parentis* to

cause him to attend for medical or psychiatric examination, treatment or assessment at a hospital, clinic or other place specified by the court.

(5) Any person who fails to comply with the terms of a supervision order or any directions given by a court under *subsection (4)* or who prevents a person from visiting a child on behalf of the health board or who obstructs or impedes any such person visiting a child in pursuance of such an order shall be guilty of an offence and shall be liable on summary conviction to a fine not exceeding £500 or, at the discretion of the court, to imprisonment for a term not exceeding 6 months or both such fine and such imprisonment.

(6) A supervision order shall remain in force for a period of 12 months or such shorter period as may be specified in the order and, in any event, shall cease to have effect when the person in respect of whom the order is made ceases to be a child.

(7) On or before the expiration of a supervision order, a further supervision order may be made on the application of the health board with effect from the expiration of the first mentioned order.

20 Proceedings under Guardianship of Infants Act, 1964, Judicial Separation and Family Law Reform Act, 1989, etc

(1) Where in any proceedings under section 7, 8, 11, 11B or Part III of the Guardianship of Infants Act, 1964, or in any case to which—

  (a) section 3(3) of the Judicial Separation and Family Law Reform Act, 1989,
  (b) section 6(b) or 10(f) of the Family Law Act, 1995, or
  (c) section 5(2), 11(b) or 41 of the Family Law (Divorce) Act, 1996,

relates, or in any other proceedings for the delivery or return of a child, it appears to the court that it may be appropriate for a care order or a supervision order to be made with respect to the child concerned in the proceedings, the court may, of its own motion or on the application of any person, adjourn the proceedings and direct the health board for the area in which the child resides or is for the time being to undertake an investigation of the child's circumstances.

(2) Where proceedings are adjourned and the court gives a direction under *subsection (1)*, the court may give such directions as it sees fit as to the care and custody of, or may make a supervision order in respect of, the child concerned pending the outcome of the investigation by the health board.

(3) When the court gives a direction under *subsection (1)*, the health board concerned shall undertake an investigation of the child's circumstances and shall consider whether it should—

  (a) apply for a care order or for a supervision order with respect to the child,
  (b) provide services or assistance for the child or his family, or
  (c) take any other action with respect to the child.

(4) Where a health board undertakes an investigation under this section and decides not to apply for a care order or a supervision order with respect to the child concerned, it shall inform the court of—

  (a) its reasons for so deciding,
  (b) any service or assistance it has provided, or it intends to provide, for the child and his family, and

(c) any other action which it has taken, or proposes to take, with respect to the child.

Amendments—Children Act 1997, s 17.

---

21   Effect of appeal from orders

An appeal from an order under this Part shall, if the court that made the order or the court to which the appeal is brought so determines (but not otherwise), stay the operation of the order on such terms (if any) as may be imposed by the court making the determination.

22   Variation or discharge of orders etc

The court, of its own motion or on the application of any person, may—

(a) vary or discharge a care order or a supervision order,

(b) vary or discharge any condition or direction attaching to the order, or

(c) in the case of a care order, discharge the care order and make a supervision order in respect of the child.

23   Powers of court in case of invalidity of orders

Where a court finds or declares in any proceedings that a care order for whatever reason is invalid, that court may of its own motion or on the application of any person refuse to exercise any power to order the delivery or return of the child to a parent or any other person if the court is of opinion that such delivery or return would not be in the best interests of the child and in any such case the court, of its own motion or on the application of any person, may—

(a) make a care order as if it were a court to which an application had been made by a health board under *section 18,*

(b) make an order remitting the matter to a justice of the District Court for the time being assigned to the district court district where the child resides or is for the time being or was residing or was at the time that the invalid order was made or the application therefor was made, and where the matter has been so remitted the health board shall be deemed to have made an application under *section 18,*

(c) direct that any order under *paragraph (a)* shall, if necessary, be deemed for the purposes of this Act to have been made by a justice of the District Court for the time being assigned to a district court district, specified by the court, or

(d) where it makes an order under *paragraph (b),* make a temporary order under *paragraph (a)* pending the making of an order by the court to which the matter or question has been remitted.

PART V

JURISDICTION AND PROCEDURE

24   Welfare of child to be paramount

In any proceedings before a court under this Act in relation to the care and protection of a child, the court, having regard to the rights and duties of parents, whether under the Constitution or otherwise, shall—

(a) regard the welfare of the child as the first and paramount consideration, and

(b) in so far as is practicable, give due consideration, having regard to his age and understanding, to the wishes of the child.

25 Power of court to join child as a party and costs of child as a party

(1) If in any proceedings under *Part IV* or *VI* the child to whom the proceedings relate is not already a party, the court may, where it is satisfied having regard to the age, understanding and wishes of the child and the circumstances of the case that it is necessary in the interests of the child and in the interests of justice to do so, order that the child be joined as a party to, or shall have such of the rights of a party as may be specified by the court in, either the entirety of the proceedings or such issues in the proceedings as the court may direct. The making of any such order shall not require the intervention of a next friend in respect of the child.

(2) Where the court makes an order under *subsection (1)* or a child is a party to the proceedings otherwise than by reason of such an order, the court may, if it thinks fit, appoint a solicitor to represent the child in the proceedings and give directions as to the performance of his duties (which may include, if necessary, directions in relation to the instruction of counsel).

(3) The making of an order under *subsection (1)* or the fact that a child is a party to the proceedings otherwise than by reason of such an order shall not prejudice the power of the court under *section 30(2)* to refuse to accede to a request of a child made thereunder.

(4) Where a solicitor is appointed under *subsection (2)*, the costs and expenses incurred on behalf of a child exercising any rights of a party in any proceedings under this Act shall be paid by the health board concerned. The health board may apply to the court to have the amount of any such costs or expenses measured or taxed.

(5) The court which has made an order under *subsection (2)* may, on the application to it of a health board, order any other party to the proceedings in question to pay to the board any costs or expenses payable by that board under *subsection (4)*.

26 Appointment of guardian *ad litem* for a child

(1) If in any proceedings under *Part IV* or *VI* the child to whom the proceedings relate is not a party, the court may, if it is satisfied that it is necessary in the interests of the child and in the interests of justice to do so, appoint a guardian *ad litem* for the child.

(2) Any costs incurred by a person in acting as a guardian *ad litem* under this section shall be paid by the health board concerned. The health board may apply to the court to have the amount of any such costs or expenses measured or taxed.

(3) The court which has made an order under *subsection (1)* may, on the application to it of a health board, order any other party to the proceedings in question to pay to the board any costs or expenses payable by that board under *subsection (2)*.

(4) Where a child in respect of whom an order has been made under *subsection (1)* becomes a party to the proceedings in question (whether by virtue of an order under *section 25 (1)* or otherwise) then that order shall cease to have effect.

27 Power to procure reports on children

(1) In any proceedings under *Part IV* or *VI* the court may, of its own motion or on the application of any party to the proceedings, by an order under this section give such

directions as it thinks proper to procure a report from such person as it may nominate on any question affecting the welfare of the child.

(2) In deciding whether or not to request a report under *subsection (1)* the court shall have regard to the wishes of the parties before the court where ascertainable but shall not be bound by the said wishes.

(3) A copy of any report prepared under *subsection (1)* shall be made available to the counsel or solicitor, if any, representing each party in the proceedings or, if any party is not so represented, to that party and may be received in evidence in the proceedings.

(4) Where any person prepares a report pursuant to a request under *subsection (1)*, the fees and expenses of that person shall be paid by such party or parties to the proceedings as the court shall order.

(5) The court, if it thinks fit, or any party to the proceedings, may call the person making the report as a witness.

28 Jurisdiction

(1) The District Court and the Circuit Court on appeal from the District Court shall have jurisdiction to hear and determine proceedings under *Part III, IV* or *VI*.

(2) Proceedings under *Part III, IV* or *VI* may be brought, heard and determined before and by a justice of the District Court for the time being assigned to the district court district where the child resides or is for the time being.

29 Hearing of proceedings

(1) Proceedings under *Part III, IV* or *VI* shall be heard otherwise than in public.

(2) The provisions of sections 33(1), 33(2) and 45 of the Judicial Separation and Family Law Reform Act, 1989, shall apply to proceedings under *Part III, IV* or *VI* as they apply to proceedings to which those provisions relate.

(3) The District Court and the Circuit Court on appeal from the District Court shall sit to hear and determine proceedings under *Part III, IV* or *VI* at a different place or at different times or on different days from those at or on which the ordinary sittings of the Court are held.

(4) Proceedings before the High Court in relation to proceedings under *Part III, IV* or *VI* shall be as informal as is practicable and consistent with the administration of justice.

30 Power to proceed in absence of child

(1) It shall not be necessary in proceedings under *Part III, IV* or *VI* for the child to whom the proceedings relate to be brought before the court or to be present for all or any part of the hearing unless the court, either of its own motion or at the request of any of the parties to the case, is satisfied that this is necessary for the proper disposal of the case.

(2) Where the child requests to be present during the hearing or a particular part of the hearing of the proceedings the court shall grant the request unless it appears to the court that, having regard to the age of the child or the nature of the proceedings, it would not be in the child's interests to accede to the request.

31 Prohibition on publication or broadcast of certain matters

(1) No matter likely to lead members of the public to identify a child who is or has been the subject of proceedings under *Part III, IV* or *VI* shall be published in a written publication available to the public or be broadcast.

(2) Without prejudice to *subsection (1)*, the court may, in any case if satisfied that it is appropriate to do so in the interest of the child, by order dispense with the prohibitions of that subsection in relation to him to such extent as may be specified in the order.

(3) If any matter is published or broadcast in contravention of *subsection (1)*, each of the following persons, namely—

- (a) in the case of publication in a newspaper or periodical, any proprietor, any editor and any publisher of the newspaper or periodical,
- (b) in the case of any other publication, the person who publishes it, and
- (c) in the case of a broadcast, any body corporate who transmits or provides the programme in which the broadcast is made and any person having functions in relation to the programme corresponding to those of an editor of a newspaper,

shall be guilty of an offence and shall be liable on summary conviction to a fine not exceeding £1,000 or to imprisonment for a term not exceeding 12 months or both.

(4) Nothing in this section shall affect the law as to contempt of court.

(5) In this section—

'broadcast' means the transmission, relaying or distribution by wireless telegraphy of communications, sounds, signs, visual images or signals, intended for direct reception by the general public whether such communications, sounds, signs, visual images or signals are actually received or not,

'written publication' includes a film, a sound track and any other record in permanent form (including a record that is not in a legible form but which is capable of being reproduced in a legible form) but does not include an indictment or other document prepared for use in particular legal proceedings.

32 Presumption and determination of age

(1) In any application for an order under *Part III, IV* or *VI*, the court shall make due inquiry as to the age of the person to whom the application relates and the age presumed or declared by the court to be the age of that person shall, until the contrary is proved, for the purposes of this Act, be deemed to be the true age of that person.

33 Rules of court

(1) For the purpose of ensuring the expeditious hearing of applications under *Part III, IV* or *VI*, rules of court may make provision for the service of documents otherwise than under section 7 of the Courts Act, 1964 (as amended by section 22 of the Courts Act, 1971) in circumstances to which the said section 7 relates.

(2) Rules of court may make provision for the furnishing of information and documents by parties to proceedings under *Part III, IV* or *VI* to each other or to solicitors acting for them.

(3) This section is without prejudice to section 17 of the Interpretation Act, 1937, which provides for rules of court.

34 Failure or refusal to deliver up a child

(1) Without prejudice to the law as to contempt of court, where the District Court has made an order under *Part III* or *IV* directing that a child be placed or maintained in the care of a health board, any person having the actual custody of the child who, having been given or shown a copy of the order and having been required, by or on behalf of the health board, to give up the child to that board, fails or refuses to comply with the requirement shall be guilty of an offence and shall be liable on summary conviction to a fine not exceeding £500 or, at the discretion of the court, to imprisonment for a term not exceeding 6 months or both such fine and such imprisonment.

(2) For the purposes of this section, a person shall be deemed to have been given or shown a copy of an order made under *Part III* or *IV* if that person was present at the sitting of the court at which such an order was made.

35 Warrant to search for and deliver up a child

Where a justice has made an order under *Part IV* directing that a child be placed or maintained in the care of a health board, a justice may for the purpose of executing that order issue a warrant authorising a member of the Garda Síochána, accompanied by such other members of the Garda Síochána or such other persons as may be necessary, to enter (if need be by force) any house or other place specified in the warrant (including any building or part of a building, tent, caravan, or other temporary or moveable structure, vehicle, vessel, aircraft or hovercraft) where the child is or where there are reasonable grounds for believing that he is and to deliver the child into the custody of the health board.

PART VI

CHILDREN IN THE CARE OF HEALTH BOARDS

36 Accommodation and maintenance of children in care

(1) Where a child is in the care of a health board, the health board shall provide such care for him, subject to its control and supervision, in such of the following ways as it considers to be in his best interests—

(a) by placing him with a foster parent, or
(b) by placing him in residential care (whether in a children's residential centre registered under *Part VIII*, in a residential home maintained by a health board or in a school or other suitable place of residence), or
(c) in the case of a child who may be eligible for adoption under the Adoption Acts, 1952 to 1988, by placing him with a suitable person with a view to his adoption, or
(d) by making such other suitable arrangements (which may include placing the child with a relative) as the health board thinks proper.

(2) In this Act, 'foster parent' means a person other than a relative of a child who is taking care of the child on behalf of a health board in accordance with regulations made under *section 39* and 'foster care' shall be construed accordingly.

(3) Nothing in this section shall prevent a health board sending a child in its care to any hospital or to any institution which provides nursing or care for children suffering from physical or mental disability.

37   Access to children in care

(1) Where a child is in the care of a health board whether by virtue of an order under *Part III* or *IV* or otherwise, the board shall, subject to the provisions of this Act, facilitate reasonable access to the child by his parents, any person acting *in loco parentis*, or any other person who, in the opinion of the board, has a *bona fide* interest in the child and such access may include allowing the child to reside temporarily with any such person.

(2) Any person who is dissatisfied with arrangements made by a health board under *subsection (1)* may apply to the court, and the court may—

    (a) make such order as it thinks proper regarding access to the child by that person, and

    (b) vary or discharge that order on the application of any person.

(3) The court, on the application of a health board, and if it considers that it is necessary to do so in order to safeguard or promote the child's welfare, may—

    (a) make an order authorising the board to refuse to allow a named person access to a child in its care, and

    (b) vary or discharge that order on the application of any person.

(4) This section is without prejudice to *section 4(2)*.

38   Provision of residential care by health boards

(1) A health board shall make arrangements with the registered proprietors of children's residential centres or with other suitable persons to ensure the provision of an adequate number of residential places for children in its care.

(2) A health board may, with the approval of the Minister, provide and maintain a residential centre or other premises for the provision of residential care for children in care.

(3) The Minister shall make regulations with respect to the conduct of homes or other premises provided by health boards under this section and for securing the welfare of children maintained therein.

(4) Without prejudice to the generality of *subsection (3)*, regulations under this section may—

    (a) prescribe requirements as to the maintenance, care and welfare of children while being maintained in centres,

    (b) prescribe requirements as to the numbers, qualifications and availability of members of the staffs of centres,

    (c) prescribe requirements as to the design, maintenance, repair, cleaning and cleanliness, ventilation, heating and lighting of centres,

    (d) prescribe requirements as to the accommodation (including the amount of space in bedrooms, the washing facilities and the sanitary conveniences) provided in centres,

    (e) prescribe requirements as to the food provided for children while being maintained in centres,

    (f) prescribe requirements as to the records to be kept in centres and for the examination and copying of any such records or of extracts therefrom by officers of the Minister.

39   Regulations as to foster care

(1) The Minister shall make regulations in relation to the placing of children in foster care by health boards under *section 36* and for securing generally the welfare of such children.

(2) Without prejudice to the generality of *subsection (1)*, regulations under this section may—

(a) fix the conditions under which children may be placed in foster care,

(b) prescribe the form of contract to be entered into by a health board with foster parents,

(c) provide for the supervision and visiting by a health board of children in foster care.

40   Regulations as to residential care

(1) The Minister shall make regulations in relation to the placing of children in residential care (whether in children's residential centres or in other institutions) by health boards under *section 36* and for securing generally the welfare of such children.

(2) Without prejudice to the generality of *subsection (1)*, regulations under this section may—

(a) fix the conditions under which children may be placed in residential care,

(b) prescribe the form of contract to be entered into by a health board with persons providing residential care,

(c) provide for the supervision and visiting by a health board of children in residential care.

41   Regulations as to placement with relatives

(1) The Minister shall make regulations in relation to the making of arrangements by health boards under *section 36(1)(d)* for the care of children and for securing generally the welfare of such children.

(2) Without prejudice to the generality of *subsection (1)*, regulations under this section may—

(a) fix the conditions under which children may be placed by health boards with relatives,

(b) prescribe the form of contract to be entered into by a health board with relatives,

(c) provide for the supervision and visiting by a health board of children placed with relatives.

42   Review of cases of children in care

(1) The Minister shall make regulations requiring the case of each child in the care of a health board to be reviewed in accordance with the provisions of the regulations.

(2) Without prejudice to the generality of *subsection (1)*, regulations under this section may make provision—

(a) as to the manner in which each case is to be reviewed,

(b) as to the frequency of reviews, and

(c) requiring the board to consider whether it would be in the best interests of the child to be given into the custody of his parents.

43 Removal from placement

(1) A health board may, in accordance with regulations made by the Minister, remove a child in its care from the custody of any person with whom he has been placed by the board under *section 36.*

(2) Where a person refuses or neglects to comply with a request of a health board to deliver up a child in accordance with regulations made under *subsection (1)*, the board may apply to the District Court for an order directing that person to deliver up the child to the custody of the board and the justice may, if he considers that it is in the best interests of the child so to do, make such an order.

(3) Without prejudice to the law as to contempt of court, where the District Court has made an order under *subsection (2)* (requiring that a child be delivered up to the custody of a health board), any person having the actual custody of the child who, having been given or shown a copy of the order and having been required, by or on behalf of the health board, to give up the child to that board, fails or refuses to comply with the requirement shall be guilty of an offence and shall be liable on summary conviction to a fine not exceeding £500 or, at the discretion of the court, to imprisonment for a term not exceeding 6 months or both such fine and such imprisonment.

(4) For the purposes of this section, a person shall be deemed to have been given or shown a copy of an order made under *subsection (2)* if that person was present at the sitting of the court at which such an order was made.

(5) Where a child is removed from the custody of a person in pursuance of this section, any contract between the board and that person in respect of the child shall terminate immediately upon the removal.

(6) The provisions of this section are without prejudice to the power of a health board to apply for an order under *Part III* or *IV*.

44 Children who become adopted

(1) Where a child becomes adopted under the Adoption Acts, 1952 to 1988, and the child was, immediately before the adoption, being maintained in foster care by a health board with the adopter or adopters, the health board may, subject to any general directions given by the Minister and subject to such conditions as the health board sees fit, contribute to the maintenance of the child as if he continued to be in foster care.

(2) Where a child becomes adopted under the Adoption Acts, 1952 to 1988, any care order in force in respect of the child shall cease to have effect.

45 Aftercare

(1) (a) Where a child leaves the care of a health board, the board may, in accordance with *subsection (2)*, assist him for so long as the board is satisfied as to his need for assistance and, subject to *paragraph (b)*, he has not attained the age of 21 years.

(b) Where a health board is assisting a person in accordance with *subsection (2)(b)*, and that person attains the age of 21 years, the board may continue to provide such assistance until the completion of the course of education in which he is engaged.

(2) A health board may assist a person under this section in one or more of the following ways—

(a) by causing him to be visited or assisted,

(b) by arranging for the completion of his education and by contributing towards his maintenance while he is completing his education,

(c) by placing him in a suitable trade, calling or business and paying such fee or sum as may be requisite for that purpose,

(d) by arranging hostel or other forms of accommodation for him,

(e) by co-operating with housing authorities in planning accommodation for children leaving care on reaching the age of 18 years.

(3) Any arrangement made by a health board under section 55(4) or (5) of the Health Act, 1953, in force immediately before the commencement of this section shall continue in force as if made under this section.

(4) In providing assistance under this section, a health board shall comply with any general directions given by the Minister.

46 Recovery of children removed from care etc

(1) The provisions of this section shall apply to any child who is in the care of a health board and who is, without lawful authority, removed from the custody of the board or from the custody of any person who is taking care of him on behalf of the board or prevented from returning to such custody at the end of any period of leave.

(2) The health board may request the Garda Síochána to search for the child and to deliver him up to the custody of the board and the Garda Síochána may take all reasonable measures to comply with such a request.

(3) A justice of the District Court may, if satisfied by information on oath that there are reasonable grounds for believing that a person specified in the information can produce the child named in the application, make an order directing that person to deliver up the child to the custody of the board.

(4) Without prejudice to the law as to contempt of court where the District Court has made an order under *subsection (3)* directing that a child be delivered up to the care of a health board, any person having the actual custody of the child who, having been given or shown a copy of the order and having been required, by or on behalf of the health board, to give up the child to that board, fails or refuses to comply with the requirement shall be guilty of an offence and shall be liable on summary conviction to a fine not exceeding £500 or, at the discretion of the court, to imprisonment for a term not exceeding 6 months or both such fine and such imprisonment.

(5) For the purposes of this section, a person shall be deemed to have been given or shown a copy of an order made under *subsection (3)* if that person was present at the sitting of the court at which such an order was made.

(6) A justice of the District Court may, if satisfied by information on oath that there are reasonable grounds for believing that the child named in the application is in any house or other place (including any building or part of a building, tent, caravan or other temporary or moveable structure, vehicle, vessel, aircraft or hovercraft) specified in the information, issue a warrant authorising a member of the Garda Síochána, accompanied by such other members of the Garda Síochána or such other persons as may be necessary to enter (if need be by force) and to search the house or other place for the child, and if the child is found he shall be returned to the custody of the board.

(7) An application for an order under *subsection (3)* may, if the justice is satisfied that the urgency of the matter so requires, be made *ex parte.*

(8) An application for an order under *subsection (3)* or for a warrant under *subsection (6)* may, if the justice is satisfied that the urgency of the matter so requires, be heard and an order made thereon elsewhere than at a public sitting of the District Court.

(9) Without prejudice to *section 28—*

   (a) an order under *subsection (3)* may be made by a justice of the District Court for the time being assigned to the district court district where the person specified in the information resides or is for the time being, and

   (b) a warrant under *subsection (6)* may be issued by a justice for the time being assigned to the district where the house or other place specified in the information is situated,

and, in either case, where such justice is not immediately available the order may be made, or the warrant issued, by any justice of the District Court.

47 Application for directions

Where a child is in the care of a health board, the District Court may, of its own motion or on the application of any person, give such directions and make such order on any question affecting the welfare of the child as it thinks proper and may vary or discharge any such direction or order.

48 Transitional provisions

(1) On the commencement of *Part IV* any child who is in the care of a health board pursuant to an order made under *Part II* or *IV* of the Children Act, 1908 shall be deemed to be the subject of a care order committing him to the care of that health board and the provisions of *Part IV* shall apply with the necessary modifications.

(2) Where, on the commencement of *Part IV*, a child is in the care of a health board pursuant to an order made under section 21 or 24 of the Children Act, 1908 in respect of the commission of an offence against him and the person charged with the commission of the offence is acquitted of the charge or the charge is dismissed for want of prosecution, any care order to which the child is deemed to be subject under *subsection (1)* shall forthwith be void, but without prejudice to anything that may have been lawfully done under it.

(3) Nothing in this Act shall affect an order made under *Part II* or *IV* of the Children Act, 1908 committing a child to the care of a relative or fit person other than a health board.

(4) On the commencement of *Part III*, any child who is being detained in a place of safety under any provision of the Children Act, 1908 shall be deemed to have been received into that place pursuant to an emergency care order on the date of such commencement.

(5) Where, on the commencement of *Part II*, a child is in the care of a health board otherwise than by virtue of a court order, he shall be deemed to have been taken into care under *section 4* on the date of such commencement.

(6) Where, on the commencement of *Part VI*, a child is boarded-out by a health board, he shall be deemed to have been placed by the health board in foster care under an arrangement made under *section 36*.

(7) Where, on the commencement of *Part VI*, a health board is contributing towards the maintenance of a child in accordance with section 55(9)(c) of the Health Act, 1953, the

board may, subject to such conditions as it sees fit, continue to contribute to the maintenance of the child as if he were in foster care.

(8) Where, on the commencement of *Part VI*, a child is being maintained by a health board in a home or school approved by the Minister for the purposes of section 55 of the Health Act, 1953, he shall be deemed to have been placed in residential care by the health board under an arrangement made under *section 36.*

(9) Nothing in *section 67* shall affect the operation of an order committing a child to a certified industrial school to which that section applies.

PART VII

SUPERVISION OF PRE-SCHOOL SERVICES

49   Definitions for *Part VII*

In this Part—

'authorised person' means a person appointed under *section 54* to be an authorised person for the purposes of this Part,

'national school' has the meaning assigned to it in the School Attendance Act, 1926,

'pre-school child' means a child who has not attained the age of six years and who is not attending a national school or a school providing an educational programme similar to a national school,

'pre-school service' means any pre-school, play group, day nursery, crèche, day-care or other similar service which caters for pre-school children, including those grant-aided by health boards,

'relevant health board' means the health board for the area in which a pre-school service is being or is proposed to be carried on.

50   Regulations as to pre-school services

(1) The Minister shall, after consultation with the Minister for Education and the Minister for the Environment, make regulations for the purpose of securing the health, safety and welfare and promoting the development of pre-school children attending pre-school services.

(2) Without prejudice to the generality of *subsection (1)*, regulations may—

(a) prescribe requirements as to the heating, lighting, ventilation, cleanliness, repair and maintenance of premises in which pre-school services are carried on and as to the equipment and facilities to be provided,

(b) provide for the enforcement and execution of the regulations by health boards,

(c) prescribe the annual fees to be paid to health boards by persons carrying on pre-school services towards the cost of inspections under this Part.

(3) Regulations under this section may—

(a) make different provision for different classes of pre-school services,

(b) prescribe different requirements for different classes of pre-school services,

(c) provide for exemptions from any provision or provisions of the regulations for a specified class or classes of pre-school services.

(4) The Public Offices Fees Act, 1879, shall not apply in respect of any fees paid under regulations under this section.

51 Giving of notice to health board

(1) A person carrying on a pre-school service on the commencement of this Part shall give notice to the relevant health board in the prescribed manner.

(2) A person who, after the commencement of this Part, proposes to carry on a pre-school service shall give notice to the relevant health board in the prescribed manner.

52 Duty of person carrying on pre-school service

It shall be the duty of every person carrying on a pre-school service to take all reasonable measures to safeguard the health, safety and welfare of pre-school children attending the service and to comply with regulations made by the Minister under this Part.

53 Supervision of pre-school services

A health board shall cause to be visited from time to time each pre-school service in its area in order to ensure that the person carrying on the service is fulfilling the duties imposed on him under *section 52.*

54 Authorised persons

(1) A health board shall appoint such and so many of its officers as it thinks fit to be authorised persons for the purposes of this Part.

(2) A health board may, with the consent of the Minister for Education, appoint an officer of that Minister to be an authorised person for the purposes of this Part.

(3) Every authorised person shall be furnished with a warrant of his appointment as an authorised person, and, when exercising any power conferred on an authorised person under this Part, shall, if requested by any person affected, produce the warrant to that person.

55 Inspection by authorised persons

(1) Where the relevant health board has received notification in accordance with *section 51* in respect of a pre-school service, an authorised person shall be entitled at all reasonable times to enter any premises (including a private dwelling) in which the service is being carried on.

(2) A justice of the District Court may, if satisfied on information on oath that there are reasonable grounds for believing that a pre-school service is being carried on in any premises (including a private dwelling) in respect of which notice has not been received by the relevant health board in accordance with *section 51*, issue a warrant authorising a person appointed by the health board in accordance with *section 54* to enter and inspect the premises.

(3) An authorised person who enters any premises in accordance with *subsection (1)* or *(2)* may make such examination into the condition of the premises and the care and attention which the pre-school children are receiving as may be necessary for the purposes of this Part.

(4) A warrant under *subsection (2)* may be issued by a justice of the District Court for the time being assigned to the district court district where the premises are situated.

56   Provision by health boards of pre-school services and information

(1) A health board may, subject to any general directions given by the Minister, provide pre-school services in its area and provide and maintain premises for that purpose.

(2) The Minister may, after consultation with the Minister for Education and the Minister for the Environment, make regulations for the purpose of securing the health, safety and welfare and promoting the development of children attending pre-school services provided by health boards.

(3) A health board shall make available to any interested person information on pre-school services in its area, whether provided by the board or otherwise.

57   Offences under *Part VII*

(1) A person who—

   (a) refuses to allow an authorised person to enter any premises in accordance with *subsection (1)* or *(2)* of *section 55* or who obstructs or impedes an authorised person in the exercise of any of his powers under *subsection (3)* of that section, or

   (b) contravenes the requirements of this Part or of any regulations made thereunder,

shall be guilty of an offence and shall be liable on summary conviction to a fine not exceeding £1,000.

(2) Where a person is convicted of an offence under this Part the court may, either in addition to or in substitution for the imposition of a fine, by order declare that the person shall be prohibited for such period as may be specified in the order from carrying on a pre-school service.

(3) A person who contravenes an order made under *subsection (2)* shall be guilty of an offence and shall be liable on summary conviction to a fine not exceeding £1,000 or to imprisonment for a term not exceeding 12 months or both.

58   Exemptions from provisions of this Part

For the avoidance of doubt it is hereby declared that the provisions of this Part shall not apply to—

   (a) the care of one or more pre-school children undertaken by a relative of the child or children or the spouse of such relative,

   (b) a person taking care of one or more pre-school children of the same family and no other such children (other than that person's own such children) in that person's home,

   (c) a person taking care of not more than 3 pre-school children of different families (other than that person's own such children) in that person's home.

PART VIII

CHILDREN'S RESIDENTIAL CENTRES

59 Definitions for *Part VIII*

In this Part—

'children's residential centre' means any home or other institution for the residential care of children in the care of health boards or other children who are not receiving adequate care and protection excluding—

(a) an institution managed by or on behalf of a Minister of the Government or a health board,

(b) an institution in which a majority of the children being maintained are being treated for acute illnesses,

(c) an institution for the care and maintenance of physically or mentally handicapped children,

(d) a mental institution within the meaning of the Mental Treatment Acts, 1945 to 1966,

(e) an institution which is a 'certified school' within the meaning of Part IV of the Children Act, 1908, functions in relation to which stand vested in the Minister for Education,

'centre' means a children's residential centre,

'register' means a register of children's residential centres established under *section 61* and, in relation to a particular health board, means the register established by that board and cognate words shall be construed accordingly,

'registered proprietor', in relation to a registered children's residential centre, means the person whose name is entered in the register as the person carrying on the centre,

'the regulations' means the regulations under *section 63.*

60 Prohibition of unregistered children's residential centres

(1) A person shall not carry on a children's residential centre unless the centre is registered and the person is the registered proprietor thereof.

(2) A person shall not be in charge of a centre unless the centre is registered.

(3) Any person who contravenes a provision of this section shall be guilty of an offence.

61 Registration of children's residential centres

(1) Each health board shall establish and maintain a register of children's residential centres in its functional area (referred to subsequently in this Act as 'a register').

(2) (a) There shall be entered in a register in respect of each centre registered therein the name of the person by whom it is carried on, the name of the person who is in charge of it, the address of the premises in which it is carried on, a statement of the number of children who can be accommodated in the centre, the date on which the registration is to take effect (referred to subsequently in this section as 'the date of registration') and such other (if any) particulars as may be prescribed.

(b) A register maintained under this section shall be made available for inspection free of charge by members of the public at all reasonable times.

(3) (a) A health board may, on application to it in that behalf by a person who
proposes to carry on a centre in its functional area, register or refuse to register
the centre.

(b) Subject to the provisions of this section, the period of a registration shall be 3
years from the date of registration.

(4) A health board may remove a centre from the register.

(5) A health board shall not—

(a) refuse to register a centre in relation to which an application for its registration
has been duly made, or

(b) remove a centre from the register,

unless—

(i) it is of opinion that—

(I) the premises to which the application or, as the case may be, the
registration relates do not comply with the regulations, or

(II) the carrying on of the centre will not be or is not in compliance with the
regulations, or

(ii) the applicant or the registered proprietor, as the case may be, or the person
in charge or, as the case may be, proposed to be in charge of the centre has
been convicted of an offence under this Part or of any other offence that is
such as to render the person unfit to carry on or, as the case may be, to be in
charge of the centre, or

(iii) the applicant or the registered proprietor, as the case may be, has failed or
refused to furnish the board with information requested by it pursuant to
subsection (8) or has furnished the board with information that is false or
misleading in a material particular, or

(iv) the registered proprietor has, not more than one year before the date from
which the registration or removal from the register would take effect,
contravened a condition under *subsection (6)*.

(6) (a) A health board may—

(i) at the time of registration or subsequently attach to the registration
conditions in relation to the carrying on of the centre concerned and
such other matters as it considers appropriate having regard to its
functions under this Part,

(ii) attach different conditions to the registration of different centres, and

(iii) amend or revoke a condition of registration.

(b) Conditions imposed under this subsection or amendments and revocations
under this subsection shall be notified in writing to the registered proprietor of
the centre concerned.

(7) An application for registration shall be in the prescribed form or in a form to the like
effect.

(8) (a) A health board may request an applicant for registration or, as the case may be,
a registered proprietor to furnish it with such information as it considers
necessary for the purposes of its functions under this Part.

(b) A person who, whether in pursuance of a request or otherwise, furnishes
information to a health board for the purposes of this Part that is false or
misleading in a material particular shall be guilty of an offence unless he shows
that, at the time the information was furnished to the board, he was not aware
that it was false or misleading in a material particular.

(9) The registered proprietor of a centre who proposes to carry on the centre immediately after the expiration of the period of registration of the centre may apply under *subsection (3)* to the health board concerned not less than 2 months before such expiration for the registration of the centre and, if the board does not notify him before such expiration that it proposes to refuse to register the centre, it shall register the centre and its date of registration shall be the day following the day of such expiration.

(10)(a) Where a registered children's residential centre commences to be carried on by a person other than the registered proprietor—

    (i) the centre shall thereupon cease to be registered,

    (ii) the person shall (if he has not done so before such commencement) apply not later than 4 weeks after it to the health board concerned for the registration of the centre, and, if the application is granted, the date of registration of the centre shall be that of the day following the day of the cesser aforesaid,

    (iii) if the application aforesaid is duly made, and is not refused then, during the period from the commencement aforesaid until the centre is registered, it shall be deemed, for the purposes of *section 60* to be registered and there shall be deemed to be attached to the registration any conditions attached to the previous registration.

  (b) A person who contravenes *paragraph (a)(ii)* shall be guilty of an offence.

(11)(a) Where a health board proposes to refuse to register a children's residential centre, to remove a centre from the register, to attach a condition to, or amend or revoke a condition attached to, a registration, it shall notify in writing the applicant or the registered proprietor, as the case may be, of its proposal and of the reasons for it.

  (b) A person who has been notified of a proposal under *paragraph (a)* may, within 21 days of the receipt of the notification, make representations in writing to the health board concerned and the board shall—

    (i) before deciding the matter, take into consideration any representations duly made to it under this paragraph in relation to the proposal, and

    (ii) notify the person in writing of its decision and of the reasons for it.

(12) A notification of a proposal of a health board under *subsection (11)* shall include a statement that the person concerned may make representations to the board within 21 days of the receipt by him of the notification and a notification of a decision of a health board under *subsection (11)* shall include a statement that the person concerned may appeal to the District Court under *section 62* against the decision within 21 days from the receipt by him of the notification.

(13) Where, in relation to a children's residential centre, there is a contravention of a condition of registration, the registered proprietor and the person in charge of the centre shall be guilty of an offence.

62 Appeals

(1) A person, being the registered proprietor or, as the case may be, the person intending to be the registered proprietor, of a children's residential centre, may appeal to the District Court against a decision of a health board to refuse to register the centre, to remove the centre from the register or to attach a condition, or to amend or revoke a condition attached, to the registration of the centre and such an appeal shall be brought within 21 days of the receipt by the person of the notification of the decision under *section 61* and that court may, as it thinks proper, confirm the decision or direct the

health board, as may be appropriate, to register, or to restore the registration of, the centre, to withdraw the condition or the amendment to or revocation of a condition, to attach a specified condition to the registration or to make a specified amendment to a condition of the registration.

(2) The jurisdiction conferred on the District Court by this section shall be exercised by the justice of the District Court for the time being assigned to the district court district in which the centre concerned is situated.

(3) A decision of the District Court under this section on a question of fact shall be final.

(4) Where a notification of a decision specified in *subsection (1)* (other than a decision to refuse to register a centre which was not registered or deemed to be registered at the time of the relevant application for registration) is given under *section 61*, then—

    (a) during such period from such notification (not being less than 21 days) as the health board concerned considers reasonable and specifies in the notification, the centre shall be treated as if the decision had not been made and, if the decision was to refuse an application under *paragraph (a)* of *section 61(10)* for registration, be treated as if it had been registered and the registration had attached to it any conditions attached to the relevant registration that had ceased by virtue of *subparagraph (i)* of the said *paragraph (a)*, and

    (b) if an appeal against the decision is brought under this section, during—

        (i) the period from the end of the period aforesaid until the determination or withdrawal of the appeal or any appeal therefrom or from any such appeal, and

        (ii) such further period (if any) as the court concerned considers reasonable and specifies in its decision,

    the centre shall—

        (I) be treated for the purposes of *section 61* as if the appeal had been upheld, and

        (II) if the appeal was against a decision of the health board to refuse an application under *paragraph (a)* of *section 61(10)* for registration, be treated as if the registration had attached to it any conditions attached to the relevant registration that had ceased by virtue of *subparagraph (i)* of the said *paragraph (a)*.

(5) The health board concerned shall be given notice of an appeal under this section and shall be entitled to appear, be heard and adduce evidence on the hearing of the appeal.

63 Regulations in relation to children's residential centres

(1) The Minister shall, for the purpose of ensuring proper standards in relation to children's residential centres, including adequate and suitable accommodation, food and care for children while being maintained in centres, and the proper conduct of centres, make such regulations as he thinks appropriate in relation to centres.

(2) Without prejudice to the generality of *subsection (1)*, regulations under this section may—

    (a) prescribe requirements as to the maintenance, care and welfare of children while being maintained in centres,

    (b) prescribe requirements as to the numbers, qualifications and availability of members of the staffs of centres,

(c) prescribe requirements as to the design, maintenance, repair, cleaning and cleanliness, ventilation, heating and lighting of centres,

(d) prescribe requirements as to the accommodation (including the amount of space in bedrooms, the washing facilities and the sanitary conveniences) provided in centres,

(e) prescribe requirements as to the food provided for children while being maintained in centres,

(f) prescribe requirements as to the records to be kept in centres and for the examination and copying of any such records or of extracts therefrom by officers of health boards,

(g) provide for the inspection of premises in which centres are being carried on or are proposed to be carried on or that are reasonably believed by a health board to be premises in which a centre is being carried on and otherwise for the enforcement and execution of the regulations by the appropriate health boards and their officers.

(3) (a) Where, in relation to a centre, there is a failure or refusal to comply with a provision of the regulations, the registered proprietor and the person in charge of the centre shall be guilty of an offence.

(b) A person who fails or refuses to comply with a provision of the regulations shall be guilty of an offence.

(4) (a) Where a person is convicted of an offence under this section, the Circuit Court may, on the application of the health board concerned, brought not more than six months after the conviction or, in the case of an appeal against the conviction, the final determination of it or of any further appeal (if it is a determination affirming the conviction) or the withdrawal of any such appeal therefrom, by order declare that the person shall be disqualified during such period as may be specified in the order from carrying on, being in charge, or concerned with the management, of the centre to which the conviction related or, at the discretion of that Court, any centre.

(b) A person in respect of whom an order is made under this subsection shall not during the period specified in the order carry on, be in charge, or concerned with the management, of the centre specified in the order or, if the order so specifies, of any centre.

(c) A person who contravenes *paragraph (b)* shall be guilty of an offence.

(d) Notice of an application under this subsection shall be given to the person convicted of the offence concerned and he shall be entitled to appear, be heard and adduce evidence on the hearing of the application.

(e) The jurisdiction conferred on the Circuit Court by this subsection shall be exercised by the judge of the Circuit Court for the time being assigned to the circuit in which the premises concerned are situated.

(5) A person who wilfully obstructs or interferes with a health board or an officer of a health board in the performance of functions under the regulations or who fails or refuses to comply with a requirement of a health board or an officer of a health board under such regulations shall be guilty of an offence.

64 Offences under *Part VIII*

A person guilty of an offence under this Part shall be liable on summary conviction to a fine not exceeding £1,000 or to imprisonment for a term not exceeding 12 months or to both.

65 Discontinuance of centre

(1) Where the registered proprietor of a children's residential centre intends to cease to carry on the centre, he shall give six months' notice in writing to the health board for the area in which the centre is situated and at the expiration of six months from the date of the notice (unless before that time the notice is withdrawn or the period of registration has expired) the centre shall cease to be registered under this Part.

(2) A health board may, if it so thinks fit, accept a shorter period of notice for the purposes of *subsection (1)* and the provisions of that subsection shall apply with the necessary modifications.

66 Superannuation of certain staff

(1) An employee of a children's residential centre to which this section applies shall, for the purposes of the Local Government (Superannuation) Act, 1980, be deemed to be employed by the health board for the area in which the centre is situated subject to any modifications (including modifications to any scheme or regulations made under the said Act of 1980 and modifications as to service reckonable as pensionable service) which may, with the consent of the Minister for the Environment, be specified in an order made by the Minister.

(2) In this section, 'employee' means a person employed by a children's residential centre who is the holder in a wholetime capacity of a position, the establishment, remuneration and conditions of service of which have been approved by the health board for the area in which the centre is situated, with the consent of the Minister.

(3) This section applies to a children's residential centre which—

    (a) is not directly operated or administered by a health board,

    (b) is funded by a health board, and

    (c) is specified by the Minister for the purpose of this section.

67 Transitional provisions

(1) On the commencement of this Part, every institution which, immediately before such commencement, was an industrial school certified in accordance with Part IV of the Children Act, 1908, functions in relation to which stood vested in the Minister, shall cease to be so certified and shall be deemed to be registered under this Part as a children's residential centre.

(2) On the commencement of this Part, every school which, immediately before such commencement, was a school approved (or deemed to be approved) for the purposes of section 55 of the Health Act, 1953 shall be deemed to be registered under this Part as a children's residential centre.

PART IX

ADMINISTRATION

68 Regulations

(1) The Minister may make regulations—

    (a) for any purpose in relation to which regulations are provided for by any of the provisions of this Act, and

(b) for prescribing any matter or thing referred to in this Act as prescribed or to be prescribed.

(2) Every order and regulation made under any provision of an enactment repealed by this Act and in force immediately before such repeal shall continue in force under the corresponding provision, if any, of this Act, subject to such adaptations and modifications as the Minister may by regulations make to enable any such order or regulation to have effect in conformity with this Act.

(3) Every regulation made under this Act shall be laid before each House of the Oireachtas as soon as may be after it is made and, if a resolution annulling the regulation is passed by either House within the next 21 days on which that House has sat after the regulation is laid before it, the regulation shall be annulled accordingly but without prejudice to the validity of anything previously done thereunder.

69 Powers of the Minister

(1) The Minister may give general directions to a health board in relation to the performance of the functions assigned to it by or under this Act and the health board shall comply with any such direction.

(2) The Minister may cause to be inspected any service provided or premises maintained by a health board under this Act.

(3) An inspection under this section shall be conducted by a person authorised in that behalf by the Minister (in this section referred to as an authorised person).

(4) An authorised person conducting an inspection under this section may—

(a) enter any premises maintained by a health board under this Act and make such examination into the state and management of the premises and the treatment of children therein as he thinks fit, and

(b) examine such records and interview such members of the staff of the board as he thinks fit.

(5) The Minister may direct a health board to supply him with such reports and statistics in relation to the performance of the functions assigned to it by or under this Act as he may require and a health board shall comply with any such direction.

70 Charges for certain services

(1) In making available a service under *section 3, 4* or *56*, the health board shall from time to time determine in each case whether such service shall be provided without charge or at such charge as it considers appropriate.

(2) In making a determination in accordance with *subsection (1)* a health board shall comply with any general directions given by the Minister with the consent of the Minister for Finance.

(3) For the purposes of determining what charge, if any, should be made on any person for a service, a health board may require that person to make a declaration in such form as it considers appropriate in relation to his means and may take such steps as it thinks fit to verify the declaration.

(4) Where a person is recorded by a health board as entitled, because of specified circumstances, to a service without charge, he shall notify the board of any relevant change in those circumstances.

(5) Any charge which may be made by a health board under this Act may, in default of payment, be recovered as a simple contract debt in any court of competent jurisdiction from the person on whom the charge is made or, where the person has died, from his legal personal representative.

71   Prosecution of offences

(1) Summary proceedings for an offence under this Act may be brought and prosecuted by the health board for the area in which the offence is alleged to have been committed or by any other person.

(2) Notwithstanding section 10(4) of the Petty Sessions (Ireland) Act, 1851, summary proceedings for an offence under this Act may be instituted within 12 months from the date of the offence.

(3) Where an offence under this Act is committed by a body corporate or by a person purporting to act on behalf of a body corporate or an unincorporated body of persons and is proved to have been committed with the consent or approval of, or to have been attributable to any neglect on the part of, any person who, when the offence was committed, was director, member of the committee of management or other controlling authority of the body concerned, or the manager, secretary or other officer of the body, that person shall also be deemed to have committed the offence and may be proceeded against and punished accordingly.

72   Functions of chief executive officer

(1) The following functions relating to a health board shall be functions of the chief executive officer of the board:

  (a) any function with respect to a decision as to whether or not to provide a service or make facilities available to any particular person,
  (b) any function with respect to a decision as to the making or recovery of a charge or the amount of any charge for a service provided in a particular case under *section 3, 4* or *56,*
  (c) any function in relation to whether or not to receive a child into care under *section 4,*
  (d) any function in relation to the payment of a grant or allowance to a voluntary body or any other person,
  (e) any function with respect to legal proceedings in relation to the care and protection of a child,
  (f) any function in relation to a particular child in the care of the board or in relation to the provision of aftercare,
  (g) any function in relation to the supervision of pre-school services,
  (h) any function in relation to the registration and regulation of children's residential centres,
  (i) such other functions as may be prescribed.

(2) Any question as to whether or not a particular function is a function of the chief executive officer shall be determined by the Minister.

(3) In this section 'chief executive officer' includes a person acting as deputy chief executive officer in accordance with section 13 of the Health Act, 1970.

73   Expenses

The expenses incurred by the Minister in the administration of this Act shall, to such extent as may be sanctioned by the Minister for Finance, be paid out of moneys provided by the Oireachtas.

PART X

MISCELLANEOUS AND SUPPLEMENTARY

74   Sale etc of solvents

(1) It shall be an offence for a person to sell, offer or make available a substance to a person under the age of eighteen years or to a person acting on behalf of that person if he knows or has reasonable cause to believe that the substance is, or its fumes are, likely to be inhaled by the person under the age of eighteen years for the purpose of causing intoxication.

(2) In proceedings against any person for an offence under *subsection (1)*, it shall be a defence for him to prove that at the time he sold, offered or made available the substance he was under the age of eighteen years and was acting otherwise than in the course of or furtherance of a business.

(3) In proceedings against any person for an offence under *subsection (1)* it shall be a defence for him to prove that he took reasonable steps to assure himself that the person to whom the substance was sold, offered or made available, or any person on whose behalf that person was acting, was not under the age of eighteen years.

(4) A person who is guilty of an offence under *subsection (1)* shall be liable on summary conviction to a fine not exceeding £1,000 or to imprisonment for a term not exceeding 12 months or to both.

(5) Subject to *subsection (6)*, a court by which a person is convicted of an offence under this section may order anything shown to the satisfaction of the court to relate to the offence to be forfeited and either destroyed or dealt with in such other manner as the court thinks fit.

(6) A court shall not order anything to be forfeited under this section unless an opportunity is given to any person appearing to the court to be the owner of or otherwise interested in it to show cause why the order should not be made.

(7) A member of the Garda Síochána may seize any substance which is in the possession of a child in any public place and which the member has reasonable cause to believe is being inhaled by that child in a manner likely to cause him to be intoxicated. Any substance so seized may be destroyed or otherwise disposed of in such a manner as a member of the Garda Síochána not below the rank of Superintendent may direct.

(8) This section is without prejudice to the provisions of the Misuse of Drugs Acts, 1977 and 1984.

75   (Amends s 17 of the School Attendance Act, 1926)

76   (Amends s 15 of the Guardianship of Infants Act, 1964)

77   (Amends s 16 of the Guardianship of Infants Act, 1964)

78   Maintenance—saver in relation to members of Defence Forces

(1) Section 98 of the Defence Act, 1954 (which provides for deductions from pay of members of the Permanent Defence Force and reservists called out on permanent service in respect of court orders under sections 75, 82 or 99 of the Children Act, 1908) shall apply in like manner to an order made under *section 18.*

(2) Section 107 of the Defence Act, 1954 (which provides that court orders made under the aforementioned sections against a member of the Permanent Defence Force or a reservist during any period when he is called out on permanent service shall not be enforceable by imprisonment) shall apply in like manner in the case of an order made under *section 18.*

79   Repeals

The enactments specified in the *Schedule* are hereby repealed to the extent specified in the *third column.*

SCHEDULE   Section 79

ENACTMENTS REPEALED

Session and Chapter or Number and Year	Short Title	Extent of Repeal
4 Edw 7, c 15	Prevention of Cruelty to Children Act, 1904.	The whole Act.
8 Edw 7, c 67.	Children Act, 1908.	Part 1, Sections 13 and 15, Sections 20 to 26, Sections 34, 36 and 38(1), Section 58(1), (5), (6), (7) and (8), Section 59, Section 74(11), Sections 118, 119, 122 and 126.
3 & 4 Geo 5, c 7.	Children (Employment Abroad) Act, 1913.	The whole Act.
No 15 of 1934.	Children Act, 1934.	The whole Act.
No 12 of 1941.	Children Act, 1941.	Section 10(1).
No 25 of 1952.	Adoption Act, 1952.	Section 31(2).
No 26 of 1953.	Health Act, 1953.	Sections 55, 56, 57 and 65(2).
No 28 of 1957.	Children (Amendment) Act, 1957.	Sections 2, 3 and 10.
No 2 of 1964.	Adoption Act, 1964.	Section 10.

Children Act, 1941

(1941 No 12)

ARRANGEMENT OF SECTIONS

An Act to amend and extend the Children Act, 1908   [3 June 1941]

1 Definitions

(1) In this Act—
> the expression 'the Minister' means the Minister for Education;
> the expression 'the Principal Act' means the Children Act, 1908.

(2) Subject to the provisions of the next following section, every word and expression to which a particular meaning is given by the Principal Act for the purposes of that Act has in this Act the meaning so given to it.

2   Extension of meaning of certified school

In the Principal Act and this Act every reference to a certified school shall be construed as including a reference to any building, camp, or other premises, wheresoever situate, which is used for the time being with the approval of the Minister for the purpose of giving a holiday to persons detained in such school.

3   Regulations for the conduct of certified schools

(1) The Minister may make regulations for the conduct of certified schools and, in particular and without prejudice to the generality of the foregoing, such regulations may make provision in relation to the education and training to be given to persons detained in such schools and the safeguarding of the health of such persons.

(2) Regulations under this section may be so framed as to apply in respect of all or one or more certified schools or of any class or classes of certified schools.

(3) Where the Minister has made regulations under this section, he shall send by post a copy thereof to the managers of the certified school or of each certified school in relation to which such regulations apply.

(4) It shall be the duty of the managers of the certified school or of each certified school in relation to which regulations made under this section apply to comply with such regulations and to make such variations (if any) in the rules under section 54 of the Principal Act for the time being in force in relation to such school as may be necessary to bring the said rules into conformity with such regulations.

4   Regulations prescribing remuneration of officers of certified schools

(1) The Minister may make regulations prescribing the remuneration of officers of certified schools or of any class or classes of such officers.

(2) Where the Minister has made regulations under this section, he shall send by post a copy thereof to the managers of every certified school.

(3) It shall be the duty of the managers of every certified school to comply with any regulations made under this section.

5   Resident manager of certified school

(1) The managers of a certified school shall, from time to time as occasion requires, appoint a person to be responsible for the immediate control and supervision of such school, and every person so appointed shall be known and is in this section referred to as the resident manager of such school.

(2) The resident manager of a certified school shall reside ordinarily on the school premises.

(3) The managers of a certified school may authorise the resident manager of such school to exercise and perform such of their powers, functions, and duties (including in particular their powers, functions, and duties under sections 52, 53, 67 and 68 of the Principal Act) as they think fit.

(4) If the Minister is satisfied that the resident manager of a certified school has failed or neglected to discharge efficiently the duties of his position or that he is unsuitable or unfit to discharge those duties, the Minister may request the managers of the school to

remove such resident manager from his position and the managers shall comply with such request (unless withdrawn) within one month after receipt thereof.

(5) Every appointment of the resident manager of a certified school shall be made either—

   (a) if the appointment is a first appointment and the school is a certified school upon the passing of this Act—within one month after the passing of this Act,

   (b) if the appointment is a first appointment and the school becomes a certified school after the passing of this Act—within one month after the school becomes a certified school, or

   (c) if the appointment is not a first appointment—within one month after the occurrence of the vacancy calling for such appointment.

(6) The managers of a certified school shall, within ten days after appointing a resident manager, notify his name to the Minister.

6   (Amends s 44 of the Principal Act)

7   (Amends s 49 of the Principal Act)

8   (Amends s 55 of the Principal Act)

9   (Amends s 57 of the Principal Act)

10   (Amends s 58(1) of the Principal Act; sub-sections (a)–(c) repealed)

Amendments—Child Care Act, 1991, s 79, Sch 1.

---

11   (Amends s 65 of the Principal Act)

12   Extension of detention in industrial school

(1) The Minister may direct that the time for which any child shall be detained in an industrial school under a detention order shall be extended, to such extent as the Minister thinks proper, for the purpose of the completion by such child of any course of education or training and thereupon such detention order shall, notwithstanding anything contained in section 65 of the Principal Act, have effect as if altered so as to conform with the terms of such direction and such child shall be detained accordingly.

(2) The Minister shall not give a direction under this section save with the consent of the parents, surviving parent, mother (in the case of an illegitimate child), or guardian of the child to whom such direction relates.

(3) The Minister shall not give a direction under this section having the effect of extending the detention of the child to whom such direction relates beyond the time when such child will, in the opinion of the Minister, attain the age of seventeen years.

13   (Amends s 67 of the Principal Act)

14   (Amends s 68 of the Principal Act)

15   Supervision certificates

(1) The documents referred to as licences in sections 67 and 68 of the Principal Act shall be known as supervision certificates and the said documents shall be framed accordingly.

(2) This section shall be construed as effecting no more than a change in the name of the documents to which it relates.

16   (Amends s 69(1) of the Principal Act)

17   (Amends s 71(1) of the Principal Act)

18   (Amends s 72 of the Principal Act)

19   (*repealed*)

Amendments—Children (Amendment) Act, 1957, s 11, Sch.

---

20   (Amends s 74 of the Principal Act)

21   Payments in respect of inmates of certified schools

(1) The Minister, with the consent of the Minister for Finance and the Minister for Local Government and Public Health, may make regulations prescribing the payments to be made by local authorities to the managers of certified schools for the maintenance of such children and youthful offenders as such local authorities are liable under section 74 of the Principal Act to maintain.

(2) Regulations under this section may prescribe different rates of payment in respect of different certified schools or different classes of certified schools and may prescribe such rates by reference to fixed amounts or by reference to maximum and minimum amounts.

(3) Where any regulations under this section are for the time being in force, it shall be the duty of every local authority to comply with such regulations and such duty shall lie on such local authority notwithstanding anything contained in any contract made (whether before or after the commencement of this section) by them under paragraph (a) of sub-section (8) of section 74 of the Principal Act and every such contract shall accordingly be deemed to be void to the extent (if any) to which it is inconsistent with such regulations.

(4) Every sum payable by a local authority in accordance with regulations under this section to the managers of a certified school shall, in default of payment, be recoverable as a simple contract debt in any court of competent jurisdiction.

(5) Every regulation made under this section shall be laid before each House of the Oireachtas as soon as may be after it is made, and, if a resolution annulling such regulation is passed by either such House within the next twenty-one days on which such

House has sat after such regulation is laid before it, such regulation shall be annulled accordingly but without prejudice to the validity of anything previously done thereunder.

22   (Amends s 75 of the Principal Act; subss (d)–(f) repealed)

Amendments—Children (Amendment) Act, 1957, s 11, Sch.

---

23   (Amends s 84 of the Principal Act)

24   (Amends s 94 of the Principal Act)

25   (Amends s 95 of the Principal Act)

26   (Amends s 111 of the Principal Act)

27   (Amends s 123(1) of the Principal Act)

28   (Amends s 128(1) of the Principal Act)

29   (Amends s 131 of the Principal Act)

30   Repeal

The Children Act, 1929 (No 24 of 1929), is hereby repealed.

31   Short title, collective citation, and commencement

(1) This Act may be cited as the Children Act, 1941.

(2) This Act and the Children Act, 1908, the Children Act (1908) Amendment Act, 1910, the Children (Employment Abroad) Act, 1913, and the Children Act, 1934 (No 15 of 1934), may be cited together as the Children Acts, 1908 to 1941.

(3) This Act shall come into operation on such day or days as may be fixed therefor by order or orders of the Minister either generally or with reference to any particular section or sections and different days may be so fixed for different sections of this Act.

PART TWO

Children (Amendment) Act, 1957

(1957 No 28)

ARRANGEMENT OF SECTIONS

An Act to amend and extend the Children Acts, 1908 to 1949 [17 December 1957]

1 Interpretation

(1) In this Act 'the Principal Act' means the Children Act, 1908, as amended by subsequent enactments.

(2) This Act shall be construed as one with the Principal Act.

2 (*repealed*)

Amendments—Child Care Act, 1991, s 79, Sch.

3 (*repealed*)

Amendments—Child Care Act, 1991, s 79, Sch.

4   (Amends s 12 of the Principal Act)

5   Discharge of child committed to industrial school

(1) Where—

(a)   a child has been committed to an industrial school under section 58 of the Principal Act, and

(b)   an application is made to the Minister for Education by a parent or guardian for the release of the child, and

(c)   the Minister is satisfied that the circumstances which led to the making of the committal order have ceased and are not likely to recur if the child is released, and that the parent or guardian is able to support the child,

the Minister shall order the discharge of the child.

(2) The Minister may, if he so thinks proper, refer the application to the court.

(3) If the Minister refuses the application, the parent or guardian may refer it to the court.

(4) The court, if satisfied in regard to the matters referred to in paragraph (c) of subsection (1), shall have jurisdiction to order the discharge of the child.

(5) A reference to the court under this section shall be made to the District Court in the District in which the committal order was made or, if the applicant resides in another District, in that District.

(6) The order for the discharge of the child, whether made by the Minister or the court, shall operate to revoke the detention order.

(7)   (a)   Where the District Court or, on appeal, the Circuit Court, orders the discharge of a child, the court may award costs and expenses to the successful applicant and the Minister shall defray out of moneys provided by the Oireachtas such sum as the court may certify in respect thereof.

(b)   The costs and expenses which may be certified by the court shall not exceed the maximum amounts which may be awarded as between party and party in an action for tort in the District Court.

6   Leave of absence from certified school

(1) At any time during the period of detention of a youthful offender or child in a certified school the managers of the school may grant him leave to be absent from the school in charge of such person and for such period as the managers shall think fit or to attend a course of instruction at another school, either as a boarder or as a day pupil, but during such leave of absence he shall be deemed to be under detention and under the care of the managers who may at any time require him to return to the school.

(2) A youthful offender or child absent without permission from such person or school or refusing or failing to return to the certified school when his leave of absence has expired or when required by the managers to do so shall be deemed to have escaped from the certified school.

7   Contributions out of voted moneys

(1) There shall be paid out of moneys to be provided by the Oireachtas such sums on such conditions as the Minister for Education may, with the approval of the Minister for

Finance, recommend towards the expenses of any youthful offender or child throughout the time when he is subject to an order for detention in a certified school, including any period of absence from the school with the consent of the managers of the school for the purpose of home or casual leave or of attending a course of instruction outside the school premises but, except as aforesaid, not including any period during which he is absent in pursuance of a supervision certificate under section 67 of the Principal Act.

(2) The expenses payable under this section may include the expenses of removal in the case of any youthful offender or child ordered to be transferred from one school to another.

(3) This section is in lieu of section 73 of the Principal Act, as amended by section 19 of the Act of 1941, which sections are repealed by this Act.

8　Contributions by local authority in respect of periods of absence from certified school

The payments to be made in pursuance of section 21 of the Act of 1941 by a local authority to the managers of a certified school for the maintenance of a youthful offender or child shall be and be deemed always to have been payable throughout the time when he is subject to an order for detention, including any period of absence from the school with the consent of the managers of the school for the purpose of home or casual leave or of attending a course of instruction outside the school premises but, except as aforesaid, not including any period during which he is absent in pursuance of a supervision certificate under section 67 of the Principal Act.

9　(Amends s 75 of the Principal Act)

10　(*repealed*)

Amendments—Child Care Act, 1991, s 79, Sch.

11　Repeals

The enactments referred to in the Schedule to this Act are, to the extent specified in column (3), hereby repealed.

12　Short title and collective citation

(1) This Act may be cited as the Children (Amendment) Act, 1957.

(2) The Children Acts, 1908 to 1949 and this Act may be cited together as the Children Acts, 1908 to 1957.

SCHEDULE

Section 11

ENACTMENTS REPEALED

Session and Chapter or Number and Year (1)	Short title (2)	Extent of repeal (3)
8 Edw VII, c 67.	Children Act, 1908.	Sections 1 and 73; sub-sections (7) and (12) of section 75.
No 15 of 1934.	Children Act, 1934.	Section 3.
No 12 of 1941.	Children Act, 1941.	Section 19; paragraphs (d), (e) and (f) of section 22.

Children Act, 1997

(1997 No 40)

ARRANGEMENT OF SECTIONS

PART I

PRELIMINARY AND GENERAL

PART II

GUARDIANSHIP, CUSTODY AND MAINTENANCE

PART III

EVIDENCE OF CHILDREN

PART I

PRELIMINARY AND GENERAL

1 Short title, commencement and collective citation

(1) This Act may be cited as the Children Act, 1997.

(2) This Act, except *section 11* (insofar as it inserts sections 20, 21, 22, 26, 28 and 29 into the Act of 1964) and *Part III* shall come into operation one month after the date of its passing.

(3) *Section 11* (insofar as it inserts sections 20, 21, 22, 26, 28 and 29 into the Act of 1964) and *Part III* shall come into operation on such day or days as may be fixed by the Minister by order or orders, either generally or with reference to a particular purpose or provision, and different days may be so fixed for different purposes and different provisions.

(4) An order under *subsection (3)* relating to *section 11*, insofar as that order relates to section 47(1)(b) of the Family Law Act, 1995, shall not be made without the consent of the Minister for Health and Children.

(5) The Act of 1964 (as amended by the Succession Act, 1965, the Courts Act, 1981, the Age of Majority Act, 1985, the Status of Children Act, 1987, the Judicial Separation and Family Law Reform Act, 1989, the Child Care Act, 1991, and the Court Act, 1991) and this Act (except *Part III*) may be cited together as the Guardianship of Children Acts, 1964 to 1997, and shall be construed together as one Act.

Commencement—9 January 1998, 1 January 1999 (Part III and section 11)

---

2 Interpretation

(1) In this Act—

'the Act of 1964' means the Guardianship of Infants Act, 1964;
'the Minister' means the Minister for Justice, Equality and Law Reform.

(2) In this Act—

(a) a reference to a Part or section is a reference to a Part or section of this Act, unless it is indicated that a reference to some other enactment is intended,
(b) a reference to a subsection or paragraph is a reference to the subsection or paragraph of the provision in which the reference occurs, unless it is indicated that a reference to some other provision is intended, and
(c) a reference to any enactment shall be construed as a reference to that enactment as amended by or under any subsequent enactment.

3 Expenses

Any expenses incurred by the Minister, the Minister for Health and Children or the Minister for Social, Community and Family Affairs in the administration of this Act shall, to such extent as may be sanctioned by the Minister for Finance, be paid out of moneys provided by the Oireachtas.

PART II

GUARDIANSHIP, CUSTODY AND MAINTENANCE

4   (Amends s 2 of the Act of 1964)

5   (Amends s 6 of the Act of 1964)

6   (Amends s 6A of the Act of 1964)

7   (Amends s 8 of the Act of 1964)

8   (Amends s 11 of the Act of 1964)

9   (Amends the Act of 1964)

10   (Amends s 17 of the Act of 1964)

11   (Amends the Act of 1964)

12   (Amends the Act of 1964)

13   (Amends the Civil Legal Aid Act, 1995)

14   (Amends the Courts (No 2) Act, 1986)

15   (Amends the Family Law (Maintenance of Spouses and Children) Act, 1976))

16   (Amends the Judicial Separation and Family Law Reform Act, 1989)

17   (Amends the Child Care Act, 1991)

18   (Amends the Child Abduction and Enforcement of Custody Orders Act, 1991)

PART III

EVIDENCE OF CHILDREN

19   Interpretation

(1) In this Part, unless the context otherwise requires—
  'child' means a person who is not of full age,
  'statement' means any representation of fact or opinion however made,

'video-recorded' means recorded on any medium (including a film) from which a moving image may by any means be produced, and includes the accompanying soundtrack, if any, and 'video-recording' has a corresponding meaning.

(2) Where the age of a person at any time is material for the purpose of any proceedings to which this Part applies, his or her age at that time shall, for the purposes of such proceedings, be deemed, unless the contrary is proved, to be or to have been that which appears to the court to be his or her age at that time.

20   Application of Part III

(a) civil proceedings before any court, commenced after the commencement of this Part, concerning the welfare of a child; or

(b) with the necessary modifications, in the same manner as it applies to a child, to civil proceedings before any court, commenced after the commencement of this Part, concerning the welfare of a person who is of full age but who has a mental disability to such an extent that it is not reasonably possible for the person to live independently.

21   Evidence through television link

(1) In any proceedings to which this Part applies a child may, with the leave of the court, give evidence (whether from within or outside the State) through a live television link.

(2) Evidence given under *subsection (1)* shall be video-recorded.

(3) Any child who, in giving evidence under *subsection (1)* from outside the State, makes a statement material in the proceedings which the child knows to be false or does not believe to be true shall be guilty of perjury, or, if *section 28* applies, shall be guilty of an offence specified in *subsection (2)* of that section.

(4) Proceedings for an offence under *subsection (3)* may be taken, and the offence may, for the purposes of the jurisdiction of the court, be treated as having been committed, in any place in the State.

(5) Where evidence is given by a child under *subsection (1)* that any person was known to him or her before the date of commencement of the proceedings, the child shall not be required to identify the person during the course of those proceedings, unless the court directs otherwise.

22   Evidence through intermediary

(1) Where in proceedings to which this Part applies the evidence of a child is being given or to be given through a live television link, the court may, of its own motion or on the application of a party to the proceedings, if satisfied that, having regard to the age or mental condition of the child, any questions to be put to the child should be put through an intermediary, direct that any such question be so put.

(2) Questions put to a child through an intermediary under this section shall be either in the words used by the questioner or in words that convey to the child, in a way that is appropriate to his or her age or mental condition, the meaning of the questions being asked.

(3) An intermediary referred to in *subsection (1)* shall be appointed by the court and shall be a person who, in its opinion, is competent to act as such.

23 Admissibility of hearsay evidence

(1) Subject to *subsection (2)*, a statement made by a child shall be admissible as evidence of any fact therein of which direct oral evidence would be admissible in any proceeding to which this Part applies, notwithstanding any rule of law relating to hearsay, where the court considers that—

- (a) the child is unable to give evidence by reason of age, or
- (b) the giving of oral evidence by the child, either in person or under *section 21*, would not be in the interest of the welfare of the child.

(2) (a) Any statement referred to in *subsection (1)* or any part thereof shall not be admitted in evidence if the court is of the opinion that, in the interests of justice, the statement or that part of the statement ought not to be so admitted.

(b) In considering whether the statement or any part of the statement ought to be admitted, the court shall have regard to all the circumstances, including any risk that the admission will result in unfairness to any of the parties to the proceedings.

(3) A party proposing to adduce evidence admissible in proceedings to which this Part applies by virtue of *subsection (1)*, shall give to the other party or parties to the proceedings—

- (a) such notice, if any, of that fact, and
- (b) such particulars of or relating to the evidence,

as is reasonable and practicable in the circumstances for the purpose of enabling such party or parties to deal with any matter arising from its being hearsay.

(4) *Subsection (3)* shall not apply where the parties concerned agree that it should not apply.

24 Weight of hearsay evidence

(1) In estimating the weight, if any, to be attached to any statement admitted in evidence pursuant to *section 23*, regard shall be had to all the circumstances from which any inference can reasonably be drawn as to its accuracy or otherwise.

(2) Regard may be had, in particular, as to whether—

- (a) the original statement was made contemporaneously with the occurrence or existence of the matters stated,
- (b) the evidence involves multiple hearsay,
- (c) any person involved has any motive to conceal or misrepresent matters,
- (d) the original statement was an edited account or was made in collaboration with another for a particular purpose, and
- (e) the circumstances in which the evidence is adduced as hearsay are such as to suggest an attempt to prevent proper evaluation of its weight.

25 Evidence as to credibility

Where information is given in a statement admitted in evidence pursuant to *section 23*—

- (a) any evidence which, if the child who originally supplied the information had been called as a witness, would have been admissible as relevant to his or her credibility as a witness shall be admissible for that purpose,

(b) evidence may, with the leave of the court, be given of any matter which, if that child had been called as a witness, could have been put to him or her in cross-examination as relevant to his or her credibility as a witness but of which evidence could not have been adduced by the cross-examining party, and

(c) evidence tending to prove that the child, whether before or after supplying the information, made (whether orally or not) a statement which is inconsistent with it shall, if not already admissible, be admissible for the purpose of showing that the witness has contradicted himself or herself.

26 Copies of documents in evidence

(1) Where information contained in a document is admissible in evidence in proceedings to which this Part applies, the information may be given in evidence, whether or not the document is still in existence, by producing a copy of the document, or of the material part of it, authenticated in such manner as the court may approve.

(2) It is immaterial for the purposes of *subsection (1)* how many removes there are between the copy and the original, or by what means (which may include facsimile transmission) the copy was produced or any intermediate copy was made.

(3) In this section 'document' includes a sound recording and a video-recording.

27 Transfer of proceedings

Where in proceedings to which this Part applies the court is of the opinion that it is desirable that evidence be taken by live television link or by means of a video-recording and facilities for doing so are not available, it may, by order, transfer the proceedings to a court where those facilities are available and, where such an order is made, the jurisdiction of the court to which the proceedings have been transferred may be exercised—

(a) in the case of the Circuit Court, by the judge of the circuit concerned, and

(b) in the case of the District Court, by the judge of that court for the time being assigned to the district court district concerned.

28 Oath or affirmation not necessary for child witnesses

(1) Notwithstanding any rule of law, in any civil proceedings (whether or not they are proceedings to which this Part applies) the evidence of a child who has not attained the age of 14 years may be received otherwise than on oath or affirmation if the court is satisfied that the child is capable of giving an intelligible account of events which are relevant to the proceedings.

(2) Any child whose evidence is received in accordance with *subsection (1)* and who makes a statement material in the proceedings concerned which the child knows to be false or does not believe to be true, shall be guilty of an offence and on conviction shall be liable to be dealt with as if guilty of perjury.

(3) *Subsection (1)* shall apply to a person with mental disability who has attained the age of 14 years as it applies to a child who has not attained that age.

(4) Unsworn evidence received by virtue of this section may corroborate evidence (sworn or unsworn) given by any other person.

Domestic Violence Act, 1996

(1996 No 1)

ARRANGEMENT OF SECTIONS

ACTS REFERRED TO

PART TWO

Housing (Private Rented Dwellings) Acts, 1982 and 1983
Interpretation Act, 1937   No 38 of 1937
Judicial Separation and Family Law Reform Act, 1989   No 6 of 1989
Landlord and Tenant Acts, 1967 to 1994
Offences against the Person Act, 1861   24 & 25 Vict. c. 100
Status of Children Act, 1987   No 26 of 1987
Statutes of Limitation, 1957 and 1991

*An Act to make provision for the protection of a spouse and any children or other dependent persons,
and of persons in other domestic relationships, whose safety and welfare requires it because of the
conduct of another person in the domestic relationship concerned and for that purpose to repeal
and re-enact with amendments the provisions of the Family Law (Protection of Spouses and
Children) Act, 1981, to provide for arrest without warrant in certain circumstances, to provide
for the hearing at the same time of certain applications to a court under more than one enactment
for orders relating to domestic relationships and to provide for other connected matters.*[27
February 1996]

1   Interpretation

(1) In this Act, except where the context otherwise requires—

    'applicant', where appropriate, has the meaning assigned by either *section 2* or *3* or
        by both of those sections and where an interim barring order has been made the
        applicant for the barring order to which the interim barring order relates shall be
        deemed to be the applicant for the interim barring order and where a protection
        order has been made the applicant for the safety order or the barring order to
        which the protection order relates shall be deemed to be the applicant for that
        protection order;
    'barring order' has the meaning assigned by *section 3*;
    'civil proceedings under this Act' means—

    (a) proceedings for the making, variation or discharge of a safety order or a
        barring order,
    (b) proceedings, consequent on the making of an application for a barring
        order, for the making, variation or discharge of an interim barring order
        which relates to the application,
    (c) proceedings, consequent on the making of an application for a safety order
        or barring order, for the making, variation or discharge of a protection
        order which relates to the application,
    (d) any proceedings by way of appeal or case stated which are related to
        proceedings to which *paragraph (a), (b)* or *(c)* applies;

    'the court' means the Circuit Court or the District Court;
    'dependent person', in relation to the applicant or the respondent or both of them,
        as the case may be, means any child—

    (a) of the applicant and the respondent or adopted by both the applicant and
        the respondent under the Adoption Acts 1952 to 1991, or under an
        adoption deemed to have been effected by a valid adoption order by virtue
        of section 2, 3, 4 or 5 of the Adoption Act, 1991, or in relation to whom both
        the applicant and the respondent are *in loco parentis,* or
    (b) of the applicant or adopted by the applicant under the Adoption Acts, 1952
        to 1991, or under an adoption deemed to have been effected by a valid
        adoption order by virtue of section 2, 3, 4 or 5 of the Adoption Act, 1991, or
        in relation to whom the applicant is *in loco parentis,* or

(c) of the respondent or adopted by the respondent under the Adoption Acts, 1952 to 1991, or under an adoption deemed to have been effected by a valid adoption order by virtue of section 2, 3, 4 or 5 of the Adoption Act, 1991, or in relation to whom the respondent is *in loco parentis*, and the applicant, while not in the same relationship to that child for the purposes of this paragraph as the respondent is in, is in respect of that child a person to whom *paragraph (b)* of this definition relates,

who is not of full age or if the child has attained full age has a physical or mental disability to such extent that it is not reasonably possible for the child to live independently of the applicant;

'full age' has the same meaning as it has in the Age of Majority Act, 1985;

'functions' includes powers and duties;

'health board' means a health board established under the Health Act, 1970;

'interim barring order' has the meaning assigned by *section 4*;

'protection order' has the meaning assigned by *section 5*;

'respondent', where appropriate, has the meaning assigned by either *section 2* or *3* or by both of those sections and where an interim barring order has been made the respondent to the application for the barring order to which the interim barring order relates shall be deemed to be the respondent to the interim barring order and where a protection order has been made the respondent to the application for the safety order or the barring order to which the protection order relates shall be deemed to be the respondent to that protection order;

'safety order' has the meaning assigned by *section 2*;

'welfare' includes the physical and psychological welfare of the person in question.

(2) (a) A reference in this Act to a section is a reference to a section of this Act unless it is indicated that a reference to some other Act is intended.

(b) A reference in this Act to a subsection or to a paragraph is to the subsection or paragraph of the provision in which the reference occurs unless it is indicated that reference to some other provision is intended.

(3) Any reference in this Act to any other enactment shall, except where the context otherwise requires, be construed as a reference to that enactment as amended by or under any other enactment including this Act.

2   Safety order

(1)(a) In this section—

'the applicant' means a person, other than a health board, who has applied or on whose behalf a health board has applied by virtue of *section 6* for a safety order against another person (in this section referred to as 'the respondent') and the person so applying or on whose behalf the health board has so applied—

    (i) is the spouse of the respondent, or

    (ii) is not the spouse of the respondent but has lived with the respondent as husband or wife for a period of at least six months in aggregate during the period of twelve months immediately prior to the application for the safety order, or

    (iii) is a parent of the respondent and the respondent is a person of full age who is not, in relation to the parent, a dependent person, or

    (iv) being of full age resides with the respondent in a relationship the basis of which is not primarily contractual, 'kindred', in respect of two or more persons, means the relationship of each of those persons to the other person or to the rest of those persons by blood, adoption or marriage.

   (b) In deciding whether or not a person is residing with another person in a relationship the basis of which is not primarily contractual, the court shall have regard to—
      (i)   the length of time those persons have been residing together,
      (ii) the nature of any duties performed by either person for the other person or for any kindred person of that other person,
      (iii) the absence of any profit or of any significant profit made by either person from any monetary or other consideration given by the other person in respect of residing at the place concerned,
      (iv) such other matters as the court considers appropriate in the circumstances.

(2) Where the court, on application to it, is of the opinion that there are reasonable grounds for believing that the safety or welfare of the applicant or any dependent person so requires, it may, subject to *section 7*, by order (in this Act referred to as a 'safety order') direct that the respondent to the application—

   (a) shall not use or threaten to use violence against, molest or put in fear the applicant or that dependent person, and
   (b) if he or she is residing at a place other than the place where the applicant or that dependent person resides, shall not watch or beset the place where the applicant or that dependent person resides,

and the court may make such order subject to such exceptions and conditions as it may specify.

(3) Where a safety order has been made, any of the following may apply to have it varied, that is to say:

   (a) if the application for the order was made by a health board in respect of any dependent person by virtue of *section 6*—
      (i)   the health board,
      (ii) the person referred to in *subsection (1)(c)* of that section, or
      (iii) the respondent to that application,
   (b) if the application for the order was made by a health board in any other case by virtue of *section 6*—
      (i)   the health board,
      (ii) the person who was the applicant for the order, or
      (iii) the respondent to that application,
   (c) in any other case—
      (i)   the person who was the applicant for the order, or
      (ii) the person who was the respondent to the application for the order,

and the court upon hearing any such application shall make such order as it considers appropriate in the circumstances.

(4) For the purposes of *subsection (3)*, a safety order made by a court on appeal from another court shall be treated as if it had been made by that other court.

(5) A safety order, if made by the District Court or by the Circuit Court on appeal from the District Court, shall subject to *subsection (6)(a)* and *section 13*, expire five years after the date of its making or on the expiration of such shorter period as the court may provide for in the order.

(6) (a) On or before the expiration of a safety order to which *subsection (5)* relates, a further safety order may be made by the District Court or by the Circuit Court on appeal from the District Court for a period of five years, or such shorter period as the court may provide for in the order, with effect from the expiration of the first-mentioned order.

(b) On or before the expiration of a safety order to which *paragraph (a)* does not relate, a further safety order may be made with effect from the expiration of the first-mentioned safety order.

(7) Notwithstanding *subsection (5)*, so much of a safety order as was made for the benefit of a dependent person shall expire in accordance with such order or upon such person ceasing to be a dependent person, whichever first occurs.

(8) The court shall not make a safety order on an application for a barring order unless there is also an application for a safety order before the court concerning the same matter.

Note: reference in this section to a spouse includes an ex-spouse; see Family Law (Divorce) Act, 1996, s 51.

---

3 Barring order

(1) In this section 'the applicant' means a person, other than a health board, who has applied or on whose behalf a health board has applied by virtue of *section 6* for a barring order against another person (in this section referred to as 'the respondent') and the person so applying or on whose behalf the health board has so applied—

(a) is the spouse of the respondent, or

(b) is not the spouse of the respondent but has lived with the respondent as husband or wife for a period of at least six months in aggregate during the period of nine months immediately prior to the application for the barring order, or

(c) is a parent of the respondent and the respondent is a person of full age who is not, in relation to the parent, a dependent person.

(2) (a) Where the court, on application to it, is of the opinion that there are reasonable grounds for believing that the safety or welfare of the applicant or any dependent person so requires, it may, subject to *section 7* and having taken into account any order made or to be made to which *paragraph (a)* or *(d)* of *subsection (2)* of *section 9* relates, by order (in this Act referred to as a 'barring order')—

(i) direct the respondent, if residing at a place where the applicant or that dependent person resides, to leave such place, and

(ii) whether the respondent is or is not residing at a place where the applicant or that dependent person resides, prohibit that respondent from entering such place until further order of the court or until such other time as the court shall specify.

(b) In deciding whether or not to grant a barring order the court shall have regard to the safety and welfare of any dependent person in respect of whom the respondent is a parent or *in loco parentis*, where such dependent person is residing at the place to which the order, if made, would relate.

(3) A barring order may, if the court thinks fit, prohibit the respondent from doing one or more of the following, that is to say:

(a) using or threatening to use violence against the applicant or any dependent person,

(b) molesting or putting in fear the applicant or any dependent person,

(c) attending at or in the vicinity of, or watching or besetting a place where, the applicant or any dependent person resides,

and shall be subject to such exceptions and conditions as the court may specify.

(4) (a) In respect of a person who is an applicant by virtue of *paragraph (b)* or *(c)* of *subsection (1)*, the court shall not make a barring order in respect of the place where the applicant or dependent person resides where the respondent has a legal or beneficial interest in that place but—

    (i) the applicant has no such interest, or

    (ii) the applicant's interest is, in the opinion of the court, less than that of the respondent.

  (b) Where in the proceedings to which this section applies the applicant states the belief, in respect of the place to which *paragraph (a)* relates, that he or she has a legal or beneficial interest in that place which is not less than that of the respondent, then such belief shall be admissible in evidence.

(5) Without prejudice to *section 22*, nothing in this Act shall be construed as affecting the rights of any person, other than the applicant or the respondent, who has a legal or beneficial interest in a place in respect of which the court has made an order under this section.

(6) Where a barring order has been made, any of the following may apply to have it varied, that is to say:

(a) if the application for the order was made by a health board in respect of any dependent person by virtue of *section 6*—

    (i) the health board,

    (ii) the person referred to in *subsection (1)(c)* of that section, or

    (iii) the respondent to that application,

(b) if the application for the order was made by a health board in any other case by virtue of *section 6*—

    (i) the health board,

    (ii) the person who was the applicant for the order, or

    (iii) the respondent to that application,

(c) in any other case—

    (i) the person who was the applicant for the order, or

    (ii) the person who was the respondent to the application for the order,

and the court upon hearing any such application shall make such order as it considers appropriate in the circumstances.

(7) For the purposes of *subsection (6)*, a barring order made by a court on appeal from another court shall be treated as if it had been made by that other court.

(8) A barring order, if made by the District Court or by the Circuit Court on appeal from the District Court, shall, subject to *subsection (9)(a)* and *section 13*, expire three years after the date of its making or on the expiration of such shorter period as the court may provide for in the order.

(9) (a) On or before the expiration of a barring order to which *subsection (8)* relates, a further barring order may be made by the District Court or by the Circuit Court on appeal from the District Court for a period of three years, or such shorter

period as the court may provide for in the order, with effect from the expiration of the first-mentioned order.

(b) On or before the expiration of a barring order to which *paragraph (a)* does not relate, a further barring order may be made with effect from the expiration of the first-mentioned barring order.

(10) Notwithstanding *subsection (8)*, so much of a barring order as was made for the benefit of a dependent person shall expire in accordance with such order or upon such person ceasing to be a dependent person, whichever first occurs.

(11) The court shall not make a barring order on an application for a safety order unless there is also an application for a barring order before the court concerning the same matter.

Note: reference in this section to a spouse includes an ex-spouse; see Family Law (Divorce) Act, 1996, s 51.

---

(12) For the purposes of *subsections (2)* and *(3)*, an applicant or a dependent person who would, but for the conduct of the respondent, be residing at a place shall be treated as residing at such place.

(13) Where, by reason only of either or both of the following, that is to say, a barring order and an interim barring order, an applicant who is not the spouse of the respondent has not lived with the respondent as husband or wife for a period of at least six months in aggregate during the period of nine months immediately prior to the application for a further barring order under *subsection (9)*, the applicant shall be deemed, for the purposes of this section, to have lived with the respondent as husband or wife for a period of at least six months in aggregate during the period of nine months immediately prior to the application.

Amendments—Family Law (Miscellaneous Provisions) Act, 1997, s 4.

4   Interim barring order

(1) If, on the making of an application for a barring order or between the making of such application and its determination, the court is of the opinion that there are reasonable grounds for believing that—

(a) there is an immediate risk of significant harm to the applicant or any dependent person if the order is not made immediately, and

(b) the granting of a protection order would not be sufficient to protect the applicant or any dependent person,

the court may, subject to *section 7* and having taken into account any order made or to be made to which *paragraph (a)* or *(d)* of *subsection (2)* of *section 9* relates, by order (in this Act referred to as an 'interim barring order')—

(i) direct the respondent, if residing at a place where the applicant or that dependent person resides, to leave such place, and

(ii) whether the respondent is or is not residing at a place where the applicant or that dependent person resides, prohibit that respondent from entering such place until further order of the court or until such other time as the court shall specify.

(2) *Subsections (3), (4), (5), (6), (7)* and *(12)* of *section 3* shall apply to an interim barring order as they apply to a barring order.

(3) Where the court in exceptional cases considers it necessary or expedient in the interests of justice, an interim barring order may be made *ex parte* or notwithstanding the fact that the originating document or other notice of the application required to be duly served on the respondent to the application for a barring order has not been so served.

(4) An interim barring order shall cease to have effect on the determination by the court of the application for a barring order.

(5) Notwithstanding *subsection (4)*, so much of an interim barring order as was made for the benefit of a dependent person shall cease to have effect in accordance with that subsection or upon such person ceasing to be a dependent person, whichever first occurs.

5 Protection order

(1) If, on the making of an application for a safety order or a barring order or between the making of such an application and its determination, the court is of the opinion that there are reasonable grounds for believing that the safety or welfare of the applicant for the order concerned or of any dependent person so requires, the court may by order (in this Act referred to as a 'protection order') direct that the respondent to the application—

(a) shall not use or threaten to use violence against, molest or put in fear the applicant or that dependent person, and

(b) if he or she is residing at a place other than the place where the applicant or that dependent person resides, shall not watch or beset the place where the applicant or that dependent person resides,

and the court may make the protection order subject to such exceptions and conditions as it may specify.

(2) Where a protection order has been made, any of the following may apply to have it varied, that is to say:

(a) if the application for the order was made by a health board in respect of any dependent person by virtue of *section 6*—
    (i)   the health board;
    (ii) the person referred to in *subsection (1)(c)* of that section; or
    (iii) the respondent to that application;

(b) if the application for the order was made by a health board in any other case by virtue of *section 6*—
    (i)   the health board;
    (ii) the person who was the applicant for the order; or
    (iii) the respondent to that application;

(c) in any other case—
    (i)   the person who was the applicant for the order; or
    (ii) the person who was the respondent to the application for the order,

and the court upon hearing any such application shall make such order as it considers appropriate in the circumstances.

(3) For the purposes of *subsection (2)*, a protection order made by a court on appeal from another court shall be treated as if it had been made by that other court.

(4) A protection order may be made notwithstanding the fact that the originating document or other notice of the application required to be duly served on the

respondent to the application for a safety order or a barring order has not been so served.

(5) A protection order shall cease to have effect on the determination by the court of the application for a safety order or a barring order.

(6) Notwithstanding *subsection (5)*, so much of a protection order as was made for the benefit of a dependent person shall cease to have effect in accordance with that subsection or upon such person ceasing to be a dependent person, whichever first occurs.

(7) For the purposes of this section, an applicant or a dependent person who would, but for the conduct of the respondent, be residing at a place shall be treated as residing at such place.

6   Power of health board to apply for certain orders

(1) Subject to *subsections (2), (3)* and *(4)*, this section shall apply where a health board—

- (a) becomes aware of an alleged incident or series of incidents which in its opinion puts into doubt the safety or welfare of a person (in this section referred to as the 'aggrieved person'),
- (b) has reasonable cause to believe that the aggrieved person has been subjected to molestation, violence or threatened violence or otherwise put in fear of his or her safety or welfare,
- (c) is of the opinion that there are reasonable grounds for believing that, where appropriate in the circumstances, a person would be deterred or prevented as a consequence of molestation, violence or threatened violence by the respondent or fear of the respondent from pursuing an application for a safety order or a barring order on his or her own behalf or on behalf of a dependent person, and
- (d) considers, having ascertained as far as is reasonably practicable the wishes of the aggrieved person or, where the aggrieved person is a dependent person, of the person to whom *paragraph (c)* relates in respect of such dependent person, that it is appropriate in all the circumstances to apply for a safety order or a barring order or both in accordance with this Act on behalf of the aggrieved person.

(2) A health board may apply to the court on behalf of the aggrieved person for a safety order or a barring order for which the aggrieved person or, where the aggrieved person is a dependent person, the person to whom *subsection (1)(c)* relates in respect of such dependent person could have applied.

(3) Where an application is made by a health board by virtue of this section, the court shall, in determining whether, and if so to what extent, to exercise any of its functions under *section 2, 3, 4, 5* or *13*, have regard to any wishes expressed by—

- (a) the aggrieved person, or
- (b) where the aggrieved person is a dependent person, the person to whom *subsection (1)(c)* relates in respect of such dependent person and, where the court considers it appropriate, such dependent person.

(4) The provisions of *paragraphs (a)* and *(b)* of *subsection (1)* need not be complied with—

- (a) where the application relates to an aggrieved person who is a dependent person, or
- (b) in respect of so much of an application as relates to an aggrieved person where such person is a dependent person,

if the court is of the opinion that there is reasonable cause to believe that—

(i)   such dependent person has been or is being assaulted, ill-treated, sexually abused or seriously neglected, or

(ii) such dependent person's health, development or welfare has been is being or is likely to be avoidably impaired or seriously neglected,

and that if the order is made the likelihood of harm to such dependent person will not arise or will be materially diminished.

(5) The court shall not make a barring order or an interim barring order where the aggrieved person is a dependent person unless the health board satisfies the court that the person to whom *subsection (1)(c)* relates in respect of such dependent person is willing and able to provide reasonable care for such dependent person.

(6) (a) The functions of a health board by virtue of this section shall be functions of the chief executive officer of the board.

     (b) In this subsection 'chief executive officer' includes a person acting as deputy chief executive officer in accordance with section 13 of the Health Act, 1970.

7   Power to make orders, etc, under Child Care Act, 1991

(1) Where in proceedings for any order under this Act, other than proceedings to which *section 6* relates, it appears to the court that it may be appropriate for a care order or a supervision order to be made under the Child Care Act, 1991, with respect to a dependent person concerned in the proceedings, the court may, of its own motion or on the application of any person concerned, adjourn the proceedings and direct the health board for the area in which such dependent person resides or is for the time being to undertake an investigation or, as the case may be, further investigations of such dependent person's circumstances.

(2) Where proceedings are adjourned and the court gives a direction under *subsection (1)*, the court may give such directions under the Child Care Act, 1991, as it sees fit as to the care and custody of, and may make a supervision order under that Act in respect of, the dependent person concerned pending the outcome of the investigation by the health board concerned.

(3) Where the court gives a direction under *subsection (1)* in respect of a dependent person, the health board concerned shall undertake an investigation of such dependent person's circumstances and shall consider if it should—

(a) apply for a care order or a supervision order under the Child Care Act, 1991,

(b) provide services or assistance for such dependent person's family, or

(c) take any other action in respect of such dependent person.

(4) Where a health board undertakes an investigation under this section and decides not to apply for a care order or supervision order under the Child Care Act, 1991, with respect to the dependent person concerned, it shall inform the court of—

(a) its reasons for so deciding,

(b) any service or assistance it has provided, or intends to provide, for such dependent person and his or her family, and

(c) any other action which it has taken, or proposes to take, with respect to such dependent person.

8 Application of section 9(2) of Family Home Protection Act, 1976, to certain orders

(1)Subsection (2) of section 9 (which restricts the right of a spouse to dispose of or remove household chattels pending the determination of matrimonial proceedings) of the Family Home Protection Act, 1976, shall apply between the making of an application, against the spouse of the applicant, for a barring order or a safety order and its determination, and if an order is made, while such order is in force, as it applies between the institution and final determination of matrimonial proceedings to which that section relates.

(2) For the avoidance of doubt, it is hereby declared that the court which is empowered under *subsection (2)(b)* of *section 9* of the Family Home Protection Act, 1976, to grant permission for any disposition or removal of household chattels (being household chattels within the meaning of that section) is, notwithstanding anything in section 10 of that Act, the court before which the proceedings (including any proceedings for a barring order or a safety order) have been instituted.

9 Hearing of applications under various Acts together

(1) Where an application is made to the court for an order under this Act, the court may, on application to it in the same proceedings and without the institution of proceedings under the Act concerned, if it appears to the court to be proper to do so, make one or more of the orders referred to in *subsection (2)*.

(2) The provisions to which *subsection (1)* relates are as follows, that is to say:

- (a) an order under section 11 (as amended by the Status of Children Act, 1987) of the Guardianship of Infants Act, 1964,
- (b) an order under *section 5, 5A, 6, 7* or *21A* of the Family Law (Maintenance of Spouses and Children) Act, 1976 (as amended by the Status of Children Act, 1987),
- (c) an order under *section 5* or *9* of the Family Home Protection Act, 1976,
- (d) an order under the Child Care Act, 1991.

10 Taking effect of orders

(1) A safety order, barring order, interim barring order or protection order shall take effect on notification of its making being given to the respondent.

(2) Oral communication to the respondent by or on behalf of the applicant of the fact that a safety order, barring order, interim barring order or protection order has been made, together with production of a copy of the order, shall, without prejudice to the sufficiency of any other form of notification, be taken to be sufficient notification to the respondent of the making of the order.

(3) If the respondent is present at a sitting of the court at which the safety order, barring order, interim barring order or protection order is made, that respondent shall be taken for the purposes of *subsection (1)* to have been notified of its making.

(4) An order varying a safety order, barring order, interim barring order or protection order shall take effect on notification of its making being given to the person who was the other party in the proceedings for the making of the safety order or barring order and for this purpose *subsections (2)* and *(3)* shall apply with the necessary modifications.

11 Copies of orders to be given to certain persons

(1) The court, on making, varying or discharging a safety order or a protection order, shall cause a copy of the order in question to be given or sent as soon as practicable—

(a) to the applicant for the safety order or, in respect of a protection order, the applicant for the safety order or barring order concerned,

(b) to the respondent to the application for the safety order or, in respect of a protection order, the respondent to the application for the safety order or barring order concerned,

(c) where a health board by virtue of *section 6* made the application for the safety order or, in respect of a protection order, for the safety order or barring order, to the health board,

(d) to the member of the Garda Síochána in charge of the Garda Síochána station for the area in which the person for whose benefit the safety order or protection order was made resides, and

(e) where the order in question is a variation or discharge of a safety order or a protection order and the person for whose benefit the order was made had previously resided elsewhere, to the member of the Garda Síochána in charge of the Garda Síochána station for the area in which is situated that place but only if that member had previously been sent under this subsection a copy of such barring order or interim barring order or any order relating thereto.

(2) The court on making, varying or discharging a barring order or an interim barring order shall cause a copy of the order in question to be given or sent as soon as practicable to—

(a) the applicant for the barring order,

(b) the respondent to the application for the barring order,

(c) where a health board by virtue of *section 6* made the application for the barring order concerned, the health board,

(d) the member of the Garda Síochána in charge of the Garda Síochána station for the area in which is situate the place in relation to which the application for the barring order was made, and

(e) where the order in question is a variation or discharge of a barring order or an interim barring order and the place in respect of which the previous order was made is elsewhere, to the member of the Garda Síochána in charge of the Garda Síochána station for the area in which is situated that place but only if that member had previously been sent under this subsection a copy of such barring order or interim barring order or any order relating thereto.

(3) The Court—

(a) on making a barring order, a safety order, an interim barring order or a protection order on the application of, or on behalf of, a person who is not of full age, or

(b) on varying or discharging an order to which *paragraph (a)* relates,

shall cause a copy of the order in question to be given or sent as soon as practicable to the health board for the area in which the person resides.

(4) The validity of any order to which this section relates shall not be affected by non-compliance with the other provisions of this section.

12 Effect of appeal from order

(1) An appeal from a safety order or a barring order shall, if the court that made the order or the court to which the appeal is brought so determines (but not otherwise), stay the operation of the order on such terms (if any) as may be imposed by the court making the determination.

(2) An appeal from a protection order or an interim barring order shall not stay the operation of the order.

13 Discharge of orders

(1) Where a safety order, barring order, interim barring order or protection order has been made, any of the following may apply to the court that made the order to have the order discharged, that is to say:

  (a) if the application for the order was made by a health board in respect of any dependent person by virtue of *section 6*—
    (i) the health board,
    (ii) the person referred to in *subsection (1)(c)* of that section; or
    (iii) the respondent to that application;
  (b) if the application for the order was made by a health board in any other case by virtue of *section 6*—
    (i) the health board,
    (ii) the person who was the applicant for the order, or
    (iii) the respondent to that application,
  (c) in any other case—
    (i) the person who was the applicant for the order, or
    (ii) the person who was the respondent to the application for the order,

and thereupon the court shall discharge the order if it is of the opinion that the safety and welfare of the applicant or such dependent person for whose protection the order was made does not require that the order should continue in force.

(2) On determination of any matrimonial cause or matter between the applicant and the respondent or of any proceedings between them under the Guardianship of Infants Act, 1964, the court determining any such cause, matter or proceedings may, if it thinks fit, discharge any safety order, barring order, interim barring order or protection order.

(3) For the purposes of this section, an order made by a court on appeal from another court shall be treated as if it had been made by that other court.

14 Exercise of jurisdiction by court

(1) The jurisdiction of the court in respect of civil proceedings under this Act may be exercised—

  (a) as regards the Circuit Court, by the judge of the circuit, and
  (b) as regards the District Court, by the judge of the District Court for the time being assigned to the district court district,

where the applicant resides or, if the application is for a barring order, where there is situate the place in relation to which that application was made.

(2) For the purposes of *subsection (1)*, the court may treat any person concerned as residing at a place where that person would, but for the conduct of the respondent, be residing at.

PART TWO

(3) Where a judge of the District Court to whom *subsection (1)* relates is not immediately available, the jurisdiction of the District Court under that subsection may be exercised by any judge of the District Court.

15 Rules of court

(1) For the purpose of ensuring the expeditious hearing of applications under this Act, rules of the court may make provision for the service of documents otherwise than under section 7 (as amended by section 22 of the Courts Act, 1971) of the Courts Act, 1964, in circumstances to which that section relates.

(2) This section is without prejudice to section 17 of the Interpretation Act, 1937, which provides for rules of court.

16 Hearing of civil proceedings, etc

(1) Civil proceedings under this Act shall be heard otherwise than in public.

(2) Where under *section 9* the court hears together applications under several enactments, then the court shall as far as is practicable comply with the requirements relating to the hearing of applications under each of those enactments and the other relevant provisions of those Acts shall apply accordingly.

(3) (a) Civil proceedings under this Act before the District Court shall be as informal as is practicable and consistent with the administration of justice.
 (b) District Court judges hearing and determining civil proceedings under this Act and barristers and solicitors appearing in such proceedings shall not wear wigs or gowns.

(4) Civil proceedings under this Act before the Circuit Court shall be heard by the Circuit Family Court and, accordingly, the provisions of section 32 and subsection (1) and (2) of section 33 of the Judicial Separation and Family Law Reform Act, 1989, shall apply to such proceedings.

(5) The proceedings to which subsections (3) and (4) of section 33 of the Judicial Separation and Family Law Reform Act, 1989, apply shall be deemed to include civil proceedings under this Act.

17 Offences

(1) A respondent who—

 (a) contravenes a safety order, a barring order, an interim barring order or a protection order, or
 (b) while a barring order or interim barring order is in force refuses to permit the applicant or any dependent person to enter in and remain in the place to which the order relates or does any act for the purpose of preventing the applicant or such dependent person from so doing,

shall be guilty of an offence and shall be liable on summary conviction to a fine not exceeding £1,500 or, at the discretion of the court, to imprisonment for a term not exceeding 12 months, or to both.

(2) *Subsection (1)* is without prejudice to the law as to contempt of court or any other liability, whether civil or criminal, that may be incurred by the respondent concerned.

18   Arrest without warrant

(1) (a) Where a member of the Garda Síochána has reasonable cause for believing that, in respect of an order under this Act, an offence is being or has been committed under *section 17* the member may, on complaint being made to him or her by or on behalf of the person who was the applicant to which the order relates, arrest the respondent concerned without warrant.

(b) For the purpose of arresting a respondent under *paragraph (a)*, a member of the Garda Síochána may enter, if need be by force, and search any place where the member, with reasonable cause, suspects the respondent to be.

(2) Where a member of the Garda Síochána has reasonable cause for believing that a person (in this section referred to as 'the first-mentioned person') is committing or has committed—

(a) an assault occasioning actual bodily harm, or

(b) an offence under section 20 (which relates to unlawfully and maliciously wounding or inflicting any grievous bodily harm) of the Offences against the Person Act, 1861,

against a person (in this section referred to as 'the second-mentioned person') in circumstances which in the opinion of the member could give rise to the second-mentioned person applying for, or on whose behalf another person could in accordance with this Act apply for, a safety order or a barring order, then the member may—

(i)   arrest the first-mentioned person without warrant, and

(ii) for the purpose of making such an arrest, enter, if need by by force, and search any place where the member, with reasonable cause, suspects the first-mentioned person to be.

19   Costs

The costs of any civil proceedings under this Act shall be in the discretion of the court.

20   (Amends the Judicial Separation and Family Law Reform Act, 1989)

21   (Amends the Family Law Act, 1995)

22   Saving provisions

(1) Where, by reason only of an interim barring order or a barring order, a person is not residing at a place during any period, that person shall be deemed, for the purposes of any rights under the Statutes of Limitation 1957 and 1991, the Landlord and Tenant Acts 1967 to 1994, and the Housing (Private Rented Dwellings) Acts 1982 and 1983, to be residing at that place during that period.

(2) Except in so far as the exercise by a respondent of a right to occupy the place to which a barring order or an interim barring order relates is suspended by virtue of the order, the order shall not affect any estate or interest in that place of that respondent or any other person.

23 Repeal and transitional provisions

(1) The Family Law (Protection of Spouses and Children) Act, 1981 (in this section referred to as 'the Act of 1981'), is hereby repealed.

(2) (a) Subject to *paragraph (b)*, this Act shall apply to a barring order made under the Act of 1981 and which is in force, or stayed by virtue of section 10 of that Act, at the commencement of this Act as if it were an order made under *section 3*.

    (b) For the purposes of a barring order to which *paragraph (a)* relates, the reference in *section 3(8)* to the expiration of three years after the date of its making shall be construed as a reference to twelve months after the date of its making.

(3) An application made to the court under the Act of 1981 for a barring order and not determined before the commencement of this Act shall be treated as if it had been made under *section 3*.

(4) This Act shall apply to a protection order made under the Act of 1981 and which is in force at the commencement of this Act as if it were an order made under *section 5*.

24 Expenses

The expenses incurred by the Minister for Equality and Law Reform, the Minister for Health and the Minister for Justice in the administration of this Act shall, to such extent as may be sanctioned by the Minister for Finance, be paid out of moneys provided by the Oireachtas.

25 Commencement

(1) Subject to *subsection (2)*, this Act shall come into operation one month after the date of its passing.

(2) *Section 6* and so much of the other provisions of this Act as relate to that section shall come into operation on the 1st day of January, 1997.

26 Short title

This Act may be cited as the Domestic Violence Act, 1996.

Domicile and Recognition of Foreign Divorces Act, 1986

(1986 No 24)

ARRANGEMENT OF SECTIONS

An Act to amend the law relating to domicile and the recognition of foreign divorces [2 July 1986]

1 Abolition of wife's dependent domicile

(1) From the commencement of this Act the domicile of a married woman shall be an independent domicile and shall be determined by reference to the same factors as in the case of any other person capable of having an independent domicile and, accordingly, the rule of law whereby upon marriage a woman acquires the domicile of her husband and is during the subsistence of the marriage incapable of having any other domicile is hereby abolished.

(2) This section applies to the parties to every marriage, irrespective of where and under what law the marriage takes place and irrespective of the domicile of the parties at the time of the marriage.

2 Domicile before commencement of Act

The domicile that a person had at any time before the commencement of this Act shall be determined as if this Act had not been passed.

3 Domicile after commencement of Act

The domicile that a person has at any time after the commencement of this Act shall be determined as if this Act had always been in force.

4 Dependent domicile of minor

(1) The domicile of a minor at any time when his father and mother are living apart shall be that of his mother if—

    (a) the minor then has his home with her and has no home with his father, or

    (b) the minor has at any time had her domicile by virtue of *paragraph (a)* of this subsection and has not since had a home with his father.

(2) The domicile of a minor whose mother is dead shall be that which she last had before she died if at her death the minor had her domicile by virtue of *subsection (1)* of this section and has not since had a home with his father.

(3) This section shall not affect any existing rule of law as to the cases in which a minor's domicile is regarded as being, by dependence, that of his mother.

(4) In the application of this section to a minor who has been adopted, references to the father or mother of such minor shall be construed as references to the adoptive father or adoptive mother of such minor.

5   Recognition of foreign divorces

(1) For the rule of law that a divorce is recognised if granted in a country where both spouses are domiciled, there is hereby substituted a rule that a divorce shall be recognised if granted in the country where either spouse is domiciled.

(2) In relation to a country which has in matters of divorce two or more systems applying in different territorial units, this section shall, without prejudice to *subsection (3)* of this section, have effect as if each territorial unit were a separate country.

(3) A divorce granted in any of the following jurisdictions—

    (a)   England and Wales,
    (b)   Scotland,
    (c)   Northern Ireland,
    (d)   the Isle of Man,
    (e)   the Channel Islands,

shall be recognised if either spouse is domiciled in any of those jurisdictions.

(4) In a case where neither spouse is domiciled in the State, a divorce shall be recognised if, although not granted in the country where either spouse is domiciled, it is recognised in the country or countries where the spouses are domiciled.

(5) This section shall apply to a divorce granted after the commencement of this Act.

(6) Nothing in this section shall affect a ground on which a court may refuse to recognise a divorce, other than such a ground related to the question whether a spouse is domiciled in a particular country, or whether the divorce is recognised in a country where a spouse is domiciled.

(7) In this section—

    'divorce' means divorce *a vinculo matrimonii*;
    'domiciled' means domiciled at the date of the institution of the proceedings for
      divorce.

6   Short title and commencement

(1) This Act may be cited as the Domicile and Recognition of Foreign Divorces Act 1986.

(2) This Act shall come into operation on the day that is three months after the date of the passing of this Act.

Commencement—2 October 1986.

Family Home Protection Act, 1976

(1976 No 27)

ARRANGEMENT OF SECTIONS

An Act to provide for the protection of the family home and for related matters   [12 July 1976]

1   Interpretation

(1) In this Act, except where the context otherwise requires—

'conduct' includes an act and a default or other omission;

'conveyance' includes a mortgage, lease, assent, transfer, disclaimer, release and any other disposition of property otherwise than by a will or a *donatio mortis causa* and also includes an enforceable agreement (whether conditional or unconditional) to make any such conveyance, and 'convey' shall be construed accordingly;

'the court' means the court having jurisdiction under section 10;

'dependent child of the family', in relation to a spouse or spouses, means any child—

    (a) of both spouses, or adopted by both spouses under the Adoption Acts, 1952 to 1974, or in relation to whom both spouses are in *loco parentis,* or

    (b) of either spouse, or adopted by either spouse under the Adoption Acts, 1952 to 1974, or in relation to whom either spouse is in *loco parentis,* where the other spouse, being aware that he is not the parent of the child, has treated the child as a member of the family,

who is under the age of sixteen years, or, if he has attained that age—

(i)   is receiving full-time education or instruction at any university, college, school or other educational establishment and is under the age of twenty-one years, or

(ii) is suffering from mental or physical disability to such extent that it is not reasonably possible for him to maintain himself fully;

'family home' has the meaning assigned by section 2;

'household chattels' has the meaning assigned by section 9(7);

'interest' means any estate, right, title or other interest, legal or equitable;

'mortgage' includes an equitable mortgage, a charge on registered land and a chattel mortgage, and cognate words shall be construed accordingly;

'rent' includes a conventional rent, a rentcharge within the meaning of section 2(1) of the Statute of Limitations, 1957, and a terminable annuity payable in respect of a loan for the purchase of a family home.

(2) References in this Act to any enactment shall be construed as references to that enactment as amended or extended by any subsequent enactment, including this Act.

(3) (a) A reference in this Act to a section is a reference to a section of this Act, unless it is indicated that reference to some other enactment is intended.

     (b) A reference in this Act to a subsection is a reference to the subsection of the section in which the reference occurs unless it is indicated that reference to some other section is intended.

2   Family home

(1) In this Act 'family home' means, primarily, a dwelling in which a married couple ordinarily reside. The expression comprises, in addition, a dwelling in which a spouse whose protection is in issue ordinarily resides or, if that spouse has left the other spouse, ordinarily resided before so leaving.

(2) In subsection (1), 'dwelling' means any building or part of a building occupied as a separate dwelling and includes any garden or other land usually occupied with the dwelling, being land that is subsidiary and ancillary to it, is required for amenity or convenience and is not being used or developed primarily for commercial purposes, and includes a structure that is not permanently attached to the ground and a vehicle, or vessel, whether mobile or not, occupied as a separate dwelling.

Amendments—Family Law Act, 1995, s 54(1)(a).

---

3   Alienation of interest in family home

(1) Where a spouse, without the prior consent in writing of the other spouse, purports to convey any interest in the family home to any person except the other spouse, then, subject to subsections (2), (3) and (8) and section 4, the purported conveyance shall be void.

(2) Subsection (1) does not apply to a conveyance if it is made by a spouse in pursuance of an enforceable agreement made before the marriage of the spouses.

(3) No conveyance shall be void by reason only of subsection (1)—

(a) if it is made to a purchaser for full value,

(b) if it is made, by a person other than the spouse making the purported conveyance referred to in subsection (1), to a purchaser for value, or

(c) if its validity depends on the validity of a conveyance in respect of which any of the conditions mentioned in subsection (2) or paragraph (a) or (b) is satisfied.

(4) If any question arises in any proceedings as to whether a conveyance is valid by reason of subsection (2) or (3), the burden of proving that validity shall be on the person alleging it.

(5) In subsection (3), 'full value' means such value as amounts or approximates to the value of that for which it is given.

(6) In this section, 'purchaser' means a grantee, lessee, assignee, mortgagee, chargeant or other person who in good faith acquires an estate or interest in property.

(7) For the purposes of this section, section 3 of the Conveyancing Act, 1882, shall be read as if the words 'as such' wherever they appear in paragraph (ii) of subsection (1) of that section were omitted.

(8) (a) (i) Proceedings shall not be instituted to have a conveyance declared void by reason only of subsection (1) after the expiration of 6 years from the date of the conveyance.

　　　 (ii) Subparagraph (i) does not apply to any such proceedings instituted by a spouse who has been in actual occupation of the land concerned from immediately before the expiration of 6 years from the date of the conveyance concerned until the institution of the proceedings.

　　　 (iii) Subparagraph (i) is without prejudice to any right of the other spouse referred to in subsection (1) to seek redress for a contravention of that subsection otherwise than by proceedings referred to in that subparagraph.

　 (b) A conveyance shall be deemed not to be and never to have been void by reason of subsection (1) unless—

　　　 (i) it has been declared void by a court by reason of subsection (1) in proceedings instituted—
　　　　 (I) before the passing of the Family Law Act, 1995, or
　　　　 (II) on or after such passing and complying with paragraph (a), or

　　　 (ii) subject to the rights of any other person concerned, it is void by reason of subsection (1) and the parties to the conveyance or their successors in title so state in writing before the expiration of 6 years from the date of the conveyance.

　 (c) A copy of a statement made for the purpose of subparagraph (ii) of paragraph (b) and certified by, or by the successor or successors in title of, the party or parties concerned ('the person or persons') to be a true copy shall, before the expiration of the period referred to in that subparagraph, as appropriate, be lodged by the person or persons in the Land Registry for registration pursuant to section 69(1) of the Registration of Title Act, 1964, as if statements so made had been prescribed under paragraph (s) of the said section 69(1) or be registered by them in the Registry of Deeds.

　 (d) Rules of court shall provide that a person who institutes proceedings to have a conveyance declared void by reason of subsection (1) shall, as soon as may be, cause relevant particulars of the proceedings to be entered as a *lis pendens* under and in accordance with the Judgments (Ireland) Act, 1844.

(9) If, whether before or after the passing of the Family Law Act, 1995, a spouse gives a general consent in writing to any future conveyance of any interest in a dwelling that is or was the family home of that spouse and the deed for any such conveyance is executed

after the date of that consent, the consent shall be deemed, for the purposes of subsection (1), to be a prior consent in writing of the spouse to that conveyance.

Amendments—Family Law Act, 1995, s 54(1) (b).

---

4 Consent of spouse

(1) Where the spouse whose consent is required under section 3(1) omits or refuses to consent, the court may, subject to the provisions of this section, dispense with the consent.

(2) The court shall not dispense with the consent of a spouse unless the court considers that it is unreasonable for the spouse to withhold consent, taking into account all the circumstances, including—

    (a) the respective needs and resources of the spouses and of the dependent children (if any) of the family, and

    (b) in a case where the spouse whose consent is required is offered alternative accommodation, the suitability of that accommodation having regard to the respective degrees of security of tenure in the family home and in the alternative accommodation.

(3) Where the spouse whose consent is required under section 3(1) has deserted and continues to desert the other spouse, the court shall dispense with the consent. For this purpose, desertion includes conduct on the part of the former spouse that results in the other spouse, with just cause, leaving and living separately and apart from him.

(4) Where the spouse whose consent is required under section 3(1) is incapable of consenting by reason of unsoundness of mind or other mental disability or has not after reasonable inquiries been found, the court may give the consent on behalf of that spouse, if it appears to the court to be reasonable to do so.

5 Conduct leading to loss of family home

(1) Where it appears to the court, on the application of a spouse, that the other spouse is engaging in such conduct as may lead to the loss of any interest in the family home or may render it unsuitable for habitation as a family home with the intention of depriving the applicant spouse or a dependent child of the family of his residence in the family home, the court may make such order as it considers proper, directed to the other spouse or to any other person, for the protection of the family home in the interest of the applicant spouse or such child.

(2) Where it appears to the court, on the application of a spouse, that the other spouse has deprived the applicant spouse or a dependent child of the family of his residence in the family home by conduct that resulted in the loss of any interest therein or rendered it unsuitable for habitation as a family home, the court may order the other spouse or any other person to pay to the applicant spouse such amount as the court considers proper to compensate the applicant spouse and any such child for their loss or make such other order directed to the other spouse or to any other person as may appear to the court to be just and equitable.

6 Payment of outgoings on family home

(1) Any payment or tender made or any other thing done by one spouse in or towards satisfaction of any liability of the other spouse in respect of rent, rates, mortgage

payments or other outgoings affecting the family home shall be as good as if made or done by the other spouse, and shall be treated by the person to whom such payment is made or such thing is done as though it were made or done by the other spouse.

(2) Nothing in subsection (1) shall affect any claim by the first-mentioned spouse against the other to an interest in the family home by virtue of such payment or thing made or done by the first-mentioned spouse.

7   Adjournment of proceedings by mortgagee or lessor for possession or sale of family home

(1) Where a mortgagee or lessor of the family home brings an action against a spouse in which he claims possession or sale of the home by virtue of the mortgage or lease in relation to the non-payment by that spouse of sums due thereunder, and it appears to the court—

    (a) that the other spouse is capable of paying to the mortgagee or lessor the arrears (other than arrears of principal or interest or rent that do not constitute part of the periodical payments due under the mortgage or lease) of money due under the mortgage or lease within a reasonable time, and future periodical payments falling due under the mortgage or lease, and that the other spouse desires to pay such arrears and periodical payments; and

    (b) that it would in all the circumstances, having regard to the terms of the mortgage or lease, the interests of the mortgagee or lessor and the respective interests of the spouses, be just and equitable to do so,

the court may adjourn the proceedings for such period and on such terms as appear to the court to be just and equitable.

(2) In considering whether to adjourn the proceedings under this section and, if so, for what period and on what terms they should be adjourned, the court shall have regard in particular to whether the spouse of the mortgagor or lessee has been informed (by or on behalf of the mortgagee or lessor or otherwise) of the non-payment of the sums in question or of any of them.

8   Modification of terms of mortgage or lease as to payment of capital sum

(1) Where, on an application by a spouse, after proceedings have been adjourned under section 7, it appears to the court that—

    (a) all arrears (other than arrears of principal or interest or rent that do not constitute part of the periodical payments due under the mortgage or lease) of money due under the mortgage or lease, and

    (b) all the periodical payments due to date under the mortgage or lease,

have been paid off and that the periodical payments subsequently falling due will continue to be paid, the court may by order declare accordingly.

(2) If the court makes an order under subsection (1), any term in a mortgage or lease whereby the default in payment that gave rise to the proceedings under section 7 has, at any time before or after the initial hearing of such proceedings, resulted or would have resulted in the capital sum advanced thereunder (or part of such sum or interest thereon) or any sum other than the periodical payments, as the case may be, becoming due, shall be of no effect for the purpose of such proceedings or any subsequent proceedings in respect of the sum so becoming due.

9   Restriction on disposal of household chattels

(1) Where it appears to the court, on the application of a spouse, that there are reasonable grounds for believing that the other spouse intends to sell, lease, pledge, charge or otherwise dispose of or to remove such a number or proportion of the household chattels in a family home as would be likely to make it difficult for the applicant spouse or a dependent child of the family to reside in the family home without undue hardship, the court may by order prohibit, on such terms as it may see fit, the other spouse from making such intended disposition or removal.

(2) Where matrimonial proceedings have been instituted by either spouse, neither spouse shall sell, lease, pledge, charge or otherwise dispose of or remove any of the household chattels in the family home until the proceedings have been finally determined, unless—

(a) the other spouse has consented to such sale, lease, pledge, charge or other disposition or removal, or

(b) the court before which the proceedings have been instituted, on application to it by the spouse who desires to make such disposition or removal, permits that spouse to do so, which permission may be granted on such terms as the court may see fit.

(3) In subsection (2) 'matrimonial proceedings' includes proceedings under section 12 of the Married Women's Status Act, 1957, under the Guardianship of Infants Act, 1964, or under section 21 or 22 of the Family Law (Maintenance of Spouses and Children) Act, 1976.

(4) A spouse who contravenes the provisions of subsection (2) shall, without prejudice to any other liability, civil or criminal, be guilty of an offence and shall be liable on summary conviction to a fine not exceeding £100 or to imprisonment for a term not exceeding six months or to both.

(5) Where it appears to the court, on application to it by either spouse, that the other spouse—

(a) has contravened an order under subsection (1) or the provisions of subsection (2), or

(b) has sold, leased, pledged, charged or otherwise disposed of or removed such a number or proportion of the household chattels in the family home as has made or is likely to make it difficult for the applicant spouse or a dependent child of the family to reside in the family home without undue hardship,

the court may order that other spouse to provide household chattels for the applicant spouse, or a sum of money in lieu thereof, so as to place the applicant spouse or the dependent child of the family as nearly as possible in the position that prevailed before such contravention, disposition or removal.

(6) Where a third person, before a sale, lease, pledge, charge or other disposition of any household chattel to him by a spouse, is informed in writing by the other spouse that he intends to take proceedings in respect of such disposition or intended disposition, the court in proceedings under this section may make such order, directed to the former spouse or the third person, in respect of such chattel as appears to it to be proper in the circumstances.

(7) For the purposes of this section 'household chattels' means furniture, bedding, linen, china, earthenware, glass, books and other chattels of ordinary household use or

ornament and also consumable stores, garden effects and domestic animals, but does not include any chattels used by either spouse for business or professional purposes or money or security for money.

10 Jurisdiction

(1) The jurisdiction conferred on a court by this Act may be exercised by the High Court.

(2) Subject to subsections (3) and (4), the Circuit Court shall concurrently with the High Court have all the jurisdiction of the High Court to hear and determine proceedings under this Act.

(3) Where either spouse is a person of unsound mind and there is a committee of the spouse's estate, the jurisdiction conferred by this Act may, subject to subsection (4), be exercised by the court that has appointed the committee.

(4) Where the rateable value of the land to which the proceedings relate exceeds £200 and the proceedings are brought in the Circuit Court, that Court shall, if a defendant so requires before the hearing thereof, transfer the proceedings to the High Court, but any order made or act done in the course of such proceedings before such transfer shall be valid unless discharged or varied by order of the High Court.

(5) (a) The District Court shall, subject to subsection (3), have all the jurisdiction of the High Court to hear and determine proceedings under this Act where the rateable valuation of the land to which the proceedings relate does not exceed £20.

(b) The District Court shall, subject to subsection (3), have jurisdiction to deal with a question arising under section 9 where the value of the household chattels intended to be disposed of or removed or actually disposed of or removed, as the case may be, does not exceed £5,000 or where such chattels are or immediately before such disposal or removal, were in a family home the rateable valuation of which does not exceed £20.

(c) The District Court may, for the purpose of determining whether it has jurisdiction in proceedings under this Act in relation to a family home that has not been given a rateable valuation or is the subject with other land of a rateable valuation, determine that its rateable valuation would exceed, or would not exceed, £20.

(6) Proceedings under or referred to in this Act in which each spouse is a party (whether by joinder or otherwise) shall be conducted in a summary manner and shall be heard otherwise than in public.

(7) Proceedings in the High Court and in the Circuit Court under or referred to in this Act in which each spouse is a party (whether by joinder or otherwise) shall be heard in chambers.

Amendments—Courts Act, 1981, s 13(a) and (b); Courts Act, 1991, s 8; Family Law Act, 1995, s 54(c).

---

11 Joinder of parties

In any proceedings under or referred to in this Act each of the spouses as well as any third person who has or may have an interest in the proceedings may be joined—

(a) by service upon him of a third-party notice by an existing party to the proceedings, or

(b) by direction of the court.

12   Registration of notice of existence of marriage

(1) A spouse may register in the Registry of Deeds pursuant to the Registration of Deeds Act, 1707 (in the case of unregistered property) or under the Registration of Title Act, 1964 (in the case of registered land) a notice stating that he is married to any person, being a person having an interest in such property or land.

(2) The fact that notice of a marriage has not been registered under subsection (1) shall not give rise to any inference as to the non-existence of a marriage.

(3) No stamp duty, Registry of Deeds fee or land registration fee shall be payable in respect of any such notice.

13   Restriction of section 59(2) of Registration of Title Act, 1964

Section 59(2) of the Registration of Title Act, 1964 (which refers to noting upon the register provisions of any enactment restricting dealings in land) shall not apply to the provisions of this Act.

14   Creation of joint tenancy in family home, exemption from stamp duty and fees

No stamp duty, land registration fee, Registry of Deeds fee or court fee shall be payable on any transaction creating a joint tenancy between spouses in respect of a family home where the home was immediately prior to such transaction owned by either spouse or by both spouses otherwise than as joint tenants.

15   Offences

Where any person having an interest in any premises, on being required in writing by or on behalf of any other person proposing to acquire that interest to give any information necessary to establish if the conveyance of that interest requires a consent under section 3(1), knowingly gives information which is false or misleading in any material particular, he shall be guilty of an offence and shall be liable—

(a) on summary conviction, to a fine not exceeding £200 or to imprisonment for a term not exceeding twelve months or to both, or

(b) on conviction on indictment, to imprisonment for a term not exceeding five years,

without prejudice to any other liability, civil or criminal.

16   Short title

This Act may be cited as the Family Home Protection Act, 1976.

Commencement—12 June 1976.

PART TWO

Family Law Act, 1981

(1981 No 22)

ARRANGEMENT OF SECTIONS

ACTS REFERRED TO

An Act to abolish actions for criminal conversation, enticement and harbouring of a spouse and breach of promise of marriage, to make provision in relation to the property of, and gifts to and between, persons who have been engaged to be married and in relation to the validity of the consent of a minor spouse for the purposes of the Family Home Protection Act, 1976, and to provide for related matters [23 June 1981]

1 Abolition of actions for criminal conversation, enticement and harbouring of spouse

(1) After the passing of this Act, no action shall lie for criminal conversation, for inducing a spouse to leave or remain apart from the other spouse or for harbouring a spouse.

(2) Subsection (1) shall not have effect in relation to any action that has been commenced before the passing of this Act.

2 Engagements to marry not enforceable at law

(1) An agreement between two persons to marry one another, whether entered into before or after the passing of this Act, shall not under the law of the State have effect as a contract and no action shall be brought in the State for breach of such an agreement, whatever the law applicable to the agreement.

(2) Subsection (1) shall not have effect in relation to any action that has been commenced before the passing of this Act.

3 Gifts to engaged couples by other persons

Where two persons have agreed to marry one another and any property is given as a wedding gift to either or both of them by any other person, it shall be presumed, in the absence of evidence to the contrary, that the property so given was given—

(a) to both of them as joint owners, and

(b) subject to the condition that it should be returned at the request of the donor or his personal representative if the marriage for whatever reason does not take place.

4 Gifts between engaged couples

Where a party to an agreement to marry makes a gift of property (including an engagement ring) to the other party, it shall be presumed, in the absence of evidence to the contrary, that the gift—

(a) was given subject to the condition that it should be returned at the request of the donor or his personal representative if the marriage does not take place for any reason other than the death of the donor, or

(b) was given unconditionally, if the marriage does not take place on account of the death of the donor.

5 Property of engaged couples

(1) Where an agreement to marry is terminated, the rules of law relating to the rights of spouses in relation to property in which either or both of them has or have a beneficial interest shall apply in relation to any property in which either or both of the parties to the agreement had a beneficial interest while the agreement was in force as they apply in relation to property in which either or both spouses has or have a beneficial interest.

(2) Where an agreement to marry is terminated, section 12 of the Married Women's Status Act, 1957 (which relates to the determination of questions between husband and wife as to property) shall apply, as if the parties to the agreement were married, to any dispute between them, or claim by one of them, in relation to property in which either or both had a beneficial interest while the agreement was in force.

6 Application to the court in case of substantial benefit to a party to a broken engagement

Where an agreement to marry is terminated and it appears to the court, on application made to it in a summary manner by a person other than a party to the agreement, that a party to the agreement has received a benefit of a substantial nature (not being a gift to which section 3 applies) from the applicant in consequence of the agreement, the court may make such order (including an order for compensation) as appears to it just and equitable in the circumstances.

7 Application to the court in case of substantial expenditure incurred by or on behalf of a party to a broken engagement

Where an agreement to marry is terminated and it appears to the court, on application made to it in a summary manner by a party to the agreement or another person, that, by reason of the agreement—

(a) in the case of the party to the agreement, expenditure of a substantial nature has been incurred by him, or

(b) in the case of the other person, expenditure of a substantial nature has been incurred by him on behalf of a party to the agreement,

and that the party by whom or on whose behalf the expenditure was incurred has not benefited in respect of the expenditure, the court may make such order (including an order for the recovery of the expenditure) as appears to it just and equitable in the circumstances.

8 Jurisdiction (sections 6 and 7)

(8) The Circuit Court shall, concurrently with the High Court, have jurisdiction to hear and determine proceedings under section 6 or 7 subject, in the case of a claim exceeding £30,000, to the like consents as are required for the purposes of section 22 of the Courts (Supplemental Provisions) Act, 1961.

(2) The District Court shall have jurisdiction to hear and determine proceedings under section 6 or 7 where the amount claimed does not exceed £5,000.

Amendments—Courts Act, 1991, s 13.

9 Limitation period for proceedings under this Act

Proceedings to enforce a right conferred by this Act arising out of the termination for whatever reason of an agreement to marry shall not be brought after the expiration of three years from the date of the termination of the agreement.

10 Consent by minor spouse to disposal of family home, etc

(1) No consent given by a spouse, whether before or after the passing of this Act, for the purposes of section 3(1) of the Family Home Protection Act, 1976 (which provides that a conveyance by one spouse of an interest in the family home without the written consent of the other spouse shall be void) or of section 9(2) of that Act (which restricts the right of a spouse to dispose of household chattels without the consent of the other spouse) shall be, or shall be taken to have been, invalid by reason only that it is or was given by a spouse who has not or had not attained the age of majority.

(2) Subsection (1) shall apply to a consent given for the aforesaid purposes before the passing of this Act by a guardian or a court on behalf of a spouse who had not attained the age of majority as if the consent had been given by the spouse.

11 Short title

This Act may be cited as the Family Law Act, 1981.

Commencement—23 June 1982.

PART TWO

Family Law Act, 1988

(1988 No 31)

ARRANGEMENT OF SECTIONS

An Act to abolish proceedings for restitution of conjugal rights   [23 November 1988]

1 Abolition of proceedings for restitution of conjugal rights

After the passing of this Act, no person shall be entitled to institute proceedings for restitution of conjugal rights.

2 Short title

This Act may be cited as the Family Law Act, 1988.

PART TWO

Family Law Act, 1995

(1995 No 26)

ARRANGEMENT OF SECTIONS

PART I

PRELIMINARY AND GENERAL

PART II

PRELIMINARY AND ANCILLARY ORDERS IN OR AFTER PROCEEDINGS FOR JUDICIAL SEPARATION

PART III

RELIEF AFTER DIVORCE OR SEPARATION OUTSIDE STATE

PART IV

DECLARATIONS AS TO MARITAL STATUS

PART V

MARRIAGE

PART VI

MISCELLANEOUS

SCHEDULE

ACTS REFERRED TO

Adoption Acts, 1952 to 1991
Capital Acquisitions Tax Act, 1976	1976 No 8
Child Abduction and Enforcement of Custody Orders Act, 1991	1991 No 6
Defence Act, 1954	1954 No 18
Enforcement of Court Orders Act, 1940	1940 No 23
Family Home Protection Act, 1976	1976 No 27
Family Law Act, 1981	1981 No 22
Family Law (Maintenance of Spouses and Children) Act, 1976	1976 No 11
Family Law (Protection of Spouses and Children) Act, 1981	1981 No 21
Finance (1909–10) Act, 1910	10 Edw 7 c 8
Finance Act, 1972	1972 No 19
Finance Act, 1983	1983 No 15
Finance Act, 1993	1993 No 13
Finance Act, 1994	1994 No 13
Guardianship of Infants Act, 1964	1964 No 7
Income Tax Act, 1967	1967 No 6
Insurance Act, 1989	1989 No 3
Judgments (Ireland) Act, 1844	1844 c 90
Judicial Separation and Family Law Reform Act, 1989	1989 No 6

Jurisdiction of Courts and Enforcement of Judgments Acts, 1988 and 1993
Legitimacy Declaration Act, (Ireland), 1868	1868 c 20
Maintenance Act, 1994	1994 No 28
Marriages Act, 1972	1972 No 30
Marriages (Ireland) Act, 1844	1844 c 81
Marriage Law (Ireland) Amendment Act, 1863	1863 c 27
Married Women's Status Act, 1957	1957 No 5
Matrimonial Causes and Marriage Law (Ireland) Amendment Act, 1870	1870 c 110
Partition Act, 1868	1868 c 40
Partition Act, 1876	1876 c 17
Pensions Act, 1990	1990 No 25
Registration of Marriages (Ireland) Act, 1863	1863 c 90
Registration of Title Act, 1964	1964 No 16
Status of Children Act, 1987	1987 No 26
Succession Act, 1965	1965 No 27

An Act to make further provision in relation to the jurisdiction of the courts to make preliminary and ancillary orders in or after proceedings for judicial separation, to enable such orders to be made in certain cases where marriages are dissolved, or as respects which the spouses become judicially separated, under the law of another State, to make further provision in relation to maintenance under the Family Law (Maintenance of Spouses and Children) Act, 1976, and in relation to marriage and to provide for connected matters   [2 October 1995]

PART TWO

PART I

PRELIMINARY AND GENERAL

1 Short title and commencement

(1) This Act may be cited as the Family Law Act, 1995.

(2) (a) This Act shall come into operation on such day or days as, by order or orders made by the Minister for Equality and Law Reform under this section, may be fixed therefor either generally or with reference to any particular purpose or provision and different days may be so fixed for different purposes and different provisions.

    (b) An order under *paragraph (a)* relating to, or in so far as it relates to, *section 32* shall not be made without the consent of the Minister for Health.

Commencement—1 August 1996.

---

2 Interpretation

(1) In this Act, save where the context otherwise requires—

'the Act of 1964' means the Guardianship of Infants Act, 1964;
'the Act of 1965' means the Succession Act, 1965;
'the Act of 1976' means the Family Law (Maintenance of Spouses and Children) Act, 1976;
'the Act of 1989' means the Judicial Separation and Family Law Reform Act, 1989;
'the Act of 1996' means the Domestic Violence Act, 1996;
'conveyance' includes a mortgage, lease, assent, transfer, disclaimer, release and any other disposition of property otherwise than by a will or a *donatio mortis causa* and also includes an enforceable agreement (whether conditional or unconditional) to make any such disposition;
'the court' shall be construed in accordance with *section 38*;
'decree of judicial separation' means a decree under section 3 of the Act of 1989;
'decree of nullity' means a decree granted by a court declaring a marriage to be null and void;
'dependent member of the family', in relation to a spouse, or the spouses, concerned, means any child—

    (a) of both spouses or adopted by both spouses under the Adoption Acts, 1952 to 1991, or in relation to whom both spouses are *in loco parentis*, or

    (b) of either spouse or adopted by either spouse under those Acts or in relation to whom either spouse is *in loco parentis*, where the other spouse, being aware that he or she is not the parent of the child, has treated the child as a member of the family,

who is under the age of 18 years or if the child has attained that age—

    (i) is or will be or, if an order were made under this Act providing for periodical payments for the benefit of the child or for the provision of a lump sum for the child, would be receiving full-time education or instruction at any university, college, school or other educational establishment and is under the age of 23 years, or

(ii) has a mental or physical disability to such extent that it is not reasonably possible for the child to maintain himself or herself fully;

'family home' has the meaning assigned to it by section 2 of the Family Home Protection Act, 1976, with the modification that the references to a spouse in that section shall be construed as references to a spouse within the meaning of this Act;

'financial compensation order' has the meaning assigned to it by *section 11*;

'Land Registry' and 'Registry of Deeds' have the meanings assigned to them by the Registration of Title Act, 1964;

'lump sum order' means an order under *section 8(1)(c)*;

'maintenance pending suit order' means an order under *section 7*;

'maintenance pending relief order' means an order under *section 24*;

'member', in relation to a pension scheme, means any person who, having been admitted to membership of the scheme under its rules, remains entitled to any benefit under the scheme;

'pension adjustment order' means an order under *section 12*;

'pension scheme' means—

(a) an occupational pension scheme (within the meaning of the Pensions Act, 1990), or

(b) (i) an annuity contract approved by the Revenue Commissioners under section 235 of the Income Tax Act, 1967, or a contract so approved under section 235A of that Act,

(ii) a trust scheme, or part of a trust scheme, so approved under subsection (4) of the said section 235 or subsection (5) of the said section 235A, or

(iii) a policy or contract of assurance approved by the Revenue Commissioners under Chapter II of Part I of the Finance Act, 1972, or

(c) any other scheme or arrangement (including a personal pension plan and a scheme or arrangement established by or pursuant to statute or instrument made under statute other than under the Social Welfare Acts) that provides or is intended to provide either or both of the following, that is to say:

(i) benefits for a person who is a member of the scheme or arrangement ('the member') upon retirement at normal pensionable age or upon earlier or later retirement or upon leaving, or upon the ceasing of, the relevant employment,

(ii) benefits for the widow, widower or dependants of the member, or for any other persons, on the death of the member;

'periodical payments order' and 'secured periodical payments order' have the meanings assigned to them by *section 8(1)*;

'property adjustment order' has the meaning assigned to it by *section 9*;

'relief order' means an order under *Part II* made by virtue of *section 23*;

'trustees', in relation to a scheme that is established under a trust, means the trustees of the pension scheme and, in relation to a pension scheme not so established, means the persons who administer the scheme.

(2) In this Act, where the context so requires—

(a) a reference to a marriage includes a reference to a marriage that has been dissolved under the law of a country or jurisdiction other than the State,

(b) a reference to a remarriage includes a reference to a marriage that takes place after a marriage that has been dissolved under the law of a country or jurisdiction other than the State,

(c) a reference to a spouse includes a reference to a person who is a party to a marriage that has been dissolved under the law of a country or jurisdiction other than the State,

(d) a reference to a family includes a reference to a family as respects which the marriage of the spouses concerned has been dissolved under the law of a country or jurisdiction other than the State,

(e) a reference to an application to a court by a person on behalf of a dependent member of the family includes a reference to such an application by such a member and a reference to a payment, the securing of a payment, or the assignment of an interest, to a person for the benefit of a dependent member of the family includes a reference to a payment, the securing of a payment, or the assignment of an interest, to such a member,

and cognate words shall be construed accordingly.

(3) In this Act—

(a) a reference to any enactment shall, unless the context otherwise requires, be construed as a reference to that enactment as amended or extended by or under any subsequent enactment including this Act,

(b) a reference to a Part or section is a reference to a Part or section of this Act unless it is indicated that reference to some other enactment is intended,

(c) a reference to a subsection, paragraph, subparagraph or clause is a reference to the subsection, paragraph, subparagraph or clause of the provision in which the reference occurs unless it is indicated that reference to some other provision is intended.

Amendments—Domestic Violence Act, 1996, s 21.

---

3 Repeals

(1) The enactments specified in the *Schedule* to this Act are hereby repealed to the extent specified in the *third column* of that Schedule.

(2) Notwithstanding *subsection (1)*—

(a) orders made before the commencement of *Part II* under a provision of the Act of 1989 repealed by *subsection (1)* shall continue in force and be treated after such commencement as if made under the corresponding provision of this Act,

(b) (i) orders or decrees made or exceptions granted under section 1 of the Legitimacy Declaration Act (Ireland), 1868, section 1 of the Marriages Act, 1972, or section 12 of the Married Women's Status Act, 1957, before such commencement shall continue in force after such commencement,

(ii) proceedings instituted under any of those sections before such commencement may be continued and determined after such commencement; and

(iii) orders or decrees made or exceptions granted after such commencement in those proceedings shall be in force,

(c) proceedings instituted before such commencement under a provision of the Act of 1989 repealed by *subsection (1)* may be continued and determined as if instituted under the corresponding provision of this Act and orders made in those proceedings after such commencement shall be in force and be treated as if made under the corresponding provision of this Act.

4   Expenses

The expenses incurred by the Minister for Equality and Law Reform, the Minister for Health or the Minister for Justice in the administration of this Act shall, to such extent as may be sanctioned by the Minister for Finance, be paid out of moneys provided by the Oireachtas.

PART II

PRELIMINARY AND ANCILLARY ORDERS IN OR AFTER PROCEEDINGS FOR
JUDICIAL SEPARATION

5   Application (*sections 6 to 14*)

Each of the following sections, that is to say, *sections 6* to *14,* applies to a case in which proceedings for the grant of a decree of judicial separation are instituted after the commencement of that section.

6   Preliminary orders in proceedings for judicial separation

Where an application is made to the court for the grant of a decree of judicial separation, the court, before deciding whether to grant or refuse to grant the decree, may, in the same proceedings and without the institution of proceedings under the Act concerned, if it appears to the court to be proper to do so, make one or more of the following orders—

    (a)   an order under section 2, 3, 4 or 5 of the Act of 1996,

    (b)   an order under section 11 of the Act of 1964,

    (c)   an order under section 5 or 9 of the Family Home Protection Act, 1976.

Amendments—Domestic Violence Act, 1996, s 21.

7   Maintenance pending suit orders

(1) Where an application is made to the court for the grant of a decree of judicial separation, the court may make an order for maintenance pending suit, that is to say, an order requiring either of the spouses concerned to make to the other spouse such periodical payments or lump sum payments for his or her support and, where appropriate, to make to such person as may be specified in the order such periodical payments for the benefit of such (if any) dependent member of the family and, as respects periodical payments, for such period beginning not earlier than the date of the application and ending not later than the date of its determination, as the court considers proper and specifies in the order.

(2) The court may provide that payments under an order under this section shall be subject to such terms and conditions as it considers appropriate and specifies in the order.

8   Periodical payments and lump sum orders

(1) On granting a decree of judicial separation or at any time thereafter, the court, on application to it in that behalf by either of the spouses concerned or by a person on behalf of a dependent member of the family, may, during the lifetime of the other

spouse or, as the case may be, the spouse concerned, make one or more of the following orders, that is to say:

    (a) a periodical payments order, that is to say—

        (i) an order that either of the spouses shall make to the other spouse such periodical payments of such amount, during such periods and at such times as may be specified in the order, or

        (ii) an order that either of the spouses shall make to such person as may be so specified for the benefit of such (if any) dependent member of the family such periodical payments of such amount, during such period and at such times as may be so specified,

    (b) a secured periodical payments order, that is to say—

        (i) an order that either of the spouses shall secure, to the satisfaction of the court, to the other spouse such periodical payments of such amounts during such period and at such times as may be so specified, or

        (ii) an order that either of the spouses shall secure, to the satisfaction of the court, to such person as may be so specified for the benefit of such (if any) dependent member of the family such periodical payments of such amounts, during such period and at such times as may be so specified,

    (c) (i) an order that either of the spouses shall make to the other spouse a lump sum payment or lump sum payments of such amount or amounts and at such time or times as may be so specified, or

        (ii) an order that either of the spouses shall make to such person as may be so specified for the benefit of such (if any) dependent member of the family a lump sum payment or lump sum payments of such amount or amounts and at such time or times as may be so specified.

(2) The court may—

    (a) order a spouse to pay a lump sum to the other spouse to meet any liabilities or expenses reasonably incurred by that other spouse before the making of an application by that other spouse for an order under *subsection (1)* in maintaining himself or herself or any dependent member of the family, or

    (b) order a spouse to pay a lump sum to such person as may be specified to meet any liabilities or expenses reasonably incurred by or for the benefit of a dependent member of the family before the making of an application on behalf of the member for an order under *subsection (1)*.

(3) An order under this section for the payment of a lump sum may provide for the payment of the lump sum by instalments of such amounts as may be specified in the order and may require the payment of the instalments to be secured to the satisfaction of the court.

(4) The period specified in an order under *paragraph (a)* or *(b)* of *subsection (1)* shall begin not earlier than the date of the application for the order and shall end not later than the death of the spouse, or any dependent member of the family, in whose favour the order is made or the other spouse concerned.

    (5) (a) Upon the remarriage of the spouse in whose favour an order is made under *paragraph (a)* or *(b)* of *subsection (1)*, the order shall, to the extent that it applies to that spouse, cease to have effect, except as respects payments due under it on the date of the remarriage.

        (b) If, after the grant of a decree of judicial separation, either of the spouses concerned remarries, the court shall not, by reference to that decree, make an order under *subsection (1)* in favour of that spouse.

(6) (a) Where a court makes an order under *subsection (1)(a)*, it shall in the same proceedings, subject to *paragraph (b)*, make an attachment of earnings order (within the meaning of the Act of 1976) to secure payments under the first-mentioned order if it is satisfied that the person against whom the order is made is a person to whom earnings (within the meaning aforesaid) fall to be paid.

(b) Before deciding whether to make or refuse to make an attachment of earnings order by virtue of *paragraph (a)*, the court shall give the spouse concerned an opportunity to make the representations specified in *paragraph (c)* in relation to the matter and shall have regard to any such representations made by that spouse.

(c) The representations referred to in *paragraph (b)* are representations relating to the questions—

    (i) whether the spouse concerned is a person to whom such earnings as aforesaid fall to be paid, and

    (ii) whether he or she would make the payments to which the relevant order under *subsection (1)(a)* relates.

(d) References in this subsection to an order under *subsection (1)(a)* include references to such an order as varied or affirmed on appeal from the court concerned or varied under *section 18*.

Amendments—Family Law (Divorce) Act, 1996, s 52(a).

---

9   Property adjustment orders

(1) On granting a decree of judicial separation or at any time thereafter, the court, on application to it in that behalf by either of the spouses concerned or by a person on behalf of a dependent member of the family, may, during the lifetime of the other spouse or, as the case may be, the spouse concerned, make a property adjustment order, that is to say, an order providing for one or more of the following matters:

(a) the transfer by either of the spouses to the other spouse, to any dependent member of the family or to any other specified person for the benefit of such a member of specified property, being property to which the first-mentioned spouse is entitled either in possession or reversion,

(b) the settlement to the satisfaction of the court of specified property, being property to which either of the spouses is so entitled as aforesaid, for the benefit of the other spouse and of any dependent member of the family or of any or all of those persons,

(c) the variation for the benefit of either of the spouses and of any dependent member of the family or of any or all of those persons of any ante-nuptial or post-nuptial settlement (including such a settlement made by will or codicil) made on the spouses,

(d) the extinguishment or reduction of the interest of either of the spouses under any such settlement.

(2) An order under *paragraph (b)*, *(c)* or *(d)* may restrict to a specified extent or exclude the application of *section 18* in relation to the order.

(3) If, after the grant of a decree of judicial separation, either of the spouses concerned remarries, the court shall not, by reference to that decree, make a property adjustment order in favour of that spouse.

(4) Where a property adjustment order is made in relation to land, a copy of the order certified to be a true copy by the registrar or clerk of the court concerned shall, as appropriate, be lodged by him or her in the Land Registry for registration pursuant to section 69(1)(h) of the Registration of Title Act, 1964, in a register maintained under that Act or be registered in the Registry of Deeds.

(5) Where—

(a) a person is directed by an order under this section to execute a deed or other instrument in relation to land, and

(b) the person refuses or neglects to comply with the direction or, for any other reason, the court considers it necessary to do so,

the court may order another person to execute the deed or instrument in the name of the first-mentioned person, and a deed or other instrument executed by a person in the name of another person pursuant to an order under this subsection shall be as valid as if it had been executed by that other person.

(6) Any costs incurred in complying with a property adjustment order shall be borne, as the court may determine, by either of the spouses concerned, or by both of them in such proportions as the court may determine, and shall be so borne in such manner as the court may determine.

(7) This section shall not apply in relation to a family home in which, following the grant of a decree of judicial separation either of the spouses concerned, having remarried, ordinarily resides with his or her spouse.

Amendments—Family Law (Divorce) Act, 1996, s 52(b).

---

10   Miscellaneous ancillary orders

(1) On granting a decree of judicial separation or at any time thereafter, the court, on application to it in that behalf by either of the spouses concerned or by a person on behalf of a dependent member of the family, may, during the lifetime of the other spouse or, as the case may be, the spouse concerned, make one or more of the following orders:

(a) an order—

(i) providing for the conferral on one spouse either for life or for such other period (whether definite or contingent) as the court may specify the right to occupy the family home to the exclusion of the other spouse, or

(ii) directing the sale of the family home subject to such conditions (if any) as the court considers proper and providing for the disposal of the proceeds of the sale between the spouses and any other person having an interest therein,

(b) an order under *section 36*,

(c) an order under section 4, 5, 7 or 9 of the Family Home Protection Act, 1976,

(d) an order under section 2, 3, 4 or 5 of the Act of 1996,

(e) an order for the partition of property or under the Partition Act, 1868, and the Partition Act, 1876,

(f) an order under section 11 of the Act of 1964.

(2) The court, in exercising its jurisdiction under *subsection (1)(a)*, shall have regard to the welfare of the spouses and any dependent member of the family and, in particular, shall take into consideration—

(a) that, where a decree of judicial separation is granted, it is not possible for the spouses concerned to continue to reside together, and

(b) that proper and secure accommodation should, where practicable, be provided for a spouse who is wholly or mainly dependent on the other spouse and for any dependent member of the family.

(3) Subsection 1(a) shall not apply in relation to a family home in which, following the grant of a decree of judicial separation, either of the spouses concerned, having remarried, ordinarily resides with his or her spouse.

Amendments—Family Law (Divorce) Act, 1996, s 52(c); Domestic Violence Act, 1996, s 21.

11   Financial compensation orders

(1) Subject to the provisions of this section, on granting a decree of judicial separation or at any time thereafter, the court, on application to it in that behalf by either of the spouses concerned or by a person on behalf of a dependent member of the family, may, during the lifetime of the other spouse or, as the case may be, the spouse concerned, if it considers—

(a) that the financial security of the spouse making the application ('the applicant') or the dependent member of the family ('the member') can be provided for either wholly or in part by so doing, or

(b) that the forfeiture, by reason of the decree of judicial separation, by the applicant or the dependent, as the case may be, of the opportunity or possibility of acquiring a benefit (for example, a benefit under a pension scheme) can be compensated for wholly or in part by so doing,

make a financial compensation order, that is to say, an order requiring either or both of the spouses to do one or more of the following:

(i) to effect such a policy of life insurance for the benefit of the applicant or the member as may be specified in the order,

(ii) to assign the whole or a specified part of the interest of either or both of the spouses in a policy of life insurance effected by either or both of the spouses to the applicant or to such person as may be specified in the order for the benefit of the member,

(iii) to make or to continue to make to the person by whom a policy of life insurance is or was issued the payments which either or both of the spouses is or are required to make under the terms of the policy.

(2) (a) The court may make a financial compensation order in addition to or in substitution in whole or in part for orders under *sections 8* to *10* and *12* and in deciding whether or not to make such an order it shall have regard to whether proper provision, having regard to the circumstances, exists or can be made for the spouse concerned or the dependent member of the family concerned by orders under those sections.

(b) An order under this section shall cease to have effect on the remarriage or death of the applicant in so far as it relates to the applicant.

(c) The court shall not make an order under this section if the spouse who is applying for the order has remarried.

(d) An order under *section 18* in relation to an order under *paragraph (i)* or *(ii)* of *subsection (1)* may make such provision (if any) as the court considers appropriate in relation to the disposal of—

(i)   an amount representing any accumulated value of the insurance policy effected pursuant to the order under the said *paragraph (i)*, or

(ii) the interest or the part of the interest to which the order under the said *paragraph (ii)* relates.

Amendments—Family Law (Divorce) Act, 1996, s 52(d).

---

12   Pension adjustment orders

(1) In this section, save where the context otherwise requires—

'the Act of 1990' means the Pensions Act, 1990;

'active member', in relation to a scheme, means a member of the scheme who is in reckonable service;

'actuarial value' means the equivalent cash value of a benefit (including, where appropriate, provision for any revaluation of such benefit) under a scheme calculated by reference to appropriate financial assumptions and making due allowance for the probability of survival to normal pensionable age and thereafter in accordance with normal life expectancy on the assumption that the member concerned of the scheme, at the effective date of calculation, is in a normal state of health having regard to his or her age;

'approved arrangement', in relation to the trustees of a scheme, means an arrangement whereby the trustees, on behalf of the person for whom the arrangement is made, effect policies or contracts of insurance that are approved of by the Revenue Commissioners with, and make the appropriate payments under the policies or contracts to, one or more undertakings;

'contingent benefit' means a benefit payable under a scheme, other than a payment under *subsection (7)* to or for one or more of the following, that is to say, the widow or the widower and any dependants of the member spouse concerned and the personal representative of the member spouse, if the member spouse dies while in relevant employment and before attaining any normal pensionable age provided for under the rules of the scheme;

'defined contribution scheme' means a scheme which, under its rules, provides retirement benefit, the rate or amount of which is in total directly determined by the amount of the contributions paid by or in respect of the member of the scheme concerned and includes a scheme the contributions under which are used, directly or indirectly, to provide—

(a) contingent benefit, and

(b) retirement benefit the rate or amount of which is in total directly determined by the part of the contributions aforesaid that is used for the provision of the retirement benefit;

'designated benefit', in relation to a pension adjustment order, means an amount determined by the trustees of the scheme concerned, in accordance with relevant guidelines, and by reference to the period and the percentage of the retirement benefit specified in the order concerned under *subsection (2)*;

'member spouse', in relation to a scheme, means a spouse who is a member of the scheme;

'normal pensionable age' means the earliest age at which a member of a scheme is entitled to receive benefits under the rules of the scheme on retirement from relevant employment, disregarding any such rules providing for early retirement on grounds of ill health or otherwise;

'occupational pension scheme' has the meaning assigned to it by section 2(1) of the Act of 1990;

'reckonable service' means service in relevant employment during membership of any scheme;

'relevant guidelines' means any relevant guidelines for the time being in force under paragraph (c) or (cc) of section 10(1) of the Act of 1990;

'relevant employment', in relation to a scheme, means any employment (or any period treated as employment) or any period of self employment to which a scheme applies;

'retirement benefit', in relation to a scheme, means all benefits (other than contingent benefits) payable under the scheme;

'rules', in relation to a scheme, means the provisions of the scheme, by whatever name called;

'scheme' means a pension scheme;

'transfer amount' shall be construed in accordance with *subsection (4)*;

'undertaking' has the meaning assigned to it by the Insurance Act, 1989.

(2) Subject to the provisions of this section, where a decree of judicial separation ('the decree') has been granted, the court, if it so thinks fit, may, in relation to retirement benefit under a scheme, of which one of the spouses concerned is a member, on application to it in that behalf at the time of the making of the order for the decree or at any time thereafter during the lifetime of the member spouse by either of the spouses or by a person on behalf of a dependent member of the family, make an order providing for the payment, in accordance with the provisions of this section, to either of the following, as the court may determine, that is to say:

(a) the other spouse and, in the case of the death of that spouse, his or her personal representative, and

(b) such person as may be specified in the order for the benefit, of a person who is, and for so long only as he or she remains, a dependent member of the family,

of a benefit consisting, either, as the court may determine, of the whole, or such part as the court considers appropriate, of that part of the retirement benefit that is payable (or which, but for the making of the order for the decree, would have been payable) under the scheme and has accrued at the time of the making of the order for the decree and, for the purpose of determining the benefit, the order shall specify—

(i) the period of reckonable service of the member spouse prior to the granting of the decree to be taken into account, and

(ii) the percentage of the retirement benefit accrued during that period to be paid to the person referred to in *paragraph (a)* or *(b)*, as the case may be.

(3) Subject to the provisions of this section, where a decree of judicial separation ('the decree') has been granted, the court, if it so thinks fit, may, in relation to a contingent benefit under a scheme of which one of the spouses concerned is a member, on application to it in that behalf not more than one year after the making of the order for the decree by either of the spouses or by a person on behalf of a dependent member of the family concerned, make an order providing for the payment, upon the death of the member spouse, to either of the following, or to both of them in such proportions as the court may determine, that is to say:

(a) the other spouse, and

(b) such person as may be specified in the order for the benefit of a dependent member of the family, of, either, as the court may determine, the whole, or such part (expressed as a percentage) as the court considers appropriate, of that part of any contingent benefit that is payable (or which, but for the making of the order for the decree, would have been payable) under the scheme.

(4) Where the court makes an order under *subsection (2)* in favour of a spouse and payment of the designated benefit concerned has not commenced, the spouse in whose favour the order is made shall be entitled to the application in accordance with *subsection (5)* of an amount of money from the scheme concerned (in this section referred to as a 'transfer amount') equal to the value of the designated benefit, such amount being determined by the trustees of the scheme in accordance with relevant guidelines.

(5) Subject to *subsection (17)*, where the court makes an order under *subsection (2)* in favour of a spouse and payment of the designated benefit concerned has not commenced, the trustees of the scheme concerned shall, for the purpose of giving effect to the order—

(a) on application to them in that behalf at the time of the making of the order or at any time thereafter by the spouse in whose favour the order was made ('the spouse'), and

(b) on the furnishing to them by the spouse of such information as they may reasonably require,

apply in accordance with relevant guidelines the transfer amount calculated in accordance with those guidelines either—

(i) if the trustees and the spouse so agree, in providing a benefit for or in respect of the spouse under the scheme aforesaid that is of the same actuarial value as the transfer amount concerned, or

(ii) in making a payment either to—

    (I) such other occupational pension scheme, being a scheme the trustees of which agree to accept the payment, or

    (II) in the discharge of any payment falling to be made by the trustees under any such other approved arrangement,

as may be determined by the spouse.

(6) Subject to *subsection (17)*, where the court makes an order under *subsection (2)* in relation to a defined contribution scheme and an application has not been brought under *subsection (5)*, the trustees of the scheme may, for the purpose of giving effect to the order, if they so think fit, apply in accordance with relevant guidelines the transfer amount calculated in accordance with those guidelines in making a payment to—

(a) such other occupational pension scheme, being a scheme the trustees of which agree to accept the payment, or

(b) in the discharge of any payment falling to be made by the trustees under such other approved arrangement,

as may be determined by the trustees.

(7) Subject to *subsection (17)*, where—

(a) the court makes an order under *subsection (2)*, and

(b) the member spouse concerned dies before payment of the designated benefit concerned has commenced,

the trustees shall, for the purpose of giving effect to the order, within 3 months of the death of the member spouse, provide for the payment to the person in whose favour the order is made of an amount that is equal to the transfer amount calculated in accordance with relevant guidelines.

(8) Subject to *subsection (17)*, where—

    (a) the court makes an order under *subsection (2)*, and

    (b) the member spouse concerned ceases to be a member of the scheme otherwise than on death,

the trustees may, for the purpose of giving effect to the order, if they so think fit, apply, in accordance with relevant guidelines, the transfer amount calculated in accordance with those guidelines either, as the trustees may determine—

    (i) if the trustees and the person in whose favour the order is made ('the person') so agree, in providing a benefit for or in respect of the person under the scheme aforesaid that is of the same actuarial value as the transfer amount concerned, or

    (ii) in making a payment, either to—

        (I) such other occupational pension scheme, being a scheme the trustees of which agree to accept the payment, or

        (II) in the discharge of any payment falling to be made under such other approved arrangement,

    as may be determined by the trustees.

(9) Subject to *subsection (17)*, where—

    (a) the court makes an order under *subsection (2)* in favour of a spouse ('the spouse'), and

    (b) the spouse dies before payment of the designated benefit has commenced,

the trustees shall, within 3 months of the death of the spouse, provide for the payment to the personal representative of the spouse of an amount equal to the transfer amount calculated in accordance with relevant guidelines.

(10) Subject to *subsection (17)*, where—

    (a) the court makes an order under *subsection (2)* in favour of a spouse ('the spouse'), and

    (b) the spouse dies after payment of the designated benefit has commenced,

the trustees shall, within 3 months of the death of the spouse, provide for the payment to the personal representative of the spouse of an amount equal to the actuarial value, calculated in accordance with relevant guidelines, of the part of the designated benefit which, but for the death of the spouse, would have been payable to the spouse during the lifetime of the member spouse.

(11) Where—

    (a) the court makes an order under *subsection (2)* for the benefit of a dependent member of the family ('the person'), and

    (b) the person dies before payment of the designated benefit has commenced,

the order shall cease to have effect in so far as it relates to that person.

(12) Where—

    (a) the court makes an order under *subsection (2)* or *(3)* in relation to an occupational pension scheme, and

    (b) the trustees of the scheme concerned have not applied the transfer amount concerned in accordance with *subsection (5)*, *(6)*, *(7)*, *(8)* or *(9)*, and

(c) after the making of the order, the member spouse ceases to be an active member of the scheme,

the trustees shall, within 12 months of the cessation, notify the registrar or clerk of the court concerned and the other spouse of the cessation.

(13) Where the trustees of a scheme apply a transfer amount under *subsection (6)* or *(8)*, they shall notify the spouse (not being the spouse who is the member spouse) or other person concerned and the registrar or clerk of the court concerned of the application and shall give to that spouse or other person concerned particulars of the scheme or undertaking concerned and of the transfer amount.

(14) Where the court makes an order under *subsection (2)* or *(3)* for the payment of a designated benefit or a contingent benefit, as the case may be, the benefit shall be payable or the transfer amount concerned applied out of the resources of the scheme concerned and, unless otherwise provided for in the order or relevant guidelines, shall be payable in accordance with the rules of the scheme or, as the case may be, applied in accordance with relevant guidelines.

(15) Where the court makes an order under *subsection (2)*, the amount of the retirement benefit payable, in accordance with the rules of the scheme concerned to, or to or in respect of, the member spouse shall be reduced by the amount of the designated benefit payable pursuant to the order.

(16)(a) Where the court makes an order under *subsection (3)*, the amount of the contingent benefit payable, in accordance with the rules of the scheme concerned in respect of the member spouse shall be reduced by an amount equal to the contingent benefit payable pursuant to the order.

(b) Where the court makes an order under *subsection (2)* and the member spouse concerned dies before payment of the designated benefit concerned has commenced, the amount of the contingent benefit payable in respect of the member spouse in accordance with the rules of the scheme concerned shall be reduced by the amount of the payment made under *subsection (7)*.

(17) Where, pursuant to an order under *subsection (2)*, the trustees of a scheme make a payment or apply a transfer amount under *subsections (5), (6), (7), (8), (9)* or *(10)*, they shall be discharged from any obligation to make any further payment or apply any transfer amount under any other of those subsections in respect of the benefit payable pursuant to the order.

(18) A person who makes an application under *subsection (2)* or *(3)* or an application for an order under *section 18(2)* in relation to an order under *subsection (2)* shall give notice thereof to the trustees of the scheme concerned and, in deciding whether to make the order concerned and in determining the provisions of the order, the court shall have regard to any representations made by any person to whom notice of the application has been given under this section or *section 40*.

(19) An order under *subsection (3)*, shall cease to have effect on the death or remarriage of the person in whose favour it was made in so far as it relates to that person.

(20) The court may, in a pension adjustment order or by order made under this subsection after the making of a pension adjustment order, give to the trustees of the scheme concerned such directions as it considers appropriate for the purposes of the pension adjustment order including directions compliance with which occasions non-compliance with the rules of the scheme concerned or the Act of 1990, and a trustee of a scheme shall not be liable in any court or other tribunal for any loss or damage caused by his or her non-compliance with the rules of the scheme or with the Act of 1990

if the non-compliance was occasioned by his or her compliance with a direction of the court under this section.

(21) The registrar or clerk of the court concerned shall cause a copy of a pension adjustment order to be served on the trustees of the scheme concerned.

(22)(a) Any costs incurred by the trustees of a scheme under *subsection (18)* or in complying with a pension adjustment order or a direction under *subsection (20)* or *(25)* shall be borne, as the court may determine, by the member spouse or by the other person concerned or by both, of them in such proportion as the court may determine and, in the absence of such determination, those costs shall be borne by them equally.

   (b) Where a person fails to pay an amount in accordance with *paragraph (a)* to the trustees of the scheme concerned, the court may, on application to it in that behalf by the trustees, order that the amount be deducted from the amount of any benefit payable to the person under the scheme or pursuant to an order under *subsection (2)* or *(3)* and be paid to the trustees.

(23)(a) The court shall not make a pension adjustment order if the spouse who applies for the order has remarried.

   (b) The court may make a pension adjustment order in addition to or in substitution in whole or in part for an order or orders under *section 8, 9, 10* or *11* and, in deciding whether or not to make a pension adjustment order, the court shall have regard to the question whether proper provision, having regard to the circumstances, exists or can be made for the spouse concerned or the dependent member of the family concerned by an order or orders under any of those sections.

(24) Section 54 of the Act of 1990 and any regulations under that section shall apply with any necessary modifications to a scheme if proceedings for the grant of a decree of judicial separation to which a member spouse is a party have been instituted and shall continue to apply notwithstanding the grant of a decree of judicial separation in the proceedings.

(25) For the purposes of this Act, the court may, of its own motion, and shall, if so requested by either of the spouses concerned or any other person concerned, direct the trustees of the scheme concerned to provide the spouses or that other person and the court, within a specified period of time—

   (a) with a calculation of the value and the amount, determined in accordance with relevant guidelines, of the retirement benefit, or contingent benefit, concerned that is payable (or which, but for the making of the order for the decree of judicial separation concerned, would have been payable) under the scheme and has accrued at the time of the making of that order, and

   (b) with a calculation of the amount of the contingent benefit concerned that is payable (or which, but for the making of the order for the decree of judicial separation concerned, would have been payable) under the scheme.

(26) An order under this section may restrict to a specified extent or exclude the application of *section 18* in relation to the order.

Amendments—Family Law (Divorce) Act, 1996, s 52(d)(e).

13 Preservation of pension entitlements after judicial separation

(1) Subject to the provisions of this section, on granting a decree of judicial separation or at any time thereafter, the court may, in relation to a pension scheme, on application to it in that behalf by either of the spouses concerned, make during the lifetime of the spouse who is a member of the scheme ('the member spouse') an order directing the trustees of the scheme not to regard the separation of the spouses resulting from the decree as a ground for disqualifying the other spouse for the receipt of a benefit under the scheme a condition for the receipt of which is that the spouses should be residing together at the time the benefit becomes payable.

(2) Notice of an application under *subsection (1)* shall be given by the spouse concerned to the trustees of the pension scheme concerned and, in deciding whether to make an order under *subsection (1)*, the court shall have regard to any representations made by any person to whom notice of the application has been given under this section or section 40.

(3) Any costs incurred by the trustees of a pension scheme under *subsection (2)* or in complying with an order under *subsection (1)* shall be borne, as the court may determine, by either of the spouses concerned or by both of the spouses and in such proportion and manner as the court may determine.

(4) The court may make an order under this section in addition to or in substitution in whole or in part for orders under *sections 8* to *11* and, in deciding whether or not to make such an order, it shall have regard to the question whether adequate and reasonable financial provision exists or can be made for the spouse concerned by orders under those sections.

14 Orders extinguishing succession rights on judicial separation

On granting a decree of judicial separation or at any time thereafter, the court may, on application to it in that behalf by either of the spouses concerned, make an order extinguishing the share that either of the spouses would otherwise be entitled to in the estate of the other spouse as a legal right or on intestacy under the Act of 1965 if—

    (a) it is satisfied that adequate and reasonable financial provision exists or can be made under *section 8, 9, 10(1)(a), 11, 12* or *13* for the spouse whose succession rights are in question ('the spouse concerned'),

    (b) the spouse concerned is a spouse for the support of whom the court refused to make an order under *section 8, 9, 10(1)(a), 11, 12* or *13*, or

    (c) it is satisfied that the spouse concerned is not a spouse for whose benefit the court would, if an application were made to it in that behalf, make an order under *section 8, 9, 10(1)(a), 11, 12* or *13*.

15 Orders for sale of property

(1) Where the court makes a secured periodical payments order, a lump sum order or a property adjustment order, thereupon, or at any time thereafter, it may make an order directing the sale of such property as may be specified in the order, being property in which, or in the proceeds of sale of which, either or both of the spouses concerned has or have a beneficial interest, either in possession or reversion.

(2) The jurisdiction conferred on the court by *subsection (1)* shall not be so exercised as to affect a right to occupy the family home of the spouse concerned that is enjoyed by virtue of an order under this Part.

(3) (a) An order under *subsection (1)* may contain such consequential or supplementary provisions as the court considers appropriate.

    (b) Without prejudice to the generality of *paragraph (a)*, an order under *subsection (1)* may contain—

       (i) a provision specifying the manner of sale and some or all of the conditions applying to the sale of the property to which the order relates,

       (ii) a provision requiring any such property to be offered for sale to a person, or a class of persons, specified in the order,

       (iii) a provision directing that the order, or a specified part of it, shall not take effect until the occurrence of a specified event or the expiration of a specified period,

       (iv) a provision requiring the making of a payment or payments (whether periodical payments or lump sum payments) to a specified person or persons out of the proceeds of the sale of the property to which the order relates, and

       (v) a provision specifying the manner in which the proceeds of the sale of the property concerned shall be disposed of between the following persons or such of them as the court considers appropriate, that is to say, the spouses concerned and any other person having an interest therein.

(4) A provision in an order under *subsection (1)* providing for the making of periodical payments to one of the spouses concerned out of the proceeds of the sale of property shall, on the death or remarriage of that spouse, cease to have effect except as respects payments due on the date of the death or remarriage.

(5) Where a spouse has a beneficial interest in any property, or in the proceeds of the sale of any property, and a person (not being the other spouse) also has a beneficial interest in that property or those proceeds, then, in considering whether to make an order under this section or *section 9* or *10(1)(a)* in relation to that property or those proceeds, the court shall give to that person an opportunity to make representations with respect to the making of the order and the contents thereof, and any representations made by such a person shall be deemed to be included among the matters to which the court is required to have regard under *section 16* in any relevant proceedings under a provision referred to in that section after the making of those representations.

(6) This section shall not apply in relation to a family home in which, following the grant of a decree of judicial separation, either of the spouses concerned, having remarried, ordinarily resides with his or her spouse.

Amendments—Family Law (Divorce) Act, 1996, s 52(f).

15A Orders for provision for spouse out of estate of other spouse

(1) Subject to the provisions of this section, where, following the grant of a decree of judicial separation, a court makes an order under section 14 in relation to the spouses concerned and one of the spouses dies, the court, on application to it in that behalf by the other spouse ('the applicant') not more than 6 months after representation is first granted under the Act of 1965 in respect of the estate of the deceased spouse, may by order make such provision for the applicant out of the estate of the deceased spouse as it considers appropriate having regard to the rights of any other person having an interest in the matter and specifies in the order if it is satisfied that proper provision in the circumstances was not made for the applicant during the lifetime of the deceased

spouse under *section 8, 9, 10(1)(a), 11* or *12* for any reason (other than conduct referred to in *subsection (2)(i)* of *section 16* of the applicant).

(2) The court shall not make an order under this section if the applicant concerned has remarried since the granting of the decree of judicial separation concerned.

(3) In considering whether to make an order under this section the court shall have regard to all the circumstances of the case including—

   (a) any order under *paragraph (c)* of *section 8(1)* or a property adjustment order in favour of the applicant, and
   (b) any devise or bequest made by the deceased spouse to the applicant.

(4) The provision made for the applicant concerned by an order under this section together with any provision made for the applicant by an order referred to in *subsection 3(a)* (the value of which for the purposes of this subsection shall be its value on the date of the order) shall not exceed in total the share (if any) of the applicant in the estate of the deceased spouse to which the applicant was entitled or (if the deceased spouse died intestate as to the whole or part of his or her estate) would have been entitled under the Act of 1965 if the court had not made an order under section 14.

(5) Notice of an application under this section shall be given by the applicant to the spouse (if any) of the deceased spouse concerned and to such other persons as the court may direct and, in deciding whether to make the order concerned and in determining the provisions of the order, the court shall have regard to any representations made by the spouse of the deceased spouse and any other such persons as aforesaid.

(6) The personal representative of a deceased spouse in respect of whom a decree of judicial separation has been granted shall make a reasonable attempt to ensure that notice of his or her death is brought to the attention of the other spouse concerned and, where an application is made under this section, the personal representative of the deceased spouse shall not, without the leave of the court, distribute any of the estate of that spouse until the court makes or refuses to make an order under this section.

(7) Where the personal representative of a deceased spouse in respect of whom a decree of judicial separation has been granted gives notice of his or her death to the other spouse concerned ('the spouse') and—

   (a) the spouse intends to apply to the court for an order under this section,
   (b) the spouse has applied for such an order and the application is pending, or
   (c) an order has been made under this section in favour of the spouse,

the spouse shall, not later than one month after the receipt of the notice, notify the personal representative of such intention, application or order, as the case may be, and, if he does not do so, the personal representative shall be at liberty to distribute the assets of the deceased spouse, or any part thereof, amongst the parties entitled thereto.

(8) The personal representative shall not be liable to the spouse for the assets or any part thereof so distributed unless, at the time of such distribution, he or she had notice of the intention, application or order aforesaid.

(9) Nothing in subsection (7) or (8) shall prejudice the right of the spouse to follow any such assets into the hands of any person who may have received them.

(10) On granting a decree of judicial separation or at any time thereafter, the court, on application to it in that behalf by either of the spouses concerned, may, during the lifetime of the other spouse or, as the case may be, the spouse concerned, if it considers it

just to do so, make an order that either or both spouses shall not, on the death of either of them, be entitled to apply for an order under this section.

Amendments—Inserted by Family Law (Divorce) Act, 1996, s 52(g).

16 Provisions relating to certain orders under *sections 7* to *13* and *18*

(1) In deciding whether to make an order under *section 7, 8, 9, 10(1)(a), 11, 12, 13, 14, 15A, 18* or *25* and in determining the provisions of such an order, the court shall endeavour to ensure that such provision exists or will be made for each spouse concerned and for any dependent member of the family concerned as is proper having regard to all the circumstances of the case.

(2) Without prejudice to the generality of *subsection (1)*, in deciding whether to make such an order as aforesaid and in determining the provisions of such an order, the court shall, in particular, have regard to the following matters—

   (a) the income, earning capacity, property and other financial resources which each of the spouses concerned has or is likely to have in the foreseeable future,
   (b) the financial needs, obligations and responsibilities which each of the spouses has or is likely to have in the foreseeable future (whether in the case of the remarriage of the spouse or otherwise),
   (c) the standard of living enjoyed by the family concerned before the proceedings were instituted or before the spouses separated, as the case may be,
   (d) the age of each of the spouses and the length of time during which the spouses lived together,
   (e) any physical or mental disability of either of the spouses,
   (f) the contributions which each of the spouses has made or is likely in the foreseeable future to make to the welfare of the family, including any contribution made by each of them to the income, earning capacity, property and financial resources of the other spouse and any contribution made by either of them by looking after the home or caring for the family,
   (g) the effect on the earning capacity of each of the spouses of the marital responsibilities assumed by each during the period when they lived together and, in particular, the degree to which the future earning capacity of a spouse is impaired by reason of that spouse having relinquished or foregone the opportunity of remunerative activity in order to look after the home or care for the family,
   (h) any income or benefits to which either of the spouses is entitled by or under statute,
   (i) the conduct of each of the spouses, if that conduct is such that in the opinion of the court it would in all the circumstances of the case be unjust to disregard it,
   (j) the accommodation needs of either of the spouses,
   (k) the value to each of the spouses of any benefit (for example, a benefit under a pension scheme) which by reason of the decree of judicial separation concerned that spouse will forfeit the opportunity or possibility of acquiring,
   (l) the rights of any person other than the spouses but including a person to whom either spouse is remarried.

   (3) (a) The court shall not make an order under a provision referred to in *subsection (1)* for the support of a spouse if the spouse had deserted the other spouse before the institution of proceedings for the decree or, as the case may be, a decree, specified in that provision and had continued such desertion up to the time of

the institution of such proceedings unless, having regard to all the circumstances of the case (including the conduct of the other spouse), the court is of
opinion that it would be unjust not to make the order.

  (b) A spouse who, with just cause, leaves and lives apart from the other spouse
      because of conduct on the part of that other spouse shall not be regarded for
      the purposes of *paragraph (a)* as having deserted that spouse.

(4) Without prejudice to the generality of *subsection (1)*, in deciding whether to make an
order referred to in that subsection in favour of a dependent member of the family
concerned and in determining the provisions of such an order, the court shall, in
particular, have regard to the following matters:

  (a) the financial needs of the member,
  (b) the income, earning capacity (if any), property and other financial resources of
      the member,
  (c) any physical or mental disability of the member,
  (d) any income or benefits to which the member is entitled by or under statute,
  (e) the manner in which the member was being and in which the spouses concerned
      anticipated that the member would be educated or trained,
  (f) the matters specified in *paragraphs (a), (b)* and *(c)* of subsection (2),
  (g) the accommodation needs of the member.

(5) The court shall not make an order under a provision referred to in *subsection (1)*
unless it would be in the interests of justice to do so.

(6) In this section 'desertion' includes conduct on the part of one of the spouses
concerned that results in the other spouse, with just cause, leaving and living apart from
the first-mentioned spouse.

Amendments—Family Law (Divorce) Act, 1996, s 52(h).

---

17 Retrospective periodical payments orders

(1) Where, having regard to all the circumstances of the case, the court considers it
appropriate to do so, it may, in a periodical payments order, direct that—

  (a) the period in respect of which payments under the order shall be made shall
      begin on such date before the date of the order, not being earlier than the time of
      the institution of the proceedings concerned for the grant of a decree of judicial
      separation, as may be specified in the order,
  (b) any payments under the order in respect of a period before the date of the order
      be paid in one sum and before a specified date, and
  (c) there be deducted from any payments referred to in *paragraph (b)* made to the
      spouse concerned an amount equal to the amount of such (if any) payments
      made to that spouse by the other spouse as the court may determine, being
      payments made during the period between the making of the order for the grant
      of the decree aforesaid and the institution of the proceedings aforesaid.

(2) The jurisdiction conferred on the court by *subsection (1)(b)* is without prejudice to the
generality of *section 8(1)(c)*.

18 Variation, etc, of certain orders under this Part

(1) This section applies to the following orders—

  (a) a maintenance pending suit order,

  (b) a periodical payments order,

  (c) a secured periodical payments order,

  (d) a lump sum order if and in so far as it provides for the payment of the lump sum concerned by instalments or requires the payment of any such instalments to be secured,

  (e) an order under *paragraph (b), (c)* or *(d)* of *section 9(1)* in so far as such application is not restricted or excluded, pursuant to *section 9(2)*,

  (f) an order under *subparagraph (i)* or *(ii)* of *section 10(1)(a)*,

  (g) a financial compensation order,

  (h) an order under *subsection (2)* of *section 12* insofar as such application is not restricted or excluded by section 12(26),

  (i) an order under *section 13,*

  (j) an order under this section.

PART TWO

(2) Subject to the provisions of this section and *section 16* and any restriction pursuant to *section 9(2)* and without prejudice to *section 11(2)(d)*, the court may, on application to it in that behalf by either of the spouses concerned or, in the case of the death of either of the spouses, by any other person who, in the opinion of the court, has a sufficient interest in the matter or by a person on behalf of a dependent member of the family concerned, if it considers it proper to do so having regard to any change in the circumstances of the case and to any new evidence, by order vary or discharge an order to which this section applies, suspend any provision of such an order or any provision of such an order temporarily, revive the operation of such an order or provision so suspended, further vary an order previously varied under this section or further suspend or revive the operation of an order or provision previously suspended or revived under this section, and, without prejudice to the generality of the foregoing, an order under this section may require the divesting of any property vested in a person under or by virtue of an order to which this section applies.

(3) Without prejudice to the generality of *section 7* or *8*, that part of an order to which this section applies which provides for the making of payments for the support of a dependent member of the family shall stand discharged if the member ceases to be a dependent member of the family by reason of his or her attainment of the age of 18 years or 23 years, as may be appropriate, and shall be discharged by the court, on application to it under *subsection (2)*, if it is satisfied that the member has for any reason ceased to be a dependent member of the family.

(4) The power of the court under *subsection (2)* to make an order varying, discharging or suspending an order referred to in *subsection (1)(e)* shall be subject to any restriction or exclusion specified in that order and shall (subject to the limitation aforesaid) be a power—

  (a) to vary the settlement to which the order relates in any person's favour or to extinguish or reduce any person's interest under that settlement, and

  (b) to make such supplemental provision (including a further property adjustment order or a lump sum order) as the court thinks appropriate in consequence of any variation, extinguishment or reduction made pursuant to *paragraph (a),*

and *section 15* shall apply to a case where the court makes such an order as aforesaid under *subsection (2)* as it applies to a case where the court makes a property adjustment order with any necessary modifications.

(5) The court shall not make an order under *subsection (2)* in relation to an order referred to in *subsection (1)(e)* unless it appears to it that the order will not prejudice the interests of any person who—

(a) has acquired any right or interest in consequence of the order referred to in *subsection (1)(e)*, and

(b) is not a party to the marriage concerned or a dependent member of the family concerned.

(6) This section shall apply, with any necessary modifications, to instruments executed pursuant to orders to which this section applies as it applies to those orders.

(7) Where the court makes an order under *subsection (2)* in relation to a property adjustment order relating to land a copy of the order under *subsection (2)* certified to be a true copy by the registrar or clerk of the court concerned shall, as appropriate, be lodged by him or her in the Land Registry for registration pursuant to section 69(1)(h) of the Registration of Title Act, 1964, in a register maintained under that Act or be registered in the Registry of Deeds.

Amendments—Family Law (Divorce) Act, 1998, s 52(i).

---

19 Restriction in relation to orders for benefit of dependent members of the family

In deciding whether—

(a) to include in an order under *section 7* a provision requiring the making of periodical payments for the benefit of a dependent member of the family,

(b) to make an order under *paragraph (a)(ii)*, *(b)(ii)* or *(c)(ii)* of *section 8(1)*,

(c) to make an order under *section 18* varying, discharging or suspending a provision referred to in *paragraph (a)* or an order referred to in *paragraph (b)*,

the court shall not have regard to conduct by the spouse or spouses concerned of the kind specified in *subsection (2)(i)* of *section 16* or desertion referred to in *subsection (3)* of that section.

20 Transmission of periodical payments through District Court clerk

Notwithstanding anything in this Act, section 9 of the Act of 1976 shall apply in relation to an order ('the relevant order'), being a maintenance pending suit order, a periodical payments order or a secured periodical payments order or any such order as aforesaid as affected by an order under *section 18*, with the modifications that—

(a) the reference in subsection (4) of the said section 9 to the maintenance creditor shall be construed as a reference to the person to whom payments under the relevant order concerned are required to be made,

(b) the other references in the said section 9 to the maintenance creditor shall be construed as references to the person on whose application the relevant order was made, and

(c) the reference in subsection (3) of the said section 9 to the maintenance debtor shall be construed as a reference to the person to whom payments under the relevant order are required by that order to be made,

and with any other necessary modifications.

21   Application of maintenance pending suit and periodical payment orders to certain members of Defence Forces

The reference in section 98(1)(h) of the Defence Act, 1954, to an order for payment of alimony shall be construed as including a reference to a maintenance pending suit order, a periodical payments order and a secured periodical payments order.

22   (Amends s 8 of the Enforcement of Court Orders Act, 1940)

PART III

RELIEF AFTER DIVORCE OR SEPARATION OUTSIDE STATE

23   Relief orders where marriage dissolved, or spouses legally separated outside State

(1) This section applies to a marriage that has been dissolved, or as respects which the spouses have been legally separated, after the commencement of this section under the law of a country or jurisdiction other than the State, being a divorce or legal separation that is entitled to be recognised as valid in the State.

(2) (a)   Subject to the provisions of this Part, the court may, in relation to a marriage to which this section applies, on application to it in that behalf by either of the spouses concerned or by a person on behalf of a dependent member of the family concerned, make any order under *Part II* (other than an order under *section 6* or a maintenance pending suit order) (in this Act referred to as a relief order) that it could have made if the court had granted a decree of judicial separation in relation to the marriage.

   (b)   *Part II* shall apply and have effect in relation to relief orders and applications therefor as it applies and has effect in relation to orders under *Part II* and applications therefor with the modifications that—

   (i)   *subsections (4)* and *(5)* of *section 8, section 10(1)(c)* and *section 13* shall not apply in relation to a marriage that has been dissolved under the law of a country or jurisdiction other than the State,

   (ii)   *section 15* shall not apply in relation to a family home in which, following the dissolution of the marriage under such a law, either spouse, having remarried, ordinarily resides with his or her spouse, and

   (iii)   the modifications specified in *paragraph (c)* and any other necessary modifications.

   (c)   *Section 16* shall apply in relation to a relief order subject to the modifications that—

   (i)   it shall be construed as including a requirement that the court should have regard to the duration of the marriage,

   (ii)   the reference in *subsection (2)(k)* to the forfeiture of the opportunity or possibility of acquiring any benefit shall be construed as a reference to such forfeiture by reason of the divorce or legal separation concerned, and

   (iii)   the reference in *subsection (3)* to proceedings shall be construed as a reference to the proceedings for the divorce concerned or, as the case may be, for the legal separation concerned.

   (d)   Where a spouse whose marriage has been dissolved in a country or jurisdiction other than the State has remarried, the court may not make a relief order in favour of that spouse in relation to a previous marriage of that spouse.

(3) (a) An application shall not be made to the court by a person for a relief order unless, prior to the application, the court, on application to it *ex parte* in that behalf by that person, has by order granted leave for the making of the first-mentioned application and the court shall not grant such leave unless it considers that there is a substantial ground for so doing and a requirement specified in *section 27* is satisfied.

(b) The court may make the grant of leave under this subsection subject to such (if any) terms and conditions as it considers appropriate and specifies in its order.

(c) The court may grant leave under this subsection to a person notwithstanding that an order has been made by a court of a country or jurisdiction other than the State requiring the spouse concerned to make a payment or transfer property to the person.

(d) This subsection does not apply to an application for a relief order made pursuant to a request under section 14 of the Maintenance Act, 1994.

(4) In determining, for the purposes of this section, the financial resources of a spouse or a dependent member of the family in a case in which payments are required to be made or property is required to be transferred to the spouse or to the member by the other spouse under an order of a court of a country or jurisdiction other than the State or an agreement in writing, the court shall have regard to the extent to which the order or agreement has been complied with or, if payments are required to be made, or property is required to be transferred, after the date of the order made by virtue of this section under *Part II*, is likely to be complied with.

(5) The period specified in a periodical payments order made by virtue of this section under *paragraph (a)* or *(b)* of *section 8(1)* shall begin not earlier than the date of the application for the order and shall end not later than the death of either of the spouses concerned or, if the order is made on or after the dissolution of the marriage, the remarriage of the spouse in whose favour the order was made.

(6) (a) Where, by virtue of this section, the court makes a periodical payments order or a secured periodical payments order on or after the dissolution of the marriage concerned, it may direct that the person in whose favour the order is made shall not apply for an order under *section 18* extending the period specified in the order and, if the court so directs, such an order under *section 18* shall not be made.

(b) Where, by virtue of this section, the court makes a periodical payments order or a secured periodical payments order in favour of a spouse other than on or after the dissolution of the marriage of the spouse and the marriage is dissolved subsequently, the order, if then in force, shall cease to have effect on the remarriage of that spouse, except as respects payments due under it on the date of the remarriage.

(c) If, after the dissolution of a marriage to which this section, applies, either of the spouses concerned remarries, the court shall not, by reference to that dissolution, make by virtue of this section such an order as aforesaid, or a property adjustment order, in favour of that spouse.

24   Maintenance pending relief orders

(1) Where leave is granted to a person under *section 23(3)* for the making of an application for a relief order, the court may, subject to *subsection (3)*, on application to it in that behalf by the person, if it appears to it that a spouse, or a dependent member of the family, concerned is in immediate need of financial assistance, make an order for

maintenance pending relief, that is to say, an order requiring the other spouse or either of the spouses, as may be appropriate, to make to the person such periodical payments or lump sum payments for his or her support or, as may be appropriate, for the benefit of the dependent member of the family as it considers proper and, as respects any periodical payments, for such period beginning not earlier than the date of such grant and ending not later than the date of the determination of the application as it considers proper.

(2) The court may, on application to it in that behalf, provide that payments under an order under this section shall be subject to such terms and conditions as it considers appropriate and specifies in the order.

(3) The court shall not make an order under this section in a case where neither of the requirements specified in *paragraphs (a)* and *(b)* of *section 27(1)* is satisfied.

25 Orders for provision for spouse out of estate of other spouse

(1) Subject to the provisions of this section, where a spouse whose marriage has been dissolved in a country or jurisdiction other than the State dies, the court, on application to it in that behalf by the other spouse ('the applicant') not more than 6 months after representation is first granted under the Act of 1965 in respect of the estate of the deceased spouse, may by order make such provision for the applicant out of the estate of the deceased spouse as it considers appropriate having regard to the rights of any other person having an interest in the matter and specifies in the order if it is satisfied that it was not possible to provide proper provision, having regard to the circumstances, for the applicant during the lifetime of the deceased spouse under *sections 8* to *12* for any reason (other than conduct referred to in *subsection (2)(i)* of *section 16* or desertion referred to in *subsection (3)* of that section by the applicant).

(2) The court shall not make an order under this section if the applicant concerned has remarried since the granting of the decree of divorce concerned.

(3) In considering whether to make an order under this section, the court shall have regard to all the circumstances of the case including—

    (a) any order under *paragraph (c)* of *section 8(1)* or a property adjustment order in favour of the applicant, and

    (b) any devise or bequest made by the deceased spouse to the applicant.

(4) The provision made for the applicant concerned by an order under this section together with any provision made for the applicant by an order referred to in *subsection (3)(a)* (the value of which for the purposes of this subsection shall be its value on the date of the order) shall not exceed in total the share (if any) of the applicant in the estate of the deceased spouse to which the applicant was entitled or (if the deceased spouse died intestate as to the whole or part of his or her estate) would have been entitled under the Act of 1965 if the marriage had not been dissolved.

(5) Section 121 of the Act of 1965 shall apply with any necessary modifications to a disposition referred to in subsection (1) of that section in respect of which the court is satisfied that it was made for the purpose of defeating or substantially diminishing the provision which the court would make for the applicant concerned under this section if the disposition had not been made.

(6) Notice of an application under this section shall be given by the applicant to the spouse (if any) of the deceased spouse concerned and to such (if any) other persons as the court may direct and, in deciding whether to make the order concerned and in determining the provisions of the order, the court shall have regard to any represen-

tations made by the spouse of the deceased spouse and any other such persons as aforesaid.

(7) The personal representative of a deceased spouse in respect of whom a decree of divorce has been granted in a country or jurisdiction other than the State shall make a reasonable attempt to ensure that notice of his or her death is brought to the attention of the other spouse concerned and, where an application is made under this section, the personal representative of the deceased spouse shall not, without the leave of the court, distribute any of the estate of that spouse until the court makes or refuses to make an order under this section.

(8) Where the personal representative of a deceased spouse in respect of whom a decree of divorce has been granted in a country or jurisdiction other than the State gives notice of his or her death to the other spouse concerned ('the spouse') and—

(a) the spouse intends to apply to the court for an order under this section,
(b) the spouse has applied for such an order and the application is pending, or
(c) an order has been made under this section in favour of the spouse,

the spouse shall, not later than one month after the receipt of the notice, notify the personal representative of such intention, application or order, as the case may be, and, if he or she does not do so, the personal representative shall be at liberty to distribute the assets of the deceased spouse, or any part thereof, amongst the parties entitled thereto.

(9) The personal representative shall not be liable to the spouse for the assets or any part thereof so distributed unless, at the time of such distribution, he or she had notice of the intention, application or order aforesaid.

(10) Nothing in subsection (8) or (9) shall prejudice the right of the spouse to follow any such assets into the hands of any person who may have received them.

Amendments—Family Law (Divorce) Act, 1996, s 52(d) and (j).

---

26 Appropriateness of making relief orders in State

The court shall not make a relief order unless it is satisfied that in all the circumstances of the particular case it is appropriate that such an order should be made by a court in the State and, without prejudice to the generality of the foregoing, in deciding whether to make a relief order, the court shall, in particular, have regard to the following matters:

(a) the connection which the spouses concerned have with the State,
(b) the connection which the spouses have with the country or jurisdiction other than the State in which the marriage concerned was dissolved or in which they were legally separated,
(c) the connection which the spouses have with any country or jurisdiction other than the State,
(d) any financial benefit which the spouse applying for the making of the order ('the applicant') or a dependent member of the family has received, or is likely to receive, in consequence of the divorce or legal separation concerned or by virtue of any agreement or the operation of the law of a country or jurisdiction other than the State,
(e) in a case where an order has been made by a court in a country or jurisdiction other than the State requiring a spouse, or the spouses, concerned to make any payment or transfer any property for the benefit of the applicant or a dependent

member of the family, the financial relief given by the order and the extent to which the order has been complied with or is likely to be complied with,

(f) any right which the applicant or a dependent member of the family has, or has had, to apply for financial relief from a spouse or the spouses under the law of any country or jurisdiction other than the State and, if the applicant or dependent member of the family has omitted to exercise any such right, the reason for that omission,

(g) the availability in the State of any property in respect of which a relief order in favour of the applicant or dependent member of the family could be made,

(h) the extent to which the relief order is likely to be enforceable,

(i) the length of time which has elapsed since the date of the divorce or legal separation concerned.

27 Jurisdiction of court to make relief orders

(1) Subject to *subsection (2)*, the court may make a relief order if, but only if, at least one of the following requirements is satisfied:

(a) either of the spouses concerned was domiciled in the State on the date of the application for an order under *section 23(3)* in relation to the relief order or was so domiciled on the date on which the divorce or judicial separation concerned took effect in the country or jurisdiction in which it was obtained,

(b) either of the spouses was ordinarily resident in the State throughout the period of one year ending on either of the dates aforesaid,

(c) on the date of the institution of the proceedings aforesaid either or both of the spouses had a beneficial interest in land situated in the State.

(2) *Subsection (1)* does not apply in relation to a case to which the Jurisdiction of Courts and Enforcement of Judgments Acts, 1988 and 1993, apply or to a relief order that is the subject of a request under section 14 of the Maintenance Act, 1994.

28 Restriction of jurisdiction of court to make relief orders

(1) Where the jurisdiction of the court to make a relief order is conferred by virtue only of *section 27(1)(c)*, the court may make any of the following relief orders, but no others:

(a) a lump sum order,

(b) a property adjustment order providing for one or more of the matters specified in *paragraphs (b)*, *(c)* and *(d)* of *section 9(1)*,

(c) an order under *section 14*,

(d) an order under *section 25*,

(e) an order directing the sale of the interest of either of the spouses concerned in the family home concerned.

(2) Where, in the circumstances referred to in *subsection (1)*, the court makes one or more lump sum orders, the amount or aggregate amount of the sum or sums to which the order or orders relate shall not exceed—

(a) in case the interest of the spouse liable to make the payment or payments under the order or orders in the family home concerned is sold whether in pursuance of an order of the court or otherwise, the amount of the proceeds of the sale after deduction therefrom of the costs thereof, or

(b) in any other case, such amount as, in the opinion of the court, represents the value of that interest.

(3) The reference in *subsection (1)(e)* to the interest of either of the spouses concerned shall, in relation to a case where the interest of a spouse in the family home concerned is held under a joint tenancy or a tenancy in common with another person or other persons, be construed as including a reference to the interest of the other person or persons in the home.

PART IV

DECLARATIONS AS TO MARITAL STATUS

29 Declarations as to marital status

(1) The court may, on application to it in that behalf by either of the spouses concerned or by any other person who, in the opinion of the court, has a sufficient interest in the matter, by order make one or more of the following declarations in relation to a marriage, that is to say:

    (a) a declaration that the marriage was at its inception a valid marriage,

    (b) a declaration that the marriage subsisted on a date specified in the application,

    (c) a declaration that the marriage did not subsist on a date so specified, not being the date of the inception of the marriage,

    (d) a declaration that the validity of a divorce, annulment or legal separation obtained under the civil law of any other country or jurisdiction in respect of the marriage is entitled to recognition in the State,

    (e) a declaration that the validity of a divorce, annulment or legal separation so obtained in respect of the marriage is not entitled to recognition in the State.

(2) The court may grant an order under *subsection (1)* if, but only if, either of the spouses concerned—

    (a) is domiciled in the State on the date of the application,

    (b) has been ordinarily resident in the State throughout the period of one year ending on that date, or

    (c) died before that date and either—

        (i) was at the time of death domiciled in the State, or

        (ii) had been ordinarily resident in the State throughout the period of one year ending on that date.

(3) The other spouse or the spouses concerned or the personal representative of the spouse or each spouse, within the meaning of the Act of 1965, shall be joined in proceedings under this section.

(4) The court may, at any stage of proceedings under this section of its own motion or on application to it in that behalf by a party thereto, order that notice of the proceedings be given to the Attorney General or any other person and that such documents relating to the proceedings as may be necessary for the purposes of his or her functions shall be given to the Attorney General.

(5) The court shall, on application to it in that behalf by the Attorney General, order that he or she be added as a party to any proceedings under this section and, in any such proceedings, he or she shall, if so requested by the court, whether or not he or she is so added to the proceedings, argue any question arising in the proceedings specified by the court.

(6) Where notice of proceedings under this section is given to a person (other than the Attorney General), the court may, of its own motion or on application to it in that behalf

by the person or a party to the proceedings, order that the person be added as a party to the proceedings.

(7) Where a party to proceedings under this section alleges that the marriage concerned is or was void, or that it is voidable, and should be annulled, the court may treat the application under *subsection (1)* as an application for a decree of nullity of marriage and may forthwith proceed to determine the matter accordingly and may postpone the determination of the application under *subsection (1)*.

(8) A declaration under this section shall be binding on the parties to the proceedings concerned and on any person claiming through such a party and, if the Attorney General is a party to the proceedings, the declaration shall also be binding on the State.

(9) A declaration under this section shall not prejudice any person if it is subsequently proved to have been obtained by fraud or collusion.

(10) Where proceedings under this section, and proceedings in another jurisdiction, in relation to the same marriage have been instituted but have not been finally determined, the court may stay the first-mentioned proceedings until the other proceedings have been finally determined.

(11) In this section a reference to a spouse includes a reference to a person who is a party to a marriage that has been dissolved under the Family Law (Divorce) Act, 1996.

Amendments—Family Law (Divorce) Act, 1996, s 52(k).

30 Provisions supplementary to *section 29*

(1) Rules of court may make provision as to the information to be given in an application under *section 29(1)* including particulars of any previous or pending proceedings in relation to any marriage concerned or to the matrimonial status of a party to any such marriage.

(2) The court may make such order (if any) as it considers just for the payment of all or part of any costs incurred by the Attorney General in proceedings under this section by other parties to the proceedings.

(3) Without prejudice to the law governing the recognition of decrees of divorce granted by courts outside the State, a declaration under *section 29* conflicting with a previous final judgment or decree of a court of competent jurisdiction of a country or jurisdiction other than the State shall not be made unless the judgment or decree was obtained by fraud or collusion.

(4) Notification of a declaration under *section 29* (other than a declaration relating to a legal separation) shall be given by the registrar of the court to an tArd Chláraitheoir.

PART V

MARRIAGE

31 Age of marriage

(1) (a) (i) A marriage solemnised, after the commencement of this section, between persons either of whom is under the age of 18 years shall not be valid in law.

(ii) *Subparagraph (i)* applies to any marriage solemnised—

      (I)   in the State, irrespective of where the spouses or either of them are or is ordinarily resident, or

     (II) outside the State, if at the time of the solemnisation of the marriage, the spouses or either of them are or is ordinarily resident in the State.

  (b) *Paragraph (a)* does not apply if exemption from it was granted under *section 33* before the marriage concerned.

  (c) The requirement in relation to marriage arising by virtue of *paragraph (a)* is hereby declared to be a substantive requirement for marriage.

(2) Any person to whom application is made in relation to the solemnisation of an intended marriage may, if he or she so thinks fit, request the production of evidence of age with respect to either or both of the parties concerned.

(3) Where a request is made under *subsection (2)*—

  (a) refusal or failure to comply with the request shall be a proper reason for refusal of the application concerned, and

  (b) if the request is complied with and the evidence shows that either or both of the parties is or are under the age of 18 years, the application shall be refused.

(4) Where a person knowingly—

  (a) solemnises or permits the solemnisation of a marriage which, consequent on the provisions of this section, is not valid in law, or

  (b) is a party to such a marriage,

the person shall be guilty of an offence and shall be liable on summary conviction to a fine not exceeding £500.

32 Notification of intention to marry

(1) (a) A marriage solemnised, after the commencement of this section, in the State between persons of any age shall not be valid in law unless—

     (i)   the persons concerned notify the Registrar in writing of their intention to so marry not less than 3 months prior to the date on which the marriage is to be solemnised, or

    (ii) exemption from this section was granted before the marriage under *section 33*.

  (b) The requirement specified in *paragraph (a)* is hereby declared to be a substantive requirement for marriage.

(2) The Registrar shall notify each of the persons concerned in writing of the receipt by him or her of a notification under *subsection (1)*.

(3) A notification under *subsection (2)* shall not be construed as indicating the approval of the Registrar concerned of the proposed marriage concerned.

(4) (a) The Minister for Health may make regulations for the purposes of this section and, in particular, in relation to the notifications provided for by *subsections (1)* and *(2)*.

  (b) A regulation under this section shall be laid before each House of the Oireachtas as soon as may be after it is made and, if a resolution annulling the regulation is passed by either such House within the next 21 days on which that House has sat after the regulation is laid before it, the regulation shall be annulled accordingly, but without prejudice to anything previously done thereunder.

(5) (a) Where the Registrar receives a notification under subsection (1)—

(i)   the health board in whose functional area the District of the Registrar is situated shall pay to the Registrar a fee of such amount as may stand specified for the time being by regulations under subsection (4), and

(ii) if the District of the Registrar is situated in the functional area of more than one health board, each health board concerned shall pay to the Registrar so much of the fee aforesaid as is proportionate to the part of the District aforesaid in the functional area of that board.

(6) In this section—

'the Act of 1844' means the Marriages (Ireland) Act, 1844,

'the Act of 1863' means the Registration of Marriages (Ireland) Act, 1863,

'District' means a District formed under the Act of 1844 or the Act of 1863, as may be appropriate,

'the Registrar'—

(a)   in relation to a marriage to which section 11 of the Act of 1863 applies, means the Registrar appointed under section 10 of that Act for the District in which the marriage is intended to be solemnised or a person authorised by that Registrar to act on his or her behalf, and

(b)   in relation to any other marriage, means the Registrar appointed under section 57 of the Act of 1844 for the District in which the marriage is intended to be solemnised or a person authorised by that Registrar to act on his or her behalf.

Amendments—Family Law (Miscellaneous Provisions) Act, 1997, s 2(1)(a)(b).

33   Exemption of certain marriages from *sections 31(1)* and *32(1)*

(1) The court may, on application to it in that behalf by both of the parties to an intended marriage, by order exempt the marriage from the application of *section 31(1)(a)* or *32(1)(a)* or both of those provisions.

(2) The following provisions shall apply in relation to an application under *subsection (1)*:

(a)   it may be made informally,

(b)   it may be heard and determined otherwise than in public,

(c)   a court fee shall not be charged in respect of it, and

(d)   it shall not be granted unless the applicant shows that its grant is justified by serious reasons and is in the interests of the parties to the intended marriage.

34   Abolition of right to petition for jactitation of marriage

No person shall after the commencement of this Act be entitled to petition a court for jactitation of marriage.

PART VI

MISCELLANEOUS

35 Powers of court in relation to transactions intended to prevent or reduce relief

(1) In this section—

'disposition' means any disposition of property howsoever made other than a disposition made by a will or codicil,

'relief' means the financial or other material benefits conferred by—

(a) an order under *section 7, 8* or *9, paragraph (a)* or *(b)* of *section 10(1)* or *section 11, 12, 13, 15A, 17, 18* (other than an order affecting an order referred to in *subsection (1)(e)* thereof), *24* or *25,* or

(aa) an order under section 11(2)(b) of the Act of 1964 or section 5, 5A or 7 of the Act of 1976, or

(b) a relief order (other than an order under *section 18* affecting an order referred to in *subsection (1)(e)* thereof),

and references to defeating a claim for relief are references to—

(i) preventing relief being granted to the person concerned, whether for the benefit of the person or a dependent member of the family concerned,

(ii) limiting the relief granted, or

(iii) frustrating or impeding the enforcement of an order granting relief,

'reviewable disposition', in relation to proceedings for the grant of relief brought by a spouse, means a disposition made by the other spouse concerned or any other person but does not include such a disposition made for valuable consideration (other than marriage) to a person who, at the time of the disposition acted in good faith and, without notice of an intention on the part of the respondent to defeat the claim for relief.

(2) (a) The court, on the application of a person ('the applicant') who—

(i) has instituted proceedings that have not been determined for the grant of relief,

(ii) has been granted leave under *section 23(3)* to institute such proceedings, or

(iii) intends to apply for such leave upon the completion of one year's ordinary residence in the State—

may—

(I) if it is satisfied that the other spouse concerned or any other person, with the intention of defeating the claim for relief, proposes to make any disposition of or to transfer out of the jurisdiction or otherwise deal with any property, make such order as it thinks fit for the purpose of restraining that other spouse or other person from so doing or otherwise for protecting the claim,

(II) if it is satisfied that that other spouse or other person has, with that intention, made a reviewable disposition and that, if the disposition were set aside, relief or different relief would be granted to the applicant, make an order setting aside the disposition.

(b) Where relief has been granted by the court and the court is satisfied that the other spouse concerned or another person has, with the intention aforesaid, made a reviewable disposition, it may make an order setting aside the disposition.

(c) An application under *paragraph (a)* shall, in a case in which proceedings for relief have been instituted, be made in those proceedings.

(3) Where the court makes an order under *paragraph (a)* or *(b)* of *subsection (2)*, it shall include in the order such provisions (if any) as it considers necessary for its implementation (including provisions requiring the making of any payments or the disposal of any property).

(4) In a case where neither of the conditions specified in *paragraphs (a)* and *(b)* of *section 27(1)* is satisfied, the court shall not make an order under *subsection (2)* in respect of any property other than the family home concerned.

(5) Where an application is made under *subsection (2)* with respect to a disposition that took place less than 3 years before the date of the application or with respect to a disposition or other dealing with property that the other spouse concerned or any other person proposes to make and the court is satisfied—

(a) in case the application is for an order under *subsection (2)(a)(I)*, that the disposition or other dealing concerned would (apart from this section) have the consequence, or

(b) in case the application is for an order under *paragraph (a)(II)* or *(b)* of *subsection (2)*, that the disposition has had the consequence,

of defeating the applicant's claim for relief, it shall be presumed, unless the contrary is shown, that that other spouse or other person disposed of or otherwise dealt with the property concerned, or, as the case may be, proposes to do so, with the intention of defeating the applicant's claim for relief.

Amendments—Family Law (Divorce) Act, 1996, s 52(I).

---

36 Determination of questions between spouses in relation to property

(1) Either spouse may apply to the court in a summary manner to determine any question arising between them as to the title to or possession of any property.

(2) On application to it under *subsection (1)*, the court may—

(a) make such order with respect to the property in dispute (including an order that it be sold or partitioned) and as to the costs consequent upon the application, and

(b) direct such inquiries, and give such other directions, in relation to the application,

as the court considers proper.

(3) Either spouse or a child of a deceased spouse (in this section referred to subsequently as 'the plaintiff spouse') may make an application specified in *subsection (1)* where it is claimed that the other spouse (in this section referred to subsequently as 'the defendant spouse') has had in his or her possession or under his or her control—

(a) money to which, or to a share of which, the plaintiff spouse was beneficially entitled whether by reason of the fact that it represented the proceeds of property to which, or to an interest in which, the plaintiff spouse was beneficially entitled or for any other reason, or

(b) property (other than money) to which, or to an interest in which, the plaintiff spouse was beneficially entitled,

and that either that money or other property has ceased to be in the possession or under the control of the defendant spouse or that the plaintiff spouse does not know whether it is still in the possession or under the control of the defendant spouse.

(4) Where an application under *subsection (1)* is made by virtue of *subsection (3)* and the court is satisfied that—

(a) (i) the defendant spouse concerned has had in his or her possession or under his or her control money or other property to which *paragraph (a)* or *(b)* of *subsection (3)* relates, or

   (ii) the defendant spouse has in his or her possession or under his or her control property that represents the whole or part of the money or other property aforesaid,

   and

(b) the defendant spouse has not made to the plaintiff spouse concerned such payment or disposition (not being a testamentary disposition) as would have been appropriate in all the circumstances,

the court may make an order under *subsection (2)* in relation to the application and may, in addition to or in lieu of such an order, make an order requiring the defendant spouse to pay to the plaintiff spouse either, as the case may be—

(i) such sum in respect of the money to which the application relates, or the plaintiff spouse's share thereof, or

(ii) such sum in respect of the value of the property (other than money) referred to in *paragraph (a)*, or the plaintiff spouse's interest therein,

as the court considers proper.

(5) In any proceedings under this section, a person (other than the plaintiff spouse concerned or the defendant spouse concerned) who is a party thereto shall, for the purposes of costs or any other matter, be treated as a stakeholder only.

(6) This section is without prejudice to section 2 (which prescribes the legal capacity of married women) of the Married Women's Status Act, 1957.

(7) (a) Where a marriage—
   (i) has been annulled or dissolved under the law of the State, or
   (ii) has been annulled or dissolved under the law of a country or jurisdiction other than the State and is, by reason of that annulment or divorce, not or no longer a subsisting valid marriage under the law of the State,
   an application under this section shall not be made by either of the spouses more than 3 years after the date of the annulment or divorce.

   (b) Where a marriage is void but has not been so declared under the law of the State or another state, an application shall not be made under this section by either of the spouses more than 3 years after the parties have ceased to be ordinarily resident together.

(8) In this section references to a spouse include references to—

(a) a personal representative of a deceased spouse,

(b) either of the parties to a void marriage, whether or not it has been declared to be void under the law of the State or a country or jurisdiction other than the State,

(c) either of the parties to a voidable marriage that has been annulled under the law of the State,

(cc) either of the parties to a marriage that has been dissolved under the law of the State,

(d) either of the parties to a marriage that has been annulled under the law of another state and that is, by reason of the annulment, not a subsisting valid marriage under the law of the State, and

(e) either of the parties to a marriage that has been dissolved under the law of another state and that is, by reason of the divorce, no longer a subsisting valid marriage under the law of the State.

Amendments—Family Law (Divorce) Act, 1996, s 52(m).

37 Payments to be made without deduction of income tax

Payments of money pursuant to an order under this Act (other than under *section 12*) shall be made without deduction of income tax.

38 Jurisdiction of courts and venue

(1) Subject to the provisions of this section, the Circuit Court shall, concurrently with the High Court, have jurisdiction to hear and determine proceedings under this Act and shall, in relation to that jurisdiction, be known as the Circuit Family Court.

(2) Subject to the other provisions of this section, the Circuit Family Court shall, concurrently with the High Court, have jurisdiction to hear and determine proceedings for a decree of nullity.

(3) Where the rateable valuation of any land to which proceedings in the Circuit Family Court under this Act relate exceeds £200, that Court shall, if an application is made to it in that behalf by any person having an interest in the proceedings, transfer the proceedings to the High Court, but any order made or act done in the course of such proceedings before the transfer shall be valid unless discharged or varied by the High Court by order.

(4) The jurisdiction conferred on the Circuit Family Court by this Act may be exercised—

(a) in the case of an application under section 33, by the judge of any circuit, and

(b) in any other case, by the judge of the circuit in which any of the parties to the proceedings ordinarily resides or carries on any business, profession or occupation.

(5) The Circuit Family Court may, for the purposes of *subsection (3)* and section 31(3) of the Act of 1989 in relation to land that has not been given a rateable valuation or is the subject with other land of a rateable valuation, determine that its rateable valuation would exceed, or would not exceed, £200.

(6) Section 32 of the Act of 1989 shall apply to proceedings under this Act in the Circuit Family Court and sections 33 to 36 of that Act shall apply to proceedings under this Act in that Court and in the High Court.

(7) In proceedings under *section 8, 9, 10(1)(a), 11, 12, 13, 14, 15A, 18, 23* or *25*—

(a) each of the spouses concerned shall give to the other spouse and to, or to a person acting on behalf of, any dependent member of the family concerned, and

(b) any dependent member of the family concerned shall give to, or to a person acting on behalf of, any other such member and to each of the spouses concerned,

such particulars of his or her property and income as may reasonably be required for the purposes of the proceedings.

(8) Where a person fails or refuses to comply with *subsection (7)*, the court, on application to it in that behalf by a person having an interest in the matter, may direct the person to comply with that subsection.

Amendments—Family Law (Divorce) Act, 1996, s 52(n); Family Law (Miscellaneous Provisions) Act, 1997, s 2(2).

39 Exercise of jurisdiction by court in relation to nullity

(1) The court may grant a decree of nullity if, but only if, one of the following requirements is satisfied:

(a) either of the spouses concerned was domiciled in the State on the date of the institution of the proceedings concerned,

(b) either of the spouses was ordinarily resident in the State throughout the period of one year ending on that date,

(c) either of the spouses died before that date and—

(i) was at the time of death domiciled in the State, or

(ii) had been ordinarily resident in the State throughout the period of one year ending on that date.

(2) Where proceedings are pending in a court in respect of an application for the grant of a decree of nullity or in respect of an appeal from the determination of such an application and the court has or had, by virtue of *subsection (1)*, jurisdiction to determine the application, the court, notwithstanding section 31 (4) of the Act of 1989, shall have jurisdiction to determine an application for the grant of a decree of judicial separation in respect of the marriage concerned.

40 Notice of proceedings under Act

Notice of any proceedings under this Act shall be given by the person bringing the proceedings to—

(a) the other spouse concerned or, as the case may be, the spouses concerned, and

(b) any other person specified by the court.

41 Secured maintenance orders

Where, in proceedings under any other Act, the court or the District Court makes or has made an order providing for the payment—

(a) by a spouse to the other spouse of periodical payments for the support or maintenance of that other spouse, or

(b) by a parent to the other parent or to another person specified in the order of periodical payments for the support or maintenance of a child—

(i) of both parents or adopted by both parents under the Adoption Acts, 1952 to 1991, or in relation to whom both parents are *in loco parentis*, or

(ii) of either parent or adopted by either parent under those Acts or in relation to whom either parent is *in loco parentis* where the other parent being aware that he or she is not the parent of the child has treated the child as a member of the family,

the court by which the order was made may in those proceedings or subsequently, on application to it by any person having an interest in the proceedings, order the spouse or parent liable to make the payments under the order to secure them to the other spouse or parent or the other person specified in the order to the satisfaction of the court.

42 Lump sum maintenance orders

(1) Where, in proceedings under any other Act, an order providing for the periodical payments referred to in *paragraph (a)* or *(b)* of *section 41* would, apart from this section, fall to be made, the court may in addition to, or instead of such an order, make an order providing for the making by the person concerned to the person concerned of a lump sum payment or lump sum payments of such amount or amounts and at such time or times as may be specified in the order.

(2) The amount or aggregate amount of a lump sum payment or of lump sum payments to a person under an order under this section shall be—

(a) if the order is instead of an order for the making of periodical payments to the person, such amount as the court considers appropriate having regard to the amount of the periodical payments that would have been made, and the periods during which and the times at which they would have been made, but for this section, and

(b) if the first-mentioned order is in addition to an order for the making of periodical payments to the person, such amount as the court considers appropriate having regard to the amount of the periodical payments and the periods during which and the times at which they will be made.

(3) In this section 'the court' includes the District Court.

(4) The amount or aggregate amount of a lump sum payment or of lump sum payments provided for in an order of the District Court under this section shall not exceed £5,000.

43 (Amends the Act of 1976)

44 Discharge of orders under Act of 1976

Where, while a maintenance order, an order varying a maintenance order, or an interim order, under the Act of 1976 is in force, an application is made to the court by a spouse to whom the order aforesaid relates for an order granting a decree of judicial separation or an order under *Part II* or *III*, the court may by order discharge the order aforesaid under the Act of 1976 as on and from such date as may be specified in the order.

45 (Amends ss 3, 4 and 14 of the Maintenance Act, 1994)

46 Custody of dependent members of the family after decree of nullity

Where the court makes an order for the grant of a decree of nullity, it may declare either of the spouses concerned to be unfit to have custody of any dependent member of the family who is a minor and, if it does so and the spouse to whom the declaration relates is a parent of any dependent member of the family who is a minor, that spouse shall not, on the death of the other spouse, be entitled as of right to the custody of that minor.

47   Social reports in family law proceedings

(1) In proceedings to which this section applies, the court may, of its own motion or on application to it in that behalf by a party to the proceedings, by order give such directions as it thinks proper for the purpose of procuring a report in writing on any question affecting the welfare of a party to the proceedings or any other person to whom they relate from—

   (a)   such probation and welfare officer (within the meaning of the Child Abduction and Enforcement of Custody Orders Act, 1991) as the Minister for Justice may nominate,
   (b)   such person nominated by a health board specified in the order as that board may nominate, being a person who, in the opinion of that board, is suitably qualified for the purpose, or
   (c)   any other person specified in the order.

(2) In deciding whether or not to make an order under *subsection (1)*, the court shall have regard to any submission made to it in relation to the matter by or on behalf of a party to the proceedings concerned or any other person to whom they relate.

(3) A copy of a report under *subsection (1)* shall be given to the parties to the proceedings concerned and (if he or she is not a party to the proceedings) to the person to whom it relates and may be received in evidence in the proceedings.

(4) The fees and expenses incurred in the preparation of a report under *subsection (1)* shall be paid by such parties to the proceedings concerned and in such proportions, or by such party to the proceedings, as the court may determine.

(5) The court or a party to proceedings to which this section applies may call as a witness in the proceedings a person who prepared a report under *subsection (1)* pursuant to an order under that subsection in those proceedings.

(6) This section applies to proceedings—

   (a)   under the Act of 1964,
   (b)   under the Act of 1976,
   (c)   under the Family Home Protection Act, 1976,
   (d)   under the Act of 1996,
   (e)   under the Status of Children Act, 1987,
   (f)   under the Act of 1989,
   (g)   under the Child Abduction and Enforcement of Custody Orders Act, 1991,
   (h)   in relation to an application for a decree of nullity, and
   (i)   under this Act.

(7) The function conferred on a health board by *subsection (1)(b)* shall be a function of the chief executive officer of the board.

Amendments—Family Law (Divorce) Act, 1996, s 52(p); Domestic Violence Act, 1996, s 21(d).

---

48   Property of engaged couples

For the avoidance of doubt, it is hereby declared that the reference in section 5(1) of the Family Law Act, 1981, to the rules of law relating to the rights of spouses in relation to property in which either or both of them has or have a beneficial interest shall relate and be deemed always to have related only to the rules of law for the determination of disputes between spouses, or a claim by one of them, in relation to the beneficial ownership of property in which either or both of them has or have a beneficial interest and, in particular, does not relate, and shall be deemed never to have related, to the rules of law relating to the rights of spouses under the Act of 1965, the Family Home Protection Act, 1976, the Act of 1989 or this Act.

49 Income tax treatment of persons divorced outside State

Where a payment to which section 3 of the Finance Act, 1983, applies is made in a year of assessment (within the meaning of the Income Tax Acts) by a spouse who is a party to a marriage, that has been dissolved, for the benefit of the other spouse and—

(a) the dissolution was under the law of a country or jurisdiction other than the State, being a divorce that is entitled to be recognised as valid in the State,

(b) both spouses are resident in the State for tax purposes for that year of assessment, and

(c) neither spouse has entered into another marriage,

then, the provisions of section 4 of the Finance Act, 1983, shall, with any necessary modifications, have effect in relation to the spouses for that year of assessment as if their marriage had not been dissolved.

50 (*Repealed*)

51 Exemption of certain transfers from capital acquisitions tax

(1) Notwithstanding the provisions of the Capital Acquisitions Tax Act, 1976, a gift or inheritance (within the meaning, in each case, of that Act) taken by virtue or in consequence of an order to which this subsection applies by a spouse who was a party to the marriage concerned shall be exempt from any capital acquisitions tax under that Act and shall not be taken into account in computing such a tax.

(2) *Subsection (1)* applies to—

(a) a relief order or an order under *section 25* made following the dissolution of a marriage,

(b) a maintenance pending relief order made following the granting of leave under *section 23(3)* to a spouse whose marriage has been dissolved, and

(c) an order referred to in *section 41(a)*, or an order under *section 42(1)* made in addition to or instead of an order under *section 41(a)*, in favour of a spouse whose marriage has been dissolved.

52 Capital gains tax treatment of certain disposals by spouses

(1) Notwithstanding the provisions of the Capital Gains Tax Acts, where, by virtue or in consequence of—

(a) an order made under *Part II* on or following the granting of a decree of judicial separation, or

(b) a deed of separation, or

(c) a relief order made following the dissolution of a marriage,

either of the spouses concerned disposes of an asset to the other spouse, both spouses shall be treated for the purposes of those Acts as if the asset was acquired from the spouse making the disposal for a consideration of such amount as would secure that on the disposal neither a gain nor a loss would accrue to the spouse making the disposal:

Provided that this subsection shall not apply if, until the disposal, the asset formed part of the trading stock of a trade carried on by the spouse making the disposal or if the asset is acquired as trading stock for the purposes of a trade carried on by the spouse acquiring the asset.

(2) Where *subsection (1)* applies in relation to a disposal of an asset by a spouse to the other spouse, then, in relation to a subsequent disposal of the asset (not being a disposal to which *subsection (1)* applies), the spouse making the disposal shall be treated for the purposes of the Capital Gains Tax Acts as if the other spouse's acquisition or provision of the asset had been his or her acquisition or provision of the asset.

(3) This section shall not apply to disposals made before its commencement.

53   Abatement and postponement of probate tax on property the subject of an order under *section 25*

Subsection (1) of section 115A of the Finance Act, 1993 (which was inserted by the Finance Act, 1994, and provides for the abatement or postponement of probate tax payable by a surviving spouse)—

(a)   shall apply to a spouse in whose favour an order has been made under *section 25* as it applies to a spouse referred to in the said section 115A, and

(b)   shall apply to property or an interest in property the subject of such an order as it applies to the share of a spouse referred to in the said section 115A in the estate of a deceased referred to in that section or the interest of such a spouse in property referred to in that section,

with any necessary modifications.

54   Amendment of Family Home Protection Act, 1976, and Act of 1989

(1) (Amends ss 2, 3 and 10 of the Family Home Protection Act, 1976)

(2) The amendment effected by *subsection (1)(a)* does not apply in relation to—

(a)   any conveyances referred to in section 3 of the Family Home Protection Act, 1976, the dates of which are,

(b)   any proceedings under or referred to in that Act which are instituted,

(c)   any thing referred to in section 6 of that Act which is done, and

(d)   any transactions referred to in section 14 of that Act which occur,

before the commencement of this section.

(3) Where a court, when granting a decree of judicial separation under the Act of 1989, orders that the ownership of the family home shall be vested in one of the spouses, it shall, unless it sees reason to the contrary, order that section 3(1) (prior consent of spouse to conveyance of interest in family home) of the Family Home Protection Act, 1976, shall not apply to any conveyance by that spouse of an interest in the home and, if the court so orders, the said section 3(1) shall have effect accordingly.

55 (Amends s 2 of the Child Abduction and Enforcement of Custody Orders Act, 1991)

SCHEDULE   Section 3

ENACTMENTS REPEALED

Year and Chapter or Number and Year	Short Title	Extent of Repeal
1844, c 81	Marriages (Ireland) Act 1844	In section 9, ', and that they are both of the full age of twenty-one years, or, when either of the parties shall be under the age of twenty-one years, that the consent of the person or persons whose consent to such marriage is required by law has been obtained thereto, or that there is no person having authority to give such consent, or that such party is a widower or widow, as the case may be'
		Sections 19 and 25
		In section 22, ', and that they are both of the full age of twenty-one years, or, where either of the parties shall be under the age of twenty-one years, that the consent of the person or persons whose consent to such marriage is required by law has been obtained thereto, or that there is no person having authority to give such consent, or that such party is a widower or widow, as the case may be'
1868, c 20	Legitimacy Declaration Act (Ireland) 1868	Section 1
1863, c 27	Marriage Law (Ireland) Amendment Act 1863	In section 4, the words from 'and when either of the Parties intending marriage' to 'whose consent to such Marriage is by Law required;'
		In Schedule (B), the fourth paragraph

Year and Chapter or Number and Year	Short Title	Extent of Repeal
1870, c 110	Matrimonial Causes and Marriage Law (Ireland) Amendment Act 1870	In section 35, the words 'Whenever a marriage shall not be had within three calendar months after the notice shall have been so given to the person so appointed as aforesaid, the notice, and any licence which may have been granted thereupon, shall be utterly void.' and the words ', and that they are both of the full age of twenty-one years, or, where either of the parties shall be under the age of twenty-one years, that the consent of the person or persons whose consent to such marriage is required by law has been obtained thereto, or that there is no person having authority to give such consent, or that such person is a widower or widow, as the case may be' Section 41
No 5 of 1957	Married Women's Status Act, 1957	Section 12
No 30 of 1972	Marriages Act, 1972	Sections 1 and 18
No 6 of 1989	Judicial Separation and Family Law Reform Act, 1989	Part II (other than section 25) and sections 39 and 40

Family Law (Divorce) Act, 1996

(1996 No 33)

ARRANGEMENT OF SECTIONS

PART I

PRELIMINARY AND GENERAL

PART II

THE OBTAINING OF A DECREE OF DIVORCE

PART III

PRELIMINARY AND ANCILLARY ORDERS IN OR AFTER PROCEEDINGS FOR DIVORCE

PART IV

INCOME TAX, CAPITAL ACQUISITIONS TAX, CAPITAL GAINS TAX, PROBATE TAX AND STAMP DUTY

PART V

MISCELLANEOUS

ACTS REFERRED TO

Adoption Acts 1952 to 1991
Capital Acquisitions Tax Act, 1976   1976, No 8

Capital Gains Tax Acts	
Censorship of Publications Act, 1929	1929, No 21
Criminal Damage Act, 1991	1991, No 31
Criminal Evidence Act, 1992	1992, No 12
Defence Act, 1954	1954, No 18
Domestic Violence Act, 1996	1996, No 1
Enforcement of Court Orders Act, 1940	1940, No 23
Family Home Protection Act, 1976	1976, No 27
Family Law Act, 1995	1995, No 26
Family Law (Maintenance of Spouses and Children) Act, 1976	1976, No 11
Finance (1909–10) Act, 1910	1920, c 8
Finance Act, 1972	1972, No 19
Finance Act, 1983	1983, No 15
Finance Act, 1993	1993, No 13
Finance Act, 1994	1994, No 13
Guardianship of Infants Act, 1964	1964, No 7
Income Tax Act, 1967	1967, No 6
Income Tax Acts	
Insurance Act, 1989	1989, No 3
Judicial Separation and Family Law Reform Act, 1989	1989, No 6
Maintenance Act, 1994	1994, No 28
Partition Act 1868	1868, c 40
Partition Act 1876	1876, c 17
Pensions Act, 1990	1990, No 25
Pensions (Amendment) Act, 1996	1996, No 18
Powers of Attorney Act, 1996	1996, No 12
Registration of Title Act, 1964	1964, No 16
Social Welfare Acts	
Status of Children Act, 1987	1987, No 26
Succession Act, 1965	1965, No 27

An Act to make provision for the exercise by the courts of the jurisdiction conferred by the Constitution to grant decrees of divorce, to enable the courts to make certain preliminary and ancillary orders in or after proceedings for divorce, to provide, as respects transfers of property of divorced spouses, for their exemption from, or for the abatement of certain taxes (including stamp duty) and to provide for related matters. [27 November 1996]

PART I

PRELIMINARY AND GENERAL

1 Short title and commencement

(1) This Act may be cited as the Family Law (Divorce) Act, 1996.

(2) This Act shall come into operation on the day that is 3 months after the date of its passing.

2 Interpretation

(1) In this Act, save where the context otherwise requires—

'the Act of 1964' means the Guardianship of Infants Act, 1964;
'the Act of 1965' means the Succession Act, 1965;

'the Act of 1976' means the Family Law (Maintenance of Spouses and Children) Act, 1976;

'the Act of 1989' means the Judicial Separation and Family Law Reform Act, 1989;

'the Act of 1995' means the Family Law Act, 1995;

'the Act of 1996' means the Domestic Violence Act, 1996;

'conveyance' includes a mortgage, lease, assent, transfer, disclaimer, release and any other disposition of property otherwise than by a will or a *donatio mortis causa* and also includes an enforceable agreement (whether conditional or unconditional) to make any such disposition;

'the court' shall be construed in accordance with section 38;

'decree of divorce' means a decree under section 5;

'decree of judicial separation' means a decree under section 3 of the Act of 1989;

'decree of nullity' means a decree granted by a court declaring a marriage to be null and void;

'dependent member of the family', in relation to a spouse, or the spouses, concerned, means any child—

(a) of both spouses or adopted by both spouses under the Adoption Acts 1952 to 1991, or in relation to whom both spouses are *in loco parentis*, or

(b) of either spouse or adopted by either spouse under those Acts, or in relation to whom either spouse is in *loco parentis*, where the other spouse, being aware that he or she is not the parent of the child, has treated the child as a member of the family,

who is under the age of 18 years or if the child has attained that age—

(i) is or will be or, if an order were made under this Act providing for periodical payments for the benefit of the child or for the provision of a lump sum for the child, would be receiving full-time education or instruction at any university, college, school or other educational establishment and is under the age of 23 years, or

(ii) has a mental or physical disability to such extent that it is not reasonably possible for the child to maintain himself or herself fully;

'family home' has the meaning assigned to it by section 2 of the Family Home Protection Act, 1976, with the modification that the references to a spouse in that section shall be construed as references to a spouse within the meaning of this Act;

'financial compensation order' has the meaning assigned to it by section 16;

'Land Registry' and 'Registry of Deeds' have the meanings assigned to them by the Registration of Title Act, 1964;

'lump sum order' means an order under section 13(1)(c);

'maintenance pending suit order' means an order under section 12;

'member', in relation to a pension scheme, means any person who, having been admitted to membership of the scheme under its rules, remains entitled to any benefit under the scheme;

'pension adjustment order' means an order under section 17;

'pension scheme' means—

(a) an occupational pension scheme (within the meaning of the Pensions Act, 1990), or

(b) (i) an annuity contract approved by the Revenue Commissioners under section 235 of the Income Tax Act, 1967, or a contract so approved under section 235A of that Act,

(ii) a trust scheme, or part of a trust scheme, so approved under subsection (4) of the said section 235 or subsection (5) of the said section 235A, or

(iii) a policy or contract of assurance approved by the Revenue Commissioners under Chapter II of Part I of the Finance Act, 1972, or

(c) any other scheme or arrangement (including a personal pension plan and a scheme or arrangement established by or pursuant to statute or instrument made under statute other than under the Social Welfare Acts) that provides or is intended to provide either or both of the following, that is to say:

(i) benefits for a person who is a member of the scheme or arrangement ('the member') upon retirement at normal pensionable age or upon earlier or later retirement or upon leaving, or upon the ceasing of, the relevant employment,

(ii) benefits for the widow, widower or dependents of the member, or for any other persons, on the death of the member;

'periodical payments order' and 'secured periodical payments order' have the meanings assigned to them by section 13;

'property adjustment order' has the meaning assigned to it by section 14;

'trustees', in relation to a scheme that is established under a trust, means the trustees of the scheme and, in relation to a pension scheme not so established, means the persons who administer the scheme.

(2) In this Act, where the context so requires—

(a) a reference to a marriage includes a reference to a marriage that has been dissolved under this Act,

(b) a reference to a remarriage includes a reference to a marriage that takes place after a marriage that has been dissolved under this Act,

(c) a reference to a spouse includes a reference to a person who is a party to a marriage that has been dissolved under this Act,

(d) a reference to a family includes a reference to a family as respects which the marriage of the spouses concerned has been dissolved under this Act,

(e) a reference to an application to a court by a person on behalf of a dependent member of the family includes a reference to such an application by such a member and a reference to a payment, the securing of a payment, or the assignment of an interest, to a person for the benefit of a dependent member of the family includes a reference to a payment, the securing of a payment, or the assignment of an interest, to such a member,

and cognate words shall be construed accordingly.

(3) In this Act—

(a) a reference to any enactment shall, unless the context otherwise requires, be construed as a reference to that enactment as amended or extended by or under any subsequent enactment including this Act,

(b) a reference to a Part or section is a reference to a Part or section of this Act unless it is indicated that reference to some other enactment is intended,

(c) a reference to a subsection, paragraph, subparagraph or clause is a reference to the subsection, paragraph, subparagraph or clause of the provision in which the reference occurs unless it is indicated that reference to some other provision is intended.

3   Repeal

Section 14(2) of the Censorship of Publications Act, 1929, is hereby repealed.

4 Expenses

The expenses incurred by the Minister for Equality and Law Reform, the Minister for Health or the Minister for Justice in the administration of this Act shall, to such extent as may be sanctioned by the Minister for Finance, be paid out of moneys provided by the Oireachtas.

PART II

THE OBTAINING OF A DECREE OF DIVORCE

5 Grant of decree of divorce and custody etc, of children

(1) Subject to the provisions of this Act, where, on application to it in that behalf by either of the spouses concerned, the court is satisfied that—

    (a) at the date of the institution of the proceedings, the spouses have lived apart from one another for a period of, or periods amounting to, at least four years during the previous five years,

    (b) there is no reasonable prospect of a reconciliation between the spouses, and

    (c) such provision as the court considers proper having regard to the circumstances exists or will be made for the spouses and any dependent members of the family,

the court may, in exercise of the jurisdiction conferred by Article 41.3.2° of the Constitution, grant a decree of divorce in respect of the marriage concerned.

(2) Upon the grant of a decree of divorce, the court may, where appropriate, give such directions under section 11 of the Act of 1964 as it considers proper regarding the welfare (within the meaning of that Act), custody of, or right of access to, any dependent member of the family concerned who is an infant (within the meaning of that Act) as if an application has been made to it in that behalf under that section.

6 Safeguards to ensure applicant's awareness of alternatives to divorce proceedings and to assist attempts at reconciliation

(1) In this section 'the applicant' means a person who has applied, is applying or proposes to apply to the court for the grant of a decree of divorce.

(2) If a solicitor is acting for the applicant, the solicitor shall, prior to the institution of the proceedings concerned under section 5—

    (a) discuss with the applicant the possibility of a reconciliation and give to him or her the names and addresses of persons qualified to help to effect a reconciliation between spouses who have become estranged,

    (b) discuss with the applicant the possibility of engaging in mediation to help to effect a separation (if the spouses are not separated) or a divorce on a basis agreed between the applicant and the other spouse and give to the applicant the names and addresses of persons qualified to provide a mediation service for spouses who have become estranged, and

    (c) discuss with the applicant the possibility (where appropriate) of effecting a separation by means of a deed or agreement in writing executed or made by the applicant and the other spouse and providing for their separation.

(3) Such a solicitor shall also ensure that the applicant is aware of judicial separation as an alternative to divorce where a decree of judicial separation in relation to the applicant and the other spouse is not in force.

(4) If a solicitor is acting for the applicant—

   (a) the originating document by which the proceedings under section 5 are instituted shall be accompanied by a certificate signed by the solicitor indicating, if it be the case, that he or she has complied with subsection (2) and, if appropriate, subsection (3) in relation to the matter and, if the document is not so accompanied, the court may adjourn the proceedings for such period as it considers reasonable to enable the solicitor to engage in the discussions specified in subsection (2), and, if appropriate, to make the applicant aware of judicial separation,

   (b) if the solicitor has complied with paragraph (a), any copy of the originating document aforesaid served on any person or left in an office of the court shall be accompanied by a copy of the certificate aforesaid.

(5) A certificate under subsection (4)(a) shall be in a form prescribed by rules of court or a form to the like effect.

(6) The Minister may make regulations to allow for the establishment of a Register of Professional Organisations whose members are qualified to assist the parties involved in effecting a reconciliation, such register to show the names of members of those organisations and procedures to be put in place for the organisations involved to regularly update the membership lists.

7   Safeguards to ensure respondent's awareness of alternatives to divorce proceedings and to assist at reconciliation

(1) In this section 'the respondent' means a person who is the respondent in proceedings in the court under section 5.

(2) If a solicitor is acting for the respondent, the solicitor shall, as soon as may be after receiving instructions from the respondent in relation to the proceedings concerned under section 5—

   (a) discuss with the respondent the possibility of a reconciliation and give to him or her the names and addresses of persons qualified to effect a reconciliation between spouses who have become estranged,

   (b) discuss with the respondent the possibility of engaging in mediation to help to effect a separation (if the spouses are not separated) or a divorce on a basis agreed between the respondent and the other spouse and give to the respondent the names and addresses of persons qualified to provide a mediation service for spouses who have become estranged, and

   (c) discuss with the respondent the possibility (where appropriate) of effecting a separation by means of a deed or agreement in writing executed or made by the applicant and the other spouse and providing for their separation.

(3) Such a solicitor shall also ensure that the respondent is aware of judicial separation as an alternative to divorce where a decree of judicial separation is not in force in relation to the respondent and the other spouse.

(4) If a solicitor is acting for the respondent—

   (a) the memorandum or other document delivered to the appropriate officer of the court for the purpose of the entry of an appearance by the respondent in proceedings under section 5 shall be accompanied by a certificate signed by the solicitor indicating, if it be the case, that the solicitor has complied with subsection (2) and, if appropriate, subsection (3) in relation to the matter and, if the document is not so accompanied, the court may adjourn the proceedings for such period as it considers reasonable to enable the solicitor to engage in the discussions specified in subsection (2) and, if appropriate, to make the applicant aware of judicial separation,

  (b) if paragraph (a) is complied with, any copy of the document aforesaid given or sent to the other party to the proceedings or his or her solicitor shall be accompanied by a copy of the relevant certificate aforesaid.

(5) A certificate under subsection (4)(a) shall be in a form prescribed by rules of court or a form to the like effect.

8 Adjournment of proceedings to assist reconciliation or agreements on the terms of the divorce

(1) Where an application is made to the court for the grant of a decree of divorce, the court shall give consideration to the possibility of a reconciliation between the spouses concerned and, accordingly, may adjourn the proceedings at any time for the purpose of enabling attempts to be made by the spouses, if they both so wish, to effect such a reconciliation with or without the assistance of a third party.

(2) Where, in proceedings under section 5, it appears to the court that a reconciliation between the spouses cannot be effected, it may adjourn or further adjourn the proceedings for the purpose of enabling attempts to be made by the spouses, if they both so wish, to reach agreement, with or without the assistance of a third party, on some or all of the terms of the proposed divorce.

(3) If proceedings are adjourned pursuant to subsection (1) or (2), either or both of the spouses may at any time request that the hearing of the proceedings be resumed as soon as may be and, if such a request is made, the court shall, subject to any other power of the court to adjourn proceedings, resume the hearing.

(4) The powers conferred by this section are additional to any other power of the court to adjourn proceedings.

(5) Where the court adjourns proceedings under this section, it may, at its discretion, advise the spouses concerned to seek the assistance of a third party in relation to the effecting of a reconciliation between the spouses or the reaching of agreement between them on some or all of the terms of the proposed divorce.

9 Non-admissibility as evidence of certain communications relating to reconciliation, separation or divorce

An oral or written communication between either of the spouses concerned and a third party for the purpose of seeking assistance to effect a reconciliation or to reach agreement between them on some or all of the terms of a separation or a divorce (whether or not made in the presence or with the knowledge of the other spouse), and any record of such a communication, made or caused to be made by either of the spouses concerned or such a third party, shall not be admissible as evidence in any court.

10 Effect of decree of divorce

(1) Where the court grants a decree of divorce, the marriage, the subject of the decree, is thereby dissolved and a party to that marriage may marry again.

(2) For the avoidance of doubt, it is hereby declared that the grant of a decree of divorce shall not affect the right of the father and mother of an infant, under section 6 of the Act of 1964, to be guardians of the infant jointly.

PART III

PRELIMINARY AND ANCILLARY ORDERS IN OR AFTER PROCEEDINGS FOR DIVORCE

11   Preliminary orders in proceedings for divorce

Where an application is made to the court for the grant of a decree of divorce, the court, before deciding whether to grant or refuse to grant the decree, may, in the same proceedings and without the institution of proceedings under the Act concerned, if it appears to the court to be proper to do so, make one or more of the following orders—

   (a)   a safety order, a barring order, an interim barring order or a protection order under the Act of 1996,
   (b)   an order under section 11 of the Act of 1964,
   (c)   an order under section 5 or 9 of the Family Home Protection Act, 1976.

12   Maintenance pending suit orders

(1) Where an application is made to the court for the grant of a decree of divorce, the court may make an order for maintenance pending suit, that is to say, an order requiring either of the spouses concerned to make to the other spouse such periodical payments or lump sum payments for his or her support and, where appropriate, to make to such person as may be specified in the order such periodical payments for the benefit of such (if any) dependent member of the family and, as respects periodical payments, for such period beginning not earlier than the date of the application and ending not later than the date of its determination, as the court considers proper and specifies in the order.

(2) The court may provide that payments under an order under this section shall be subject to such terms and conditions as it considers appropriate and specifies in the order.

13   Periodical payments and lump sum orders

(1) On granting a decree of divorce or at any time thereafter, the court, on application to it in that behalf by either of the spouses concerned or by a person on behalf of a dependent member of the family, may, during the lifetime of the other spouse, or, as the case may be, the spouse concerned, make one or more of the following orders, that is to say—

   (a) a periodical payments order, that is to say—
      (i)   an order that either of the spouses shall make to the other spouse such periodical payments of such amount, during such period and at such times as may be specified in the order, or
      (ii) an order that either of the spouses shall make to such person as may be so specified for the benefit of such (if any) dependent member of the family such periodical payments of such amount, during such period and at such times as may be so specified,
   (b) a secured periodical payments order, that is to say—

    (i)   an order that either of the spouses shall secure, to the satisfaction of the court, to the other spouse such periodical payments of such amounts, during such period and at such times as may be so specified, or

    (ii)   an order that either of the spouses shall secure, to the satisfaction of the court, to such persons as may be so specified for the benefit of such (if any) dependent member of the family such periodical payments of such amounts, during such period and at such times as may be so specified,

(c) (i)   an order that either of the spouses shall make to the other spouse a lump sum payment or lump sum payments of such amount or amounts and at such time or times as may be so specified, or

    (ii)   an order that either of the spouses shall make to such person as may be so specified for the benefit of such (if any) dependent member of the family a lump sum payment or lump sum payments of such amount or amounts and at such time or times as may be so specified.

(2) The court may—

  (a) order a spouse to pay a lump sum to the other spouse to meet any liabilities or expenses reasonably incurred by that other spouse before the making of an application by that other spouse for an order under subsection (1) in maintaining himself or herself or any dependent member of the family, or

  (b) order a spouse to pay a lump sum to such person as may be specified to meet any liabilities or expenses reasonably incurred by or for the benefit of a dependent member of the family before the making of an application on behalf of the member for an order under subsection (1).

(3) An order under this section for the payment of a lump sum may provide for the payment of the lump sum by instalments of such amounts as may be specified in the order and may require the payment of the instalments to be secured to the satisfaction of the court.

(4) The period specified in an order under paragraph (a) or (b) of subsection (1) shall begin not earlier than the date of the application for the order and shall end not later than the death of the spouse, or any dependent member of the family, in whose favour the order is made or the other spouse concerned.

(5) (a) Upon the remarriage of the spouse in whose favour an order is made under paragraph (a) or (b) of subsection (1), the order shall, to the extent that it applies to that spouse, cease to have effect, except as respects payments due under it on the date of the remarriage.

  (b) If, after the grant of a decree of divorce, either of the spouses concerned remarries, the court shall not, by reference to that decree, make an order under subsection (1) in favour of that spouse.

(6) (a) Where a court makes an order under subsection (1)(a), it shall in the same proceedings, subject to paragraph (b), make an attachment of earnings order (within the meaning of the Act of 1976) to secure payments under the first mentioned order if it is satisfied that the person against whom the order is made is a person to whom earnings (within the meaning aforesaid) fall to be paid.

  (b) Before deciding whether to make or refuse to make an attachment of earnings order by virtue of paragraph (a), the court shall give the spouse concerned an opportunity to make the representations specified in paragraph (c) in relation to the matter and shall have regard to any such representations made by that spouse.

(c) The representations referred to in paragraph (b) are representations relating to the questions—
  (i) whether the spouse concerned is a person to whom such earnings as aforesaid fall to be paid, and
  (ii) whether he or she would make the payments to which the relevant order under subsection (1)(a) relates.
(d) References in this subsection to an order under subsection (1)(a) include references to such an order as varied or affirmed on appeal from the court concerned or varied under section 22.

14   Property adjustment orders

(1) On granting a decree of divorce or at any time thereafter, the court, on application to it in that behalf by either of the spouses concerned or by a person on behalf of a dependent member of the family, may, during the lifetime of the other spouse or, as the case may be, the spouse concerned, make a property adjustment order, that is to say, an order providing for one or more of the following matters:

(a) the transfer by either of the spouses to the other spouse, to any dependent member of the family or to any other specified person for the benefit of such a member of specified property, being property to which the first-mentioned spouse is entitled either in possession or reversion,
(b) the settlement to the satisfaction of the court of specified property, being property to which either of the spouses is so entitled as aforesaid, for the benefit of the other spouse and of any dependent member of the family or of any or all of those persons,
(c) the variation for the benefit of either of the spouses and of any dependent member of the family or of any or all of those persons of any ante-nuptial or post-nuptial settlement (including such a settlement made by will or codicil) made on the spouses,
(d) the extinguishment or reduction of the interest of either of the spouses under any such settlement.

(2) An order under paragraph (b), (c) or (d) may restrict to a specified extent or exclude the application of section 22 in relation to the order.

(3) If, after the grant of a decree of divorce, either of the spouses concerned remarries, the court shall not, by reference to that decree, make a property adjustment order in favour of that spouse.

(4) Where a property adjustment order is made in relation to land, a copy of the order certified to be a true copy by the registrar or clerk of the court concerned shall, as appropriate, be lodged by him or her in the Land Registry for registration pursuant to section 69(1)(h) of the Registration of Title Act, 1964, in a register maintained under that Act or be registered in the Registry of Deeds.

(5) Where—

(a) a person is directed by an order under this section to execute a deed or other instrument in relation to land, and
(b) the person refuses or neglects to comply with the direction or, for any other reason, the court considers it necessary to do so,

the court may order another person to execute the deed or instrument in the name of the first-mentioned person, and a deed or other instrument executed by a person in the name of another person pursuant to an order under this subsection shall be as valid as if it had been executed by that other person.

(6) Any costs incurred in complying with a property adjustment order shall be borne, as the court may determine, by either of the spouses concerned, or by both of them in such proportions as the court may determine, and shall be so borne in such manner as the court may determine.

(7) This section shall not apply in relation to a family home in which, following the grant of a decree of divorce, either of the spouses concerned, having remarried, ordinarily resides with his or her spouse.

15   Miscellaneous ancillary orders

(1) On granting a decree of divorce or at any time thereafter, the court, on application to it in that behalf by either of the spouses concerned or by a person on behalf of a dependent member of the family, may, during the lifetime of the other spouse or, as the case may be, the spouse concerned, make one or more of the following orders:

- (a) an order—
  - (i)   providing for the conferral on one spouse either for life or for such other period (whether definite or contingent) as the court may specify of the right to occupy the family home to the exclusion of the other spouse, or
  - (ii) directing the sale of the family home subject to such conditions (if any) as the court considers proper and providing for the disposal of the proceeds of the sale between the spouses and any other person having an interest therein,
- (b) an order under section 36 of the Act of 1995,
- (c) an order under section 5, 7 or 9 of the Family Home Protection Act, 1976,
- (d) an order under section 2, 3, 4 or 5 of the Act of 1996,
- (e) an order for the partition of property or under the Partition Act 1868, and the Partition Act 1876,
- (f) an order under section 11 of the Act of 1964,

and, for the purposes of this section, in paragraphs (b), (c) and (d), a reference to a spouse in a statute referred to in paragraph (b), (c) or (d) shall be construed as including a reference to a person who is a party to a marriage that has been dissolved under this Act.

(2) The court, in exercising its jurisdiction under subsection (1) (a), shall have regard to the welfare of the spouses and any dependent member of the family and, in particular, shall take into consideration—

- (a) that, where a decree of divorce is granted, it is not possible for the spouses concerned to reside together, and
- (b) that proper and secure accommodation should, where practicable, be provided for a spouse who is wholly or mainly dependent on the other spouse and for any dependent member of the family.

(3) Subsection (1) (a) shall not apply in relation to a family home in which, following the grant of a decree of divorce, either of the spouses concerned, having remarried, ordinarily resides with his or her spouse.

16   Financial compensation orders

(1) Subject to the provisions of this section, on granting a decree of divorce or at any time thereafter, the court, on application to it in that behalf by either of the spouses concerned or by a person on behalf of a dependent member of the family, may, during the lifetime of the other spouse or, as the case may be, the spouse concerned, if it considers—

  (a) that the financial security of the spouse making the application ('the applicant') or the dependent member of the family ('the member') can be provided for either wholly or in part by so doing, or
  (b) that the forfeiture, by reason of the decree of divorce, by the applicant or the member, as the case may be, of the opportunity or possibility of acquiring a benefit (for example, a benefit under a pension scheme) can be compensated for wholly or in part by so doing,

make a financial compensation order, that is to say, an order requiring the other spouse to do one or more of the following:

  (i)   to effect such a policy of life insurance for the benefit of the applicant or the member as may be specified in the order,
  (ii) to assign the whole or a specified part of the interest of the other spouse in a policy of life insurance effected by that other spouse or both of the spouses to the applicant or to such person as may be specified in the order for the benefit of the member,
  (iii) to make or to continue to make to the person by whom a policy of life insurance is or was issued the payments which that other spouse or both of the spouses is or are required to make under the terms of the policy.

(2) (a) The court may make a financial compensation order in addition to or in substitution in whole or in part for orders under section 13, 14, 15 or 17 and in deciding whether or not to make such an order it shall have regard to whether proper provision having regard to the circumstances exists or can be made for the spouse concerned or the dependent member of the family concerned by orders under those sections.
   (b) An order under this section shall cease to have effect on the re-marriage or death of the applicant in so far as it relates to the applicant.
   (c) The court shall not make an order under this section in favour of a spouse who has remarried.
   (d) An order under section 22 in relation to an order under paragraph (i) or (ii) of subsection (1) may make such provision (if any) as the court considers appropriate in relation to the disposal of—
      (i)   an amount representing any accumulated value of the insurance policy effected pursuant to the order under the said paragraph (i), or
      (ii) the interest or the part of the interest to which the order under the said paragraph (ii) relates.

17   Pension adjustment orders

(1) In this section, save where the context otherwise requires—

   'the Act of 1990' means the Pensions Act, 1990;
   'active member' in relation to a scheme, means a member of the scheme who is in reckonable service;

'actuarial value' means the equivalent cash value of a benefit (including, where appropriate, provision for any revaluation of such benefit) under a scheme calculated by reference to appropriate financial assumptions and making due allowance for the probability of survival to normal pensionable age and thereafter in accordance with normal life expectancy on the assumption that the member concerned of the scheme, at the effective date of calculation, is in a normal state of health having regard to his or her age;

'approved arrangement', in relation to the trustees of a scheme, means an arrangement whereby the trustees, on behalf of the person for whom the arrangement is made, effect policies or contracts of insurance that are approved of by the Revenue Commissioners with, and make the appropriate payments under the policies or contracts to, one or more undertakings;

'contingent benefit' means a benefit payment under a scheme, other than a payment under subsection (7) to or for one or more of the following, that is to say, the widow or the widower and any dependents of the member spouse concerned and the personal representative of the member spouse, if the member spouse dies while in relevant employment and before attaining any normal pensionable age provided for under the rules of the scheme;

'defined contribution scheme' means a scheme which, under its rules, provides retirement benefit, the rate or amount of which is in total directly determined by the amount of the contributions paid by or in respect of the member of the scheme concerned and includes a scheme the contributions under which are used, directly or indirectly, to provide—

(a) contingent benefit, and

(b) retirement benefit the rate or amount of which is in total directly determined by the part of the contributions aforesaid that is used for the provision of the retirement benefit,

'designated benefit', in relation to a pension adjustment order, means an amount determined by the trustees of the scheme concerned, in accordance with relevant guidelines, and by reference to the period and the percentage of the retirement benefit specified in the order concerned under subsection (2);

'member spouse', in relation to a scheme, means a spouse who is a member of the scheme;

'normal pensionable age' means the earliest age at which a member of a scheme is entitled to receive benefits under the rules of the scheme on retirement from relevant employment, disregarding any such rules providing for early retirement on grounds of ill health or otherwise;

'occupational pension scheme' has the meaning assigned to it by section 2(1) of the Act of 1990;

'reckonable service' means service in relevant employment during membership of any scheme;

'relevant guidelines' means any relevant guidelines for the time being in force under paragraph (c) or (cc) of section 10(1) of the Act of 1990;

'relevant employment', in relation to a scheme, means any employment (or any period treated as employment) or any period of self-employment to which a scheme applies;

'retirement benefit', in relation to a scheme, means all benefits (other than contingent benefits) payable under the scheme;

'rules', in relation to a scheme, means the provisions of the scheme, by whatever name called;

'scheme' means a pension scheme;

'transfer amount' shall be construed in accordance with subsection (4);

'undertaking' has the meaning assigned to it by the Insurance Act, 1989.

(2) Subject to the provisions of this section, where a decree of divorce ('the decree') has been granted, the court, if it so thinks fit, may, in relation to retirement benefit under a scheme of which one of the spouses concerned is a member, on application to it in that behalf at the time of the making of the order for the decree or at any time thereafter during the lifetime of the member spouse by either of the spouses or by a person on behalf of a dependent member of the family, make an order providing for the payment, in accordance with the provisions of this section, to either of the following, as the court may determine, that is to say—

(a) the other spouse and, in the case of the death of that spouse, his or her personal representative, and

(b) such person as may be specified in the order for the benefit of a person who is, and for so long only as he or she remains, a dependent member of the family,

of a benefit consisting, either, as the court may determine, of the whole, or such part as the court considers appropriate, of that part of the retirement benefit that is payable (or which, but for the making of the order for the decree, would have been payable) under the scheme and has accrued at the time of the making of the order for the decree and, for the purpose of determining the benefit, the order shall specify—

(i) the period of reckonable service of the member spouse prior to the granting of the decree to be taken into account, and

(ii) the percentage of the retirement benefit accrued during that period to be paid to the person referred to in paragraph (a) or (b), as the case may be.

(3) Subject to the provisions of this section, where a decree of divorce ('the decree') has been granted, the court, if it so thinks fit, may, in relation to a contingent benefit under a scheme of which one of the spouses concerned is a member, on application to it in that behalf not more than one year after the making of the order for the decree by either of the spouses or by a person on behalf of a dependent member of the family concerned, make an order providing for the payment, upon the death of the member spouse, to either of the following, or to both of them in such proportions as the court may determine, that is to say—

(a) the other spouse, and

(b) such person as may be specified in the order for the benefit of a dependent member of the family,

of, either, as the court may determine, the whole, or such part (expressed as a percentage) as the court considers appropriate, of that part of any contingent benefit that is payable (or which, but for the making of the order for the decree, would have been payable) under the scheme.

(4) Where the court makes an order under subsection (2) in favour of a spouse and payment of the designated benefit concerned has not commenced, the spouse in whose favour the order is made shall be entitled to the application in accordance with subsection (5) of an amount of money from the scheme concerned (in this section referred to as a 'transfer amount') equal to the value of the designated benefit, such amount being determined by the trustees of the scheme in accordance with relevant guidelines.

(5) Subject to subsection (17), where the court makes an order under subsection (2) in favour of a spouse and payment of the designated benefit concerned has not

commenced, the trustees of the scheme concerned shall, for the purpose of giving effect to the order—

(a) on application to them in that behalf at the time of the making of the order or at any time thereafter by the spouse in whose favour the order was made ('the spouse'), and

(b) on the furnishing to them by the spouse of such information as they may reasonably require,

apply in accordance with relevant guidelines the transfer amount calculated in accordance with those guidelines either—

(i) if the trustees and the spouse so agree, in providing a benefit for or in respect of the spouse under the scheme aforesaid that is of the same actuarial value as the transfer amount concerned, or

(ii) in making a payment either to—

(I) such other occupational pension scheme, being a scheme the trustees of which agree to accept the payment, or

(II) in the discharge of any payment falling to be made by the trustees under any such other approved arrangement,

as may be determined by the spouse.

(6) Subject to subsection (17), where the court makes an order under subsection (2) in relation to a defined contribution scheme and an application has not been brought under subsection (5), the trustees of the scheme may, for the purpose of giving effect to the order, if they so think fit, apply in accordance with relevant guidelines the transfer amount calculated in accordance with those guidelines, in making a payment to—

(a) such other occupational pension scheme, being a scheme the trustees of which agree to accept the payment, or

(b) in the discharge of any payment falling to be made by the trustees under such other approved arrangement,

as may be determined by the trustees.

(7) Subject to subsection (17), where—

(a) the court makes an order under subsection (2), and

(b) the member spouse concerned dies before payment of the designated benefit concerned has commenced,

the trustees shall, for the purpose of giving effect to the order, within 3 months of the death of the member spouse, provide for the payment to the person in whose favour the order was made of an amount that is equal to the transfer amount calculated in accordance with relevant guidelines.

(8) Subject to subsection (17), where—

(a) the court makes an order under subsection (2), and

(b) the member spouse concerned ceases to be a member of the scheme otherwise than on death,

the trustees may, for the purpose of giving effect to the order, if they so think fit, apply, in accordance with relevant guidelines, the transfer amount calculated in accordance with those guidelines either, as the trustees may determine—

    (i) if the trustees and the person in whose favour the order is made ('the person') so agree, in providing a benefit for or in respect of the person under the scheme aforesaid that is of the same actuarial value as the transfer amount concerned, or

    (ii) in making a payment, either to—

      (I) such other occupational pension scheme, being a scheme the trustees of which agree to accept the payment, or

      (II) in the discharge of any payment falling to be made under such other approved arrangement,

    as may be determined by the trustees.

(9) Subject to subsection (17), where—

  (a) the court makes an order under subsection (2) in favour of a spouse ('the spouse'),

  (b) the spouse dies before the payment of the designated benefit has commenced,

the trustees shall, within 3 months of the death of the spouse, provide for the payment to the personal representative of the spouse of an amount equal to the transfer amount calculated in accordance with relevant guidelines.

(10) Subject to subsection (17), where—

  (a) the court makes an order under subsection (2) in favour of a spouse ('the spouse'), and

  (b) the spouse dies after payment of the designated benefit has commenced,

the trustees shall, within 3 months of the death of the spouse, provide for the payment to the personal representative of the spouse of an amount equal to the actuarial value, calculated in accordance with relevant guidelines, of the part of the designated benefit which, but for the death of the spouse, would have been payable to the spouse during the lifetime of the member spouse.

(11) Where—

  (a) the court makes an order under subsection (2) for the benefit of a dependent member of the family ('the person'), and

  (b) the person dies before payment of the designated benefit has commenced,

the order shall cease to have effect in so far as it relates to that person.

(12) Where—

  (a) the court makes an order under subsection (2) or (3) in relation to an occupational pension scheme, and

  (b) the trustees of the scheme concerned have not applied the transfer amount concerned in accordance with subsection (5), (6), (7), (8) or (9), and

  (c) after the making of the order, the member spouse ceases to be an active member of the scheme,

the trustees shall, within 12 months of the cessation, notify the registrar or clerk of the court concerned and the other spouse of the cessation.

(13) Where the trustees of a scheme apply a transfer amount under subsection (6) or (8), they shall notify the spouse (not being the spouse who is the member spouse) or other person concerned and the registrar or clerk of the court concerned of the application and shall give to that spouse or other person concerned particulars of the scheme or undertaking concerned and of the transfer amount.

(14) Where the court makes an order under subsection (2) or (3) for the payment of a designated benefit or a contingent benefit, as the case may be, the benefit shall be payable or the transfer amount concerned applied out of the resources of the scheme concerned and, unless otherwise provided for in the order or relevant guidelines, shall be payable in accordance with the rules of the scheme or, as the case may be, applied in accordance with relevant guidelines.

(15) Where the court makes an order under subsection (2), the amount of the retirement benefit payable, in accordance with the rules of the scheme concerned to, or to or in respect of, the member spouse shall be reduced by the amount of the designated benefit payable pursuant to the order.

(16) (a) Where the court makes an order under subsection (3), the amount of the contingent benefit payable, in accordance with the rules of the scheme concerned in respect of the member spouse shall be reduced by an amount equal to the contingent benefit payable pursuant to the order.

   (b) Where the court makes an order under subsection (2) and the member spouse concerned dies before payment of the designated benefit concerned has commenced, the amount of the contingent benefit payable in respect of the member spouse in accordance with the rules of the scheme concerned shall be reduced by the amount of the payment made under subsection (7).

(17) Where, pursuant to an order under subsection (2), the trustees of a scheme make a payment or apply a transfer amount under subsection (5), (6), (7), (8), (9) or (10), they shall be discharged from any obligation to make any further payment or apply any transfer amount under any other of those subsections in respect of the benefit payable pursuant to the order.

(18) A person who makes an application under subsection (2) or (3) or an application for an order under section 22(2) in relation to an order under subsection (2) shall give notice thereof to the trustees of the scheme concerned and, in deciding whether to make the order concerned and in determining the provisions of the order, the court shall have regard to any representations made by any person to whom notice of the application has been given under this section or section 40.

(19) An order under subsection (3) shall cease to have effect on the death or remarriage of the person in whose favour it was made in so far as it relates to that person.

(20) The court may, in a pension adjustment order or by order made under this subsection after the making of a pension adjustment order, give to the trustees of the scheme concerned such directions as it considers appropriate for the purposes of the pension adjustment order including directions compliance with which occasions non-compliance with the rules of the scheme concerned or the Act of 1990, and a trustee of a scheme shall not be liable in any court or other tribunal for any loss or damage caused by his or her non-compliance with the rules of the scheme or with the Act of 1990 if the non-compliance was occasioned by his or her compliance with a direction of the court under this subsection.

(21) The registrar or clerk of the court concerned shall cause a copy of a pension adjustment order to be served on the trustees of the scheme concerned.

(22) (a) Any costs incurred by the trustees of a scheme under subsection (18) or in complying with a pension adjustment order or a direction under subsection (20) or (25) shall be borne, as the court may determine, by the member spouse or by the other person concerned or by both of them in such

proportion as the court may determine and, in the absence of such determination, those costs shall be borne by them equally.

(b) Where a person fails to pay an amount in accordance with paragraph (a) to the trustees of the scheme concerned, the court may, on application to it in that behalf by the trustees, order that the amount be deducted from the amount of any benefit payable to the person under the scheme or pursuant to an order under subsection (2) or (3) and be paid to the trustees.

(23) (a) The court shall not make a pension adjustment order in favour of a spouse who has remarried.

(b) The court may make a pension adjustment order in addition to or in substitution in whole or in part for an order or orders under section 13, 14, 15 or 16 and, in deciding whether or not to make a pension adjustment order, the court shall have regard to the question whether proper provision, having regard to the circumstances, exists or can be made for the spouse concerned or the dependent member of the family concerned by an order or orders under any of those sections.

(24) Section 54 of the Act of 1990 and any regulations under that section shall apply with any necessary modifications to a scheme if proceedings for the grant of a decree of divorce to which a member spouse is a party have been instituted and shall continue to apply notwithstanding the grant of a decree of divorce in the proceedings.

(25) For the purposes of this Act, the court may, of its own motion, and shall, if so requested by either of the spouses concerned or any other person concerned, direct the trustees of the scheme concerned to provide the spouses or that other person and the court, within a specified period of time—

(a) with a calculation of the value and the amount, determined in accordance with relevant guidelines, of the retirement benefit, or contingent benefit, concerned that is payable (or which, but for the making of the order for the decree of divorce concerned, would have been payable) under the scheme and has accrued at the time of the making of that order, and

(b) with a calculation of the amount of the contingent benefit concerned that is payable (or which, but for the making of the order for the decree of divorce concerned, would have been payable) under the scheme.

(26) An order under this section may restrict to a specified extent or exclude the application of section 22 in relation to the order.

18   Orders for provision for spouse out of estate of other spouse

(1) Subject to the provisions of this section, where one of the spouses in respect of whom a decree of divorce has been granted dies, the court, on application to it in that behalf by the other spouse ('the applicant') not more than 6 months after representation is first granted under the Act of 1965 in respect of the estate of the deceased spouse, may by order make such provision for the applicant out of the estate of the deceased spouse as it considers appropriate having regard to the rights of any other person having an interest in the matter and specifies in the order if it is satisfied that proper provision in the circumstances was not made for the applicant during the lifetime of the deceased spouse under section 13, 14, 15, 16 or 17 for any reason (other than conduct referred to in subsection (2)(i) of section 20 of the applicant).

(2) The court shall not make an order under this section in favour of a spouse who has remarried since the granting of the decree of divorce concerned.

(3) In considering whether to make an order under this section the court shall have regard to all the circumstances of the case including—

    (a) any order under paragraph (c) of section 13(1) or a property adjustment order in favour of the applicant, and

    (b) any devise or bequest made by the deceased spouse to the applicant.

(4) The provision made for the applicant concerned by an order under this section together with any provision made for the applicant by an order referred to in subsection (3)(a) (the value of which for the purposes of this subsection shall be its value on the date of the order) shall not exceed in total the share (if any) of the applicant in the estate of the deceased spouse to which the applicant was entitled or (if the deceased spouse died intestate as to the whole or part of his or her estate) would have been entitled under the Act of 1965 if the marriage had not been dissolved.

(5) Notice of an application under this section shall be given by the applicant to the spouse (if any) of the deceased spouse concerned and to such (if any) other persons as the court may direct and, in deciding whether to make the order concerned and in determining the provisions of the order, the court shall have regard to any representations made by the spouse of the deceased spouse and any other such persons as aforesaid.

(6) The personal representative of a deceased spouse in respect of whom a decree of divorce has been granted shall make a reasonable attempt to ensure that notice of his or her death is brought to the attention of the other spouse concerned and, where an application is made under this section, the personal representative of the deceased spouse shall not, without the leave of the court, distribute any of the estate of that spouse until the court makes or refuses to make an order under this section.

(7) Where the personal representative of a deceased spouse in respect of whom a decree of divorce has been granted gives notice of his or her death to the other spouse concerned ('the spouse') and—

    (a) the spouse intends to apply to the court for an order under this section,

    (b) the spouse has applied for such an order and the application is pending, or

    (c) an order has been made under this section in favour of the spouse,

the spouse shall, not later than one month after the receipt of the notice, notify the personal representative of such intention, application or order, as the case may be, and, if he or she does not do so, the personal representative shall be at liberty to distribute the assets of the deceased spouse, or any part thereof, amongst the parties entitled thereto.

(8) The personal representative shall not be liable to the spouse for the assets or any part thereof so distributed unless, at the time of such distribution, he or she had notice of the intention, application or order aforesaid.

(9) Nothing in subsection (7) or (8) shall prejudice the right of the spouse to follow any such assets into the hands of any person who may have received them.

(10) On granting a decree of divorce or at any time thereafter, the court, on application to it in that behalf by either of the spouses concerned, may, during the lifetime of the other spouse or, as the case may be, the spouse concerned, if it considers it just to do so, make an order that either or both spouses shall not, on the death of either of them, be entitled to apply for an order under this section.

19   Orders for sale of property

(1) Where the court makes a secured periodical payments order, a lump sum order or a property adjustment order, thereupon, or at any time thereafter, it may make an order directing the sale of such property as may be specified in the order, being property in which, or in the proceeds of sale of which, either or both of the spouses concerned has or have a beneficial interest, either in possession or reversion.

(2) The jurisdiction conferred on the court by subsection (1) shall not be so exercised as to affect a right to occupy the family home of the spouse concerned that is enjoyed by virtue of an order under this Part.

(3) (a)   An order under subsection (1) may contain such consequential or supplementary provisions as the court considers appropriate.

    (b)   Without prejudice to the generality of paragraph (a), an order under subsection (1) may contain—

      (i)   a provision specifying the manner of sale and some or all of the conditions applying to the sale of the property to which the order relates,

      (ii)   a provision requiring any such property to be offered for sale to a person, or a class of persons, specified in the order,

      (iii)   a provision directing that the order, or a specified part of it, shall not take effect until the occurrence of a specified event or the expiration of a specified period,

      (iv)   a provision requiring the making of a payment or payments (whether periodical payments or lump sum payments) to a specified person or persons out of the proceeds of the sale of the property to which the order relates, and

      (v)   a provision specifying the manner in which the proceeds of the sale of the property concerned shall be disposed of between the following persons or such of them as the court considers appropriate, that is to say, the spouses concerned and any other person having an interest therein.

(4) A provision in an order under subsection (1) providing for the making of periodical payments to one of the spouses concerned out of the proceeds of the sale of property shall, on the death or remarriage of that spouse, cease to have effect except as respects payments due on the date of the death or remarriage.

(5) Where a spouse has a beneficial interest in any property, or in the proceeds of the sale of any property, and a person (not being the other spouse) also has a beneficial interest in that property or those proceeds, then, in considering whether to make an order under this section or section 14 or 15(1)(a) in relation to that property or those proceeds, the court shall give to that person an opportunity to make representations with respect to the making of the order and the contents thereof, and any representations made by such a person shall be deemed to be included among the matters to which the court is required to have regard under section 20 in any relevant proceedings under a provision referred to in that section after the making of those representations.

(6) This section shall not apply in relation to a family home in which, following the grant of a decree of divorce, either of the spouses concerned, having remarried, ordinarily resides with his or her spouse.

20   Provisions relating to certain orders under sections 12 to 18 and 22

(1) In deciding whether to make an order under section 12, 13, 14, 15(1)(a), 16, 17, 18 or 22 and in determining the provisions of such an order, the court shall ensure that such provision as the court considers proper having regard to the circumstances exists or will be made for the spouses and any dependent member of the family concerned.

(2) Without prejudice to the generality of subsection (1), in deciding whether to make such an order as aforesaid and in determining the provisions of such an order, the court shall, in particular, have regard to the following matters:

(a) the income, earning capacity, property and other financial resources which each of the spouses concerned has or is likely to have in the foreseeable future,

(b) the financial needs, obligations and responsibilities which each of the spouses has or is likely to have in the foreseeable future (whether in the case of the remarriage of the spouse or otherwise),

(c) the standard of living enjoyed by the family concerned before the proceedings were instituted or before the spouses commenced to live apart from one another, as the case may be,

(d) the age of each of the spouses, the duration of their marriage and the length of time during which the spouses lived with one another,

(e) any physical or mental disability of either of the spouses,

(f) the contributions which each of the spouses has made or is likely in the foreseeable future to make to the welfare of the family, including any contribution made by each of them to the income, earning capacity, property and financial resources of the other spouse and any contribution made by either of them by looking after the home or caring for the family,

(g) the effect on the earning capacity of each of the spouses of the marital responsibilities assumed by each during the period when they lived with one another and, in particular, the degree to which the future earning capacity of a spouse is impaired by reason of that spouse having relinquished or foregone the opportunity of remunerative activity in order to look after the home or care for the family,

(h) any income or benefits to which either of the spouses is entitled by or under statute,

(i) the conduct of each of the spouses, if that conduct is such that in the opinion of the court it would in all the circumstances of the case be unjust to disregard it,

(j) the accommodation needs of either of the spouses,

(k) the value to each of the spouses of any benefit (for example, a benefit under a pension scheme) which by reason of the decree of divorce concerned, that spouse will forfeit the opportunity or possibility of acquiring,

(l) the rights of any person other than the spouses but including a person to whom either spouse is remarried.

(3) In deciding whether to make an order under a provision referred to in subsection (1) and in determining the provisions of such an order, the court shall have regard to the terms of any separation agreement which has been entered into by the spouses and is still in force.

(4) Without prejudice to the generality of subsection (1), in deciding whether to make an order referred to in that subsection in favour of a dependent member of the family concerned and in determining the provisions of such an order, the court shall, in particular, have regard to the following matters:

(a) the financial needs of the member,

(b) the income, earning capacity (if any), property and other financial resources of the member,

(c) any physical or mental disability of the member,

(d) any income or benefits to which the member is entitled by or under statute,

(e) the manner in which the member was being and in which the spouses concerned anticipated that the member would be educated or trained,

(f) the matters specified in paragraphs (a), (b) and (c) of subsection (2) and in subsection (3),

(g) the accommodation needs of the member.

(5) The court shall not make an order under a provision referred to in subsection (1) unless it would be in the interests of justice to do so.

21   Retrospective periodical payments orders

(1) Where, having regard to all the circumstances of the case, the court considers it appropriate to do so, it may, in a periodical payments order, direct that—

(a) the period in respect of which payments under the order shall be made shall begin on such date before the date of the order, not being earlier than the time of the institution of the proceedings concerned for the grant of a decree of divorce, as may be specified in the order,

(b) any payments under the order in respect of a period before the date of the order be paid in one sum and before a specified date, and

(c) there be deducted from any payments referred to in paragraph (b) made to the spouse concerned an amount equal to the amount of such (if any) payments made to that spouse by the other spouse as the court may determine, being payments made during the period between the making of the order for the grant of the decree aforesaid and the institution of the proceedings aforesaid.

(2) The jurisdiction conferred on the court by subsection (1)(b) is without prejudice to the generality of section 13(1)(c).

22   Variation, etc, of certain orders under this Part

(1) This section applies to the following orders:

(a) a maintenance pending suit order,

(b) a periodical payments order,

(c) a secured periodical payments order,

(d) a lump sum order if and insofar as it provides for the payment of the lump sum concerned by instalments or requires the payment of any such instalments to be secured,

(e) an order under paragraph (b), (c) or (d) of section 14(1) insofar as such application is not restricted or excluded pursuant to section 14(2),

(f) an order under subparagraph (i) or (ii) of section 15(1)(a),

(g) a financial compensation order,

(h) an order under section 17(2) insofar as such application is not restricted or excluded pursuant to section 17(26),

(i) an order under this section.

(2) Subject to the provisions of this section and section 20 and to any restriction or exclusion pursuant to section 14(2) or 17(26) and without prejudice to section 16(2)(d), the court may, on application to it in that behalf—

   (a) by either of the spouses concerned,

   (b) in the case of the death of either of the spouses, by any other person who has, in the opinion of the court, a sufficient interest in the matter or by a person on behalf of a dependent member of the family concerned, or

   (c) in the case of the remarriage of either of the spouses, by his or her spouse,

if it considers it proper to do so having regard to any change in the circumstances of the case and to any new evidence, by order vary or discharge an order to which this section applies, suspend any provision of such an order or any provision of such an order temporarily, revive the operation of such an order or provision so suspended, further vary an order previously varied under this section or further suspend or revive the operation of an order or provision previously suspended or revived under this section, and, without prejudice to the generality of the foregoing, an order under this section may require the divesting of any property vested in a person under or by virtue of an order to which this section applies.

(3) Without prejudice to the generality of section 12 or 13, that part of an order to which this section applies which provides for the making of payments for the support of a dependent member of the family shall stand discharged if the member ceases to be a dependent member of the family by reason of his or her attainment of the age of 18 years or 23 years, as may be appropriate, and shall be discharged by the court, on application to it under subsection (2), if it is satisfied that the member has for any reason ceased to be a dependent member of the family.

(4) The power of the court under subsection (2) to make an order varying, discharging or suspending an order referred to in subsection (1)(e) shall be subject to any restriction or exclusion specified in that order and shall (subject to the limitation aforesaid) be a power—

   (a) to vary the settlement to which the order relates in any person's favour or to extinguish or reduce any person's interest under that settlement, and

   (b) to make such supplemental provision (including a further property adjustment order or a lump sum order) as the court thinks appropriate in consequence of any variation, extinguishment or reduction made pursuant to paragraph (a),

and section 19 shall apply to a case where the court makes such an order as aforesaid under subsection (2) as it applies to a case where the court makes a property adjustment order with any necessary modifications.

(5) The court shall not make an order under subsection (2) in relation to an order referred to in subsection (1)(e) unless it appears to it that the order will not prejudice the interests of any person who—

   (a) has acquired any right or interest in consequence of the order referred to in subsection (1)(e), and

   (b) is not a party to the marriage concerned or a dependent member of the family concerned.

(6) This section shall apply, with any necessary modifications, to instruments executed pursuant to orders to which this section applies as it applies to those orders.

(7) Where the court makes an order under subsection (2) in relation to a property adjustment order relating to land, a copy of the order under subsection (2) certified to be a true copy by the registrar or clerk of the court concerned shall, as appropriate, be lodged by him or her in the Land Registry for registration pursuant to section 69(1)(h) of the Registration of Title Act, 1964, in a register maintained under that Act or be registered in the Registry of Deeds.

23 Restriction in relation to orders for benefit of dependent members of family

In deciding whether—

    (a) to include in an order under section 12 a provision requiring the making of periodical payments for the benefit of a dependent member of the family,

    (b) to make an order under paragraph (a)(ii), (b)(ii) or (c)(ii) of section 13(1),

    (c) to make an order under section 22 varying, discharging or suspending a provision referred to in paragraph (a) or an order referred to in paragraph (b),

the court shall not have regard to conduct by the spouse or spouses concerned of the kind specified in subsection (2)(i) of section 20.

24 Method of making payments under certain orders

(1) The court may by order provide that a payment under an order to which this section applies shall be made by such method as is specified in the order and be subject to such terms and conditions as it considers appropriate and so specifies.

(2) This section applies to an order under—

    (a) section 11(2)(b) of the Act of 1964,

    (b) section 5, 5A or 7 of the Act of 1976,

    (c) section 7, 8 or 24 of the Act of 1995, and

    (d) section 12, 13, 19 or 22.

25 Stay on certain orders the subject of appeal

Where an appeal is brought from an order under—

    (a) section 11(2)(b) of the Act of 1964,

    (b) section 5, 5A or 7 of the Act of 1976,

    (c) section 7, paragraph (a) or (b) of section 8(1) or section 24 of the Act of 1995, or

    (d) section 12, paragraph (a) or (b) of section 13(1) or paragraph (a), (b) or (c) of section 22(1),

the operation of the order shall not be stayed unless the court that made the order or to which the appeal is brought directs otherwise.

26 Orders under Acts of 1976, 1989 and 1995

(1) Where, while an order ('the first-mentioned order'), being—

    (a) a maintenance order, an order varying a maintenance order, or an interim order under the Act of 1976,

    (b) an order under section 14, 15, 16, 18 or 22 of the Act of 1989,

    (c) an order under section 8, 9, 10, 11, 12, 13, 14, 15 or 18 of the Act of 1995,

is in force, an application is made to the court by a spouse to whom the first-mentioned order relates for an order granting a decree of divorce or an order under this Part, the court may by order discharge the first-mentioned order as on and from such date as may be specified in the order.

(2) Where, on the grant of a decree of divorce an order specified in subsection (1) is in force, it shall, unless it is discharged by an order under subsection (1), continue in force as if it were an order made under a corresponding provision of this Act and section 22 shall apply to it accordingly.

27 (Amends s 3 of the Act of 1976)

28 Transmission of periodical payments through District Court clerk

Notwithstanding anything in this Act, section 9 of the Act of 1976 shall apply in relation to an order ('the relevant order'), being a maintenance pending suit order, a periodical payments order or a secured periodical payments order or any such order as aforesaid as affected by an order under section 22, with the modifications that—

   (a) the reference in subsection (4) of the said section 9 to the maintenance creditor shall be construed as a reference to the person to whom payments under the relevant order concerned are required to be made,

   (b) the other references in the said section 9 to the maintenance creditor shall be construed as references to the person on whose application the relevant order was made, and

   (c) the reference in subsection (3) of the said section 9 to the maintenance debtor shall be construed as a reference to the person to whom payments under the relevant order are required by that order to be made,

and with any other necessary modifications.

29 Application of maintenance pending suit and periodical payment orders to certain members of Defence Forces

The reference in section 98(1)(h) of the Defence Act, 1954, to an order for payment of alimony shall be construed as including a reference to a maintenance pending suit order, a periodical payments order and a secured periodical payments order.

30 Amendment of Enforcement of Court Orders Act, 1940

The references in subsections (1) and (7) of section 8 of the Enforcement of Court Orders Act, 1940 (as amended by section 29 of the Act of 1976 and section 22 of the Act of 1995), to an order shall be construed as including references to a maintenance pending suit order and a periodical payments order.

PART IV

INCOME TAX, CAPITAL ACQUISITIONS TAX, CAPITAL GAINS TAX, PROBATE TAX AND STAMP DUTY

31 Payments to be made without deduction of income tax

Payments of money pursuant to an order under this Act (other than under section 17) shall be made without deduction of income tax.

32 Income tax treatment of divorced persons

Where a payment to which section 3 of the Finance Act, 1983, applies is made in a year of assessment (within the meaning of the Income Tax Acts) by a spouse who was a party to a marriage that has been dissolved for the benefit of the other spouse and—

   (a) both spouses are resident in the State for tax purposes for that year of assessment, and

   (b) neither spouse has entered into another marriage,

then, the provisions of section 4 of the Finance Act, 1983, shall, with any necessary modifications, have effect in relation to the spouses for that year of assessment as if their marriage had not been dissolved.

33   (*Repealed*)

34   Exemption of certain transfers from capital acquisitions tax

Notwithstanding the provisions of the Capital Acquisitions Tax Act, 1976, a gift or inheritance (within the meaning, in each case, of that Act) taken by virtue or in consequence of an order under Part III by a spouse who was a party to the marriage concerned shall be exempt from any capital acquisitions tax under that Act and shall not be taken into account in computing such a tax.

35   Capital gains tax treatment of certain disposals by divorced persons

(1) Notwithstanding the provisions of the Capital Gains Tax Acts, where, by virtue or in consequence of an order made under Part III on or following the granting of a decree of divorce either of the spouses concerned disposes of an asset to the other spouse, both spouses shall be treated for the purpose of those Acts as if the asset was acquired from the spouse making the disposal for a consideration of such amount as would secure that on the disposal neither a gain nor a loss would accrue to the spouse making the disposal:

Provided that this subsection shall not apply if, until the disposal, the asset formed part of the trading stock of a trade carried on by the spouse making the disposal or if the asset is acquired as trading stock for the purposes of a trade carried on by the spouse acquiring the asset.

(2) Where subsection (1) applies in relation to a disposal of an asset by a spouse to the other spouse, then, in relation to a subsequent disposal of the asset (not being a disposal to which subsection (1) applies), the spouse making the disposal shall be treated for the purposes of the Capital Gains Tax Acts as if the other spouse's acquisition or provision of the asset had been his or her acquisition or provision of the asset.

36   Abatement and postponement of probate tax on property the subject of an order under section 18

Subsection (1) of section 115A of the Finance Act, 1993 (which was inserted by the Finance Act, 1994, and provides for the abatement or postponement of probate tax payable by a surviving spouse)—

(a) shall apply to a spouse in whose favour an order has been made under section 18 as it applies to a spouse referred to in the said section 115A, and

(b) shall apply to property or an interest in property the subject of such an order as it applies to the share of a spouse referred to in the said section 115A in the estate of a deceased referred to in that section or the interest of such a spouse in property referred to in that section,

with any necessary modifications.

PART V

MISCELLANEOUS

37   Powers of court in relation to transactions intended to prevent or reduce relief

(1) In this section—

'disposition' means any disposition of property howsoever made other than a disposition made by a will or codicil;

'relief' means the financial or other material benefits conferred by an order under section 12, 13 or 14, paragraph (a) or (b) of section 15(1) or section 16, 17, 18 or 22 other than an order affecting an order referred to in subsection (1)(e) thereof and references to defeating a claim for relief are references to—

(a) preventing relief being granted to the person concerned, whether for the benefit of the person or a dependent member of the family concerned,

(b) limiting the relief granted, or

(c) frustrating or impeding the enforcement of an order granting relief,

'reviewable disposition', in relation to proceedings for the grant of relief brought by a spouse, means a disposition made by the other spouse concerned or any other person but does not include such a disposition made for valuable consideration (other than marriage) to a person who, at the time of the disposition, acted in good faith and without notice of an intention on the part of the respondent to defeat the claim for relief.

(2) (a) The court, on the application of a person ('the applicant') who has instituted proceedings that have not been determined for the grant of relief, may—

(i) if it is satisfied that the other spouse concerned or any other person, with the intention of defeating the claim for relief, proposes to make any disposition of or to transfer out of the jurisdiction or otherwise deal with any property, make such order as it thinks fit for the purpose of restraining that other spouse or other person from so doing or otherwise for protecting the claim,

(ii) if it is satisfied that that other spouse or other person has, with that intention, made a reviewable disposition and that, if the disposition were set aside, relief or different relief would be granted to the applicant, make an order setting aside the disposition.

(b) Where relief has been granted by the court and the court is satisfied that the other spouse concerned or another person has, with the intention aforesaid, made a reviewable disposition, it may make an order setting aside the disposition.

(c) An application under paragraph (a) shall be made in the proceedings for the grant of the relief concerned.

(3) Where the court makes an order under paragraph (a) or (b) of subsection (2), it shall include in the order such provisions (if any) as it considers necessary for its implementation (including provisions requiring the making of any payments or the disposal of any property).

(4) Where an application is made under subsection (2) with respect to a disposition that took place less than 3 years before the date of the application or with respect to a

disposition or other dealing with property that the other spouse concerned or any other person proposes to make and the court is satisfied—

- (a) in case the application is for an order under subsection (2)(a)(i), that the disposition or other dealing concerned would (apart from this section) have the consequence, or
- (b) in case the application is for an order under paragraph (a)(ii) or (b) of subsection (2), that the disposition has had the consequence,

of defeating the applicant's claim for relief, it shall be presumed, unless the contrary is shown, that that other spouse or other person disposed of or otherwise dealt with the property concerned, or, as the case may be, proposes to do so, with the intention of defeating the applicant's claim for relief.

38 Jurisdiction of courts and venue

(1) Subject to the provisions of this section, the Circuit Court shall, concurrently with the High Court, have jurisdiction to hear and determine proceedings under this Act and shall, in relation to that jurisdiction, be known as the Circuit Family Court.

(2) Where the rateable valuation of any land to which proceedings in the Circuit Family Court under this Act relate exceeds £200, that Court shall, if an application is made to it in that behalf by any person having an interest in the proceedings, transfer the proceedings to the High Court, but any order made or act done in the course of such proceedings before the transfer shall be valid unless discharged or varied by the High Court by order.

(3) The jurisdiction conferred on the Circuit Family Court by this Act may be exercised by the judge of the circuit in which any of the parties to the proceedings ordinarily resides or carries on any business, profession or occupation.

(4) The Circuit Family Court may, for the purposes of subsection (2) in relation to land that has not been given a rateable valuation or is the subject with other land of a rateable valuation, determine that its rateable valuation would exceed, or would not exceed, £200.

(5) Section 32 of the Act of 1989 shall apply to proceedings under this Act in the Circuit Family Court and sections 33 to 36 of that Act shall apply to proceedings under this Act in that Court and in the High Court.

(6) In proceedings under section 13, 14, 15(1)(a), 16, 17, 18 or 22—

- (a) each of the spouses concerned shall give to the other spouse and to, or to a person acting on behalf of, any dependent member of the family concerned, and
- (b) any dependent member of the family concerned shall give to, or to a person acting on behalf of, any other such member and to each of the spouses concerned,

such particulars of his or her property and income as may reasonably be required for the purposes of the proceedings.

(7) Where a person fails or refuses to comply with subsection (6), the court on application to it in that behalf by a person having an interest in the matter, may direct the person to comply with that subsection.

PART TWO

39   Exercise of jurisdiction by court in relation to divorce

(1) The court may grant a decree of divorce if, but only if, one of the following requirements is satisfied—

(a) either of the spouses concerned was domiciled in the State on the date of the institution of the proceedings concerned,

(b) either of the spouses was ordinarily resident in the State throughout the period of one year ending on that date.

(2) Where proceedings are pending in a court in respect of an application for the grant of a decree of divorce or in respect of an appeal from the determination of such an application and the court has or had, by virtue of subsection (1), jurisdiction to determine the application, the court shall, notwithstanding section 31(4) of the Act of 1989 or section 39 of the Act of 1995, as the case may be, have jurisdiction to determine an application for the grant of a decree of judicial separation or a decree of nullity in respect of the marriage concerned.

(3) Where proceedings are pending in a court in respect of an application for the grant of a decree of nullity or in respect of an appeal from the determination of such an application and the court has or had, by virtue of section 39 of the Act of 1995, jurisdiction to determine the application, the court shall, notwithstanding subsection (1), have jurisdiction to determine an application for the grant of a decree of divorce in respect of the marriage concerned.

(4) Where proceedings are pending in a court in respect of an application for the grant of a decree of judicial separation or in respect of an appeal from the determination of such an application and the court has or had, by virtue of section 31(4) of the Act of 1989, jurisdiction to determine the application, the court shall, notwithstanding subsection (1), have jurisdiction to determine an application for the grant of a decree of divorce in respect of the marriage concerned.

40   Notice of proceedings under Act

Notice of any proceedings under this Act shall be given by the person bringing the proceedings to—

(a) the other spouse concerned or, as the case may be, the spouses concerned, and

(b) any other person specified by the court.

41   Custody of dependent members of family after decree of divorce

Where the court makes an order for the grant of a decree of divorce, it may declare either of the spouses concerned to be unfit to have custody of any dependent member of the family who is a minor and, if it does so and the spouse to whom the declaration relates is a parent of any dependent member of the family who is a minor, that spouse shall not, on the death of the other spouse, be entitled as of right to the custody of that minor.

42   Social reports in family law proceedings

Section 47 of the Act of 1995 shall apply to proceedings under this Act.

43   Cost of mediation and counselling services

The cost of any mediation services or counselling services provided for a spouse who is or becomes a party to proceedings under this Act, the Act of 1964 or the Act of 1989 or for a dependent member of the family of such a spouse shall be in the discretion of the court concerned.

44   Determination of questions between persons formerly engaged to each other in relation to property

Where an agreement to marry is terminated, section 36 of the Act of 1995 shall apply, as if the parties to the agreement were married to each other, to any dispute between them, or claim by one of them, in relation to property in which either or both of them had a beneficial interest while the agreement was in force.

45   (Amends the Act of 1989)

46   (Amends s 117(6) of the Act of 1965)

47   (Amends the Pensions Act, 1990)

48   (Amends the Criminal Damage Act, 1991)

49   (Amends the Criminal Evidence Act, 1992)

50   (Amends the Powers of Attorney Act, 1996)

51   (Amends the Act of 1996)

52   (Amends the Act of 1995)

53   (Amends the Maintenance Act, 1994)

PART TWO

Family Law (Maintenance of Spouses and Children) Act, 1976

(1976 No 11)

ARRANGEMENT OF SECTIONS

PART I

PRELIMINARY AND GENERAL

PART II

MAINTENANCE OF SPOUSES AND DEPENDENT CHILDREN

PART III

ATTACHMENT OF EARNINGS

PART IV

MISCELLANEOUS

An Act to make provision for periodical payments by a spouse for the support of the other spouse and any dependent children of the family of the spouses in certain cases of failure by the spouse to provide reasonable maintenance, to enable payments to be made by an employer, by deductions from an employee's earnings, to a person entitled under certain court orders to periodic payments for maintenance from the employee, to provide for other matters connected with the matters aforesaid and to amend in other respects the law relating to parents and children.

[6 April 1976]

PART I

PRELIMINARY AND GENERAL

1   Short title

This Act may be cited as the Family Law (Maintenance of Spouses and Children) Act, 1976.

2   Commencement

This Act shall come into operation on the day that is one month after the date of its passing.

3   Interpretation

(1) In this Act, save where the context otherwise requires—

'allowance' means deserted wife's allowance under section 195, lone parent's allowance under section 198B or supplementary welfare allowance under section 200 of the Social Welfare (Consolidation) Act, 1981;
'antecedent order' means—

(a) a maintenance order,
(b) a variation order,
(c) an interim order,
(d) an order under section 8 of this Act (in so far as it is deemed under that section to be a maintenance order),
(e) an order deemed under section 30 of this Act to be a maintenance order,

(f) an order providing for a periodical payment under the Illegitimate Children (Affiliation Orders) Act, 1930,

(g) an order for maintenance under section 11(2)(b) of the Guardianship of Infants Act, 1964,

(h) an enforceable maintenance order under the Maintenance Orders Act, 1974,

(i) an order for alimony pending suit,

(j) an order for maintenance pending suit under the Judicial Separation and Family Law Reform Act, 1989, or a periodical payments order under that Act,

(k) a maintenance pending suit order under the Family Law Act, 1995, or a periodical payments order under that Act,

(l) a maintenance pending suit order under the Family Law (Divorce) Act, 1996, or a periodical payments order under that Act,

'attachment of earnings order' means an order under section 10 of this Act;

'benefit' means deserted wife's benefit under section 100 of the Social Welfare (Consolidation) Act, 1981;

'competent authority' has the meaning assigned to it by section 314 of the Social Welfare (Consolidation) Act, 1981;

'Court' shall be construed in accordance with section 23 of this Act;

'dependent child' means any child (including a child whose parents are not married to each other) who is under the age of 18 years, or, if he has attained that age—

(a) is or will be or, if an order were made under this Act providing for periodical payments for his support, would be receiving full-time education or instruction at any university, college, school or other educational establishment and is under the age of 23 years, or

(b) is suffering from mental or physical disability to such extent that it is not reasonably possible for him to maintain himself fully;

'dependent child of the family', in relation to a spouse or spouses, means any dependent child—

(a) of both spouses, or adopted by both spouses under the Adoption Acts, 1952 to 1976, or in relation to whom both spouses are *in loco parentis*, or

(b) of either spouse, or adopted by either spouse under the Adoption Acts, 1952 to 1976, or in relation to whom either spouse is *in loco parentis*, where the other spouse, being aware that he is not the parent of the child, has treated the child as a member of the family;

'desertion' includes conduct on the part of one spouse that results in the other spouse, with just cause, leaving and living separately and apart from him, and cognate words shall be construed accordingly;

'earnings' means any sums payable to a person—

(a) by way of wages or salary (including any fees, bonus, commission, overtime pay or other emoluments payable in addition to wages or salary or payable under a contract of service);

(b) by way of pension or other like benefit in respect of employment (including an annuity in respect of past services, whether or not rendered to the person paying the annuity, and including periodical payments by way of compensation for the loss, abolition or relinquishment, or diminution in the emoluments, of any office or employment);

'interim order' means an order under section 7 of this Act;

'lump sum order' means an order under section 21A of this Act;

'maintenance creditor', in relation to an order under this Act (other than an order under section 22 of this Act), or to proceedings arising out of such an order, means a person on whose application there has been made such an order;

'maintenance debtor', in relation to an attachment of earnings order, or to proceedings in which a Court has power to make such an order, or to proceedings arising out of such an order, means the spouse by whom payments are required by the relevant antecedent order to be made and, in relation to any other order under this Act (other than an order under section 22 of this Act) or to proceedings in which a Court has power to make such an order, or to proceedings arising out of such an order, means a spouse who is or, if it were made, would be required by such an order to make periodical payments for the support of persons named in the order;

'maintenance order' means, where the context requires, an order under either section 5 or 5A of this Act;

'normal deduction rate' and 'protected earnings rate' have the meanings respectively assigned to them by section 10 of this Act;

'parent', in relation to a dependent child, includes a person who has adopted the child under the Adoption Acts, 1952 to 1976, but does not include a person who is a parent of the child adopted under those Acts where the person is not an adopter of the child;

'variation order' means an order under section 6 of this Act varying a maintenance order.

(2) Subject to section 16 of this Act, the relationship of employer and employee shall be regarded as subsisting between two persons if one of them as a principal and not as a servant or agent pays earnings to the other.

(3) References in this Act to a District Court clerk include references to his successor in the office of District Court clerk and to any person acting on his behalf.

(4) References in this Act to any enactment shall be construed as references to that enactment as amended by any subsequent enactment, including this Act.

Amendments—Status of Children Act, 1987, s 16(a)–(e); Judicial Separation and Family Law Reform Act, 1989, s 25(1); Social Welfare Act, 1989, s 13(1)(a); Social Welfare Act, 1990, s 15; Family Law Act, 1995, s 43(a)(i)(ii); Family Law (Divorce) Act, 1996, s 27, s 52(o)(i).

---

4 Commencement of periodical payments

A periodical payment under an order under this Act shall commence on such date, not being earlier than the date on which the order is made, as may be specified in the order.

PART II

MAINTENANCE OF SPOUSES AND DEPENDENT CHILDREN

5 Maintenance order

(1) (a) Subject to subsection (4) of this section, where it appears to the Court, on application to it by a spouse, that the other spouse has *failed* to provide such maintenance for the applicant spouse and any dependent children of the

family as is proper in the circumstances, the Court may make an order (in this Act referred to as a maintenance order) that the other spouse make to the applicant spouse periodical payments, for the support of the applicant spouse and of each of the dependent children of the family, for such period during the lifetime of the applicant spouse, of such amount and at such times, as the Court may consider proper.

(b) Subject to subsection (4) of this section, where a spouse—

    (i)   is dead,

    (ii) has deserted, or has been deserted by, the other spouse, or

    (iii) is living separately and apart from the other spouse,

and there are dependent children of the family (not being children who are being fully maintained by either spouse), then, if it appears to the Court, on application to it by any person, that the surviving spouse or, as the case may be, either spouse has failed to provide such maintenance for any dependent children of the family as is proper in the circumstances, the Court may make an order (in this Act referred to as a maintenance order) that that spouse make to that person periodical payments, for the support of each of those dependent children, for such period during the lifetime of that person, of such amount and at such times, as the Court may consider proper.

(c) A maintenance order under this section or a variation order shall specify each part of a payment under the order that is for the support of a dependent child of the family and may specify the period during the lifetime of the person applying for the order for which so much of a payment under the order as is for the support of a dependent child of the family shall be made.

(2) The court shall not make a maintenance order for the support of a spouse where the spouse has deserted and continues to desert the other spouse unless, having regard to all the circumstances (including the conduct of the other spouse), the Court is of opinion that it would be repugnant to justice not to make a maintenance order.

(3) (*deleted*)

(4) The Court, in deciding whether to make a maintenance order under this section and, if it decides to do so, in determining the amount of any payment, shall have regard to all the circumstances of the case and, in particular, to the following matters—

(a) the income, earning capacity (if any), property and other financial resources of—

    (i)   the spouses and any dependent children of the family, and

    (ii) any other dependent children of which either spouse is a parent,

including income or benefits to which either spouse or any such children are entitled by or under statute with the exception of a benefit or allowance or any increase in such benefit or allowance in respect of any dependent children granted to either parent of such children; and

(b) the financial and other responsibilities of—

    (i)   the spouses towards each other and towards any dependent children of the family, and

    (ii) each spouse as a parent towards any other dependent children,

and the needs of any such children, including the need for care and attention;

(c) the conduct of each of the spouses, if that conduct is such that in the opinion of the Court it would in all the circumstances be repugnant to justice to disregard it.

PART TWO

Amendments—Status of Children Act, 1987, s 17 (a) (i) (ii) (b); Social Welfare Act, 1989, s 13 (1) (b); Judicial Separation and Family Law Reform Act, 1989, s 38 (2) (a) (b) (c).

5A   Maintenance order (provision for certain dependent children)

(1) Subject to subsection (3) of this section, where, in respect of a dependent child whose parents are not married to each other, it appears to the Court on application to it by either parent of the child that the other parent has *failed* to provide such maintenance for the child as is proper in the circumstances, the Court may make an order (in this Act referred to as a maintenance order) that the other parent make to the applicant parent periodical payments, for the support of the child as aforesaid, for such period during the lifetime of the applicant parent, of such amount and at such times, as the Court may consider proper.

(2) Subject to subsections (3) and (4) of this section, where in respect of a dependent child whose parents are not married to each other it appears to the Court, on application to it by any person other than a parent, that a parent of the child (not being a child who is being fully maintained by the other parent) has failed to provide such maintenance for the child as is proper in the circumstances, the Court may make an order (in this Act referred to as a maintenance order) that the parent make to that person periodical payments for the support of the child for such period during the lifetime of that person, of such amount and at such times as the Court may consider proper.

(3) The Court, in deciding whether to make a maintenance order under this section and, if it decides to do so, in determining the amount of any payment, shall have regard to all the circumstances of the case and, in particular, to the following matters—

  (a) the income, earning capacity (if any), property and other financial resources of—

     (i)   each parent,

     (ii) the dependent child in respect of whom the order is sought, and

     (iii) any other dependent children of either parent,

    including income or benefits to which either parent, the dependent child as aforesaid or such other dependent children are entitled by or under statute with the exception of a benefit or allowance or any increase in such benefit or allowance in respect of any dependent children granted to either parent of such children, and

  (b) the financial and other responsibilities of each parent towards—

     (i)   a spouse,

     (ii) the dependent child in respect of whom the order is sought, and

     (iii) any other dependent children of either parent,

    and the needs of any dependent child as aforesaid or of any such other dependent children, including the need for care and attention.

(4) The Court shall not make a maintenance order under subsection (2) of this section in relation to a parent of a dependent child if a maintenance order under subsection (1) of this section requiring that parent to make periodical payments for the support of the child is in force or that parent has made provision for the child by an agreement under which, at or after the time of the hearing of the application for the order under the said

subsection (2) payments fall to be made and in relation to which an order under section 8A of this Act has been made unless—

(a) the parent is not complying with the order under the said subsection (1) or the agreement, as the case may be, and

(b) the Court, having regard to all the circumstances, thinks it proper to do so,

but if the Court makes the order under the said subsection (2), any amounts falling due for payment under the order under the said subsection 91) or the agreement, as the case may be, on or after the date of the making of the order under the said subsection (2) shall not be payable.

Amendments—Inserted by Status of Children Act, 1987, s 18; Social Welfare Act, 1989, s 13(1)(c).

6 Discharge, variation and termination of maintenance order

(1) The court may—

(a) discharge a maintenance order at any time after one year from the making thereof, on the application of the maintenance debtor, where it appears to the Court that, having regard to the maintenance debtor's record of payments pursuant to the order and to the other circumstances of the case, the persons for whose support it provides will not be prejudiced by the discharge thereof, or

(b) discharge or vary a maintenance order at any time, on the application of either party, if it thinks it proper to do so having regard to any circumstances not existing when the order was made (including the conduct of each of the spouses, if that conduct is such that in the opinion of the Court it would in all the circumstances be repugnant to justice to disregard it) or, if it has been varied, when it was last varied, or to any evidence not available to that party when the maintenance order was made or, if it has been varied, when it was last varied.

(2) Notwithstanding anything contained in subsection (1) of this section, the Court shall, on application to it under that subsection, discharge that part of a maintenance order which provides for the support of a maintenance creditor where it appears to it that the maintenance creditor, being the spouse of the maintenance debtor, has deserted and continues to desert the maintenance debtor unless, having regard to all the circumstances (including the conduct of the other spouse), the Court is of opinion that it would be repugnant to justice to do so.

(3) That part of a maintenance order which provides for the support of a dependent child shall stand discharged when the child ceases to be a dependent child by reason of his attainment of the age of 18 years or 23 years, as the case may be, and shall be discharged by the Court, on application to it under subsection (1) of this section, if it is satisfied that the child has for any reason ceased to be a dependent child for the purposes of the order.

(4) (*deleted*)

(5) Desertion by or conduct of a spouse shall not be a ground for discharging or varying any part of a maintenance order that provides for the support of dependent children of the family.

Amendments—Status of Children Act, 1987, s 19; Judicial Separation and Family Law Reform Act, 1989, s 38(3); Family Law Act, 1995, s 43(b).

7 Interim order

On an application to the Court for a maintenance order, the Court, before deciding whether to make or refuse to make the order, may, if it appears to the Court proper to do so having regard to the needs of the persons for whose support the maintenance order is sought and the other circumstances of the case, make an order (in this Act referred to as an interim order) for the payment to the applicant by the maintenance debtor, for a definite period specified in the order or until the application is adjudicated upon by the Court, of such periodical sum as, in the opinion of the Court, is proper.

8 Orders in respect of certain marital agreements

Where—

 (a) the parties to a marriage enter into an agreement in writing (including a separation agreement) after the commencement of this Act that includes either or both of the following provisions, that is to say—
   (i) a provision whereby one spouse undertakes to make periodical payments towards the maintenance of the other spouse or of any dependent children of the family or of both that other spouse and any dependent children of the family,
   (ii) a provision governing the rights and liabilities of the spouses towards one another in respect of the making or securing of payments (other than payments specified in paragraph (a)(i) of this section), or the disposition or use of any property, and
 (b) an application is made by one or both of the spouses to the High Court or the Circuit Court or, in relation to an agreement other than a separation agreement, the District Court for an order making the agreement a rule of court,

the Court may make such an order if it is satisfied that the agreement is a fair and reasonable one which in all the circumstances adequately protects the interests of both spouses and the dependent children (if any) of the family, and such order shall, in so far as it relates to a provision specified in paragraph (a)(i) of this section, be deemed, for the purpose of section 9 and Part III of this Act, to be a maintenance order.

Amendments—Children Act, 1997, s 15.

8A Orders in respect of certain other agreements

Where—

 (a) the parents of a dependent child who are not married to each other enter into an agreement in writing after the commencement of *Part IV* of the Status of Children Act, 1987, that includes either or both of the following provisions, that is to say—
   (i) a provision whereby a parent undertakes to make periodical payments towards the maintenance of the child,
   (ii) a provision affecting the interests of the child which governs the rights and liabilities of the parents towards one another in respect of the making or securing of payments (other than payments specified in paragraph (a)(i) of this section), or the disposition or use of any property,
  and

(b) an application is made by one or both of the parents to the High Court or the Circuit Court or, in relation to an agreement other than a separation agreement, the District Court for an order making the agreement a rule of court,

that Court may make such an order if it is satisfied that the agreement is a fair and reasonable one which in all the circumstances adequately protects the interests of the child and such order shall, in so far as it relates to a provision specified in paragraph (a) (i) of this section, be deemed, for the purposes of section 9 and Part III of this Act, to be a maintenance order.

Amendments—Inserted by Status of Children Act, 1987, s 20; amended by Children Act, 1997, s 15.

8B Preservation of pension entitlements in separation agreements

(1) Subject to the provisions of this section, on an application to the High Court or the Circuit Court under section 8 of this Act, the Court may, on application to it in that behalf by either of the spouses concerned, make an order directing the trustees of a pension scheme of which either or both of the spouses are members, not to regard the separation of the spouses by agreement as a ground for disqualifying either of them for the receipt of a benefit under the scheme a condition for the receipt of which is that the spouses should be residing together at the time when the benefit becomes payable.

(2) Notice of an application under subsection (1) shall be given by the spouse concerned to the trustees of the pension scheme concerned and, in deciding whether to make an order under subsection (1), the Court shall have regard to any order made, or proposed to be made, by it in relation to the application by the spouse or spouses concerned under section 8 of this Act and any representations made by those trustees in relation to the matter.

(3) Any costs incurred by the trustees of a pension scheme under subsection (2) or in complying with an order under subsection (1) shall be borne, as the court may determine, by either of the spouses concerned or by both of the spouses and in such proportions and such manner as the Court may determine.

(4) In this section 'pension scheme' has the meaning assigned to it by the Family Law Act, 1995.

Amendments—Inserted by Family Law Act, 1995, s 43(c).

9 Transmission of payments through District Court clerk

(1) Where the Court makes a maintenance order, a variation order or an interim order under this Act, the Court shall—

(a) thereupon direct that payments under the order shall be made to the District Court clerk, unless the maintenance creditor requests it not to do so and the Court considers that it would be proper not to do so, and

(b) in a case in which the Court has not given a direction under paragraph (a) of this subsection, direct, at any time thereafter on the application of the maintenance creditor, that the payments aforesaid shall be made to the District Court clerk.

(2) Where payments to the District Court clerk under this section are in arrear, the District Court clerk shall, if the maintenance creditor so requests in writing, take such

steps as he considers reasonable in the circumstances to recover the sums in arrear whether by proceeding in his own name for an attachment of earnings order or otherwise.

(3) Where a direction has been given under subsection (1) of this section, the Court, on the application of the maintenance debtor and having afforded the maintenance creditor an opportunity to oppose the application, may, if it is satisfied that, having regard to the record of the payments made to the District Court clerk and all the other circumstances, it would be proper to do so, discharge the direction.

(4) The District Court clerk shall transmit any payments made to him by virtue of this section to the maintenance creditor or, where appropriate, to the competent authority.

(5) Nothing in this section shall affect any right of a person to take proceedings in his own name for the recovery of any sum payable, but not paid, to the District Court clerk by virtue of this section.

(6) References in this section, in relation to any proceedings, to the District Court clerk are references to such District Court clerk in such District Court district as may be determined from time to time by the Court concerned.

(7) Nothing in subsection (1) or (2) of this section shall affect paragraph (a) or (b) of section 14(8) of the Maintenance Orders Act, 1974.

(8) Section 14(8) of the Maintenance Orders Act, 1974, is hereby amended by the insertion in paragraph (b) after 'application under' of 'section 10 of the Family Law (Maintenance of Spouses and Children) Act, 1976, or' and by the substitution of 'the said section 8' for 'that section' and the said paragraph (b), as so amended, is set out in the Table to this section.

TABLE

(b) The district court clerk shall, if any sum payable by virtue of an enforceable maintenance order is not duly paid and if the maintenance creditor so requests in writing, make an application under section 10 of the Family Law (Maintenance of Spouses and Children) Act, 1976, or section 8 (which relates to the enforcement of certain maintenance orders) of the Enforcement of Court Orders Act, 1940, and for that purpose the references in the said section 8 (other than subsections (4) and (5)) to the applicant shall be construed as references to the district court clerk.

Amendments—Social Welfare Act, 1989, s 13(1)(d).

PART III

ATTACHMENT OF EARNINGS

10 Attachment of earnings order

(1) (a) On application—
   (i)   to the High Court by a person on whose application the High Court has made an antecedent order,
   (ii) to the Circuit Court by a person on whose application the Circuit Court has made an antecedent order,
   (iii) to the District Court—

(I) by a person on whose application the District Court has made an antecedent order, or

(II) by a District Court clerk to whom payments under an antecedent order are required to be made,

the Court to which the application is made (subsequently referred to in this section as 'the Court') may, to secure payments under the antecedent order, if it is satisfied that the maintenance debtor is a person to whom earnings fall to be paid, make an attachment of earnings order.

(b) References in this subsection to an antecedent order made by any Court include references to such an order made, varied or affirmed on appeal from that Court.

(1A)(a) Where a court has made an antecedent order, it shall in the same proceedings, subject to subsection (3), make an attachment of earnings order in order to secure payments under the antecedent order if it is satisfied that the maintenance debtor is a person to whom earnings fall to be paid.

(b) References in this subsection to an antecedent order made by a court include references to such an order made, varied or affirmed on appeal from that court.

(2) An attachment of earnings order shall be an order directed to a person who (at the time of the making of the order or at any time thereafter) has the maintenance debtor in his employment or is a trustee (within the meaning of the Family Law Act, 1995) of a pension scheme (within the meaning aforesaid) under which the maintenance debtor is receiving periodical pension benefits and shall operate as a direction to that person to make, at such times as may be specified in the order, periodical deductions of such amounts (specified in the order) as may be appropriate, having regard to the normal deduction rate and the protected earnings rate, from the maintenance debtor's earnings and to pay the amounts deducted, at such times as the Court may order—

(a) in case the relevant antecedent order or, where appropriate, to the competent authority is an enforceable maintenance order, to the District Court clerk specified by the attachment of earnings order for transmission to the person entitled to receive payments made under the relevant antecedent order,

(b) in any other case, to the person referred to in paragraph (a) of this subsection or, if the Court considers proper, to the District Court clerk specified by the attachment of earnings order for transmission to that person or, where appropriate, to the competent authority.

(3) (a) Before deciding whether to make or refuse to make an attachment of earnings order, the court shall give the maintenance debtor concerned an opportunity to make the representations specified in paragraph (b) in relation to the matter and shall have regard to any such representations made by the maintenance debtor.

(b) The representations referred to in paragraph (a) are representations relating to the questions—

(i) whether the spouse concerned is a person to whom such earnings as aforesaid fall to be paid, and

(ii) whether he or she would make the payments to which the relevant order relates.

(4) An attachment of earnings order shall—

(a) specify the normal deduction rate, that is to say, the rate at which the Court considers it reasonable that the earnings to which the order relates should be applied in satisfying the relevant antecedent order, not exceeding the rate appearing to the Court to be necessary for the purpose of—

    (i) securing payment of the sums falling due from time to time under the relevant antecedent order, and

    (ii) securing payment within a reasonable period of any sums already due and unpaid under the relevant antecedent order and any costs incurred in proceedings relating to the relevant antecedent order which are payable by the maintenance debtor,

(b) specify the protected earnings rate, that is to say, the rate below which, having regard to the resources and the needs of the maintenance debtor, the Court considers it proper that the relevant earnings should not be reduced by a payment made in pursuance of the attachment of earnings order,

(c) contain so far as they are known to the Court such particulars as it considers appropriate for the purpose of enabling the maintenance debtor to be identified by the person to whom the order is directed.

(5) Payments under an attachment of earnings order shall be in lieu of payments of the like total amount under the relevant antecedent order that have not been made and that, but for the attachment of earnings order, would fall to be made under the relevant antecedent order.

Amendments—Social Welfare Act, 1989, s 13(1)(e) and (f); Family Law Act, 1995, s 43(d).

---

11 Compliance with attachment of earnings order

(1) Where an attachment of earnings order or an order varying it is made, the employer for the time being affected by it shall, if it has been served upon him, comply with it; but he shall be under no liability for non-compliance therewith before ten days have elapsed since the service.

(2) Where an attachment of earnings order is served on any person and the maintenance debtor is not in his employment or the maintenance debtor subsequently ceases to be in his employment, that person shall (in either case), within ten days from the date of service or, as the case may be, the cesser, give notice of that fact to the Court.

(3) On any occasion when a person makes, in compliance with an attachment of earnings order, a deduction from a maintenance debtor's earnings, he shall give to the maintenance debtor a statement in writing of the total amount of the deduction.

(4) Such court registrar or court clerk as may be specified by an attachment of earnings order shall cause the order to be served on the employer to whom it is directed and on any subsequent employer of the maintenance debtor concerned of whom the registrar or clerk so specified becomes aware and such service may be effected by leaving the order or a copy of the order at, or sending the order or a copy of the order by registered prepaid post to, the residence or place of business in the State of the person to be served.

12 Application of sums received by District Court clerk

Any payments made to a District Court clerk under an attachment of earnings order shall, when transmitted by him to the person entitled to receive those payments or, where appropriate, to the competent authority, be deemed to be payments made by the maintenance debtor so as to discharge—

(a) firstly, any sums payable under the relevant antecedent order, and
(b) secondly, any costs in proceedings relating to the relevant antecedent order payable by the maintenance debtor when the attachment of earnings order was made or last varied.

Amendments—Social Welfare Act, 1989, s 13(1)(g).

---

13 Statement as to earnings

(1) In relation to an attachment of earnings order or an application for such an order, the Court that made the order or to which the application is made may, before or at the hearing or while the order is in force—

(a) order the maintenance debtor to give to the Court, within a specified period, a statement in writing signed by him of—
  (i) the name and address of any person by whom earnings are paid to him,
  (ii) specified particulars as to his earnings and expected earnings and as to his resources and needs, and
  (iii) specified particulars for enabling the maintenance debtor to be identified by any employer of his,
(b) order any person appearing to the Court to have the maintenance debtor in his employment to give to the Court, within a specified period, a statement signed by that person, or on his behalf, of specified particulars of the maintenance debtor's earnings and expected earnings.

(2) Notice of an application for an attachment of earnings order served on a maintenance debtor may include a requirement that he shall give to the Court, within the period and in the manner specified in the notice, a statement in writing of the matters referred to in subsection (1)(a) of this section and of any other matters which are or may be relevant to the determination of the normal deduction rate and the protected earnings rate to be specified in the order.

(3) In any proceedings in relation to an attachment of earnings order, a statement given to the Court in compliance with an order under paragraph (a) or (b) of subsection (1) of this section or with a requirement under subsection (2) of this section shall be admissible as evidence of the facts stated therein, and a document purporting to be such a statement shall be deemed, unless the contrary is shown, to be a statement so given.

14 Notification of changes of employment and earnings

Where an attachment of earnings order is in force:

(a) the maintenance debtor shall notify in writing the Court that made the order of every occasion on which he leaves any employment, or becomes employed or re-employed, not later (in each case) than ten days from the date on which he does so,
(b) the maintenance debtor shall, on any occasion on which he becomes employed or re-employed, include in his notification under paragraph (a) of this section particulars of his earnings and expected earnings from the relevant employment,
(c) any person who becomes an employer of the maintenance debtor and knows that the order is in force and by what Court it was made shall, within ten days of his becoming the maintenance debtor's employer or of acquiring that knowledge (whichever is the later), notify that Court in writing that he is the debtor's

employer, and include in his notification a statement of the debtor's earnings and expected earnings.

15 Power to determine whether particular payments are earnings

(1) Where an attachment of earnings order is in force, the Court that made the order shall, on the application of the employer concerned or the maintenance debtor or the person to whom payments are being made under the order, determine whether payments (or any portions thereof) to the maintenance debtor of a particular class or description specified by the application are earnings for the purpose of the order, and the employer shall give effect to any determination for the time being in force under this section.

(2) Where an application under this section is made by the employer, he shall not incur any liability for non-compliance with the order as respects any payments (or any portions thereof) of the class or description specified by the application which are made by him to the maintenance debtor while the application or any appeal in consequence thereof or any decision in relation to the application or appeal is pending, but this shall not, unless the Court otherwise orders, apply as respects such payments (or any portions thereof) if the employer subsequently withdraws the application or, as the case may be, abandons the appeal.

16 Persons in service of State, local authority etc

(1) Where a maintenance debtor is in the service of the State, a local authority for the purposes of the Local Government Act, 1941, a harbour authority within the meaning of the Harbours Act, 1946, a health board, a vocational education committee established by the Vocational Education Act, 1930, or a committee of agriculture established by the Agriculture Act, 1931, or is a member of either House of the Oireachtas—

(a) in a case where a maintenance debtor in the service of the State is employed in a department, office, organisation, service, undertaking or other body, its chief officer (or such other officer as the Minister of State by whom the department, office, organisation, service, undertaking or other body is administered may from time to time designate) shall, for the purposes of this Act, be regarded as having the maintenance debtor in his employment,

(b) in a case where a maintenance debtor is in the service of such an authority, board or committee, its chief officer shall, for the purposes of this Act, be regarded as having the maintenance debtor in his employment,

(c) in any other case, where a maintenance debtor is paid out of the Central Fund or out of moneys provided by the Oireachtas, the Secretary of the Department of Finance (or such other officer of the Minister for Finance as that Minister may from time to time designate) shall, for the purposes of this Act, be regarded as having the maintenance debtor in his employment, and

(d) any earnings of a maintenance debtor paid out of the Central Fund or out of moneys provided by the Oireachtas shall be regarded as paid by the chief officer referred to in paragraph (a) or (b), as the case may be, of this subsection, the Secretary of the Department of Finance or such other officer as may be designated under paragraph (a) or (c), as the case may be, of this subsection, as may be appropriate.

(2) If any question arises in proceedings for or arising out of an attachment of earnings order as to what department, office, organisation, service, undertaking or other body a

maintenance debtor in the service of the State is employed in for the purposes of this section, the question may be referred to and determined by the Minister for the Public Service, but that Minister shall not be under any obligation to consider a reference under this subsection unless it is made by the Court.

(3) A document purporting to contain a determination of the Minister for the Public Service under subsection (2) of this section and to be signed by an officer of the Minister for the Public Service shall, in any such proceedings as are mentioned in that subsection, be admissible in evidence and be deemed, unless the contrary is shown, to contain an accurate statement of that determination.

(4) In this section references to a maintenance debtor in the service of the State include references to a maintenance debtor to whom earnings are paid directly out of moneys provided by the Oireachtas.

17   Discharge, variation and lapse of attachment of earnings order

(1) The Court that made an attachment of earnings order may, if it thinks fit, on the application of the maintenance creditor, the maintenance debtor or the District Court clerk on whose application the order was made, make an order discharging or varying that order.

(2) Where an order varying an attachment of earnings order is made under this section, the employer shall, if it has been served upon him, comply with it, but he shall be under no liability for non-compliance before ten days have elapsed since the service.

(3) Where an employer affected by an attachment of earnings order ceases to have the maintenance debtor in his employment, the order shall, in so far as that employer is concerned, lapse (except as respects deductions from earnings paid after the cesser by that employer and payment to the person in whose favour the order was made of deductions from earnings made at any time by that employer).

(4) The lapse of an order under subsection (3) of this section shall not prevent its remaining in force for other purposes.

18   Cesser of attachment of earnings order

(1) An attachment of earnings order shall cease to have effect upon the discharge of the relevant antecedent order, except as regards payments under the attachment of earnings order in respect of any time before the date of the discharge.

(2) Where an attachment of earnings order ceases to have effect, the clerk or registrar of the Court that made the order shall give notice of the cesser to the employer.

19   Provisions in relation to alternative remedies

(1) Where an attachment of earnings order has been made, any proceedings commenced under section 8(1) of the Enforcement of Court Orders Act, 1940, for the enforcement of the relevant antecedent order shall lapse and any warrant or order issued or made under that section in any such proceedings shall cease to have effect.

(2) An attachment of earnings order shall cease to have effect upon the making of an order under section 8(1) of the Enforcement of Court Orders Act, 1940, for the enforcement of the relevant antecedent order.

20   Enforcement

(1) Where, without reasonable excuse, a person—

- (a) fails to comply with subsection (1) or (2) of section 11 or section 14 or an order under section 13 or section 17(2) of this Act, or
- (b) gives to a Court a statement pursuant to section 13(1) of this Act, or a notification under section 14 of this Act, that is false or misleading,

and a maintenance creditor as a result fails to obtain a sum of money due under an attachment of earnings order, that sum may be sued for as a simple contract debt in any court of competent jurisdiction by the maintenance creditor or the District Court clerk to whom such sum falls to be paid, and that court may order the person to pay to the person suing such amount (not exceeding the sum aforesaid) as in all the circumstances the court considers proper for distribution in such manner and in such amounts as the court may specify amongst the persons for whose benefit the attachment of earnings order was made.

(2) Where a person gives to a Court—

- (a) a statement pursuant to section 13 of this Act, or
- (b) a notification under section 14 of this Act,

that is to his knowledge false or misleading, he shall be guilty of an offence and shall be liable on summary conviction to a fine not exceeding £200 or, at the discretion of the court, to imprisonment for a term not exceeding six months or to both.

(3) A person who contravenes section 11(3) of this Act shall be guilty of an offence and shall be liable on summary conviction to a fine not exceeding £50.

PART IV

MISCELLANEOUS

21   Property in household allowance

Any allowance made by one spouse to the other spouse after the commencement of this Act for the purpose of meeting household expenses, and any property or interest in property acquired out of such allowance, shall, in the absence of any agreement, whether express or implied, between them to the contrary, belong to the spouses as joint owners.

21A   Birth and funeral expenses of dependent child

(1) The Court may make an order (in this Act referred to as a lump sum order) where it appears to the Court on application by—

- (a) in relation to a dependent child of the family, a spouse, or
- (b) in relation to a dependent child whose parents are not married to each other, a parent,

that the other spouse or parent, as the case may be, has failed to make such contribution as is proper in the circumstances towards the expenses incidental to either or both—

- (i) the birth of a child who is a dependent child or who would have been a dependent child were he alive at the time of the application for a lump sum order,

(ii) the funeral of a child who w̄as a dependent child or who would have been a dependent child had he been born alive,

any lump sum order shall direct the respondent spouse or parent, as the case may be, to pay to the applicant a lump sum not exceeding £1,500, but no such order shall direct the payment of an amount exceeding £750 in respect of the birth of a child to whom this section relates or £750 in respect of the funeral of such a child.

(2) Section 5(4) or 5A(3) of this Act, as may be appropriate, shall apply for the purpose of determining the amount of any lump sum under this section as it applies for the purpose of determining the amount of any payment under section 5 or 5A of this Act, as appropriate.

(3) (a) Nothing in this section, apart from this subsection, shall prejudice any right of a person otherwise to recover moneys expended in relation to the birth or funeral of a child.

(b) Where an application for a lump sum order has been determined, the applicant shall not be entitled otherwise to recover from the respondent moneys in relation to matters so determined.

Amendments—Inserted by Status of Children Act, 1987, s 21(1).

22 (*repealed*)

Amendments—Family Law (Protection of Spouses and Children) Act, 1981, s 17(1).

23 Jurisdiction of Courts

(1) Subject to subsection (2) of this section, the Circuit Court and the District Court shall have jurisdiction to hear and determine proceedings under sections 5, 5A, 6, 7, 9 and 21A of this Act.

(2) (a) The District Court and the Circuit Court, on appeal from the District Court, shall not have jurisdiction to make an order under this Act for the payment of a periodical sum at a rate greater than £200 per week for the support of a spouse or £60 per week for the support of a child.

(b) Subject to paragraph (d) of this subsection, nothing in subsection (1) of this section shall be construed as conferring on the District Court or the Circuit Court jurisdiction to make an order or direction under section 5, 5A, 6, 7, 9 or 21A of this Act in any matter in relation to which the High Court has made an order or direction under any of those sections.

(c) Subject to paragraph (d) of this subsection, nothing in subsection (1) of this section shall be construed as conferring on the District Court jurisdiction to make an order or direction under section 5, 5A, 6, 7, 9 or 21A of this Act in any matter in relation to which the Circuit Court (except on appeal from the District Court) has made an order or direction under any of those sections.

(d) The District Court and the Circuit Court may vary or revoke an order or direction made by the High Court under section 5, 5A, 6, 7, 9 or 21A of this Act before the commencement of section 12 of the Courts Act, 1981, if—

(i) the circumstances to which the order or direction of the High Court related have changed other than by reason of such commencement, and

      (ii)   in the case of a variation or revocation of such an order or direction by the District Court, the provisions of the order or direction would have been within the jurisdiction of that Court if the said section 12 had been in operation at the time of the making of the order or direction.

(3) In proceedings under this Act—

  (a) each of the spouses concerned shall give to the other spouse and to, or to a person acting on behalf of, any dependent member of the family concerned, and

  (b) any dependent member of the family concerned shall give to, or to a person acting on behalf of, any other such member and to each of the spouses concerned,

such particulars of his or her property and income as may reasonably be required for the purpose of the proceedings.

(4) Where a person fails or refuses to comply with subsection (3), the Court, on application to it in that behalf by a person having an interest in the matter, may direct the person to comply with that subsection.

Amendments—Courts Act, 1981, s 12; Status of Children Act, 1987, s 22; Courts Act, 1991, s 11; Family Law Act, 1995, s 43(e); Family Law (Divorce) Act, 1996, s 52(o)(ii).

24   Payments to be without deduction of income tax

A periodical payment of money pursuant to a maintenance order, a variation order, an interim order, an order under section 8 or 8A of this Act (in so far as it is deemed under that section to be a maintenance order), or an attachment of earnings order shall be made without deduction of income tax.

Amendments—Status of Children Act, 1987, s 23.

25   Conduct of Court proceedings

(1) Proceedings under this Act shall be conducted in a summary manner and shall be heard otherwise than in public.

(2) Proceedings in the High Court and the Circuit Court under this Act shall be heard in chambers.

26   Costs

The costs of any proceedings under this Act shall be in the discretion of the Court.

27   Voidance of certain provisions of agreements

An agreement shall be void in so far as it would have the effect of excluding or limiting the operation of any provision of this Act (other than section 21).

28   (Amends the Illegitimate Children (Affiliation Orders) Act, 1930 and Courts Act, 1971)

29   (Amends s 8(1) and (7) of the Enforcement of Court Orders Act, 1940)

30   Repeals

(1) The Married Women (Maintenance in case of Desertion) Act, 1886, section 13 of the Illegitimate Children (Affiliation Orders) Act, 1930, section 7 of the Enforcement of Court Orders Act, 1940, and section 18 of the Courts Act, 1971, are hereby repealed, and the reference in section 98(1)(a) of the Defence Act, 1954, to an order made by a civil court under section 1 of the said Married Women (Maintenance in case of Desertion) Act, 1886, shall be construed as a reference to an order under section 5, 6, or 7 of this Act or an order under section 8 of this Act (in so far as it is deemed under that section to be a maintenance order).

(2) (a) Any order made by a Court under the provisions repealed by this section and in force immediately before the commencement of this Act shall continue in force as if it was, and shall be deemed for all purposes to be, a maintenance order or an attachment of earnings order, as the case may be.

   (b) Any proceedings initiated under the provisions repealed by this section and not completed before the repeal shall be deemed for all purposes to be proceedings under the corresponding provisions of this Act and may be continued accordingly.

Family Law (Miscellaneous Provisions) Act, 1997

(1997 No 18)

ARRANGEMENT OF SECTIONS

ACTS REFERRED TO

An Act to amend the law in relation to notification of intention to marry, the law in relation to barring orders, the law in relation to irrevocable powers of attorney and the law in relation to the distribution of disclaimed estates   [5 May 1997]

1 Definition

In this Act 'the Act of 1995' means the Family Law Act, 1995.

2 (Amends the Act of 1995)

3 Validity in law of certain marriages

(1) Where, in relation to a marriage solemnised after the commencement of section 32 (whether before or after the passing of this Act) of the Act of 1995, the notification provided for in subsection (1) of that section is or was given to a Registrar appointed under section 57 of the Marriages (Ireland) Act, 1844, or section 10 of the Registration of Marriages (Ireland) Act, 1863, or a person authorised by that Registrar to act on his or her behalf and that Registrar is or was not the Registrar (within the meaning of section 32 of the Act of 1995) in relation to that marriage, the marriage shall be and shall be deemed always to have been valid in law if it would have been so valid if the notification had been given to the Registrar (within the meaning aforesaid) in relation to that marriage.

(2) Where, in relation to a marriage, exemption from section 31(1)(a) or 32(1)(a) of the Act of 1995, or both of those provisions, was granted, before the passing of this Act, by a judge of the Circuit Family Court who, in relation to the application concerned, was

not the appropriate judge having regard to section 38(4) of the Act of 1995, the marriage shall be and shall be deemed always to have been valid in law if it would have been so valid if the exemption aforesaid had been granted by the judge who, in relation to the application, was the appropriate judge having regard to the said section 38(4).

4   (Amends s 3 of the Domestic Violence Act, 1996)

5   (Amends the Powers of Attorney Act, 1996)

6   (Amends the Succession Act, 1965)

7   Short title

This Act may be cited as the Family Law (Miscellaneous Provisions) Act, 1997.

Finance Act, 1997

(1997 No 22)

ARRANGEMENT OF SECTIONS

127 Exemption of certain transfers from stamp duty following the dissolution of a marriage

(1) Subject to *subsection (3)*, stamp duty shall not be chargeable on an instrument by which property is transferred pursuant to an order to which this subsection applies by either or both of the spouses who were parties to the marriage concerned to either or both of them.

(2) Section 74(2) of the Finance (1909–10) Act, 1910, shall not apply to a transfer to which *subsection (1)* applies.

(3) (a) *Subsection (1)* applies—
      (i)   to a relief order, within the meaning of section 23 of the Family Law Act, 1995, made following the dissolution of a marriage, or
      (ii) to an order under Part III of the Family Law (Divorce) Act, 1996.
    (b) *Subsection (1)* does not apply in relation to an instrument referred to in that subsection by which any part of or beneficial interest in the property concerned is transferred to a person other than the spouses concerned.

(4) Section 50 of the Family Law Act, 1995 and section 33 of the Family Law (Divorce) Act, 1996, are hereby repealed.

Guardianship of Infants Act, 1964

(1964 No 7)

ARRANGEMENT OF SECTIONS

PART I

PRELIMINARY AND GENERAL

PART II

GUARDIANSHIP

PART III

ENFORCEMENT OF RIGHT OF CUSTODY

PART IV

SAFEGUARDING INTERESTS OF CHILDREN

SCHEDULE

An Act to consolidate with amendments the enactments relating to the custody and guardianship of infants   [25 March 1964]

PART I

PRELIMINARY AND GENERAL

1   Short title

This Act may be cited as the Guardianship of Infants Act, 1964.

2   Interpretation

(1) In this Act, unless the context otherwise requires—

'the Act of 1987' means the Status of Children Act, 1987;
'adoption order' means—

(a) an adoption order made under the Adoption Acts, 1952 to 1991, or
(b) an order made or decree granted outside the State, providing for the
    adoption of a person, which is recognised by virtue of the law for the time
    being in force in the State,

and for the time being in force;
'child' means a person who has not attained full age;
'father' includes a male adopter under an adoption order, but, subject to *section
11(4)*, does not include the father of a child who has not married that child's
mother unless either—

(a) an order under *section 6A* (inserted by the Act of 1987) is in force in respect of that child,

(b) the circumstances set out in *subsection (3)* of this section apply, or

(c) the circumstances set out in *subsection (4)* of this section apply;

'maintenance' includes education;

'mother' includes a female adopter under an adoption order;

'parent' means a father or mother as defined by this subsection;

'testamentary guardian' means a guardian appointed by deed or will;

'welfare', in relation to an child, comprises the religious, moral, intellectual, physical and social welfare of the child.

(2) A reference, however expressed, in this Act to a child whose father and mother have not married each other shall, except in a case to which *subsection (3)* relates, be construed in accordance with *section 4* of the Act of 1987.

(3) (a) The circumstances referred to in *paragraph (b)* of the definition of 'father' in *subsection (1)* are that the father and mother of the child concerned have at some time gone through a ceremony of marriage and the ceremony resulted in—

   (i) a voidable marriage in respect of which a decree of nullity was granted after, or at some time during the period of 10 months before, the birth of the child, or

   (ii) a void marriage which the father reasonably believed (whether or not such belief was due to a mistake of law or of fact) resulted in a valid marriage—

     (I) where the ceremony occurred before the birth of the child, at some time during the period of 10 months before that birth, or

     (II) where the ceremony occurred after the birth of the child, at the time of that ceremony.

   (b) It shall be presumed for the purposes of *subparagraph (ii)* of *paragraph (a)*, unless the contrary is shown, that the father reasonably believed that the ceremony of marriage to which that subparagraph relates resulted in a valid marriage.

(4) The circumstances referred to in *paragraph (c)* of the definition of 'father' in *subsection (1)* are that the father and mother of the child concerned, not being a father or mother to whom the circumstances set out in *subsection (3)* apply—

(a) have not married each other,

(b) declare that they are the father and mother of the child concerned,

(c) agree to the appointment of the father as a guardian of the child,

(d) have entered into arrangements regarding the custody of and, as the case may be, access to the child, and

(e) have made a statutory declaration to that effect as may be prescribed by the Minister for Justice, Equality and Law Reform.

(5) In this Act—

(a) a reference to a Part or section is a reference to a Part or section of this Act, unless it is indicated that a reference to some other enactment is intended,

(b) a reference to a subsection or paragraph is a reference to the subsection or paragraph of the provision in which the reference occurs, unless it is indicated that a reference to some other provision is intended, and

(c) a reference to any enactment shall be construed as a reference to that enactment as amended by or under any subsequent enactment.

Amendments—Inserted by the Children Act, 1997, s 4.

3 Welfare of child to be paramount

Where in any proceedings before any court the custody, guardianship or upbringing of a child, or the administration of any property belonging to or held on trust for a child, or the application of the income thereof, is in question, the court, in deciding that question, shall regard the welfare of the child as the first and paramount consideration.

Amendments—Children Act, 1997, s 12.

3A Proof of paternity in certain proceedings

Where in any proceedings before any court on an application for an order under this Act (other than so much of any proceedings as *section 15* of the Act of 1987 relates to) in respect of a child whose father and mother have not married each other, a person (being a party to the proceedings) is alleged to be, or alleges that he is, the father of the child but that allegation is not admitted by a party to the proceedings, the court shall not on that application make any final order which imposes any obligation or confers any right on that person unless it is proved on the balance of probabilities that he is the father of the child:

Provided that this section applies only where the fact that that person is or is not the father of the child is material to the proceedings.

Amendments—Inserted by Status of Children Act, 1987, s 10; amended by Children Act, 1997, s 12.

4 Repeals

Each enactment specified in the Schedule is hereby repealed to the extent indicated in the third column of the Schedule.

PART II

GUARDIANSHIP

5 Jurisdiction in guardianship matters

(1) Subject to *subsection (2)* of this section, the jurisdiction conferred on a court by this Part may be exercised by the Circuit Court or the District Court.

(2) The District Court and the Circuit Court, on appeal from the District Court, shall not have jurisdiction to make an order under this Act for the payment of a periodical sum at a rate greater than £60 per week towards the maintenance of a child.

(3) The jurisdiction conferred by this Part is in addition to any other jurisdiction to appoint or remove guardians or as to the wardship of children or the care of children's estates.

Amendments—Courts Act, 1981, s 15(1)(a); Courts Act, 1991, s 12; Children Act, 1997, s 12.

6   Rights of parents to guardianship

(1) The father and mother of a child shall be guardians of the child jointly.

(2) On the death of the father of a child the mother, if surviving, shall be guardian of the child, either alone or jointly with any guardian appointed by the father or by the court.

(3) On the death of the mother of a child the father, if surviving, shall be guardian of the child, either alone or jointly with any guardian appointed by the mother or by the court.

(4) Where the mother of a child has not married the child's father, she, while living, shall alone be the guardian of the child, unless the circumstances set out in *section 2(4)* apply or there is in force an order under *section 6A* (inserted by the Act of 1987) or a guardian has otherwise been appointed in accordance with this Act.

Amendments—Status of Children Act, 1987, s 11; Children Act, 1997, s 12.

6A   Power of court to appoint certain fathers as guardians

(1) Where the father and mother of a child have not married each other and have not made a declaration under *section 2(4)*, or where the father was a guardian of the child by virtue of a declaration under *section 2(4)* but was removed from office under *section 8(4)*, the court may, on the application of the father, by order, appoint the father to be a guardian of the child.

(2) Without prejudice to the provisions of *sections 5(3)* (inserted by the Courts Act, 1981), 8(4) and 12 of this Act, the appointment by the court under this section of the father of a child as his guardian shall not affect the prior appointment of any person as a guardian of the child under *section 8(1)* of this Act unless the court otherwise orders.

Amendments—Inserted by Status of Children Act, 1987, s 12; amended by Children Act, 1997, s 6, s 12.

7   Power of father and mother to appoint testamentary guardians

(1) The father of a child may by deed or will appoint a person or persons to be guardian or guardians of the child after his death.

(2) The mother of a child may by deed or will appoint a person or persons to be guardian or guardians of the child after her death.

(3) A testamentary guardian shall act jointly with the surviving parent of the child so long as the surviving parent remains alive unless the surviving parent objects to his so acting.

(4) If the surviving parent so objects or if a testamentary guardian considers that the surviving parent is unfit to have the custody of the child, the testamentary guardian may apply to the court for an order under this section.

(5) The court may—

  (a) refuse to make an order (in which case the surviving parent shall remain sole guardian), or

  (b) make an order that the testamentary guardian shall act jointly with the surviving parent, or

(c)   make an order that he shall act as guardian of the infant to the exclusion, so far as the court thinks proper, of the surviving parent.

(6) In the case mentioned in *paragraph (c)* of *subsection (5)* the court may make such order regarding the custody of the child and the right of access to the child of the surviving parent as the court thinks proper, and the court may further order that the surviving parent shall pay to the guardian or guardians, or any of them, towards the maintenance of the child such weekly or other periodical sum as, having regard to the means of the surviving parent, the court considers reasonable.

(7) (*repealed*)

(8) An appointment of a guardian by deed may be revoked by a subsequent deed or by will.

Amendments—Succession Act, 1965, s 8, Second Sch, Pt IV; Children Act, 1997, s 12.

8   Appointment and removal of guardians by court

(1) Where a child has no guardian, the court, on the application of any person or persons, may appoint the applicant or applicants or any of them to be the guardian or guardians of the child.

(2) When no guardian has been appointed by a deceased parent or if a guardian so appointed dies or refuses to act, the court may appoint a guardian or guardians to act jointly with the surviving parent.

(3) A guardian appointed by the court to act jointly with a surviving parent shall continue to act as guardian after the death of the surviving parent.

(4) A guardian appointed by will or deed or order of court, or holding office by virtue of the circumstances set out in *section 2(4)* (inserted by the Children Act, 1997) applying to him, may be removed from office only by the court.

(5) The court may appoint another guardian in place of a guardian so removed or in place of a guardian appointed by any such order who dies.

Amendments—Children Act, 1997, s 7, s 12.

9   Provisions where two or more guardians appointed

(1) Where two or more persons are appointed to be guardians they shall act jointly and on the death of any of them the survivor or survivors shall continue to act.

(2) Where guardians are appointed by both parents the guardians so appointed shall after the death of the surviving parent act jointly.

Amendments—Children Act, 1997, s 12.

10   Powers and duties of guardians

(1) Every guardian under this Act shall be a guardian of the person and of the estate of the child unless, in the case of a guardian appointed by deed, will or order of the court, the terms of his appointment otherwise provide.

(2) Subject to the terms of any such deed, will or order, a guardian under this Act—

(a) as guardian of the person, shall, as against every person not being, jointly with him, a guardian of the person, be entitled to the custody of the child and shall be entitled to take proceedings for the restoration of his custody of the child against any person who wrongfully takes away or detains the child and for the recovery, for the benefit of the child, of damages for any injury to or trespass against the person of the child;

(b) as guardian of the estate, shall be entitled to the possession and control of all property, real and personal, of the child and shall manage all such property and receive the rents and profits on behalf and for the benefit of the child until the child attains the age of twenty-one years or during any shorter period for which he has been appointed guardian and may take such proceedings in relation thereto as may by law be brought by any guardian of the estate of a child.

(3) The provisions of this section are without prejudice to the provisions of any other enactment or to any other powers or duties conferred or imposed by law on parents, guardians or trustees of the property of children.

Amendments—Children Act, 1997, s 12.

---

11   Applications to court

(1) Any person being a guardian of a child may apply to the court for its direction on any question affecting the welfare of the child and the court may make such order as it thinks proper.

(2) The court may by an order under this section—

(a) give such directions as it thinks proper regarding the custody of the child and the right of access to the child of his father or mother;

(b) order the father or mother to pay towards the maintenance of the child such weekly or other periodical sum as, having regard to the means of the father or mother, the court considers reasonable.

(3) An order under this section may be made on the application of either parent notwithstanding that the parents are then residing together, but an order made under *paragraph (a)* of *subsection (2)* shall not be enforceable and no liability thereunder shall accrue while they reside together, and the order shall cease to have effect if for a period of three months after it is made they continue to reside together.

(4) In the case of a child whose father and mother have not married each other, the right to make an application under this section regarding the custody of the child and the right of access thereto of his father or mother shall extend to the father who is not a guardian of the child, and for this purpose references in this section to the father or parent of a child shall be construed as including him.

(5) A reference in *subsection (2)(b)* to a child shall include a reference to a person who—

(a) has not attained the age of 18 years, or

(b) has attained the age of 18 years and is or will be, or if any order were made under this Act providing for payment of maintenance for the benefit of the person, would be, receiving full-time education or instruction at a university, college, school or other educational establishment, and who has not attained the age of 23 years.

(6) *Subsection (2)(b)* shall apply to and in relation to a person who has attained the age of 18 years and has a mental or physical disability to such extent that it is not reasonably possible for the person to maintain himself or herself fully, as it applies to a child.

(7) A copy of any report prepared under *subsection (5)* shall be made available to the barrister or solicitor, if any, representing each party in the proceedings or, if any party is not so represented, to that party and may be received in evidence in the proceedings.

(8) Where any person prepares a report pursuant to a request under *subsection (5)* of this section, the fees and expenses of that person shall be paid by such party or parties to the proceedings as the court shall order.

(9) The court may, if it thinks fit, or either party to the proceedings may, call the person making the report as a witness.

Amendments—Inserted by Age of Majority Act, 1985, s 6(a); Status of Children Act, 1987, s 13; Judicial Separation and Family Law Reform Act, 1989, s 40; Children Act, 1997, s 8, s 12.

11A   Custody may be granted to father and mother jointly

For the avoidance of doubt, it is hereby declared that the court, in making an order under *section 11*, may, if it thinks it appropriate, grant custody of a child to the child's father and mother jointly.

11B   Relatives may apply for access to child

(1) Any person who—

    (a)   is a relative of a child, or,
    (b)   has acted *in loco parentis* to a child,

and to whom *section 11* does not apply may, subject to *subsection (3)*, apply to the court for an order giving that person access to the child on such terms and conditions as the court may order.

(2) A person may not make an application under *subsection (1)* unless the person has first applied for and has been granted by the court leave to make the application.

(3) In deciding whether to grant leave under *subsection (1)*, the court shall have regard to all the circumstances, including in particular—

    (a)   the applicant's connection with the child,
    (b)   the risk, if any, of the application disrupting the child's life to the extent that the child would be harmed by it,
    (c)   the wishes of the child's guardians.

(4) In this section, a relative of a child who is the subject of an adoption order includes—

    (a)   a relative of the child's adoptive parents,
    (b)   the adoptive parents of the child's parents, or
    (c)   a relative of the adoptive parents of the child's parents.

11C Operation of order not to be stayed pending appeal unless so ordered

The operation of an order under this Act shall not be stayed pending the outcome of an appeal against the order unless the court that made the order or the court to which the appeal is brought directs otherwise.

11D Provision relating to orders under *sections 6A, 11, 14 and 16*

In considering whether to make an order under *section 6A, 11, 14* or *16* the court shall have regard to whether the child's best interests would be served by maintaining personal relations and direct contact with both his or her father and mother on a regular basis.

Amendments—Sections 11A–11D are inserted by the Children Act, 1997, s 9.

12 Variation and discharge of court orders

The court may vary or discharge any order previously made by the court under this Part.

PART III

ENFORCEMENT OF RIGHT OF CUSTODY

13 Definitions for Part III

In this Part—

'the court' means the Circuit Court or the District Court;
'health authority' has the meaning assigned to it by *subsection (1)* of *section 2* of the Health Act, 1947, as amended by *section 9* of the Health Authorities Act, 1960;
'parent' includes a guardian of the person and any person at law liable to maintain a child or entitled to his custody;
'person' includes any school or institution.

Amendments—Courts Act, 1981, s 15(1)(b); Children Act, 1997, s 12.

14 Power of court as to production of child

Where a parent of a child applies to the court for an order for the production of the child and the court is of opinion that that parent has abandoned or deserted the child or that he has otherwise so conducted himself that the court should refuse to enforce his right to the custody of the child, the court may in its discretion decline to make the order.

Amendments—Children Act, 1997, s 12.

15 Power to court to order repayment of costs of bringing up child

Where, upon application by a parent for the production of a child, the court finds—

(a) that the child is being brought up at the expense of another person, or

(b) that at any time assistance has been provided for the infant by a health authority under *section 55* of the Health Act, 1953 or that at any time the child has been maintained in the care of a health board under *section 4* of the Child Care Act, 1991,

the court may, in its discretion, if it orders the child to be given up to the parent, further order that the parent shall pay to that person or health authority the whole of the costs properly incurred by the person or health authority in bringing up or providing assistance for the child or such portion thereof as the court considers reasonable, having regard to all the circumstances of the case, including, in particular, the means of the parent.

Amendments—Child Care Act, 1991, s 76; Children Act, 1997, s 12.

16   Court in making order to have regard to conduct of parent

Where a parent has—

(a) abandoned or deserted a child, or
(b) allowed a child to be brought up by another person at that person's expense, or to be provided with assistance by a health authority under *section 55* of the Health Act, 1953 or to be maintained in the care of a health board under *section 4* of the Child Care Act, 1991, for such a length of time and under such circumstances as to satisfy the court that the parent was unmindful of his parental duties,

the court shall not make an order for the delivery of the child to the parent unless the parent has satisfied the court that he is a fit person to have the custody of the child.

Amendments—Child Care Act, 1991, s 77; Children Act, 1997, s 12.

17   Power of court as to child's religious education

(1) Upon any application by a parent for the production or custody of a child, if the court is of opinion that that parent ought not to have the custody of the infant, the court shall have power to make such order as it thinks fit to secure that the infant be brought up in the religion in which the parents, or a parent, have or has a legal right to require that the child should be brought up.

Amendments—Children Act, 1997, s 10, s 12.

18   Custody where parents are separated

(1) In any case where a decree for divorce *a mensa et thoro* is pronounced, the Circuit Court may thereby declare the parent by reason of whose misconduct the decree is made to be a person unfit to have the custody of the children (if any) of the marriage or of any children adopted under the Adoption Act, 1952, by the parents jointly; and in such case, the parent so declared to be unfit shall not, on the death of the other parent, be entitled as of right to the custody of the children.

(2) A provision contained in any separation agreement made between the father and mother of a child shall not be invalid by reason only of its providing that one of them shall give up the custody or control of the child to the other.

Amendments—Courts Act, 1981, s 15(1)(c); Children Act, 1997, s 12.

PART IV

SAFEGUARDING INTERESTS OF CHILDREN

19   Definitions

In this Part—

'the Act of 1976' means the Family Law (Maintenance of Spouses and Children) Act, 1976;'

'the Act of 1989' means the Judicial Separation and Family Law Reform Act, 1989;

'the Act of 1995' means the Family Law Act, 1995;

'the Act of 1996' means the Family Law (Divorce) Act, 1996.

20   Safeguards to ensure applicant's awareness of alternatives to custody, access and guardianship proceedings and to assist attempts at agreement

(1) In this section 'the applicant' means a person who has applied, is applying or proposes to apply to the court for directions under *section 6A, 11* or *11B.*

(2) If a solicitor is acting for the applicant, the solicitor shall, before the institution of proceedings under *section 6A, 11* or *11B,* discuss with the applicant the possibility of the applicant—

(a) engaging in counselling to assist in reaching an agreement with the respondent about the custody of the child, the right of access to the child or any other question affecting the welfare of the child and give to the applicant the name and address of persons qualified to give counselling on the matter.

(b) engaging in mediation to help to effect an agreement between the applicant and the respondent about the custody of the child, the right of access to the child or any question affecting the welfare of the child, and give to the applicant the name and addresses of persons qualified to provide an appropriate mediation service, and

(c) where appropriate, effecting a deed or agreement in writing executed or made by the applicant and the respondent and providing for the custody of the child, the right of access to the child or any question affecting the welfare of the child.

(3) If a solicitor is acting for the applicant—

(a) the original documents by which the proceedings under *section 6A, 11* or *11B* are instituted shall be accompanied by a certificate signed by the solicitor indicating, if it be the case, that the solicitor has complied with *subsection (2)* in relation to the matter and, if the document is not so accompanied, the court may adjourn the proceedings for such period as it considers reasonable to enable the solicitor to engage in the discussions referred to in *subsection (2),*

(b) if the solicitor has complied with *paragraph (a),* any copy of the original document served on any person or left in an office of the court shall be accompanied by a copy of that certificate.

(4) The solicitor shall be deemed to have complied with *subsection (3)* in relation to the requirement of a certificate where the application under *section 6A, 11* or *11B* is made in proceedings for the grant of—

    (a) a decree of judicial separation under the Act of 1989 and *section 5(2)* of that Act has been complied with by the solicitor, or

    (b) a decree of divorce under the Act of 1996 and *section 6(4)* of that Act has been complied with by the solicitor.

21   Safeguards to ensure respondent's awareness of alternatives to custody, access and guardianship proceedings and to assist attempts at agreement

(1) In this section 'the respondent' means a respondent in proceedings in the court under *section 6A, 11* or *11B.*

(2) If a solicitor is acting for the respondent, the solicitor shall, as soon as practicable after receiving instructions from the respondent in relation to proceedings under *section 6A, 11* or *11B* discuss with the respondent the possibility of the respondent—

    (a) engaging in counselling to assist in reaching an agreement with the applicant about the custody of the child, the right of access to the child or any other question affecting the welfare of the child and give to the respondent the name and addresses of persons qualified to give counselling on the matter,

    (b) engaging in mediation to help to effect an agreement between the respondent and the applicant about the custody of the child, the right of access to the child or any question affecting the welfare of the child and where appropriate give to the respondent the name and addressses of persons qualified to provide an appropriate mediation service, and

    (c) where appropriate, effecting a deed or agreement in writing executed or made by the respondent and the applicant and providing for the custody of the child, the right of access to the child or any question affecting the welfare of the child.

(3) If a solicitor is acting for the respondent—

    (a) the memorandum or other documents delivered to the appropriate officer of the court for the purpose of the entry of an appearance by the respondent in proceedings under *section 6A, 11* or *11B* shall be accompanied by a certificate signed by the solicitor indicating, if it be the case, that the solicitor has complied with *subsection (2)* in relation to the matter and, if the document is not so accompanied, the court may adjourn the proceedings for such period as it considers reasonable to enable the solicitor to engage in the discussions referred to in *subsection (2),*

    (b) if the solicitor has complied with *paragraph (a)*, any copy of the original document given or sent to the applicant or his solicitor shall be accompanied by a copy of that certificate.

(4) The solicitor shall be deemed to have complied with *subsection (3)* in relation to the requirement of a certificate where the application under *section 6A, 11* or *11B* is made in proceedings for the grant of—

    (a) a decree of judicial separation under the Act of 1989 and *section 6(2)* of that Act has been complied with by the solicitor, or

    (b) a decree of divorce under the Act of 1996 and *section 7(4)* of that Act has been complied with by the solicitor.

22 Adjournment of proceedings to assist agreement on custody or guardianship of or access to child

(1) Where, in proceedings under *section 6A, 11* or *11B* it appears to the court that agreement between the parties on the subject matter of the proceedings may be affected, it may adjourn or further adjourn the proceedings for the purpose of enabling attempts to be made by the parties, if they wish, to reach agreement, with or without the assistance of a third party, on some or all of the issues which are in dispute.

(2) If proceedings are adjourned pursuant to *subsection (1)*, any party may at any time request that the hearing of the proceedings be resumed as soon as practicable and, if such a request is made, the court shall, subject to any other power of the court to adjourn proceedings, resume the hearing.

(3) The powers conferred by this section are additional to any other power of the court to adjourn proceedings.

(4) Where the court adjourns proceedings under this section, it may, at its discretion, advise the parties concerned to seek the assistance of a third party in relation to the effecting of an agreement between them on all or any of its terms.

23 Non-admissibility as evidence of certain communications relating to agreement

An oral or written communication between any of the parties concerned and a third party for the purpose of seeking assistance to reach agreement between them regarding the custody of the child, the right of access to the child or any question affecting the welfare of the child (whether or not made in the presence or with the knowledge of the other party) and any record of such communication, made or caused to be made by any of the parties concerned or such a third party, shall not be admissible as evidence in any court.

24 Orders in respect of custody or access agreements

Where—

(a) the parties to a dispute relating to the welfare of a child enter into an agreement in writing that includes—
   (i) a provision whereby one party undertakes, or both parties undertake, to take custody of the child, or
   (ii) a provision governing the rights of access of parties, and
(b) an application is made by any party to the court for an order making the agreement a rule of court,

the court may make such an order if it is satisfied that the agreement is a fair and reasonable one which in all the circumstances adequately protects the interests of the parties and the child, and such order shall, insofar as it relates to a provision specified in *subparagraph (i)* or *(ii)* of *paragraph (a)*, be deemed to be an order under *section 11(2)(a)* or *11B* as appropriate.

25 Wishes of child

In any proceedings to which *section 3* applies, the court shall, as it things appropriate and practicable having regard to the age and understanding of the child, take into account the child's wishes in the matter.

26   Social reports

For the purposes of the application of *section 47* of the Act of 1995 to proceedings under this Act, 'court' includes the District Court.

27   Power to proceed in absence of child

(1) It shall not be necessary in proceedings under *section 6A, 11* or *11B* for the child to whom the proceedings relate to be brought before the court or to be present for all or any part of the hearing unless the court, either of its own motion or at the request of any of the parties to the proceedings, is satisfied that it is necessary for the proper disposal of the proceedings.

(2) Where the child requests to be present during the hearing or a particular part of the hearing of the proceedings, the court shall grant the request unless it appears to it that, having regard to the age of the child or the nature of the proceedings, it would not be in the child's best interests to accede to the request.

28   Appointment of guardian *ad litem* for a child and provision for separate representation

(1) If in proceedings under *section 6A, 11* or *11B* the child to whom the proceedings relate is not a party, the court may, if satisfied that having regard to the special circumstances of the case it is necessary in the best interests of the child to do so, appoint a guardian *ad litem* for the child.

(2) Without prejudice to the generality of *subsection (1)*, in deciding whether to appoint a guardian *ad litem*, the court shall, in particular, have regard to—

    (a) the age and understanding of the child,
    (b) any report on any question affecting the welfare of the child that is furnished to the court under *section 47* of the Act of 1995,
    (c) the welfare of the child,
    (d) whether and to what extent the child should be given the opportunity to express the child's wishes in the proceedings, taking into account any statement in relation to those matters in any report under *section 47* of the Act of 1995, and
    (e) any submission made in relation to the matter of the appointment as a guardian *ad litem* that is made to the court by or on behalf of a party to the proceedings or any other person to whom they relate.

(3) For the purposes of this section, the court may appoint as a guardian *ad litem* the person from whom, under *section 47(1)* of the Act of 1995, a report on any question affecting the welfare of the child was procured, or such other persons as it thinks fit.

(4) If having regard to the gravity of the matters that may be in issue or any other special circumstances relating to the particular case, it appears to the court that it is necessary in the best interests of the child that the guardian *ad litem* ought to be legally represented, the court may order that the guardian *ad litem* be so represented in the proceedings.

(5) The fees and expenses of a guardian *ad litem* appointed pursuant to *subsection (1)* and the costs of obtaining legal representation pursuant to an order under *subsection (4)* shall be paid by such parties to the proceedings concerned, and in such proportions, or by such party to the proceedings, as the court may determine.

29   Cost of mediation and counselling services

The cost of any mediation or counselling services provided for an applicant or respondent who is or becomes a party to proceedings under this Act, or for the child to whom the proceedings relate, shall be in the discretion of the court concerned.

30   Jurisdiction

(1) Subject to *subsection (2)*, the jurisdiction conferred on a court by this Part may be exercised by the Circuit Court or the District Court.

(2)Where the agreement referred to in *section 24* is a separation agreement, the application for an order in respect of that agreement shall be made to the Circuit Court.

(3) Where an application is made to the court for an order under *section 24*, the court may, in the same proceedings, if it appears to it to be proper to do so, make an order under *section 8* or *8A* of the Act of 1976 without the institution of proceedings under that Act.

(4) Where an application is made to the court for an order under *section 8* or *8A* of the Act of 1976, the court may, in the same proceedings, if it appears to it to be proper to do so, make an order under *section 24* without the institution of proceedings under this Act.

Amendments—Children Act, 1997, s 11.

SCHEDULE   Section 4

REPEALS

Session and Chapter	Short Title	Extent of Repeal
14 & 15 Chas 2, sess 4, c 19.	Tenures Abolition Act, 1662.	Sections 6, 7, 15 and 16.
36 Vict, c 12.	Custody of Infants Act 1873.	The whole Act.
49 & 50 Vict, c 27.	Guardianship of Infants Act 1886.	The whole Act.
54 Vict, c 3.	Custody of Children Act 1891.	The whole Act.

Judicial Separation and Family Law Reform Act, 1989

(1989 No 6)

ARRANGEMENT OF SECTIONS

PART I

THE OBTAINING OF A DECREE OF SEPARATION

PART II

ANCILLARY FINANCIAL, PROPERTY, CUSTODY AND OTHER ORDERS

PART III

COURT JURISDICTION

PART TWO

PART IV

MISCELLANEOUS

ACTS REFERRED TO

An Act to amend the grounds for judicial separation: to facilitate reconciliation between estranged spouses: to provide for the making of ancillary orders in separation proceedings: to amend the law relating to the courts' family law jurisdiction and to provide for connected matters.

[19 April, 1989]

PART I

THE OBTAINING OF A DECREE OF SEPARATION

1   Definition

In this Act, except where the context otherwise requires—

'the court' means the court having jurisdiction under *Part III* of this Act.

2   Application for a decree of judicial separation

(1) An application by a spouse for a decree of judicial separation from the other spouse may be made to the court having jurisdiction to hear and determine proceedings under *Part III* of this Act on one or more of the following grounds—

(a) that the respondent has committed adultery;

(b) that the respondent has behaved in such a way that the applicant cannot reasonably be expected to live with the respondent;

(c) subject to *subsection (2)* of this section, that there has been desertion by the respondent of the applicant for a continuous period of at least one year immediately preceding the date of the application;

(d) subject to *subsection (2)* of this section, that the spouses have lived apart from one another for a continuous period of at least one year immediately preceding the date of the application and the respondent consents to a decree being granted;

(e) subject to *subsection (2)* of this section, that the spouses have lived apart from one another for a continuous period of at least three years immediately preceding the date of the application;

(f) that the marriage has broken down to the extent that the court is satisfied in all the circumstances that a normal marital relationship has not existed between the spouses for a period of at least one year immediately preceding the date of the application.

(2) In considering for the purposes of *subsection (1)* of this section, whether—

(a) in the case of *paragraph (c)* of that subsection, the period for which the respondent has deserted the applicant, or

(b) in the case of *paragraph (d)* or *(e)* of that subsection, the period for which the spouses have lived apart,

has been continuous, no account shall be taken of any one period (not excluding 6 months) or of any two or more periods (not exceeding 6 months in all) during which the spouses resumed living with each other, but no such period or periods during which the spouses lived with each other shall count as part of the period of desertion or the period for which the spouses have lived apart, as the case may be.

Provided that this subsection shall only apply where the spouses are not living with each other at the time the application is made.

(3) (a) In this section spouses shall be treated as living apart from each other unless they are living with each other in the same household, and references to spouses living with each other shall be construed as references to their living with each other in the same household.

(b) In this section 'desertion' includes conduct on the part of one spouse that results in the other spouse, with just cause, leaving and living apart from that other spouse.

3 Grant of decree of judicial separation, custody, etc of children

(1) Where, on an application under *section 2* of this Act, the court is satisfied that any of the grounds referred to in *subsection (1)* of that section which have been relied on by the applicant have been proved on the balance of probabilities, the court shall, subject to *subsection (2)* of this section and *sections 5* and *6* of this Act, grant a decree of judicial separation in respect of the spouses concerned.

(2) (a) Where there are, in respect of the spouses concerned, any dependent children of the family, the court shall not grant a decree of judicial separation unless the court—

(i) is satisfied that such provision exists or has been made, or

(ii) intends by order upon the granting of the decree to make such provision, for the welfare of those children as is proper in the circumstances.

(b) In this subsection—
'dependent children of the family' has the same meaning as it has for the purposes of *Part II* of this Act;
'welfare' comprises the religious and moral, intellectual, physical and social welfare of the children concerned.

(3) Upon the granting of a decree of judicial separation by the court, the court may, where appropriate, by order give such directions under *section 11* of the Guardianship of Infants Act, 1964, as it thinks proper regarding the welfare or custody of, or right of access to, an infant (being an infant within the meaning of that Act) as if an application had been made under that section.

Amendments—Family Law (Divorce) Act, 1996, s 45.

---

4 Supplemental provisions as to proof of adultery and unreasonable behaviour

(1) Where the spouses have lived with each other for more than 1 year after it became known to the applicant that the respondent had committed adultery the applicant shall not be entitled to rely on that adultery for the purposes of *section 2(1)(a)* although that adultery may be one of the factors that the applicant may rely on for the purposes of *section 2(1)(b)* together with other matters.

(2) Where the applicant alleges that the respondent has behaved in such a way that the applicant cannot reasonably be expected to cohabit with him but the spouses have cohabited for a period or periods after the date of the occurrence of the final incident relied on by the applicant and held by the court to support his allegation, such cohabitation shall be disregarded in determining for the purpose of *section 2(1)(b)* of this Act whether the applicant cannot be reasonably expected to live with the respondent if the length of the period or of those periods of cohabitation together was or were 6 months or less.

5 Safeguards to ensure applicant's awareness of alternatives to separation proceedings and to assist attempts at reconciliation

(1) A solicitor, if any, acting for an applicant for a decree of judicial separation shall, prior to the making of an application for a decree of judicial separation—

(a) discuss with the applicant the possibility of reconciliation and give to him the names and addresses of persons qualified to help effect a reconciliation between spouses who have become estranged, and
(b) discuss with the applicant the possibility of engaging in mediation to help effect a separation on an agreed basis with an estranged spouse and give to him the names and addresses of persons and organisations qualified to provide a mediation service, and
(c) discuss with the applicant the possibility of effecting a separation by the negotiation and conclusion of a separation deed or written separation agreement.

(2) An application for judicial separation shall be accompanied by a certificate by the solicitor, if any, acting on behalf of the applicant that he has complied with the provisions of *subsection (1)* of this section and, where a solicitor does not so certify, the court may adjourn the proceedings for such period as it deems reasonable for the

applicant's solicitor to discuss with the applicant the matters referred to in that subsection.

(3) Provision shall be made by rules of court for the certification required for the purposes of *subsection (2)* of this section.

6 Safeguards to ensure respondent's awareness of alternatives to separation proceedings and to assist attempts at reconciliation

(1) A solicitor, if any, acting for a respondent in an application for a decree of judicial separation shall, as soon as possible after receiving instructions from the respondent—

(a) discuss with the respondent the possibility of reconciliation and give to him the names and addresses of persons qualified to help effect a reconciliation between parties to a marriage who have become estranged, and

(b) discuss with the respondent the possibility of engaging in mediation to help effect a separation on an agreed basis with an estranged spouse and give to him the names and addresses of persons and organisations qualified to provide a mediation service, and

(c) discuss with the respondent the possibility of effecting a separation by the negotiation and conclusion of a separation deed or written separation agreement.

(2) An Entry of Appearance or a Notice of Intention to Defend an application for judicial separation shall be accompanied by a certificate by the solicitor, if any, acting on behalf of the respondent, that he has complied with the provisions of *subsection (1)* of this section and where a solicitor does not so certify, the court may adjourn the proceedings for such period as it deems reasonable for the respondent's solicitor to discuss with the respondent the matters referred to in that subsection.

(3) Provision shall be made by rules of court for the certification required for the purposes of this section.

7 Adjournment of proceedings to assist reconciliation or agreements on separation

(1) Where an application is made under this Act to the court for a decree of judicial separation, the court shall give consideration to the possibility of a reconciliation of the spouses concerned and, accordingly, may adjourn the proceedings at any time for the purpose of affording the spouses an opportunity, if they both so wish, to consider a reconciliation between themselves with or without the assistance of a third party.

(2) If during any adjournment of proceedings to which *subsection (1)* of this section relates the spouses resume living with each other, no account shall be taken of that fact for the purposes of those proceedings.

(3) Where on an application made under this Act for a decree of judicial separation it appears to the court that no reconciliation of the spouses concerned is possible, it may adjourn or further adjourn the proceedings for the purpose of affording the spouses an opportunity, if they both so wish, to establish agreement (with or without the assistance of a third party) on the terms, so far as is possible, of the separation.

(4) If an adjournment has taken place by virtue of *subsection (1)* or *(3)* of this section, either or both of the spouses may request that the hearing of the application be proceeded with and, without prejudice to *subsection (5)* of this section, the court shall resume hearing the application as soon as is practicable.

(5) The power of adjournment exercisable under *subsections (1)* and *(3)* of this section is in addition to and not in substitution for any other power of adjournment exercisable by the court.

(6) Where the court adjourns proceedings under *subsection (1)* or *(3)* of this section, it may at its discretion advise the spouses concerned to seek the assistance of a third party for the purpose set out in the appropriate subsection.

Amendments—Family Law (Divorce) Act, 1996, s 45.

7A   Non-admissibility as evidence of certain communications relating to reconciliation or separation

An oral or written communication between either of the spouses concerned and a third party for the purpose of seeking assistance to effect a reconciliation or to reach agreement between them on some or all of the terms of a separation (whether or not made in the presence or with the knowledge of the other spouse), and any record of such a communication, made or caused to be made by either of the spouses concerned or such a third party, shall not be admissible as evidence in any court.

Amendments—Family Law (Divorce) Act, 1996, s 45.

---

8   Effect of judicial separation and rescission of decree of separation and ancillary orders upon reconciliation

(1) Where the court grants a decree of judicial separation it shall no longer be obligatory for the spouses who were the parties to such proceedings to cohabit.

(2) Following the granting of a decree of judicial separation the applicant and the respondent in the separation proceedings may at any future date by consent apply to the court to rescind the decree of separation granted and such order of rescission shall be made by the court upon it being satisfied that a reconciliation has taken place between the applicant and the respondent and that they have already resumed or again wish to resume cohabiting as husband and wife.

(3) Upon making an order of rescission under *subsection (2)* of this section the court may also make such necessary ancillary order or orders as it deems proper in the circumstances with regard to any orders previously made under *Part II* of this Act.

9   Abolition of decree of divorce *a mensa et thoro*, etc

(1) After the commencement of this Act, no action shall lie for divorce *a mensa et thoro*.

(2) *Subsection (1)* of this section shall not have effect in relation to any action instituted before the commencement of this Act.

PART II

ANCILLARY FINANCIAL, PROPERTY, CUSTODY AND OTHER ORDERS

10–24   (*repealed*)

25   (Amends Family Law (Maintenance of Spouses and Children) Act, 1976, s 3.)

26–29   (*repealed*)

PART III

COURT JURISDICTION

30   Definition (*Part III*)

In this Part 'family law proceedings', in relation to a court, means proceedings before a court of competent jurisdiction under—

(a) this Act,
(b) the Adoption Acts, 1952 to 1988,
(c) the Family Home Protection Act, 1976,
(d) the Family Law (Maintenance of Spouses and Children) Act, 1976,
(e) the Family Law (Protection of Spouses and Children) Act, 1981,
(f) the Family Law Act, 1981,
(g) the Guardianship of Infants Act, 1964,
(h) the Legitimacy Declaration Act (Ireland), 1868,
(i) the Married Women's Status Act, 1957, or
(j) the Status of Children Act, 1987,

or between spouses under the Partition Act, 1868, and the Partition Act, 1876, where the fact that they are married to each other is of relevance to the proceedings.

31   Courts, jurisdiction and venue

(1) The Circuit Court shall be known as 'the Circuit Family Court' when exercising its jurisdiction to hear and determine family law proceedings or, where provided for, when transferring family law proceedings to the High Court.

(2) Subject to the other provisions of this section, the Circuit Family Court shall, concurrently with the High Court, have jurisdiction to hear and determine proceedings under this Act for a decree of judicial separation.

(3) Where in proceedings under this Act for a decree of judicial separation an order could be made in respect of land whose rateable valuation exceeds £200 and an application commencing those proceedings is made to the Circuit Family Court, that Court shall, if the respondent so requires before the hearing thereof, transfer those proceedings to the High Court, but any order made (including an interim order) or act done in the course of those proceedings before such transfer shall be valid unless discharged or varied by order of the High Court.

(4) The jurisdiction referred to in *subsection (2)* of this section shall only be exercisable where either of the spouses is domiciled in the State on the date of the application

commencing proceedings or is ordinarily resident in the State throughout the period of one year ending on that date.

(5) The jurisdiction referred to in *subsection (2)* of this section shall, in the Circuit Family Court, be exercised by the judge of the circuit where either spouse to the proceedings ordinarily resides or carries on any profession, business or occupation.

32   Hearing of proceedings

The Circuit Family Court shall sit to hear and determine proceedings instituted under this Act and under the Acts referred to in *section 30* of this Act in a different place or at different times or on different days from those on which the ordinary sittings of the Circuit Court are held.

33   Conduct of family proceedings in Circuit and High Courts

(1) Circuit Family Court proceedings shall be as informal as is practicable and consistent with the administration of justice.

(2) Neither judges sitting in the Circuit Family Court nor barristers nor solicitors appearing in such courts shall wear wigs or gowns.

(3) Family law proceedings before the High Court shall be as informal as is practicable and consistent with the administration of justice.

(4) In hearing and determining such proceedings as are referred to in *subsection (3)* of this section neither judges sitting in the High Court nor barristers nor solicitors appearing in such proceedings shall wear wigs or gowns.

34   Privacy

Proceedings under this Act shall be heard otherwise than in public.

35   Costs

The costs of any proceedings under this Act shall be at the discretion of the court.

36   Rules of court

(1) Rules of court shall provide for the documentation required for the commencement of proceedings under this Act in a summary manner.

(2) The rules of court, and any established form or course of pleading, practice or procedure, for the purposes of any enactment or jurisdiction affected by this Act shall, pending the due making of rules of court, apply for such purposes with such adaptations as may be necessary.

PART IV

MISCELLANEOUS

37   Saver for existing law

Save in so far as otherwise provided in this Act, the law relating to proceedings for divorce *a mensa et thoro* shall, so far as applicable, apply in relation to proceedings for judicial separation.

38   (Amends ss 5 and 6 of the Family Law (Maintenance of Spouses and Children) Act, 1976)

39–40   (*repealed*)

41   Custody of dependent children

(1) In this section 'dependent member of the family' has the meaning assigned to it by *section 2* of the Family Law Act, 1995.

(2) Where the court grants a decree of judicial separation, it may declare either of the spouses concerned to be unfit to have custody of any dependent member of the family who is a minor and, if it does so and the spouse to whom the declaration related is a parent of a dependent member of the family who is a minor, that spouse shall not, on the death of the other spouse, be entitled as of right to the custody of that minor.

(3) *Section 18(1)* of the Guardianship of Infants Act, 1964, is hereby repealed to an action instituted before the commencement of this Act.

Amendments—Children Act, 1997, s 16.

---

42   Amendment of *section 120(2)* of Succession Act, 1965

(1) (Amends s 120(2) of the Succession Act, 1965).

(2) *Subsection (1)* of this section shall not have effect in relation to a decree of divorce *a mensa et thoro* granted in proceedings instituted before the commencement of this Act.

43   Divorce *a mensa et thoro* decrees and alimony orders

Any order made by either the Circuit Court or the High Court granting a decree of divorce *a mensa et thoro* in proceedings issued before the commencement of this Act shall not be affected by this Act save that any alimony order made subsequent to the granting of such decree shall be deemed for all purposes to be an order made under *section 14(1)(a)* of this Act.

44   Collusion, condonation, recrimination, connivance

(1) Collusion between the spouses in connection with an application for a judicial separation or, subject to *subsection (2)* of this section, any conduct (including condonation or recrimination) on the part of the applicant shall not be a bar to the grant of a decree of judicial separation.

(2) Where an application for a decree of judicial separation is made on the ground of adultery and the respondent proves that the adultery was committed with the connivance of the applicant the court may refuse the application.

45   Conduct of District Court family proceedings

(1) Proceedings before the District Court under the Guardianship of Infants Act, 1964, the Family Law (Maintenance of Spouses and Children) Act, 1976, the Family Home Protection Act, 1976, *section 9* of the Family Law Act, 1981, the Family Law (Protection of Spouses and Children) Act, 1981, the Status of Children Act, 1987 and the Child Abduction and Enforcement of Custody Orders Act, 1991, shall be as informal as is practicable and consistent with the administration of justice.

(2) Neither district justices hearing and determining such proceedings as are referred to in *subsection (1)* of this section nor barristers nor solicitors appearing in such proceedings shall wear wigs or gowns.

Amendments—Child Abduction and Enforcement of Custody Orders Act, 1991, s 39.

46   Short title and commencement

(1) This Act may be cited as the Judicial Separation and Family Law Reform Act, 1989.

(2) This Act shall come into operation on the day that is 6 months after the date of the passing of this Act.

Maintenance Act, 1994

(1994 No 28)

ARRANGEMENT OF SECTIONS

PART I

PRELIMINARY

PART II

RECOVERY OF MAINTENANCE (RECIPROCATING JURISDICTIONS)

PART III

RECOVERY OF MAINTENANCE (DESIGNATED JURISDICTIONS)

PART IV

PROVISIONS COMMON TO RECIPROCATING AND DESIGNATED JURISDICTIONS

PART TWO

PART V

MISCELLANEOUS

FIRST SCHEDULE

SECOND SCHEDULE

ACTS REFERRED TO

Central Bank Act, 1989	1989, No 16
Courts Act, 1971	1971, No 36
Enforcement of Court Orders Act, 1940	1940, No 23
Family Law (Maintenance of Spouses and Children) Act, 1976	1976, No 11
Jurisdiction of Courts and Enforcement of Judgments Act, 1993	1993, No 9
Jurisdiction of Courts and Enforcement of Judgments (European Communities) Act, 1988	1988, No 3
Maintenance Orders Act, 1974	1974, No 16
Social Welfare (Consolidation) Act, 1993	1993, No 27
Status of Children Act, 1987	1987, No 26

An Act to enable effect to be given to the Convention between the Member States of the European Communities on the simplification of procedures for the recovery of maintenance payments done at Rome on the 6th day of November, 1990, and the Convention on the recovery abroad of maintenance done at New York on the 20th day of June, 1956, and to provide for other matters related to the recovery of maintenance. [23rd November, 1994]

PART I

PRELIMINARY

1 Short title

This Act may be cited as the Maintenance Act, 1994.

2 Commencement

This Act shall come into operation on such day or days as the Minister shall fix by order or orders either generally or with reference to any particular purpose or provision and different days may be so fixed for different purposes and different provisions.

3   Interpretation

(1) In this Act, unless the context otherwise requires—

'the Act of 1976' means the Family Law (Maintenance of Spouses and Children) Act, 1976;

'the Act of 1988' means the Jurisdiction of Courts and Enforcement of Judgments (European Communities) Act, 1988;

'the Act of 1993' means the Jurisdiction of Courts and Enforcement of Judgments Act, 1993;

'the Act of 1995' means the Family Law Act, 1995;

'the Central Authority' has the meaning assigned to it by *section 4*;

'court', in relation to a jurisdiction other than the State, means any authority competent under the law of that jurisdiction to make an order for the recovery of maintenance;

'designated jurisdiction' has the meaning assigned to it by *section 13*;

'the Minister' means the Minister for Equality and Law Reform;

'the New York Convention' has the meaning assigned to it by *section 13*;

'reciprocating jurisdiction' has the meaning assigned to it by *section 6*;

'the Rome Convention' has the meaning assigned to it by *section 6*.

(2) In this Act a reference to a Part or section is to a Part or section of this Act, unless it is indicated that reference to some other enactment is intended.

(3) In this Act a reference to a subsection or paragraph is to the subsection or paragraph of the provision in which the reference occurs, unless it is indicated that reference to some other provision is intended.

(4) In this Act a reference to any enactment includes a reference to that enactment as amended or adapted by any other enactment including this Act.

(5) This Act is without prejudice to the provisions of the Maintenance Orders Act, 1974.

Amendments—Family Law Act, 1995, s 45.

---

4   Central Authority

(1) (a) The Minister may by order appoint a Central Authority ('the Central Authority') to discharge the functions required of it under this Act or required of a central authority under the Rome Convention or of a transmitting agency or receiving agency under the New York Convention.

   (b) Pending the appointment of a Central Authority the Minister shall discharge its functions, and references in this Act to the Central Authority shall be construed accordingly as references to the Minister.

   (c) The Minister may by order amend or revoke an order made under this section.

(2) (a) For the purposes of *section 8* of the Enforcement of Court Orders Act, 1940, of the Acts of 1976, 1988 and 1993 (as amended by this Act), 1995 and of this Act the Central Authority shall have authority to act on behalf of, as the case may be, a maintenance creditor or claimant, within the meaning of *section 13(1)*, and references in those enactments to a maintenance creditor or claimant shall be construed as including references to the Central Authority.

(b) Where the Central Authority so acts, payments of maintenance shall be made directly to the maintenance creditor or claimant unless the Central Authority requests that they be made to a public authority in the jurisdiction where the maintenance creditor or claimant resides.

PART II

RECOVERY OF MAINTENANCE (RECIPROCATING JURISDICTIONS)

5 Construction of *Part II*

This Part shall be construed as one with the Jurisdiction of Courts and Enforcement of Judgments Acts, 1988 and 1993.

6 Interpretation of *Part II*

(1) In this Part—

'the Brussels Convention' means the Convention on jurisdiction and the enforcement of judgments in civil and commercial matters (including the Protocol annexed to that Convention), done at Brussels on the 27th day of September, 1968, as subsequently amended, and given the force of law in the State by the Acts of 1988 and 1993 and a reference to an Article of that Convention shall be construed as including a reference to the corresponding Article of the Lugano Convention;

'central authority of a reciprocating jurisdiction' means—

(a) the central authority of such a jurisdiction which has been designated pursuant to *paragraph 1* or, where appropriate, *paragraph 2* of *Article 2* of the Rome Convention; or

(b) an authority of such a jurisdiction with functions corresponding to those exercisable by the Central Authority within the State;

'the Lugano Convention' has the meaning assigned to it by the Act of 1993;

'maintenance creditor' includes any body which, under the law of a reciprocating jurisdiction, is entitled to exercise the rights of redress of, or to represent, the creditor;

'reciprocating jurisdiction' means a Contracting State (within the meaning of the Acts of 1988 and 1993) which is declared by order of the Minister for Foreign Affairs to be a reciprocating jurisdiction;

'the Rome Convention' means the Convention between the Member States of the European Communities on the simplification of procedures for the recovery of maintenance payments done at Rome on the 6th day of November, 1990, the text of which in the English language is set out, for convenience of reference, in the First Schedule to this Act.

(2) (a) The Minister for Foreign Affairs may by order declare that any Contracting State (within the meaning of the Acts of 1988 and 1993) specified in the order is a reciprocating jurisdiction.

(b) An order that is in force under this subsection shall be evidence that any state specified in the order is a reciprocating jurisdiction.

(c) The Minister for Foreign Affairs may by order amend or revoke an order under this subsection.

(3) If a judgment or an instrument or settlement referred to in *article 50* or *51* of the Brussels Convention does not relate solely to maintenance, this Part shall apply only to those parts that relate to maintenance.

(4) A word or expression in this Part which is used in the Rome Convention has the same meaning as it has in that Convention and for this purpose the report by Mr. J. Martin and Mr. C. ÓhUiginn on the Convention, a copy of which has been placed in the Oireachtas Library, may be considered by any court when interpreting such word or expression and shall be given such weight as is appropriate in the circumstances.

7   Application from reciprocating jurisdiction

(1) The Central Authority may, on receipt of an application for the recognition or enforcement in the State of a maintenance order which has been transmitted by a central authority of a reciprocating jurisdiction, send the application to the Master of the High Court for determination in accordance with *section 5* of the Act of 1988.

(2) The Master shall consider the application privately and shall make an enforcement order unless it appears to the Master from the application and accompanying documents or from the Master's own knowledge that its recognition and enforcement are prohibited by the Brussels Convention or the Lugano Convention.

(3) The Master shall cause the decision on the request to be brought to the notice of the Central Authority and, if an enforcement order has been made, shall cause notice thereof to be served on the maintenance debtor.

(4) (a)   The notice to be served on a maintenance debtor uner *subsection (3)* shall include a statement of the provisions of *Article 36* (right of appeal against enforcement order) of the Brussels Convention.

   (b)   Service of the notice may be effected personally or in any manner in which service of a superior court document within the meaning of *section 23* of the Courts Act 1971, may be effected.

(5) The Master may—

   (a)   accept an application under *subsection (1)* as having been transmitted by the central authority of the reciprocating jurisdiction concerned, and
   (b)   accept the documents accompanying the application, namely—
      (i)   a request that the application be processed in accordance with the provisions of the Rome Convention,
      (ii)   a letter delegating to the Central Authority to act, or cause action to be taken, on behalf of the maintenance creditor, including specific authority to enable enforcement proceedings to be taken,
      (iii) a document containing the name, date of birth, nationality and description of the maintenance debtor and all other relevant information regarding the identity, whereabouts or location of the assets, of the maintenance debtor,
      (iv)   a document required under *Article 46* or *47* of the Brussels Convention to be produced by a party seeking recognition or applying for enforcement of a judgment, and
      (v)   any translation of such a document,
   as being such request, letter, document or translation, as the case may be.

(6) If any of the documents mentioned in *subsection (5)(b)* are not produced, the Master may allow time for their production, accept equivalent documents or, if the Master considers that there is sufficient information available, dispense with their production.

(7) The Central Authority may, on receipt of an application for the recognition or enforcement of an instrument or settlement referred to *Article 50* or *51* of the Brussels Convention which provides for the payment of maintenance and has been transmitted by a central authority of a reciprocating jurisdiction, apply to the High Court under *Article 31* of that Convention for the recognition or enforcement of the whole or part of the instrument or settlement concerned.

8　Evidence in proceedings

Subject to *section 21(4)*, in any proceedings under this Part, unless the court sees good reason to the contrary—

(a) a document purporting to be an application for the recognition or enforcement in the State of a maintenance order and to have been transmitted by a central authority of a reciprocating jurisdiction may be admitted as evidence that it is such an application and has been so transmitted, and

(b) a document purporting to be a document accompanying such an application and to be—

    (i) a request that the application be processed in accordance with the provisions of the Rome Convention,

    (ii) a letter delegating to the Central Authority to act, or cause action to be taken, on behalf of the maintenance creditor, including specific authority to enable enforcement proceedings to be taken, and

    (iii) a document containing the name, date of birth, nationality and description of the maintenance debtor and all other relevant information regarding the identity, whereabouts, or location of the assets, of the maintenance debtor,

may be admitted as evidence of any matter to which it relates.

9　(Amends s 1 of the Act of 1988)

10　(Amends s 6 of the Act of 1988)

11　(Amends s 7 of the Act of 1988)

12　(Amends s 11 of the Act of 1993)

PART III

RECOVERY OF MAINTENANCE (DESIGNATED JURISDICTIONS)

13　Interpretation of *Part III*

(1) In this Part, unless the context otherwise requires—

'central authority of a designated jurisdiction' means—

(a) a transmitting agency or receiving agency in a state which is a contracting party to the New York Convention, or

(b) an authority of a designated jurisdiction with functions corresponding to those exercisable by the Central Authority within the State;

'claimant' means, according to the context, either—

(a) a person residing in a designated jurisdiction (including any body which under the law of that jurisdiction is entitled to exercise the rights of redress of, or to represent, that person) and claiming pursuant to this Part to be entitled to receive maintenance from a person residing in the State, or

(b) a person residing in the State (including a competent authority within the meaning of Part IX (Liability to Maintain Family) of the Social Welfare (Consolidation) Act 1993) and claiming pursuant to this Part to be entitled to recover maintenance from a person residing in a designated jurisdiction;

'designated jurisdiction' means—

(a) any state which is a contracting party to the New York Convention, or

(b) any other state or jurisdiction which is declared by order of the Minister for Foreign Affairs to be a designated jurisdiction for the purposes of this Part;

'the New York Convention' means the Convention on the recovery abroad of maintenance done at New York on the 20th day of June, 1956, the text of which in the English language is set out, for convenience of reference, in the Second Schedule to this Act;

'respondent' means, according to the context, either—

(a) a person residing in the State from whom maintenance is sought to be recovered pursuant to this Part by a person residing in a designated jurisdiction, or

(b) a person residing in a designated jurisdiction from whom maintenance is sought to be recovered pursuant to this Part by a person residing in the State.

(2) (a) The Minister for Foreign Affairs may by order declare that any state or jurisdiction specified in the order is a designated jurisdiction.

(b) An order that is in force under this subsection shall be evidence that any state or jurisdiction specified in the order is a designated jurisdiction.

(c) The Minister for Foreign Affairs may by order amend or revoke an order under this subsection.

(3) Subject to *subsection (1)*, a word or expression in this Part which is used in the New York Convention has the same meaning as it has in that Convention.

14 Application for maintenance from designated jurisdiction

(1) On receipt of a request by the Central Authority from a central authority of a designated jurisdiction on behalf of a claimant for the recovery of maintenance from a person for the time being residing in the State ('the respondent') the Central Authority may—

(a) if the request is accompanied by an order of a court in a Contracting State (within the meaning of the Acts of 1988 and 1993), transmit the request to the Master of the High Court for determination in accordance with *section 5* of the Act of 1988 and Part II and the other provisions of those Acts shall apply accordingly, with any necessary modifications,

(b) if the request is accompanied by an order made by any other court and the Central Authority is of opinion that the order may be enforceable in the State, apply to the District Court for the enforcement of the order, or

(c) if either the request is not accompanied by such an order or enforcement of the order is refused—

(i) if the amount of maintenance sought to be recovered exceeds the maximum amount which the District Court has jurisdiction to award under the Act of 1976 or, if the request is for a relief order within the meaning of the Act of 1995, make an application to the Circuit Court,

(ii) in any other case, make an application to the District Court,

for the recovery of maintenance in accordance with the request.

(2) The District Court, on an application to it under *subsection (1)(b)*, may, if it considers that the order of the court in the designated jurisdiction for the recovery of maintenance is enforceable in the State, make an order for its enforcement and thereupon—

(a) the order of the said court shall be deemed to be an enforceable maintenance order within the meaning of *section 7* of the Act of 1988, and

(b) *sections 6, 7* and *8* of that Act shall apply in relation to the order, with any necessary modifications.

(3) An application referred to in *subsection (1)(c)* shall be deemed to be an application for a maintenance order under *seciton 5* or *section 5A* or *21A* (inserted by the Status of Children Act, 1987) of the Act of 1976 or a relief order made within the meaning of the Act of 1995, as may be appropriate, and to have been made on the date on which the request of the claimant for the recovery of maintenance was received by the central authority of the designated jurisdiction concerned.

(4) The court, on an application to it under *subsection (1)(c)* may, subject to *subsection (5)*—

(a) take evidence from the respondent by way of affidavit or on sworn deposition,

(b) cause a copy of the affidavit or deposition to be sent to the Central Authority for transmission to the central authority of the designated jurisdiction with a request that the claimant provide an answering affidavit,

(c) send letters of request pursuant to *section 17* for the taking of further evidence in a designated jurisdiction,

(d) take the evidence of the claimant or of any witness residing in a designated jurisdiction through a live television link,

(e) pending the final determination of the application, make an interim order under *section 7* of the Act of 1976 or an order under *section 24* of the Act of 1995.

(5) Where it appears to the court that the claimant or respondent *bona fide* desires to cross-examine a witness and the witness is available for the cross-examination, whether through a live television link or otherwise, the court shall decline to permit the evidence of the witness to be given by affidavit.

(6) Notice of an application under *paragraph (b)* or *(c)* of *subsection (1)* shall be given to the respondent by the Central Authority and shall be accompanied by a copy of the documents proposed to be given in evidence by the Central Authority at the hearing of the application.

(7) Where—

(a) on an application pursuant to *subsection (1)(c)* it is necessary to take the evidence of the claimant or of any witness through a live television link, and

(b) facilities for doing so are not available in the circuit or district court district concerned,

the court may by order transfer the proceedings to a circuit or district court district where those facilities are available.

(8) The provisions of this section shall also apply as appropriate to a request made to the Central Authority to vary or discharge an order made on an application under *subsection (1)(c)*.

(9) Where an order of a court which accompanies a request referred to in *subsection (1)* includes provision for matters other than those relating to maintenance, this section shall apply to the order only in so far as it relates to maintenance.

(10) *Section 8* and *section 8A* (inserted by the Status of Children Act, 1987) of the Act of 1976 shall apply and have effect in relation to any agreement in writing which contains a provision mentioned in *paragraph (a)* of either section and is made—

(a) between a claimant and respondent, notwithstanding that one of them may at the time of the making of the agreement be resident outside the State, and

(b) between a respondent and a person or body in the State where such a person or body has been authorised to enter into such an agreement on behalf of the claimant,

and an application may be made by the Central Authority to the Circuit Court under *paragraph (b)* of either section for an order making such an agreement a rule of court.

(11) The jurisdiction conferred by this section may be exercised—

(a) in the case of the Circuit Court, by the judge of the circuit, and

(b) in the case of the District Court, by the judge of the District Court assigned to the district court district,

in which the respondent resides or carries on any profession, business or occupation or, as the case may be, to which proceedings have been transferred under *subsection (7)*.

Amendments—Family Law Act, 1995, s 45.

---

15 Application for maintenance in designated jurisdiction

(1) A claimant who wishes to recover maintenance from a respondent residing in a designated jurisdiction may apply to the Central Authority to have the claim transmitted to the central authority in that jurisdiction notwithstanding the existence of a maintenance order made against the respondent by a court in the State.

(2) (a) Such a claimant may give evidence on sworn deposition before the District Court as to the facts relating to the claim, and the Court, if satisfied that the deposition sets forth facts from which it may be determined that the respondent concerned owes a duty to maintain the claimant, may certify accordingly.

(b) The district court clerk concerned shall give to the claimant a certified copy of the deposition and certificate.

(c) The jurisdiction conferred on the District Court by this subsection may be exercised by the judge of the District Court assigned to the district court district in which the claimant resides or carries on any profession, business or occupation.

(3) As respects an order for the recovery of maintenance or an order varying such an order made by a court in the State on the application of the claimant, the registrar or clerk of the court shall, at the request of the claimant and subject to any conditions that may be specified by rules of court, give to the claimant—

(a) a copy of the order duly authenticated,

(b) a certificate signed by the registrar or clerk stating—
   (i)   the date on which the time for lodging an appeal against the order will expire or, if it has expired, the date on which it expired,
   (ii) whether notice of appeal against the order has been entered,
   (iii) the amount of any arrears under the order, and
   (iv) such other particulars (if any) as may be specified by rules of court, and

(c) in case the order was made in default of appearance, the original or a copy, certified by the registrar or clerk to be a true copy, of a document establishing that notice of the institution of proceedings was served on the respondent.

16   Evidence in proceedings

Subject to *section 21(4)*, in any proceedings under this Part, unless the court sees good reason to the contrary—

(a) a document purporting to be an application by a claimant who is residing in a designated jurisdiction to the central authority of that jurisdiction for the recovery of maintenance from a respondent residing in the State, or for the variation or revocation of an order made on such an application, and to have been transmitted by that authority to the Central Authority may be admitted as evidence that it is such an application and has been so transmitted;

(b) a document purporting to be signed by or on behalf of the claimant and to authorise the Central Authority to act, or to appoint some other person to act, on behalf of the claimant may be admitted as evidence of such authorisation;

(c) a document purporting to be an order for the payment of maintenance by the respondent, or an order varying or discharging such an order, made by a court in a designated jurisdiction and to be signed by a judge, magistrate or officer of that court may be admitted as evidence that the order was so made and—
   (i)   that the respondent is liable to maintain the claimant and, where appropriate, a child of the claimant, and
   (ii) that the claimant was resident or present in that jurisdiction at the date of the commencement of the relevant proceedings;

(d) a document purporting to be—
   (i)   a petition which has been filed in a court in a designated jurisdiction seeking an order for the recovery of maintenance against a person alleged in the petition to have a duty of support,
   (ii) a certificate by a judge, magistrate or officer of that court to the effect that the petition sets forth facts from which it may be determined that the person owes such a duty of support,
   may be admitted as evidence of the matters to which the document relates;

(e) a document purporting to be signed by a judge, magistrate or officer of a court in a designated jurisdiction and to be—
   (i)   a document setting out or summarising evidence given in proceedings in that court or evidence taken in that jurisdiction for the purpose of maintenance proceedings in that jurisdiction or elsewhere,
   (ii) a document which has been received in evidence in proceedings in that court, or
   (iii) if an order for the recovery of maintenance from the respondent has been made in default of the respondent's appearance by a court in that jurisdiction, a document which establishes that notice of the institution of proceedings was served on the respondent,
   may be admitted as evidence of the matters to which the document relates;

(f) a document purporting to be signed on behalf of a central authority of a designated jurisdiction and to certify that the request of a specified claimant for the recovery of maintenance from a specified repsondent residing in the State was received by that central authority on a specified date may be admitted as evidence that the request was so received on that date.

17 Obtaining of evidence from designated jurisdiction

(1) A court may, for the purpose of any proceedings under this Part, address letters of request for further evidence, documentary or otherwise, either to the appropriate court of a designated jurisdiction or to any other authority or institution designated in that behalf by that jurisdiction.

(2) Letters of request under *subsection (1)* may also be sent to the Central Authority for transmission to the court, authority or institution concerned.

18 Provisional, including protective, measures

Where the Central Authority has received a request under this Part from a central authority of a designated jurisdiction for the recovery of maintenance, the High Court may, on application to it by the Central Authority, grant provisional, including protective, measures of any kind that the Court has power to grant in proceedings that are within its jurisdiction.

19 Taking of evidence for proceedings in designated jurisdiction

(1) Where a request is made to the Central Authority by or on behalf of a court in a designated jurisdiction ('the requesting authority') to obtain the evidence of a person residing in the State for the purposes of any proceedings in that jurisdiction for the recovery of maintenance the provisions of this section shall have effect.

(2) If the request is in order the Central Authority shall refer the request to the Master of the High Court, who shall request a judge of the District Court to take the evidence.

(3) The judge shall cause notice of the time and place at which evidence is to be taken to be given to the person concerned, to the Central Authority for communication to the requesting authority, to the Master of the High Court and to such other persons as the judge thinks fit.

(4) The judge shall take the evidence and cause a record thereof to be sent to the Central Authority for transmission to the requesting authority.

(5) If it is not possible to take the evidence within four months of the receipt of the request by the Central Authority, the judge shall cause the reasons for the non-execution of the request or for the delay in executing it to be sent to the Central Authority for transmission to the requesting authority.

(6) The judge shall have the same powers in relation to compelling the attendance of persons and the production of documents and in relation to the taking of evidence as the District Court has on the hearing of an action.

(7) Where any person, not being a party to proceedings referred to in *subsection (1)*, attends pursuant to a request under that subsection, the judge may order that there shall be paid to that person out of public funds such sum by way of expenses as the District Court may order to be paid in respect of a witness on the hearing of an action.

(8) If the Central Authority or the judge is of the view that the authenticity of the request is not established or that the execution of the request would compromise the sovereignty or safety of the State the execution of the request shall not be proceeded with.

(9) Where the requesting authority makes a request for the taking of evidence directly to a court in the State—

(a) if that court is the District Court, the evidence shall be taken by a judge of that Court, and

(b) in any other case, the court addressed may refer the request to the Master of the High Court,

and this section shall apply in relation to such a request with the necessary modifications.

PART IV

PROVISIONS COMMON TO RECIPROCATING AND DESIGNATED JURISDICTIONS

20 Obtaining information on debtor

(1) The Central Authority may, for the purposes of obtaining any information that is necessary or expedient for the performance of its functions, require any holder of a public office or body financed wholly or partly by means of moneys provided by the Oireachtas to provide it with any information in the possession on procurement of the holder or body as to the whereabouts, place of work, or location and extent of the assets, of a maintenance debtor (within the meaning of the Act of 1988) or respondent and the holder or body shall, as soon as practicable, comply with the requirement.

(2) If the District Court, on application to it by the Central Authority, is of opinion that any person or body (not being a person or body mentioned in *subsection (1)*) is likely to have information as to the matters referred to in that subsection and that the Central Authority requires the information for the purposes so referred to, the Court may order that person or body to provide it to the Central Authority within such period as may be specified in the order.

(3) The jurisdiction conferred on the District Court by *subsection (2)* may be exercised by the judge of the District Court for the time being assigned to the district court district in which the person or body to whom the order sought is to be directed resides or carries on any profession, business or occupation.

21 Evidence in proceedings

(1) Subject to *subsection (4)*, in any proceedings under *Part II* or *III*, unless the court sees good reason to the contrary, a document—

(a) purporting to be signed by a judge, magistrate or officer of a court in a reciprocating jurisdiction or designated jurisdiction and to be a statement of arrears under an order of that court for the recovery of maintenance, or

(b) purporting to be—
    (i)   a tax assessment or other statement or certificate relating to tax,
    (ii) a statement or certificate of earnings,
    (iii) a medical certificate,

(iv) a statement or certificate that a person was employed or was unemployed for a specified period,

(v) a letter written by a party to maintenance proceedings who is residing in a reciprocating jurisdiction or designated jurisdiction,

(vi) an affidavit or other document made or signed by such a party, or a witness, residing in such a jurisdiction,

(vii) a document establishing a marital relationship between parties to such proceedings or a relationship between the parties, or one of the parties, and a child for whom maintenance is sought in the proceedings, or

(viii) a document establishing that a person or body is entitled to exercise, under the law of the state in which that party resides, the rights of the party seeking maintenance,

may, unless the contrary is proved, be admitted as evidence that it is such a document and as evidence of any matter to which it relates subject to such authentication, if any, as the court may require.

(2) A document purporting to be—

(a) a translation of a document mentioned in *subsection (1)* or in *section 8* or *16*, and

(b) certified as correct by a person competent to do so,

may be admitted as evidence of any matter to which it relates.

(3) (a) Where a document is admissible in evidence by virtue of *subsection (1)* or of *section 8* or *16*, it may be given in evidence, whether or not the document is still in existence, by producing a copy of the document, or of the material part of it, authenticated in such manner as the court may approve.

(b) It is immaterial for the purposes of *paragraph (a)* how many removes there are between the copy and the original or by what means (which may include facsimile transmission) the copy produced or any intermediate copy was made.

(4) In estimating in the weight (if any) to be attached to a statement in a document admitted in evidence by virtue of *subsection (1)* or of *section 8* or *16*, regard shall be had to any other evidence available to the court and to any circumstances from which any inference can reasonably be drawn as to the accuracy or otherwise of the statement, including (except in the case of a court order or a certificate or other document prepared by or on behalf of a court or public authority) the question whether the maker of the statement had any incentive to conceal or misrepresent facts and whether or not it was made on oath.

PART V

MISCELLANEOUS

22 Enforceability of foreign maintenance orders

Recognition or enforcement of an order (other than a provisional order) for recovery of maintenance made by a court in a jurisdiction other than the State may not be refused—

(a) by reason only of the fact that the court which made the order had power to vary or revoke it, or

(b) on the ground that, under the rules of private international law of the State, the court concerned had not jurisdiction by reason of the fact that the respondent was not resident or present in that jurisdiction at the date of the commencement of the relevant proceedings, provided that at that date the claimant was resident there.

23   Currency of payments under foreign maintenance orders

(1) An amount payable in the State under an order for recovery of maintenance which is made by a court in a jurisdiction other than the State and is enforceable in the State shall be paid in the currency of the State and, if the amount is stated in the order in a currency other than the currency of the State, the payment shall be made on the basis of the exchange rate prevailing, on the date of the making of an order by a court in the State for the enforcement of the order, between that currency and the currency of the State.

(2) For the purposes of this section, a certificate purporting to be signed by an officer of a bank in the State and to state the exchange rate prevailing on a specified date between a specified currency and the currency of the State shall be evidence of the facts stated in the certificate.

(3) In this section 'bank' means the holder of a banker's licence within the meaning of the Central Bank Act, 1989.

24   Saving

Nothing in this Act shall prevent the recognition or enforcement of an order for recovery of maintenance which is made in a reciprocating jurisdiction or designated jurisdiction and which, apart from this Act, would be recognised or enforceable in the State.

25   Expenses

The expenses incurred in the administration of this Act shall, to such extent as may be sanctioned by the Minister for Finance, be paid out of moneys provided by the Oireachtas.

Section 6   FIRST SCHEDULE

TEXT OF ROME CONVENTION

CONVENTION BETWEEN THE MEMBER STATES OF THE EUROPEAN
COMMUNITIES ON THE SIMPLIFICATION OF PROCEDURES FOR THE
RECOVERY OF MAINTENANCE PAYMENTS

PREAMBLE

The Member States of the European Communities, hereinafter referred to as 'The Member States',

Mindful of the close links existing between their peoples,

Having regard to the developments tending to the elimination of obstacles to the free movement of persons between Member States,

Convinced of the need to simplify among the Member States the procedures for securing the reciprocal recognition and enforcement of judgments relating to maintenance,

Desiring for this purpose to complement with administrative arrangements the provisions of the Brussels Convention of 27 September 1968 on jurisdiction and the enforcement of judgments in civil and commercial matters, as amended by the Accession Conventions under the successive enlargements of the European Communities,

Have agreed as follows:

Article 1

SCOPE AND APPLICATION

1. This Convention may be applied to any judgment relating to maintenance which comes within the scope of the Convention on jurisdiction and the enforcement of judgments in civil and commercial matters signed at Brussels on 27 September 1968 and as subsequently amended (hereinafter referred to as 'the Brussels Convention').

2. The judgment may be a judgment given before or after this Convention enters into force provided it is a judgment that is enforceable in the State addressed under the Brussels Convention or a convention concluded between the State of origin and the State addressed.

3. If the judgment does not relate solely to maintenance the Convention shall only apply to those parts of the judgment which relate to maintenance.

4. For the purpose of this Convention 'judgment' shall include an authentic instrument or court settlement within the meaning of *Articles 50* and *51* of the Brussels Convention.

5. Any body which, under the law of a Contracting State, is entitled to exercise the rights of redress of the creditor or to represent him shall benefit from the provisions of this Convention.

Article 2

CENTRAL AUTHORITIES

1. Each Contracting State shall designate a Central Authority to carry out or arrange to have carried out the functions provided for by this Convention.

2. Federal States and States with more than one legal system shall be free to appoint more than one Central Authority. Where a State has appointed more than one Central Authority it shall designate the Central Authority to which applications under this Convention may be addressed for transmission to the appropriate Central Authority within that State.

3. Central Authorities shall not charge any fees in respect of services rendered by them under this Convention.

Article 3

1. The Central Authorities shall cooperate with each other and promote cooperation between the competent authorities in their respective states in order to facilitate the recovery of maintenance payments due.

2. On receipt of the application mentioned in *Article 5* the Central Authority in the State addressed shall take or cause to be taken without delay all appropriate and useful measures to:

   (i)   seek out and locate the debtor or his assets;

(ii) obtain, where appropriate, relevant information from Government Departments or agencies in relation to the debtor;

(iii) have the judgment registered or declared enforceable, where appropriate;

(iv) facilitate the transfer of maintenance payments to the creditor or body referred to in *Article 1(5)*; and

(v) ensure, where the payments due to the maintenance creditor are not made, the use of all appropriate means of enforcement provided for in the State addressed which are applicable and which might permit recovery of these sums.

3. The Central Authority in the State addressed shall keep the Central Authority in the State of origin informed of the measures taken under *paragraph 2* and their results.

Article 4

Each Contracting State shall take the necessary administrative and legal measures, including the provision of effective enforcement measures, to enable the Central Authority to fulfil its obligations under this Convention.

Article 5

APPLICATIONS

1. Where a maintenance creditor or body referred to in *Article 1(5)* obtains in a Contracting State a judgment relating to maintenance and wishes to have that judgment recognised or enforced in another Contracting State, the maintenance creditor or body may submit a request for this purpose to the Central Authority in the State of origin.

2. Before transmitting an application to the State addressed, the Central Authority in the State of origin shall ensure that the application and the accompanying documents are in accordance with *paragraph 3* of this Article and with *Article 6*.

3. The application shall contain:

(i) a request that it be processed in accordance with the provisions of this Convention;

(ii) a letter delegating to the Central Authority addressed authority to act, or cause action to be taken, on behalf of the maintenance creditor including specific authority to enable enforcement proceedings to be taken;

(iii) the name, date of birth, nationality and description of the debtor and all other relevant information regarding his identity or whereabouts or the location of his assets;

(iv) the documentation required under *Section 3* of Title III of the Brussels Convention.

Article 6

LANGUAGE

The documentation referred to in *Article 5* and any correspondence between the Central Authorities relating to the application shall, unless otherwise agreed between the Central Authorities concerned, be in, or shall be accompanied by a translation into, the official language or one of the official languages of the State addressed or any other language that the State addressed has declared it will accept.

Article 7

RELATIONSHIP WITH OTHER CONVENTIONS

The provisions of this Convention are in addition to the provisions of the Brussels Convention and are without prejudice to other existing international instruments.

Article 8

STANDING COMMITTEE

1. A Standing Committee shall be set up for the purposes of exchanging views on the functioning of the Convention and resolving any difficulties which arise in practice. The Committee may issue recommendations on the implementation of the Convention or recommend changes in the Convention.

2. The Committee shall be composed of representatives appointed by each Member State. The Commission of the European Communities may attend meetings as observers.

3. The Presidency of European Political Cooperation shall convene meetings of the Committee at least once every two years and otherwise at its discretion. In this regard it shall pay due regard to any requests made by other Member States.

Article 9

FINAL PROVISIONS

1. This Convention shall be open for signature by the Member States. It shall be subject to ratification, acceptance or approval. The instruments of ratification, acceptance or approval shall be deposited with the Ministry of Foreign Affairs of the Italian Republic.

2. This Convention shall enter into force 90 days after the date of deposit of the instruments of ratification, acceptance or approval by all the States which are members of the European Communities on the date on which it is opened for signature.

3. Each Member State may, when depositing its instrument of ratification, acceptance or approval, or at any later date, declare that the Convention shall apply to it in its relations with other states which have made the same declaration 90 days after the date of deposit.

4. A Member State which has not made such a declaration may apply the Convention with other contracting Member States on the basis of bilateral agreements.

5.   (i)   Each Member State shall at the time of the deposit of its instrument of ratification, acceptance or approval inform the Ministry of Foreign Affairs of the Italian Republic of the following—
       (a)   the designation of a Central Authority pursuant to *Article 2* and
       (b)   any declarations pursuant to *Article 6.*
     (ii)   Any such designation or declaration may at a later date be changed, and any new declaration may be made, by notification addressed to the Ministry of Foreign Affairs of the Italian Republic.

6. The Ministry of Foreign Affairs of the Italian Republic shall notify all the Member States of any signature, deposit of instruments, declaration or designation.

Article 10

1. This Convention shall be open to accession by any State which becomes a member of the European Communities. The instruments of accession shall be deposited with the Ministry of Foreign Affairs of the Italian Republic.

2. This Convention shall enter into force in respect of any State which accedes to it 90 days after the date of deposit of that State's instrument of accession.

Done at Rome on the sixth day of November in the year one thousand nine hundred and ninety, in the Danish, Dutch, English, French, German, Greek, Irish, Italian, Portuguese and Spanish languages, each text being equally authentic, in a single original which shall be deposited in the archives of the Ministry of Foreign Affairs of the Italian Republic.

The Ministry of Foreign Affairs of the Italian Republic shall transmit certified copies of the Convention to the Government of each Member State.

Section 13   SECOND SCHEDULE

TEXT OF NEW YORK CONVENTION

CONVENTION ON THE RECOVERY ABROAD OF MAINTENANCE DONE AT NEW YORK ON 20 JUNE 1956

PREAMBLE

Considering the urgency of solving the humanitarian problem resulting from the situation of persons in need dependent for their maintenance on persons abroad,

Considering that the prosecution or enforcement abroad of claims for maintenance gives rise to serious legal and practical difficulties, and

Determined to provide a means to solve such problems and to overcome such difficulties,

The Contracting Parties have agreed as follows:

Article 1

SCOPE OF THE CONVENTION

1. The purpose of this Convention is to facilitate the recovery of maintenance to which a person, hereinafter referred to as claimant, who is in the territory of one of the Contracting Parties, claims to be entitled from another person, hereinafter referred to as respondent, who is subject to the jurisdiction of another Contracting Party. This purpose shall be effected through the offices of agencies which will hereinafter be referred to as Transmitting and Receiving Agencies.

2. The remedies provided for in this Convention are in addition to, and not in substitution for, any remedies available under municipal or international law.

Article 2

DESIGNATION OF AGENCIES

1. Each Contracting Party shall, at the time when the instrument of ratification or accession is deposited, designate one or more judicial or administrative authorities which shall act in its territory as Transmitting Agencies.

2. Each Contracting Party shall, at the time when the instrument of ratification or accession is deposited, designate a public or private body which shall act in its territory as Receiving Agency.

3. Each Contracting Party shall promptly communicate to the Secretary-General of the United Nations the designations made under *paragraphs 1* and *2* and any changes made in respect thereof.

4. Transmitting and Receiving Agencies may communicate directly with Transmitting and Receiving Agencies of other Contracting Parties.

Article 3

APPLICATION TO TRANSMITTING AGENCY

1. Where a claimant is in the territory of one Contracting Party, hereinafter referred to as the State of the claimant, and the respondent is subject to the jurisdiction of another Contracting Party, hereinafter referred to as the State of the respondent, the claimant may make application to a Transmitting Agency in the State of the claimant for the recovery of maintenance from the respondent.

2. Each Contracting Party shall inform the Secretary-General as to the evidence normally required under the law of the State of the Receiving Agency for the proof of maintenance claims, of the manner in which such evidence should be submitted, and of other requirements to be complied with under such law.

3. The application shall be accompanied by all relevant documents, including, where necessary, a power of attorney authorising the Receiving Agency to act, or to appoint some other person to act, on behalf of the claimant. It shall also be accompanied by a photograph of the claimant and, where available, a photograph of the respondent.

4. The Transmitting Agency shall take all reasonable steps to ensure that the requirements of the law of the State of the Receiving Agency are complied with; and subject to the requirements of such law, the application shall include:

(a) the full name, address, date of birth, nationality, and occupation of the claimant, and the name and address of any legal representative of the claimant;

(b) the full name of the respondent, and, so far as known to the claimant, his addresses during the preceding five years, date of birth, nationality, and occupation;

(c) particulars of the grounds upon which the claim is based and of the relief sought, and any other relevant information such as the financial and family circumstances of the claimant and the respondent.

Article 4

TRANSMISSION OF DOCUMENTS

1. The Transmitting Agency shall transmit the documents to the Receiving Agency of the State of the respondent, unless satisfied that the application is not made in good faith.

Before transmitting such documents, the Transmitting Agency shall satisfy itself that they are regular as to form, in accordance with the law of the State of the claimant.

3. The Transmitting Agency may express to the Receiving Agency an opinion as to the merits of the case and may recommend that free legal aid and exemption from costs be given to the claimant.

Article 5

TRANSMISSION OF JUDGMENTS AND OTHER JUDICIAL ACTS

1. The Transmitting Agency shall, at the request of the claimant, transmit under the provisions of *Article 4*, any order, final or provisional, and any other judicial act, obtained by the claimant for the payment of maintenance in a competent tribunal of any of the Contracting Parties, and, where necessary and possible, the record of the proceedings in which such order was made.

2. The orders and judicial acts referred to in the preceding paragraph may be transmitted in substitution for or in addition to the documents mentioned in *Article 3*.

3. Proceedings under *Article 6* may include, in accordance with the law of the State of the respondent, exequatur or registration proceedings or an action based upon the act transmitted under *paragraph 1*.

Article 6

FUNCTIONS OF THE RECEIVING AGENCY

1. The Receiving Agency shall, subject always to the authority given by the claimant, take, on behalf of the claimant, all appropriate steps for the recovery of maintenance, including the settlement of the claim and, where necessary, the institution and prosecution of an action for maintenance and the execution of any order or other judicial act for the payment of maintenance.

2. The Receiving Agency shall keep the Transmitting Agency currently informed. If it is unable to act, it shall inform the Transmitting Agency of its reasons and return the documents.

3. Notwithstanding anything in this Convention, the law applicable in the determination of all questions arising in any such action or proceedings shall be the law of the State of the respondent, including its private international law.

Article 7

LETTERS OF REQUEST

If provision is made for letters of request in the laws of the two Contracting Parties concerned, the following rules shall apply:

(a) A tribunal hearing an action for maintenance may address letters of request for further evidence, documentary or otherwise, either to the competent tribunal of the other Contracting Party or to any other authority or institution designated by the other Contracting Party in whose territory the request is to be executed.

(b) In order that the parties may attend or be represented, the requested authority shall give notice of the date on which and the place at which the proceedings requested are to take place to the Receiving Agency and the Transmitting Agency concerned, and to the respondent.

(c) Letters of request shall be executed with all convenient speed; in the event of such letters of request not being executed within four months from the receipt of the letters by the requested authority, the reasons for such non-execution or for such delay shall be communicated to the requesting authority.

(d) The execution of letters of request shall not give rise to reimbursement of fees or costs of any kind whatsoever.

(e) Execution of letters of request may only be refused:

(1) If the authenticity of the letters is not established;

(2) If the Contracting Party in whose territory the letters are to be executed deems that its sovereignty or safety would be compromised thereby.

Article 8

VARIATION OF ORDERS

The provisions of this Convention apply also to applications for the variation of maintenance orders.

Article 9

EXEMPTIONS AND FACILITIES

1. In proceedings under this Convention, claimants shall be accorded equal treatment and the same exemptions in the payment of costs and charges as are given to residents or nationals of the State where the proceedings are pending.

2. Claimants shall not be required, because of their status as aliens or non-residents, to furnish any bond or make any payment or deposit as security for costs or otherwise.

3. Transmitting and Receiving Agencies shall not charge any fees in respect of services rendered under this Convention.

Article 10

TRANSFER OF FUNDS

A Contracting Party, under whose law the transfer of funds abroad is restricted, shall accord the highest priority to the transfer of funds payable as maintenance or to cover expenses in respect of proceedings under this Convention.

Article 11

FEDERAL STATE CLAUSE

In the case of a Federal or non-unitary State, the following provisions shall apply:

(a) With respect to those articles of this Convention that come within the legislative jurisdiction of the federal legislative authority, the obligations of the Federal Government shall to this extent be the same as those of Parties wihch are not Federal States;

(b) With respect to those articles of this Convention that come within the legislative jurisdiction of constituent States, provinces or cantons which are not, under the constitutional system of the Federation, bound to take legislative action, the Federal Government shall bring such articles with a favourable recommendation to the notice of the appropriate authorities of States, provinces or cantons at the earliest possible moment;

(c) A Federal State Party to this Convention shall, at the request of any other Contracting party transmitted through the Secretary-General, supply a statement of the law and practice of the Federation and its constituent units in regard to any particular provision of the Convention, showing the extent to which effect has been given to that provision by legislative or other action.

Article 12

TERRITORIAL APPLICATION

The provisions of this Convention shall extend or be applicable equally to all non-self-governing, trust or other territories for the international relations of which a contracting Party is responsible, unless the latter, on ratifying or acceding to this Convention, has given notice that the Convention shall not apply to any one or more of such territories. Any Contracting Party making such a declaration may, at any time thereafter, by notification to the Secretary-General, extend the application of the Convention to any or all of such territories.

Article 13

SIGNATURE, RATIFICATION AND ACCESSION

1. This Convention shall be open for signature until 31 December 1956 on behalf of any Member of the United Nations, any non-Member State which is a Party to the Statute of the International Court of Justice, or member of a specialised agency, and any other non-Member State which has been invited by the Economic and Social Council to become a Party to the Convention.

2. This Convention shall be ratified. The instruments of ratification shall be deposited with the Secretary-General.

3. This Convention may be acceded to at any time on behalf of any of the States referred to in *paragraph 1* of this article. The instruments of accession shall be deposited with the Secretary-General.

Article 14

ENTRY INTO FORCE

1. This Convention shall come into force on the thirtieth day following the date of deposit of the third instrument of ratification or accession in accordance with *Article 13*.

2. For each State ratifying or acceding to the Convention after the deposit of the third instrument of ratification or accession, the Convention shall enter into force on the thirtieth day following the date of the deposit by such State of its instrument of ratification or accession.

Article 15

DENUNCIATION

1. Any Contracting Party may denounce this Convention by notification to the Secretary-General. Such denunciation may also apply to some or all of the territories mentioned in *Article 12*.

2. Denunciation shall take effect one year after the date of receipt of the notification by the Secretary-General, except that it shall not prejudice cases pending at the time it becomes effective.

Article 16

SETTLEMENT OF DISPUTES

If a dispute should arise between Contracting Parties relating to the interpretation or application of this Convention, and if such dispute has not been settled by other means, it shall be referred to the International Court of Justice. The dispute shall be brought before the Court either by the notification of a special agreement or by a unilateral application of one of the parties to the dispute.

Article 17

RESERVATIONS

1. In the event that any State submits a reservation to any of the articles of this Convention at the time of ratification or accession, the Secretary-General shall communicate the text of the reservation to all States which are Parties to this Convention, and to the other States referred to in *Article 13*. Any Contracting Party which objects to the reservation may, within a period of ninety days from the date of the communication, notify the Secretary-General that it does not accept it, and the Convention shall not then enter into force as between the objecting State and the State making the reservation. Any State thereafter acceding may make such notification at the time of its accession.

2. A Contracting Party may at any time, withdraw a reservation previously made and shall notify the Secretary-General of such withdrawal.

Article 18

RECIPROCITY

A Contracting Party shall not be entitled to avail itself of this Convention against other Contracting Parties except to the extent that it is itself bound by the Convention.

Article 19

NOTIFICATION BY THE SECRETARY-GENERAL

1. The Secretary-General shall inform all Members of the United Nations and the non-Member States referred to in *Article 13*:

    (a) of communications under *paragraph 3* of *Article 2*;
    (b) of information received under *paragraph 2* of *Article 3*;
    (c) of declarations and notifications made under *Article 12*;
    (d) of signatures, ratifications and accessions under *Article 13*;
    (e) of the date on which the Convention has entered into force under *paragraph 1* of *Article 14*;
    (f) of denunciations made under *paragraph 1* of *Article 15*;
    (g) of reservations and notifications made under *Article 17*.

2. The Secretary-General shall also inform all Contracting Parties of requests for revision and replies thereto received under *Article 20*.

Article 20

REVISION

1. Any Contracting Party may request revision of this Convention at any time by a notification addressed to the Secretary-General.

2. The Secretary-General shall transmit the notification to each Contracting Party with a request that such Contracting Party reply within four months whether it desires the convening of a Conference to consider the proposed revision. If a majority of the Contracting Parties favour the convening of a Conference it shall be convened by the Secretary-General.

Article 21

LANGUAGES AND DEPOSIT OF CONVENTION

The original of this Convention, of which the Chinese, English, French, Russian and Spanish texts are equally authentic, shall be deposited with the Secretary-General, who shall transmit certified true copies thereof to all States referred to in *Article 13*.

Maintenance Orders Act, 1974

(1974 No 16)

ARRANGEMENT OF SECTIONS

PART I

PRELIMINARY AND GENERAL

PART II

RECIPROCAL RECOGNITION AND ENFORCEMENT OF MAINTENANCE ORDERS

Maintenance orders made in a reciprocating jurisdiction

Maintenance orders made in the State

Evidence

An Act to make provision in relation to the reciprocal recognition and enforcement of maintenance orders as between the State and Northern Ireland, England and Wales and Scotland.

[9th July, 1974]

PART I

PRELIMINARY AND GENERAL

1 Short title

This Act may be cited as the Maintenance Orders Act, 1974.

2 Commencement

This Act shall come into operation on such day as the Minister for Justice by order appoints.

3 Interpretation

(1) In this Act—

'appropriate authority' means the person who, in a reciprocating jurisdiction, has a function corresponding to that of the Master of the High Court under *section 19(3)*;

'enforcement order' has the meaning assigned to it in *section 6*;

'maintenance creditor', in relation to a maintenance order, means the person entitled to the payments for which the order provides;

'maintenance debtor', in relation to a maintenance order, means the person liable to make payments under the order;

'maintenance order' means—

(a) an order (including an affiliation order or an order consequent thereon) which provides for the periodical payment of sums of money towards the maintenance of any person, being a person whom the person liable to make payments under the order is, in accordance with the law of the jurisdiction in which the order was made, liable to maintain, or

(b) an affiliation order or an order consequent thereon, being an order which provides for the payment by a person adjudged, found or declared to be a child's father of expenses incidental to the birth of the child or, where the child has died, of the funeral expenses,

and, in the case of a maintenance order which has been varied, means that order as varied;

'maintenance proceedings' means proceedings in relation to the making, variation or revocation of a maintenance order;

'notice of the institution of the proceedings', in relation to maintenance proceedings, means—

(a) where the proceedings were instituted in the State, a copy of the summons or other originating document served in the State or a notice of the issue of the summons or other originating document,

(b) where the proceedings were instituted in Northern Ireland or in England and Wales, a copy of the summons or other originating document served in a reciprocating jurisdiction, a notice that a provisional maintenance order has been made or a notice of an application to a court for a maintenance order,

(c) where the proceedings were instituted in Scotland, a copy of the writ, summons or other originating document, together with a copy of the warrant for service and a copy of the citation;

'reciprocating jurisdiction' means Northern Ireland, England and Wales or Scotland;

'revocation', in relation to a maintenance order, includes the discharge of such order or the termination of a weekly sum payable thereunder and cognate words shall be construed accordingly.

(2) For the avoidance of doubt, a maintenance order includes—

(a) such an order which is incidental to a decision as to the status of natural persons,

(b) such an order obtained by or in favour of a public authority in connection with the provision of maintenance or other benefits in respect of a person whom the maintenance debtor is, in accordance with the law of the jurisdiction in which the order was made, liable to maintain, and

(c) a provision in an agreement in writing between spouses for the making by one spouse of periodical payments towards the maintenance of the other or of any of their children or of any child to whom either is *in loco parentis*, being an agreement which has been embodied in or approved by a court order or made a rule of court.

(3) A reference in this Act to a section is to a section of this Act unless it is indicated that reference to some other enactment is intended.

(4) A reference in this Act to a subsection, paragraph or other division is to the subsection, paragraph or other division of the provision in which the reference occurs unless it is indicated that reference to some other provision is intended.

4   Scope of Act

This Act shall have effect in relation to maintenance orders whether made before or after the commencement of this Act but shall not have effect in relation to arrears accrued before such commencement.

5   Expenses

The expenses incurred in the administration of this Act shall, to such extent as may be sanctioned by the Minister for Finance, be paid out of moneys provided by the Oireachtas.

PART II

RECIPROCAL, RECOGNITION AND ENFORCEMENT OF MAINTENANCE ORDERS

Maintenance orders made in a reciprocating jurisdiction

6   Recognition and enforcement

Subject to and in accordance with this Act, a maintenance order made in a reciprocating jurisdiction and enforceable therein shall be recognised and enforceable in the State when, on receipt by the Master of the High Court from an appropriate authority of a request for the enforcement of the order, an order is made under *subsection (4)*.

(2) The documents referred to in *section 13(1)* shall be attached to the request.

(3) The maintenance debtor shall not, at this stage, be entitled to make any submission on the request.

(4) The Master shall consider the request privately and shall make an order (in this Act referred to as an enforcement order) for the enforcement of the maintenance order to which the request relates, unless it appears to him from the documents before him or from his own knowledge that its recognition and enforcement is prohibited by *section 9*.

(5) The Master shall cause his decision on the request to be brought to the notice of the maintenance creditor and, if an enforcement order has been made, shall cause notice thereof to be served on the maintenance debtor.

(6) (a) The notice to be served on a maintenance debtor under *subsection (5)* shall include a statement of his right of appeal under *section 7(1)*, the restriction imposed by *section 7(3)* on the taking of measures of execution against his property and the provisions of *section 9*.

(b) Service of the notice may be effected personally or in any manner in which service of a superior court document within the meaning of *section 23* of the Courts Act, 1971, may be effected.

7 Appeal against enforcement order

(1) Where an enforcement order is made, the maintenance debtor may appeal to the High Court against the order within one month of service of notice thereof on him.

(2) The Court may, on the application of the appellant, stay the proceedings if either enforcement of the maintenance order has been suspended in the reciprocating jurisdiction in which it was made pending the determination of any form of appeal or the time for an appeal has not yet expired and enforcement has been suspended pending the making of an appeal; in the latter case, the Court may lay down the time for which it will stay the proceedings.

(3) During the time allowed for an appeal under *subsection (1)* and until the appeal is determined, no measures of execution may be taken against the property of the maintenance debtor other than measures ordered by a court and designed to protect the interests of the maintenance creditor.

(4) The judgment given on the appeal may be contested only on a point of law.

8 Appeal against refusal of enforcement order

(1) If a request to which *section 6(1)* relates is refused, the maintenance creditor may appeal to the High Court against the refusal.

(2) Notice of the appeal shall be served on the maintenance debtor.

(3) The judgment given on the appeal may be contested only on a point of law.

9 Prohibition of recognition and enforcement

A maintenance order made in a reciprocating jurisdiction shall not be recognised or enforceable if, but only if—

(a) recognition or enforcement would be contrary to public policy,

(b) where it was made in default of appearance, the person in default was not served with notice of the institution of the proceedings in sufficient time to enable him to arrange for his defence, or

(c) it is irreconcilable with a judgment given in a dispute between the same parties in the State.

10 Jurisdiction, substance not to be examined

In any proceedings under this Act for the recognition and enforcement of a maintenance order—

(a) the jurisdiction of the court which made the order may not be examined, and

(b) the order may not be examined as to its substance.

11 Partial enforcement

(1) Where, in a maintenance order made in a reciprocating jurisdiction, there are provisions in respect of which enforcement cannot be ordered, an enforcement order may be made in respect of any other provision of the maintenance order.

(2) Where partial enforcement of a maintenance order is sought in a request to which *section 6(1)* relates, the enforcement order may provide accordingly.

12 Restriction on security for costs

No security or deposit, however described, may be required from a person seeking enforcement of a maintenance order made in a reciprocating jurisdiction solely on the ground that he is not residing in the State.

13 Documents required to accompany request for enforcement order

(1) Subject to *subsection (2)*, the documents which shall be attached to a request to which *section 6(1)* relates are—

(a) a certified copy of the maintenance order concerned,

(b) in the case of a maintenance order made in default of appearance, the original or a certified copy of the document which establishes that notice of the institution of the proceedings was served on the person in default,

(c) documents which establish that the order is enforceable according to the law of the jurisdiction in which it was made and that notice of the order has been served on the maintenance debtor outside the State or sent by registered post to him at an address within the State, and

(d) where appropriate, a document showing that the maintenance creditor is receiving legal aid in that jurisdiction.

(2) If the documents specified in *subsection (1)(b)* or *(1)(d)* are not produced, the Master of the High Court may allow time for their production, accept equivalent documents or, if he considers that there is sufficient information available, dispense with their production.

(3) If the Master so requires, a translation of the documents shall be produced; the translation shall be certified as correct by a person competent to do so.

(4) Where the Master receives a document containing a request for the enforcement in the State of a maintenance order made in a reciprocating jurisdiction and purporting to have been transmitted by or at the instance of an appropriate authority, he may, without further proof, accept the document as being a request to which *section 6(1)* relates and as having been received from an appropriate authority.

(5) A document which purports to be—

    (a) a copy of a maintenance order made by a court in a reciprocating jurisdiction, or of the document specified in *subsection (1)(b)*, and to be certified by a judge, magistrate or officer of that court to be a true copy thereof,

    (b) any other document specified in *subsection (1)*, or any equivalent document to which *subsection (2)* relates, and to be signed by a judge, magistrate or officer of such court, or

    (c) a translation required under *subsection (3)* and to be certified as correct by a person competent to do so,

may, without further proof, be accepted by the Master as being such copy, document or translation, as the case may be.

14   Enforcement by District Court

(1) In this section 'enforceable maintenance order' means—

    (a) a maintenance order in respect of which an enforcement order has been made, or

    (b) in the case of a maintenance order to which *section 11* relates, the maintenance order to the extent to which it is ordered to be enforced in accordance with that section.

(2) (a) The District Court shall have jurisdiction to enforce an enforceable maintenance order and for that purpose the order shall, from the date on which the maintenance order was made, be deemed to be an order made by the District Court under *section 1* of the Married Women (Maintenance in case of Desertion) Act, 1886, or *section 3* of the Illegitimate Children (Affiliation Orders) Act, 1930, as the case may be.

    (b) *Paragraph (1)* shall have effect notwithstanding that any amount payable under the enforceable maintenance order concerned exceeds the maximum amount which the District Court has jurisdiction to award under the said Acts.

(3) Notwithstanding anything contained in the Acts referred to in *subsection (2)*, as extended by that subsection, an enforceable maintenance order may not be varied or revoked by a court in the State.

(4) Where an enforceable maintenance order is varied by a court in a reciprocating jurisdiction and a certified copy of the variation order is sent to the District Court, the enforceable maintenance order shall, from the date on which the variation order takes effect, be enforceable in the State as so varied.

(5) Where an enforceable maintenance order is revoked by a court in a reciprocating jurisdiction and a certified copy of the revocation order is sent to the District Court, the enforceable maintenance order shall, from the date on which the revocation order takes effect, cease to be enforceable in the State except in relation to any arrears accrued at that date.

(6) Any arrears under an enforceable maintenance order and any costs in respect of such order awarded against the maintenance debtor by a court in a reciprocating

jurisdiction shall, for the purposes of *subsection (2)* and subject to *section 4*, be regarded as a sum payable by virtue of an order made under the enactments referred to in the said *subsection (2)*, as extended by that subsection.

(7) The jurisdiction vested in the District Court by this section shall be exercised by the justice of the District Court for the time being assigned to the district court district in which the maintenance debtor under the maintenance order concerned resides.

(8) (a) Any sum payable by virtue of an enforceable maintenance order shall, notwithstanding anything to the contrary therein, be paid by the maintenance debtor to the district court clerk for the district court area in which the debtor for the time being resides for transmission to the maintenance creditor or, where a public authority has been authorised by the creditor to receive such sum, to that public authority.

(b) The district court clerk shall, if any sum payable by virtue of an enforceable maintenance order is not duly paid and if the maintenance creditor so requests in writing, make an application under *section 10* of the Family Law (Maintenance of Spouses and Children) Act, 1976 or *section 8* (which relates to the enforcement of certain maintenance orders) of the Enforcement of Court Orders Act, 1940, and for that purpose the references in the said *section 8* (other than *subsections (4)* and *(5)*) to the applicant shall be construed as references to the district court clerk.

(c) Nothing in this subsection shall affect the right of a maintenance creditor to proceed for the recovery of any sum payable to a district court clerk under *paragraph (a)*.

(9) A maintenance debtor under an enforceable maintenance order shall give notice to the district court clerk for the district court area in which he has been residing of any change of address and, if he fails without reasonable cause to do so, he shall be guilty of an offence and shall be liable on summary conviction to a fine not exceeding twenty pounds.

(10) In this section, a reference to a district court clerk shall, where there are two or more district court clerks for the district court area concerned, be construed as a reference to any of those clerks.

(11) For the purposes of this section, the Dublin Metropolitan District shall be deemed to be a district court area.

Amendments—Family Law (Maintenance of Spouses and Children) Act, 1976, s 9.

15 Service of certain documents

Service of a document relating to maintenance proceedings in a reciprocating jurisdiction which is received by the Master of the High Court from an appropriate authority for service on the person against whom the proceedings have been instituted may be effected in any manner in which service of a District Court document within the meaning of *section 7* of the Courts Act, 1964, may be effected.

16 Saving

Nothing in this Act (other than *section 9*) shall be taken as preventing the recognition of a maintenance order which is made in a reciprocating jurisdiction and which, apart from this Act, would be recognised in the State.

Maintenance orders made in the State

17 Jurisdiction where defendant resides in reciprocating jurisdiction and transmission of documents

(1) Where proceedings are instituted under the Married Women (Maintenance in case of Desertion) Act, 1886, or the Illegitimate Children (Affiliation Orders) Act, 1930, against a person residing in a reciprocating jurisdiction for the making, variation or revocation of a maintenance order, the court shall have the like jurisdiction to hear and determine the proceedings as it would have if that person were residing in the State and a summons to appear before the court had been served on him.

(2) The jurisdiction conferred by *subsection (1)* shall, in so far as it vests in the District Court, be exercised by the justice of the District Court for the time being assigned to the district court district in which the person instituting the proceedings resides.

(3) (a) On the institution of proceedings to which *subsection (1)* relates, the registrar or clerk of the court shall send the documents specified in *paragraph (b)* to the Master of the High Court, who shall transmit them to the appropriate authority in the reciprocating jurisdiction concerned if it appears to him that the statement referred to in *paragraph (b)(ii)* gives sufficient information to justify that being done.

(b) The documents referred to in *paragraph (a)* are—
   (i)   notice of the institution of the proceedings, which shall include a statement of the substance of the complaint or application, as the case may be,
   (ii) a statement signed by the registrar or clerk giving such information as he possesses as to the whereabouts of the person against whom the proceedings have been instituted,
   (iii) a statement signed by the registrar or clerk giving such information as he possesses for facilitating the identification of that person,
   (iv) where available, a photograph of that person, and
   (v)   any other relevant document.

18 Restriction on making, etc, of maintenance orders

In any proceedings under the enactments referred to in *section 17(1)* against a person residing in a reciprocating jurisdiction, a maintenance order shall not be made, varied or revoked unless—

(a) notice of the institution of the proceedings has been served on him in accordance with the law of that jurisdiction and in sufficient time to enable him to arrange for his defence, and
(b) the notice included a statement of the substance of the complaint or application, as the case may be.

19 Transmission of maintenance order to reciprocating jurisdiction for enforcement

(1) Where the maintenance debtor under a maintenance order made in the State is residing in a reciprocating jurisdiction, the maintenance creditor may apply to have the order transmitted to that jurisdiction for enforcement.

(2) The application shall be made to the registrar or clerk of the court which made the order.

(3) (a) If it appears to the registrar or clerk that the maintenance debtor is residing in a reciprocating jurisdiction,

    (i) notice of the order shall be sent by him to such debtor by registered post, and

    (ii) the documents specified in *paragraph (b)* shall be sent by him to the Master of the High Court, who shall transmit them to the appropriate authority in that jurisdiction if it appears to him that the statement referred to in *paragraph (b)(v)* gives sufficient information to justify that being done.

(b) The documents referred to in *paragraph (a)(ii)* are—

    (i) a certified copy of the maintenance order,

    (ii) in the case of a maintenance order made in default of appearance, the original or a certified copy of the document which establishes that notice of the institution of the proceedings was served on the person in default,

    (iii) a certificate signed by the registrar or clerk certifing that the maintenance order is enforceable in the State and that notice thereof has been sent to the maintenance debtor by registered post,

    (iv) a certificate signed by the registrar or clerk of any arrears under the order,

    (v) a statement signed by the registrar or clerk giving such information as he possesses as to the whereabouts of the maintenance debtor,

    (vi) a statement signed by the registrar or clerk giving such information as he possesses for facilitating the identification of the maintenance debtor,

    (vii) where available, a photograph of the maintenance debtor, and

    (viii) any other relevant document.

Evidence

20 Obtaining of evidence from reciprocating jurisdiction

A court may, for the purpose of any proceedings under this Act or proceedings to which *section 17(1)* relates, send to the Master of the High Court for transmission to the appropriate authority in a reciprocating jurisdiction a request for the taking in that jurisdiction of the evidence of a person residing therein in relation to such matters as may be specified in the request.

21 Taking of evidence for court in reciprocating jurisdiction

(1) Where, for the purpose of any maintenance proceedings in a court in a reciprocating jurisdiction or proceedings in such court for the enforcement of a maintenance order, a request is received by the Master of the High Court from an appropriate authority for the taking in the State of the evidence of a person residing therein relating to matters specified in the request, the Master shall request a justice of the District Court to take such evidence.

(2) The justice shall, after giving notice of the time and place at which the evidence is to be taken to such persons and in such manner as he thinks fit, take the evidence and cause a record thereof to be sent to the Master for transmission to the appropriate authority from which the request was received.

(3) The justice shall have the same powers in relation to compelling the attendance of persons and the production of documents and in relation to the taking of evidence as the District Court has on the hearing of an action.

(4) A person whose evidence is requested to be taken under *subsection (1)* shall, in relation to the taking of the evidence, have the same rights as he would have on the hearing of an action in the District Court.

(5) Where any person, not being a party to proceedings referred to in *subsection (1)*, attends pursuant to a request under that subsection, the justice concerned may order that there shall be paid to him out of public funds such sum by way of expenses as the District Court may order to be paid in respect of a witness on the hearing of an action.

22   Evidence in proceedings

(1) In any proceedings under this Act or proceedings to which *section 17(1)* relates, unless the court sees good reason to the contrary—

   (a) a document containing a request for the enforcement in the State of a maintenance order made in a reciprocating jurisdiction and purporting to have been transmitted to the Master of the High Court by or at the instance of an appropriate authority may, without further proof, be admitted as evidence that it is a request to which *section 6(1)* relates and has been received by the Master from an appropriate authority;

   (b) a document which purports to be a copy of a maintenance order, or of an order varying or revoking a maintenance order, made by a court in a reciprocating jurisdiction and to be certified by a judge, magistrate or officer of that court to be a true copy hereof may, without further proof, be admitted as evidence of the order;

   (c) a statement contained in a document which purports to be certified by a judge, magistrate or officer of a court in a reciprocating jurisdiction to be—

      (i)   a document setting out or summarising evidence given in proceedings in that court or evidence taken in that jurisdiction for the purpose of maintenance proceedings in the State, whether in response to a request made under *section 20* or otherwise, or a true copy of such document.

      (ii) a document which has been received in evidence in proceedings in that court, or a true copy of a document so received, or

      (iii) a true copy of the document specified in *section 13(1)(b)*,

   may, without further proof, be admitted as evidence of any fact stated therein to the same extent as oral evidence of that fact by the maker of the statement would be admissible in those proceedings;

   (d) a statement contained in a document which purports to be signed by a judge, magistrate or officer of a court in a reciprocating jurisdiction and to be—

      (i)   a document specified in *section 13(1)* (other than *paragraph (a)*),

      (ii) an equivalent document to which *section 13(2)* relates,

      (iii) a document which establishes that notice of the institution of proceedings in a reciprocating jurisdiction for the variation or revocation of a maintenance order made in that jurisdiction was served on the person against whom the proceedings were instituted, or

      (iv) a certificate of any arrears under a maintenance order,

   may, without further proof, be admitted as evidence of any fact stated or certified therein to the same extent as oral evidence of that fact by the maker of the statement would be admissible in those proceedings;

   (e) a statement contained in a document which purports to be—

      (i)   a tax assessment or other statement or certificate relating to tax,

      (ii) a statement or certificate of earnings,

      (iii) a medical certificate,

(iv) a statement or certificate that a person was employed or was unemployed for a specified period,

(v) a statement or certificate that the notice referred to in *section 18(a)* has been served in accordance with the law of the reciprocating jurisdiction concerned,

(vi) a letter written by a party to maintenance proceedings who is residing in a reciprocating jurisdiction, or

(vii) an affidavit or other document made or signed by such a party,

may, without further proof, be admitted as evidence of any fact stated or certified therein to the same extent as oral evidence of that fact by the maker of the statement would be admissible in those proceedings.

(2) The provisions of *subsection (1)* shall apply to a translation of any document referred to therein if it purports to be certified as correct by a person competent to do so.

(3) A statement which is admissible as evidence by virtue of *subsection (1)(d), (1)(e)* or *(2)* may be proved by the production of a copy (authenticated in such manner as the court may approve) of the document which contains the statement or of the material part thereof, whether or not the document is still in existence.

(4) In estimating the weight (if any) to be attached to a statement admitted as evidence by virtue of *subsection (1)(c), (1)(d)* or *(1)(e)*, regard shall be had to any other evidence available to the court and to any circumstances from which any inference can reasonably be drawn as to the accuracy or otherwise of the statement, including the question whether the maker of the statement had any incentive to conceal or misrepresent facts and whether or not the statement was made on oath.

Marriages Act, 1972

(1972 No 30)

ARRANGEMENT OF SECTIONS

An Act to amend the law relating to marriages   [20 December 1972]

1   (*repealed*)

Amendments—Family Law Act, 1995, s 3, Sch.

---

2   Validity as to form of certain marriages

(1) This section applies to a marriage—

- (a) which was solemnised before the passing of this Act solely by a religious ceremony in the département of Hautes Pyrénées, France, and
- (b) was between persons both or either of whom were or was citizens or a citizen of Ireland on the day of the marriage.

(2) A marriage to which this section applies shall be and shall be deemed always to have been valid as to form if it would have been so valid had it been solemnised in the State.

(3) An tArd-Chláraitheoir may, on production of such evidence as appears to him to be satisfactory, cause a marriage to which this section applies to be registered in a register to be maintained in Oifig and Ard-Chláraitheora.

(4) The register in which a marriage is entered under subsection (3) of this section shall be deemed to be a register maintained under the Registration of Marriages (Ireland) Act, 1863, and that Act shall apply and have effect accordingly.

3   Provisions for certain marriages where neither party was resident in appropriate parish or district

No marriage which was solemnised before the commencement of this section in—

    (a) a church of the Church of Ireland, being a church which existed immediately before the passing of the Marriages (Ireland) Act, 1844, or

    (b) a church or chapel licensed under section 33 of the Marriages (Ireland) Act, 1844, or section 34 of the Matrimonial Causes and Marriage Law (Ireland) Amendment Act, 1870,

shall be or be deemed ever to have been invalid or ineffective by reason only of the fact that neither of the parties was resident in—

    (i) in the case of a marriage solemnised in a church referred to in paragraph (a) of this section—the parish or district attached to the church, or

    (ii) in the case of a marriage solemnised in a church or chapel referred to in paragraph (b) of this section—the district specified in the licence of the church or chapel.

4   Deputy for secretary of synagogue

(1) In case of the absence from illness or other reasonable cause of a person who is certified under section 63 of the Marriages (Ireland) Act, 1844, to be the secretary of a synagogue, he may, with the approval of the Chief Rabbi of the Jewish Communities in Ireland and subject to the obligation of notifying an tArd-Chláraitheoir, appoint a deputy to discharge his duties under that Act and the other Acts relating to marriages during any period not exceeding twelve months.

(2) The approval referred to in the foregoing subsection may, in case of the absence of the Chief Rabbi or in case the office of Chief Rabbi is vacant, be given by the person or persons for the time being performing the functions of the Chief Rabbi.

(3) References in the Marriages (Ireland) Act, 1844, to a secretary of a synagogue shall be construed as including references to a deputy appointed under this section.

5   Secretary of synagogue (Dublin Jewish Progressive Congregation)

(1) Where the governing body of the Dublin Jewish Progressive Congregation notify and tArd-Chláraitheoir that a person has been appointed by them to be the secretary of their synagogue, that person shall be deemed to be a person who is certified under section 63 of the Marriages (Ireland) Act, 1844, to be the secretary of a synagogue, and until an tArd-Chláraithceoir is notified by the governing body that that person has ceased to be the secretary of their synagogue, he shall continue to be so deemed.

(2) In case of the absence from illness or other reasonable cause of any such person, he may, with the approval of the governing body and subject to the obligation of notifying an tArd-Chláraitheoir, appoint a deputy to discharge his duties under the Marriages

(Ireland) Act, 1844, and the other Acts relating to marriages during any period not exceeding twelve months.

(3) References in the Marriages (Ireland) Act, 1844, to a secretary of a synagogue shall be construed as including references both to a person who is deemed under this section to be certified as aforesaid and to a deputy appointed under this section.

6 (Amends s 13 of Marriages (Ireland) Act, 1844, and s 2 of Marriage Law (Ireland) Amendment Act, 1863)

7 (Amends ss 19 and 20 of Marriages (Ireland) Act, 1844)

8 (Amends the Marriages (Ireland) Act, 1844)

9 (Amends s 10 of the Registration of Births and Deaths (Ireland) Act, 1863)

10 (Amends s 3 of the Marriage Law (Ireland) Amendment Act, 1863 and s 41 of the Matrimonial Causes and Marriage Law (Ireland) Amendment Act, 1870)

11 (Amends s 33 of the Matrimonial Causes and Marriage Law (Ireland) Amendment Act, 1870)

12 Amendment of section 35 of Matrimonial Causes and Marriage Law (Ireland) Amendment Act, 1870

(1) (Amends s 35 of the Matrimonial Causes and Marriage Law (Ireland) Amendment Act, 1870)

(2) A licence under section 33 of the Marriages (Ireland) Act, 1844, or section 34 of the Matrimonial Causes and Marriage Law (Ireland) Amendment Act, 1870, shall operate to licence the church or chapel for the celebration of marriages licensed under section 35 of the latter Act as amended by this section.

13 (Amends s 36 of the Matrimonial Causes and Marriage Law (Ireland) Amendment Act, 1870)

14 (Amends s 37 of the Matrimonial Causes and Marriage Law (Ireland) Amendment Act, 1870)

15 Licensing and registration of buildings in which marriages may be solemnised

(1) A building may be licensed for the celebration of marriages, or, as the case may be, registered, two or more times under any of the following enactments, and may be so licensed or registered under more than one of them:

  (a) section 7 of the Marriages (Ireland) Act, 1844,
  (b) section 27 of that Act,
  (c) section 12 of the Marriage Law (Ireland) Amendment Act, 1863,
  (d) section 34 of the Matrimonial Causes and Marriage Law (Ireland) Amendment Act, 1870,

if it satisfies the conditions specified in the section in question.

(2) The words 'is being used by them' are hereby substituted for the words from 'has been used' to 'least' in the said section 27 and in the said section 12.

16   Special marriage licence where one party is seriously ill

(1) An tArd-Chláraitheoir may grant a special licence to marry on being satisfied that one of the persons to be married is, for reasons of health certified by a registered medical practitioner, unable to attend at the office of a registrar of marriages for the ceremony.

(2) A marriage authorised by a licence under this section may be solemnised, in the presence of two witnesses, at any time and place by the registrar of marriages for the registration district in which that place is situate provided that, in some part of the ceremony, and in the presence of such registrar and witnesses, each of the parties declares:

> 'I do solemnly declare that I know not of any lawful impediment why I, A.B., may not be joined in matrimony to C.D.'

and that each of the persons says to the other:

> 'I call upon these persons here present to witness that I, A.B., do take thee, C.D., to be my lawful wedded wife (*or* husband).'

(3) Section 66 of the Marriages (Ireland) Act, 1844, is hereby amended by the insertion of 'or pursuant to a special licence granted by an tArd-Chláraitheoir,' after 'in his office,'.

17   Hours of solemnisation—repeals and amendment

(1) There are hereby repealed:

  (a) the words 'between the hours of eight in the morning and three in the afternoon' and 'between the same hours' in section 4 of the Marriages (Ireland) Act, 1844, as amended by the Marriages (Ireland) Act, 1918,
  (b) the words 'between the hours of eight in the forenoon and three in the afternoon' in section 29 of the Marriages (Ireland) Act, 1844, as so amended,
  (c) the words 'between the hours of eight in the morning and three in the afternoon' in section 7 of the Marriage Law (Ireland) Amendment Act, 1863, as so amended,
  (d) the words 'save only that such marriages may be celebrated at any time between the hours of eight o'clock in the forenoon and three o'clock in the afternoon' in section 33 of the Matrimonial Causes and Marriage Law (Ireland) Amendment Act, 1870, as so amended,
  (e) the words 'between the hours of eight in the forenoon and three in the afternoon' in section 38 of the Matrimonial Causes and Marriage Law (Ireland) Act, 1870, as so amended,
  (f) the Marriages (Ireland) Act, 1918,
  (g) any incorporation in any enactment of the requirement repealed by the foregoing paragraphs.

(2) Section 30 of the Marriages (Ireland) Act, 1844, is hereby amended by the substitution of 'between the hours of eight in the forenoon and five in the afternoon' for 'between the hours aforesaid'.

(3) The forms of marriage licences shall be altered so as to be in conformity with the provisions of the foregoing subsections of this section.

18   (*repealed*)

Amendments—Family Law Act, 1995, s 3, Sch.

---

19   Short title and commencement

(1) This Act may be cited as the Marriages Act, 1972.

(2) This Act shall come into operation on such day or days as may be fixed therefor by order or orders of the Minister for Health either generally or with reference to any particular purpose or provision and different days may be so fixed for different purposes and different provisions of this Act.

Married Women's Status Act, 1957

(1957 No 5)

ARRANGEMENT OF SECTIONS

An Act to consolidate with amendments the law relating to the status of married women and the liabilities of husbands [30 April 1957]

1 Application of Act

Save where otherwise appears, this Act applies to persons whether married before or after the commencement of this Act.

2 Capacity of married women

(1) Subject to this Act, a married woman shall—

  (a) be capable of acquiring, holding, and disposing (by will or otherwise) of, any property, and

  (b) be capable of contracting, and

  (c) be capable of rendering herself, and being rendered, liable in respect of any tort, contract, debt or obligation, and in respect of any tort, contract, debt or obligation, and

  (d) be capable of suing and being sued, and
  (e) be subject to the law relating to bankruptcy and to the enforcement of judgments and orders,

as if she were unmarried.

(2) Subsection (1) shall apply as between a married woman and her husband in like manner as it applies as between her and any other person.

(3) A married woman may act as a trustee or personal representative as if she were unmarried.

(4) The provisions of the Settled Land Acts, 1882 to 1890, referring to a tenant for life and a settlement and settled land shall apply to a married woman as if she were unmarried.

(5) A married woman may be the protector of a settlement as if she were unmarried.

3 Property of married women

All property which—

  (a) immediately before the commencement of this Act was the separate property of a married woman or held for her separate use in equity, or
  (b) belongs at the time of her marriage to a woman married after such commencement, or
  (c) after such commencement is acquired by or devolves upon a married woman,

shall belong to her as if she were unmarried and may be disposed of accordingly.

4 Joint capacity of husband and wife

A husband and wife shall—

  (a) be capable of acquiring, holding and disposing of any property jointly or as tenants in common, and
  (b) be capable of rendering themselves, and being rendered, jointly liable in respect of any tort, contract, debt or obligation, and
  (c) be capable of suing and being sued, and
  (d) be capable of exercising any joint power given to them,

in like manner as if they were not married.

5 Property right of husband and wife

A husband and wife shall, for all purposes of acquisition of any property, under a disposition made or coming into operation after the commencement of this Act, be treated as two persons.

6 Abolition of restraint upon anticipation

A restriction upon anticipation or alienation attached (whether before or after the commencement of this Act) to the enjoyment of any property by a woman which could not have been attached to the enjoyment of that property by a man shall be of no effect.

7 Insurance for benefit of spouse or children

(1) This section applies to a policy of life assurance or endowment expressed to be for the benefit of, or by its express terms purporting to confer a benefit upon, the wife, husband or child of the insured.

(2) The policy shall create a trust in favour of the objects therein named.

(3) The moneys payable under the policy shall not, so long as any part of the trust remains unperformed, form part of the estate of the insured or be subject to his or her debts.

(4) If it is proved that the policy was effected and the premiums paid with intent to defraud the creditors of the insured, they shall be entitled to receive, on account of their debts, payment out of the moneys payable under the policy, so, however, that the total amount of such payments shall not exceed the amount of the premiums so paid.

(5) The insured may by the policy, or by any memorandum under his or her hand, appoint a trustee or trustees of the moneys payable under the policy, and may from time to time appoint a new trustee or new trustees thereof, and may make provision for the appointment of a new trustee or trustees thereof and for the investment of the moneys payable under the policy.

(6) In default of any such appointment of a trustee, the policy, immediately on its being effected, shall vest in the insured and his or her legal personal representatives in trust for the purposes aforesaid.

(7) The receipt of a trustee or trustees duly appointed or, in default either of any such appointment or of notice thereof to the insurer, the receipt of the legal personal representative of the insured shall be a good discharge to the insurer for any sum paid by him under the policy.

(8) In this section 'child' includes stepchild, illegitimate child, adopted person (within the meaning of the Adoption Act, 1952 (No. 25 of 1952)), and a person to whom the insured is *in loco parentis*.

(9) This section applies whether the policy was effected before or after the commencement of this Act.

8 Contracts for benefit of spouse, or children

(1) Where a contract (other than a contract to which section 7 applies) is expressed to be for the benefit of, or by its express terms purports to confer a benefit upon, a third person being the wife, husband or child of one of the contracting parties, it shall be enforceable by the third person in his or her own name as if he or she were a party to it.

(2) The right conferred on a third person by this section shall be subject to any defence that would have been valid between the parties to the contract.

(3) Unless the contract otherwise provides, it may be rescinded by agreement of the contracting parties at any time before the third person has adopted it either expressly or by conduct.

(4) This section applies whether the contract was made before or after the commencement of this Act.

(5) In this section, 'child' includes stepchild, illegitimate child, adopted person (within the meaning of the Adoption Act, 1952 (No 25 of 1952)), and a person to whom the contracting party is *in loco parentis*.

9   Criminal proceedings for protection of property of married persons

(1) Subject to subsection (3), every married woman shall have in her own name against all persons whomsoever, including her husband, the same remedies and redress by way of criminal proceedings for the protection and security of her property as if she were unmarried.

(2) Subject to subsection (3), a husband shall have against his wife the same remedies and redress by way of criminal proceedings for the protection and security of his property as if she were not his wife.

(3) No criminal proceedings concerning any property claimed by one spouse (in this subsection referred to as the claimant) shall, by virtue of subsection (1) or subsection (2), be taken by the claimant against the other spouse while they are living together, nor, while they are living apart, concerning any act done while living together by the other spouse, unless such property was wrongfully taken by the other spouse when leaving or deserting or about to leave or desert the claimant.

(4) (*repealed*)

(5) In any indictment or process grounding criminal proceedings in relation to the property of a married woman, it shall be sufficient to allege the property to be her property.

Amendments—Criminal Evidence Act, 1992, s 3, Sch.

10   Wife's antenuptial debts and liabilities

A woman after her marriage shall continue to be liable for all debts contracted and all contracts entered into or torts committed by her before her marriage, including any sums for which she may be liable as contributory, either before or after she has been placed on the list of contributories under and by virtue of the Companies (Consolidation) Act, 1908, and she may be sued for any such debt and for any liability in damages or otherwise under any such contract or in respect of any such tort.

11   Abolition of husband's liability for wife's torts, contracts, debts and obligations

(1) The husband of a woman shall not, by reason only of his being her husband—

   (a) be liable in respect of any tort committed by her, whether before or after the marriage, or

   (b) be sued, or made a party to any legal proceedings brought, in respect of any such tort, or

   (c) be liable in respect of any contract entered into, or debt or obligation incurred by her before the marriage, or

   (d) be liable in respect of any contract entered into, or debt or obligation incurred by her (otherwise than as agent) after the marriage, or

   (e) be sued, or made a party to any legal proceedings brought, in respect of any such contract, debt or obligation.

(2) Notwithstanding subsection (1), where alimony has been ordered by a court to be paid and has not been duly paid by the husband, he shall be liable for necessaries supplied for the use of the wife.

12 (*repealed*)

Amendments—Courts Act, 1981, s 3; Family Law Act, 1995, s 3, Sch.

13 Saving for settlements

(1) Subject to section 6 and to subsection (2) of this section, nothing in this Act shall interfere with or invalidate any settlement or agreement for a settlement made or to be made, whether before or after marriage, respecting the property of a married woman, but no settlement or agreement for a settlement shall have any greater force or validity against creditors of such woman than a like settlement or agreement for a settlement made by a man would have against his creditors.

(2) (a) The provisions of this subsection shall have effect in relation to a settlement or agreement for a settlement made on or after the 1st day of January, 1908, whether before or after marriage, by the husband or intended husband, respecting the property of any woman he may marry or have married.

  (b) It shall not be valid unless it was or is executed by her if of full age or, if she was or is not of full age, confirmed by her after she attains full age.

  (c) If she dies an infant, any covenant or disposition by her husband contained in the settlement or agreement for a settlement shall bind or pass any interest in any property of hers to which he may become entitled on her death and which he could have bound or disposed or if the Married Women's Property Act, 1907, and this Act had not been passed.

  (d) (*repealed*)

Amendments—Age of Majority Act, 1985, s 8(d).

14 Breaches of trust by married women

The provisions of this Act as to the liabilities of married women shall extend to any liability arising out of a breach of trust or devastavit committed by a married woman, whether before or after her marriage, in her capacity as trustee or personal representative and her husband shall not, by reason only of his being her husband, be liable in respect thereof.

15 Will of married woman

Section 24 (which provides for the cases in which a will is to be construed as speaking from the death of the testator) of the Wills Act, 1837, shall apply to the will of a married woman made during coverture whether she is or is not possessed of or entitled to any property at the time of making it and such will shall not require to be re-executed or republished after the death of her husband.

16 Power of attorney of married woman

A married woman, whether an infant or not, shall have power, as if she were unmarried and of full age, by deed, to appoint an attorney on her behalf for the purpose of executing any deed or doing any other act which she might herself execute or do; and the provisions of the Conveyancing Acts, 1881 to 1911, relating to instruments creating powers of attorney shall apply thereto.

PART TWO

17 Savings as to pending proceedings and enforcement of certain judgments

(1) Nothing in this Act shall affect any legal proceedings in respect of any tort if proceedings in respect thereof had been instituted before the commencement of this Act.

(2) Nothing in this Act shall enable any judgment or order against a married woman in respect of a contract entered into, or debt or obligation incurred before the commencement of this Act, to be enforced in bankruptcy or to be enforced otherwise than against her property.

18 Gifts in fraud of creditors

(1) Nothing in this Act shall be construed as validating, as against creditors of the husband, any gift, by a husband to his wife of any property which, after such gift, continues to be in the order or disposition or reputed ownership of the husband or any deposit or other investment of moneys of the husband made by or in the name of his wife in fraud of his creditors, and any such moneys so deposited or invested may be followed as if this Act had not been passed.

(2) Nothing in this Act shall be construed as validating, as against creditors of the wife, any gift, by a wife to her husband, of any property which, after such gift, continues to be in the order or disposition or reputed ownership of the wife or any deposit or other investment of moneys of the wife made by or in the name of her husband in fraud of her creditors, and any such moneys so deposited or invested may be followed as if this Act had not been passed.

19 Consequential repeals

The enactments mentioned in the *Schedule* are hereby repealed to the extent specified in the third column.

20 Short title and commencement

(1) This Act may be cited as the Married Women's Status Act, 1957.

(2) This Act shall come into operation on the first day of June, 1957.

Commencement—1 July 1957.

SCHEDULE   Section 19

ENACTMENTS REPEALED

Session and Chapter or Number and Year (1)	Short Title (2)	Extent of Repeal (3)
11 Geo 4 & 1 Will 4. c 65.	The Infants' Property Act, 1830 (extended to Ireland by the Infants' Property (Ireland) Act, 1835).	Section 16, so far as it refers to married women.

Session and Chapter or Number and Year (1)	Short Title (2)	Extent of Repeal (3)
4 & 5 Will 4. c 92.	The Fines and Recoveries (Ireland) Act, 1834.	Section 21; In section 38, the words from 'and if the tenant in tail' to the end of the section; Section 43; Sections 68 to 81.
4 & 5 Vic c 20.	The Excise Management Act, 1841.	In section 7, the words 'whose husband shall become insane or idiot, or be otherwise incapable of transacting his affairs, or whose husband shall be separated from her and be out of the limits of the United Kingdom'; The proviso to section 7.
8 & 9 Vic c 106.	The Real Property Act, 1845.	In section 6, the words from 'and every such disposition by a married woman' to the end of the section.
18 & 19 Vic c 39.	The Leasing Powers Act for Religious Worship in Ireland, 1855.	In paragraph (5) of section 3, the words 'for their separate use'; Paragraphs (6) and (7) of section 3.
20 & 21 Vic c 57.	The Married Women's Reversionary Interests Act, 1857.	The whole Act.
28 & 29 Vic c 43.	The Married Women's Property (Ireland) Act, 1865.	The whole Act.
33 & 34 Vic c 46.	The Landlord and Tenant (Ireland) Act, 1870.	Section 60.
40 & 41 Vic c 18.	The Settled Estates Act, 1877.	Sections 50 and 51; In section 52, the words 'Subject to such examination as aforesaid'.
40 & 41 Vic c 56.	The County Officers and Courts (Ireland) Act, 1877.	Section 65.

PART TWO

Session and Chapter or Number and Year (1)	Short Title (2)	Extent of Repeal (3)
44 & 45 Vic c 41.	The Conveyancing Act, 1881.	Section 40; In subsection (1) of section 50, the words from 'and may, in like manner' to the end of the subsection; In paragraph (i) of sub-section (2) of section 65, the words from 'but, in the case of a married woman' to the end of the paragraph.
44 & 45 Vic c 49.	The Land Law (Ireland) Act, 1881.	Paragraph (4) of section 38.
44 & 45 Vic c 65.	The Leases for Schools (Ireland) Act, 1881.	In paragraph (d) of section 2, the words 'for their separate use, and whether restrained or not from anticipation'; Paragraphs (e) and (f) of section 2.
45 & 46 Vic c 38.	The Settled Land Act, 1882.	Section 61.
45 & 46 Vic c 39.	The Conveyancing Act, 1882.	Section 7.
45 & 46 Vic c 75.	The Married Women's Property Act, 1882.	The whole Act.
47 & 48 Vic c 14.	The Married Women's Property Act, 1884.	The whole Act.
54 & 55 Vic c 66.	The Registration of Title Act, 1891.	In subsection (1) of section 73, the words 'Subject to the provisions of this section'; Subsection (2) of section 73.
56 & 57 Vic c 53.	The Trustee Act, 1893.	Section 16; In subsection (1) of section 45, the words from 'and notwithstanding' to 'anticipation'.
56 & 57 Vic c 63.	The Married Women's Property Act, 1893.	The whole Act.
7 Edw 7. c 18.	The Married Women's Property Act, 1907.	The whole Act.

Session and Chapter or Number and Year (1)	Short Title (2)	Extent of Repeal (3)
8 Edw 7. c 24.	The Summary Jurisdiction (Ireland) Act, 1908.	In paragraph (a) of sub-section (1) of section 1 the word 'separate'.
8 Edw 7. c 69.	The Companies (Consolidation) Act, 1908.	Section 128.
1 & 2 Geo 5. c 37.	The Conveyancing Act, 1911.	Section 7.
6 & 7 Geo 5. c 50.	The Larceny Act, 1916.	Section 36.
No 16 of 1927.	The Industrial and Commercial Property (Protection) Act, 1927.	In subsection (4) of section 166, the word 'separate'.

PART TWO

Registration of Births Act, 1996

(1996 No 36)

ARRANGEMENT OF SECTIONS

ACTS REFERRED TO

Births and Deaths Registration Act (Ireland), 1880	43 & 44 Vict c 13
Births and Deaths Registration Acts, 1863 to 1994	
Births, Deaths and Marriages Registration Act, 1972	1972, No 25
Defence (Amendment) (No 2) Act, 1960	1960, No 44
Garda Síochána Act, 1989	1989, No 1
Legitimacy Act, 1931	1931, No 13
Registration of Births and Deaths (Ireland) Act, 1863	26 & 27 Vict c 11
Status of Children Act, 1987	1987, No 26

An Act to amend the law in relation to the registration and re-registration of births and to provide for related matters   [19 December 1996]

1   Particulars required concerning births registered or re-registered after commencement of Act

(1) The registration of a birth registered, after the commencement of this Act, under—

(a) the Births and Deaths Registration Acts, 1863 to 1994,

(b) section 6 of the Defence (Amendment) (No 2) Act, 1960, or

(c) section 4 of the Garda Síochána Act, 1989,

shall comprise information of the particulars concerning such birth specified in the *Schedule* to this Act.

(2) The re-registration of a birth re-registered, after the commencement of this Act, under—

(a) the Births and Deaths Registration Acts, 1863 to 1994, or

(b) the Legitimacy Act, 1931,

shall comprise information of the particulars concerning such birth specified in the *Schedule* to this Act.

(3) When the birth of any child is being registered, after the commencement of this Act, under any of the enactments mentioned in *subsection (1)* of this section, the surname of the child to be entered in the register shall be, subject to any necessary linguistic modifications—

(a) that of the mother or father of the child as shown in the register or of both, or

(b) such other surname requested by either the mother or father as an tÁrd Chláraitheoir or a person authorised by him or her may permit if he or she is satisfied that the circumstances so warrant, or

(c) in any case where no information of the particulars of parentage of the child is registered, such surname as the informant may specify.

(4) When the birth of any child is being re-registered, after the commencement of this Act, under any of the enactments mentioned in *subsection (2)* of this section, being a birth which has been registered after the commencement of this Act, the surname of the child shall be that which has been so registered.

(5) The following provisions do not apply to the particulars specified in the *Schedule* to this Act—

(a) section 6 of the Registration of Births and Deaths (Ireland) Act, 1863,

(b) section 34 of the Births and Deaths Registration Act (Ireland), 1880, and

(c) section 5 of the Births, Deaths and Marriages Registration Act, 1972.

(6) Section 1(4) of the Legitimacy Act, 1931, does not apply where the entry in the register relating to the birth to be re-registered, being either—

(a) a registration under section 7 (inserted by section 49 of the Status of Children Act, 1987), or

(b) a re-registration under section 7A (inserted by the said section 49),

of the Births and Deaths Registration Act (Ireland), 1880, is made, after the commencement of this Act, and which contains the name of the father of the child.

(7) This section does not affect the registration or re-registration of any birth which has been registered or re-registered, as the case may be, before the commencement of this Act.

2 Forms

An tÁrd Chláraitheoir may provide forms for use for the purposes of this Act.

3 Delivery and provision of register books

Notwithstanding the provisions of sections 16, 30 and 47 of the Registration of Births and Deaths (Ireland) Act, 1863, an tÁrd Chláraitheoir may make such arrangements, as he or she considers necessary, for—

(a) the delivery of register books by registrars, and

(b) the provision of register books to registrars,

for the purposes of this Act.

4 (Amends the Registration of Births and Deaths (Ireland) Act, 1863)

5 (Amends the Births and Deaths Registration Act (Ireland), 1880)

6 Consequential amendments

(1) (Amends s 6(3)(c) of the Defence (Amendment) (No. 2) Act, 1960)

(2) (Amends s 48 of the Status of Children Act, 1987)

(3) (Amends s 4(3)(c) of the Garda Síochána Act, 1989)

7 Short title, collective citation, construction and commencement

(1) This Act may be cited as the Registration of Births Act, 1996.

(2) The Births and Deaths Registration Acts, 1863 to 1994, section 1(4) of, and the Schedule to, the Legitimacy Act, 1931, and this Act may be cited together as the Births and Deaths Registration Acts, 1863 to 1996, and shall be construed together as one.

(3) This Act shall come into operation on such day as the Minister for Equality and Law Reform may appoint by order.

Commencement—1 October 1997.

SCHEDULE

PARTICULARS TO BE REGISTERED IN A REGISTER BOOK

Number.

Date and Place of Birth.

Sex of Child.

Forename(s) and Surname of Child.

Mother's Forename and Surname, Address and Occupation.

Any former Surname(s) of Mother.

Father's Forename and Surname, Address and Occupation.

Any former Surname(s) of Father.

Signature, Qualification and Address of Informant.

When Registered.

Signature of Registrar.

Forename(s) of Child if added after Registration of Birth, and Date.

Status of Children Act, 1987

(1987 No 26)

ARRANGEMENT OF SECTIONS

PART I

PRELIMINARY AND GENERAL

PART II

AMENDMENT OF THE ACT OF 1931

PART III

GUARDIANSHIP

PART IV

MAINTENANCE

PART TWO

PART IX

REGISTRATION AND RE-REGISTRATION OF BIRTHS

ACTS REFERRED TO

An Act to equalise the rights of children and amend the law relating to their status and for those purposes to amend the law relating to legitimacy and to guardianship of infants, to amend and extend the Family Law (Maintenance of Spouses and Children) Act, 1976, in relation to certain children and to amend further the law relating to maintenance, to amend the law relating to succession and other property rights, to provide for declarations of parentage and for the use of blood tests to assist in the determination of parentage, to amend the law relating to certain presumptions and evidence, to make further provision for the registration and re-registration of births and to provide for connected matters [14 December 1987]

PART I

PRELIMINARY AND GENERAL

1   Short title and commencement

(1) This Act may be cited as the Status of Children Act, 1987.

(2) (a) This Part (other than *sections 3* and *4*) shall come into operation on the passing
of this Act and the said *sections 3* and *4* shall come into operation one month
after such passing.

   (b) *Parts II* to *IX* shall come into operation six months after the passing of this Act
or on such earlier day or days (not being earlier than one month after such
passing) as may be fixed therefor by order or orders of the Minister for Justice,
either generally or with reference to any particular Part or Parts.

Commencement—14 December 1987 (Part I (except s 3 and s 4)), 14 January 1988 (s 3 and s 4), 14
June 1988 (Parts II–IX).

---

2   Interpretation

In this Act, a reference to a Part is to a Part of this Act unless the context requires that a
reference to some other enactment is intended.

3   Marital status of parents to be of no effect on relationships

(1) In deducing any relationship for the purposes of this Act or of any Act of the
Oireachtas passed after the commencement of this section, the relationship between
every person and his father and mother (or either of them) shall, unless the contrary
intention appears, be determined irrespective of whether his father and mother are or
have been married to each other, and all other relationships shall be determined
accordingly.

(2) (a) An adopted person shall, for the purposes of *subsection (1)* of this section, be
deemed from the date of the adoption to be the child of the adopter or
adopters and not the child of any other person or persons.

   (b) In this subsection 'adopted person' means a person who has been adopted
under the Adoption Acts, 1952 to 1976, or, where the person has been adopted
outside the State, whose adoption is recognised by virtue of the law for the time
being in force in the State.

4   Construction of references to persons whose parents have or have not married each other, etc

In this Act and in every Act of the Oireachtas passed after the commencement of this
section—

   (a) a reference, however expressed, to a person whose parents have not married
each other shall, unless the contrary intention appears, be construed as
including a reference to a person whose parents are or have been married to
each other but between whom there has been no subsisting marriage at any time
during the period of ten months before the person's birth, or during the
person's lifetime, and

(b) a reference, however expressed, to a person whose parents have married each other shall, unless the contrary intention appears, be construed as excluding a reference to a person in respect of whom *paragraph (a)* of this section applies.

5   Meaning of father, mother, parent in Irish Nationality and Citizenship Acts, 1956 and 1986

It is hereby declared that, in relation to a child, any reference to 'father', 'mother' or 'parent' in the Irish Nationality and Citizenship Acts, 1956 and 1986, includes and shall be deemed always to have included the father, mother or parent, as the case may require, who was not married to the child's other parent at the time of the child's birth or at any time during the period of ten months preceding the birth.

PART II

AMENDMENT OF THE ACT OF 1931

6   Definition (*Part II*)

In this Part 'the Act of 1931' means the Legitimacy Act, 1931.

7   (Amends s 1 of the Act of 1931)

8   Definition (*Part III*)

In this Part 'the Act of 1964' means the Guardianship of Infants Act, 1964.

9   (Amends s 2 of the Act of 1964)

10   (Amends the Act of 1964)

11   (Amends s 6 of the Act of 1964)

12   (Amends the Act of 1964)

13   (Amends s 11 of the Act of 1964)

PART IV

MAINTENANCE

14   Definition (*Part IV*)

In this Part 'the Act of 1976' means the Family Law (Maintenance of Spouses and Children) Act, 1976.

15   Disputed parentage in maintenance proceedings, etc

Where, in any proceedings before a court relating to the maintenance of a child or the payment of a lump sum in respect of the expenses for the birth or funeral of a child, the making of an order for the purpose of granting such maintenance or the payment of such a lump sum, as the case may be, depends on a finding that a person is a parent of the child, the court shall not in those proceedings make any such order unless it is proved on the balance of probabilities that that person is a parent of the child.

16   (Amends s 3 of the Act of 1976)

17   (Amends s 5 of the Act of 1976)

18   (Amends the Act of 1976)

19   (Amends s 6 of the Act of 1976)

20   (Amends the Act of 1976)

21   (Amends the Act of 1976, s 64 of the Health Act, 1970 and s 28 of the Social Welfare (Consolidation) Act, 1981)

22   (Amends s 23 of the Act of 1976)

23   (Amends s 24 of the Act of 1976)

24   (Amends the Defence Act, 1954)

25   (Repeals the Illegitimate Children (Affiliation Orders) Act, 1930)

PART V

PROPERTY RIGHTS

26   Definition (*Part V*)

In this Part 'the Act of 1965' means the Succession Act, 1965.

27   Construction of dispositions, etc

(1) In any disposition (including a disposition creating an entailed estate) made after the commencement of this Part, references, however expressed, to relationships between persons shall be construed in accordance with *section 3* of this Act.

(2) The following provisions of section 3 of the Legitimacy Act, 1931, namely—

    (a) subsection (1)(b) (which relates to the effect of dispositions where a person has been legitimated),

    (b) subsection (1)(c) (which relates to the effect of legitimation on entailed estates), and

    (c) subsection (2) (which provides that, where the right to any property depends on the relative seniority of the children of any person, legitimated persons shall rank as if born on the date of legitimation).

shall not apply—

    (i) in the case of the said subsection (1)(b), to a disposition made after the commencement of this Part,

(ii) in the case of the said subsection (1)(c), in relation to any entitlement under an entailed estate created by a disposition made after the commencement of this Part, and

(iii) in the case of the said subsection (2), in relation to any right conferred by a disposition made after the commencement of this Part,

except as respects any interest in relation to which the disposition refers only to persons who are, or whose relationship is deduced through, legitimate persons.

(3) For the purpose of any property right to which this section or section 4A (inserted by this Act) of the Act of 1965 relates, the provisions of section 26 of the Adoption Act, 1952 (which relates to the property rights of persons adopted under the Adoption Acts, 1952 to 1976) shall be construed as applying also to any person adopted outside the State whose adoption is recognised by virtue of the law for the time being in force in the State.

(4) (a) Subject to *paragraph (b)* of this subsection, this section is without prejudice to section 26 (as construed in accordance with *subsection (3)* of this section) of the Adoption Act, 1952.

(b) An adopted person shall, unless the contrary intention appears, be entitled to take under a disposition made after the commencement of this Part in the same manner as he would have been entitled to so take if, at the date of the adoption order, he had been born in lawful wedlock to the person or persons who so adopted him.

(5) Any rule of law that a disposition in favour of illegitimate children not in being when the disposition takes effect is void as contrary to public policy is hereby abrogated as respects such dispositions made after the commencement of this Part.

(6) In relation to any disposition made before the commencement of this Part—

(a) nothing in this section shall affect the operation or construction of, or any entitlement under, any disposition so made, and

(b) where such a disposition creates a special power of appointment, nothing in this section shall be interpreted as extending the class of persons in whose favour the appointment may be made so as to include any person who is not a member of that class.

(7) (a) In this section 'disposition' means a disposition, including an oral disposition, of real or personal property whether *inter vivos* or by will or codicil.

(b) Notwithstanding any rule of law, a disposition made by will or codicil executed before the commencement of this Part shall not be treated for the purposes of this section as made on or after that date by reason only that the will or codicil is confirmed by a codicil executed on or after that date.

28   (Amends s 3 of the Act of 1965)

29   (Amends the Act of 1965)

30   (Amends the Act of 1965)

31   (Amends s 117 of the Act of 1965)

32   Repeals relating to property rights

The provisions of the following enactments are hereby repealed to the extent specified:

(a) in the Provident Nominations and Small Intestacies Act, 1883, section 8;

(b) in the Savings Banks Act, 1887, the words ', or in case of any illegitimacy of the deceased person or his children, to or among such person or persons as may be directed by the said regulations,' in section 3(2);

(c) in the Superannuation Act, 1887, the words ', or in case of the illegitimacy of the deceased person or his children, to or among such persons as the department may think fit,' in section 8;

(d) in the Industrial and Provident Societies Act, 1893, section 27(2);

(e) in the Friendly Societies Act, 1896, section 58(2);

(f) in the Legitimacy Act, 1931, sections 1(3) and 9;

(g) in the Local Government (Superannuation) Act, 1956, the words 'or, in the case of the illegitimacy of the deceased, to or among such persons as the local authority think fit,' in section 61(1)(e);

(h) in the Act of 1965, section 110.

PART VI

DECLARATIONS OF PARENTAGE

33   Definitions (*Part VI*)

In this Part—

'the Court' means the Circuit Court;
'prescribed' means prescribed by rules of court.

34   Jurisdiction and venue (*Part VI*)

(1) The Court shall have jurisdiction to grant a declaration under this Part.

(2) The jurisdiction conferred on the Court by this section shall be exercised by the judge of the circuit where any party to the proceedings ordinarily resides or carries on any profession, business or occupation or, where no party to the proceedings ordinarily resides or carries on any profession, business or occupation in the State, by a judge assigned to the Dublin Circuit.

(3) The jurisdiction conferred by this section is in addition to any other jurisdiction to grant a declaration of parentage or to make an order which has the effect of such a declaration.

35 Declaration of parentage

(1) (a) A person (other than an adopted person) born in the State, or

  (b) any other person (other than an adopted person),

may apply to the Court in such manner as may be prescribed for a declaration under this section that a person named in the application is his father or mother, as the case may be, or that both the persons so named are his parents.

(2) An application may be made under *subsection (1)* of this section notwithstanding the fact that any person named in the application as the father or the mother or a parent, as the case may be, is not, or may not be, alive.

(3) Where a person not born in the State makes an application for a declaration by virtue of *subsection (1)(b)* of this section, he shall specify in the application the reasons for seeking the declaration from the Court, and the Court shall refuse to hear or refuse to continue hearing, as the case may be, the application if at any stage it considers that there are no good and proper reasons for seeking the declaration.

(4) Where a person makes an application for a declaration under this section by his next friend the Court shall refuse to hear or refuse to continue hearing, as the case may be, the application if at any stage the Court considers that it would be against the interests of the applicant to determine the application.

(5) On an application under this section the Court may at any stage of the proceedings, of its own motion or on the application of any party to the proceedings, direct that all necessary papers in the matter be sent to the Attorney General.

(6) Where on an application under this section the Attorney General requests to be made a party to the proceedings, the Court shall order that he shall be added as a party, and, whether or not he so requests, the Attorney General may argue before the Court any question in relation to the application which the Court considers necessary to have fully argued and take such other steps in relation thereto as he thinks necessary or expedient.

(7) The Court may direct that notice of any application under this section shall be given in the prescribed manner to such other persons as the Court thinks fit and where notice is so given to any person the Court may, either of its own motion or on the application of that person or any party to the proceedings, order that that person shall be added as a party to those proceedings.

(8) Where on an application under this section it is proved on the balance of probabilities that—

  (a) a person named in the application is the father, or
  (b) a person so named is the mother, or
  (c) persons so named are the parents,

of the applicant, the Court shall make the declaration accordingly.

(9) Any declaration made under this section shall be in a form to be prescribed and shall be binding on the parties to the proceedings and any person claiming through a party to the proceedings, and where the Attorney General is made a party to the proceedings the declaration shall also be binding on the State.

36   Supplementary provisions to section 35

(1) Rules of court may provide that any application for a declaration under *section 35* of this Act shall contain such information as may be prescribed.

(2) Where any costs are incurred by the Attorney General in connection with any application for a declaration under *section 35* of this Act, the court may make such order as it considers just as to the payment of those costs by other parties to the proceedings.

(3) No proceedings on an application under *section 35* of this Act shall affect any final judgment or decree already pronounced or made by any court of competent jurisdiction.

(4) On the hearing of an application under *section 35* of this Act the Court may direct that the whole or any part of the proceedings shall be heard otherwise than in public, and an application for a direction under this subsection shall be so heard unless the Court otherwise directs.

(5) Where a declaration is made by the Court under *section 35* of this Act, notification of that decision shall be given to an tArd-Chláraitheoir and shall be given in such manner as may be prescribed.

PART VII

BLOOD TESTS IN DETERMINING PARENTAGE IN CIVIL PROCEEDINGS

37   Definitions (Part VII)

In this Part—

'blood samples' means blood taken for the purpose of blood tests;
'blood test' means any test carried out under this Part and made with the object of ascertaining inheritable characteristics;
'excluded' means excluded subject to the occurrence of mutation;
'the Minister' means the Minister for Justice.

38   Direction by court on blood tests

(1) In *any* civil proceedings before *a court* in which the parentage of any person is in question, the court may, either of its own motion or on an application by any party to the proceedings, give a direction for the use of blood tests for the purpose of assisting the court to determine whether a person named in the application or a party to the proceedings, as the case may be, is or is not a parent of the person whose parentage is in question, and for the taking, within a period to be specified in the direction, of blood samples from the person whose parentage is so questioned, from any person alleged to be a parent of that person and from any other person who is a party to the proceedings, or from any of those persons.

(2) Where, on the application of any party to proceedings—

(a) a direction is given under *subsection (1)* of this section, such party shall pay the costs of taking and testing blood samples for the purpose of giving effect to the direction (including any expenses reasonably incurred by any person in taking any steps required of him for that purpose) and of making a report to the court under *section 40(2)* of this Act,

(b) such party obtains, under *section 40(4)* of this Act, a written statement explaining or supplementing any statement made in a report under the said *section 40(2)*, that party shall, subject to any direction by the court, pay the costs (if any) of obtaining the written statement (including any expenses reasonably incurred by any person in taking any steps required by him for that purpose),

but any amount paid or to be paid by virtue of this subsection shall be treated as costs incurred by such party in the proceedings.

(3) The court may at any time revoke or vary a direction previously given by it under this section.

39   Consent to, and taking of, blood samples

(1) *Subject to subsection (3)* of this section, a blood sample which is required to be taken from any person for the purpose of giving effect to a direction under *section 38* of this Act *shall not be taken from that person except with his consent.*

(2) Where for the purpose of giving effect to a direction under *section 38* of this Act a blood sample is required to be taken from a person who is *not of full age* and the court considers that he is in the *circumstances capable of giving or refusing the necessary* consent, any consent given or refused by him shall be as effective as it would be if he were of full age.

(3) For the purpose of giving effect to a direction under *section 38* of this Act—

(a) a blood sample may be taken from a minor, other than one to whom *subsection (2)* of this section relates, if the person having charge of or control over the minor consents:

Provided that where more than one person has charge of or control over the minor and they disagree as to whether consent should be given, the minor shall be treated as not having consented;

(b) a blood sample may be taken from a person of full age who is, in the opinion of the court, incapable of understanding the nature and purpose of blood tests if the person having charge of or control over him consents and any medical practitioner in whose care he may be has certified that the taking of a blood sample from him will not be prejudicial to his proper care and treatment:

Provided that where more than one person has charge of or control over the person concerned and they disagree as to whether consent should be given, the person concerned shall be treated as not having consented.

40   Blood tests and reports

(1) Where blood samples are taken for the purpose of giving effect to a direction of a court under *section 38(1)* of this Act, they shall be tested—

(a) under the control of such person (including a person to whom *subsection (6)* of this section relates) as all the parties to the proceedings before the court agree to, or

(b) where the parties are not in agreement,
   (i) under the control of such person to whom *subsection (6)* of this section relates, or
   (ii) under the control of such other person,

as the court shall direct.

(2) The person under whose control blood samples are to be tested by virtue of *subsection (1)* of this section shall make to the court by which the direction was given a report in which he shall state—

   (a) in relation to each person from whom blood samples were so taken, the results of the tests, and

   (b) in relation to each person (other than the person whose parentage is in question) from whom blood samples were so taken—

       (i)   whether the person to whom the report relates is or is not excluded by the results from being a parent of the person whose parentage is in question, and

      (ii)   if the person to whom the report relates is not so excluded, the value, if any, of the results in determining whether that person is a parent of the person whose parentage is in question,

and the report shall be received by the court as evidence in the proceedings of the matters stated therein.

(3) A report under *subsection (2)* of this section shall be in the form prescribed by regulations made under *section 41* of this Act.

(4) Where a report has been made to a court under *subsection (2)* of this section, any party may, with the leave of the court, or shall, if the court so directs, obtain from the person who made the report a written statement explaining or supplementing any statement made in the report, and that statement shall be deemed for the purposes of this section (other than *subsections (3)* and *(6)*) to form part of the report made to the court.

(5) Where a direction is given under *section 38(1)* of this Act in any proceedings and the blood samples to which the direction relates have been tested by virtue of this section, a party to the proceedings, unless the court otherwise directs, shall not be entitled to call as a witness the person under whose control the blood samples were tested for the purpose of giving effect to that direction, or any person by whom any thing necessary for the purpose of enabling those tests to be carried out was done, unless within 14 days after receiving a copy of the report he serves notice on the other parties to the proceedings, or on such of them as the court may direct, of his intention to call that person as a witness and, where that person is so called, the party who called him shall be entitled to cross-examine him.

(6) (a) The Minister may, for the purpose of *subsection (1)* of this section, appoint a person or category of persons under whose control blood tests may be carried out.

    (b) The Minister may at any time amend or revoke an appointment under this subsection but such amendment or revocation shall not affect any blood test carried out, or the testing of any blood sample for the purpose of this Part which was submitted for testing, before such amendment or revocation.

    (c) Notice of an appointment, or the amendment or revocation of any appointment, shall be published by the Minister in the *Iris Oifigiúil.*

41   Regulations for purpose of giving effect to this Part

(1) The Minister may make regulations for the purpose of giving effect to this Part.

(2) Without prejudice to the generality of *subsection (1)* of this section, regulations made under this section may in particular—

(a) regulate the taking, identification and transport of blood samples;

(b) require the production at the time when a blood sample is to be taken of such evidence of the identity of the person from whom it is to be taken as may be prescribed by the regulations;

(c) require any person from whom a blood sample is to be taken, or, in such cases as may be prescribed by the regulations, such other person as may be so prescribed, to state in writing whether he or the person from whom the sample is to be taken, as the case may be, had during such period as may be specified in the regulations suffered from any such illness as may be so specified or received a transfusion of blood;

(d) prescribe the form of any report to be made to a court under this Part.

(3) Every regulation made under this section shall be laid before each House of the Oireachtas as soon as may be after it is made and, if a resolution annulling the regulation is passed by either such House within the next 21 days on which that House has sat after the regulation is laid before it, the regulation shall be annulled accordingly, but without prejudice to the validity of anything previously done thereunder.

42 Failure to comply with direction on blood tests

(1) Where a court gives a direction under *section 38* of this Act and any person fails to take any step required of him for the purpose of giving effect to the direction, the court may draw such inferences, if any, from that fact as appear proper in the circumstances.

(2) Where in proceedings on an application under *section 35* of this Act a court gives a direction under *section 38* of this Act for the taking of blood samples then, if any person named in the direction fails, within such period as may be specified by the court, to take any step required of him for the purpose of giving effect to the direction, the court may dismiss the application.

(3) Where in any civil proceedings in which the parentage of any person falls to be determined by the court hearing those proceedings there is, by virtue of *section 46* of this Act, a presumption of paternity relating to such person, then if—

(a) a direction is given under *section 38* of this Act in those proceedings, and

(b) any party who is claiming any relief in the proceedings and who for the purpose of obtaining that relief is entitled to rely on the presumption fails to take any step required of him for the purpose of giving effect to the direction,

the court may adjourn the hearing for such period as it thinks fit to enable that party to take that step, and if at the end of that period he has failed without reasonable cause to take it the court may, without prejudice to *subsection (1)* of this section, dismiss his claim for relief notwithstanding the absence of evidence to rebut the presumption.

(4) Where any person named in a direction under *section 38* of this Act fails to consent to the taking of a blood sample from himself or from any person named in the direction whom he has charge of or control over, he shall be deemed for the purposes of this section to have failed to take a step required of him for the purpose of giving effect to the direction.

43 Penalty for personation for blood test purposes

If, for the purpose of providing a blood sample for a test under *section 40* of this Act, any person personates another or proffers another knowing him not to be the person named in the direction, he shall be liable—

  (a)   on summary conviction, to a fine not exceeding £1,000 or to imprisonment for a term not exceeding 12 months, or to both;

  (b)   on conviction on indictment, to a fine not exceeding £2,500 or to imprisonment for a term not exceeding two years, or to both.

PART VIII

PRESUMPTIONS AND EVIDENTIAL PROVISIONS

44   Abrogation of presumption of legitimacy or illegitimacy

Any presumption of law as to the legitimacy or illegitimacy of any person is hereby abrogated.

45   Finding of parentage as evidence in other proceedings

(1) Where, either before or after the commencement of this Part, a person has been found or adjudged to be a parent of a child in any civil proceedings before a court relating to guardianship of infants or maintenance (including affiliation) or under section 215 of the Social Welfare (Consolidation) Act, 1981, such a finding or adjudication shall, notwithstanding the fact that that person did or did not offer any defence to the allegation of parentage or was or was not a party to those proceedings, be admissible in evidence in any subsequent civil proceedings for the purpose of proving that that person is or, where not alive, was a parent of that child:

  Provided that no finding or adjudication as aforesaid other than a subsisting one shall be admissible in evidence by virtue of this section.

(2) Where evidence that a person has been found or adjudged to be a parent of a child has been submitted in subsequent proceedings by virtue of *subsection (1)* of this section, then—

  (a)   that person shall be taken to be or, where he is not alive, to have been a parent of that child, unless the contrary is proved on the balance of probabilities, and

  (b)   in relation to the prior proceedings the contents of any document which was before that court, or which contains any pronouncement of that court, shall, without prejudice to the submission of any other admissible evidence for the purpose of identifying the facts on which the finding or adjudication was based, be admissible for that purpose.

(3) Where in subsequent civil proceedings the contents of any document are admissible in evidence by virtue of *subsection (2)* of this section, a copy of that document, or of the material part thereof, purporting to be certified or otherwise authenticated by or on behalf of the court or authority having custody of that document shall be admissible in evidence and shall be taken to be a true copy of that document or part unless the contrary is shown.

46   Presumptions of paternity and non-paternity

(1) Where a woman gives birth to a child—

  (a)   during a subsisting marriage to which she is a party, or

  (b)   within the period of ten months after the termination, by death or otherwise, of a marriage to which she is a party, then the husband of the marriage shall be presumed to be the father of the child unless the contrary is proved on the balance of probabilities.

(2) Notwithstanding *subsection (1)* of this section, where a married woman, being a woman who is living apart from her husband under—

(a) a decree of divorce *a mensa et thoro,* or

(b) a deed of separation,

gives birth to a child more than ten months after the decree was granted or the deed was executed, as the case may be, then her husband shall be presumed not to be the father of the child unless the contrary is proved on the balance of probabilities.

(3) Notwithstanding *subsection (1)* of this section, where—

(a) the birth of a child is registered in a register maintained under the Births and Deaths Registration Acts, 1863 to 1987, and

(b) the name of a person is entered as the father of the child on the register so maintained,

then the person whose name is so entered shall be presumed to be the father of the child unless the contrary is proved on the balance of probabilities.

(4) For the purposes of *subsection (1)* of this section 'subsisting marriage' shall be construed as including a voidable marriage and the expression 'the termination, by death or otherwise, of a marriage' shall be construed as including the annulment of a voidable marriage.

47 Admissibility of certain evidence

(1) The evidence of a husband or wife shall be admissible in any proceedings to prove that marital intercourse did or did not take place between them during any period.

(2) The proviso to section 3 of the Evidence Further Amendment Act, 1869, is hereby repealed.

PART IX

REGISTRATION AND RE-REGISTRATION OF BIRTHS

48 Re-registration of birth after declaration of parentage

The Minister for Health may, in relation to declarations of parentage made under *section 35* of this Act which render births registrable, or concern births registered, under the Births and Deaths Registration Acts, 1863 to 1987, by regulations prescribe the place where, and the manner in which, any such birth is to be registered or re-registered, as the case may be.

Amendments—Registration of Births Act, 1996, s 6(2).

---

49   (Amends the Births and Deaths Registration Act (Ireland), 1880)

50   Construction and citation

The Births and Deaths Registration Acts, 1863 to 1972, and his Part shall be construed together as one and may be cited together as the Births and Deaths Registration Acts, 1863 to 1987.

Succession Act, 1965

(1965 No 27)

ARRANGEMENT OF SECTIONS

Section   *page*
...

PART V

ADMINISTRATION OF ASSETS

PART IX

LEGAL RIGHT OF TESTATOR'S SPOUSE AND PROVISION FOR CHILDREN

PART X

UNWORTHINESS TO SUCCEED AND DISINHERITANCE

55   Powers of personal representatives as to appropriation

(1) The personal representatives may, subject to the provisions of this section, appropriate any part of the estate of a deceased person in its actual condition or state of

investment at the time of appropriation in or towards satisfaction of any share in the estate, whether settled or not, according to the respective rights of the persons interested in the estate.

(2) Except in a case to which *section 56* applies, an appropriation shall not be made under this section so as to affect prejudicially any specific devise or bequest.

(3) Except in a case to which *section 56* applies, an appropriation shall not be made under this section unless notice of the intended appropriation has been served on all parties entitled to a share in the estate (other than persons who may come into existence after the time of the appropriation or who cannot after reasonable enquiry be found or ascertained at that time) any one of which parties may within six weeks from the service of such notice on him apply to the court to prohibit the appropriation.

(4) An appropriation of property, whether or not being an investment authorised by law or by the will, if any, of the deceased, shall not (save as in this section mentioned) be made under this section except with the following consents:

(a) when made for the benefit of a person absolutely and beneficially entitled in possession, the consent of that person;
(b) when made in respect of any settled share, the consent of either the trustee thereof, if any (not being also the personal representative), or the person who may for the time being be entitled to the income.

(5) If the person whose consent is so required is an infant or a person of unsound mind, the consent shall be given on his behalf by his parents or parent, guardian, committee or receiver, or if, in the case of an infant there is no such parent or guardian, by the court on the application of his next friend.

(6) No consent (save of such trustee as aforesaid) shall be required on behalf of a person who may come into existence after the time of appropriation, or who cannot after reasonable enquiry be found or ascertained at that time.

(7) If no committee or receiver of a person of unsound mind has been appointed, then, if the appropriation is of an investment authorised by law or by the will, if any, of the deceased, no consent shall be required on behalf of the person of unsound mind.

(8) If, independently of the personal representatives there is no trustee of a settled share, and no person of full age and capacity entitled to the income thereof, no consent shall be required to an appropriation in respect of such share provided that the appropriation is of an investment authorised as aforesaid.

(9) Any property duly appropriated under the powers conferred by this section shall thereafter be treated as an authorised investment, and may be retained or dealt with accordingly.

(10) For the purposes of such appropriation, the personal representatives may ascertain and fix the values of the respective parts of the estate and the liabilities of the deceased person as they may think fit, and may for that purpose employ a duly qualified valuer in any case where such employment may be necessary; and may make any conveyance which may be requisite for giving effect to the appropriation.

(11) Unless the court on an application made to it under *subsection (3)* otherwise directs, an appropriation made pursuant to this section shall bind all persons interested in the property of the deceased whose consent is not hereby made requisite.

(12) The personal representatives shall, in making the appropriation, have regard to the rights of any person who may thereafter come into existence, or who cannot after

reasonable enquiry be found or ascertained at the time of appropriation, and of any other person whose consent is not required by this section.

(13) This section does not prejudice any other power of appropriation conferred by law or by the will, if any, of the deceased, and takes effect with any extended powers conferred by the will, if any, of the deceased, and, where an appropriation is made under this section, in respect of a settled share, the property appropriated shall remain subject to all trusts for sale and powers of leasing, disposition and management or varying investments which would have been applicable thereto or to the share in respect of which the appropriation is made, if no such appropriation had been made.

(14) If, after any property has been appropriated in purported exercise of the powers conferred by this section, the person to whom it was conveyed disposes of it or any interest therein, then, in favour of a purchaser, the appropriation shall be deemed to have been made in accordance with the requirements of this section and after all requisite notices and consents, if any, had been given.

(15) In this section, a settled share includes any share to which a person is not absolutely entitled in possession at the date of the appropriation and also an annuity.

(16) This section applies whether the deceased died intestate or not, and whether before or after the commencement of this Act, and extends to property over which a testator exercises a general power of appointment, and authorises the setting apart of a fund to answer an annuity by means of the income of that fund or otherwise.

(17) Where any property is appropriated under the provisions of this section, a conveyance thereof by the personal representatives to the person to whom it is appropriated shall not, by reason only that the property so conveyed is accepted by the person to whom it is conveyed in or towards the satisfaction of a legacy or a share in residuary estate, be liable to any higher stamp duty than that payable on a transfer of personal property for the like purpose.

(18) The powers conferred by this section may be exercised by the personal representatives in their own favour.

56　Right of surviving spouse to require dwelling and household chattels to be appropriated

(1) Where the estate of a deceased person includes a dwelling in which, at the time of the deceased's death, the surviving spouse was ordinarily resident, the surviving spouse may, subject to *subsection (5)*, require the personal representatives in writing to appropriate the dwelling under *section 55* in or towards satisfaction of any share of the surviving spouse.

(2) The surviving spouse may also require the personal representatives in writing to appropriate any household chattels in or towards satisfaction of any share of the surviving spouse.

(3) If the share of a surviving spouse is insufficient to enable an appropriation to be made under *subsection (1)* or *(2)*, as the case may be, the right conferred by the relevant subsection may also be exercised in relation to the share of any infant for whom the surviving spouse is a trustee under *section 57* or otherwise.

(4) It shall be the duty of the personal representatives to notify the surviving spouse in writing of the rights conferred by this section.

(5) A right conferred by this section shall not be exercisable—

(a) after the expiration of six months from the receipt by the surviving spouse of such notification or one year from the first taking out of representation of the deceased's estate, whichever is the later, or

(b) in relation to a dwelling, in any of the cases mentioned in *subsection (6)*, unless the court, on application made by the personal representatives or the surviving spouse, is satisfied that the exercise of that right is unlikely to diminish the value of the assets of the deceased, other than the dwelling, or to make it more difficult to dispose of them in due course of administration and authorises its exercise.

(6) *Paragraph (b)* of *subsection (5)* and *paragraph (d)* of *subsection (10)* apply to the following cases:

(a) where the dwelling forms part of a building, and an estate or interest in the whole building forms part of the estate;

(b) where the dwelling is held with agricultural land an estate or interest in which forms part of the estate;

(c) where the whole or a part of the dwelling was, at the time of the death, used as a hotel, guest house or boarding house;

(d) where a part of the dwelling was, at the time of the death, used for purposes other than domestic purposes.

(7) Nothing in *subsection (12)* of *section 55* shall prevent the personal representatives from giving effect to the rights conferred by this section.

(8) (a) So long as a right conferred by this section continues to be exercisable, the personal representatives shall not, without the written consent of the surviving spouse or the leave of the court given on the refusal of an application under *paragraph (b)* of *subsection (5)*, sell or otherwise dispose of the dwelling or household chattels except in the course of administration owing to want of other assets.

(b) This subsection shall not apply where the surviving spouse is a personal representative.

(c) Nothing in this subsection shall confer any right on the surviving spouse against a purchaser from the personal representatives.

(9) The rights conferred by this section on a surviving spouse include a right to require appropriation partly in satisfaction of a share in the deceased's estate and partly in return for a payment of money by the surviving spouse on the spouse's own behalf and also on behalf of any infant for whom the spouse is a trustee under *section 57* or otherwise.

(10)(a) In addition to the rights to require appropriation conferred by this section, the surviving spouse may, so long as a right conferred by this section continues to be exercisable, apply to the court for appropriation on the spouse's own behalf and also on behalf of any infant for whom the spouse is a trustee under *section 57* or otherwise.

(b) On any such application, the court may, if of opinion that, in the special circumstances of the case, hardship would otherwise be caused to the surviving spouse or to the surviving spouse and any such infant, order that appropriation to the spouse shall be made without the payment of money provided for in *subsection (9)* or subject to the payment of such amount as the court considers reasonable.

(c) The court may make such further order in relation to the administration of the deceased's estate as may appear to the court to be just and equitable having regard to the provisions of this Act and to all the circumstances.

(d) The court shall not make an order under this subsection in relation to a dwelling in any of the cases mentioned in *subsection (6)*, unless it is satisfied that the order would be unlikely to diminish the value of the assets of the deceased, other than the dwelling, or to make it more difficult to dispose of them in due course of administration.

(11) All proceedings in relation to this section shall be heard in chambers.

(12) Where the surviving spouse is a person of unsound mind, a requirement or consent under this section may, if there is a committee of the spouse's estate, be made or given on behalf of the spouse by the committee by leave of the court which has appointed the committee or, if there is no committee, be given or made by the High Court or, in a case within the jurisdiction of the Circuit Court, by that Court.

(13) An appropriation to which this section applies shall for the purposes of succession duty be deemed to be a succession derived from the deceased.

(14) In this section—

'dwelling' means an estate or interest in a building occupied as a separate dwelling or a part, so occupied, of any building and includes any garden or portion of ground attached to and usually occupied with the dwelling or otherwise required for the amenity or convenience of the dwelling;

'household chattels' means furniture, linen, china, glass, books and other chattels of ordinary household use or ornament and also consumable stores, garden effects and domestic animals, but does not include any chattels used at the death of the deceased for business or professional purposes or money or security for money.

...

PART IX

LEGAL RIGHT OF TESTATOR'S SPOUSE AND PROVISION FOR CHILDREN

109 Application of Part IX

(1) Where, after the commencement of this Act, a person dies wholly or partly testate leaving a spouse or children or both spouse and children, the provisions of this Part shall have effect.

(2) In this Part, references to the estate of the testator are to all estate to which he was beneficially entitled for an estate or interest not ceasing on his death and remaining after payment of all expenses, debts, and liabilities (other than estate duty) properly payable thereout.

110 Legitimated, illegitimate and adopted persons

In deducing any relationship for the purposes of this Part, the provisions of the Legitimacy Act, 1931, and of *section 26* of the Adoption Act, 1952, shall apply as they apply in relation to succession on intestacy.

111 Right of surviving spouse

(1) If the testator leaves a spouse and no children, the spouse shall have a right to one-half of the estate.

PART TWO

(2) If the testator leaves a spouse and children, the spouse shall have a right to one-third of the estate.

112 Priority of legal right

The right of a spouse under *section 111* (which shall be known as a legal right) shall have priority over devises, bequests and shares on intestacy.

113 Renunciation of legal right

The legal right of a spouse may be renounced in an ante-nuptial contract made in writing between the parties to an intended marriage or may be renounced in writing by the spouse after marriage and during the lifetime of the testator.

114 Effect of devise or bequest to spouse

(1) Where property is devised or bequeathed in a will to a spouse and the devise or bequest is expressed in the will to be in addition to the share as a legal right of the spouse, the testator shall be deemed to have made by the will a gift to the spouse consisting of—

    (a) a sum equal to the value of the share as a legal right of the spouse, and
    (b) the property so devised or bequeathed.

(2) In any other case, a devise or bequest in a will to a spouse shall be deemed to have been intended by the testator to be in satisfaction of the share as a legal right of the spouse.

115 Election between legal right and rights under a will and on partial intestacy

(1) (a) Where, under the will of a deceased person who dies wholly testate, there is a devise or bequest to a spouse, the spouse may elect to take either that devise or bequest or the share to which he is entitled as a legal right.

    (b) In default of election, the spouse shall be entitled to take under the will, and he shall not be entitled to take any share as a legal right.

(2) (a) Where a person dies partly testate and partly intestate, a spouse may elect to take either—

      (i) his share as a legal right, or
      (ii) his share under the intestacy, together with any devise or bequest to him under the will of the deceased.

    (b) In default of election, the spouse shall be entitled to take his share under the intestacy, together with any devise or bequest to him under the will, and he shall not be entitled to take any share as a legal right.

(3) A spouse, in electing to take his share as a legal right, may further elect to take any devise or bequest to him less in value than the share in partial satisfaction thereof.

(4) It shall be the duty of the personal representatives to notify the spouse in writing of the right of election conferred by this section. The right shall not be exercisable after the expiration of six months from the receipt by the spouse of such notification or one year from the first taking out of representation of the deceased's estate, whichever is the later.

(5) Where the surviving spouse is a person of unsound mind, the right of election conferred by this section may, if there is a committee of the spouse's estate, be exercised on behalf of the spouse by the committee by leave of the court which has appointed the committee or, if there is no committee, be exercised by the High Court or, in a case within the jurisdiction of the Circuit Court, by that Court.

(6) In this section, but only in its application to a case to which *subsection (1)* of *section 114* applies, 'devise or bequest' means a gift deemed under that subsection to have been made by the will of the testator.

116   Provision in satisfaction of legal right

(1) Where a testator, during his lifetime, has made permanent provision for his spouse, whether under contract or otherwise, all property which is the subject of such provision (other than periodical payments made for her maintenance during his lifetime) shall be taken as being given in or towards satisfaction of the share as a legal right of the surviving spouse.

(2) The value of the property shall be reckoned as at the date of the making of the provision.

(3) If the value of the property is equal to or greater than the share of the spouse as a legal right, the spouse shall not be entitled to take any share as a legal right.

(4) If the value of the property is less than the share of the spouse as a legal right, the spouse shall be entitled to receive in satisfaction of such share so much only of the estate as, when added to the value of the property, is sufficient, as nearly as can be estimated, to make up the full amount of that share.

(5) This section shall apply only to a provision made before the commencement of this Act.

117   Provision for children

(1) Where, on application by or on behalf of a child of a testator, the court is of opinion that the testator has failed in his moral duty to make proper provision for the child in accordance with his means, whether by his will or otherwise, the court may order that such provision shall be made for the child out of the estate as the court thinks just.

(1A)(a) An application made under this section by virtue of Part V of the Status of Children Act, 1987, shall be considered in accordance with *subsection (2)* irrespective of whether the testator executed his will before or after the commencement of the said Part V.

(b) Nothing in *paragraph (a)* shall be construed as conferring a right to apply under this section in respect of a testator who dies before the commencement of the said Part V.

(2) The court shall consider the application from the point of view of a prudent and just parent, taking into account the position of each of the children of the testator and any other circumstances which the court may consider of assistance in arriving at a decision that will be as fair as possible to the child to whom the application relates and to the other children.

(3) An order under this section shall not affect the legal right of a surviving spouse or, if the surviving spouse is the mother or father of the child, any devise or bequest to the spouse or any share to which the spouse is entitled on intestacy.

(4) Rules of court shall provide for the conduct of proceedings under this section in a summary manner.

(5) The costs in the proceedings shall be at the discretion of the court.

(6) An order under this section shall not be made except on an application made within twelve months from the first taking out of representation of the deceased's estate.

Amendments—Status of Children Act, 1987, s 31.

---

118 Estate duty

Property representing the share of a person as a legal right and property which is the subject of an order under *section 117* shall bear their due proportions of the estate duty payable on the estate of the deceased.

119 Proceedings to be in chambers

All proceedings in relation to this Part shall be heard in chambers.

PART X

UNWORTHINESS TO SUCCEED AND DISINHERITANCE

120 Exclusion of persons from succession

(1) A sane person who has been guilty of the murder, attempted murder or manslaugher of another shall be precluded from taking any share in the estate of that other, except a share arising under a will made after the act constituting the offence, and shall not be entitled to make an application under *section 117*.

(2) A spouse who failed to comply with a decree of restitution of conjugal rights obtained by the deceased and a spouse guilty of desertion which has continued up to the death for two years or more shall be precluded from taking any share in the estate of the deceased as a legal right or on intestacy.

(3) A spouse who was guilty of conduct which justified the deceased in separating and living apart from him shall be deemed to be guilty of desertion within the meaning of *subsection (2)*.

(4) A person who has been found guilty of an offence against the deceased, or against the spouse or any child of the deceased (including a child adopted under the Adoption Acts, 1952 and 1964, and a person to whom the deceased was *in loco parentis* at the time of the offence), punishable by imprisonment for a maximum period of at least two years or by a more severe penalty, shall be precluded from taking any share in the estate as a legal right or from making an application under *section 117*.

(5) Any share which a person is precluded from taking under this section shall be distributed as if that person had died before the deceased.

Amendments—Judicial Separation and Family Law Reform Act, 1989, s 42.

---

121 Dispositions for purpose of disinheriting spouse or children

(1) This section applies to a disposition of property (other than a testamentary disposition or a disposition to a purchaser) under which the beneficial ownership of the property vests in possession in the donee within three years before the death of the person who made it or on his death or later.

(2) If the court is satisfied that a disposition to which this section applies was made for the purpose of defeating or substantially diminishing the share of the disponer's spouse, whether as a legal right or on intestacy, or the intestate share of any of his children, or of leaving any of his children insufficiently provided for, then, whether the disponer died testate or intestate, the court may order that the disposition shall, in whole or in part, be deemed, for the purposes of Parts VI and IX, to be a devise or bequest made by him by will and to form part of his estate, and to have had no other effect.

(3) To the extent to which the court so orders, the disposition shall be deemed never to have had effect as such and the donee of the property, or any person representing or deriving title under him, shall be a debtor of the estate for such amount as the court may direct accordingly.

(4) The court may make such further order in relation to the matter as may appear to the court to be just and equitable having regard to the provisions and the spirit of this Act and to all the circumstances.

(5) Subject to *subsections (6)* and *(7)*, an order may be made under this section—

    (a)   in the interest of the spouse, on the application of the spouse or the personal representative of the deceased, made within one year from the first taking out of representation,

    (b)   in the interest of a child, on an application under *section 117*.

(6) In the case of a disposition made in favour of the spouse of the disponer, an order shall not be made under this section on an application by or on behalf of a child of the disponer who is also a child of the spouse.

(7) An order shall not be made under this section affecting a disposition made in favour of any child of the disponer, if—

    (a)   the spouse of the disponer was dead when the disposition was made, or

    (b)   the spouse was alive when the disposition was made but was a person who, if the disponer had then died, would have been precluded under any of the provisions of *section 120* from taking a share in his estate, or

    (c)   the spouse was alive when the disposition was made and consented in writing to it.

(8) If the donee disposes of the property to a purchaser, this section shall cease to apply to the property and shall apply instead to the consideration given by the purchaser.

(9) Accrual by survivorship on the death of a joint tenant of property shall, for the purposes of this section, be deemed to be a vesting of the beneficial ownership of the entire property in the survivor.

(10) In this section 'disposition' includes a *donatio mortis causa*.

122 Proceedings to be in chambers

All proceedings in relation to this Part shall be heard in chambers.

Taxes Consolidation Act, 1997

(1997 No 39)

ARRANGEMENT OF SECTIONS

Section   *page*
...

PART 44

MARRIED, SEPARATED AND DIVORCED PERSONS

CHAPTER 1

Income Tax

PART 44

MARRIED, SEPARATED AND DIVORCED PERSONS

CHAPTER 1

Income tax

1015 Interpretation Chapter 1

(1) In this Chapter, 'the inspector', in relation to a notice, means any inspector who might reasonably be considered by the person giving notice to be likely to be concerned with the subject matter of the notice or who declares himself or herself ready to accept the notice.

(2) A wife shall be treated for income tax purposes as living with her husband unless either—

    (a) they are separated under an order of a court of competent jurisdiction or by deed of separation, or

    (b) they are in fact separated in such circumstances that the separation is likely to be permanent.

(3) (a) In this Chapter, references to the income of a wife include references to any sum which apart from this Chapter would be included in computing her total income, and this Chapter shall apply in relation to any such sum notwithstanding that some enactment (including, except in so far as the contrary is expressly provided, an enactment passed after the passing of this Act) requires that that sum should not be treated as income of any person other than her.

    (b) In the Income Tax Acts, a reference to a person who has duly elected to be assessed to tax in accordance with a particular section includes a reference to a person who is deemed to have elected to be assessed to tax in accordance with that section, and any reference to a person who is assessed to tax in accordance with *section 1017* for a year of assessment includes a reference to a case where the person and his or her spouse are assessed to tax for that year in accordance with *section 1023*.

(4) Any notice required to be served under any section in this Chapter may be served by post.

1016 Assessment as single persons

(1) Subject to *subsection (2)* in any case in which a wife is treated as living with her husband, income tax shall be assessed, charged and recovered, except as is otherwise provided by the Income Tax Acts, on the income of the husband and on the income of the wife as if they were not married.

(2) Where an election under *section 1018* has effect in relation to a husband and wife for a year of assessment, this section shall not apply in relation to that husband and wife for that year of assessment.

1017 Assessment of husband in respect of income of both spouses

(1) Where in the case of a husband and wife an election under *section 1018* to be assessed to tax in accordance with this section has effect for a year of assessment—

(a) the husband shall be assessed and charged to income tax, not only in respect of his total income (if any) for that year, but also in respect of his wife's total income (if any) for any part of that year of assessment during which she is living with him, and for this purpose and for the purposes of the Income Tax Acts that last-mentioned income shall be deemed to be his income,

(b) the question whether there is any income of the wife chargeable to tax for any year of assessment and, if so, what is to be taken to be the amount of that income for tax purposes shall not be affected by this section, and

(c) any tax to be assessed in respect of any income which under this section is deemed to be income of a woman's husband shall, instead of being assessed on her, or on her trustees, guardian or committee, or on her executors or administrators, be assessable on him or, in the appropriate cases, on his executors or administrators.

(2) Any relief from income tax authorised by any provision of the Income Tax Acts to be granted to a husband by reference to the income or profits or gains or losses of his wife or by reference to any payment made by her shall be granted to a husband for a year of assessment only if he is assessed to tax for that year in accordance with this section.

1018 Election for assessment under *section 1017*

(1) A husband and his wife, where the wife is living with the husband, may at any time during a year of assessment, by notice in writing given to the inspector, jointly elect to be assessed to income tax for that year of assessment in accordance with *section 1017* and, where such election is made, the income of the husband and the income of the wife shall be assessed to tax for that year in accordance with that section.

(2) Where an election is made under *subsection (1)* in respect of a year of assessment, the election shall have effect for that year and for each subsequent year of assessment.

(3) Notwithstanding *subsections (1)* and *(2)*, either the husband or the wife may, in relation to a year of assessment, by notice in writing given to the inspector before the end of the year, withdraw the election in respect of that year and, on the giving of that notice, the election shall not have effect for that year or for any subsequent year of assessment.

(4) (a) A husband and his wife, where the wife is living with the husband and where an election under *subsection (1)* has not been made by them for a year of assessment (or for any prior year of assessment) shall be deemed to have duly elected to be assessed to tax in accordance with *section 1017* for that year unless before the end of that year either of them gives notice in writing to the inspector that he or she wishes to be assessed to tax for that year as a single person in accordance with *section 1016.*

   (b) Where a husband or his wife has duly given notice under *paragraph (a)* that paragraph shall not apply in relation to that husband and wife for the year of assessment for which the notice was given or for any subsequent year of assessment until the year of assessment in which the notice is withdrawn, by the person who gave it, by further notice in writing to the inspector.

1019 Assessment of wife in respect of income of both spouses

(1) In this section—

   'the basis year', in relation to a husband and wife, means the year of marriage or, if earlier, the latest year of assessment preceding that year of marriage for which details of the total incomes of both the husband and the wife are available to the inspector at the time they first elect, or are first deemed to have duly elected, to be assessed to tax in accordance with *section 1017.*

'year of marriage', in relation to a husband and wife, means the year of assessment in which their marriage took place.

(2) *Subsection (3)* shall apply for a year of assessment where, in the case of a husband and wife who are living together—

- (a) (i) an election (including an election deemed to have been duly made) by the husband and wife to be assessed to income tax in accordance with *section 1017* has effect in relation to the year of assessment, and
  - (ii) the husband and the wife by notice in writing jointly given to the inspector before the 6th day of July in the year of assessment elect that the wife should be assessed to income tax in accordance with *section 1017,* or
- (b) (i) the year of marriage is the year 1993–94 or a subsequent year of assessment,
  - (ii) not having made an election under *section 1018(1)* to be assessed to income tax in accordance with *section 1017,* the husband and wife have been deemed for that year of assessment, in accordance with *section 1018(4)* to have duly made such an election, but have not made an election in accordance with *paragraph (a)(ii)* for that year, and
  - (iii) the inspector, to the best of his or her knowledge and belief, considers that the total income of the wife for the basis year exceeded the total income of her husband for that basis year.

(3) Where this subsection applies for a year of assessment, the wife shall be assessed to income tax in accordance with *section 1017* for that year, and accordingly references in *section 1017* or in any other provision of the Income Tax Acts, however expressed—

- (a) to a husband being assessed, assessed and charged or chargeable to income tax for a year of assessment in respect of his own total income (if any) and his wife's total income (if any), and
- (b) to income of a wife being deemed for income tax purposes to be that of her husband,

shall, subject to this section and the modifications set out in *subsection (6)* and any other necessary modifications, be construed respectively for that year of assessment as references—

- (i) to a wife being assessed, assessed and charged or chargeable to income tax in respect of her own total income (if any) and her husband's total income (if any), and
- (ii) to the income of a husband being deemed for income tax purposes to be that of his wife.

(4) (a) Where in accordance with *subsection (3)* a wife is by virtue of *subsection (2)(b)* to be assessed and charged to income tax in respect of her total income (if any) and her husband's total income (if any) for a year of assessment—

- (i) in the absence of a notice given in accordance with *subsection (1)* or *(4)(a)* of *section 1018* or an application made under *section 1023* the wife shall be so assessed and charged for each subsequent year of assessment, and
- (ii) any such charge shall apply and continue to apply notwithstanding that her husband's total income for the basis year may have exceeded her total income for that year.

- (b) Where a notice under *section 1018(4)(a)* or an application under *section 1023* is withdrawn and, but for the giving of such a notice or the making of such an application in the first instance, a wife would have been assessed to income tax in respect of her own total income (if any) and the total income (if any) of her husband for the year of assessment in which the notice was given or the application was made, as may be appropriate, then, in the absence of an election made in accordance with *section 1018(1)* (not being such an election deemed to have been duly made in accordance with *section 1018(4)*), the wife shall be so assessed to income tax for the year of assessment in which that notice or application is withdrawn and for each subsequent year of assessment.

(5) Where an election is made in accordance with *subsection (2)(a)(ii)* for a year of assessment, the election shall have effect for that year and each subsequent year of assessment unless it is withdrawn by further notice in writing given jointly by the husband and the wife to the inspector before the 6th day of July in a year of assessment and the election shall not then have effect for the year for which the further notice is given or for any subsequent year of assessment.

(6) For the purposes of the other provisions of this section and as the circumstances may require—

    (a) a reference in the Income Tax Acts, however expressed, to an individual or a claimant, being a man, a married man or a husband shall be construed respectively as a reference to a woman, a married woman or a wife, and a reference in those Acts, however expressed, to a woman, a married woman or a wife shall be construed respectively as a reference to a man, a married man or a husband, and

    (b) any provision of the Income Tax Acts shall, in so far as it may relate to the treatment of any husband and wife for the purposes of those Acts, be construed so as to give effect to this section.

1020   Special provisions relating to year of marriage

(1) In this section—

    'income tax month' means a month beginning on the 6th day of any of the months of April to March in any year of assessment;

    'year of marriage', in relation to a husband and wife, means the year of assessment in which their marriage took place.

(2) *Section 1018* shall not apply in relation to a husband and his wife for the year of marriage.

(3) Where, on making a claim in that behalf, a husband and his wife prove that the amount equal to the aggregate of the income tax paid and payable by the husband on his total income for the year of marriage and the income tax paid and payable by his wife on her total income for the year of marriage is in excess of the income tax which would have been payable by the husband on his total income and the total income of his wife for the year of marriage if—

    (a) he had been charged to income tax for the year of marriage in accordance with *section 1017*, and

    (b) he and his wife had been married to each other throughout the year of marriage,

they shall be entitled, subject to *subsection (4)*, to repayment of income tax of an amount determined by the formula—

$$A \times \frac{B}{12}$$

where—

A is the amount of the aforementioned excess, and

B is the number of income tax months in the period between the date on which the marriage took place and the end of the year of marriage, part of an income tax month being treated for this purpose as an income tax month in a case where the period consists of part of an income tax month or of one or more income tax months and part of an income tax month.

(4) Any repayment of income tax under *subsection (3)* shall be allocated to the husband and to the wife concerned in proportion to the amounts of income tax paid and payable by them, having regard to *subsection (2)*, on their respective total incomes for the year of marriage.

(5) Any claim for a repayment of income tax under *subsection (3)* shall be made in writing to the inspector after the end of the year of marriage and shall be made by the husband and wife concerned jointly.

(6) (a) *Subsections (1)* and *(2)* of *section 459* and *section 460* shall apply to a repayment of income tax under this section as they apply to any allowance, deduction, relief or reduction under the provisions specified in the Table to *section 458*.

(b) *Subsections (3)* and *(4)* of *section 459* and *paragraph 8* of *Schedule 28* shall, with any necessary modifications, apply in relation to a repayment of tax under this section.

1021 Repayment of tax in case of certain husbands and wives

(1) This section shall apply for a year of assessment in the case of a husband and wife one of whom is assessed to income tax for the year of assessment in accordance with *section 1017* and to whom *section 1023* does not apply for that year.

(2) Where for a year of assessment this section applies in the case of a husband and wife, any repayment of income tax to be made in respect of the aggregate of the net tax deducted or paid under any provision of the Tax Acts (including a tax credit in respect of a distribution from a company resident in the State) in respect of the total income (if any) of the husband and of the total income (if any) of the wife shall be allocated to the husband and the wife concerned in proportion to the net amounts of tax so deducted or paid in respect of their respective total incomes; but this subsection shall not apply where a repayment, which but for this subsection would not be made to a spouse, is less than £20.

(3) Notwithstanding *subsection (2)*, where the inspector, having regard to all the circumstances of a case, is satisfied that a repayment or a greater part of a repayment of income tax arises by reason of some allowance or relief which, if *sections 1023* and *1024* had applied for the year of assessment, would have been allowed to one spouse only, the inspector may make the repayment to the husband and the wife in such proportions as the inspector considers just and reasonable.

1022 Special provisions relating to tax on wife's income

(1) Where—

    (a) an assessment to income tax (in this section referred to as 'the original assessment') has been made for any year of assessment on a man, or on a man's trustee, guardian or committee, or on a man's executors or administrators,

    (b) the Revenue Commissioners are of the opinion that, if an application for separate assessment under *section 1023* had been in force with respect to that year of assessment, an assessment in respect of or of part of the same income would have been made on, or on the trustee, guardian or committee of, or on the executors or administrators of, a woman who is the man's wife or was his wife in that year of assessment, and

    (c) the whole or part of the amount payable under the original assessment has remained unpaid at the expiration of 28 days from the time when it became due.

the Revenue Commissioners may give to that woman, or, if she is dead, to her executors or administrators, or, if an assessment referred to in *paragraph (b)* could in the circumstances referred to in that paragraph have been made on her trustee, guardian or committee, to her or to her trustee, guardian or committee, a notice stating—

    (i) particulars of the original assessment and of the amount remaining unpaid under that assessment, and

    (ii) to the best of their judgment, particulars of the assessment which would have been so made,

and requiring the person to whom the notice is given to pay the amount which would have been payable under the last-mentioned assessment if it conformed with those particulars, or the amount remaining unpaid under the original assessment, whichever is the less.

(2) The same consequences as respects—

    (a) the imposition of a liability to pay, and the recovery of, the tax with or without interest,

    (b) priority for the tax in bankruptcy or in the administration of the estate of a deceased person,

    (c) appeals to the Appeal Commissioners, the rehearing of such appeals and the stating of cases for the opinion of the High Court, and

    (d) the ultimate incidence of the liability imposed,

shall follow on the giving of a notice under *subsection (1)* to a woman, or to her trustee, guardian or committee, or to her executors or administrators, as would have followed on the making on her, or on her trustee, guardian or committee, or on her executors or administrators, as the case may be, of an assessment referred to in *subsection (1)(b)*, being an assessment which—

    (i) was made on the day of the giving of the notice,

    (ii) charged the same amount of tax as is required to be paid by the notice,

    (iii) fell to be made and was made by the authority who made the original assessment, and

    (iv) was made by that authority to the best of that authority's judgment,

and the provisions of the Income Tax Acts relating to the matters specified in *paragraphs (a)* to *(d)* shall, with the necessary modifications, apply accordingly.

(3) Where a notice is given under *subsection (1)*, tax up to the amount required to be paid by the notice shall cease to be recoverable under the original assessment and, where the tax charged by the original assessment carried interest under *section 1080*, such adjustment shall be made of the amount payable under that section in relation to that assessment and such repayment shall be made of any amounts previously paid under that section in relation to that assessment as are necessary to secure that the total sum, if any, paid or payable under that section in relation to the assessment is the same as it would have been if the amount which ceases to be recoverable had never been charged.

(4) Where the amount payable under a notice under *subsection (1)* is reduced as the result of an appeal or of a case stated for the opinion of the High Court—

(a) the Revenue Commissioners shall, if having regard to that result they are satisfied that the original assessment was excessive, cause such relief to be given by means of repayment or otherwise as appears to them to be just; but

(b) subject to any relief so given, a sum equal to the reduction in the amount payable under the notice shall again become recoverable under the original assessment.

(5) The Revenue Commissioners and the inspector or other proper officer shall have the like powers of obtaining information with a view to the giving of, and otherwise in connection with, a notice under *subsection (1)* as they would have had with a view to the making of, and otherwise in connection with, an assessment referred to in *subsection (1)(b)* if the necessary conditions had been fulfilled for the making of such an assessment.

(6) Where a woman dies who at any time before her death was a wife living with her husband, he or, if he is dead, his executors or administrators may, not later than 2 months from the date of the grant of probate or letters of administration in respect of her estate or, with the consent of her executors or administrators, at any later date, give to her executors or administrators and to the inspector a notice in writing declaring that, to the extent permitted by this section, he disclaims or they disclaim responsibility for unpaid income tax in respect of all income of hers for any year of assessment or part of a year of assessment, being a year of assessment or part of a year of assessment for which any income of hers was deemed to be his income and in respect of which he was assessed to tax under *section 1017*.

(7) A notice given to the inspector pursuant to *subsection (6)* shall be deemed not to be a valid notice unless it specifies the names and addresses of the woman's executors or administrators.

(8) Where a notice under *subsection (6)* has been given to a woman's executors or administrators and to the inspector—

(a) it shall be the duty of the Revenue Commissioners and the Appeal Commissioners to exercise such powers as they may then or thereafter be entitled to exercise under *subsections (1)* to *(5)* in connection with any assessment made on or before the date when the giving of that notice is completed, being an assessment in respect of any of the income to which that notice relates; and

(b) the assessments (if any) to tax which may be made after that date shall, in all respects and in particular as respects the persons assessable and the tax payable, be the assessments which would have been made if—

(i) an application for separate assessment under *section 1023* had been in force in respect of the year of assessment in question, and

(ii) all assessments previously made had been made accordingly.

1023 Application for separate assessments

(1) In this section and in *section 1024*, 'personal reliefs' means relief under any of the provisions specified in the Table to *section 458*, apart from relief under *sections 462* and *463*.

(2) Where an election by a husband and wife to be assessed to income tax in accordance with *section 1017* has effect in relation to a year of assessment and, in relation to that year of assessment, an application is made for the purpose under this section in such manner and form as may be prescribed by the Revenue Commissioners, either by the husband or by the wife, income tax for that year shall be assessed, charged and recovered on the income of the husband and on the income of the wife as if they were not married and the provisions of the Income Tax Acts with respect to the assessment, charge and recovery of tax shall, except where otherwise provided by those Acts, apply as if they were not married except that—

    (a) the total deductions from total income allowed to the husband and wife by means of personal reliefs shall be the same as if the application had not had effect with respect to that year,

    (b) the total tax payable by the husband and wife for that year shall be the same as the total tax which would have been payable by them if the application had not had effect with respect to that year, and

    (c) *section 1024* shall apply.

(3) An application under this section in respect of a year of assessment may be made—

    (a) in the case of persons marrying during the course of that year, before the 6th day of July in the following year, and

    (b) in any other case, within 6 months before the 6th day of July in that year.

(4) Where an application is made under *subsection (2)* that subsection shall apply not only for the year of assessment for which the application was made, but also for each subsequent year of assessment; but, in relation to a subsequent year of assessment, the person who made the application may, by notice in writing given to the inspector before the 6th day of July in that year, withdraw that election and, on the giving of that notice, *subsection (2)* shall not apply for the year of assessment in relation to which the notice was given or any subsequent year of assessment.

(5) A return of the total incomes of the husband and of the wife may be made for the purposes of this section either by the husband or by the wife but, if the Revenue Commissioners are not satisfied with any such return, they may require a return to be made by the wife or by the husband, as the case may be.

(6) The Revenue Commissioners may by notice require returns for the purposes of this section to be made at any time.

1024 Method of apportioning reliefs and charging tax in cases of separate assessments

(1) This section shall apply where pursuant to an application under *section 1023* a husband and wife are assessed to tax for a year of assessment in accordance with that section.

    (2) (a) Subject to *subsection (3)*, the benefit flowing from the personal reliefs for a year of assessment may be given either by means of reduction of the amount of the tax to be paid or by repayment of any excess of tax which has been paid, or by

both of those means, as the case requires, and shall be allocated to the husband and the wife, in so far as it flows from—

(i)   relief under *sections 244, 328, 337, 349, 364* and *371*, in the proportions in which they incurred the expenditure giving rise to the relief;

(ii)   relief under *sections 461, 464, 465* (other than *subsection (3)*) and *468*, in the proportions of one-half and one-half;

(iii) relief in respect of a child under *section 465(3)* and relief in respect of a dependent relative under *section 466*, to the husband or to the wife according as he or she maintains the child or dependent relative;

(iv)   relief under *section 467*, in the proportions in which they bear the cost of employing the person in respect of whom the relief is given;

(v)   relief under *section 469*, in the proportions in which they bore the expenditure giving rise to the relief;

(vi)   relief under *sections 470* and *473*, to the husband or to the wife according as he or she made the payment giving rise to the relief;

(vii) relief under *section 471*, in the proportions in which they incurred the expenditure giving rise to the relief;

(viii) relief under *section 472*, to the husband or to the wife according as the emoluments from which the deduction under that section is made are emoluments of the husband or of the wife;

(ix)   relief under *sections 474, 475, 476, 477, 478* and *479*, in the proportions in which they incurred the expenditure giving rise to the relief;

(x)   relief under *section 481*, in the proportions in which they made the relevant investment giving rise to the relief;

(xi)   relief under *Part 16*, in the proportions in which they subscribed for the eligible shares giving rise to the relief;

(xii) relief under *paragraphs 12* and *20* of *Schedule 32*, in the proportions in which they incurred the expenditure giving rise to the relief.

(b) Any reduction of income tax to be made under *section 187(4)(b)* or *188(5)* for a year of assessment shall be allocated to the husband and to the wife in proportion to the amounts of income tax which but for *section 187(4)(b)* or *188(5)* would have been payable by the husband and by the wife for that year.

(c) Subject to *subsection (4)*, *section 15* shall apply for the year of assessment in relation to each of the spouses concerned as if the part of the taxable income specified in *Part 2* of the Table to that section which is to be charged to tax at the standard rate were one-half of the part so specified.

(3) Where the amount of relief allocated to the husband under *subsection (2)(a)* exceeds the income tax chargeable on his income for the year of assessment, the balance shall be applied to reduce the income tax chargeable on the income of the wife for that year, and where the amount of relief allocated to the wife under that paragraph exceeds the income tax chargeable on her income for the year of assessment, the balance shall be applied to reduce the income tax chargeable on the income of the husband for that year.

(4) Where the part of the taxable income of a spouse chargeable to tax in accordance with *subsection (2)(c)* at the standard rate is less than that of the other spouse and is less than the part of taxable income specified in *column (1)* of *Part 2* of the Table to *section 15* (in this subsection referred to as 'the appropriate part') in respect of which the first-mentioned spouse is so chargeable to tax at that rate, the part of taxable income of the other spouse which by virtue of that subsection is to be charged to tax at that rate shall be increased by the amount by which the taxable income of the first-mentioned spouse chargeable to tax at that rate is less than the appropriate part.

1025   Maintenance in case of separated spouses

(1) In this section—

'maintenance arrangement' means an order of a court, rule of court, deed of separation, trust, covenant, agreement, arrangement or any other act giving rise to a legally enforceable obligation and made or done in consideration or in consequence of—

    (a)   the dissolution or annulment of a marriage; or

    (b)   such separation of the parties to a marriage as is referred to in *section 1015(2)*,

and a maintenance arrangement relates to the marriage in consideration or in consequence of the dissolution or annulment of which, or of the separation of the parties to which, the maintenance arrangement was made or arises;

'payment' means a payment or part of a payment, as the case may be;

a reference to a child of a person includes a child in respect of whom the person was at any time before the making of the maintenance arrangement concerned entitled to a deduction under *section 465*.

(2) (a)   This section shall apply to payments made directly or indirectly by a party to a marriage under or pursuant to a maintenance arrangement relating to the marriage for the benefit of his or her child, or for the benefit of the other party to the marriage, being payments—

      (i)   which are made at a time when the wife is not living with the husband,

      (ii)   the making of which is legally enforceable, and

      (iii) which are annual or periodical;

but this section shall not apply to such payments made under a maintenance arrangement made before the 8th day of June, 1983, unless and until such time as one of the following events occurs, or the earlier of such events occurs where both occur—

      (I)   the maintenance arrangement is replaced by another maintenance arrangement or is varied, and

      (II)   both parties to the marriage to which the maintenance arrangement relates, by notice in writing to the inspector, jointly elect that this section shall apply,

and where such an event occurs in either of those circumstances, this section shall apply to all such payments made after the date on which the event occurs.

    (b)   For the purposes of this section and of *section 1026* but subject to *paragraph (c)*, a payment, whether conditional or not, which is made directly or indirectly by a party to a marriage under or pursuant to a maintenance arrangement relating to the marriage (other than a payment of which the amount, or the method of calculating the amount, is specified in the maintenance arrangement and from which, or from the consideration for which, neither a child of the party to the marriage making the payment nor the other party to the marriage derives any benefit) shall be deemed to be made for the benefit of the other party to the marriage.

    (c)   Where the payment, in accordance with the maintenance arrangement, is made or directed to be made for the use and benefit of a child of the party to the marriage making the payment, or for the maintenance, support, education or other benefit of such a child, or in trust for such a child, and the amount or the method of calculating the amount of such payment so made or directed to be made is specified in the maintenance arrangement, that payment shall be deemed to be made for the benefit of such child, and not for the benefit of any other person.

(3) Notwithstanding anything in the Income Tax Acts but subject to *section 1026,* as respects any payment to which this section applies made directly or indirectly by one party to the marriage to which the maintenance arrangement concerned relates for the benefit of the other party to the marriage—

- (a) the person making the payment shall not be entitled on making the payment to deduct and retain out of the payment any sum representing any amount of income tax on the payment,
- (b) the payment shall be deemed for the purposes of the Income Tax Acts to be profits or gains arising to the other party to the marriage, and income tax shall be charged on that other party under Case IV of Schedule D in respect of those profits or gains, and
- (c) the party to the marriage by whom the payment is made, having made a claim in that behalf in the manner prescribed by the Income Tax Acts, shall be entitled for the purposes of the Income Tax Acts to deduct the payment in computing his or her total income for the year of assessment in which the payment is made.

(4) Notwithstanding anything in the Income Tax Acts, as respects any payment to which this section applies made directly or indirectly by a party to the marriage to which the maintenance arrangement concerned relates for the benefit of his or her child—

- (a) the person making the payment shall not be entitled on making the payment to deduct and retain out of the payment any sum representing any amount of income tax on the payment,
- (b) the payment shall be deemed for the purposes of the Income Tax Acts not to be income of the child,
- (c) the total income for any year of assessment of the party to the marriage who makes the payment shall be computed for the purposes of the Income Tax Acts as if the payment had not been made, and
- (d) for the purposes of *section 465(7),* the payment shall be deemed to be an amount expended on the maintenance of the child by the party to the marriage who makes the payment and, notwithstanding that the payment is made to the other party to the marriage to be applied for or towards the maintenance of the child and is so applied, it shall be deemed for the purposes of that section not to be an amount expended by that other party on the maintenance of the child.
- (5) (a) *Subsections (1)* and *(2)* of *section 459* and *section 460* shall apply to a deduction under *subsection (3)(c)* as they apply to any allowance, deduction, relief or reduction under the provisions specified in the Table to *section 458.*
  - (b) *Subsections (3)* and *(4)* of *section 459* and *paragraph 8* of *Schedule 28* shall, with any necessary modifications, apply in relation to a deduction under *subsection (3)(c).*

1026   Separated and divorced persons: adaptation of provisions relating to married persons

(1) Where a payment to which *section 1025* applies is made in a year of assessment by a party to a marriage (being a marriage which has not been dissolved or annulled) and both parties to the marriage are resident in the State for that year, *section 1018* shall apply in relation to the parties to the marriage for that year of assessment as if—

(a) in *subsection (1)* of that section ', where the wife is living with the husband,' were deleted, and

(b) *subsection (4)* of that section were deleted.

(2) Where by virtue of *subsection (1)* the parties to a marriage elect as provided for in *section 1018(1)*, then, as respects any year of assessment for which the election has effect—

(a) subject to *subsection (1)* and *paragraphs (b)* and *(c)*, the Income Tax Acts shall apply in the case of the parties to the marriage as they apply in the case of a husband and wife who have elected under *section 1018(1)* and whose election has effect for that year of assessment,

(b) the total income or incomes of the parties to the marriage shall be computed for the purposes of the Income Tax Acts as if any payments to which *section 1025* applies made in that year of assessment by one party to the marriage for the benefit of the other party to the marriage had not been made; and

(c) income tax shall be assessed, charged and recovered on the total income or incomes of the parties to the marriage as if an application under *section 1023* had been made by one of the parties and that application had effect for that year of assessment.

(3) Notwithstanding *subsection (1)*, where a payment to which *section 1025* applies is made in a year of assessment by a spouse who is a party to a marriage, that has been dissolved, for the benefit of the other spouse, and—

(a) the dissolution was under either—

   (i) *section 5* of the Family Law (Divorce) Act, 1996, or

   (ii) the law of a country or jurisdiction other than the State, being a divorce that is entitled to be recognised as valid in the State,

(b) both spouses are resident in the State for tax purposes for that year of assessment, and

(c) neither spouse has entered into another marriage,

then, *subsections (1)* and *(2)* shall, with any necessary modifications, apply in relation to the spouses for that year of assessment as if their marriage had not been dissolved.

1027 Payments pursuant to certain orders under Judicial Separation and Family Law Reform Act, 1989, Family Law Act, 1995, and Family Law (Divorce) Act, 1996, to be made without deduction of income tax

Payment of money pursuant to—

(a) an order under Part II of the Judicial Separation and Family Law Reform Act, 1989,

(b) an order under the Family Law Act, 1995 (other than section 12 of that Act), and

(c) an order under the Family Law (Divorce) Act, 1996 (other than section 17 of that Act),

shall be made without deduction of income tax.

CHAPTER 2

Capital gains tax

1028   Married persons

(1) Subject to this section, the amount of capital gains tax on chargeable gains accruing to a married woman in a year of assessment or part of a year of assessment during which she is a married woman living with her husband shall be assessed and charged on the husband and not otherwise; but this subsection shall not affect the amount of capital gains tax chargeable on the husband apart from this subsection or result in the additional amount of capital gains tax charged on the husband by virtue of this subsection being different from the amount which would otherwise have remained chargeable on the married woman.

(2) (a)   Subject to *paragraph (b)*, *subsection (1)* shall not apply in relation to a husband and wife in any year of assessment where, before the 6th day of July in the year following that year of assessment, an application is made by either the husband or wife that *subsection (1)* shall not apply, and such an application duly made shall have effect not only as respects the year of assessment for which it is made but also for any subsequent year of assessment.

(b)   Where the applicant gives, for any subsequent year of assessment, a notice withdrawing an application under *paragraph (a)*, that application shall not have effect with respect to the year for which the notice is given or any subsequent year; but such notice of withdrawal shall not be valid unless it is given before the 6th day of July in the year following the year of assessment for which the notice is given.

(3) In the case of a woman who during a year of assessment or part of a year of assessment is a married woman living with her husband, any allowable loss which under *section 31* would be deductible from the chargeable gains accruing in that year of assessment to the one spouse but for an insufficiency of chargeable gains shall for the purposes of that section be deductible from chargeable gains accruing in that year of assessment to the other spouse; but this subsection shall not apply in relation to losses accruing in a year of assessment to either spouse where an application that this subsection shall not apply is made by the husband or the wife before the 6th day of July in the year following that year of assessment.

(4) Where apart from *subsection (1)* the amount on which an individual is chargeable to capital gains tax under *section 31* for a year of assessment (in this subsection referred to as 'the first-mentioned amount') is less than £1,000 and the spouse of the individual (being, at any time during that year of assessment, a married woman living with her husband, or that husband) is apart from *subsection (1)* chargeable to capital gains tax on any amount for that year, *section 601(1)* shall apply in relation to the spouse as if the sum of £1,000 mentioned in that section were increased by an amount equal to the difference between the first-mentioned amount and £1,000.

(5) Where in any year of assessment in which or in part of which the married woman is a married woman living with her husband, the husband disposes of an asset to the wife, or the wife disposes of an asset to the husband, both shall be treated as if the asset was acquired from the spouse making the disposal for a consideration of such amount as would secure that on the disposal neither a gain nor a loss would accrue to the spouse making the disposal; but this subsection shall not apply if until the disposal the asset

formed part of trading stock of a trade carried on by the spouse making the disposal, or if the asset is acquired as trading stock for the purposes of a trade carried on by the spouse acquiring the asset.

(6) *Subsection (5)* shall apply notwithstanding *section 596* or any other provision of the Capital Gains Tax Acts fixing the amount of the consideration deemed to be given on a disposal or acquisition.

(7) Where *subsection (5)* is applied in relation to a disposal of an asset by a husband to his wife, or by his wife to him, then, in relation to a subsequent disposal of the asset (not within that subsection), the spouse making the disposal shall be treated for the purposes of the Capital Gains Tax Acts as if the other spouse's acquisition or provision of the asset had been his or her acquisition or provision of the asset.

(8) An application or notice of withdrawal under this section shall be in such form and made in such manner as may be prescribed.

1029   Application of *section 1022* for purposes of capital gains tax

Section 1022 shall apply with any necessary modifications in relation to capital gains tax as it applies in relation to income tax.

1030   Separated spouses: transfers of assets

(1) In this section, 'spouse' shall be construed in accordance with *section 2(2)(c)* of the Family Law Act, 1995.

(2) Notwithstanding any other provision of the Capital Gains Tax Acts, where by virtue or in consequence of—

(a) an order made under Part II of the Family Law Act, 1995, on or following the granting of a decree of judicial separation within the meaning of that Act,

(b) an order made under Part II of the Judicial Separation and Family Law Reform Act, 1989, on or following the granting of a decree of judicial separation where such order is treated, by virtue of *section 3* of the Family Law Act, 1995, as if made under the corresponding provision of the Family Law Act, 1995,

(c) a deed of separation, or

(d) a relief order (within the meaning of the Family Law Act, 1995) made following the dissolution of a marriage,

either of the spouses concerned disposes of an asset to the other spouse, then, subject to *subsection (3)*, both spouses shall be treated for the purposes of the Capital Gains Tax Acts as if the asset was acquired from the spouse making the disposal for a consideration of such amount as would secure that on the disposal neither a gain nor a loss would accrue to the spouse making the disposal.

(3) *Subsection (2)* shall not apply if until the disposal the asset formed part of the trading stock of a trade carried on by the spouse making the disposal or if the asset is acquired as trading stock for the purposes of a trade carried on by the spouse acquiring the asset.

(4) Where *subsection (2)* applies in relation to a disposal of an asset by a spouse to the other spouse, then, in relation to a subsequent disposal of the asset (not being a disposal to which *subsection (2)* applies), the spouse making the disposal shall be treated for the purposes of the Capital Gains Tax Acts as if the other spouse's acquisition or provision of the asset had been his or her acquisition or provision of the asset.

1031 Divorced persons: transfers of assets

(1) In this section, 'spouse' shall be construed in accordance with *section 2(2)(c)* of the Family Law (Divorce) Act, 1996.

(2) Notwithstanding any other provision of the Capital Gains Tax Acts, where by virtue or in consequence of an order made under Part III of the Family Law (Divorce) Act, 1996, on or following the granting of a decree of divorce, either of the spouses concerned disposes of an asset to the other spouse, then, subject to *subsection (3)*, both spouses shall be treated for the purpose of the Capital Gains Tax Acts as if the asset was acquired from the spouse making the disposal for a consideration of such amount as would secure that on the disposal neither a gain nor a loss would accrue to the spouse making the disposal.

(3) *Subsection (2)* shall not apply if until the disposal the asset formed part of the trading stock of a trade carried on by the spouse making the disposal or if the asset is acquired as trading stock for the purposes of a trade carried on by the spouse acquiring the asset.

(4) Where *subsection (2)* applies in relation to a disposal of an asset by a spouse to the other spouse, then, in relation to a subsequent disposal of the asset (not being a disposal to which *subsection (2)* applies), the spouse making the disposal shall be treated for the purposes of the Capital Gains Tax Acts as if the other spouse's acquisition or provision of the asset had been his or her acquisition or provision of the asset.

PART THREE: STATUTORY INSTRUMENTS

PART THREE

Circuit Court Rules (No 1) of 1997 (Judicial Separation and Family Law Reform Act, 1989 and Family Law Act, 1995 and Family Law (Divorce) Act, 1996)

(SI 84/1997)

1. These Rules may be cited as the Circuit Court Rules (No 1), 1997 and shall come into operation on the 27th day of February, 1997.

2. The Order referred to in these Rules shall be added to and construed together with those orders contained in the Circuit Court Rules, 1950, as amended.

ORDER 78

JUDICIAL SEPARATION AND FAMILY LAW REFORM ACT, 1989 AND FAMILY LAW ACT, 1995 AND FAMILY LAW (DIVORCE) ACT, 1996

1 Introduction, Substitution and Revocation

In this Order 'the 1996 Act' means the Family Law (Divorce) Act, 1996 (No 33 of 1996) and 'the 1995 Act' means the Family Law Act, 1995 (No 26 of 1995) and 'the 1989 Act' means the Judicial Separation and Family Law Reform Act, 1989 (No 6 of 1989). These Rules shall be substituted for the Rules contained in Circuit Court Rules (No 1) of 1989 (SI 289/1989) and Circuit Court Rules (No 1) of 1994 (SI 225/1994) which are hereby revoked, subject only to the provisions contained in Rule 2 hereof.

2 Transitional

All applications made or proceedings taken before these Rules shall have come into operation but which are in accordance with the then existing Rules and practice of the Court shall have the same validity as applications made or proceedings taken in accordance with these Rules.

3 Venue

Any proceedings under this Order shall be brought in the County where any party to the proceedings ordinarily resides or carries on any profession, business or occupation.

4 Commencement

(a) All proceedings for divorce, judicial separation, relief after foreign divorce or separation outside the State, nullity, declarations of marital status, the determination of property issues between spouses pursuant to section 36 of the 1995 Act/formerly engaged couples pursuant to section 44 of the 1996 Act and relief pursuant to section 25 of the 1995 Act, section 18 of the 1996 Act or section 15A of the 1995 Act under this Order, shall be instituted by the issuing out of the Office of the County Registrar for the appropriate County (hereinafter referred

PART THREE

to as 'the appropriate Office') of the appropriate Family Law Civil Bill in the format and manner hereinafter provided save that no Family Law Civil Bill for relief after foreign divorce or separation outside the State shall be issued until requirements set down in Rule 4(b) of these Rules have been complied with. Upon issue, the Family Law Civil Bill shall be served in a manner provided for hereunder.

(b) No proceedings for a relief order after foreign divorce or separation outside the State shall issue without the leave of the appropriate Court in accordance with section 23(3) of the 1995 Act. Such application for leave to issue proceedings shall be made *ex parte* by way of *ex parte* docket grounded upon the Affidavit of the Applicant or another appropriate person. The aforementioned Affidavit shall exhibit a draft of the Family Law Civil Bill for relief after divorce or separation outside the State which the Applicant seeks leave to issue as well as the foreign divorce or separation decree, shall set forth fully the reasons why relief is being sought and shall make specific averment to the fact that, to the knowledge, information and belief of the Applicant, the jurisdictional requirements of section 27 of the 1995 Act are complied with in the particular case, specifying the particular basis of jurisdiction being relied upon.

5 Form of Proceedings

Every Family Law Civil Bill shall be in numbered paragraphs setting out the relief sought and the grounds relied upon in support of the application. The Civil Bill shall be in accordance with the form set out in Form 1 herein or such modification thereof as may be appropriate, subject to the requirements hereinafter set out.

(a) A Family Law Civil Bill for a Decree of Divorce shall, in all cases, include the following details:
  (i) the date and place of marriage of the parties;
  (ii) the length of time the parties have lived apart, including the date upon which the parties commenced living apart, and the addresses of both of the parties during that time, where known;
  (iii) details of any previous matrimonial relief sought and/or obtained and details of any previous separation agreement entered into between the parties (where appropriate a certified copy of any relevant court order and/or deed of separation/separation agreement should be annexed to the Civil Bill);
  (iv) the names and ages and dates of birth of any dependent children of the marriage;
  (v) details of the family home(s) and/or other residences of the parties including, if relevant, details of any former family home/residence to include details of the manner of occupation/ownership thereof;
  (vi) where reference is made in the Civil Bill to any immovable property, whether it is registered or unregistered land and a description of the land/premises so referred to;
  (vii) the basis of jurisdiction under the 1996 Act;
  (viii) the occupation(s) of each party;
  (ix) the grounds relied upon for the relief sought;
  (x) each section of the 1996 Act under which relief is sought.
(b) A Family Law Civil Bill for a Decree of Judicial Separation shall, in all cases, include the following details:
  (i) the date and place of marriage of the parties;

   (ii) the names and ages and dates of birth of any dependent children of the marriage;

   (iii) details of the family home(s) and/or other residences of the parties including, if relevant, details of any former family home/residence to include details of the manner of occupation/ownership thereof;

   (iv) where reference is made in the Civil Bill to any immovable property, whether it is registered or unregistered land and a description of the land/premises so referred to;

   (v) the basis of jurisdiction under the Act;

   (vi) the occupation(s) of each party;

   (vii) the grounds relied upon for the decree and any other relief sought;

   (viii) each section of the Act under which relief is sought including whether or not an Order pursuant to section 54(3) of the 1995 Act is sought.

(c) A Family Law Civil Bill for relief after foreign divorce or separation outside the State pursuant to section 23 of the 1995 Act shall, in all cases, include the following details:

   (i) the date and place of marriage and divorce/separation of the parties (a certified copy of the decree absolute or final decree of divorce/separation together with, where appropriate an authenticated translation thereof shall be annexed to the Family Law Civil Bill);

   (ii) financial and property and custodial/access arrangements operating ancillary to the said decree, whether such arrangements were made by agreement or by Order of the Court or otherwise and whether such arrangements were made contemporaneous to the decree or at another time and the extent of compliance therewith;

   (iii) the names and ages and dates of birth of any dependent children of the marriage;

   (iv) details of the family home(s) and/or other residences of the parties including, if relevant, details of any former family home/residence to include details of the manner of occupation/ownership thereof;

   (v) where reference is made in the Civil Bill to any immovable property within the State, whether it is registered or unregistered land and a description of the land/premises so referred to;

   (vi) the basis of jurisdiction under section 27 of the 1995 Act;

   (vii) the present marital status and occupation(s) of each party;

   (viii) the grounds relied upon for the relief sought;

   (ix) each section of the 1995 Act under which relief is sought;

   (x) details relevant to the matters referred to in section 26 of the 1995 Act.

(d) A Family Law Civil Bill for nullity shall, in all cases, include the following details:

   (i) the date and place of marriage of the parties;

   (ii) the domicile of the spouses on the date of the marriage and on the date of the institution of proceedings and, where either spouse has died prior to the institution of proceedings, the domicile of the said spouse at the date of death;

   (iii) whether or not the spouses or either of them has been ordinarily resident in the State throughout the period of one year prior to the date of institution of proceedings and, where either spouse has died prior to the institution of proceedings, whether or not the said spouse was ordinarily resident in the State throughout the period of one year prior to his/her death;

   (iv) the address and description of each party;

   (v) the number of children of the marriage;

   (vi) the grounds upon which the decree and any other relief is sought;

(vii) the relief sought (including whether or not a declaration relating to the custody of a dependent member of the family pursuant to section 46 of the 1995 Act is being sought) and the issues to be tried.

(e) A Family Law Civil Bill for Declaration of Marital Status shall, in all cases, include the following details:

   (i) the nature of the Applicant's reason for seeking such a declaration;

   (ii) full details of the marriage/divorce/annulment/legal separation in respect of which the declaration is sought including the date and place of such marriage/divorce/annulment/legal separation (where possible, a certified copy of the marriage certificate/decree of divorce/annulment/legal separation should be annexed to the Civil Bill);

   (iii) the manner in which the jurisdictional requirements of section 29(2) of the 1995 Act are satisfied;

   (iv) particulars of any previous or pending proceedings in relation to any marriage concerned or to the matrimonial status of a party to any such marriage in accordance with section 30 of the 1995 Act;

   (v) the relief being sought;

   (vi) any other relevant facts.

(f) A Family Law Civil Bill for the determination of property issues between spouses, pursuant to section 36 of the 1995 Act/formerly engaged couples, pursuant to section 44 of the 1996 Act, shall, in all cases, include the following details:

   (i) the description, nature and extent of the disputed property or monies;

   (ii) the state of knowledge of the Applicant spouse in relation to possession and control of the disputed property or monies at all relevant times;

   (iii) the nature and extent of the interest being claimed by the Applicant in the property or monies and the basis upon which such a claim is made;

   (iv) the nature and extent of any claim for relief being made and the basis upon which any such claim for relief is being made;

   (v) where reference is made in the Civil Bill to any immovable property, whether it is registered or unregistered land and a description of the land/premises so referred to;

   (vi) the manner in which it is claimed that the Respondent spouse has failed, neglected or refused to make to the Applicant spouse such appropriate payment or disposition in all of the circumstances and details of any payment or disposition made;

   (vii) that the time limits referred to at section 36(7) of the 1995 Act have been complied with;

   (viii) any other relevant matters.

(g) A Family Law Civil Bill for relief pursuant to section 18 of the Family Law (Divorce) Act, 1996 or section 15A or section 25 of the Family Law Act, 1995 shall, in all cases include the following details:

   (i) the date and place of marriage and the date of any decree of divorce/judicial separation and the marriage certificate and a certified copy of the decree of divorce/separation shall be annexed to the Civil Bill (with authenticated translations, where appropriate);

   (ii) details of previous matrimonial relief obtained by the Applicant and in particular lump sum maintenance orders and property adjustment orders, if any;

   (iii) details of any benefits previously received from or on behalf of the deceased spouse whether by way of agreement or otherwise and details of any benefits accruing to the Applicant under the terms of the Will of the deceased spouse or otherwise;

(iv) the date of death of the deceased spouse, the date on which representation was first granted in respect of the estate of the said spouse and, if applicable, the date upon which notice of the death of the deceased spouse was given to the Applicant spouse and the date upon which the Applicant spouse notified the personal representative of his/her intention to apply for relief pursuant to section 18(7) of the 1996 Act and section 15A(7) of the 1995 Act;

(v) the nature and extent of any claim for relief being made and the basis upon which any such claim for relief is being made;

(vi) the marital status of the deceased spouse at the date of death and the marital status of the Applicant at the date of the application and whether the Applicant has remarried since the dissolution of the marriage between the Applicant and the deceased spouse;

(vii) details of all dependents of the deceased spouse at the date of death and of all dependents of the Applicant at the date of the application together with details of any other interested persons;

(viii) that no Order pursuant to section 18(10) of the 1996 Act or section 15A(10) of the 1995 Act has previously been made;

(ix) details of the value of the estate of the deceased spouse, where known;

(x) any other relevant facts.

Applications pursuant to section 15A(6) or section 25(7) of the 1995 Act or section 18(6) of the 1996 Act by the personal representative in relation to the distribution of the estate shall be by motion, grounded on Affidavit, on notice to the Applicant spouse and such other persons as the Court shall direct.

6   All Family Law Civil Bills shall be dated and shall bear the name, address and description of the Applicant and an address for service of proceedings, and shall be signed by the party's solicitor, if any, or, where the Applicant does not have a solicitor, by that party personally. The address to which a Respondent should apply in order to receive information in relation to legal aid shall also be included in such Civil Bills.

7   Issuing and Entry

On the issuing of a Family Law Civil Bill the original thereof shall be filed, together with the appropriate certificate (pursuant to section 5 of the 1989 Act or section 6 of the 1996 Act), an Affidavit of Means in the intended action sworn by the Applicant in compliance with Rules 18 and 19 hereof and, in all circumstances where there are dependent children, an Affidavit of Welfare in the intended action in compliance with Rule 20 hereof, and the County Registrar shall thereupon enter same.

8   Service

(a) All Family Law Civil Bills shall be served by registered post on the Respondent at his/her last-known address or alternatively shall be served personally on the Respondent by any person over the age of eighteen years together with the appropriate certificate in the form set out in Forms 7 and 9 herein (pursuant to section 5 of the 1989 Act or section 6 of the 1996 Act), an Affidavit of Means in compliance with Rules 18 and 19 hereof in the form set out in Form 2 herein or such modification thereof as may be appropriate and in all cases where there are dependent children, an Affidavit of Welfare in compliance with Rule 20 hereof in the form set out in Form 3 herein. Where relief pursuant to section 12 and/or section 13 of the 1995 Act or section 17 of the 1996 Act is sought, notice thereof in accordance with Form 4 herein shall also be served on the trustees of the pension scheme in question by registered post at their registered office or other appropriate address and an Affidavit of such service shall be sworn and filed within fourteen days of service of the Civil Bill. Service shall be endorsed upon all Family Law Civil Bills in accordance with the provisions of Order 10, Rule 22 of the Circuit Court Rules, 1950, as amended. All other pleadings may be served by ordinary pre-paid post.

(b) In all cases in which a declaration of marital status under section 29 of the 1995 Act is sought, the Family Law Civil Bill shall, in addition to the provisions of Rule 8(a) hereof, be served upon the parties to the marriage or, where no longer living, their personal representatives (all of whom shall be parties to the proceedings) and to such other persons as the Court may direct, including the Attorney General, in accordance with the provisions as to service of Family Law Civil Bills hereinbefore set out in respect of the Respondent to proceedings which said persons (excepting the Attorney General) may be made parties to the application in accordance with section 29(6) of the 1995 Act. The Attorney General shall, however, be entitled to interplead in such proceedings.

(c) Where relief is sought pursuant to sections 15A or 25 of the 1995 Act or section 18 of the 1996 Act, the Family Law Civil Bill shall be served in accordance with these Rules on the personal representative of the deceased and on the spouse (if any) of the deceased and on such other person or persons as the Court shall direct.

9   Appearance

If a Respondent intends to contest the application, or participate in proceedings, or any part thereof, he/she shall enter an Appearance in the Office within 10 days of the service upon him/her of the Family Law Civil Bill and shall serve a copy of the Appearance on the Applicant's solicitors or, where appropriate, on the Applicant. The Appearance shall bear an address for service of any interlocutory applications and shall be signed by the Respondent's solicitor or, if the Respondent does not have a solicitor, by the Respondent personally.

10   Defence

(a) A Respondent shall at the same time as entering an Appearance, or within 10 dear days from the date of service of the Appearance, or such further time as may be agreed between the parties or allowed by the Court, file and serve a Defence, together with the appropriate certificate in the form set out in Forms 8 and 10 herein (pursuant to section 6 of the 1989 Act and section 7 of the 1996 Act), an Affidavit of Means in compliance with Rules 18 and 19 hereof and, in all cases where there are dependent children, an Affidavit of Welfare in compliance with Rule 20 hereof in the form set out in Form 3 herein, on the Applicant, or the Applicant's solicitor, if any, and on the County Registrar in the form set out in Form 2 herein or such modification thereof as may be appropriate. Where relief pursuant to section 12 and/or section 13 of the 1995 Act or section 17 of the 1996 Act is sought by way of Counterclaim, notice thereof in accordance with Form 4 herein shall also be served on the trustees of the pension scheme in question by registered post at their registered office and an Affidavit of such service shall be sworn and filed within 7 days of service of the Defence and Counterclaim.

(b) No Appearance or Defence shall be entered after the time specified in these Rules without the leave of the Court or of the County Registrar or the agreement of the parties, and no Defence shall be entered unless the Respondent has previously entered an Appearance as required by these Rules.

(c) Whether or not a Defence is filed and served in any proceedings, the Respondent shall, where appropriate, in any event be obliged to file and serve an Affidavit of Means and a Welfare Statement in accordance with these Rules of Court within 20 days after the service of the Family Law Civil Bill upon him/her subject to Rule 36 hereof.

(d) Without prejudice to the entitlement of the Court to permit representations in relation to the making or refusal of an attachment of earnings order at the hearing of the action, such representations for the purposes of section 8(6)(b) of the 1995 Act or section 13(6)(b) of the 1996 Act may be included in the Defence and for the purposes of section 10(3)(a) of the Family Law (Maintenance of Spouses and Children) Act, 1976 may be included in the Answer provided for by Rule 15 of the Circuit Court Rules (No 6) of 1982 (SI 158/1982) and Form 9 scheduled thereto.

11 Motions for Judgment

(a) In any case in which a Respondent has made default in entering an Appearance or filing a Defence, as the case may be, the Applicant may, subject to the provisions of the following sub-rules of this Rule, at any time after such default, on notice to be served on the Respondent and, where relief pursuant to section 12 and/or 13 of the 1995 Act and section 17 of the 1996 Act is sought, on the trustees of the pension scheme concerned, not less than fourteen clear days before the hearing, apply to the Court for judgment in default of appearance/defence.

(b) No notice of motion for Judgment in default of defence shall be served unless the Applicant has, at least fourteen days prior to the service of such notice, written to the Respondent giving him/her notice of his/her intention to serve a notice of motion for Judgment in default of appearance/defence and at the same time consenting to the late filing of a Defence within fourteen days from the date of the letter.

(c) If no defence is delivered within the said period the Applicant shall be at liberty to serve a notice of motion for Judgment in default of defence which shall be returnable to a date not less than fourteen clear days from the date of the service of the notice, such notice of motion to be filed not later than six days before the return date.

(d) If, not later than seven days after the service of such notice of motion for Judgment in default of appearance/defence, the defendant delivers a Defence to the Applicant and not less than six days before the return date lodges a copy thereof in the appropriate Office with a certified copy of the said notice of motion attached thereto, the said motion for Judgment shall not be put in the Judge's List but shall stand struck out and the Respondent shall pay to the Applicant the appropriate sum for his/her costs of the said motion for Judgment.

(e) If in any case the Applicant can establish special reasons for making it necessary to serve a notice of motion for Judgment in default of appearance/defence in the cases provided for by this Rule with greater urgency than in accordance with the provisions hereinbefore contained, he/she may apply *ex parte* to the Court or the County Registrar for an Order giving him/her liberty to serve a notice of motion for Judgment in default of appearance/defence giving not less than four clear days' notice to the Respondent, or in the alternative the Judge or the County

Registrar may deem good the service of a Notice of Motion giving not less than four clear days' notice to the Respondent.

(f) Upon the hearing of such application the Court may, on proof of such default as aforesaid, and upon hearing such evidence, oral or otherwise, as may be adduced, give judgment upon the Applicant's claim endorsed upon the Family Law Civil Bill, or may give leave to the Respondent to defend the whole or part of the claim upon such terms as he or she may consider just.

(g) Upon the hearing of an application for judgment under this Order the Court may make such order as to costs as the Court considers just.

(h) In any case in which the parties are agreed in respect of all of the reliefs being sought and a Defence in accordance with Rule 10 hereof has been filed and served by the Respondent which reflects this agreement, the Applicant or the Respondent may, subject to the provisions of the following sub-rules of this Rule, at any time after such Defence has been filed and served, on notice to be served on the other party and, where relief pursuant to section 12 and/or 13 of the 1995 Act and section 17 of the 1996 Act is sought, on the trustees of the pension scheme concerned, not less than fourteen clear days before the hearing, apply to the Court for judgment, the application to be by way of motion on notice.

(i) Upon the hearing of such application the Court may, upon hearing such evidence, oral or otherwise, as may be adduced

   (i) give judgment in the terms agreed between the parties or,

   (ii) give such directions in relation to the service of a Notice of Trial/Notice to fix a date for Trial as to the Court appears just.

(j) Upon the hearing of an application for judgment under this Order the Court may make such order as to costs as the Court considers just.

12 Notice of trial/Notice to fix a date for trial

Subject to Rule 11(h), (i) and (j) herein, when a Defence has been duly entered and served, the Applicant may serve a notice of trial or a notice to fix a date for trial, as appropriate.

13 Notice of trial (Circuits other than Dublin Circuit)

Not less than ten days' notice of trial shall be served upon the Respondent and all other necessary parties and, where relief is sought under sections 12 and/or 13 of the 1995 Act or section 17 of the 1996 Act, upon the trustees of the pension scheme in question, and shall be for the Sittings next ensuing after the expiration of the time mentioned in the said notice, and same shall be filed at the appropriate Office not later than seven days before the opening of such Sittings. Such notice of trial and filing thereof shall operate to set down the action or matter (including Counterclaim if any) for hearing at the next ensuing Sittings. This Rule shall not apply to the Dublin Circuit.

14 Notice to fix a date for trial (Dublin Circuit)

This Rule shall apply only to the Dublin Circuit. Ten days' notice to fix a date for trial shall be necessary and sufficient and shall be served upon the Respondent and all other necessary parties and, where relief is sought under sections 12 and/or 13 of the 1995 Act or section 17 of the 1996 Act, upon the trustees of the pension scheme in question, and filed at the appropriate Office. Such notice to fix a date for a trial shall set out the date upon which a date for hearing shall be fixed by the County Registrar and shall operate to set down the action or matter (including a Counterclaim if any) for hearing upon such date as may be fixed by the County Registrar. A notice to fix a date for trial shall be in accordance with Form 5 herein.

15 Service by Respondent

Where the Applicant has failed to serve a notice of trial or notice to fix a date for trial, as appropriate, within ten days after the service and entry of the Defence, the Respondent may do so and may file the same in accordance with these Rules.

16 Joinder

The Court, if it considers it desirable, may order that two or more actions be tried together, and on such terms as to costs as the Court shall deem just.

17 Affidavits of Representation

(a) Save where the Court shall otherwise direct, any notice party, including the trustees of a pension scheme, who wishes to make representations to the Court pursuant to section 12(18) and/or section 13(2) of the 1995 Act or section 17(18) of the 1996 Act shall make such representations by Affidavit of Representation to be filed and served on all parties to the proceedings within 28 days of service upon them of notice of the application for relief under section 12 and/or 13 of the 1995 Act or section 17 of the 1996 Act in accordance with Rules 8 and 10 hereof or within such time or in such manner as the Court may direct.

(b) Without prejudice to the entitlement of the Court to permit representations by persons having a beneficial interest in property (not being the other spouse) pursuant to section 15(5) of the 1995 Act and section 19(5) of the 1996 Act or by interested persons pursuant to section 15A(5) or section 25(6) of the 1995 Act and section 18(5) of the 1996 Act at the hearing of the action, such representations may be made by way of Affidavit of Representation to be filed and served on all parties to the proceedings as directed by the Court.

18 Affidavit of Means

Without prejudice to the right of each party to make application to the Court for an Order of Discovery pursuant to the Rules of this Honourable Court and without prejudice to the jurisdiction of the Court pursuant to section 12(25) of the 1995 Act and section 17(25) of the 1996 Act, in any case where financial relief under the Acts is sought, the parties shall file Affidavits of Means in accordance with Rules 7 and 10 hereof in respect of which the following Rules shall be applicable:

(a) either party may request the other party to vouch any or all items referred to therein within 14 days of the request;

(b) in the event of a party failing to properly comply with the provisions in relation to the filing and serving of Affidavits of Means as set down in these Rules or failing to properly vouch the matters set out therein the Court may on application grant an Order for Discovery and/or may make such Orders as the Court deems appropriate and necessary (including an Order that such party shall not be entitled to pursue or defend as appropriate such claim for any ancillary reliefs under the Acts save as permitted by the Court upon such terms as the Court may determine are appropriate and/or adjourning the proceedings for a specified period of time to enable compliance) and furthermore and/or in the alternative relief pursuant to section 38(8) of the 1995 Act or section 38(7) of the 1996 Act may be sought in accordance with Rule 24 hereof.

19   The Affidavit of Means shall set out in schedule form details of the party's income, assets, debts, expenditure and other liabilities wherever situated and from whatever source and, to the best of the deponent's knowledge, information and belief the income, assets, debts, expenditure and other liabilities wherever situated and from whatever source of any dependent member of the family and shall be in accordance with the form set out in Form 2 herein or such modification thereof as may be appropriate. Where relief pursuant to section 12 of the 1995 Act is sought, the Affidavit of Means shall also state to the best of the deponent's knowledge, information and belief, the nature of the scheme, the benefits payable thereunder, the normal pensionable age and the period of reckonable service of the member spouse and where information relating to the pension scheme has been obtained from the trustees of the scheme under the Pensions Acts 1990–1996, such information should be exhibited in the Affidavit of Means and where such information has not been obtained a specific averment shall be included in the Affidavit of Means as to why such information has not been obtained.

20   Affidavit of Welfare

An Affidavit of Welfare shall be in the form set out in Form 3 herein. In circumstances in which the Respondent agrees with the facts as averred to in the Affidavit of Welfare filed and served by the Applicant, the Respondent may file and serve an Affidavit of Welfare in the alternative form provided for in Form 3 herein. In circumstances in which the Respondent disagrees with the Affidavit of Welfare filed and served by the Applicant, a separate Affidavit of Welfare, including the schedule provided for in the form set out in Form 3 herein shall be sworn, filed and sewed by the Respondent in accordance with Rule 10 hereof.

21   Counterclaims

Save where otherwise directed by the Court, a Counterclaim, if any, brought by a Respondent shall be included in and served with the Defence, in accordance with the provisions of these Rules relating thereto, and shall, in particular, set out in numbered paragraphs:

(a) in the case of an application for a decree of divorce
   (i)   the facts specified at Rule 5(a) hereof in like manner as in the Family Law Civil Bill;
   (ii)   outline the ground(s) for a decree of divorce, if sought;
   (iii) specify any ground upon which the Respondent intends to rely in support of any ancillary relief claimed; and
   (iv)   the relief sought pursuant to the 1996 Act;
(b) in the case of an application for a decree of judicial separation
   (i)   the facts specified at Rule 5(b) hereof in like manner as in the Family Law Civil Bill;
   (ii)   outline the ground(s) for a decree of judicial separation, if sought;
   (iii) specify any additional ground upon which the Respondent intends to rely in support of any ancillary relief claimed; and
   (iv)   the relief sought pursuant to the 1995 Act;
(c) in the case of an application for relief after divorce or separation outside the State

- (i) the facts specified at Rule 5(c) hereof in like manner as in the Family Law Civil Bill;
- (ii) specify any additional ground upon which the Respondent intends to rely in support of any ancillary relief claimed; and
- (iii) the relief sought pursuant to the 1995 Act;
- (d) in the case of an application for a decree of nullity
  - (i) outline the ground(s) for a decree of nullity, if sought;
  - (ii) specify any additional ground upon which the Respondent intends to rely in support of any relief claimed; and
  - (iii) the relief sought (including whether or not a declaration relating to the custody of a dependent member of the family pursuant to section 46 of the 1995 Act is being sought) and any additional issues to be tried;
- (e) in the case of an application for a Declaration of Marital Status
  - (i) the facts specified at Rule 5(e) hereof in like manner as in the Family Law Civil Bill;
  - (ii) specify any additional ground upon which the Respondent intends to rely in support of any relief claimed; and
  - (iii) the relief sought pursuant to the 1995 Act;
- (f) in the case of an application for the determination of property issues between spouses, pursuant to section 36 of the 1995 Act/formerly engaged couples pursuant to section 44 of the 1996 Act
  - (i) the facts specified at Rule 5(f) hereof in like manner as in the Family Law Civil Bill;
  - (ii) specify any additional ground upon which the Respondent intends to rely in support of any relief claimed; and
  - (iii) the relief sought pursuant to the 1995 Act;

and shall be in the form set out in Form 6 herein or such modification thereof as may be appropriate.

22 Evidence

Save where the Court otherwise directs and subject to Rules 17, 23 or 26 hereof, every Application under this Order shall be heard on oral evidence, such hearings to be held in camera.

23 Notwithstanding the provisions of Rule 22 hereof, where relief pursuant to section 12 of the 1995 Act or section 17 of the 1996 Act is sought by the Applicant or the Respondent, evidence of the actuarial value of a benefit under the scheme (as defined in section 12(1) of the 1995 Act and section 17(1) of the 1996 Act) may be by Affidavit filed on behalf of the Applicant/Respondent, such Affidavit to be sworn by an appropriate person and served on all parties to the proceedings and filed at least 14 days in advance of the hearing and subject to the right of the Respondent/ Applicant to serve Notice of cross-examination in relation to same. Where one of the parties has adduced evidence of the actuarial value of a benefit by Affidavit as provided for herein and the other party intends to adduce similar or contra oral evidence, notice of such intention shall be served by the disputing party upon all other parties at least 10 days in advance of the hearing.

24 Interim and Interlocutory Applications

- (a) An application for Preliminary Orders pursuant to section 6 of the 1995 Act or section 11 of the 1996 Act or for maintenance pending suit/relief pursuant to section 7 or section 24 of the 1995 Act or section 12 of the 1996 Act or for information pursuant to section 12(25) of the 1995 Act of section 17(25) of the 1996 Act or for relief pursuant to section 35 of the 1995 Act or section 37 of the 1996 Act or for relief pursuant to section 38(8) of the 1995 Act or section 38(7) of the 1996 Act or for a report pursuant to section 47 of the 1995 Act or section 42 of the 1995 Act or for any other interlocutory relief shall be by Notice of Motion to be served upon the parties to the proceedings and, in the case of applications pursuant to section 12(25) of the 1995 Act or section 17(25) of the 1996 Act, upon the trustees of the pension scheme concerned.

(b) Prior to any interlocutory application for discovery or for information pursuant to section 12(25) of the 1995 Act or section 17(25) of the 1996 Act being made, the information being sought shall be requested in writing voluntarily at least 14 days prior to the issuing of the motion for the relief concerned and upon failure to make such a request, the judge may adjourn the motion or strike out the motion or make such other order, including an order as to costs, as to the Court may appear appropriate.

(c) An application for alimony pending suit in nullity proceedings shall be by Notice of Motion grounded upon Affidavit setting out the assets, liabilities, income, debts and expenditure of the Applicant for alimony and, in so far as same is known to the Applicant, the assets, liabilities, income, debts and expenditure of the Respondent to the said Motion. In every case in which the Respondent wishes to defend such an application for alimony, the Respondent shall file a replying Affidavit setting out details of his assets, liabilities, income, debts and expenditure.

(d) Applications for the appointment of medical and/or psychiatric inspectors in respect of the Applicant and/or the Respondent shall be made by Motion on Notice to the other party and such Motion shall be issued not later than 14 days after the elapsing of the times for the entry of an Appearance and delivery of a Defence save with the leave of the Court or the County Registrar. Where medical and/or psychiatric inspectors are appointed by the Court or the County Registrar, the solicitors for the parties shall attend with the parties on the appointed day at the place in which the inspection is to take place for the purpose of identifying the parties to the County Registrar or his/her nominee. In any circumstances in which a party is unrepresented, appropriate photographic proof of identity must be produced sufficient to satisfy the County Registrar or his/her nominee of the identity of the party concerned. No inspection shall be carried out unless the procedures contained herein are satisfied. Upon completion of the inspection, a report thereof shall be sent by the inspector directly to the County Registrar for the County in which the proceedings have issued.

(e) In any case where the Court is satisfied that the delay caused by proceeding by Motion on Notice under this Order would or might entail serious harm or mischief, the Court may make an Order *ex parte* as it shall consider just. Urgent applications under this Rule may be made to a Judge at any time or place approved by him, by arrangement with the County Registrar for the County in question.

(f) Interim and interlocutory applications shall where appropriate be made to the County Registrar in accordance with the Second Schedule to the Courts and Court Officers Act, 1995 and Orders 15 and 16 of the Circuit Court Rules, 1950, as amended.

25   If on the date for hearing of any application under this Order the matter is not dealt with by the Court for any reason, and, in particular, on foot of an adjournment sought by either party, the other party, whether consenting to the adjournment or not, may apply for, and the Court may grant, such interim or interlocutory relief as to it shall seem appropriate without the necessity of service of a Notice of Motion.

26   Any interim or interlocutory application shall be heard on Affidavit, unless the Court otherwise directs, save that the Deponent of any Affidavit must be available to the Court to give oral evidence or to be cross-examined as to the Court shall seem appropriate, save that a Motion for Discovery and a Motion in the course of nullity proceedings for the appointment of medical/psychiatric inspectors shall be heard on a Notice of Motion only. Where any oral evidence is heard by the Court in the course of such applications *ex parte*, a note of such evidence shall be prepared by the Applicant or the Applicant's solicitor and approved by the judge and shall be served upon the Respondent forthwith together with a copy of the Order made (if any), unless otherwise directed by the Court.

27   Further relief and applications on behalf of dependent persons

(a)   Where either party or a person on behalf of a dependent member of the family wishes at any time after the hearing of the application to seek further relief as provided for in the 1995 Act or the 1996 Act or to vary or discharge an Order previously made by the Court, that party shall issue a Notice of Motion to re-enter or to vary or discharge as the case may be grounded upon an Affidavit seeking such relief. Such Motions shall be subject to the provisions of Rules 8, 17, 18, 19, 22 and 23 hereof, as appropriate.

(b)   Where a person on behalf of a dependent member of the family wishes to make application for ancillary reliefs at the hearing of the action, such application shall be by way of Notice of Motion to be served on all other parties to the proceedings setting out the reliefs sought grounded on Affidavit which said Motion shall be listed for hearing on the same date as the hearing of the action contemporaneously therewith. Such Motions shall be subject to the provisions of Rules 8, 17, 18, 19, 22 and 23 hereof, as appropriate.

28   Where any party to proceedings for a declaration under section 29 of the 1995 Act alleges that the marriage in question was void or voidable and the Court decides to treat the application as one for annulment of the marriage, the provisions of these Rules in relation to the procedures applicable to decrees of nullity may be adapted in such manner as the Court shall direct.

29   Relief under section 33 of the 1995 Act

Applications under section 33 of the 1995 Act for an order or orders exempting the marriage from the application of section 31(1)(a) or section 32(1)(a) of the 1995 Act may be made *ex parte* by the parties where both are over the age of 18 years, by the legal guardians of the parties to the intended marriage where both are under the age of 18 years or, where one of the parties is over the age of 18 years, by that party and the legal guardian or guardians of the other party, and further, where deemed appropriate by the Court, a guardian or guardians *ad litem* may be appointed by the Court to represent either or both of the parties. Such applications may be grounded upon Affidavit or upon oral evidence given by or on behalf of the parties, as the Court may direct, which evidence shall set out the reasons justifying the exemption and the basis upon which it is claimed that the application is in the interests of the parties to the intended marriage.

30   Applications under section 8 of the Family Law (Maintenance of Spouses and Children) Act, 1976 (as amended) (hereinafter 'the 1976 Act')

Applications pursuant to section 8 of the Family Law (Maintenance of Spouses and Children) Act, 1976 may be by way of originating Notice of Motion, grounded upon Affidavit.

31   For the purposes of Rule 30 hereof, the Notice of Motion shall be entitled in the matter of the 1976 Act (as amended) and shall state the relief sought (including whether or not relief pursuant to section 8B of the 1976 Act, as inserted by section 43 of the 1995 Act is sought); state the name and place of residence or address for service of the Applicant; the date upon which it is proposed to apply to the Court for relief and shall be filed in the appropriate Office.

32   For the purposes of Rule 30 hereof, without prejudice to the jurisdiction of the Court to make an Order for substituted service, the Motion shall be served by registered post on the Respondent at his last-known address or alternatively shall be served personally on the Respondent by any person over the age of eighteen years. Where relief pursuant to section 8B of the 1976 Act is sought, the Motion shall be served upon the trustees of the pension scheme also. There must be at least ten clear days between the service of the Notice and the day named therein for the hearing of the Motion.

33   (a) Subject to the right of the Court to give such directions as it considers appropriate or convenient, evidence at the hearing of the Motion under Rule 30 shall be by Affidavit.

   (b) Any Affidavit to be used in support of the Motion shall be filed in the appropriate Office and a copy of any such Affidavit shall be served with the Notice. Any Affidavit to be used in opposition to the application shall be filed in the appropriate Office and served upon the Applicant and, where relief pursuant to section 8B of the 1976 Act is sought, upon the trustees of the pension scheme by the Respondent following the service on him of the Applicant's Affidavit and any Affidavit of Representation to be used by the trustees of the pension scheme shall be filed in the appropriate Office and served upon the Applicant and the Respondent.

34   The plaintiff in proceedings wherein it is sought to have a conveyance declared void pursuant to the provisions of section 3 of the Family Home Protection Act, 1976 (as amended by section 54 of the Family Law Act, 1995) (which said proceedings shall be instituted by way of Equity Civil Bill seeking declaratory relief) shall forthwith and without delay following the institution of such proceedings cause relevant particulars of the proceedings to be entered as a *lis pendens* upon the property and/or premises in question under and in accordance with the Judgments (Ireland) Act, 1844.

35   Costs

   (a) The costs as between party and party may be measured by the Judge, and if not so measured shall be taxed, in default of agreement by the parties, by the County Registrar according to such scale of costs as may be prescribed. Any party aggrieved by such taxation may appeal to the Court and have the costs reviewed by it.

(b) Where necessary, the Court may make an order determining who shall bear any costs incurred by trustees of a pension scheme pursuant to section 12(22) of the 1995 Act or section 17(22) of the 1996 Act and in making such determination the Court shall have regard, *inter alia*, to the representations made by the trustees pursuant to Rule 17 hereof, if any.

36   General

The Court may, upon such terms (if any) as it may think reasonable, enlarge or abridge any of the times fixed by these Rules for taking any step or doing any act in any proceeding, and may also, upon such terms as to costs or otherwise as it shall think fit, declare any step taken or act done to be sufficient, even though not taken or done within the time or in the manner prescribed by these Rules.

37   Certificates

(a) The Certificate required by section 5 of the 1989 Act shall be in accordance with Form No 7 in the Schedule attached hereto.
(b) The Certificate required by section 6 of the 1989 Act shall be in accordance with Form No 8 in the Schedule attached hereto.
(c) The Certificate required by section 6 of the 1996 Act shall be in accordance with Form No 9 in the Schedule attached hereto.
(d) The Certificate required by section 7 of the 1996 Act shall be in accordance with Form No 10 in the Schedule attached hereto.

38   Service of orders by the Registrar of the Court

In all circumstances in which the Registrar of the Court and/or the County Registrar is required to serve or lodge a copy of an order upon any person(s) or body such service of lodgment shall be satisfied by the service of a certified copy of the said order by registered post to the said person(s) or body.

SCHEDULE

FORM NO 1

AN CHUIRT TEAGHLAIGH CHUARDA
(THE CIRCUIT FAMILY COURT)

CIRCUIT   COUNTY OF
[Insert as appropriate]

IN THE MATTER OF THE JUDICIAL SEPARATION AND FAMILY LAW REFORM ACT, 1989

IN THE MATTER OF THE FAMILY LAW ACT, 1995

IN THE MATTER OF THE FAMILY LAW (DIVORCE) ACT, 1996

BETWEEN

A.B.
Applicant
And

C.D.
Respondent

FAMILY LAW CIVIL BILL
INDORSEMENT OF CLAIM

YOU ARE HEREBY REQUIRED within ten days after the service of this Civil Bill upon you, to enter, or cause to be entered with the County Registrar, at his or her Office at
....
an Appearance to answer the Claim of ....
of .... in the County of ....
the Applicant herein as indorsed hereon.

AND TAKE NOTICE THAT unless you do enter an Appearance, you will be held to have admitted the said claim and the Applicant may proceed therein and judgment may be given against you in your absence without further notice.

AND FURTHER TAKE NOTICE THAT if you intend to defend the proceedings on any grounds, you must not only enter an Appearance as aforesaid, but also within ten days after the Appearance deliver a statement in writing showing the nature and grounds of your Defence.

The Appearance and Defence may be entered by posting same to the said Office and by giving copies to the Applicant and his/her Solicitor by post.

Dated the   day of   19 .

To: The Respondent

Signed: ....
Applicant/Solicitor for the Applicant

[Here set out in numbered paragraphs details of the relief(s) being claimed by the Applicant specifying the matters required by Rule 5 of these Rules].

AND THE APPLICANT CLAIMS:

[Here set out in numbered paragraphs the reliefs (including decrees and declarations) being claimed pursuant to the 1989 Act, the 1995 Act or the 1996 Act specifying, where appropriate, the statutory basis upon which each such relief is sought.]

AND FURTHER TAKE NOTICE that, in any cases where financial relief is sought by either party you must file with the Defence herein or in any event within 20 days after the service of this Civil Bill upon you at the aforementioned Circuit Court Office an Affidavit of Means and, where appropriate, an Affidavit of Welfare in the Manner prescribed by the Rules of this Court and serve a copy of same as provided by the Rules of this Court on the Applicant or his/her Solicitor at the address provided below.

Dated the   day of   19 .

The address for service of proceedings upon the Applicant is as follows:

(here insert address of Applicant or his/her Solicitor)

Signed: ....
Applicant or Solicitor for the Applicant

To: The Registrar Circuit Family Court
     Address

and

To: Respondent or Solicitor for Respondent
     Address

TAKE NOTICE that it is in your interest to have legal advice in regard to these proceedings. If you cannot afford a private solicitor, you may be entitled to legal aid provided by the State at a minimum cost to you. Details of this legal aid service are available at the following address:

Legal Aid Board,
St Stephen's Green House,
Dublin 2.
Telephone No (01) 6615811

where you can obtain the addresses and telephone numbers of the Legal Aid Centres in your area.

FORM NO 2

AN CHUIRT TEAGHLAIGH CHUARDA
(THE CIRCUIT FAMILY COURT)

CIRCUIT   COUNTY OF
[Insert as appropriate]

IN THE MATTER OF THE JUDICIAL SEPARATION AND FAMILY LAW REFORM ACT, 1989

IN THE MATTER OF THE FAMILY LAW ACT, 1995

IN THE MATTER OF THE FAMILY LAW (DIVORCE) ACT, 1996

BETWEEN

A.B.

Applicant

And

C.D.

Respondent

AFFIDAVIT OF MEANS

I,   , [insert occupation]

, of

aged 18 years and upwards MAKE OATH and say as follows:

1. I say that I am the Applicant/Respondent [delete as appropriate] in the above entitled proceedings and I make this Affidavit from facts within my own knowledge save where otherwise appears and where so appearing I believe the same to be true.

2. I say that I have set out in the First Schedule hereto all the assets to which I am legally or beneficially entitled and the manner in which such property is held.

3. I say that I have set out in the Second Schedule hereto all income which I receive and the source(s) of such income.

4. I say that I have set out in the Third Schedule hereto all my debts and/or liabilities and the persons to whom such debts and liabilities are due.

5. I say that my weekly outgoings amount to the sum of £   and I say that the details of such outgoings have been set out in the Fourth Schedule hereto.

6. I say that to the best of my knowledge, information and belief, all pension information known to me relevant to the within proceedings is set out in the Fifth Schedule hereto. [Where information has been obtained from the trustees of the pension scheme concerned under the Pensions Act, 1990, such information should be exhibited and where such information has not been obtained, the Deponent should depose to the reason(s) why such information has not been obtained].

FIRST SCHEDULE

[Here set out in numbered paragraphs all assets whether held in the Applicant/ Respondent's sole name or jointly with another, whether held legally or beneficially, the manner in which the assets are held, whether they are subject to a mortgage or other charge or lien and such further and other details as are appropriate.]

SECOND SCHEDULE

[Here set out in numbered paragraphs all income from whatever source(s).]

THIRD SCHEDULE

[Here set out in numbered paragraphs all debts and/or liabilities and the persons/ institutions to which such debts and/or liabilities are due.]

FOURTH SCHEDULE

[Here set out full details of weekly personal outgoings.]

FIFTH SCHEDULE

[Here full details of nature of pension scheme, benefits payable thereunder, normal pensionable age and period of reckonable service should be listed to the best of the Deponent's knowledge, information and belief.]

SWORN etc

FORM NO 3

AN CHUIRT TEAGHLAIGH CHUARDA
(THE CIRCUIT FAMILY COURT)

CIRCUIT   COUNTY OF
[Insert as appropriate]

IN THE MATTER OF THE JUDICIAL SEPARATION AND
FAMILY LAW REFORM ACT, 1989

IN THE MATTER OF THE FAMILY LAW ACT, 1995

IN THE MATTER OF THE FAMILY LAW (DIVORCE) ACT, 1996

BETWEEN

A.B.
                                                       Applicant

And

C.D.
                                                      Respondent

AFFIDAVIT OF WELFARE

I,   , [insert occupation]

        , of
aged 18 years and upwards MAKE OATH and say as follows:

1. I say that I am the Applicant/Respondent [delete as appropriate] in the above
entitled proceedings and I make this Affidavit from facts within my own knowledge save
where otherwise appears and where so appearing I believe the same to be true.

2. I say and believe that the facts set out in the Schedule hereto are true.

[In circumstances in which the Respondent does not dispute the facts as deposed to by
the Applicant in his/her Affidavit of Welfare, the following averment shall be included,
replacing Paragraph 2 hereof, and in such circumstances, the Schedule shall not be
completed by the Respondent:

3. I say that I am fully in agreement with the facts as averred to by the Applicant in
his/her Affidavit of Welfare sworn herein on the   day of   19   and I say and
believe that the facts set out in the Schedule thereto are true.]

SCHEDULE

PART I—DETAILS OF THE CHILDREN

1. Details of children born to the Applicant and the Respondent or adopted by both the Applicant and the Respondent

Forenames   Surname   Date of Birth

2. Details of other children of the family or to which the parties or either of them are in loco parentis

Forenames   Surname   Date of Birth   Relationship to
                                                            Applicant/
                                                            Respondent

PART II—ARRANGEMENTS FOR THE CHILDREN OF THE FAMILY

3. Home Details

   (a) The address or addresses at which the children now live.
   (b) Give details of the number of living rooms, bedrooms, etc at the addresses in (a) above.
   (c) Is the house rented or owned and, if so, name the tenant(s) or owner(s)?
   (d) Is the rent or mortgage being regularly paid and, if so, by whom?
   (e) Give the names of all other persons living with the children either on a full-time or part-time basis and state their relationship to the children, if any.
   (f) Will there be any change in these arrangements and, if so, give details.

PART III—EDUCATION AND TRAINING DETAILS

   (a) Give the names of the school, college or place of training attended by each child.
   (b) Do the children have any special educational needs? If so, please specify.
   (c) Is the school, college or place of training fee-paying? If so, give details of how much the fees are per term/year. Are fees being regularly paid and, if so, by whom?
   (d) Will there be any change in these circumstances? If so, give details.

PART IV—CHILDCARE DETAILS

   (a) Which parent looks after the children from day to day? If responsibility is shared, please give details.
   (b) Give details of work commitments of both parents.
   (c) Does someone look after the children when the parent is not there? If yes, give details
   (d) Who looks after the children during school holidays?
   (c) Will there be any changes in these arrangements? If yes, give details.

PART V—MAINTENANCE

   (a) Does the Applicant/Respondent pay towards the upkeep of the children? If yes, give details. Please specify any other source of maintenance.
   (b) Is the maintenance referred to at (a) above paid under court order? If yes, give details.
   (c) Has maintenance for the children been agreed? If yes, give details.

(d) If not, will you be applying for a maintenance order from the Court?

PART VI—DETAILS OF CONTACT WITH THE CHILDREN

(a) Do the children see the Applicant/Respondent? Please give details.
(b) Do the children stay overnight and/or have holiday visits with the Applicant/Respondent? Please give details.
(c) Will there be any change to these arrangements? Please give details.

PART VII—DETAILS OF HEALTH

(a) Are the children generally in good health? Please give details of any serious disability or chronic illness suffered by any of the children.
(b) Do the children or any of them have any special health needs? Please give details of the care needed and how it is to be provided.
(c) Are the Applicant or Respondent generally in good health? If not, please give details.

PART VIII—DETAILS OF CARE AND OTHER COURT PROCEEDINGS

(a) Are the children or any of them in the care of a health board or under the supervision of a social worker or probation officer? If so, please specify.
(b) Are there or have there been any proceedings in any Court involving the children or any of them? If so, please specify. (All relevant Court Orders relating to the children or any of them should be annexed hereto.)

SWORN etc

FORM NO 4

AN CHUIRT TEAGHLAIGH CHUARDA
(THE CIRCUIT FAMILY COURT)

CIRCUIT   COUNTY OF
[Insert as appropriate]

IN THE MATTER OF THE JUDICIAL SEPARATION AND FAMILY LAW REFORM ACT, 1989

IN THE MATTER OF THE FAMILY LAW ACT, 1995

IN THE MATTER OF THE FAMILY LAW (DIVORCE) ACT, 1996

BETWEEN

A.B.

Applicant

And

C.D.

Respondent

NOTICE TO TRUSTEES

TAKE NOTICE that relief has been claimed by the Applicant/Respondent in the above entitled proceedings pursuant to section(s) 12 and/or 13 of the Family Law Act, 1995 or section 17 of the Family Law (Divorce) Act, 1996 or section 8B of the Family Law (Maintenance of Spouses and Children) Act, 1976 and in particular in relation to ..... [here insert details of pension in respect of which relief is claimed].

AND FURTHER TAKE NOTICE that a Notice of Trial or a Notice to fix a date for Trial will be served upon you in due course in accordance with the Rules of the Circuit Court. Dated the   day of   19 .

Signed: ....
Solicitors for the Applicant/Respondent

To: The County Registrar

and

To: The trustees of the pension scheme concerned

and

To: Applicant/Respondent [or Solicitors where appropriate]

FORM NO 5

AN CHUIRT TEAGHLAIGH CHUARDA
(THE CIRCUIT FAMILY COURT)

CIRCUIT   COUNTY OF
[Insert as appropriate]

IN THE MATTER OF THE JUDICIAL SEPARATION AND FAMILY LAW REFORM ACT, 1989

IN THE MATTER OF THE FAMILY LAW ACT, 1995

IN THE MATTER OF THE FAMILY LAW (DIVORCE) ACT, 1996

BETWEEN

A.B.

Applicant

And

C.D.

Respondent

NOTICE TO FIX A DATE FOR TRIAL

TAKE NOTICE that the above matter will be listed before this Honourable Court/the County Registrar sitting at   on the   day of   19   at   o'clock in the forenoon for the purpose of fixing a date for the trial hereof.

Dated this   day of   19 .

Signed: ....

Solicitor for Applicant/Respondent (delete as appropriate)

To: The County Registrar

and

To: The Respondent/Applicant (delete as appropriate) or the solicitors for the Respondent/Applicant, if appropriate.

To: The trustees of the pension scheme concerned if relief is sought under sections 12 and/or 13 of the 1995 Act of section 17 of the 1996 Act.

FORM NO 6

AN CHUIRT TEAGHLAIGH CHUARDA
(THE CIRCUIT FAMILY COURT)

CIRCUIT   COUNTY OF
[Insert as appropriate]

IN THE MATTER OF THE JUDICIAL SEPARATION AND FAMILY LAW REFORM ACT, 1989

IN THE MATTER OF THE FAMILY LAW ACT, 1995

IN THE MATTER OF THE FAMILY LAW (DIVORCE) ACT, 1996

BETWEEN

A.B.

Applicant

And

C.D.

Respondent

DEFENCE AND COUNTERCLAIM

TAKE NOTICE that the Respondent   of
in the County of
disputes the claims made in the Applicant's Family Law Civil Bill pursuant to sections
of the above entitled Acts, which Civil Bill was served on the Respondent on the
day of   19 .

AND TAKE NOTICE that the Respondent will rely upon the following matters in disputing the Applicant's claim:

[Here set out in numbered paragraphs the matters disputed or denied by the Respondent. Indicate clearly the extent (if any) to which the Applicant's claim or claims are admitted]

COUNTERCLAIM

AND TAKE NOTICE that the Respondent will rely on the following matters in support of his/her Counterclaim:

[Here set out in numbered paragraphs details of the relief(s) being claimed by the Respondent specifying the matters required by Rule 21 of these Rules.]

AND THE RESPONDENT CLAIMS:

[Here set out in numbered paragraphs the reliefs (including decrees and declarations) being claimed pursuant to the 1989 Act, the 1995 Act or the 1996 Act specifying, where appropriate, the statutory basis upon which each such relief is sought.]

Dated the   day of   19 .

The address for the service of proceedings on the Respondent is as follows: [Here insert address of Respondent/Solicitor for the Respondent]

Signed: ....
Respondent/Solicitor for Respondent

PART THREE

To: The County Registrar

   Address

and

To: The Applicant/Solicitors for the Applicant

   Address

FORM NO 7

AN CHUIRT TEAGHLAIGH CHUARDA
(THE CIRCUIT FAMILY COURT)

CIRCUIT   COUNTY OF

IN THE MATTER OF THE JUDICIAL SEPARATION AND
FAMILY LAW REFORM ACT, 1989 AND IN THE MATTER OF
THE FAMILY LAW ACT, 1995

BETWEEN

A.B.

Applicant

And

C.D.

Respondent

CERTIFICATE PURSUANT TO SECTION 5 OF THE JUDICIAL
SEPARATION AND FAMILY LAW REFORM ACT, 1989

I,   , the
Solicitor acting for the above Applicant do hereby certify as follows:

1. I have discussed with the Applicant the possibility of reconciliation with the Respondent and I have given the Applicant the names and addresses of persons qualified to help effect a reconciliation between spouses who have become estranged.

2. I have discussed with the Applicant the possibility of engaging in mediation to help effect a separation on an agreed basis with the Respondent and I have given the Applicant the names and addresses of persons and organisations qualified to provide a mediation service.

3. I have discussed with the Applicant the possibility of effecting a separation by the negotiation and conclusion of a Separation Deed or written Separation Agreement with the Respondent.

Dated the   day of   , 19 .

Signed: ....

Solicitor

Address:

PART THREE

FORM NO 8

AN CHUIRT TEAGHLAIGH CHUARDA
(THE CIRCUIT FAMILY COURT)

CIRCUIT   COUNTY OF
[Insert as appropriate]

IN THE MATTER OF THE JUDICIAL SEPARATION AND
FAMILY LAW REFORM ACT, 1989 AND IN THE MATTER OF
THE FAMILY LAW ACT, 1995

BETWEEN

A.B.

Applicant

And

C.D.

Respondent

CERTIFICATE PURSUANT TO SECTION 6 OF THE JUDICIAL
SEPARATION AND FAMILY LAW REFORM ACT, 1989

I,   , the
Solicitor acting for the above Respondent do hereby certify as follows:

1. I have discussed with the Respondent the possibility of reconciliation with the Applicant and I have given the Respondent the names and addresses of persons qualified to help effect a reconciliation between spouses who have become estranged.

2. I have discussed with the Respondent the possibility of engaging in mediation to help effect a separation on an agreed basis with the Applicant and I have given the Respondent the names and addresses of persons and organisations qualified to provide a mediation service.

3. I have discussed with the Respondent the possibility of effecting a separation by the negotiation and conclusion of a Separation Deed or written Separation Agreement with the Applicant.

Dated the   day of   , 19 .

Signed: ....

Solicitor

Address:

FORM NO 9

AN CHUIRT TEAGHLAIGH CHUARDA
(THE CIRCUIT FAMILY COURT)

CIRCUIT   COUNTY OF

IN THE MATTER OF THE FAMILY LAW (DIVORCE) ACT, 1996

BETWEEN

A.B.

Applicant

And

C.D.

Respondent

CERTIFICATE PURSUANT TO SECTION 6 OF THE FAMILY LAW
(DIVORCE) ACT, 1996

I,   , the
Solicitor acting for the above Applicant do hereby certify as follows:

1. I have discussed with the Applicant the possibility of reconciliation with the Respondent and I have given the Applicant the names and addresses of persons qualified to help effect a reconciliation between spouses who have become estranged.

[The following paragraphs to be inserted where appropriate.]

2. I have discussed with the Applicant the possibility of engaging in mediation to help effect a separation on an agreed basis (the spouses the parties hereto not being separated) or a divorce on a basis agreed between the Applicant with the Respondent and I have given the Applicant the names and addresses of persons and organisations qualified to provide a mediation service for spouses who have become estranged.

3. I have discussed with the Applicant the possibility of effecting a separation by the negotiation and conclusion of a Separation Deed or written Separation Agreement with the Respondent.

4. I have ensured that the Applicant is aware of judicial separation as an alternative to divorce, no decree of judicial separation in relation to the Applicant and the Respondent being in force.

Dated the   day of   , 19 .

Signed: ....

Solicitor

Address:

FORM NO 10

AN CHUIRT TEAGHLAIGH CHUARDA
(THE CIRCUIT FAMILY COURT)

CIRCUIT　　　　　　　　　　COUNTY OF

IN THE MATTER OF THE FAMILY LAW (DIVORCE) ACT, 1996

BETWEEN

A.B.

Applicant

And

C.D.

Respondent

CERTIFICATE PURSUANT TO SECTION 7 OF THE FAMILY LAW
(DIVORCE) ACT, 1996

I,　　　　　　　　　　　　　　　　　　　　　　　　　, the
Solicitor acting for the above Respondent do hereby certify as follows:

1. I have discussed with the Respondent the possibility of reconciliation with the Applicant and I have given the Respondent the names and addresses of persons qualified to help effect a reconciliation between spouses who have become estranged.

[The following paragraphs to be inserted where appropriate.]

2. I have discussed with the Respondent the possibility of engaging in mediation to help effect a separation on an agreed basis (the spouses the parties hereto not being separated) or a divorce on a basis agreed between the Respondent with the Applicant and I have given the Respondent the names and addresses of persons and organisations qualified to provide a mediation service for spouses who have become estranged.

3. I have discussed with the Respondent the possibility of effecting a separation by the negotiation and conclusion of a Separation Deed or written Separation Agreement with the Applicant.

4. I have ensured that the Respondent is aware of judicial separation as an alternative to divorce, no decree of judicial separation in relation to the Respondent and the Applicant being in force.

Dated the　　　　day of　　　　　, 19　.

Signed: ....

Solicitor

Address:

District Court Rules 1997

(SI 93/1997)

...

ORDER 55

RECIPROCAL ENFORCEMENT OF MAINTENANCE ORDERS AS BETWEEN THE
STATE AND NORTHERN IRELAND, ENGLAND AND WALES AND SCOTLAND

1 Definition

In this Order:

'the Act' means the Maintenance Orders Act, 1974 (No 16 of 1974).

1A Order not to apply to proceedings under the EC (Judgments) Convention 1968

This Order shall not apply to proceedings brought by virtue of the Conventions defined in section 1(1) of the Jurisdiction of Courts and Enforcement of Judgments (European Communities) Act, 1988, which are provided for in Order 62 of these Rules.

ENFORCEMENT OF ENFORCEABLE MAINTENANCE ORDERS

2 Clerk to register order

(1) Where a copy of a maintenance order, in respect of which an enforcement order has been made, is received by the Clerk from the Master of the High Court such clerk shall:

(a) register particulars of such maintenance order and such enforcement order, and

Notice to maintenance debtor
(b) by notice (Form 55.1 Schedule C) inform the maintenance debtor of the days and hours during which and the place at which the payments under the order are to be made. Such notice shall be sent by registered prepaid post and a copy thereof shall also be sent by registered prepaid post to the person entitled to receive the payments.

Clerk to register particulars of variation etc

(2) Where a maintenance order has been varied or revoked by a court in a reciprocating jurisdiction and a certified copy of the variation or revocation order is received by the Clerk he or she shall register particulars thereof and shall send a copy of such variation or revocation order by registered prepaid post to the maintenance debtor.

3 Receipt for payment

The Clerk shall give a receipt to the maintenance debtor for each payment made by him or her pursuant to the order and shall transmit such payment to the person entitled to receive same.

4   Where maintenance debtor ceases to reside in court area

(1) Where the maintenance debtor ceases to reside in the district court area in which the proceedings have been entered, the Clerk for such court area shall forward to the Clerk of the court area in which the maintenance debtor is for the time being residing the following documents:

    (a) a copy of the maintenance order together with a copy of the enforcement order,
    (b) a certificate of arrears (Form 55.2, Schedule C),
    (c) a copy of the variation order (if any), and
    (d) any other relevant document.

(2) The Clerk who receives the documents referred to in *paragraph (1)* shall proceed in the same manner as if the copy maintenance order and enforcement order had been received by him or her from the Master of the High Court.

Where maintenance debtor ceases to reside in the State

(3) Where the maintenance debtor ceases to reside in the State the Clerk shall forward the documents referred to in *paragraph (1)* to the Master of the High Court together with a statement (Form 55.8 Schedule C) giving such information as he or she possesses as to the whereabouts of such maintenance debtor.

5   Recovery of arrears by Clerk

(1) Where payments to the Clerk under an enforceable maintenance order are in arrears and such clerk receives a request in writing from the maintenance creditor to take such steps as he or she considers reasonable to recover such arrears, such Clerk may make an application, under *section 10* of the Family Law (Maintenance of Spouses and Children) Act, 1976 for an attachment of earnings order or, for an order under *section 8* of the Enforcement of Court Orders Act, 1940, (as provided for in Order 56 or Order 57, as the case may be, of these Rules).

(2) Where payments referred to in *paragraph (1)* hereof are in arrears and the Clerk has received no request to recover the arrears, such Clerk may in his or her discretion, having considered the extent of the arrears and any other relevant matter, notify the maintenance creditor of the means of enforcement available in respect of the order.

INSTITUTION OF PROCEEDINGS AGAINST A PERSON RESIDING IN A RECIPROCATING JURISDICTION

6   Clerk to send documents to Master of High Court

Where proceedings are instituted against a person residing in a reciprocating jurisdiction for the making, variation or revocation of a maintenance order, pursuant to *section 17* of the Act, the Clerk to whom the application for the issue of a summons is made, shall send the following documents to the Master of the High Court by registered prepaid post:

    (a) notice of the institution of the proceedings in one of the Forms 55.3 to 55.7, Schedule C, as the case may be,
    (b) a statement (Form 55.8, Schedule C) signed by such Clerk, giving such information as he or she possesses as to the whereabouts of the person against whom the proceedings have been instituted,

(c) a statement (Form 55.9, Schedule C) signed by such Clerk giving such information as he or she possesses for facilitating the identification of that person,

(d) where available, a photograph of that person, and

(e) any other relevant document.

The Clerk shall also send with the aforesaid documents a Schedule thereof in duplicate (Form 55.10 Schedule C).

7   Listing of proceedings by Clerk

(1) When proof of service of the notice of institution of proceedings has been received by the Clerk he or she shall list the proceedings for hearing at a scheduled sitting of the Court on a day not earlier than twenty-one days after the day on which the notice of the institution of proceedings was served, and shall, by notice (Form 55.11 Schedule C) inform both parties to the proceedings by registered prepaid post of the date, time and place of such hearing.

Hearing to be otherwise than in public

(2) Such proceedings shall be heard otherwise than in public and only officers of the Court, the parties and their legal representatives, witnesses (subject to the provisions of Order 8, rule 2 of these Rules) and such other persons as the Judge in his or her discretion shall allow, shall be permitted to be present at the hearing.

8   Clerk to produce documents

On the hearing of the proceedings the Clerk shall produce to the Court any communication or correspondence received by him or her.

9   Order of Court

The order of the Court hearing the proceedings shall be in accordance with one of the Forms 55.12 to 55.17, Schedule C, as the case may be. Notice of the making of any such order (Form 55.18 Schedule C) shall be sent by the Clerk by registered prepaid post to the person against whom the order is made.

TRANSMISSION OF MAINTENANCE ORDERS TO RECIPROCATING
JURISDICTION FOR ENFORCEMENT

10   Application to enforce order

(1) An application by a maintenance creditor to have a maintenance order made by the Court enforced against a person residing in a reciprocating jurisdiction, pursuant to *section 19* of the Act, shall be by notice which shall be in accordance with Form 55.19 Schedule C.

Clerk to send documents to Master of High Court

(2) The Clerk to whom such application is made shall, if it appears to him or her that the maintenance debtor is residing in a reciprocating jurisdiction,

(a) send notice of the order (Form 55.18 Schedule C) by registered prepaid post to the maintenance debtor, and

(b) send by registered prepaid post to the Master of the High Court the following documents:

     (i)   a certified copy of the maintenance order,

     (ii) in the case of a maintenance order made in default of appearance, the original or a certified copy of the document which establishes that notice of the institution of the proceedings was served upon the person in default,

    (iii) a certificate (Form 55.20 Schedule C) signed by such Clerk certifying that the maintenance order is enforceable in the State and that the notice thereof has been sent to the maintenance debtor by registered post,

    (iv) a certificate (Form 55.21 Schedule C) signed by such Clerk of any arrears under the order,

     (v) a statement (Form 55.8 Schedule C) signed by such Clerk giving such information as he or she possesses as to the whereabouts of the maintenance debtor,

    (vi) a statement (Form 55.9 Schedule C) signed by such Clerk giving such information as he or she possesses for facilitating the identification of the maintenance debtor,

   (vii) where available, a photograph of the maintenance debtor, and

  (viii) any other relevant document.

The Clerk shall also send with the aforesaid documents a Schedule thereof in duplicate (Form 55.22 Schedule C).

Where maintenance order varied or revoked

(3) Where a maintenance order which is being enforced by a court in a reciprocating jurisdiction is varied or revoked, the Clerk shall send a certified copy of such variation order or revocation order, as the case may be, to such court.

OBTAINING OF EVIDENCE FROM COURT IN RECIPROCATING JURISDICTION

11   Request for the taking of evidence

A request for the taking of evidence of a person residing in a reciprocating jurisdiction, pursuant to *section 20* of the Act, shall be in accordance with Form 55.23 Schedule C, and shall be sent by registered prepaid post by the Clerk to the Master of the High Court for transmission by him to the appropriate authority in the reciprocating jurisdiction.

TAKING OF EVIDENCE FOR COURT IN RECIPROCATING JURISDICTION

12   Receipt of request to take evidence

(1) Where, pursuant to *section 21* of the Act, a Judge receives a request from the Master of the High Court for the taking of evidence of a person residing in such Judge's district, the Judge shall cause the Clerk for the court area in which such person resides to sign and issue a summons (Form 55.24 Schedule C) directed to such person requiring him or her to attend before such Judge at a specified date, time and place to give evidence in relation to the subject matter of the request.

Evidence on oath and in writing

(2) The evidence of such person shall be taken on oath and in writing in the Form 55.25 Schedule C.

(3) Such evidence may, at the discretion of the Judge, be taken in chambers.

Procedure on failure to attend, etc

(4) The procedure contained in Order 21 of these Rules for the purpose of procuring the attendance of a person who fails or refuses to attend or, when present in court, refuses to take the oath or refuses to give evidence, shall apply to the taking of evidence under this rule.

Clerk to transmit evidence

(5) When the evidence has been taken the Clerk shall transmit same by registered prepaid post to the Master of the High Court.

...

ORDER 57

PROCEEDINGS UNDER SECTION 8 OF THE ENFORCEMENT OF COURT ORDERS ACT, 1940

1 Definition

In this Order 'the Act' means the Enforcement of Court Orders Act, 1940 (No 23 of 1940).

2 Venue

Proceedings to which this Order relates may be brought, heard or determined at any sitting of the Court for the court area where either party to the proceedings ordinarily resides or carries on any profession, business or occupation or where the order which it is sought to enforce was made.

3 Information

An application under *section 8(1)* of the Act shall be by sworn information in one of the Forms 57.1 to 57.3 Schedule C, as the case may be.

4 Warrant

A warrant of arrest which may be issued on foot of such information shall be in one of the Forms 57.4 to 57.6 Schedule C as the case may be.

5 Summons in lieu of warrant

A Judge may, however, if he or she thinks fit, instead of issuing such warrant of arrest as is provided by *section 8(1)* of the Act, issue a summons in one of the Forms 57.7 to 57.9 Schedule C, as the case may be on foot of such information.

6 Warrant may issue notwithstanding issue of summons

Where, after the issue of the summons, it seems fit to the Judge, at any time before the date of hearing of the application to issue a warrant of arrest the Judge may issue such warrant notwithstanding the fact that a summons has already been issued.

7 Warrant of committal

A warrant of committal under *section 8(1)* of the Act shall be in accordance with Form 57.10 or 57.11 Schedule C, as the case may be.

8 Distress warrant

A warrant of distress and sale under *section 8(1)* of the Act shall be in accordance with Form 57.12 or 57.13 Schedule C, as the case may be.

9 Recognisance and warrant of detention

A recognisance under section 8(2) of the Act shall be in accordance with Form 57.14 Schedule C. A warrant of detention on refusing to enter into a recognisance shall be in accordance with Form 57.15 Schedule C.

10 Warrant of committal

A warrant of committal under *section 8(2)(d)* of the Act shall be in accordance with Form 57.16 Schedule C.

11 Clerk to produce documents

On the hearing of an application under *section 8(1)* of the Act the Clerk to whom payments under the maintenance order, variation order, interim order or enforceable maintenance order are payable shall tender as evidence:

    (a) the maintenance order, variation order, interim order, (as the case may be) and in the case of an enforceable maintenance order a copy of the maintenance order,

    (b) the request in writing received by the Clerk from the maintenance creditor,

    (c) in the case of an enforceable maintenance order, a copy of the order made by the Master of the High Court, and

    (d) any other relevant document.

The Clerk shall also prove the amount of arrears due.

12 Provisions regarding warrants to apply

The provisions contained in Order 26 of these Rules regarding warrants shall apply to warrants issued under this Order with the proviso that warrants of distress shall be addressed to and executed by the several sheriffs and county registrars.

ORDER 58

CUSTODY AND GUARDIANSHIP OF INFANTS

1 Definitions

In this Order:

    'the Act' means the Guardianship of Infants Act, 1964 (No 7 of 1964);

    'the Act of 1987' means the Status of Children Act, 1987 (No 26 of 1987);

'infant' shall be construed in accordance with *section 2* of the Age of Majority Act, 1985 (No 2 of 1985).

2 Venue

(1) Proceedings under the Act may be brought, heard or determined at any sitting of the Court for the court area where any party to the proceedings resides or carries on any profession, business or occupation.

(2) Where however the Clerk, having consulted the Judge for the time being assigned to the district within which such area is situate, certifies on a notice of application or a summons that the proceedings are urgent, the said notice or summons may, subject to the provisions of rule 9 of this Order, be issued for, and the proceedings may be heard and determined at any sitting of the Court in that district.

3 Hearing to be otherwise than in public

Proceedings under the Act shall be heard otherwise than in public and only officers of the Court, the parties and their legal representatives, witnesses (subject to the provisions of Order 8, rule 2 of these Rules) and such other persons as the Judge in his or her discretion shall allow, shall be permitted to be present at the hearing.

4 Guardianship applications and court orders

(1) (a) An application to the Court under *section 6A* (inserted by *section 12* of the Act of 1987) of the Act by the father of an infant whose father and mother have not married each other for an order appointing him to be a guardian of the infant shall be preceded by the completion by the applicant of a notice in the Form 58.1 Schedule C.

  (b) Where the mother of the infant consents in writing (Form 58.2 Schedule C) to the appointment of the father as a guardian and the applicant is registered as the father in a register maintained under the Births and Deaths Registration Acts, 1863 to 1987, the application may be made *ex parte*, subject to the prior lodgment with the Clerk of the completed notice (Form 58.1 Schedule C) together with the said consent in writing and a certified extract from the said register showing that the applicant is so registered.

  (c) In any other case, an application under the said *section 6A* shall be preceded by the issue and service of the notice (Form 58.1 Schedule C) upon the mother and upon any other guardian of the infant.

  (d) The order of the Court granting such application shall be in the Form 58.3 Schedule C.

(2) An application under section 7(4) of the Act shall be preceded by the issue and service of a notice in the Form 58.4 Schedule C upon the surviving parent and upon any other guardian of the infant. The Order of the Court on hearing the application shall be in the Form 58.5, 58.6 or 58.7 Schedule C, as appropriate.

(3) An application to appoint a guardian or guardians under *section 8(1)* of the Act shall be made *ex parte* in the first instance subject to the prior lodgment with the Clerk of a notice in the Form 58.8 Schedule C. The order of the Court thereon shall be in the Form 58.9 Schedule C.

(4) An application to appoint a guardian or guardians under *section 8(2)* of the Act shall be made *ex parte* if made by the surviving parent, subject to the prior lodgment with the

Clerk of a notice in the Form 58.10 Schedule C, and in any other case it shall be preceded by the issue and service of a notice in the Form 58.10 Schedule C upon that parent. The order of the Court thereon shall be in the Form 58.11 Schedule C.

(5) (i) An application to remove from office a guardian appointed by will or deed or order of court and to appoint another guardian in his or her place under *section 8(4)* and *8(5)* of the Act shall be preceded by the issue and service of a notice in the Form 58.12 Schedule C upon each guardian of the infant. The order of the Court thereon shall be in the Form 58.14 Schedule C.

(ii) An application to appoint a guardian in place of a deceased guardian, under *section 8(5)* of the Act, may be made *ex parte* where the infant has no guardian or where the applicant is the only guardian, subject to the prior judgment with the Clerk of a notice in the Form 58.13 Schedule C, and in any other case it shall be preceded by the issue and service of the said notice upon each guardian of the infant. The order of the Court thereon should be in the Form 58.15 Schedule C.

5 Application seeking Court's direction

Where the Court's direction is sought under *section 11(1)* or the Act or *section 11(4)* (inserted by *section 13* of the Act of 1987) of the Act, the application therefor shall be preceded by the issue and service of a notice in the form 58.16 Schedule C upon each of the other guardians or each of the guardians of the infant, as the case may be. The order of the Court thereon shall be in the Form 58.17 Schedule C.

6 Application to vary/discharge

An application under *section 12* of the Act for an order varying or discharging a previous order shall be preceded by the issue and service of a notice in the form 58.18 Schedule C upon each of the other guardians or each of the guardians of the infant as the case may be. The order of the Court thereon shall be in the Form 58.19 Schedule C.

7 Application for production of infant

An application under Part III of the Act for an order for the production of an infant shall be preceded by the issue and service of a notice in the Form 58.20 Schedule C upon the person having custody of the infant. The order of the Court thereon shall be in the Form 58.21 Schedule C which shall be served upon the said person. The order of the Court under Part III of the Act shall be in the Form 58.22, 58.23 or 58.24 Schedule C, as appropriate.

8 Custody/Right of access—non-compliance with direction

Where complaint is made to a Judge alleging an offence of failure or refusal, under *section 5* of the Courts (No 2) Act, 1986, to comply with the requirements of a direction given in an order under *section 7* or *section 11* of the Act, the summons which may be issued and served upon the person against whom the offence is alleged shall be in the Form 58.25 or 58.26 Schedule C, as appropriate. The relevant provisions of Order 15 of these Rules shall apply in such case.

9 Service and lodgment of documents

(1) A notice or court order required by this Order to be served, may be served upon the person to whom it is directed in accordance with the provisions of Order 10 of these

Rules at least fourteen days or, in the case of proceedings certified as urgent under rule 2(2) hereof, at least two days, before the date of the sitting of the Court to which it is returnable.

(2) Save where service has been effected by the Clerk, the original of every such notice or order served shall, together with a statutory declaration as to service thereof, be lodged with the Clerk at least two days before the date of the said sitting.

10 Clerk to supply copies of orders

Where the Court makes an order under the Act, the Clerk shall give, or send by ordinary post, a copy of such order to each person in whose favour or against whom the order was made.

11 The age of an infant may be proved by producing a certified extract from the Register of Births showing the date of the infant's birth.

12 Court may direct service

In any proceedings under the Act the Court may direct the service of notice upon any person not already served.

13 Effect of appeal from orders

Notwithstanding the provisions of Order 25, r (4) and Order 101 of these Rules and that an appellant has entered into a recognisance for appeal, an appeal from an order made under the Act shall stay the operation of the order only if, and to such extent and upon such terms (if any) as, the Court shall determine.

ORDER 59

DOMESTIC VIOLENCE

1 Definitions

In this Order:

'the Act' means the Domestic Violence Act, 1996;

2 Venue

Proceedings under this Order may be brought, heard and determined before a sitting of the District Court for the Court District in which the applicant resides or, if the application is for a barring order, where there is situate the place in relation to which that application is made.

3 Hearing otherwise than in public

Proceedings under the Act shall be heard otherwise than in public and only officers of the Court, the parties and their legal representatives, witnesses (subject to the provisions of Order 8, rule 2 of these Rules) and such other persons as the Judge shall in the exercise of his or her discretion allow, shall be permitted to be present at the hearing.

4 Safety Order

(1) An application to the Court under *section 2(2)* of the Act for a safety order shall be preceded by the issue and service upon the respondent of a summons in the Form 59.1, Schedule C.

(2) The order of the Court granting the application shall be in the Form 59.2, Schedule C.

5 Barring Order

(1) An application to the Court under *section 3(2)* of the Act for a barring order shall be preceded by the issue and service upon the respondent of a summons in the Form 59.3, Schedule C.

(2) The order of the Court granting the application shall be in the Form 59.4, Schedule C.

6 Interim barring order

(1) Where an interim barring order is made under the terms of *section 4* of the Act on the occasion of the making of an application for a barring order, it may be made on the evidence of applicant *viva voce* and on oath.

(2) Where an interim barring order is made under the terms of *section 4* of the Act between the making of an application for a barring order and its determination, it shall be made on the information on oath and in writing of the applicant in the Form 59.5, Schedule C.

(3) Where the Court in exceptional cases considers it necessary or expedient in the interests of justice, an interim barring order may be made *ex parte* or notwithstanding the fact that the summons referred to in rule 5 of this Order has not been served.

(4) The order of the Court shall be in the Form 59.6, Schedule C.

7 Protection Order

(1) Where a summons applying for a safety order or a barring order has been issued but the application has not been determined by the Court, an application may be made to the Court *ex parte* under *section 5(1)* of the Act for a protection order pending such determination.

(2) An application to the Court under *section 5* of the Act for a protection order, save where made in the course of the hearing of an application for a safety order or a barring order, shall be by sworn information in the Form 59.7, Schedule C.

(3) The Order of the court granting a protection order under the terms of *section 5* of the Act shall be in the Form 59.8, Schedule C.

8 Vary Safety Barring Interim Barring Protection Order

(1) An application to the Court under *section 2(3)* to vary a safety order, *section 3(6)* to vary a barring order, *section 3(6)* as applied by *section 4(2)* to vary an interim barring order or *section 5(2)* to vary a protection order, shall be preceded by the issue and service of a summons in the Form 59.9, Schedule C.

(2) The Order of the Court granting the application shall be in the Form 59.10, Schedule C.

9　Discharge Safety, Barring Interim Barring Protection Order

(1) An application to the Court under *section 13(1)* of the Act for the discharge of a safety order, a barring order, an interim barring order or a protection order shall be preceded by the issue and service of a summons in the Form 59.11, Schedule C.

(2) The order of the Court granting the application shall be in the Form 59.12, Schedule C.

10　Clerk to supply copies of orders

(1) Where the Court makes, varies or discharges a safety order or a protection order, the Clerk shall give or send a certified copy of the order in question as soon as practicable—

- (a) to the applicant for the safety order or, in respect of a protection order, the applicant for the safety order or barring order concerned,
- (b) to the respondent to the application for the safety order or in respect of a protection order, the respondent to the application for the safety order or barring order concerned,
- (c) where a health board by virtue of *section 6* of the Act made the application for the safety order or, in respect of a protection order, for the safety order or barring order, to the health board,

by ordinary prepaid post, and

- (d) to the member of the Garda Síochána in charge of the Garda Síochána station for the area in which the person for whose benefit the safety order or protection order was made resides, and
- (e) where the order in question is a variation or discharge of a safety order or a protection order and the person for whose benefit the order was made had previously resided elsewhere, to the member of the Garda Síochána in charge of the Garda Síochána station for the area in which that person had so resided but only if that member had previously been sent under this Rule a copy of such safety order or protection order or any order relating thereto

by prepaid registered post.

(2) Where the Court makes, varies or discharges a barring order or an interim barring order, the Clerk shall give or send a certified copy of the order in question as soon as practicable—

- (a) to the applicant for the barring order,
- (b) to the respondent to the application for the barring order,
- (c) where a health board by virtue of *section 6* of the Act made the application for the barring order concerned, to the health board,

by ordinary prepaid post, and

- (d) to the member of the Garda Síochána in charge of the Garda Síochána station for the area in which is situate the place in relation to which the application for the barring order was made, and
- (e) where the order in question is a variation or discharge of a barring order or an interim barring order and the place in respect of which the previous order was made is elsewhere, to the member of the Garda Síochána in charge of the Garda Síochána station for the area in which is situated that place but only if that member had previously been sent under this Rule a copy of such barring order or interim barring order or any order relating thereto,

by prepaid registered post.

11   Clerk to notify Gardaí when Interim barring order ceases to have effect

(1) Where an interim barring order has been made and the application for a barring order has been determined, the Clerk shall send notice in the Form 59.13, Schedule C that the interim barring order has ceased to have effect, by prepaid registered post to the member of the Garda Síochána referred to in Rule 10(2)(d) or (e), as the case be.

Clerk to notify Gardaí when Protection Order ceases to have effect

(2) Where a protection order has been made and the application for a safety order or a barring order has been determined, the Clerk shall send notice in the Form 59.13, Schedule C that the protection order has ceased to have effect, by prepaid registered post to the member of the Garda Síochána referred to in Rule 10(1)(d) or (e), as the case may be.

12   Service of Summonses

(1) A summons issued under these Rules shall be served by the Clerk by prepaid ordinary post upon the person to whom it is directed at least seven days before the date fixed for the hearing of the application. Where, however, the Clerk having consulted the Judge for the time being assigned to the Court District in which the summons is being issued, certifies on the summons that the proceedings are urgent, such summons may be served at least two days before the date fixed for the hearing.

(2) The Clerk shall endorse on the original of every such summons served the time, date and place of posting of the envelope containing the copy summons for service and that endorsement shall be *prima facie* evidence of such service.

(3) The summons shall be deemed to be issued when it has been signed by the Judge or the Clerk. It shall be deemed to be served at the time at which the said envelope would be delivered in the ordinary course of post.

13   Effect of appeal from orders

(1) Notwithstanding the provisions of Order 25, r 9(4) and Order 101 of these Rules and that an appellant has entered into a recognisance for appeal,

   (a) an appeal from a safety order or a barring order shall, if the court that made the order or the court to which the appeal is brought so determines (but not otherwise), stay the operation of the order on such terms (if any) as may be imposed by the court making the determination;
   (b) an appeal from a protection order or an interim barring order shall not stay the operation of the order.

(2) (a) An application to the District Court to stay the operation of a safety order or a barring order under the terms of *section 12* of the Act, may be made following the service and lodgment of a notice of appeal and lodgment of the recognizance for appeal and when made otherwise than upon the occasion of the making of those orders shall be preceded by the issue of a notice in the Form 59.14, Schedule C which shall be served upon the respondent to the application two days before the hearing of the application.

(b) Where the Court grants a stay on the operation of a safety order or a barring order under this rule, and the Clerk has supplied the copies of the orders as directed by Rule 10 of this Order, the Clerk shall send notification of the granting of the stay in the Form 59.15, Schedule C to the same persons and in the manner directed by Rule 10 of this Order.

. . .

ORDER 61

USE OF BLOOD TESTS IN DETERMINING PARENTAGE

1 Definitions

In this Order:

'the Act' means the Status of Children Act 1987 (No 26 of 1987);

'the Regulations' means the Blood Tests (Parentage) Regulations, 1988 (SI No 215 of 1988);

'direction form' means Form 1 in the Schedule to the Regulations;

'sampler' has the meaning assigned to it in Regulation 3 of the Regulations;

2 Application for a direction for the use of blood tests

(1) Where in any civil proceedings before the Court the parentage of any person is in question, an application under *section 38(1)* of the Act by a party to the proceedings for a direction for the use of blood tests shall be preceded by the issue and service of a notice in the Form 61.1, Schedule C. Such notice shall be served by registered prepaid post upon the other party or parties to the proceedings and upon each person in respect of whom the direction is sought or, where such person is a person to whom *section 39(3)* of the Act applies, upon the person having charge of or control over him or her and shall be served at least fourteen days before the date of hearing of the application.

(2) The original of every such notice served, together with statutory declaration as to service thereof, shall be lodged with the Clerk at least two days before the said date of hearing.

(3) Where the Court of its own motion proposes to give a direction for the use of blood tests or where application for such a direction is made in the course of hearing the proceedings, and if each of the parties to the proceedings and each person in respect of whom the direction is proposed or sought (or his or her legal or other representative, as the case may be) is then present in court, the Court may dispense with the requirement to serve notice of application.

(4) The direction of the Court shall be in the Form 61.2, Schedule C, and shall be served by prepaid ordinary post upon each person in respect of whom it was given or where such person is a person to whom *section 39(3)* of the Act applies, upon the person having charge of or control over him or her.

3 Order revoking or varying a direction

Where under *section 38(3)* of the Act the Court revokes or varies a direction previously given under *section 38(1)* of the Act, the order so revoking or so varying shall be in the Form 61.3, Schedule C, and shall be served by prepaid ordinary post upon each person directly affected by that order or where such person is a person to whom *section 39(3)* of the Act applies, upon the person having charge of or control over him or her.

4 Notice of intention to call witness

(1) A notice under *section 40(5)* of the Act by a party to civil proceedings of that party's intention to call a person as a witness shall be in the Form 61.4, Schedule C. Such notice shall be served by registered prepaid post upon the other parties to the proceedings or upon such of them as the Court may direct, at least fourteen days before the sitting of the Court at which is it intended to call as a witness the person named in the notice.

(2) The original of every such notice served, together with statutory declaration as to service thereof, shall be lodged with the Clerk at least two days before the said sitting of the Court.

5 Clerk to send direction form to sampler

Where the Court gives a direction under *section 38(1)* of the Act, the Clerk shall complete and sign Part I and the appropriate section of Part II of a direction form as prescribed in the Regulations and shall send that form by prepaid ordinary post to the sampler named in the direction.

ORDER 62

PROCEEDINGS UNDER

THE BRUSSELS CONVENTION OF THE EUROPEAN COMMUNITIES ON JURISDICTION AND THE ENFORCEMENT OF JUDGMENTS IN CIVIL AND COMMERCIAL MATTERS, 1968 OR

THE LUGANO CONVENTION ON JURISDICTION AND THE ENFORCEMENT OF JUDGMENTS IN CIVIL AND COMMERCIAL MATTERS BETWEEN MEMBER STATES OF THE EUROPEAN COMMUNITIES AND THE EUROPEAN FREE TRADE ASSOCIATION, 1988 OR

THE ROME CONVENTION BETWEEN THE MEMBER STATES OF THE EUROPEAN COMMUNITIES ON THE SIMPLIFICATION OF PROCEDURES FOR THE RECOVERY OF MAINTENANCE PAYMENTS OR

THE NEW YORK CONVENTION ON THE RECOVERY ABROAD OF MAINTENANCE

1 Definitions

In this Order—

'the Act of 1976' means the Family Law (Maintenance of Spouses and Children) Act, 1976 (No 11 of 1976);

'the Act of 1988' means the Jurisdiction of Courts and Enforcement of Judgments (European Communities) Act, 1988 (No 3 of 1988);

'the Act of 1993' means the Jurisdiction of Courts and Enforcement of Judgments Act, 1993 (No 9 of 1993);

'the Act of 1994' means the Maintenance Act, 1994 (No 28 of 1994);

'the Conventions' means the 1968 Convention, the 1971 Protocol, the 1978 Accession Convention, the 1982 Accession Convention and the 1989 Accession Convention as defined in *section 1* of the Act (as amended by *section 3* of the Act of 1993);

'the 1968 Convention' means the Convention on Jurisdiction and the enforcement of judgments in civil and commercial matters (including the Protocol annexed to that Convention) done at Brussels on the 27th day of September, 1968, (as adjusted by the Accession Conventions of 1978, 1982 and 1989);

'the Lugano Convention' means the Convention on jurisdiction and the enforcement of judgments in civil and commercial matters signed at Lugano on the 16th day of September, 1988, and includes Protocol 1;

'the New York Convention' means the Convention on the recovery abroad of maintenance done at New York on the 20th day of June, 1956;

'the Central Authority' means a Central Authority appointed by order of the Minister for Equality and Law Reform under *subsection (1)(a)* of *section 4* of the Act of 1994 to discharge the functions required of it under the Act of 1994 or required of a Central Authority under the Rome Convention or of a transmitting agency or receiving agency under the New York Convention, however as provided by *paragraph (b)* of that subsection, pending the appointment of a Central Authority the said Minister shall discharge its functions and references in this Order to the Central Authority shall be construed accordingly as reference to the Minister;

'central authority of a reciprocating jurisdiction', when used in the context of proceedings under Part III of the Act of 1994, means:

   (a) the central authority of such a jurisdiction which has been designated pursuant to *paragraph 1* or, where appropriate, *paragraph 2* of Article 2 of the Rome Convention, or

   (b) an authority of such a jurisdiction with functions corresponding to those exercisable by the Central Authority within the State;

'central authority of a designated jurisdiction' means:

   (a) a transmitting or receiving agency in a state which is a contracting party to the New York Convention, or

   (b) an authority of a designated jurisdiction with functions corresponding to those exercisable by the Central Authority within the State;

'Contracting State',

   (a) when used in the context of proceedings under the 1968 Convention, has the meaning assigned to it in *section 1(1)* of the Act of 1988 (as substituted by *section 3* of the Act of 1993), and,

   (b) when used in the context of proceedings under the Lugano Convention, means a State in respect of which that Convention has entered into force or taken effect in accordance with Article 61 or 62 thereof;

'reciprocating jurisdiction' means a Contracting State (within the meaning of the Acts of 1988 and 1993) which is declared by order of the Minister for Foreign Affairs to be a reciprocating jurisdiction;

'designated jurisdiction' means:

   (a) any state which is a contracting party to the New York Convention, or

   (b) any other state or jurisdiction which is declared by order of the Minister for Foreign Affairs to be a designated jurisdiction for the purposes of Part III of the Act of 1994;

'maintenance creditor' includes any body which, under the law of a reciprocating jurisdiction, is entitled to exercise their rights of redress of, or to represent, the creditor, and references in District Court Rules to a maintenance creditor or to a claimant (as defined herein) shall be construed as including references to the Central Authority;

'claimant' means, according to the context, either:

(a) a person residing in a designated jurisdiction (including any body which under the law of that jurisdiction is entitled to exercise the rights of redress of or to represent that person) and claiming pursuant to Part III of the Act of 1994 to be entitled to receive maintenance from a person residing in the State, or

(b) a person residing in the State including a competent authority within the meaning of Part IX (Liability to Maintain Family) of the Social Welfare (Consolidation) Act, 1993 and claiming pursuant to Part III of the Act of 1994 to be entitled to recover maintenance from a person residing in a designated jurisdiction;

'respondent' means, according to the context, either:

(a) a person residing in the State from whom maintenance is sought to be recovered pursuant to Part III of the Act of 1994 by a person residing in a designated jurisdiction, or

(b) a person residing in a designated jurisdiction from whom maintenance is sought to be recovered pursuant to Part III of the Act of 1994 by a person residing in the State.

'domiciled' shall be construed in accordance with *section 13* and the Fifth Schedule of the Act of 1988 (as applied by the Act of 1993) and Articles 52 and 53 of both the 1968 Convention and the Lugano Convention;

'enforceable maintenance order' has the meaning assigned to it in *section 7(1)* of the Act of 1988 (as applied by *section 11* of the Act of 1993 and as substituted by *section 11* of the Act of 1994);

the terms 'enforcement order', 'judgment' and 'maintenance debtor' have the meanings assigned to them respectively in *section 1(1)* of the Act of 1988 or, as the case may be, *section 11(2)* of the Act of 1993;

'maintenance order' has the meaning assigned to it by *section 1* of the Act of 1988 as amended by *section 9* of the Act of 1994, and includes, where the context is appropriate, an instrument or settlement referred to in Article 50 or 51 of the 1968 Convention or the Lugano Convention in so far as it provides for the payment of maintenance.

PART I—CIVIL PROVISIONS

2 Venue in insurance matters

Whenever it is proposed to bring proceedings before the District Court by virtue of Article 8.2 (which relates to insurance matters) of either the 1968 Convention or the Lugano Convention against an insurer domiciled in a Contracting State other than the State and the policyholder is domiciled in the State, such proceedings may be brought, heard and determined at any sitting of the Court for the transaction of civil business for the district court area in which the policy-holder is ordinarily resident or carries on any profession, business or occupation.

3 Venue in consumer contracts

Whenever a consumer who is domiciled in the State proposes to bring proceedings before the District Court by virtue of Article 14 (which relates to consumer contracts) of either the 1968 Convention or the Lugano Convention against the other party to a contract and that other party is domiciled in a Contracting State other than the State, such proceedings may be brought, heard and determined at any sitting of the Court for the transaction of civil business for the district court area in which the consumer is ordinarily resident or carries on any profession, business or occupation.

4 Application of The Hague Convention

(1) The provisions of The Hague Convention of 15th November 1965 on the Service Abroad of Judicial and Extrajudicial Documents in Civil or Commercial Matters (hereinafter referred to as The Hague Convention) shall apply to proceedings brought in the District Court by virtue of the Conventions.

(2) When any document for use in such proceedings is required by this Order to be served and such document is to be served upon a person in another State which is a party to The Hague Convention, service shall be effected in accordance with the provisions (including Articles 8 to 11) of that Convention and this Order.

5 Institution of proceedings against person domiciled abroad

(1) This Order shall not apply to the institution of proceedings under *section 17* of the Maintenance Orders Act, 1974 against a person residing in a reciprocating jurisdiction, which are provided for in Order 55 of these Rules.

(2) The provisions of Order 11 (Service Out of the Jurisdiction) of these Rules shall not apply to proceedings being instituted in the District Court by virtue of the Conventions or as the case may be, the Lugano Convention, against a person who is domiciled in a Contracting State other than the State, and service may be effected without prior leave of the Court.

Where defendant is not a citizen of Ireland

(3) Whenever proceedings are instituted in the District Court by virtue of the Conventions or the Lugano Convention against a person who is domiciled in the Contracting State other than the State and that person is not or is not known or believed to be a citizen of Ireland, notice of the document instituting the proceedings in the Form 62.1, Schedule C and not the document itself shall be served upon that person.

(4) A plaintiff or solicitor for a plaintiff may institute such proceedings by completing, signing, stamping (if so required) the civil summons or other document instituting the proceedings and lodging it, together with duly completed originals and copies of the notice (Form 62.1, Schedule C) and of a certificate in the Form 62.2, Schedule C with the Clerk for the area for which the proceedings are to be issued. The Clerk shall stamp them with the official stamp showing the date of lodgment and shall, having regard to the provisions of *paragraph (5)* of this rule, list the proceedings for hearing before the Court and, having recorded the place, date and time of hearing on the civil summons or other document instituting the proceedings and the notices, shall return all documents to the plaintiff or the solicitor, as the case may be.

(5) A notice and certificate returned under *paragraph (4)* of this rule shall be served as indicated in rule 4 of this Order (which may include service by post provided the State of destination has not made an objection to such service under Article 10(a) of The Hague Convention) or, where appropriate, in accordance with the provisions of Order 11 of these Rules, upon the defendant and, where the documents are to be served in the European territory of another Contracting State they shall be served at least five weeks

prior to the date of sitting of the Court before which the proceedings have been listed for hearing. Where the documents are to be served in any non-European territory of another Contracting State, they shall be served at least six weeks prior to that date.

(6) Upon receipt of the certificate of service prescribed in Article 6 of the Hague Convention the Plaintiff (or solicitor for the Plaintiff) shall lodge with the Clerk the originals of

-   the civil summons or other document instituting the proceedings,
-   (where appropriate) the notice of institution of proceedings (Form 62.1) which was served,
-   the certificate (Form 62.2) which was served, and
-   the certificate of service,

at least four days prior to the said date of sitting of the Court.

(7) Where service has been effected by registered post or insured post the following provisions shall apply:

(a) the plaintiff or plaintiff's solicitor shall, not earlier than ten days after the date of posting, lodge with the Clerk the relevant documents listed in *paragraph (6)* hereof, together with a statutory declaration as to service of the documents posted, the certificate of posting and the advice of delivery form (when returned);

(b) the documents issued for service shall be deemed to have been issued at the time at which the envelope containing the copies for service was posted;

(c) the said documents shall, subject to the provisions of Article 15 of The Hague Convention, be deemed to have been served at the time at which the said envelope would be delivered in the ordinary course of post;

(d) the statutory declaration as to service, the certificate of posting and the advice of delivery form shall, subject to the provisions of the said Article 15, together be sufficient evidence of such service.

6   Where defendant is a citizen of Ireland

Whenever proceedings are instituted in the District Court by virtue of the Conventions or the Lugano Convention against a person who is domiciled in a Contracting State other than the State, and that person is a citizen of Ireland, the civil summons or other document instituting the proceedings, with necessary modifications, may be served (rather than notice thereof). Subject to the foregoing proviso, the requirements of rule 5 of this Order shall apply in such cases and shall be construed accordingly. Two notices of intention to appear must be served in each case.

7   Notice of intention to appear

Where, in proceedings to which rule 5 or 6 of this Order relates, a defendant intends to appear or to be represented at the hearing for the purpose of defending the proceedings and/or, by virtue of Article 18 of either the 1968 Convention or the Lugano Convention for the purpose of Contesting the jurisdiction of the Court, the defendant or solicitor for the defendant shall complete, detach and send by post to the Clerk one of the Notices of Intention to Appear (and Defend) which were received so soon as to reach the Clerk's office not later than four days before the date fixed for the hearing, and shall at the same time complete, detach and send by post to the plaintiff or solicitor for the plaintiff the other such Notice received.

8 Hearing of proceedings

(1) The provisions of Order 45 (Judgment in Default) of these Rules shall not apply to proceedings to which this Order relates.

(2) At the hearing of proceedings referred to in rule 5 or 6 hereof the Clerk shall produce to the Court any communication or correspondence received from the defendant.

Where defendant does not appear

(3) Where the defendant fails to appear and is not represented at the hearing, the Court may, if it considers it necessary to do so, require the production of the advice of delivery form confirming delivery to the defendant or to the defendant's address of the envelope containing the copy documents for service referred to in rule 5(5) of this Order.

(4) Where the defendant fails to appear and is not represented at the hearing and no notice of intention to appear has been received from the defendant, it shall be necessary for the plaintiff or solicitor for the plaintiff to show to the satisfaction of the Court:

- (a) that each claim made in the document instituting the proceedings is one which, by virtue of the provisions of the Conventions or, as the case may be, the Lugano Convention, the Court has jurisdiction to hear and determine,
- (b) that no other Court has exclusive jurisdiction within the meaning of the 1968 Convention or, as the case may be, the Lugano Convention to hear and determine such claim,
- (c) that no proceedings involving the same cause of action are pending between the parties in another Contracting State,
- (d) that the defendant was duly served with the document instituting the proceedings or notice thereof, and
- (e) that the defendant has been able to receive the said document or notice in sufficient time to enable him or her to arrange for his or her defence, or all necessary steps have been taken to this end, as required by Article 20 of either the 1968 Convention or, as the case may be, the Lugano Convention.

(5) Where the defendant has not appeared or given notice to defend, judgment shall not be given until the requirements of Article 15 of The Hague Convention (as set out in Order 11, rule 10 of these Rules) have been complied with.

(6) Notwithstanding the provisions of *sub-paragraph (5)* above, the Court may give judgment even if no certificate of service or delivery as provided for by The Hague Convention has been received, if all the conditions listed in the said Article 15 (as set out in Order 11, rule 11 of these Rules) are fulfilled.

(7) Where the Court gives judgment against a defendant in proceedings to which this rule relates, the plaintiff, (or solicitor for the plaintiff) shall forthwith notify the defendant of having obtained such judgment.

(8) Where judgment has been given in such proceedings against a defendant who has not appeared and that defendant wishes to apply for an extension of time for appeal from the judgment, the provisions of Order 11, rule 12 of these Rules shall apply in every such case.

9 Enforcement of judgments abroad provision of documents

(1) An interested party who, for the purposes of Articles 46 and 47 of either the 1968 Convention or, as the case may be, the Lugano Convention, requests the provision of the

documents mentioned in *section 12* of the Act of 1988 as applied by *section 11* of the Act of 1993 in respect of a judgment given in the District Court, shall lodge with the Clerk for the district court area in which the judgment was given:

(a) an original and two copies of the judgment, duly completed.

(b) a certificate in duplicate in the Form 62.3, Schedule C, and

(c) where appropriate, an original and copy or copies of the document or documents establishing that notice of the institution of proceedings was served upon the defendant.

(2) When the judgment has been signed by the Judge and served in accordance with the provisions of rule 10 hereof, the Clerk shall give to the party requesting them a duly authenticated copy of the judgment, a certificate in the Form 62.3, Schedule C and a certified true copy or copies of the document or documents referred to in *paragraph 1(c)* of this rule, and shall retain the other documents in his or her custody.

10   Service of judgment and proof of service

(1) Where, for the purposes of Article 47 of either the 1968 Convention or the Lugano Convention, it is necessary to serve upon a defendant a judgment given at a sitting of the District Court, such service shall be effected by or on behalf of the plaintiff and in accordance with the provisions (including Articles 8 to 11) of The Hague Convention and this Order. When service has been effected and duly certified, the certificate of service or, where appropriate, the certificate of posting, statutory declaration as to service and the advice of delivery form, shall be lodged with the Clerk for retention with the original judgment.

(2) Upon the request of a party applying for enforcement of such a judgment for the provision of the documents referred to in Article 47.1 of either the 1968 Convention or the Lugano Convention, the Clerk shall give to that party a certificate in the Form 62.4, Schedule C (with any necessary modifications) and certified copy or copies of the relevant document or documents lodged under *paragraph (1)* of this rule.

PART II—ENFORCEMENT OF CERTAIN FOREIGN MAINTENANCE ORDERS
UNDER THE ACT OF 1988 AS AMENDED BY THE ACT OF 1993

11   Order not to apply to the enforcement of UK maintenance orders

This Order shall not apply to the enforcement of maintenance orders made in a reciprocating jurisdiction as provided for in *section 14* of the Maintenance Orders Act, 1974 and to which Order 55 of these Rules relates.

12   Clerk to register enforceable maintenance order, etc and to notify parties

(1) Where a copy of a maintenance order or a copy of an order varying or revoking such an order, in respect of which an enforcement order has been made, is received together with a copy of relevant enforcement order by a District Court Clerk from the Master of the High Court (or in the case of an instrument of settlement, the High Court) such Clerk shall register particulars of each document received.

(2) If the enforcement order has been made in respect of a maintenance order or an order varying a maintenance order, the Clerk shall send by registered post to the

maintenance creditor and the maintenance debtor a notice in the Form 62.5, Schedule C.

(3) If the enforcement order has been made in respect of an order revoking a maintenance order, the Clerk shall send by registered post to the maintenance debtor a copy of such revocation order and a statement of any amounts still due and payable under the maintenance order.

13 Procedure where debtor changes address

(1) Where a maintenance debtor ceases to reside in the district court area in which the proceedings have been registered and commences to reside elsewhere in the State, the Clerk for the said district court area shall forward to the Clerk for the district court area in which the maintenance debtor is for the time being residing the following documents:

    (a) a copy of the maintenance order and a copy of the relevant enforcement order,

    (b) a certificate of arrears in the Form 62.6, Schedule C,

    (c) a copy of the variation order (if any),

    (d) any other relevant document.

(2) The Clerk receiving the said documents shall proceed as if the copy of the maintenance order and the copy of the enforcement order had been received from the Master of the High Court (or in the case of an instrument or settlement, the High Court).

14 Recovery arrears by Clerk

(1) Whenever a District Court Clerk receives a request in writing from a maintenance creditor under *section 7(7)(b)* of the Act of 1988 as applied by *section 11* of the Act of 1993 and as substituted by *section 11* of the Act of 1994 in relation to any sum payable by virtue of an enforceable maintenance order but not duly paid, such Clerk may proceed in accordance with the provisions of Order 56 (Attachment of Earnings) or Order 57 (Proceedings under *section 8* of the Enforcement of Court Orders Act, 1940) of these Rules.

(2) Where it appears to a District Court Clerk that any sums payable to him or her under an enforceable maintenance order for transmission to the maintenance creditor are in arrears and he or she has received no request in writing under the said *section 7(7)(b)* in relation thereto, such Clerk may in his or her discretion, having considered the extent of the arrears and any other relevant matter, notify the maintenance creditor of the means of enforcement available in respect of the order.

15 Application by virtue of Articles 2 and 5.2 of the 1968 Convention

An application to the District Court being brought:

    (a) by virtue of Article 5.2 of either the 1968 Convention or the Lugano Convention by a maintenance creditor domiciled or habitually resident in the State against a maintenance debtor domiciled in a Contracting State other than the State for the variation of a maintenance order,

    (b) by virtue of Article 2 of either the 1968 Convention or the Lugano Convention by a maintenance creditor domiciled in a Contracting State other than the State against a maintenance debtor domiciled in the State for the variation of a maintenance order, or

(c) by virtue of Article 2 of either the 1968 Convention or the Lugano Convention by a maintenance debtor domiciled in a Contracting State other than the State against a maintenance creditor domiciled in the State for the variation or revocation of a maintenance order,

shall be preceded by the issue and service upon the defendant party of a summons in the Form 62.7, Schedule C or, where appropriate, notice thereof in the Form 62.1, Schedule C, with any necessary modifications, where the defendant party is domiciled in a Contracting State other than the State, and the provisions of this Order shall apply. The order of the Court granting the application shall be in the Form 62.8, Schedule C and shall be served upon a party within the jurisdiction by registered post and upon a party domiciled in another contracting state in accordance with the provisions (including Articles 8 to 11) of The Hague Convention and this Order.

PART III—RECOVERY OF MAINTENANCE

—MAINTENANCE ACT, 1994—PART II

—RECIPROCATING JURISDICTIONS

—THE ROME CONVENTION

16   Enforcement Order

If a judgment or an instrument or settlement referred to in Articles 50 or 51 of the Brussels Convention or the Lugano Convention does not relate solely to maintenance, these Rules shall apply only to those parts that relate to maintenance, and upon receipt of an enforcement order made by the High Court, in relation thereto, the Clerk shall proceed as indicated in rule 17 hereof.

17   Application from reciprocating jurisdiction

Where, pursuant to *section 7(1)* of the Act of 1994, the Central Authority, on receipt of an application for the recognition or enforcement in the State of a maintenance order which has been transmitted by the Central Authority of a reciprocating jurisdiction, sends the application to—

(a) the Master of the High Court for determination in accordance with *section 5* of the Act of 1988, or

(b) the High Court for determination in accordance with Article 31 of the Brussels or Lugano Conventions

and, where an enforcement order is made under *sections 7(2)* or *7(7)* of the Act of 1994, as appropriate, and the orders are sent to the appropriate District Court Clerk, such clerk shall register the documents and proceed to enforce the enforceable maintenance order in accordance with the provisions of this order.

PART IV—RECOVERY OF MAINTENANCE

—MAINTENANCE ACT, 1994

—DESIGNATED JURISDICTIONS

—THE NEW YORK CONVENTION

18   Enforcement Order—Procedure—accompanied by order

Where the Central Authority receives a request from a central authority of a designated jurisdiction on behalf of a claimant for the recovery of maintenance from a person for the time being residing in the State ('the respondent'), and [such request being accompanied by an order of a Court in a Contracting State (within the meaning of the Acts of 1988 and 1993)], the Central Authority transmits the request pursuant to *section 14(1)(a)* of the Act of 1994 to the Master of the High Court for determination in accordance with *section 5* of the Act of 1988, and where the Master, having made an enforcement order in respect of the maintenance order, sends those orders to the appropriate District Court Clerk, such Clerk shall proceed as indicated in rule 16 of these Rules.

19   Application to District court to enforce

(1) Where the Central Authority receives a request referred to in rule 18 hereof and such request is accompanied by an order made by any other Court and the Central Authority is of opinion that the order may be enforceable in the State the Central Authority may make application pursuant to *section 14(1)(b)* of the Act of 1994 at any sitting of the District Court for the relevant district court district (as set out in *section 14(11)* of the Act of 1994) for the enforcement of the order.

—on notice

(2) Such application shall be preceded by the issue and service of a notice, in the Form 62.9, Schedule C upon the respondent. The notice shall be accompanied by a copy of the documents mentioned in *section 14(6)* of the Act of 1994. Service shall be effected by registered post at least twenty-one days prior to the date of hearing of the application.

(3) When service has been effected, the applicant shall lodge with the Clerk the original of the notice, together with a statutory declaration as to service thereof and the certificate of posting, at least four days prior to the said date of hearing.

Clerk to send copy orders

(4) Where, upon hearing the application, the Court makes an order for the enforcement of the order of the court in the designated jurisdiction for the recovery of maintenance such order of the Court shall be in the Form 62.10, Schedule C and copies thereof shall be sent by the Clerk to the Central Authority and the respondent.

and enforce order

(5) When the Court makes such an order the Clerk shall proceed to enforce the enforceable maintenance order as indicated in rule 16 of these Rules.

PART THREE

20   Enforcement procedure—where not accompanied by order

(1) Where the Central Authority receives a request referred to in rule 17 hereof and either:

(a) such request is not accompanied by an order referred to in rule 17 or in rule 18 hereof, or

(b) enforcement of the order is refused,

—application to District Court

and the Central Authority intends to make an application to the District Court pursuant to *section 14(1)(c)(ii)* of the Act of 1994, for the recovery of maintenance in accordance with the request, such application may be made at any sitting of the Court for the relevant Court District (as set out in *section 14(11)* of the Act of 1994) and shall be deemed (as provided in *subsection (3)* of that section) to be an application for a maintenance order under *section 5, 5A* or *21A* of the Act of 1976, as appropriate.

—on notice

(2) The application shall be preceded by the issue and service of a notice, in the Form 62.11, Schedule C upon the respondent. The notice shall be accompanied by a copy of documents mentioned in *section 14(6)* of the Act of 1994. Service shall be effected by registered post at least twenty-one days prior to the date of hearing of the application.

(3) When service has been effected, the applicant shall lodge with the Clerk the original of the notice, together with the certificate of posting, at least four days prior to the said date of hearing.

(4) Where, upon hearing the application, the court makes a maintenance order, the Clerk shall proceed in accordance with the relevant provisions of the Order 54 and this Order, and the forms therein provided (with any necessary modifications) may be used.

21   Deposition of respondent

Where the court, on an application to it under *section 14(1)(c)* of the Act of 1994, takes evidence from the respondent on sworn deposition, such deposition shall be in the Form 62.12, Schedule C, a copy thereof shall be sent by the Clerk to the Central Authority for transmission to the central authority of the designated jurisdiction with a request that the claimant provide an answering affidavit.

22   Transfer for use of television link

Where, at the hearing of an application under *section 14(1)(c)* of the Act of 1994, the Court makes an order pursuant to *subsection (7)* of that section transferring the proceedings to a district court district where facilities are available for taking the evidence of the claimant or of any witness through a live television link, such order shall be in the Form 62.13, Schedule C. The Clerk shall forward a copy thereof, together with any other documents in his or her possession relating to the proceedings, to the appropriate District Court Clerk.

23   Deposition of claimant

A request by the claimant to give evidence on sworn deposition before the District Court pursuant to *section 15(2)(a)* of the Act of 1994 may be made at any sitting of the Court for the district court district in which the claimant resides or carries on any profession, business or occupation. A deposition, taken under that provision shall be in the Form 62.14, Schedule C and the certificate of the Court required under that provision (which may be added at the foot of the deposition) shall be in the Form 62.15, Schedule C. A certified copy of the deposition and certificate shall be given by the Clerk to the claimant.

24. The certificate to be given by the Clerk to a claimant on request, pursuant to *section 15(3)(b)* of the Act of 1994, shall be in the form 62.16, Schedule C.

25 Taking of evidence for a designated jurisdiction

(1) Subject to the provisions of *subsection (8)* of *section 19* of the Act of 1994, where on request from the Master of the High Court, pursuant to *section 19(2)* of the Act of 1994, a Judge of the District Court proposes to take the evidence of a person for the purposes of proceedings in a designated jurisdiction for the recovery of maintenance, the Clerk shall issue and serve notice, in the Form 62.17, Schedule C upon the person concerned, the Central Authority, the Master of the High Court and upon such other persons as the judge thinks fit. The notice shall be served by registered post at least twenty-one days prior to the date fixed for taking the evidence.

(2) Where such evidence is taken on sworn deposition, the deposition shall be in the Form 62.18, Schedule C. The Clerk shall send a certified copy thereof to the Central Authority for transmission to the requesting authority.

(3) Where, as provided for in *section 19(9)* of the Act of 1994, the requesting authority makes a request for the taking of evidence directly to the District Court, the provisions of this rule shall, with any necessary modifications, apply in relation to such a request.

(4) If it is not possible to take the evidence within four months of the receipt of the request by the Central Authority, the Judge shall certify in the Form 62.21, Schedule C the reasons for the non-execution of the request or of the delay in executing it and the Clerk shall send the same to the Central Authority for transmission to the requesting authority.

PART V—MISCELLANEOUS PROVISIONS APPLICABLE TO PROCEEDINGS TO WHICH PARTS II, III AND IV REFER

26 Currency of payments

An amount payable in the State under:

- (a) an enforceable maintenance order by virtue of an enforcement order as provided for in the Act of 1988, or
- (b) an order for recovery of maintenance which is made by a Court in a jurisdiction other than the State and is enforceable in the State as provided for in the Act of 1994,

shall be paid in the currency of the State and if the amount is stated in the enforceable maintenance order or order for recovery, as the case may be, in currency other than the currency of the State, the payment shall be made on the basis of the exchange rate prevailing on the date of the making of the enforcement order or of the order of a court in the State for the enforcement of the order, for the recovery of maintenance between that other currency and the currency of the State.

27 Clerk to give receipt for and transmit payments

(1) The District Court Clerk shall give, or send by ordinary post, to the maintenance debtor a receipt for each payment made by him or her under an order referred to in rule 26 hereof and shall transmit such payment forthwith by registered post, by insured post or by any other appropriate method to the person entitled to receive it, having due regard to the provisions of *subsections 2(a)* and *2(b)* of *section 4* of the Act of 1994.

(2) Before transmitting any such payment abroad the Clerk shall comply with any Exchange Control regulations for the time being in force governing the transmission of such payments and shall, where necessary for that purpose, produce the order referred to in rule 26 hereof to an authorised dealer (ie a licensed bank) for inspection.

28 Venue for proceedings by creditor

(1) Proceedings by or on behalf of the maintenance creditor being brought in the District Court under the Act of 1988 as applied by *section 11* of the Act of 1993 for the enforcement of an enforceable maintenance order, may be brought, heard and determined—

   (a) in case the maintenance debtor under the enforceable maintenance order concerned resides in the State, at any sitting of the Court for the district court district in which the maintenance debtor resides,
   (b) in case the maintenance debtor does not reside in the State but is in the employment either of a person residing or having a place of business in the State or of a corporation or association having its seat therein, at any sitting of the Court for the district court district in which that person resides or, as the case may be, the corporation or association has its seat.

(2) Proceedings being brought by the maintenance creditor by virtue of Article 2 of either the 1968 Convention or the Lugano Convention for the variation of a maintenance order made in a Contracting State other than the State may be brought, heard and determined at any sitting of the Court for the district court district in which the maintenance debtor is domiciled.

PART VI—MISCELLANEOUS PROVISIONS APPLICABLE TO PROCEEDINGS TO WHICH PARTS III AND IV REFER

29 Obtaining information on debtor

(1) An application by the Central Authority to the District Court under *section 20(2)* of the Act of 1994 for an order requiring a person or body (not being a person information or body mentioned in *subsection (1)* of that section) to provide to the Central Authority information as to the whereabouts, place of work, or location and extent of the assets of a maintenance debtor (within the meaning of the Act of 1988) or respondent may be made at any sitting of the Court for the district court district in which the person or body to whom the order sought is to be directed resides or carries on any profession, business or occupation, and notice of such application in the Form 62.19, Schedule C shall be lodged with the Clerk at least four days prior to the date of hearing.

(2) Where the Court grants the application and makes the order sought, such order shall be in the Form 62.20, Schedule C and the Central Authority shall forward a copy thereof to the person or body concerned.

. . .

SCHEDULE C

No 54.4

FAMILY LAW (MAINTENANCE OF SPOUSES AND CHILDREN) ACT, 1976

Section 5A(2)

MAINTENANCE SUMMONS

District Court Area of   District No

.... Applicant

.... Respondent

*Delete words inapplicable

WHEREAS AN APPLICATION as been made by the above-named applicant, *(residing) *(carrying on profession, business or occupation) at ....
*(in court area and district aforesaid), a person other than a parent (within the meaning of section 5A(2) of the above-mentioned Act), for the issue of a summons seeking a maintenance order against you on the grounds THAT YOU the above-named respondent, *(residing) *(carrying on profession, business or occupation) at .... *(in court area and district aforesaid), being a parent of

.... born on ....
.... born on ....

(a) dependent child(ren) whose parents are not married to each other, (and not being *(a child) *(children) who is/are being fully maintained by the other parent), HAVE FAILED TO PROVIDE SUCH MAINTENANCE as is proper in the circumstances for the said child(ren).

THIS IS TO COMMAND YOU the respondent to appear at the sitting of the District Court for the court area and district aforesaid to be held at ....
on the   date of   19   at   am/pm on the hearing of the said application for a maintenance order.

Dated this   day of   19   .

Signed ....
Judge of the District Court
(or)
Peace Commissioner
(or)
District Court Clerk

To

of

the above-named respondent

...

No 54.16

FAMILY LAW (MAINTENANCE OF SPOUSES AND CHILDREN)
ACT, 1976

Section 9(1)(b)

NOTICE OF APPLICATION TO HAVE PAYMENTS MADE TO
DISTRICT COURT CLERK

District Court Area of   District No

.... Maintenance Creditor

.... Maintenance Debtor

*Delete words
inapplicable

TAKE NOTICE that the above named maintenance creditor *(residing) *(carrying on profession, business or occupation) at ....
*(and in court area and district aforesaid) will apply at the sitting of the District Court at ....
on the   day of   19   , at   m. for a DIRECTION pursuant to section 9(1)(b) of the above Act that payments under a *mainten-ance/*variation/*interim order made by the District Court at ....
on the   day of   19   , shall be made to the District Court Clerk.

Dated this   day of   19   .

Signed ....
Maintenance Creditor

*(Solicitor for Maintenance
Creditor)

To the District Court Clerk

at

No 54.18

FAMILY LAW (MAINTENANCE OF SPOUSES AND CHILDREN)
ACT, 1976

Section 9(1)(a), 9(1)(b)

NOTICE OF DIRECTION THAT PAYMENTS BE MADE TO
DISTRICT COURT CLERK

District Court Area of   District No

.... Maintenance Creditor

.... Maintenance Debtor

*Delete words
inapplicable

YOU ARE HEREBY GIVEN NOTICE that the weekly payments of
payable by you to the above-named maintenance creditor
of ....
under a *maintenance *variation *interim order made at the sitting
of the District Court at ....
on the   day of   19 , *(together with the sum of £   for
costs and expenses) SHOULD BE MADE TO the District Court Clerk
for the above court area for transmission to the person entitled to
receive them.

The first of such payments is due on the   day of   19 .

The payments should be forwarded to

The District Court Clerk,
District Court Office

at ....

whose office hours are from .... to .... on ....

Dated this   day of   19 .

Signed ....
District Court Clerk for above
court area.

To

of

the above-named maintenance debtor.

No 58.1

GUARDIANSHIP OF INFANTS ACT, 1964

Section 6A

NOTICE OF APPLICATION BY A FATHER TO BE APPOINTED A GUARDIAN

District Court Area of   District No

.... Applicant

.... *Respondent(s)

*Delete where
inapplicable

TAKE   NOTICE   that   the   above-named   applicant,   of .... in court (area and) district aforesaid, being the father of

.... born on ....
.... born on ....

residing at ....
(an) infant(s), whose father and mother have not married each other, WILL APPLY at the sitting of the District Court to be held at ....
on the   day of   19   at am/pm FOR AN ORDER under section 6A of the above Act appointing him to be a guardian of the said infant(s).

Dated this   day of   19 .

Signed ....
Applicant/Solicitor for the
Applicant.

To   The District Court Clerk,
      District Court Office,

at   ....
          (and)

*(To

of

To

of   )

No 58.2

GUARDIANSHIP OF INFANTS ACT, 1964

Section 6A(3)(a)

CONSENT OF MOTHER TO APPOINTMENT OF FATHER AS GUARDIAN OF AN INFANT

District Court Area of   District No

In the matter of an intended application by ....

I, ... of ....

BEING THE MOTHER and sole guardian of

.... born on ....

.... born on ....

(an) infant(s) within the meaning of the above-named Act, who reside(s) with me at the above address /

at ....

AND BEING AWARE of an intended application to the Court under section 6A(1) of the said Act

by ....

of ....

the father of the said infant(s), for an order appointing him to be a guardian of the infant(s),

HEREBY CONSENT to the appointment of the said father as a guardian of the said infant(s).

Dated this   day of   19 .

Signed ....

PART THREE

. . .

No 58.16

GUARDIANSHIP OF INFANTS ACT, 1964

NOTICE OF APPLICATION UNDER SECTION *11(1) *11(4) FOR THE COURT'S DIRECTION

District Court Area of   District No

.... Applicant

.... Respondent(s)

*Delete words
inapplicable

TAKE NOTICE THAT APPLICATION will be made at the sitting of the District Court to be held at ....
on the   day of   19   at   am/pm
*(under section 11(1) of the above Act by the above-named applicant, of ....
in court (area and) district aforesaid, BEING A GUARDIAN OF

.... born on ....
.... born on ....

(an) infant(s) residing at ....
FOR THE COURT'S DIRECTION on the following question affecting the welfare of the infant(s) (eg regarding custody, access, maintenance or any other matter):

).
*(under section 11(4) of the above Act (as substituted by section 13 of the Status of Children Act, 1987) by the above-named applicant, of ....
in court (area and) district aforesaid.

BEING THE FATHER OF and not being a guardian of

.... born on ....
.... born on ....

(an) infant(s) residing at ....
whose father and mother have not married each other.

FOR THE COURT'S DIRECTION regarding the custody of the infant(s) and the right of access thereto of the applicant or the infant(s) mother).

Dated this   day of   19 .

                           Signed ....
                           Applicant/Solicitor for the
                                   Applicant.

To

of

To

of

. . .

No 59.1

DOMESTIC VIOLENCE ACT, 1996

Section 2(2)

SUMMONS FOR A SAFETY ORDER

District Court Area of   District No

.... Applicant
.... Respondent

*Delete where   YOU ARE HEREBY REQUIRED to appear at the sitting of the
inapplicable   District Court to be held at ....
on the .... day of .... 19....., at .....m. to answer the application
of the *applicant *(or the .... Health Board on behalf of the
applicant by virtue of section 6 of the above-mentioned Act) who is
* the spouse of the respondent
* not the spouse of the respondent but has lived with the respondent
  as husband or wife for a period of at least six months in aggregate
  during the period of twelve months immediately prior to this
  application
* a parent of the respondent and the respondent being of full age
  and not, in relation to the parent, a dependent person,
* of full age and residing with the respondent in a relationship which
  is not primarily contractual
and who resides at .... *(in the Court District
aforesaid) for a safety order directing that you shall not use or
threaten to use violence against, molest or put in fear the *applicant
*or any dependent person(s) *and shall not watch or beset the place
where the applicant *and that dependent person(s) reside(s).

Dated this   day of   19 .

Signed ....
Judge of the District Court
District Court Clerk

To

of

Respondent

*WARNING

IT IS AN OFFENCE under section 9 of the Family Home
Protection Act, 1976, as applied by section 8 of the Domestic
Violence Act, 1996, for a spouse to DISPOSE OF OR REMOVE ANY
OF THE HOUSEHOLD CHATTELS pending the determination of
the application herein, and if a safety order is made, while that order
is in force (unless the other spouse consents or the Court permits it).

A spouse who contravenes this provision shall be liable on conviction
to a fine not exceeding £100 or to imprisonment for a term not
exceeding six months, or to both.

. . .

No 59.3

DOMESTIC VIOLENCE ACT, 1996

Section 3(2)

SUMMONS FOR A BARRING ORDER

District Court Area of   District No

.... Applicant

.... Respondent

*Delete where
inapplicable

YOU ARE HEREBY REQUIRED to appear at the sitting of the District Court to be held at ....
on the .... day of .... 19....., at .....m. to answer the application of the *applicant *(or the .... Health Board on behalf of the applicant by virtue of section 6 of the above-mentioned Act) who is
* the spouse of the respondent
* not the spouse of the respondent but has lived with the respondent as husband or wife for a period of at least six months in aggregate during the period of nine months immediately prior to this application
* a parent of the respondent and the respondent being of full age and not, in relation to the parent, a dependent person,
for a barring order directing you to leave the place where the applicant *or any dependent person resides at .... *(in the Court District aforesaid) and prohibiting you from entering the place where the applicant *or any dependent person resides until further order of the Court, or until such other time as the Court shall specify on the grounds that the *safety/welfare of the applicant *and any dependent person so requires.

Dated this   day of   19 .

Signed ....
Judge of the District Court
District Court Clerk

To

of

Respondent

*WARNING

IT IS AN OFFENCE under section 9 of the Family Home Protection Act, 1976, as applied by section 8 of the Domestic Violence Act, 1996, for a spouse to DISPOSE OF OR REMOVE ANY OF THE HOUSEHOLD CHATTELS pending the determination of the application herein, and if a barring order is made, while that order is in force (unless the other spouse consents or the Court permits it). A spouse who contravenes that provision shall be liable on conviction to a fine not exceeding £100 or to imprisonment for a term not exceeding six months, or to both.

...

No 59.5

DOMESTIC VIOLENCE ACT, 1996

Section 4

INFORMATION

District Court Area of   District No

.... Applicant

.... Respondent

*Delete where
inapplicable

The information of *the above-named applicant of
....
*(or   of the   Health Board on behalf of the applicant by
virtue of section 6 of the above mentioned Act) who says on oath:–

On the .... day of .... 19....., I caused a
summons for hearing at ....
District Court on the ... day of ... 19 ..., at ...m, to be issued against
the above-named respondent of ....,
applying for a barring order in respect of ....
*(in the Court District aforesaid) being the place where I *and any
dependent person reside(s) and I now request an interim barring
order against the respondent pursuant to the provisions of section 4
of the above-mentioned Act on the grounds:–

and I say that there is an immediate risk of significant harm to me
*and*or any dependent person if the order is not made immediately
and the granting of a protection order would not be sufficient to
protect me *or any dependent person.

Dated this   day of   19 .

Signed ....
Informant

Sworn before me this ..... day of ..... 19...... .

Signed ....
Judge of the District Court

PART THREE

No 59.6

DOMESTIC VIOLENCE ACT, 1996

Section 4

INTERIM BARRING ORDER

District Court Area of .... District No

.... Applicant

.... Respondent

*Delete where inapplicable

WHEREAS *the applicant above named of ....
*(or the   Health Board on behalf of the applicant by virtue of section 6 of the above-mentioned Act) has issued a summons for a barring order to be heard at the District Court at ....on the .... day of .... 19....., at .....am/pm, *the Court, in this exceptional case, considers it necessary or expedient in the interests of justice to make this order ex parte or notwithstanding the fact that the summons required by Rule 5 hereof has not been served,

AND WHEREAS the Court, on the evidence given is of opinion that there is an immediate risk of significant harm to the applicant *and*or any dependent person if this order is not made immediately, and the granting of a protection order would not be sufficient to protect the applicant *and any dependent person.

NOW THE COURT HEREBY DIRECTS YOU, the respondent to leave the place where the applicant *and any dependent person reside(s) at ....
*(in the Court District aforesaid) on being notified of the making of this order, AND PROHIBITS YOU FROM entering such place until the ..... day of ....., 19..... without leave of the Court,

* SAVE AND EXCEPT

* AND FURTHER PROHIBITS YOU from

using or threatening to use violence against *the applicant/ *any dependent person; molesting or putting in fear *the applicant/*any dependent person; attending at or in the vicinity of, or watching or besetting a place where *the applicant/any dependent person reside(s)

during the period aforesaid.

Dated this   day of   19 .

Signed ....
Judge of the District Court

To

of

Respondent.

*WARNING

A respondent who contravenes this order, or who, while this order is in force refuses to permit the applicant or any dependent person to enter in and remain in the place to which this order relates or does any act for the purpose of preventing the applicant or such dependent person from so doing may be arrested without warrant by a member of the Garda Síochána, and on conviction for such an offence may be fined £1,500.00 or be sentenced to twelve months imprisonment or be both fined and imprisoned.

A copy of this order is being sent to the Garda Síochána Station at ....

Amendments—Inserted by the District Court (Domestic Violence) Rules 1998.

PART THREE

...

No 59.7

DOMESTIC VIOLENCE ACT, 1996

Section 5

INFORMATION

District Court Area of　　　　　　　　　　　　　　　District No

.... Applicant

.... Respondent

*Delete where
inapplicable

The information of *the above-named applicant, of
....
(in the Court District aforesaid)(or　　　　of the　　　　health board
on behalf of the applicant by virtue of section 6 of the above-
mentioned Act) who says on oath:–
On the .... day of .... 19..... I caused a
summons for hearing at ....
District Court on the day of 19 to be issued against the above-named
respondent of ....,
applying pursuant to the provisions of
* section 2 of the above Act for a safety order
* section 3 of the above Act for a barring order in respect
of ....
....

* (in the Court District aforesaid) being the place where I *and any
dependent person reside(s) and I now request a protection order
against the respondent pursuant to the provisions of section 5 of the
above Act on the grounds that:–

Dated this　　　　day of　　　　19　.

Signed ....

Informant

Sworn before me this ..... day of ..... 19...... .

Signed ....

Judge of the District Court

...

No 59.11

DOMESTIC VIOLENCE ACT, 1996

Section 13

SUMMONS TO DISCHARGE A *SAFETY *BARRING *INTERIM
BARRING *PROTECTION ORDER

District Court Area of   District No

.... Applicant

.... Respondent

*Delete where   YOU ARE HEREBY REQUIRED to appear at the sitting of the
inapplicable   District Court to be held at ....

on the .... day of .... 19....., at .....m. to answer the
application of the above-named *(applicant) *(......... Health Board
on behalf of the applicant by virtue of section 6 of the above-
mentioned Act) *(respondent) of .... for the discharge of the
*safety order *barring order *interim barring order *protection
order made on the .... day of .... 19..... at the District Court
at .... on
the grounds that the safety and welfare of the applicant *and*or any
dependent person for whose protection the order was made does not
require that the order should continue in force.

Dated this   day of   19 .

Signed ....
Judge of the District Court or
District Court Clerk

To

of

*applicant *respondent

PART THREE

FORM 91

DOMESTIC VIOLENCE ACT 1998

Section 13

SUMMONS TO DISCHARGE A SAFETY / BARRING / INTERIM
BARRING / PROTECTION ORDER

District Court Area of .... District No. ....

.... Applicant
.... Respondent

Take notice: YOU ARE HEREBY REQUIRED to appear at the sitting of the
(if applicable) District Court to be held at ....
on the .... day of .... 19.... at .... a.m./p.m. to answer the
application for the discharge of (appl. an) .... Health Board
(or default of the applicant by virtue of section 6 of the above
mentioned Act) *application of ...... for the discharge of the
safety order / barring order / interim barring order *protection
order made on the ...... day of .... 19.... at the District Court
....

... grounds that the safety and welfare of the applicant and/or any
dependent person in whose protection the order was made does not
require that the order should continue in force.

Dated this ...... day of ...... 19.....

Signed ....
Judge of the District Court
District Court Clerk

To ....
of ....
applicant / respondent

District Court (Family Law) Rules 1998

(SI 42/1998)

1   These Rules may be cited as the District Court (Family Law) Rules 1998.

2   These Rules shall come into operation on the 15th day of March 1998 and shall be read together with all other District Court Rules for the time being in force.

MAINTENANCE

3   (Amends Order 54 of the District Court Rules 1997 and inserts it in Schedule 1 to these Rules)

4   (Amends Order 55 of the District Court Rules 1997 and inserts it in Schedule 2 to these Rules)

ATTACHMENT

5   (Amends Order 56 of the District Court Rules 1997 and inserts it in Schedule 3 to these Rules)

6   (Amends Order 58 of the District Court Rules 1997 and inserts it in Schedule 4 to these Rules)

PROTECTION OF THE FAMILY HOME

7   (Amends Order 60 of the District Court Rules 1997 and inserts it in Schedule 5 to these Rules)

SCHEDULE 1

ORDER 54

MAINTENANCE OF SPOUSES AND CHILDREN

1   Definitions

In this Order:

'the Act' means the Family Law (Maintenance of Spouses and Children) Act, 1976 (No 11 of 1976);
'the Act of 1987' means the Status of Children Act, 1987 (No 26 of 1987);
'competent authority' has the meaning assigned to it in Order 98 of these Rules;
'the Act of 1995' means the Family Law Act, 1995 (No 26 of 1995);
'the Act of 1996' means the Family Law (Divorce) Act, 1996 (No 33 of 1996).

2   Venue

(1) Subject to the provisions of Order 62 of these Rules, proceedings under Act may be brought, heard or determined at any sitting of the Court for the court area where either party to the proceedings ordinarily resides or carries on any profession, business or occupation.

(2) Where however the Clerk, having consulted the Judge for the time being assigned to the district within which such area is situate, certifies on a summons or a notice of application that the proceedings are urgent, the summons or notice may be issued for, and the proceedings may be heard and determined at, any sitting of the Court in that district.

3   Hearings to be otherwise than in public

Proceedings under the Act shall be heard otherwise than in public and only officers of the Court, the parties and their legal representatives, witnesses (subject to the provisions of Order 8 rule 2 of these Rules) and such other persons as the Judge in his or her discretion shall allow, shall be permitted to be present at the hearing.

4   Applications for maintenance orders

(1) An application for a maintenance order under *section 5(1)(a)* or *5(1)(b)* of the Act shall be preceded by the issue and service upon the respondent of a summons in the Form 54.1 or 54.2 Schedule C, as appropriate.

(2) An application for a maintenance order under *section 5A(1)* or *5A(2)* of the Act (inserted by *section 18* of the Act of 1987) shall be preceded by the issue and service upon the respondent of a summons in the Form 54.3 or 54.4 Schedule C, as appropriate.

(3) The order of the Court granting such application shall be in the Form 54.5, 54.6, 54.7 or 54.8 Schedule C, as appropriate.

5   Application to discharge maintenance order

An application by a maintenance debtor for the discharge of a maintenance order under *section 6(1)(a)* of the act or for the discharge of part of such order under *section 6(3)* of the Act shall be preceded by the issue and service upon the maintenance creditor of a summons in the Form 54.9 Schedule C. The order of the Court granting the application shall be in the Form 54.10 Schedule C.

6   Application to discharge or vary order

An application by either party to the proceedings to discharge or vary a maintenance order under *section 6(1)(b)* of the Act shall be preceded by the issue and service upon the other party of a summons in the Form 54.11 Schedule C. The order of the Court granting the application shall be in the Form 54.12 Schedule C.

7   Interim order

An interim order made by the Court under *Section 7* of the Act shall be in the Form 54.13 Schedule C.

8   Application for lump sum order for birth/funeral expenses

An application by a spouse or parent under *section 21A(1)* of the Act (inserted by *section 21* of the Act of 1987) for a lump sum order in respect of the expenses incidental to the birth or funeral of a dependent child shall be preceded by the issue and service upon the other spouse or parent, as the case may be, of a summons in the Form 54.14 Schedule C. The order of the Court granting the application shall be in the Form 54.15 Schedule C.

9   Clerk to send copy of order

Where the Court makes a maintenance order, an order varying, discharging or discharging part of such order, an interim order or a lump sum order in respect of the birth or funeral expenses of a dependent child, the Clerk shall give to, or send by prepaid ordinary post to the maintenance debtor or the respondent party (as the case may be) a copy of the order so made.

10   Application for direction that payments be made to Clerk

An application under *section 9(1)(b)* of the Act for a direction that payments under a maintenance order, a variation order or an interim order be made to the Clerk shall be *ex parte*. Notice of such application in the Form 54.16 Schedule C, signed by the maintenance creditor or by his or her solicitor, shall be lodged with the Clerk at least 48 hours prior to the date of the intended application. The order of the Court granting the application shall be in the Form 54.17 Schedule C.

11   Payments to the Clerk

(1) Where the Court directs that payments under a maintenance order, a variation order or an interim order shall be made to the Clerk, such Clerk shall send a notice in the Form 54.18 Schedule C by prepaid ordinary post to the maintenance debtor indicating the place at which and the days and hours during which payments under the order should be made.

(2) The Clerk shall give a receipt to the maintenance debtor for each payment made by him or her and shall transmit such payment to the maintenance creditor or, if authorised in writing by the maintenance creditor so to do, the Clerk may transmit the payment to the competent authority.

12   Application to discharge direction

An application under *section 9(3)* of the Act by a maintenance debtor to have a direction under *section 9(a)* of the Act discharged shall be preceded by the issue and service upon the maintenance creditor of a summons in the Form 54.19 Schedule C. The order of the Court granting the application shall be in the Form 54.20 Schedule C.

13   Recovery of arrears by Clerk

(1) Where payments to the Clerk under a maintenance order, a variation order or an interim order are in arrears, and such Clerk receives a request in writing in the Form 54.21 Schedule C from the maintenance creditor to take such steps as he or she considers reasonable to recover such arrears, such Clerk may make application under *section 10* of the Act for an attachment of earnings order or under *section 8* of the Enforcement of Court Orders Act, 1940 (in accordance with the provisions of Order 56 or 57, as the case may be of these Rules).

(2) Where payments referred to in *paragraph (1)* hereof are in arrears and the Clerk has received no request to recover the arrears, such Clerk may in his or her discretion, having considered the extent of the arrears and any other relevant matter, notify the maintenance creditor of the means of enforcement available in respect of the order.

14   Service of summonses

(1) A summons required by this Order to be served may be served upon the person to whom it is directed in accordance with the provisions of Order 10 of these Rules at least fourteen days before the date of the sitting of the Court to which the summons is returnable.

(2) Save where service has been effected by the Clerk, the original of every such summons served, together with a statutory declaration as to service thereof, shall be lodged with the Clerk at least two days before the said date of hearing.

15   Rules to apply to orders for maintenance pending suit etc.

Where the Clerk receives a copy:

- (a) of an order for maintenance pending suit, of a periodical payments order or of a secured periodical payments order made under the Act of 1995, or of any such order as aforesaid as affected by an order under *section 18* of the Act of 1995;
- (b) of an order for maintenance pending suit, of a periodical payments order or a secured periodical payments order made under the Act of 1996 or of any such order as aforesaid as affected by an order under *section 22* of the Act of 1996,

from the Registrar of the Court which made that order, and payments under the order are directed to be made to the District Court Clerk (as provided for in *section 20* of the Act of 1995 and in *section 28* of the Act of 1996), such Clerk shall register particulars of the order and shall proceed in relation thereto as if it were a maintenance order made at a sitting of the District Court for the district court area to which that Clerk is assigned.

16   Orders to secure payments

Where the Court has made an order providing for periodical payments by way of support or maintenance by a maintenance debtor to a maintenance creditor, an application may be made to the Court on a date subsequent to the date on which such order is made pursuant to the provisions of *section 41* of the Act of 1995 by any person having an interest in the proceedings to secure the said payments to the maintenance creditor. Such application shall be preceded by the issue and service of a notice in the Form 54.22 Schedule C. The order of the Court granting such application shall be in the Form 54.23 Schedule C.

17   Lump Sum Orders

Where, under the powers conferred by *section 42* of the Act of 1995, an order is made in the District Court providing for the making of a lump sum payment or lump sum payments the order of the Court shall be in the Form 54.24, 54.25, 54.26, or 54.27 Schedule C as the case may be.

18   Stay on certain orders the subject of appeal

(1) Notwithstanding the provisions of Order 25, rule 9(4) and Order 101 of these Rules, and that an appellant has entered into a recognizance of appeal, an appeal from an order under—

- (i)   *section 11(2)(b)* of the Guardianship of Infants Act, 1964 (No 7 of 1964),
- (ii) *section 5, 5A* or *7* of the Family Law (Maintenance of Spouses and Children) Act, 1976 (No 11 of 1976)

shall, if the court that made the order or the court to which the appeal is brought so determines (but not otherwise), stay the operation of the order.

(2) An application to the District Court to stay the operation of an order such as is mentioned in *subsection (1)* of this rule, may be made following the service and lodgment of a notice of appeal and lodgment of the recognizance for appeal and when made otherwise than upon the occasion of the making of those orders shall be preceded by the issue of a notice in the Form 54.28 which shall be served upon the respondent to the application two days before the hearing of the application. The order of the Court granting the stay shall be in the Form 54.29.

. . .

Amendments—Amended and inserted by rule 3 of these Rules.

. . .

PART THREE

SCHEDULE 3

ORDER 56

ATTACHMENT OF EARNINGS

1 Definitions

In this Order:

'the Act' means the Family Law (Maintenance of Spouses and Children) Act, 1976 (No 11 of 1976);
'the Act of 1995' means the Family Law Act, 1995 (No 26 of 1995);
'competent authority' has the meaning assigned to it in Order 98 of these Rules.

2 Venue

(1) Proceedings to which this Order relates may be brought, heard or determined at any sitting of the Court for the court area where either party to the proceedings ordinarily resides, or carries on any profession, business or occupation.

Hearing to be otherwise than in public

(2) Such proceedings shall be heard otherwise than in public and only officers of the Court, the parties and their legal representatives, witnesses (subject to the provisions of Order 8, rule 2 of these Rules) and such other persons as the Judge in his or her discretion shall allow, shall be permitted to be present at the hearing.

3 Application

An application for an attachment of earnings order under *section 10* of the Act shall be preceded by the issue and service upon the maintenance debtor of a summons in the Form 56.1 or 56.2 Schedule C as the case may be. Where the Court grants the application or, where the Court, having made an antecedent order, makes, in accordance with *subsection (1A)(a)* of the Act, as inserted by the Act of 1995, an attachment of earnings order in the same proceedings in order to secure payments under the antecedent order, the order of the Court shall be in accordance with the Form 56.3 or 56.4 Schedule C, as the case may be.

4   Service of order

The Clerk specified in an attachment of earnings order or the maintenance creditor, as the case may be, shall cause the order to be served upon the employer to whom it is directed and upon any subsequent employer of the maintenance debtor concerned of whom the Clerk so specified or the maintenance creditor becomes aware.

5   Mode of service

Such service may be affected by leaving a copy of the order at, or sending a copy of the order by registered prepaid post to the residence or place of business in the State of the person to be served. A copy of the order shall also be sent by registered prepaid post to the maintenance debtor.

6   Receipt for payment

The Clerk shall issue a receipt for each payment made by any such employer and shall transmit such payment to the maintenance creditor or, if authorised in writing by the maintenance creditor so to do, may transmit the payment to the competent authority.

7   Payment by Clerk

The Clerk may send by post any payment received by him or her under an attachment of earnings order to the person entitled thereto.

8   Order requiring statement of particulars

An order under *section 13(1)(b)* of the Act requiring a statement of particulars of a maintenance debtor's earnings shall be in accordance with Form 56.5 Schedule C. The Clerk shall cause the order to be served upon the person to whom it is directed by sending a copy thereof by prepaid post to the residence or place of business in the State of such person.

9   Application for determination as to earnings

An application under *section 15* of the Act for a determination as to whether payments of a particular class or description are earnings for the purposes of an attachment of earnings order shall be preceded by the issue and service of a summons (Form 56.6 Schedule C) upon each of the other parties to the proceedings.

10   Parties to such proceedings Order of Court

The parties to proceedings in respect of an application under rule 9 shall be the employer, the maintenance debtor and the person to whom payments under the order are being made. The order of the Court hearing such application shall be in accordance with Form 56.7 Schedule C. A copy of such order shall be sent by the Clerk by prepaid post to each of the parties to the proceedings.

11   Application to vary or discharge attachment of earnings order

An application under *section 17* of the Act for the variation or discharge of an attachment of earnings order shall be preceded by the issue and service of a summons (Form 56.8 Schedule C) upon the maintenance creditor and/or the maintenance debtor, as the case may be. The order of the Court on hearing the application shall be in accordance with Form 56.9 Schedule C. The Clerk or the maintenance creditor, as the case may be, shall cause the order to be served upon the employer in the manner prescribed in rule 5 of this Order.

12   Clerk to notify employer of cessor of order

Where an attachment of earnings order ceases to have effect the Clerk shall notify (Form 56.10 Schedule C) the employer accordingly.

13   Cesser of warrant and lapse of enforcement proceedings

Where an attachment of earnings order has been made, any proceedings commenced under *section 8* of the Enforcement of Court Orders Act, 1940, shall lapse and any warrant or order issued or made under that section in any such proceedings shall cease to have effect.

14   Clerk to produce documents

On the hearing of an application for an attachment of earnings order the Clerk to whom payments under the maintenance order, variation order, interim order, or enforceable maintenance order are payable shall tender as evidence:

(a) the maintenance order, variation order, interim order (as the case may be) and in the case of an enforceable maintenance order a copy of the maintenance order,

(b) the request in writing received by the Clerk from the maintenance creditor,

(c) in the case of an enforceable maintenance order, a copy of the order made by the Master of the High Court, and

(d) any other relevant document.

The Clerk shall also prove the amount of arrears due.

No 56.1

FAMILY LAW (MAINTENANCE OF SPOUSES AND CHILDREN)
ACT, 1976

Section 10(1)(a)(iii)

ATTACHMENT OF EARNINGS SUMMONS

District Court Area of   District No

.... Maintenance Creditor
.... Maintenance Debtor

*Delete where   WHEREAS by *maintenance/*variation/*interim/order dated
inapplicable   day of   19 , made at the sitting of the District Court
                       at ....
                       *(in court area and district aforesaid) AGAINST YOU the above-
                       named maintenance debtor YOU WERE ORDERED to pay the total
                       weekly sum of £   *(together with the sum of £   for costs
                       and expenses) to the above-named maintenance creditor
                       of ....

†Delete where   †(AND WHEREAS the Court pursuant to subsection (1) of section
summons issued   9 of the above Act directed that payments under the said Order be
by maintenance   made to the District Court Clerk for the above court area),
creditor
                       AND WHEREAS the payments directed to be made by the said
                       Order have not been duly made and there is now in arrear in respect
                       of the same the sum of £   being the amount of weekly payments
                       which have become due and payable *(within the six months
                       immediately preceding the date of issue of this summons) *(together
                       with the sum of £   for costs and expenses) making in all the sum
                       of £   .

                       †(AND WHEREAS I, being the District Court Clerk for the above
                       court area and the person to whom payments under the said Order
                       were directed to be made, have, pursuant to subsection (2) of section
                       9 of the above Act, been requested in writing by the above-named
                       maintenance creditor to take such steps as I consider reasonable in
                       the circumstances to recover the sums in arrear).

                       THIS IS TO REQUIRE YOU to appear at the sitting of the District
                       Court to be held at ....
                       in court area and district aforesaid on the   day of   19 , at
                       m on the hearing of an application for an ATTACHMENT OF
                       EARNINGS ORDER.

                       AND YOU ARE ALSO REQUIRED to fill in and sign the attached
                       STATEMENT OF PARTICULARS and send it to the Clerk of the
                       District Court at ....
                       so as to reach his/her office at least forty-eight hours before the date
                       of hearing of the application.

                       Dated this   day of   19 .

Signed ....
Judge of the District Court,
(or)
Peace Commissioner,
(or)
District Court Clerk

To

of

(the above-named maintenance debtor)

*****

STATEMENT OF PARTICULARS

Name and address of Employer(s) ....
....
....
....

Weekly earnings ....
Income from any other sources ....
Place of work ....
Nature of work ....
Works number (if any) ....
Social Welfare number ....
P.A.Y.E. number ....
Liabilities ....

To the District Court Clerk

at ....

No 56.2

FAMILY LAW (MAINTENANCE OF SPOUSES AND CHILDREN) ACT, 1976

Section 10(1)(a)(iii)

ATTACHMENT OF EARNINGS SUMMONS

District Court Area of   District No

.... Maintenance Creditor

.... Maintenance Debtor

*State Court which made order

WHEREAS by the maintenance order dated   day of   19 ,
made by *...
you the above maintenance debtor residing at ....
in court area and district aforesaid were ordered to pay to the above
named maintenance creditor of ....

†Delete where inapplicable

the total weekly sum of £   †(together with the sum of £   for
costs and expenses).

AND WHEREAS the Master of the High Court on the   day of
     19 , made an enforcement order in respect of the said
maintenance order,

AND WHEREAS the payments directed to be made by the said
maintenance order as ordered to be enforced by the said enforcement order have not been duly made and there is now in arrear in
respect of same the sum of being the amount of weekly payments
which have become due and payable †(within six months immediately preceding the date of issue of this summons) †(together with
the sum of £   for costs and expenses) making in all the sum of
£   .

AND WHEREAS I, being the District Court Clerk for the above
court area, and the person to whom payments under the said
maintenance order are to be paid and the person authorised to take
these proceedings, have been requested in writing by the above
named maintenance creditor to make application under section 10
of the above Act.

THIS IS TO REQUIRE YOU to appear at the sitting of the District
Court, to be held at ....
in court area and district aforesaid on the   day of   19 , at
     m on the hearing of an application for an ATTACHMENT OF
EARNINGS ORDER.

AND YOU ARE ALSO REQUIRED to fill in and sign the attached
STATEMENT OF PARTICULARS and send it to the District Court
Clerk at ....
so as to reach his office at least forty-eight hours before the date of
hearing of the application.

Dated this   day of   19 .

Signed ....
District Court Clerk for above
court area

To

of

(the above-named maintenance debtor)

*****

STATEMENT OF PARTICULARS

Name and address of Employer(s)   ....
....
....
....

Weekly earnings   ....
Income from any other sources   ....
Place of work   ....
Nature of work   ....
Works number (if any)   ....
Social Welfare number   ....
P.A.Y.E. number   ....
Liabilities   ....

To the District Court Clerk

at ....

Amendments—Amended and inserted by rule 5 of these Rules.

...

SCHEDULE 4

No 58.17

GUARDIANSHIP OF INFANTS ACT, 1964

Section 11

ORDER ON QUESTION AFFECTING WELFARE OF INFANT(S)

District Court Area of   District No

.... Applicant

.... Respondent(s)

*Delete words
inapplicable

UPON APPLICATION made to this Court today by the above-named applicant of .... in court (area and) district aforesaid,
*(being a guardian of

.... born on ....
.... born on ....

(an) infant(s) residing at ....
for the Court's direction under section 11 of the above Act on the following question affecting the welfare of the infant(s)

*(being the father of, and not being a guardian of   ),

.... born on ....
.... born on ....

(an) infant(s) residing at ....
whose father and mother have not married each other, for the Court's direction regarding the custody of the infant(s) and the right of access thereto of the applicant or of the infant's mother, pursuant to section 11(4) of the above Act),

THE COURT being satisfied that notice of the application was duly served, and having heard the submissions made herein, and being satisfied that the welfare of the infant(s) requires the making of this Order,

HEREBY DIRECTS (regarding custody and access—for example—)
*that the custody care and control of the said infant(s) be given to the *(applicant) *(respondent) and that access to the said infant(s) by the *(respondent) *(applicant) be allowed on every ..... day between the hours of am/pm and am/pm, the *(applicant) *(respondent) to collect the infant(s) from and return the infant(s) to ....., and that access be allowed at such further or other times as may be agreed
—Provided that the party to whom custody of the said infant(s) is hereby given shall not remove the said infant(s) from the jurisdiction of this Court without having first obtained the consent in writing of the other party or the leave of this Court or of any other Court of competent jurisdiction.

(regarding maintenance—for example—)

*that the said ....

do pay to the said ....

the weekly sum of £   towards the maintenance of (each of) the said infant(s), namely,

.... born on ....

.... born on ....

until such infant shall attain the age of 18 years, and thereafter if, when the infant has attained that age, he or she

   (i) is or will be receiving full-time education or instruction at a university, college, school or other educational establishment, until he or she has attained the age of 23 years or until such education or instruction has been completed, whichever is the sooner; or

  (ii) is suffering from mental or physical disability to such extent that it is not reasonably possible for him or her to maintain himself or herself fully;

making in all the total weekly sum of £

(regarding any other question or matter)

*that

(regarding costs)

*that the above-named *(respondent) *(applicant) do pay to the above-named *(applicant) *(respondent) the sum of £   being the costs of these proceedings.

Dated this   day of   19   .

Signed ....
Judge of the District Court.

WARNING

Where this order contains a direction regarding the custody of an infant or the right of access to an infant, any person who FAILS OR REFUSES to give up the infant or to allow access to the infant as required SHALL BE GUILTY OF AN OFFENCE and shall be liable on summary conviction to a fine not exceeding £200 or to imprisonment not exceeding SIX MONTHS, or to both such fine and such imprisonment.

Amendments—Amended and inserted by rule 6 of these Rules.

SCHEDULE 5

ORDER 60

PROTECTION OF THE FAMILY HOME

1   Definition

In this Order—

'the Act' means the Family Home Protection Act, 1976 (No 27 of 1976).

2   Venue

(1) Proceedings under the Act may be brought, heard or determined at any sitting of the Court for the court area in which the family home, as defined in *section 2* of the Act, is situate.

(2) Where however the Clerk, having consulted the Judge for the time being assigned to the court district within which such court area is situate, certifies on a notice of application or a summons that the proceedings are urgent, the said notice or summons may, subject to the provisions of rule 9 hereof, be issued for, and the proceedings may be heard and determined at any sitting of the Court for that district.

3   Hearing to be otherwise than in public

Proceedings under or referred to in the Act in which each spouse is a party (whether by joinder or otherwise) shall be heard otherwise than in public and only officers of the Court, the parties and their legal representatives, witnesses (subject to the provisions of *Order 8, rule 2* of these Rules) and such other persons as the Judge in his or her discretion shall allow, shall be permitted to be present at the hearing.

4   Application under *section 9(1)*

An application by a spouse under *section 9(1)* of the Act for an order prohibiting the disposition or removal of household chattels in the family home shall be preceded by the issue and service upon the respondent spouse of a notice in the Form 60.1 Schedule C. The order of the Court granting the application shall be in the Form 60.2 Schedule C, a copy of which shall be served upon the respondent spouse.

5   Application under *section 9(2)*

An application by a spouse under *section 9(2)* of the Act for an order permitting the disposition or removal of household chattels in the family home shall be preceded by the issue and service upon the respondent spouse of a notice in the Form 60.3 Schedule C. The order of the Court granting the application shall be in the Form 60.4 Schedule C, a copy of which shall be served upon the respondent spouse.

6   Summons under *section 9(4)*

Where complaint is made by a spouse to a Judge under *section 9(4)* of the Act that the other spouse has contravened the provisions of *section 9(2)* of the Act, the summons which may be issued and served upon the other spouse shall be in the Form 60.5 Schedule C. The relevant provisions of Order 15 of these Rules shall apply in such case.

7   Application under *section 9(5)*

An application by a spouse under *section 9(5)* of the Act for an order that the respondent spouse provide household chattels for the applicant spouse or sum of money in lieu thereof shall be preceded by the issue and service upon the respondent spouse of a notice in the Form 60.6 Schedule C. The order of the Court granting the application shall be in the Form 60.7 Schedule C, a copy of which shall be served upon the respondent spouse.

8   Summons under *section 15*

Where complaint is made to a Judge under *section 15* of the Act that a person knowingly gave information which was false or misleading in any material particular, the summons which may be issued and served upon that person shall be in the Form 60.8 Schedule C. The relevant provisions of Order 15 of these Rules shall apply in such case.

9   Service and lodgment of documents

(1) A notice or summons required by this Order to be served may be served in accordance with the provisions of Order 10 of these Rules and every such notice shall be served at least fourteen days or, in the case of proceedings certified as urgent under *rule 2(2)* hereof, at least two days before the date of the sitting of the Court to which it is returnable.

(2) Save where service has been effected by the Clerk, the original of every such notice or summons served shall, together with a statutory declaration as to service thereof, be lodged with the Clerk at least two days before the date of the said sitting.

10   Joinder of parties

The provisions of Order 42 (Third Party Procedure) of these Rules shall, with necessary modifications, apply to the proceedings mentioned in *section 11* of the Act.

11   Declaring a conveyance void

(1) An application to the Court under *section 3* of the Act of 1976 to have a conveyance declared void shall be in the Form 60.9, Schedule C.

(2) The order of the Court thereon shall be in the Form 60.10, Schedule C.

Lis Pendens

(3) A person who institutes proceedings to have a conveyance declared void by reason of *subsection (1)* of *section 3* of the Act shall, as soon as may be, cause relevant particulars of the proceedings to be entered as a *lis pendens* under and in accordance with the Judgments (Ireland) Act, 1844.

12   Dispensing with consent

(1) An application under *subsection (1)* of *section 4* of the Act to dispense with the consent required under *section 3* of that Act, of a spouse to the conveyance of the family home shall be in the Form 60.11, Schedule C.

(2) The order of the Court thereon shall be in the Form 60.12, Schedule C.

(3) On granting an application under *section 4* of the Act to dispense with the consent required under *section 3* of that Act, the Court may order pursuant to *section 33* of the Trustee Act, 1893 that a person be appointed to execute the conveyance of the interest in question and the order of the Court thereon shall be in the Form 60.13, Schedule C.

13   Consent by the Court

(1) Where the spouse whose consent is required under *subsection (1)* of *section 3* of the Act is incapable of consenting by reason of unsoundness of mind or other mental disability or has not after reasonable inquiries been found, application may be made to the Court

in the Form 60.14, Schedule C under *subsection (4)* of *section 4* of that Act for the Court to give the consent on behalf of that spouse.

(2) The order of the Court thereon shall be in the Form 60.15, Schedule C.

14   Protection of Family Home

(1) An application to the Court for an order under *subsection (1)* of *section 5* of the Act for the protection of the family home in the interest of the applicant spouse of a dependent child shall be in the Form 60.16, Schedule C.

(2) The order of the Court thereon shall be in the Form 60.17, Schedule C.

15   Conduct leading to loss of Family Home

(1) An application to the Court for an order under *subsection (2)* of *section 5* of the Act to compensate the applicant spouse and any dependent child of the family for loss occasioned by the conduct of the other spouse shall be in the Form 60.18, Schedule C.

(2) The order of the Court thereon shall be in the Form 60.19, Schedule C.

Amendments—Amended and inserted by rule 7 to these Rules.

PART THREE

Guardianship of Children (Statutory Declaration) Regulations, 1998

(SI 5/1998)

1. These regulations may be cited as the Guardianship of Children (Statutory Declaration) Regulations, 1998.

2 These Regulations shall come into operation on 1st day of February, 1998.

3 A statutory declaration referred to in *paragraph (e)* of *section 2(4)* (inserted by the Children Act, 1997 (No 40 of 1997)) of the Guardianship of Infants Act, 1964 (No 7 of 1964) shall be in the form set out in the Schedule to these Regulations.

SCHEDULE

Statutory Declaration of Father and Mother in relation to Joint Guardianship of Child

THE MAKING OF THIS DECLARATION WILL SERIOUSLY AFFECT THE LEGAL POSITION OF BOTH PARENTS. IT IS ADVISABLE TO OBTAIN LEGAL ADVICE BEFORE MAKING THIS DECLARATION.

THIS DECLARATION IS AN IMPORTANT DOCUMENT AND ON COMPLETION SHOULD BE KEPT IN A SAFE PLACE.

In the matter of a declaration under *paragraph (e)* of *section 2(4)* (inserted by the Children Act, 1997) of the Guardianship of Infants Act, 1964:

We

.... of
    (father's name)

....
                      (father's address)

and

.... of
    (mother's name)

of ....
                      (mother's address)

do solemnly and sincerely declare and say as follows:

1. We have not married each other.

2. We are the father and mother of .... who was born on
                                  (child's name)
    day of   , 199 .

3. We agree to the appointment of .... as a guardian of
                            (father's name)

....

(child's name)

4. We have entered into arrangements regarding the custody of [and access to]*

....

(child's name)

*Strike out as necessary.

We make this solemn declaration conscientiously believing the same to be true by virtue of the Statutory Declarations Act, 1938, and pursuant to *paragraph (e)* of *section 2(4)* (inserted by the Children Act, 1997) of the Guardianship of Infants Act, 1964.

Signed .... (Father)

Signed .... (Mother)

DECLARED BEFORE ME BY

.... who are personally known to me or (who are identified to me by

.... who is personally known to me) at

....
this day of   , 19   .

....

(Peace Commissioner/Commissioner for Oaths/Notary Public)

Rules of the Superior Courts (No 3), 1997
(SI 343/1997)

1. These rules shall be construed together with the Rules of the Superior Courts, 1986 and 1996 and may be cited as the Rules of the Superior Courts (No 3), 1997.

2. These rules shall come into operation on the 1st day of September 1997.

3. The following Order shall be substituted for Order 70A of the Rules of the Superior Courts.

ORDER 70A

PART THREE

1 (1) In this Order family law proceedings shall include:

(a) Any proceeding pursuant to section 36 of the Family Law Act, 1995 or to that section as applied by section 44 of the Family Law (Divorce) Act, 1996.

(b) An application pursuant to section 3 of the Adoption Act, 1974 or pursuant to section 3 of the Adoption Act, 1988.

(c) An application pursuant to section 3(8), 4, 5 or 9 of the Family Home Protection Act, 1976.

(d) Any application to section 6 or 7 of the Family Law Act, 1981.

(e) Any proceeding pursuant to the Guardianship of Infants Act, 1964, the Family Law (Maintenance of Spouses and Children) Act, 1976 or pursuant to the Domestic Violence Act, 1996 which has been instituted and maintained in the High Court pursuant to Article 34.3.1 of the Constitution.

Notice of the making of this Statutory Instrument was published in 'Iris Oifigiúil' of 22nd August, 1997

(f) An application for a decree of judicial separation pursuant to section 3 of the Judicial Separation and Family Law Reform Act, 1989 and any preliminary or ancilliary application relating thereto under Part II of the Family Law Act, 1995.

(g) Any proceedings transferred to the High Court pursuant to section 31(3) of the Judicial Separation and Family Law Reform Act, 1989.

(h) An application for a decree of divorce pursuant to section 5 of the Family Law (Divorce) Act, 1996 and preliminary or ancilliary application relating thereto under Part III thereof.

(i) An application to institute proceedings for relief subsequent to a divorce or separation outside the State pursuant to section 23 of the Family Law Act, 1995.

(j) An application pursuant to section 15(A) or section 25 of the Family Law Act, 1995 or pursuant to section 18 of the Family Law (Divorce) Act, 1996.

(k) An application for a declaration as to marital status under Part IV of the Family Law Act, 1995.

1 (2) In this Order

'the 1989 Act' means the Judicial Separation and Family Law Reform Act, 1989,
'the 1995 Act' means the Family Law Act, 1995,
'the 1996 Act' means the Family Law (Divorce) Act, 1996,
'the Acts' means all in any of the Acts referred to in rule 1(1).

2 Commencement

All family law proceedings other than an application under rule 27 of this Order shall be commenced by a special summons which shall be a family law summons and shall be entitled:

'THE HIGH COURT
FAMILY LAW

In the matter of the .... Act, 19........ (as the case may be)

Between/

A.B. the Applicant

and

C.B. the Respondent'

3 The endorsement of claim shall be entitled 'Special Endorsement of Claim' and shall state specifically, with all necessary particulars, the relief sought and each section of the Act or Acts under which the relief is sought and the grounds upon which it is sought.

4 In any proceedings pursuant to rule 1(1) above an affidavit verifying such proceedings or in reply thereto shall contain the following, where applicable:

  (a) In the case of an application for a judicial separation or a decree of divorce
     (1) The date and place of the marriage of the parties.
     (2) The length of time the parties have lived apart and the address of both of the parties during that time, where known.
     (3) Full particulars of any children of the applicant or respondent stating whether each or any of them is or are a dependent child of the family and stating whether and if so what provision has been made for each and any such dependent child of the applicant or respondent as the case may be.
     (4) Whether any possibility of a reconciliation between the applicant and respondent exists and if so on what basis the same might take place.
     (5) Details of any previous matrimonial relief sought and/or obtained and details of any previous separation agreement entered into between the parties. (Where appropriate a certified copy of any relevant Court order and/or Deed of Separation/Separation Agreement should be exhibited with the affidavit).
     (6) Where each party is domiciled at the date of the application commencing the proceeding or where each party has been ordinarily resident for the year preceding the date of such application.
     (7) Details of the family home(s) and/or other residences of the parties including, if relevant, details of any former family homes/residences which should include details of the manner of occupation and ownership thereof.
     (8) Where reference is made in the summons to any immovable property whether it is registered or unregistered land and a description of the lands/premises so referred to.
  (b) In the case of an application for relief after a foreign divorce or separation outside the State, such of the particulars at (a) above as are appropriate and
     (1) The date and place of marriage and divorce/separation of the parties. (Where appropriate, a certified copy of the decree absolute or final decree of divorce/separation, (together with, where appropriate, an authenticated translation thereof) should be exhibited with the affidavit).

(2) Particulars of the financial, property and custodial/access arrangements operating ancillary to the said decree, and whether such arrangements were made by agreement or by order of the Court or otherwise, and whether such agreements were made contemporaneously with the decree or at another time and the extent of compliance therewith.

(3) The present marital status and occupation of each party.

(4) All details relevant to the matters referred to in section 26 of the 1995 Act.

(c) In the case of an application for a declaration as to marital status, such of the particulars at (a) above as are appropriate together with

(1) The nature of the applicant's reason for seeking such a declaration.

(2) Full details of the marriage/divorce/annulment/legal separation in respect of which the declaration is sought including the date and place of such marriage/divorce/annulment/legal separation. (Where appropriate a certified copy of the marriage certificate/decree of divorce/annulment/legal separation should be exhibited with the affidavit).

(3) The manner in which the jurisdictional requirements of section 29(2) of the 1995 Act are satisfied.

(4) Particulars of any previous or pending proceeding in relation to any marriage concerned or relating to the matrimonial status of a party to any such marriage in accordance with section 30 of the 1995 Act.

(d) In the case of an application for the determination of property issues between spouses pursuant to section 36 of the 1995 Act or that section as applied by section 44 of the 1996 Act to engaged persons, such particulars of (a) above as are appropriate and

(1) The description, nature and extent of the disputed property or monies.

(2) The state of knowledge of the applicant's spouse in relation to the possession or control of the disputed properties or monies at all relevant times.

(3) The nature and extent of the interest being claimed by the applicant in the property or monies and the basis upon which such claim is made.

(4) The nature and extent of any claim for relief being made and the basis upon which any such claim is made.

(5) The manner in which it is claimed that the respondent has failed, neglected or refused to make to the applicant such appropriate payment or disposition in all of the circumstances and details of any payment or disposition actually made.

(6) Sufficient particulars to show that the time limits referred to at section 36(7) of the 1995 Act have been complied with.

(e) In the case of an application for relief out of the estate of a deceased spouse pursuant to section 15(A) or section 25 of the 1995 Act or section 18 of the 1996 Act, such of the particulars at (a) above as are appropriate and

(1) The date and place of the marriage and date of any decree of divorce/judicial separation. (The marriage certificate and a certified copy of the decree of divorce/separation shall be exhibited with the affidavit (with authenticated translations where appropriate).)

(2) Details of any previous matrimonial reliefs obtained by the applicant and in particular lump sum maintenance orders and property adjustment orders, if any.

(3) Details of any benefit received from or on behalf of the deceased spouse whether by way of agreement or otherwise and details of any benefits accruing to the applicant under the terms of the will of the deceased spouse or otherwise.

(4)   The date of death of the deceased spouse, the date upon which represen-
       tation was first granted in respect of the estate of the said spouse and, if
       applicable, the date upon which notice of death of the deceased spouse was
       given to the applicant spouse and the date upon which the applicant spouse
       notified the personal representative of an intention to apply for relief
       pursuant to section 18(7) of the 1996 Act and section 15(A)(7) of the 1995
       Act, as the case may be.

(5)   The marital status of the deceased spouse at the date of death and the
       marital status of the applicant at the date of the application and whether the
       applicant has remarried since the dissolution of the marriage between the
       applicant and the deceased spouse.

(6)   Details of the dependents of the deceased spouse at the date of death and of
       all the dependents of the applicant at the date of the application together
       with details of any other interested persons.

(7)   An averment as to whether any order pursuant to section 18(10) of the 1996
       Act or section 15(A)(10) of the 1995 Act has previously been made.

(8)   Details of the value of the estate of the deceased spouse where known.

5 Any such affidavit filed under rule 4 shall, where appropriate, also exhibit the
certificate required under section 5 or, as the case may be, section 6 of the 1989 Act or
under section 6, or as the case may be, section 7 of the 1996 Act which shall be in Form
Nos 1, 2, 3 or 4 respectively as set out in the schedule hereto.

6 Affidavit of Means

(1) Without prejudice to the right of any party to seek particulars of any matter from the
other party to any proceeding or to the right of such party to make application to the
Court for an order of discovery and without prejudice to the jurisdiction of the Court
pursuant to section 12(25) of the 1995 Act or section 17(25) of the 1996 Act, in any case
where financial relief under either of the Acts is sought each party shall file and serve an
Affidavit of Means in the proceeding.

(2) The Affidavit of Means shall be in Form No 5 as set out in the Schedule hereto.

(3) An Affidavit of Means of the applicant shall be served with the verifying affidavit
grounding such proceeding and the Affidavit of Means of any respondent or any other
party shall be served with the replying affidavit in the proceeding unless otherwise
ordered by the Master or the Court. Subsequent to the service of an Affidavit of Means
either party may request the other party to vouch all or any of the items referred to
therein within 21 days of the said request.

(4) In the event of a party failing properly to comply with the provisions in relation to
the filing and serving of an Affidavit of Means as hereinbefore provided for or failing
properly to vouch the matters set out therein, the Court may, on application by notice of
motion, grant an order for discovery and/or make any such order as the Court deems
appropriate and necessary, including an order that such party shall not be entitled to
pursue or defend as appropriate such claim for any ancillary relief under the Act save as
permitted by the Court and upon such terms as the Court may determine are
appropriate or the Court may adjourn the proceeding for a specified period of time to
enable compliance with any such previous request or order of the Court.

7 Affidavit of Welfare

In any case in which there is a dependent child or children of the spouses or either of
them an Affidavit of Welfare shall be filed and served on behalf of the applicant and shall
be in Form No 6 as set out in the Schedule hereto. In a case in which the respondent

agrees with the facts as averred to in the Affidavit of Welfare filed and served by the applicant, the respondent may file and serve an Affidavit of Welfare in the alternative form provided in Form No 3 of the Schedule hereto. In a case in which the respondent disagrees with all or any of the Affidavit of Welfare served and filed by an applicant, a separate Affidavit of Welfare in the said Form No 6 herein shall be sworn, filed and served by the respondent within 21 days from the date of service of the applicant's Affidavit of Welfare.

8 Ex parte application to seek relief under section 23 of the 1995 Act

(1) An applicant for relief under section 23 of the 1995 Act may issue but not serve a special summons and shall as soon as may be after the issue of such summons apply *ex parte* to the Court for leave to make the application for the relief claimed in the summons.

(2) The applicant shall by affidavit verify the requirements specified in section 27 of the 1995 Act and shall set forth the substantial grounds relied upon for seeking relief.

(3) The Court may upon such application, if appropriate, grant or refuse such application or may, in circumstances which seem appropriate, adjourn the application to allow the applicant to put further evidence before the Court on any relevant matter.

(4) If upon application made to it the Court shall grant leave to make the application for the relief claimed in the summons, the applicant may thereupon proceed to serve the summons in the manner provided for by these rules and the matter shall thereupon proceed in accordance with the provisions of this Order.

9 Interim and Interlocutory Relief

(1) An application for:

   (a) a preliminary order pursuant to section 6 of the 1995 Act; or
   (b) a preliminary order pursuant to section 11 of the 1996 Act; or
   (c) maintenance pending suit pursuant to section 7 of the 1995 Act; or
   (d) maintenance pending relief pursuant to section 24 of the 1995 Act; or
   (e) maintenance pending suit pursuant to section 12 of the 1996 Act; or
   (f) calculations pursuant to section 12(25) of the 1995 Act; or
   (g) calculations pursuant to section 17(25) of the 1996 Act; or
   (h) relief pursuant to section 35 of the 1995 Act; or
   (i) relief pursuant to section 37 of the 1996 Act; or
   (j) relief pursuant to section 38(8) of the 1995 Act; or
   (k) relief pursuant to section 38(7) of the 1996 Act; or
   (l) a report pursuant to section 47 of the 1995 Act; or
   (m) a report pursuant to section 42 of the 1996 Act; or

for any other interlocutory relief, shall be by notice of motion to the Court. Such notice shall be served upon the other party or parties to the proceeding 14 clear days before the return date and shall, where appropriate, be grounded upon the affidavit or affidavits of the parties concerned.

(2) An application may be made *ex parte* to the Court in any case in which interim relief of an urgent and immediate nature is required by the applicant and the Court may in any case, where it is satisfied that it is appropriate, grant such relief or make such order as appears proper in the circumstances.

(3) Any interim or interlocutory application shall be heard on affidavit unless the Court otherwise directs. Where any oral evidence is heard by the Court in the course of any

such application *ex parte*, a note of such evidence shall be prepared by the applicant or the applicant's solicitor and approved by the Court and shall be served upon the respondent forthwith together with a copy of the order made, if any, unless otherwise directed by the Court.

10 Notice to Trustees

An applicant who seeks an order under Part II of the 1995 Act or under Part III of the 1996 Act affecting a pension in any way shall give notice to the trustees thereof in the Form No 7 as set out in the Schedule hereto informing them of the application and of the right to make representations in relation thereto to the Court.

11 Motion for Directions

(1) An applicant or respondent may, at any stage, bring a motion for directions to the Court:

(a) Where there are any dependent children who are *sui juris* and whose welfare or position is or is likely to be effected by the determination of the proceeding or of any issue in the proceedings;

(b) Where an order is sought concerning the sale of any property in respect of which any other party has or may have an interest;

(c) Where an order of any type is sought which will affect the rules of a pension scheme or require non-compliance therewith; or

(d) Where an application is brought seeking provision out of the estate of a deceased spouse,

or in any other case in which it is appropriate. Such notice of motion shall be grounded upon the affidavit of the applicant which shall, in particular, identify the party or parties whose interests are or are likely to be affected by the determination of the proceeding or any issue in the proceeding and who ought to be put on notice of the said proceeding and given an opportunity of being heard.

(2) The Court may, upon such motion or of its own motion, make such order or give such direction pursuant to section 40 of the 1995 Act or section 40 of the 1996 Act as appears appropriate and may, where any order affecting the rules of a pension scheme is sought, direct that further notice be given to the trustees of such pension scheme in accordance with the Form No 7 set out in the Schedule hereto or in such variation thereof as the Court may direct, as appropriate.

(3) Save where the Court shall otherwise direct, a notice party who wishes to make representations to the Court shall make such representations by affidavit which shall be filed and served on all parties to the proceeding within 28 days of service upon them of the notice of application for relief or within such further time as the Court may direct.

12 The Court may, at any stage, direct that the parties to any proceeding exchange pleadings in relation to all or any of the issues arising in the proceeding between the parties or between the parties or any of them and any third party on such terms as appears appropriate and may give such directions in relation to the matter as appear necessary.

13 Hearing

(1) Save where the Court otherwise directs, the hearing of any interim or interlocutory application brought under the Acts shall be on the affidavits of the parties subject to the right of the parties to seek to cross examine the opposing party on their affidavit. Any party may serve a notice to cross examine in relation to the deponent of any affidavit served on him.

(2) Save where the court otherwise directs the hearing of any application under the Acts shall be on the oral evidence of the parties.

(3) Where relief is sought by the applicant or the respondent pursuant to section 12 of the 1995 Act or section 17 of the 1996 Act, evidence of the actuarial value of the benefit under the scheme shall be by affidavit filed on behalf of the applicant or respondent as the case may be. Such affidavit on behalf of an applicant shall be sworn and served on all parties to the proceeding and filed at least 28 days in advance of the hearing and subject to the right to serve notice of cross examination in relation to the affidavit. When one of the parties has adduced evidence of the actuarial value of the benefit by such affidavit as provided herein which the other part intends to dispute, he shall do so by affidavit which shall be filed at least 14 days in advance of the hearing, subject to the right to serve notice of cross examination in relation to same.

14 Where any relief is sought which has not been specifically claimed, the Court may adjourn the proceedings to allow such amendments to the Family Law Summons as may be necessary and upon such terms and conditions as it seems fit.

15 (1) Where any action or proceeding is pending in the High Court which might have been commenced in the Circuit Court or the District Court any party to such action or proceeding may apply to the High Court that the action be remitted or transferred to the Circuit Court or the District Court (as the case may be) and if the High Court should, in exercise of its discretion, consider such an order to be in the interests of justice it shall remit or transfer such action or proceeding to the Circuit Court or the District Court (as the case may be) to be prosecuted before the Judge assigned to such Circuit or (as the case may require) the Judge assigned to such District as may appear to the Court suitable and convenient, upon such terms and subject to such conditions as to costs or otherwise as may appear just.

(2) An application under this rule to remit or transfer an action or proceeding may be made at any time after an appearance has been entered.

16 The provisions of Order 49, rules 1, 2, 3 and 6 shall apply to any proceeding commenced under rule 2 above.

17 Any respondent in family law proceedings may counterclaim by way of a replying affidavit and such affidavit shall clearly set out the relief claimed and the grounds upon which it is claimed in like manner as if he were an applicant and subject to the provisions of this order.

18 In any proceeding which has been transferred to the High Court pursuant to section 31(3) of the 1989 Act, the applicant and the respondent shall each within fourteen days from the making of the order or such further time as the Master may allow, file in the Central Office an affidavit or supplemental affidavits as shall appear necessary to conform to the requirements of this order as if the proceeding had commenced in the High Court, together with certified copy of the order transferring the same and the proceeding shall thereupon be listed for hearing.

19 An application by either spouse or on behalf of a dependent member pursuant to section 18 of the 1995 Act or section 22 of the 1996 Act shall be made to the Court by motion in the proceeding notice to the party concerned and shall be supported by an affidavit verifying the same and shall set out fully how, when and in what respect circumstances have changed or what new evidence exists as a result of which the Court should vary or discharge or otherwise modify in any respect an order to which the section applies.

20 An application pursuant to section 35 of the 1995 Act or pursuant to section 37 of the 1996 Act may, at any time, be made to the Court by motion on notice in the proceeding to the party concerned and shall be supported by an affidavit verifying the facts alleged in relation to the disposition complained of and shall specify the relief claimed and the way in which the disposition is said to be intended to defeat the relief claimed or to affect it in any way and the Court may make such order upon such motion as appears proper in the circumstances and may, if necessary, adjourn the motion in order to give notice of the application to any party affected by the disposition complained of or the disposal of the property concerned.

21 An application pursuant to section 8 of the 1989 Act, for the rescission of a grant of a decree of judicial separation shall be preceded by a notice of re-entry which shall have been given at least one month before the date of the application and shall be grounded on an affidavit sworn by each of the spouses seeking such rescission which shall specify the nature and extent of the reconciliation including whether they have resumed cohabiting as husband and wife and shall also specify such necessary ancillary orders (if any) as they require the Court to make or to consider making in the circumstances.

22 Subsequent Ancillary Relief

Subsequent to the grant of a decree of judicial separation or of a decree of divorce any party who seeks any or any further ancillary relief under Part II of the 1995 Act or under Part III of the 1996 Act shall do so by notice of motion in the proceeding. Such notice shall be served on any party concerned and shall be grounded on the affidavit of the moving party.

23 Service of Orders

In all cases in which the Registrar of the Court is required to serve or lodge a copy of an order upon any person or persons or body such service or lodgement may be effected by the service of a certified copy of the said order by registered post to the said person or persons or body.

24 Adoption

(1) In any proceeding pursuant to section 3 of the Adoption Act, 1974 and upon the service of a summons on An Bord Uchtála, the Board shall take the following steps:

    (a) It shall cause the person who has agreed to the placing of the child, the subject matter of the application for adoption, to be informed of the following matters:

        (i)   the fact of the institution of the proceeding under section 3 of the Adoption Act, 1974 without revealing to such person the name or identity of the applicants;

        (ii) the fact that such person is entitled to be heard and represented upon the hearing of the summons.

    (b) It shall ascertain from such person the following information:

        (i)   whether such person wishes to be heard and to be represented at the hearing of such summons;

        (ii) whether such person has available to him/her advice and is in a position from his/her own resources to be represented by solicitor or solicitor and counsel at the hearing of such summons;

        (iii) the address at which such person may be informed of the proceeding and in particular of the date of any hearing at which such person will be heard and represented.

(2) Upon the completion of the steps provided for in sub-rule (1) the Board shall apply by Motion on Notice to the applicants to the Court for directions. Such application shall,

in the first instance, be made on affidavit and in the event that it has been possible to communicate with the person involved such affidavits shall include an affidavit by the servant or officer of the Board who has actually spoken to and had communication with such person. Such person shall not be identified in the body of the affidavit but the name and address present and future of such person shall be set out in a sealed envelope exhibited in such affidavit. Such exhibit shall be opened by the Judge only and unless by special direction of the Court the name, address and identity of such person shall not be revealed to any of the other parties in the suit.

(3) Upon the hearing of such motion for directions the Court may give such directions as it shall think fit for the hearing of the action and in particular may:

(a) provide, if necessary, for the representation of such person;

(b) fix a date for the hearing *in camera* of the evidence and submissions on behalf of the applicants in the absence of such person but in the presence of the solicitor or solicitor and counsel representing such person;

(c) fix a separate date for the hearing *in camera* of the evidence and submissions by and on behalf of such person in the absence of the applicants but in the presence of the solicitor or solicitor and counsel for the applicants.

(4) If it is satisfied upon the affidavits supporting such motion or upon such further evidence, oral or otherwise, as may be adduced on behalf of the Board that it is not possible to ascertain the whereabouts of the person who has placed the child for adoption and that it is not possible to communicate with such person the Court may proceed to hear and determine the application without further notice to such person.

25 (1) In an application brought pursuant to section 3(1)(a) of the Adoption Act, 1988, the Health Board shall serve a copy of the summons on the applicants and shall verify by affidavit the reasons why it considers it proper to make the application.

(2) In any proceeding brought pursuant to section 3(1)(b) of the Adoption Act, 1988 the applicants shall serve a copy of the summons on the relevant Health Board and thereupon the Health Board shall verify by affidavit its reasons for (as the case may be):

(i) declining to apply to the Court, or

(ii) failing to apply to the Court and failing to serve the notice required by section 3(1)(b)(i) of the Act.

Such affidavit shall be sworn by the Chief Executive Officer or by a Deputy Chief Executive Officer of the Board.

(3) In an application brought under subrule (1) or (2) above, the provisions of rule 24 relating to the steps to be taken by An Bord Uchtála shall apply *mutatis mutandis* to a Health Board in relation to the parents alleged to have failed in their duty to the child or children concerned.

26 (1) In an application to Court pursuant to section 6A or section 11(4) of the Guardianship of Infants Act, 1964 (as inserted by sections 12 and 13 of the Status of Children Act, 1987, respectively) where an infant is in the care of prospective adoptive parents under the Adoption Acts, 1952 and 1988, the following procedure shall be followed:

(i) Upon the service of a summons on An Bord Uchtála, the Board shall take the following steps:

(a) It shall cause the prospective adoptive parents to be informed of the following matters:

      (i) the fact of the institution of the proceeding under section 6A or section 11(4) of the Guardianship of Infants Act, 1964 without revealing to such parents the name or identity of the applicant or of the natural mother;

      (ii) the fact that such parents are entitled to be heard and represented upon the hearing of the summons.

  (b) It shall ascertain from such parents the following information:

      (i) whether they wish to be heard and to be represented at the hearing of such summons;

      (ii) whether they have available to them advice and are in a position from their own resources to be represented by solicitor or solicitor and counsel at the hearing of such summons;

      (iii) the address at which they may be informed of the proceedings and in particular of the date of any hearing at which they will be heard and represented.

(2) Upon the completion of the steps provided for in subrule (1) the Board shall apply by Motion on Notice to the father to the Courts for directions. Such application shall, in the first instance, be made on affidavit and such affidavits shall include an affidavit by the person who has actually spoken to and had communication with such parents. Such parents shall not be identified in the body of the affidavit but their names and addresses present and future shall be set out in a sealed envelope exhibited in such affidavit. Such exhibit shall be opened by the Judge only and unless by special direction of the Court the name, address and identity of such person shall not be revealed to any of the other parties in the suit.

(3) Upon the hearing of such motion for directions the Court may give such directions as it shall think fit for the trial of the action and in particular may:

  (a) provide, if necessary, for the representation of such parents and of the father and mother of the child;

  (b) fix a date for the hearing *in camera* of the evidence and submissions on behalf of the applicant and the natural mother in the absence of such parents but in the presence of the solicitor or solicitor and counsel representing such parents;

  (c) fix a separate date for the hearing *in camera* of the evidence and submissions by and on behalf of such parents in the absence of the applicant and the natural mother but in the presence of the solicitor or the solicitor and counsel for the applicant and the natural mother.

27 An application to Court pursuant to section 6A(3) of the Guardianship of Infants Act, 1964 (as inserted by section 12 of the Status of Children Act, 1987) shall be by Motion on Notice to the mother and not by summons and shall be entitled in a similar manner as in rule 2 and shall be grounded on the affidavit of the father seeking to be appointed guardian. Such affidavit shall afford proof of the paternity of the said infant and shall exhibit the written consent of the mother to the appointment of the father as guardian (such consent having been witnessed by a registered medical practitioner or a solicitor) and a true copy of the Birth Certificate of the Infant in respect of whom the father wishes to be appointed guardian. The Court may require such proof of paternity of an infant as it thinks fit.

28 The provision of Order 119 rules 2 and 3 shall not apply to any cause, action or proceeding under Order 70 or Order 70A.

SCHEDULE OF FORMS

FORM No 1

THE HIGH COURT
FAMILY LAW

IN THE MATTER OF THE JUDICIAL SEPARATION AND FAMILY LAW REFORM
ACT, 1989 AND IN THE MATTER OF THE FAMILY LAW ACT, 1995

BETWEEN/

A.B.

Applicant

and

C.D.

Respondent

CERTIFICATE PURSUANT TO SECTION 5 OF THE JUDICIAL SEPARATION AND
FAMILY LAW REFORM ACT, 1989

I,   , the Solicitor acting for
the above Applicant do hereby certify as follows:

1. I have discussed with the Applicant the possibility of reconciliation with the
Respondent and I have given the Applicant the names and addresses of persons
qualified to help effect a reconciliation between spouses who have become estranged.

2. I have discussed with the Applicant the possibility of engaging in mediation to help
effect a separation on an agreed basis with the Respondent and I have given the
Applicant the names and addresses of persons and organisations qualified to provide a
mediation service.

3. I have discussed with the Applicant the possibility of effecting a separation by the
negotiation and conclusion of a Separation Deed or written Separation Agreement with
the Respondent.

Dated the .... day of ...., 19........

Signed: ....

Solicitor

Address: ....
....

FORM NO 2

THE HIGH COURT
FAMILY LAW

IN THE MATTER OF THE JUDICIAL SEPARATION AND FAMILY LAW REFORM
ACT, 1989 AND IN THE MATTER OF THE FAMILY LAW ACT, 1995

BETWEEN/

A.B.

Applicant

and

C.D.

Respondent

CERTIFICATE PURSUANT TO SECTION 6 OF THE JUDICIAL SEPARATION AND
FAMILY LAW REFORM ACT, 1989

I,   , the Solicitor acting for the above Respondent do hereby certify as follows:

1. I have discussed with the Respondent the possibility of reconciliation with the Applicant and I have given the Respondent the names and addresses of persons qualified to help effect a reconciliation between spouses who have become estranged.

2. I have discussed with the Respondent the possibility of engaging in mediation to help effect a separation on an agreed basis with the Applicant and I have given the Respondent the names and addresses of persons and organisations qualified to provide a mediation service.

3. I have discussed with the Respondent the possibility of effecting a separation by the negotiation and conclusion of a Separation Deed or written Separation Agreement with the Applicant.

Dated the .... day of ...., 19........

Signed: ....

Solicitor

Address: ....

....

FORM NO 3

THE HIGH COURT

FAMILY LAW

IN THE MATTER OF THE FAMILY LAW (DIVORCE) ACT, 1996

BETWEEN/

A.B.

Applicant

and

C.D.

Respondent

CERTIFICATE PURSUANT TO SECTION 6 OF THE FAMILY LAW (DIVORCE) ACT, 1996

I, , the Solicitor acting for the above Applicant do hereby certify as follows:

1. I have discussed with the Applicant the possibility of reconciliation with the Respondent and I have given the Applicant the names and addresses of persons qualified to help effect a reconciliation between spouses who have become estranged.

[The following paragraphs to be inserted where appropriate.]

2. I have discussed with the Applicant the possibility of engaging in mediation to help effect a separation on an agreed basis (the spouses the parties hereto not being separated) or a divorce on the basis agreed between the Applicant with the Respondent and I have given the Applicant the names and addresses of persons and organisations qualified to provide a mediation service for spouses who have become estranged.

3. I have discussed with the Applicant the possibility of effecting a separation by the negotiation and conclusion of a Separation Deed or written Separation Agreement with the Respondent.

4. I have ensured that the Applicant is aware of judicial separation as an alternative to divorce, no decree of judicial separation in relation to the Applicant and the Respondent being in force.

Dated the .... day of ...., 19........

Signed: ....

Solicitor

Address: ....

....

PART THREE

FORM NO 4

THE HIGH COURT

FAMILY LAW

IN THE MATTER OF THE FAMILY LAW (DIVORCE) ACT, 1996

BETWEEN/

A.B.

Applicant

and

C.D.

Respondent

CERTIFICATE PURSUANT TO SECTION 7 OF THE FAMILY LAW (DIVORCE) ACT, 1996

I, ... , the Solicitor acting for the above Respondent do hereby certify as follows:

1. I have discussed with the Respondent the possibility of reconciliation with the Applicant and I have given the Respondent the names and addresses of persons qualified to help effect a reconciliation between spouses who have become estranged.

[The following paragraphs to be inserted where appropriate.]

2. I have discussed with the Respondent the possibility of engaging in mediation to help effect a separation on an agreed basis (the spouses the parties hereto not being separated) or a divorce on the basis agreed between the Respondent with the Applicant and I have given the Respondent the names and addresses of persons and organisations qualified to provide a mediation service for spouses who have become estranged.

3. I have discussed with the Respondent the possibility of effecting separation by the negotiation and conclusion of a Separation Deed or written Separation Agreement with the Applicant.

4. I have ensured that the Respondent is aware of judicial separation as an alternative to divorce, no decree of judicial separation in relation to the Respondent and the Applicant being in force.

Dated the .... day of ...., 19........

Signed: ....

Solicitor

Address: ....

....

FORM NO 5

THE HIGH COURT

FAMILY LAW

[Insert as appropriate]

IN THE MATTER OF THE JUDICIAL SEPARATION AND FAMILY LAW REFORM ACT, 1989

IN THE MATTER OF THE FAMILY LAW ACT, 1995

IN THE MATTER OF THE FAMILY LAW (DIVORCE) ACT, 1996

BETWEEN/

A.B.

Applicant

and

C.D.

Respondent

AFFIDAVIT OF MEANS

I, , [insert occupation],

of , aged 18 years
and upwards MAKE OATH and say as follows:

1. I say that I am the Applicant/Respondent [delete as appropriate] in the above entitled proceedings and I make this Affidavit from facts within my own knowledge save where otherwise appears and where so appearing I believe the same to be true.

2. I say that I have set out in the First Schedule hereto all the assets to which I am legally or beneficially entitled and the manner in which such property is held.

3. I say that I have set out in the Second Schedule hereto all income which I receive and the source(s) of such income.

4. I say that I have set out in the Third Schedule hereto all my debts and/or liabilities and the persons to whom such debts and liabilities are due.

5. I say that my weekly outgoings amount to the sum of £ and I say that the details of such outgoings have been set out in the Fourth Schedule hereto.

6. I say that to the best of my knowledge, information and belief, all pension information known to me relevant to the within proceedings is set out in the Fifth Schedule hereto. [Where information has been obtained from the trustees of the pension scheme concerned under the Pensions Act, 1990, such information should be exhibited and where such information has not been obtained, the Deponent should depose to the reason(s) why such information has not been obtained].

FIRST SCHEDULE

[Here set out in numbered paragraphs all assets whether held in the Applicant/ Respondent's sole name or jointly with another, whether held legally or beneficially, the manner in which the assets are held, whether they are subject to a mortgage or other charge or lien and such further and other details as are appropriate].

SECOND SCHEDULE

[Here set out in numbered paragraphs all income from whatever source(s)].

THIRD SCHEDULE

[Here set out in numbered paragraphs all debts and/or liabilities and the persons/ institutions to which such debts and/or liabilities are due].

FOURTH SCHEDULE

[Here set out full details of weekly personal outings].

FIFTH SCHEDULE

[Here full details of nature of pension scheme, benefits payable thereunder, normal pensionable age and period of reckonable service should be listed to the best of the Deponent's knowledge, information and belief].

SWORN etc.

FORM NO 6

THE HIGH COURT

FAMILY LAW

[Insert as appropriate]

IN THE MATTER OF THE JUDICIAL SEPARATION AND FAMILY LAW REFORM ACT, 1989

IN THE MATTER OF THE FAMILY LAW ACT, 1995

IN THE MATTER OF THE FAMILY LAW (DIVORCE) ACT, 1996

BETWEEN/

A.B.

Applicant

and

C.D.

Respondent

AFFIDAVIT OF WELFARE

I,   , [insert occupation]

of   , aged 18 years and upwards MAKE OATH and say as follows:

1. I say that I am the Applicant/Respondent [delete as appropriate] in above entitled proceedings and I make this Affidavit from facts within my own knowledge save where otherwise appears and where so appearing I believe the same to be true.

2. I say and believe that the facts set out in the Schedule hereto are true.

[In circumstances in which the Respondent does not dispute the facts deposed to by the Applicant in his/her Affidavit of Welfare, the following averment shall be included, replacing paragraph 2 hereof, and in such circumstances, the Schedule shall not be completed by the Respondent:

2. I say that I am fully in agreement with the facts as averted to by the Applicant in his/her Affidavit of Welfare sworn herein on the   day of   19   and I say and believe that the facts set out in the Schedule hereto are true].

SCHEDULE

Part I—Details of the children

1. Details of children born to the Applicant and the Respondent or adopted by both the Applicant and the Respondent.

Forenames   Surname   Date of Birth

2. Details of other children of the family or to which the parents or either of them are *in loco parentis*

Forenames   Surname   Date of Birth

Relationship to
Applicant/Respondent

Part II—Arrangements for the children of the family

3. Home details

 (a) The address or addresses at which the children now live.
 (b) Give details of the number of living rooms, bedrooms, etc, at the addresses in (a) above.
 (c) Is the house rented or owned and, if so, name the tenant(s) or owner(s).
 (d) Is the rent or mortgage being regularly paid and, if so, by whom?
 (e) Give the name of all other persons living with the children either on a full-time or part-time basis and the state their relationship to the children, if any.
 (f) Will there be any change in these arrangements and, if so give details.

Part III—Education and training details

 (a) Give the names of the school, college or place of training attended by each child.
 (b) Do the children have any special educational needs. If so, please specify.
 (c) Is the school, college or place of training fee-paying. If so, give details of how much the fees are per term/year. Are fees regularly paid and, if so, by whom?
 (d) Will there be any change in these circumstances? If so, give details.

Part IV—Childcare details

 (a) Which parent looks after the children from day to day? If responsibility is shared, please give details.
 (b) Give details of work commitments of both parents.
 (c) Does someone look after the children when the parent is not there? If yes, give details.
 (d) Who looks after the children during school holidays?
 (e) Will there be any change in these arrangements? If yes, give details.

Part V—Maintenance

 (a) Does the Applicant/Respondent pay towards the upkeep of the children? If yes, give details. Please specify any other source of maintenance.
 (b) Is the maintenance referred to at (a) above paid under court order? If yes, give details.
 (c) Has maintenance for the children been agreed? If yes, give details.
 (d) If not, will you be applying for a maintenance order from the Court?

Part VI—Details of contact with the children

 (a) Do the children see the Applicant/Respondent? Please give details.
 (b) Do the children stay overnight and/or have holiday visits with the Applicant/Respondent? Please give details.